NW 12000250   SARP   £36-99

KU-712-106

MEMORY

WITHDRAWN

N 0147821 4

"For Hilary" — Alan Baddeley

"To Christine with love" — Michael W. Eysenck

"In memory of my mother, Geraldine Anderson, in honor of a lifetime of encouragement and respect" — Michael C. Anderson

MEMORY

NEWMAN UNIVERSITY
COLLEGE
BARTLEY GREEN
BIRMINGHAM B32 3NT

CLASS 153.12
BARCODE 01478214
AUTHOR BAD

ALAN BADDELEY,

MICHAEL W. EYSENCK,

AND MICHAEL C. ANDERSON

Psychology Press
Taylor & Francis Group

HOVE AND NEW YORK

First published 2009 by Psychology Press
27 Church Road, Hove, East Sussex, BN3 2FA

Simultaneously published in the USA and Canada
by Psychology Press
711 Third Avenue, New York, NY 10017 (8th Floor)

*Psychology Press is an imprint of the Taylor & Francis Group,
an Informa Business*

Copyright © 2009 Psychology Press

All rights reserved. No part of this book may be reprinted or
reproduced or utilised in any form or by any electronic,
mechanical, or other means, now known or hereafter invented,
including photocopying and recording, or in any information
storage or retrieval system, without permission in writing
from the publishers.

The publisher makes no representation, express or implied,
with regard to the accuracy of the information contained in this
book and cannot accept any legal responsibility or liability for
any errors or omissions that may be made.

British Library Cataloguing in Publication Data
A catalogue record for this book is available from the British Library

Library of Congress Cataloging in Publication Data
Baddeley, Alan D., 1934–
    Memory / Alan Baddeley, Michael W. Eysenck, and Michael Anderson.
        p. cm.
    Includes bibliographical references and index.
    ISBN 978–1–84872–000–8 (hardcover)—ISBN 978–1–84872–001–5 (pbk.)
    1. Memory. I. Eysenck, Michael W. II. Anderson, Mike. III. Title.
    BF371.B227 2009
    153.1'2—dc22   2008034234

ISBN: 978–1–84872–000–8 (hb)
ISBN: 978–1–84872–001–5 (pb)

Typeset by Newgen Imaging Systems (P) Ltd, Chennai, India

CONTENTS

ABOUT THE AUTHORS

Having graduated in Psychology from University College London, Alan Baddeley spent the following year at Princeton, the first of five such stays in the US. He returned to a post at the Medical Research Council Applied Psychology Unit (APU) in Cambridge, completing a Ph.D. concerned with the design of postal codes. He continued to combine applied research, for example on deep-sea diving with theoretical issues such as the distinction between long- and short-term memory. After moving to the University of Sussex, he and Graham Hitch proposed a multicomponent model of working memory. He also began working with amnesic patients, continuing both these lines of research when he moved, first to a chair at the University of Stirling, then returning to the APU in Cambridge. After 20 years as its Director, he moved first to the University of Bristol, then to his current position in York where he has resumed his collaboration with Graham Hitch. He was awarded a CBE for his contributions to the study of memory, is a Fellow of the Royal Society, of the British Academy, and of the Academy of Medical Sciences.

Michael W. Eysenck graduated from University College London. He then moved immediately to Birkbeck University of London as a lecturer, where he completed his Ph.D. on the von Restorff and "release" memory effects. His research for several years focused on various topics within memory research (e.g. levels of processing; distinctiveness). However, for many years his research has focused mainly on anxiety and cognition (including memory). Most of this research has involved healthy populations but some has dealt with cognitive biases (including memory ones) in anxious patients. This research has been carried out at Birkbeck University of London and at Royal Holloway University of London, where he has been Professor of Psychology since 1987 (Head of Department, 1987–2005). However, it was started during his time as Visiting Professor at the University of South Florida. He has published 40 books in psychology (many relating to human memory), including two research monographs on anxiety and cognition. He has been in "Who's Who" since 1989.

ichael C. Anderson received his Ph.D. in Cognitive Psychology from the University of California, Los Angeles in 1994. After completing a post-doctoral fellowship in cognitive neuroscience at the University of California, Berkeley, he joined the Psychology faculty at the University of Oregon, where he was director of the Memory Control Laboratory through 2007. Anderson is now Professor of Cognitive Neuroscience at the University of St. Andrews, Scotland. His research investigates the roles of inhibitory processes as a cause of forgetting in long-term memory. Anderson's recent work has focused on executive control as a model of motivated forgetting, and has established the existence of cognitive and neurobiological mechanisms by which we can wilfully forget past experiences. This work begins to specify the mechanisms by which people adapt the functioning of their memories in the aftermath of traumatic experience.

PREFACE

Some years ago, one of us (ADB) accepted an invitation to write a memory book for the general public. The result, *Your Memory: A User's Guide*, took the basic structure of an introductory memory course, but illustrated its points from personal observation and research on everyday memory. Although not designed as a textbook, it began to be used, in both its initial and in a somewhat modified form for introductory memory courses, proving popular with students who liked its more relaxed approach. There have, however, been substantial developments in the study of memory since it was first written. This has included a much more extensive body of research on everyday memory, leading to the suggestion of producing a new book that attempts to keep the virtues of the original, while presenting an updated and extended account of human memory, explicitly designed as a memory text. The three of us jointly agreed to take on this task. In order to keep the personal tone, we agreed that each of us would undertake a number of chapters according with our interests, rather than attempt a more corporate style. Each chapter is therefore identified with one of the three authors.

One issue in writing a memory book is the question of how it should be structured. After a good deal of thought we have opted for the standard approach of following information through the memory system, beginning with sensory memory going on to discuss short-term and working memory, followed by episodic memory, which in turn leads to semantic memory and the accumulation of knowledge. There is, of course, substantial work that depends upon this basic framework, but goes beyond it, with topics such as autobiographical memory, prospective memory, memory development and aging, amnesia; and applied issues such as eyewitness testimony and improving your memory. We have chosen to treat such topics separately, while at the same time referring back to earlier chapters. This means that a given topic may be described more than once, often by more than one author. We regard this as a form of distributed practice and hence an advantage rather than a drawback.

A more serious problem is presented by the limitations of the simple information flow structure. First of all, it has become increasingly clear that information flows in both directions, with memory reflecting an alliance of *interactive* systems. For example, working memory plays an important role in long-term learning, but is itself influenced by existing knowledge. We try to make this clear without unduly complicating the picture.

A second problem concerns the different levels of development of research and theory in different areas. In tackling a given area, we tend to approach it from a historical viewpoint, both because of the importance of the early work for subsequent development, and also because earlier work is usually conceptually simpler, providing a clear route into subsequent more complex theory. However, while this might work well *within* chapters, it does not always work for the between-chapter structure. The chapters on short-term and working memory for instance, describe an area that has developed hugely since the 1960s, in the depth and complexity of theoretical development, in the degree of involvement of neuropsychology and neuroimaging, and in breadth of application. Other areas of equal importance are easier to understand. The role of organization in long-term learning for instance is a topic where the basic phenomena and ground rules had been established by the 1970s, with little further development necessary. Many newer applications such as the study of autobiographical memory and prospective memory are still at a relatively early stage of theoretical development, and as a result probably present less of a challenge to the student than some of the earlier chapters. We have therefore tried to structure the book in such a way as to allow the user to pick a different route through the book, if preferred.

In the twenty-first century, no memory book can be complete without taking into account the implications of recent exciting developments in neuroscience. Two of us (MCA and ADB) are currently involved in neuroimaging studies, and two of us (MWE and ADB) in studies involving patients with neuropsychological or emotional difficulties. However, while taking such advances into account where appropriate, our focus is on the *psychology* of human memory, which we believe will provide a sound foundation for developments in the neuroscience of memory, as well as continuing to offer a solid basis for applying knowledge gained in the laboratory to the many problems of memory in everyday life.

This project has depended crucially on the patience, help, and support of our colleagues at Psychology Press including Lucy Kennedy who played an important role in planning the book, and Rebekah Edmondson, Veronica Lyons, and Tara Stebnicky who ensured that the plans became a reality. We are also grateful to Michael Forster who proposed the book and provided sustained enthusiasm for it through its long gestation. ADB's contribution owes a great deal to Lindsey Bowes, who not only typed his rambling dictations, but also provided invaluable help with finding references and overcoming the many IT glitches experienced by those of us whose semantic memory comes principally from a pre-computer age. Finally, I am grateful to my wife Hilary, for her support and tolerance of my excuses for not doing the manly chores expected of a husband, initially because I was writing a book on working memory, duly followed by my embarking on the present book. Ah well, back to the chores!

MCA is very grateful to Elke Geraerts, who provided highly useful comments on earlier drafts, and who was incredibly supportive during the preparation of his chapters. He was especially appreciative of the regular supply of tasty baguette sandwiches she made for lunch, and the periodic *Kinder Surprise* chocolate egg, with the prize inside. Nothing like a chocolate egg to make the writing flow. MCA is also very grateful to Justin Hulbert, who made useful comments on his chapters; preparing all figures and their captions, key terms, supplementary PowerPoints, and biographies with dizzying efficiency.

MWE is also extremely grateful to his wife, Christine, for her unflagging support. She has become used to the fact that I have been involved almost continuously in book writing for the past 25 years or so. I don't have anyone to thank for typing up my chapters because (ill-advisedly or not) I have always done my own word processing!

Alan Baddeley

CHAPTER 1

WHAT IS MEMORY?

Alan Baddeley

Memory is something we complain about. Why? Why are we quite happy to claim "I have a terrible memory!" but not to assert that "I am amazingly stupid"? Of course, we do forget; we do sometimes forget appointments and fail to recognize people we have met in the past, and rather more frequently we forget their names. We do not, however, often forget important events; if the bridegroom failed to turn up for his wedding he would not be believed if he claimed to have forgotten. Consequently, failing to recognize an old acquaintance suggests that the person was perhaps not of great importance to us. The obvious excuse is to blame one's terrible memory.

In the chapters that follow, we will try to convince you that your memory is in fact remarkably good, although fallible. We agree with Schacter (2001) who, having described what he refers to as the seven sins of memory, accepts that the sins are in fact the necessary consequences of the virtues that make our memories so rich and flexible. Our memories might be less reliable than those of the average computer but they are just as capacious, much more flexible, and a good deal more user friendly. Let us begin by considering the case of Clive Wearing who has the misfortune to have had much of his memory capacity destroyed by disease (Wilson, Baddeley, & Kapur, 1995).

WHY DO WE NEED MEMORY?

Clive is an extremely talented musician, an expert on early music who was master of a major London choir. He himself sang and was asked to perform before the Pope during a papal visit to London. In 1985, he had the misfortune to suffer a brain infection from the herpes simplex virus, a virus that exists in a large proportion of the population, typically leading to nothing worse than cold sores but very occasionally breaking through the blood–brain barrier to cause encephalitis, an inflammation of the brain that can prove fatal. In recent years, treatment has improved, with the result that patients are more likely to survive, although often having suffered from extensive brain damage, typically in areas responsible for memory.

When he eventually recovered consciousness, Clive was densely amnesic and appeared to be unable to store information for periods longer than seconds. His interpretation of his plight was to assume that he had just recovered consciousness, something that he would announce to any visitor, and something that he repeatedly recorded in a notebook, each time crossing out the previous line and writing "I have now recovered consciousness" or "consciousness has now finally been recovered," an activity that continued for many, many years.

Clive knew who he was and could talk about the broad outlines of his early life, although the detail was very sparse. He knew he had spent 4 years at Cambridge University, but could not recognize a photograph of his college. He could remember, although somewhat vaguely, important events in his life such as directing and conducting the first modern performance of Handel's *Messiah* using original instruments in an appropriate period setting, and could talk intelligently about the historical development of the role of the musical conductor. However, even this selected knowledge was sketchy; he had written a book on the early composer Lassus, but could not recall any of the content. Asked who had written *Romeo and Juliet*, Clive did not know. He had remarried, but could not remember this. However, he did greet his new wife with enormous enthusiasm every time she appeared, even though she might only have been out of the room for a few minutes; every time he declared that he had just recovered consciousness.

Clive was totally incapacitated by his amnesia. He could not read a book or follow a television program because he immediately forgot what had gone before. If he left his hospital room, he was immediately lost. He was locked into a permanent present, something he described as "hell on earth." "It's like being dead—all the bloody time!"

However, there was one aspect of Clive's memory that appeared to be unimpaired, that part concerned with music. When his choir visited him, he found that he could conduct them just as before. He was able to read the score of a song and accompany himself on the keyboard while singing it. For a brief moment he appeared to return to his old self, only to feel wretched when he stopped playing. Over 20 years later, Clive is still just as densely amnesic but now appears to have come to terms with his terrible affliction and is calmer and less distressed.

ONE MEMORY OR MANY?

Although Clive's case makes the point that memory is crucial for daily life, it does not tell us much about the nature of memory. Clive was unfortunate in having damage to a range of brain areas, with the result that he has problems that extend beyond his amnesia. Furthermore, the fact that Clive's musical memory and skills are unimpaired suggests that memory is not a single simple system. Other studies have showed that densely amnesic patients can repeat back a telephone number, suggesting preserved immediate memory, and that they can learn motor skills at a normal rate. As we will see later, amnesic patients are capable of a number of types of learning, demonstrating this by improved performance, even though they do not remember the learning experience and typically deny having encountered the situation before. The evidence suggests, therefore, that rather than having a single global memory system, the picture is more complex. The first few chapters of this book will try to unpack some of this complexity, providing a basis for later chapters that are concerned with the way in which these systems influence our lives, how memory changes as we move through childhood to adulthood and old age, and what happens when our memory systems break down.

In giving our account of memory, we are of course presenting a range of psychological theories. Theories develop and change, and different people will hold different theories to explain the same data. As a glance at any current memory journal will indicate, this is certainly the case for the study of memory. Fortunately, there is a great deal of general agreement between different groups studying the psychology of memory, even though they tend to use somewhat different terminology. At this point, it might be useful to say a little bit about the concept of theory that underpins our own approach.

THEORIES, MAPS, AND MODELS

What should a psychological theory look like? In the 1950s, many people thought they should look like theories from physics. Clark Hull studied the learning behavior of white rats and attempted to use his results to build a rather grand general theory of learning in which the learning behavior of both rats and people was predicted using a series of postulates and equations that were explicitly modeled on the example set by Isaac Newton (Hull, 1943).

By contrast, Hull's great rival, Edward Tolman (1948), thought of rats as forming "cognitive maps," internal representations of their environment that were acquired as a result of active exploration. The controversy rumbled on from the 1930s to the 1950s, and then was abandoned quite suddenly. Both sides found that they had to assume some kind of representation that went beyond the simple association between stimuli impinging on the rat and its learned behavior, but neither seemed to have a solution to the problem of how these could be investigated.

The broad view of theory that we shall take is that theories are essentially like maps. They summarize our knowledge in a simple and structured way that helps us to understand what we know. A good theory will help us to ask new questions and that in turn will help us find out more about the topic we are mapping. The nature of the theory will depend on the questions we want to answer, just as in the case of maps of a city. The map that will help you travel by *underground* around London or New York looks very different from the sort of map that you would need if you wanted to walk, with neither being a direct representation of what you would see if you stood at a given location. That does not of course mean that they are bad maps, quite the opposite, because each map is designed to serve a different purpose.

In the case of psychological theories, different theories will operate at different levels of explanation and focus on different issues. An argument between a shopkeeper and customer, for example, would be explained in very different ways by a sociologist, who might emphasize the economic and social pressures, a social psychologist interested in interpersonal relationships, a cognitive

psychologist interested in language, and a physiological psychologist who might be interested in the emotional responses of the two disputants and how these are reflected in the brain. All of these explanations are relevant and in principle should be relatable to each other, but none is the "correct" interpretation.

This is a view that contrasts with what is sometimes called **reductionism**. This assumes that the aim of science is to reduce each explanation to the level below: Social psychology to cognitive psychology, which in turn should be explained physiologically, with the physiology then being interpreted biochemically and ultimately in terms of physics. Although it is clearly valuable to be able to explain phenomena at different but related levels, this is ultimately no more sensible than for a physicist to demand that we should attempt to design bridges on the basis of subatomic particle physics, rather than Newtonian mechanics.

The aim of the present book is to outline what we know of the *psychology* of memory. We believe that an account at the psychological level will prove valuable in throwing light on accounts of human behavior at the interpersonal and social level, and will play an important role in our capacity to understand the neurobiological factors that underpin the various types of memory. We suggest that the psychology of memory is sufficiently understood to begin to interface very fruitfully with questions at both of these levels, and hope to illustrate this over the subsequent chapters.

In a surprisingly short period of time during the 1960s, the dominant focus of interest within the study of learning and memory moved from the analysis of learning in animals to the study of memory in humans. One

KEY TERM

Reductionism: The view that all scientific explanations should aim to be based on a lower level of analysis: psychology in terms of physiology, physiology in terms of chemistry, and chemistry in terms of physics.

Ebbinghaus (1850–1909) was the first person to demonstrate that it was possible to study memory experimentally. © Bettmann/Corbis.

ambitious building of grand theories such as that proposed by Clark Hull. When the grand theories appeared to collapse, however, the more staid approach that had previously been disparagingly discounted by its critics as "dust bowl empiricism" began to attract a broader range of investigators interested in studying learning and memory. This led to the founding of a new journal *The Journal of Verbal Learning and Verbal Behavior*, which, when the term "verbal learning" later became unfashionable, became *The Journal of Memory and Language*.

A second development that occurred at this point had its roots in both Europe and North America. In the 1930s, a German approach known as **Gestalt psychology** began attempting to apply ideas developed in the study of perception to the understanding of human memory. Unlike the behaviorist approaches, *Gestalt* psychologists tended to emphasize the importance of internal representations rather than observable stimuli and responses, and to stress the active role of the remember. Gestalt psychology suffered badly from Nazi persecution, but enough Gestalt psychologists moved to North America to sow the seeds of an alternative approach to verbal learning; an approach that placed much more emphasis on the activity of the learner in organizing material. This approach was typified by two investigators who had grown up in Europe but had then been trained in North America: George Mandler and Endel Tulving.

In Britain, a third approach to memory developed, based on Frederic Bartlett's (1932) book *Remembering*. Bartlett explicitly rejected the learning of meaningless material

approach that gained in popularity at this time reflected an approach to memory that had its roots in the work of Herman Ebbinghaus, a nineteenth-century German philosopher who was the first person to demonstrate that it was possible to study memory experimentally.

The Ebbinghaus tradition was subsequently most strongly developed in the US, focusing particularly on the factors and conditions surrounding the important question of how new learning interacted with what was already known. Results were interpreted in terms of associations that were assumed to be formed between stimuli and responses, using a limited range of methods that typically involved remembering lists of words or nonwords (McGeoch & Irion, 1952). This is often referred to as the **verbal learning** approach. It developed from the 1930s to the 1960s, particularly in mid-Western laboratories, and emphasized the careful mapping of phenomena rather than the

KEY TERMS

Verbal learning: A term applied to an approach to memory that relies principally on the learning of lists of words and nonsense syllables.
Gestalt psychology: An approach to psychology that was strong in Germany in the 1930s and that attempted to use perceptual principles to understand memory and reasoning.

as an appropriate way to study memory, using instead complex material such as folk tales from other cultures, and stressing the importance of the rememberer's "effort after meaning." This approach emphasized the study of the memory errors that people made, explaining them in terms of the participants' cultural assumptions about the world. Bartlett proposed that these depended on internal representations that he referred to as **schemas**. His approach differed radically from the Ebbinghaus tradition, relying on quite complex tasks but, as was the case with the later followers of Tolman and Hull, Bartlett was left with the problem of how to study these elusive inner representations of the world.

A possible answer to this problem evolved gradually during the Second World War with the development of computers. Mathematicians such as Weiner (1950) in the US, and physiologists such as Gray Walter (1953) in the UK described machines that were able to demonstrate a degree of control that resembled purposive behavior. During the 1940s, a Scottish psychologist, Kenneth Craik (1943), working with Bartlett in Cambridge produced a brief but influential book entitled *The Nature of Explanation*. Here he proposed the idea of representing theories as **models**, and using the computer to develop such models. He carried out what were probably the first psychological experiments based on this idea, using analog computers (digital computers were still being invented) and applying his computer-based theoretical model to the practical problem of gun-aiming in tanks. Tragically, in 1945 he was killed in a traffic accident while still a young man.

Fortunately, the new approach to psychology, based on the computer metaphor, was being taken up by a range of young investigators, and in the years following the war, this information-processing approach to psychology became increasingly influential. Two books were particularly important. Donald Broadbent's *Perception and Communication* (1958) developed and applied Craik's seminal ideas to a range of work carried out at the Medical Research Council Applied Psychology Unit in Cambridge, England, much of it stimulated by practical problems originating during the war. Some 9 years later, this growing field was then brilliantly synthesized and summarized by Ulric Neisser (1967) in a book whose title provided a name for this burgeoning field: *Cognitive Psychology*.

Using the digital computer as an analogy, human memory could be regarded as comprising one or more storage systems. Any memory system—whether physical, electronic, or human—requires three things, the capacity to *encode*, or enter information into the system, the capacity to *store* it, and—subsequently—the capacity to find and *retrieve* it. However, although these three stages serve different functions, they interact: The method of registering material or encoding determines what and how the information is stored, which in turn will limit what can subsequently be retrieved. Consider a simple physical memory device, a shopping list. If it is to work, you need to write legibly in a language the recipient shopper understands. If it were to get wet, the ink would blur (impaired storage) making it less distinct and harder to read (retrieval). Retrieval would be harder if your handwriting was poor (an encoding-retrieval interaction), and if the writing was smudged (a storage-retrieval interaction). The situation is further complicated by the discovery that our memories comprise not one, but several interrelated memory systems.

HOW MANY KINDS OF MEMORY?

As the influence of the cognitive approach to psychology grew, the balance of opinion

---

KEY TERMS

Schema: Proposed by Bartlett to explain how our knowledge of the world is structured and influences the way in which new information is stored and subsequently recalled.
Model: A method of expressing a theory more precisely, allowing predictions to be made and tested.

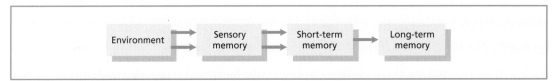

Figure 1.1 An information-processing approach to memory. Information flows from the environment through sensory storage and short-term storage to long-term memory.

moved from the assumption of a single memory system based on stimulus–response associations towards the idea that two, three, or perhaps more memory systems were involved. Figure 1.1 shows the broad view that came to be widely accepted during the 1960s. It assumed that information comes in from the environment and is first processed by a series of sensory memory systems, which could be best regarded as providing an interface between perception and memory. Information is then assumed to be passed on to a temporary short-term memory system, before being registered in long-term memory. A particularly influential version of this model was proposed by Atkinson and Shiffrin (1968). It was dubbed the **modal model** because it was representative of many similar models of the operation of human memory that were proposed at the time. As we shall see, a number of the assumptions underlying this model were subsequently questioned, causing it to be further elaborated.

The question of how many kinds of memory remains controversial. Some theorists object to the very concept of a memory *store* as too static, arguing instead that we should be concerned with *processes* (e.g. Nairne, 1990, 2002; Neath & Surprenant, 2003). They point to similarities across a range of very different memory tasks and suggest that these imply common processes, and hence a unitary memory system. Our own view is that we need to think in terms of both structures such as stores and the processes that operate on them, just as an analysis of the brain requires the contribution of both static anatomical features and a more dynamic concern with physiology. We should certainly look for similarities across domains in the way that these systems perform,

but the presence of common features should not encourage us to ignore the differences.

Fortunately, regardless of the question of whether one emphasizes similarities or differences, the broad picture remains the same. We ourselves use the distinctions between types of memory as a way of organizing and structuring our knowledge of human memory. As discussed below, we assume separate sensory, short-term, and long-term memory systems, each of which can be subdivided into separate components. We do not, however, assume the simple flow of information from the environment into long-term memory that is suggested in Figure 1.1, as there is abundant evidence that information flows in both directions. For example, our knowledge of the world, stored in long-term memory, can influence our focus of attention, which will then determine what is fed into the sensory memory systems, how it is processed, and whether it is subsequently remembered.

We begin with a brief account of **sensory memory**. This was an area of considerable activity during the 1960s and provides a good illustration of the general principles of encoding, storage, and retrieval. However, given that it relates more to perception than memory, it will not be covered in the remainder of the book. Our outline continues with introductory

KEY TERMS

Modal model: A term applied to the model of memory developed by Atkinson and Shiffrin (1968).
Sensory memory: A term applied to the brief storage of information within a specific modality.

accounts of short-term and working memory, before moving to a brief preliminary survey of long-term memory.

SENSORY MEMORY

If you wave your hand while holding a sparkler in a dark room, it leaves a trail, which rapidly fades. The fact that the image persists long enough to draw an apparent line suggests that it is being stored in some way, and the fact that the line rapidly fades implies some simple form of forgetting. This phenomenon forms the basis for movies; a sequence of static images is presented rapidly, with blank intervals in between, but is perceived as a continuous moving image. This occurs because the perceptual system stores the visual information long enough to bridge the gap between the static images, integrating each one with the next, very slightly different, image.

In the early 1960s, a number of investigators at Bell Laboratories in the US used the new information-processing approach to analyze this fleeting visual memory system (Sperling, 1960, 1963; Averbach & Sperling, 1961), which subsequently came to be known as **iconic memory**. Sperling (1960) briefly presented a visual array of twelve letters in three rows of four, and then asked for recall (Figure 1.2). People could typically remember four or five items correctly. If you try this task, however, you will have the sensation that you have seen more than four or five, but that they have gone before you can report them. One way of avoiding the problem of forgetting during reporting is to present the same array and reduce the number of items to be reported, but not tell the participant in advance which ones will be selected for recall. Sperling therefore required only one of the three lines to be reported, signaling the line to be recalled by presenting a tone; a high tone for the top line, a medium tone for line two, and a low tone for line three. As he did not tell the participants in advance which line would be cued, the report could be treated as representative of the whole

Figure 1.2 Stimulus array used by Sperling. Although 12 letters were presented, participants only had to recall the row that was cued by a high, medium, or low tone.

array; multiplying the score by three will thus give an estimate of the total number of letters stored. However, as shown in Figure 1.3, this depends on when the recall tone is presented. When recall is tested immediately, it should provide an estimate of the total capacity of the memory store, with the fall-off in performance as the tone is delayed representing the loss of information. Note that Figure 1.3 shows two curves, one with a bright field before and after the letters, and the other with the letters preceded and followed by a dark visual field. A subsequent experiment (Sperling, 1963) found that the brighter the light during the interval, the poorer the performance, suggesting that the light is interfering with the memory trace in some way, a process known as **masking**.

In fact, two separable forms of interference were found, only one of which appears to depend on the light energy of the interfering mask. A second effect depends on whether the

KEY TERMS

Iconic memory: A term applied to the brief storage of visual information.
Masking: A process by which the perception and/or storage of a stimulus is influenced by events occurring immediately before presentation (forward masking) or more commonly after (backward masking).

Figure 1.3 Estimated number of letters available using the partial report method, as a function of recall delay. From Sperling (1963). Copyright © 1963 by The Human Factors and Ergonomics Society. All rights reserved. Reproduced with permission.

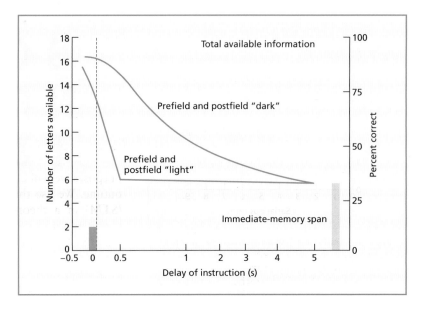

mask contains visual contours. The brightness effect occurs only when the letters and the light flash are presented to the *same* eye, suggesting that it is happening before information from the two eyes is combined. The contour-based pattern mask effect occurs even when the stimulus and mask are presented to *different* eyes, suggesting that it disrupts storage at some point after streams of information from the two eyes have been combined (Turvey, 1973).

Could it be that requiring the recall of as few as three letters causes interference that underestimates the visual storage capacity? This appears not to be the case as similar results are obtained when a single letter is probed by placing a bar underneath the item that must be reported. The visual nature of the store is reflected in the fact that it can be probed by specifying any of a range of visual features (including the color, size, or shape of the item to be reported), for example, asking for the *red* letters (Turvey & Kravetz, 1970; von Wright, 1968), but not when a nonphysical dimension is used, for example, asking for the digits from a mix of letters and digits (Sperling, 1960).

Sperling interpreted his data as suggesting that letters are read off from a peripheral visual store, at a rate of about one letter every 10 milliseconds, into a more durable store that

he termed the *recognition buffer*. This was assumed to be capable of holding information in a form that makes it possible to report, a process that Sperling suggests operates at a much slower rate than the 100 letters per second read-out from the peripheral visual store. In his subsequent account of this work, Neisser (1967) suggested the term *iconic memory* for the initial brief visual store.

The name suggested by Neisser for its auditory equivalent was **echoic memory**. If you are asked to remember a long telephone number, then your pattern of errors will differ depending on whether the number is heard or read. With visual presentation, the likelihood of an error increases systematically from the beginning to the end of the sequence, whereas, as shown in Figure 1.4, with auditory presentation the last one or two items are much more likely to be correct than are items in the middle of the list (Murdock, 1967). This recency advantage can be removed by interposing another spoken item between presentation

KEY TERM

Echoic memory: A term sometimes applied to auditory sensory memory.

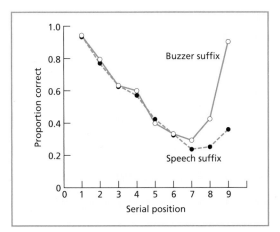

Figure 1.4 Serial recall of a nine-item list when an additional item, the suffix, is either the spoken word *zero* or a sound made by a buzzer. From Crowder (1972). Copyright © 1972 Massachusetts Institute of Technology by permission of the MIT Press.

and recall, even when this item itself does not need to be processed, and is always the same, for example a simple key press (Conrad, 1960). In an extensive series of experiments, Crowder and Morton (1969; Crowder & Raeburn, 1970; Crowder, 1971) showed that the nature of this suffix is critical. A visual or nonspeech-like auditory suffix, such as a buzzer, does not disrupt performance, whereas a spoken suffix does, regardless of its meaning.

Crowder and Morton postulated what they term a precategorical acoustic store as the basis for the auditory recency effect. However, the question of whether the process responsible for the enhanced auditory recency effect is better regarded as a form of memory or an aspect of perception remains controversial (Jones, Hughes, & Macken, 2007; but see also Baddeley & Larsen, 2007). Regardless of its interpretation, the auditory recency component is sufficiently large and robust to play a potentially significant role in studies of verbal short-term memory, and has even been proposed as an alternative to more conventional views of performance on short-term verbal memory tasks (Jones et al., 2007). We will return to this issue when discussing short-term memory. In the meantime, it seems likely that an adequate explanation of echoic memory will need to be fully integrated with a broader theory of speech perception.

SHORT-TERM AND WORKING MEMORY

As this topic, and that of long-term memory, forms a major part of the book, for present purposes we will limit ourselves to a very brief outline. We use the term **short-term memory (STM)** in a theory-neutral way to refer to the temporary storage of small amounts of material over brief delays. This leaves open the question of how this storage is achieved. In most, if not all, situations there is likely to be a contribution to performance from long-term memory that will need to be taken into account in evaluating the role of any more temporary storage systems. Much of the work in this area has used verbal material, and there is no doubt that even when the stimuli are not verbal, people will often use verbal rehearsal to help maintain their level of performance over a brief delay (see Chapter 2). It is important to bear in mind, however, that STM is not limited to verbal material, and has been studied extensively for visual and spatial information, and much less extensively for smell and touch.

The concept of **working memory** is based on the assumption that a system exists for the temporary maintenance and manipulation of information, and that this is helpful in performing many complex tasks. A number of different models of working memory have been proposed, with the nature of each model tending to depend on the particular area of interest of the theorist, and their

---

KEY TERMS

Short-term memory: A term applied to the retention of small amounts of material over periods of a few seconds.
Working memory: A memory system that underpins our capacity to "keep things in mind" when performing complex tasks.

theoretical style. However, most assume that working memory acts as a form of mental workspace, providing a basis for thought. It is usually assumed to be linked to attention, and to be able to draw on other resources within short-term and long-term memory (Miyake & Shah, 1999a). By no means all approaches, however, emphasize the role of memory rather than attention. One approach that does so is the multicomponent model proposed originally by Baddeley and Hitch in 1974 as a means of linking research on the psychology and neuropsychology of STM to its functional role in performing important cognitive activities such as reasoning, comprehension, and learning. This approach has continued to prove productive for over 30 years (Baddeley, 2007) and is the principal focus of Chapter 3, on working memory.

LONG-TERM MEMORY

We shall use the classification of **long-term memory** proposed by Squire (1992a). As shown in Figure 1.5, this classification makes a broad distinction between **explicit** or **declarative memory** and **implicit** or **nondeclarative memory**. Explicit memory refers to situations that we would generally think of as involving memory, both for specific *events*, such as meeting a friend unexpectedly on holiday last year, and remembering *facts* or information

> ### KEY TERMS
>
> **Long-term memory:** A system or systems assumed to underpin the capacity to store information over long periods of time.
> **Explicit/declarative memory:** Memory that is open to intentional retrieval, whether based on recollecting personal events (episodic memory) or facts (semantic memory).
> **Implicit/nondeclarative memory:** Retrieval of information from long-term memory through performance rather than explicit conscious recall or recognition.
> **Semantic memory:** A system that is assumed to store accumulative knowledge of the world.
> **Episodic memory:** A system that is assumed to underpin the capacity to remember specific events.

about the world, for example the meaning of the word *testify* or the color of a ripe banana. Implicit memory refers to situations in which some form of learning has occurred, but which is reflected in *performance* rather than through overt remembering: riding a bicycle for example or reading a friend's handwriting more easily because we have encountered it frequently in the past. We will briefly discuss these in turn, leaving a full exploration to subsequent chapters.

Explicit memory
As Figure 1.4 shows, this can be divided into two categories, **semantic** and **episodic**

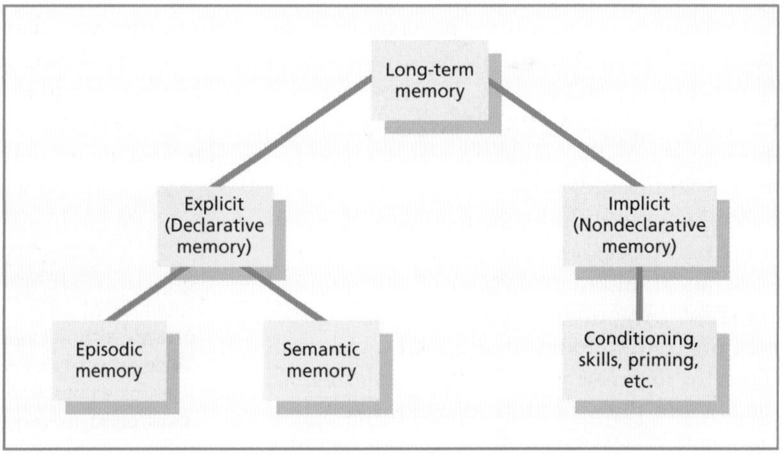

Figure 1.5 Components of long-term memory as proposed by Squire (1992a).

memory. During the 1960s, computer scientists attempting to achieve automatic language processing discovered that their computer programs needed to have built into them some kind of knowledge of the world, which could represent the meaning of the words being processed. This led psychologists to attempt to study the way in which humans store such semantic information. At a conference convened to discuss these new developments, a Canadian psychologist Endel Tulving (1972) proposed a distinction that was immediately adopted and has been used extensively ever since, that between *semantic* and *episodic* memory. Semantic memory refers to knowledge of the world. It goes beyond simply knowing the meaning of words and extends to sensory attributes such as the color of a lemon or the taste of an apple. It also includes general knowledge of how society works, what to do when you enter a restaurant, or how to book a theater seat. It is inherently general in nature, although it can in principle be acquired on a single occasion. If you heard that an old friend had died, this would be likely to become part of your general knowledge of that person, hence part of your semantic memory, although you might well forget where or when you had heard this.

Semantic memory goes beyond the meaning of words, and extends to sensory attributes such as taste and color; and to general knowledge of how society works, such as how to behave in a grocery store.

If you subsequently recall the particular occasion when and where you had learned this sad news, then this would be an instance of *episodic memory*, which underpins the capacity to remember specific single episodes or events. Hence, a given event can be registered in both types of memory. Tulving himself (2002) limits the use of the term "episodic memory" to situations in which you actually re-experience some aspect of the original episode, for example remembering how surprised you were that your informant knew your old friend. Tulving refers to this capacity as **mental time travel** and emphasizes its value, both in allowing us to recollect and "relive" individual events, and to use that information for planning a future action, for example sending a letter of condolence. It is this capacity to acquire and retrieve memories for particular events that tends to be most severely disrupted in amnesic patients, and it is this deficit that has made Clive Wearing's life so unbearably difficult.

How are semantic and episodic memory related? One possibility is that semantic memory is simply the residue of many episodes. For example, I know that Madrid is the capital of Spain, not only because I was told it at school but also because I have encountered this fact in countless news-reels and had it reinforced by visiting Madrid. Consistent with this assumed role of episodic memory in forming semantic memory is the fact that most amnesic patients have difficulty in building up new semantic knowledge. They typically would not know the name of the current President of the United States of America, or what year it is, or which teams were doing well in their favorite sport. This suggests that although semantic and episodic memory might possibly

KEY TERM

Mental time travel: A term coined by Tulving to emphasize the way in which episodic memory allows us to relive the past and use this information to imagine the future.

involve separate systems, they clearly interact (Tulving, 2002).

Implicit memory

Amnesic patients thus tend to show not only grossly disturbed episodic memory, but also a greatly impaired capacity to add to their store of knowledge of the world. There are however a number of situations in which they do appear to learn at a normal rate, and the study of these preserved capacities has had an important influence on the development of the concept of implicit or nondeclarative memory. Some of these preserved capacities are shown in Figure 1.5.

One preserved form of learning is simple **classical conditioning**. If a tone is followed by a brief puff of air to the eye, amnesic patients will learn to blink in anticipation (Weiskrantz & Warrington, 1979). Despite learning at a normal rate, they do not remember the experience and cannot explain the function of the nozzle that delivers the air puff to their eye. Amnesic patients can also learn motor skills, such as improving with practice the capacity to keep a stylus in contact with a moving spot of light (Brooks & Baddeley, 1976). Warrington and Weiskrantz (1968) demonstrated that word learning was also preserved in densely amnesic patients under certain conditions. They presented their patients with a list of unrelated words and then tested for retention in a number of different ways. When asked to recall the words or recognize which of the subsequent sequence of words had already been presented, the patients performed very poorly. However, when the nature of the test was changed to one in which the task was to "guess" a word when given the first few letters, both patients and normal participants were likely to "guess" a word that had been seen earlier (e.g. see *metal*, guess a word given *me – – –*). Patients could take full advantage of their prior experience, despite failing to remember that they had even been shown any words earlier, indicating that *something* had been stored. As we shall see, this phenomenon, known as **priming**, is found in a range of perceptual tasks, both visual and auditory, and can also be found in the progressive improvement in more complex activities such as reading mirror writing (Cohen & Squire, 1980) or assembling a jigsaw puzzle (Brooks & Baddeley, 1976).

Given that these are all examples of implicit learning and memory, do they all reflect a single memory system? While attempts continue to be made to account for them all in terms of a single system (see Neath & Surprenant, 2003), our own view is that although they have features in common, they represent a range of different learning systems using different parts of the brain that have evolved for different purposes.

EVERYDAY MEMORY

We have so far discussed the question of how to develop a theoretical understanding of human memory: how it encodes, stores, and retrieves information. However, if our theory is to be useful as well as informative, then it needs to be applicable beyond the confines of the laboratory, to tell about how our memories will work in the world. It must aim to extend beyond the student population, on which much of the research is based, and tell us about how memory functions in children and the elderly, across different cultures, and in health and disease. We tackle some of these issues in our later chapters.

KEY TERMS

Classical conditioning: A learning procedure whereby a neutral stimulus (e.g. a bell) that is paired repeatedly with a response-evoking stimulus (e.g. meat powder), will come to evoke that response (salivation).

Priming: The process whereby presentation of an item influences the processing of a subsequent item, either making it easier to process (positive priming) or more difficult (negative priming).

It is of course much more difficult to run tightly controlled experiments outside the laboratory, with the result that most of the theoretically focused studies that inform the initial chapters are laboratory based. Some investigators argue that we should confine our research to the laboratory, extending it only when we have a thorough understanding of memory. Others have followed Bartlett in suggesting that this is likely to lead to the neglect of important aspects of memory. In response to this rather conservative view, a group of psychologists in South Wales enthusiastically convened an international conference concerned with practical aspects of memory. It was a great success, with people coming from all over the world to talk about their research on topics ranging from memory for medical information to sex differences in facial memory, and from expert calculators to brain-damaged patients (Gruneberg, Morris, & Sykes, 1978).

Ulric Neisser was invited to give the opening address. In it, he lamented the laboratory-based tradition declaring that "If X is an interesting or socially significant aspect of memory, then psychologists have hardly ever studied X!" (Neisser, 1978, p. 4). He was of course preaching to an audience of the converted, whose work was already refuting his claim. However, his address was less well received in other quarters, resulting in a paper complaining of "the bankruptcy of everyday memory" (Banaji & Crowder, 1989). This led to a lively, although rather unfruitful, controversy, given that it was based on the false assumption that psychologists should limit their research to either the laboratory or the world beyond. Both approaches are valuable. It is certainly easier to develop and test our theories under controlled laboratory conditions, but if they tell us little or nothing about the way in which memory works in the world outside, they are of distinctly limited value.

In general, attempts to generalize our theories have worked well, and have in turn enriched theory. One important application of theory is to the memory performance of particular groups such as children, the elderly, and patients with memory problems. As we will see, these not only demonstrate the robustness and usefulness of cognitive theory, but have also provided ways of testing and enriching theory. A good case in point is the study of patients with a very dense but pure amnesia, which has told us about the everyday importance of episodic memory, has helped develop tests and rehabilitation techniques for clinical neuropsychologists, and has, at the same time, had a major impact on our theories of memory.

A second major benefit from moving beyond the laboratory comes from a realization that certain very important aspects of memory were not being directly covered by existing theories. Some of these have led to important new theoretical developments. This is the case with the study of semantic memory, which, as mentioned earlier, was initially prompted by the attempt of computer scientists to develop programs that could understand language (Collins & Quillian, 1969). Another area of very active research that was driven by a practical need is that of eyewitness testimony, where it became clear that the failure of the judiciary to understand the limitations of human memory was often leading to potentially very serious miscarriages of justice (Loftus, 1979). Other areas have developed as a result of identifying practical problems that have failed to be addressed by theory. A good example of this is prospective memory, remembering to do things. This use of memory is of great practical importance, but for many years was neglected because it reflects a complex interaction between attention and memory. These broader topics are covered in the latter part of the book, which will illustrate the now widely accepted view that theoretical and practical approaches to memory are allies and not rivals.

The contribution of neuroscience

Both the Ebbinghaus and Bartlett approaches to the study of memory were based on the psychological study of memory performance in normal individuals. In recent years, however, this approach has increasingly been enriched by data from neuroscience, looking at the contribution of the brain to our capacity to learn and remember. Throughout this book, you will come across cases in which the study of memory disorders in patients has thrown light on the normal functioning of human memory. In particular, the problems faced by patients with memory problems can often tell us about the function that our memories serve, and how they can be further investigated.

Neuropsychological studies of patients fall into two very broad categories. One approach is concerned with understanding specific diseases such as Alzheimer's disease, for which the memory deficit is a defining feature. However, such deficits are rarely pure. Indeed, a diagnosis of Alzheimer's disease requires that the memory deficit be accompanied by other cognitive failings. Because these can be many and varied, it is hard to tease out exactly what aspect of the patient's cognitive deficit is based on memory and what on other problems. Such disease-related studies are important for understanding the disease, how it can be diagnosed, and how the patient can be helped to cope with its consequences. However, because of the complexity of interpreting the many possible contributing factors, such patients are less valuable for developing and testing theory.

A much more theoretically powerful contribution to our understanding comes from rare cases who have a very specific and pure deficit in one particular aspect of cognition. A very good example of this comes from the case of patient HM (Milner, 1966), who became densely amnesic following brain surgery to treat his intractable epilepsy. His case was important for two reasons: First, because it identified the importance of the hippocampal region of the brain for memory; second, because HM's memory deficit was limited to episodic long-term memory. The fact that other types of memory were preserved had an important influence on subsequent theories of memory.

However, although the study of the location of lesions in specific patients has provided useful insights, it is by no means necessarily the case that a patient with a very pure deficit will show a specific anatomical location of

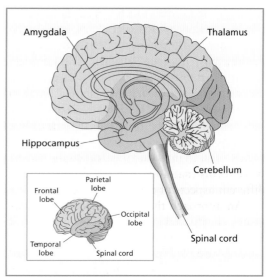

Figure 1.6 The human brain, showing those areas particularly related to memory.

damage, or vice versa. The brain is a hugely complex system, with functions often depending on more than one area, and with one part of the brain potentially allowing compensation for deficit in another. There are, however, broad generalities that have emerged from the study of brain damage as to which areas of the brain typically tend to play an important role in which type of memory. We will refer to these from time to time, usually in terms of the conventional division of the brain into the areas or lobes of the cortex and subcortical structures. Some of these are shown in Figure 1.6.

Neuroimaging human memory

In recent years, new techniques have developed, which allow the study of brain function in normal individuals when they perform different tasks, including those involved in memory (Rugg, 2002). The oldest of these is the **electroencephalogram (EEG)**, whereby the

---

KEY TERM

Electroencephalogram (EEG): A device for recording the electrical potentials of the brain through a series of electrodes placed on the scalp.

electrical activity of the brain is detected on the scalp through a series of electrodes. For many years, it has been possible to use this method to identify areas of abnormal brain activity that might be playing an important role in generating epileptic seizures. A range of techniques subsequently evolved whereby the brain activity evoked by particular stimuli can be measured. These **event-related potentials (ERPs)** result in a number of characteristic wave forms that appear to be associated with different aspects of cognitive processing.

An approach that has gained enormously in popularity and influence in recent years is that of **neuroimaging**, whereby various methods are used to monitor the functioning of the brain. The first neuroimaging studies relied on **positron emission tomography (PET)**, in which a radioactive substance is introduced into the bloodstream. The blood is taken up into the brain, with the most active brain areas absorbing most blood and showing the greatest concentration of radioactive emissions, which are then picked up by a series of detectors. This allows the sources of activation to be mapped within the brain. PET can also be used to track the operation of neurotransmitters within the brain. PET does however have some major drawbacks. Its reliance on radioactivity is expensive, and for safety reasons limits the

KEY TERMS

Event-related potentials (ERP): A method using electroencephalography, in which the electrophysiological reaction of the brain to specific stimuli is tracked over time.

Neuroimaging: A term applied to a range of methods whereby the brain can be studied, either in terms of its anatomical structure (structural imaging), or its operation (functional imaging).

Positron emission tomography (PET): A method whereby radioactively labeled substances are introduced into the bloodstream and subsequently monitored to measure physiological activation.

Magnetic resonance imaging (MRI): A method of brain imaging that relies on detecting changes induced by a powerful magnetic field.

amount of scanning that can be carried out on a single individual. It depends on averaging activation over time, which makes it unsuitable for teasing apart a sequence of rapidly changing processes of the type that typifies many cognitive tasks. Consequently, it has been overtaken as a means of functional imaging by functional **magnetic resonance imaging** (fMRI). This method depends on the fact that when the brain is placed in a strong magnetic field, different atomic nuclei align

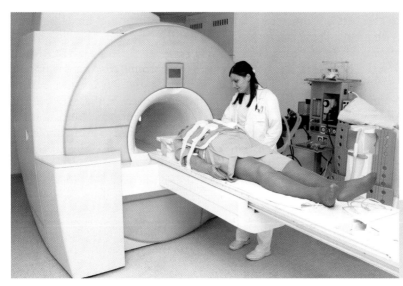

Functional magnetic resonance imaging (fMRI) scans have become an important source of data in psychology.

themselves in different orientations. It is safer than PET, being noninvasive of the body and not involving radioactivity. Unlike PET, fMRI allows brain oxygen levels to be monitored in real time, allowing individual events within the brain to be recorded as they happen, a method known as *event-related fMRI*.

An even finer temporal monitoring of brain activity is provided by a more recent development, **magnetoencephalography (MEG)**, in which the tiny magnetic forces generated by neurons within the brain are detected and located. The order in which different areas respond can be recorded very precisely,

KEY TERM

Magnetoencephalography (MEG): A system whereby the activity of neurons within the brain is detected through the tiny magnetic fields that their activity generates.

suggesting that this method has great future potential for studying the systems and processes within the brain that underpin cognitive activity. As we will see in later chapters, such methods are making a growing contribution to our understanding of human memory.

SUMMARY

Although we complain about our memories, they are remarkably efficient and flexible in storing the information we need and discarding what is less important. Many of our memory lapses result from this important need to forget, if we are to remember efficiently.

The study of memory began with Ebbinghaus, who greatly simplified the experimental situation in order to observe and quantify, an empirical tradition that continued in North America in the twentieth century. Alternative traditions developed in Germany, where the study of perception influenced the way in which Gestalt psychologists thought about memory, and in Britain, where Bartlett used a richer and less tightly constrained approach to memory.

During the 1950s and 1960s, the idea of models functioning as theories became influential with the development of the computer, resulting in an approach that became known as cognitive psychology. In the case of memory, this emphasized the need to distinguish between encoding or input into memory, memory storage, and memory retrieval. This led to the proposal of three broad types of memory: sensory memory, short-term memory, and long-term memory.

The information-processing model is very well illustrated in Sperling's model of visual sensory memory, in which the various stages were ingeniously separated and analyzed. At the same time, the auditory equivalent, echoic memory, began to be explored. These sensory systems have subsequently come to be regarded as part of the perceptual process rather than memory *per se*. They were assumed to lead into a temporary short-term or working memory. This was initially thought to be largely verbal in nature but other modalities were subsequently shown to be capable of temporary storage.

The short-term memory system was assumed to feed information into and out of long-term memory, which was further subdivided into explicit or declarative memory, and implicit or nondeclarative memory. Explicit memory was further divided into two types: The capacity to recollect individual experiences, allowing "mental time travel," became know as episodic memory, whereas our stored knowledge of the world was termed semantic memory.

A range of implicit or nondeclarative learning and memory systems were identified, including classical conditioning, the acquisition of motor skills, and various types of priming. Although there have been attempts to give a unitary explanation of implicit learning and memory, they are probably better regarded as separate systems.

An important development in recent years has been the increased interest in extending theory beyond the laboratory. This has led to controversy: It is clear that we need the laboratory to refine and develop our theories, but that we must move outside the laboratory to investigate their generality and practical importance.

The study of the relationship between memory and the brain has developed hugely over recent years. It began with amnesic patients and continues with the development of increasingly sophisticated ways of monitoring the ongoing activity of the healthy brain. Methods used include the study of the brain's electrical activity measured through scalp electrodes (*EEG* and *ERP*) and positron emission tomography (*PET*), in which the activity of the different regions of the brain can be monitored via blood flow. PET uses radioactive substances, imposing safety limitations on the amount of scanning, and is increasingly being replaced by functional magnetic resonance imaging (*fMRI*) and magnetoencephalography (*MEG*), which are less invasive and allow repeated testing of the same individual.

FURTHER READING

- **Banaji, M. R., & Crowder, R. G.** (1989). The bankruptcy of everyday memory. *American Psychologist, 44,* 1185–1193. A reply to Niesser's challenge.

- **Craik, K. J. W.** (1943). *The nature of explanation.* London: Cambridge University Press. A short but seminal book in cognitive psychology presenting the case for using models to embody theories, an approach that underpins the subsequent cognitive revolution.

- **Gruneberg, M. M., Morris, P. E., & Sykes, R. N.** (1978). *Practical aspects of memory.* London: Academic Press. The proceedings of a classic conference that can be said to have launched the everyday memory movement.

- **Neisser, U.** (1978). Memory: What are the important questions? In M. M. Gruneberg, P. E. Morris, & R. N. Sykes (Eds.), *Practical aspects of memory.* London: Academic Press. An influential paper in the movement to study everyday memory.

- **Rabbitt, P.** (2008). *Inside psychology: A science over 50 years.* New York: Oxford University Press. A series of personal views of the recent history of psychology from individuals who have been involved in a wide range of areas, including memory.

- **Roediger, H. L., Dudai, Y., & Fitzpatrick, S. M.** (2007). *Science of memory: Concepts.* Oxford: Oxford University Press. The proceedings of a conference at which leading figures in learning and memory were invited to summarize their interpretation of the basic concepts underlying the field, and to present their own views. Because available space was limited, this provides a very economical way of accessing current expert views concerning both the psychology and neuroscience of learning and memory.

- **Sperling, G.** (1963). A model for visual memory tasks. *Human Factors, 5,* 19–31. A very good example of the application of the information-processing approach to the study of sensory memory.

CHAPTER 2

SHORT-TERM MEMORY

Alan Baddeley

In 1887, John Jacobs, a schoolmaster in London, wanted to assess the abilities of his students. He devised an apparently simple test in which the student heard a sequence of digits, like a telephone number and repeated them back. The measure used was **digit span**, the longest sequence that could be repeated back without error (Jacobs, 1887). Digit span is still included in the most widely used intelligence test, the Wechsler Adult Intelligence Scale (WAIS). In this basic version, span does not correlate very highly with general intelligence but, as we will see, a somewhat more complex version, **working memory span**, does an excellent job of predicting a wide range of cognitive skills, including performance on the reasoning tasks often used to assess intelligence.

The digit span test is typically referred to as reflecting *short-term memory* (STM), and the more complex task as *working memory span*. The terms short-term memory (STM) and working memory (WM) seem often to be used interchangeably, so is there a difference?

SHORT-TERM AND WORKING MEMORY: WHAT'S THE DIFFERENCE?

The term "short-term memory" is a rather slippery one. To the general public, it refers to remembering things over a few hours or days, the sort of capacity that becomes poorer as we get older and is dramatically impaired in patients with Alzheimer's disease. To psychologists, however, these are long-term memory (LTM) problems. Remembering over a few minutes, hours, or a few years all seems to depend on the same long-term memory system.

We will use the term *short-term memory* (STM) to refer to performance on a particular type of task, one involving the simple retention of small amounts of information, tested either immediately or after a short delay. The memory system or systems responsible for STM form part of the *working memory* system. "Working memory" is the term we will use for a system that not only temporarily stores information but also manipulates it so as to allow people to perform such complex activities as reasoning, learning, and comprehension. Before going on to discuss working memory in the next chapter, we will examine the simpler concept of STM, the capacity to store small amounts of information over brief intervals, beginning with the digit span task devised by Jacobs.

We will use the term STM to describe the process of storing small amounts of

KEY TERMS

Digit span: Maximum number of sequentially presented digits that can reliably be recalled in the correct order.
Working memory span: Term applied to a range of complex memory span tasks in which simultaneous storage and processing is required.

information over a brief interval. As such, the term itself is theory-free, although there are of course theories as to how this is achieved.

In contrast to our use of STM simply to describe an experimental situation, the term *working memory* is based on a theoretical assumption, namely that tasks such as reasoning and learning depend on a system that is capable of temporarily holding and manipulating information, a system that has evolved as a mental work space. A number of different theoretical approaches to working memory have developed, some influenced strongly by the study of attention (e.g. Cowan, 2001), some on studies of individual differences in performance on complex tasks (e.g. Miyake, Friedman, Emerson, Witzki, Howerter, & Wager, 2000; Engle & Kane, 2004), and others driven by neurophysiological considerations (Goldman-Rakic, 1996). All, however, assume that WM provides a temporary workspace that is necessary for performing complex cognitive activities.

The approach used in the next two chapters reflects a multicomponent account of WM (Baddeley & Hitch, 1974) that was strongly influenced by the experimental and neuropsychological studies of human memory that form the core of the present book. It has proved durable and widely applicable, but should be seen as complementary to a range of other approaches rather than as *the* theory of working memory (Miyake & Shah, 1999a). The multicomponent model has relied heavily on studies of STM and has, as its most thoroughly explored component, the *phonological loop*, which provides a theoretical account of verbal STM. The present chapter is concerned with the major findings from studies of verbal and visual STM. It uses the phonological loop model to tie them together but also refers to other competing theories of STM. This leads on to Chapter 3, which goes beyond the study of STM, with its emphasis on short-term storage, to consider the question of why such temporary storage is needed and how it is used as part of a much broader concept, that of working memory.

MEMORY SPAN

Before proceeding, test yourself using Box 2.1.

If your digit span is rather lower than you might hope, don't worry; in this simple form, as we shall see later, it depends on a small but useful aspect of our memory system, not on general intelligence. Digit span is a classic short-term memory task, in that it involves holding a small amount of material for a short period of time.

The most obvious fact about digit span is that it is limited to about six or seven digits for most people, although some people can manage up to ten or more, whereas others have difficulty recalling more than four or five. What sets this limit and why does it vary between one person and the next?

Memory span measures require two things: (1) remembering what the *items* are; and (2) remembering the *order* in which they were presented. In the case of the digits one to nine, we already know the items very well,

---

Box 2.1 Digit span test
Read each sequence as if it were a telephone number, then close your eyes and try to repeat it back. Start with the four digit numbers, and continue until you fail on both sequences at a given length. Your span is one digit less than this.

9 7 5 4
3 8 2 5
9 4 3 1 8
6 8 2 5 9
9 1 3 8 2 5
6 4 8 3 7 1
7 9 5 8 4 2 3
5 3 1 6 8 4 2
8 6 9 5 1 3 7 2
5 1 7 3 9 8 2 6
7 1 9 3 8 4 2 6 1
1 6 3 8 7 4 9 5 2
9 1 5 2 4 3 8 1 6 2
7 1 5 4 8 5 6 1 9 3

so the test becomes principally one of memory for order. If, however, I were to present you with a sequence of digits in an unfamiliar language, Finnish for example, your span would be very much less. You would of course have much more to remember, as you would need to recall the order of the sounds comprising the Finnish digits, as well the order of the digits.

Suppose I were to use words, but not digits. Would that matter? Provided I used the same words repeatedly, you would soon become familiar with the set, and would do reasonably well. However, if I were to use a different set of words on each trial it would become somewhat harder as you would again need to remember both what the items were and their order, although this would be easier than for the unfamiliar Finnish digits.

How is order remembered? Not an easy question to answer. One might think that each number is associated or linked to the next, which is turn is linked to the next, a process known as *chaining*. The problem here is that if one link of the chain breaks, because one item is forgotten, then performance on all later items should collapse. In fact, although there is an increase in errors following a mistake, the subsequent decline is by no means as dramatic as chaining would predict. As we shall see, the simple task of explaining how the brain stores sequences remains controversial, not only for remembering words and numbers but also because learning and reproducing sequences of actions is essential for a wide range of activities, from simple reaching and grasping to the performance of a skilled athlete. Suppose we move from numbers to letters. Test yourself on the next sequence by reading each letter out loud, then close your eyes and try to repeat the letters in the order they are written.

C T A I I L T C S F R O

Now try the next sequence.

F R A C T O L I S T I C

I assume you found the second sequence easier, even though it used exactly the same letters as the first. The reason is that the order of the letters in the second sequence allowed you to break it up into pronounceable word-like subgroups or *chunks*. In a classic paper, George Miller (1956) suggested that memory capacity is limited not by the number of *items* to be recalled, but by the number of *chunks*. The first sequence comprised twelve apparently unrelated letters, making it hard to reduce the number of chunks much below twelve, whereas the second could be pronounced as a string of four syllables that, together, made a sequence that, although meaningless, could plausibly be an English word.

Chunking in this case depends on letter sequences that are consistent with long-term language habits. Grouping can also be induced by the rhythm with which a sequence of items is presented. Suppose I were to read out nine digits. If I interposed a slightly longer pause between items three and four and items six and seven, recall would be significantly improved. Hence 791-684-352 is easier than 791684352. Pauses in other locations can also be helpful, but grouping in threes seems to be best (Wickelgren, 1964; Ryan, 1969). It seems likely that the memory system is taking advantage of cues from prosody, the natural rhythms that occur in speech and that make its meaning clearer by separating into coherent phrases the continuous sequence of sounds that make up the normal speech stream.

Although remembering strings of numbers was probably of little interest to Mr Jacobs' students, it has in recent years become much more critical because of the increasing use in our culture of digit and letter sequences, initially as telephone numbers, then as zip codes, and subsequently as PINs and passwords. In the early 1960s, Dr R Conrad was tasked by the British Post and Telecommunications Service to investigate the relative advantages and disadvantages of codes based on letters and

KEY TERM

Chunking: The process of combining a number of items into a single chunk typically on the basis of long-term memory.

numbers. One of his experiments involved visually presenting strings of consonants for immediate recall. He noticed an interesting pattern in his results, namely that, despite being presented visually, errors were likely to be similar in *sound* to the item they replaced, hence *P* was more likely to be misremembered as *V* than the more visually similar letter *R* (Conrad, 1964). Conrad and Hull (1964) went on to investigate this effect further, demonstrating that memory for sequences of consonants is substantially poorer when they are similar in sound (e.g. *C V D P G T* versus *K R X L Y F*). Conrad interpreted his results in terms of a short-term memory store that relies on an acoustic code, which fades rapidly, resulting in forgetting. This was assumed to be particularly disruptive of recall of the acoustically similar letters as they had fewer distinguishing features, making each item more likely to be confused with adjacent items, resulting in errors in order of recall (e.g. *PTCVB* recalled as *PTVCB*).

TWO KINDS OF MEMORY?

Have you ever had the experience of walking from one room to another to pick something up, and by the time you arrive forgetting why you set off? If so, it is probably because you are thinking about something else, so that the original intention just slipped your mind. Lloyd and Margaret Peterson (1959), from the University of Indiana, developed a technique that could be seen as an analog of this experience. Participants were given an item to remember, a consonant triplet such as *XRQ*, and then distracted by being required to count backwards in threes from a given number (e.g. *371*: 368, 365, 362, etc.). After varying numbers of seconds of counting, they were asked to recall the triplet. Using a similar design, Murdock (1960) showed an equivalent effect for triplets of words (Figure 2.1).

How would you explain this? One possibility is that the numbers are interfering with memory of the letters. As we shall see in Chapter 9, there is abundant evidence that learning can be disrupted by subsequent activity. However, earlier research had shown that such interference depends on the *similarity* between the remembered and interfering material, and that for LTM at least, numbers do not interfere with letters (McGeogh & MacDonald, 1931). The Petersons therefore suggested their results reflected the rapid fading of a short-term memory trace. This interpretation was consistent with the

Figure 2.1 Short-term retention of consonant trigrams (Peterson & Peterson, 1959) and of one-word and three-word sequences (Murdock, 1961). From Melton (1963).

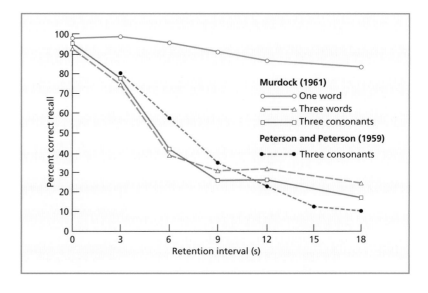

conclusion drawn by John Brown (1958) in England, based on a similar demonstration of short-term forgetting. It was however directly at odds with the widely held view at that

Forgetting, as a result of interference, depends on the similarity between the remembered and interfering material. We are more likely to forget our original intention when distracted by another similar thought or task.

time of memory as a unitary system, in which forgetting results from interference.

A simple trace decay interpretation was, however, challenged by Keppel and Underwood (1962), who showed that rapid forgetting was something that built up over the first four or five trials of the experiment. The very first triplet presented showed little or no forgetting. They argued that their results suggested the Peterson effect was attributable to interference from *earlier* triplets, which were, of course, similar in type to the remembered items. This hypothesis can be tested by changing the nature of the remembered items from one trial to the next.

As mentioned earlier, interference depends on similarity. Hence, if the previous item is not similar it should not cause forgetting. This was tested in a further experiment using word triplets in which each item in the given triplet came from the same semantic category: three birds, for example, or three colors. After five trials, all based on different examples of the same category (birds), the category was changed (e.g. to colors). As Figure 2.2 shows, performance declined steadily over the first five trials and recovered once the new category was introduced, only to decline once more until the category was changed once again (Loess, 1968).

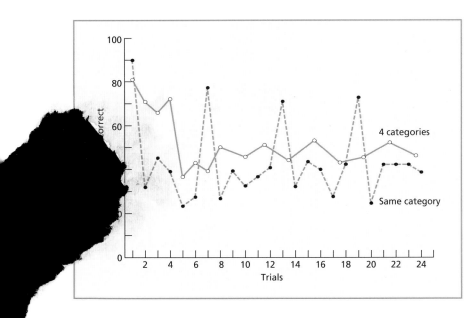

Figure 2.2 The release from the proactive interference effect. Participants were required to recall sets of four items from a single taxonomic category. After six sets, the category changed, resulting in enhanced performance on this set. Sets comprising items from all four categories show a steady decline and no release from proactive interference. From Loess (1968). Copyright © Elsevier. Reproduced with permission.

The simplest way of thinking about the **Peterson task** is in terms of the problem the participant has to solve, namely that of reproducing the *last* of a number of sequences that have been presented. The longer the delay before recall, the more difficult it is to distinguish which was the last, and which occurred slightly earlier. Considerable controversy ensued as to whether this could or could not fit into the existing stimulus–response interference theory (see Baddeley, 1993, pp. 31–37) however, there is broad agreement that the Peterson task demands on explanation in terms of retrieval processes that go beyond the initial hypothesis of simple trace decay.

Before going on to discuss further the question of trace decay versus interference, we should consider a second experimental paradigm that became both popular and theoretically controversial during the 1960s, namely **free recall**.

Free recall

In this task, participants are simply given lists of items, which they must then recall in any order they wish. Figure 2.3 shows the results of an experiment by Postman and Phillips (1965) in which 10, 20, or 30 words were presented, to be recalled immediately or after a 15-second filled delay. Their results illustrate a number of features characteristic of free recall including: (1) that the likelihood of recalling an *individual* item is less for longer lists, although the *total* number of items recalled is likely to increase; (2) that all lists showed a tendency for the first few items to be somewhat better recalled, the so-called **primacy effect**; (3) that, regardless of list length, if recall is immediate then the last few items are very well recalled, the **recency effect**; and (4) that this effect is eliminated by a brief delay filled by some activity such as counting.

How should we interpret this pattern of results? Evidence indicates that performance on the earlier items depends principally on LTM, with the primacy effect probably being due at least in part to the tendency to rehearse

the first few items as they come in, sometimes perhaps continuing to rehearse these items throughout the list (Rundus, 1971; Hockey, 1973; Tam & Ward, 2000). A whole range of variables is known to affect LTM influence performance on the early and middle part of the list (Glanzer, 1972). These include: (1) *presentation rate*: slower is better; (2) *word frequency*: familiar words are easier; (3) *imageability of the words* words that are visualizable are better; (4) *age of the participant*, young adults remember more than children or the elderly; and (5) *physiological state*: drugs such as marihuana and alcohol impair performance.

However, although these factors all influence overall performance, none of them has an equivalent impact on the recency effect. Postman and Phillips themselves offered an interpretation of their own results in terms of interference theory, although this does not readily explain why these factors influence overall retention but not recency.

The most popular interpretation during the 1960s was to assume that the recency effect reflected a temporary short-term store, which had different characteristics from the long-term store responsible for performance on earlier items (Glanzer, 1972). However, the assumption that recency simply reflects the output of a short-term store was subsequently challenged by the demonstration that recency effects can occur under conditions in which the short-term trace ought to have been disrupted. In one

KEY TERMS

The Peterson task: Short-ter
in which a small amount of ma
a brief delay filled by a rehear
Free recall: A method whe
presented with a sequence o
are subsequently required to
they wish.
Primacy effect: A tendency for th
items in a sequence to be better recalled
most of the following items.
Recency effect: A tendency for the last few
items in a list to be well recalled.

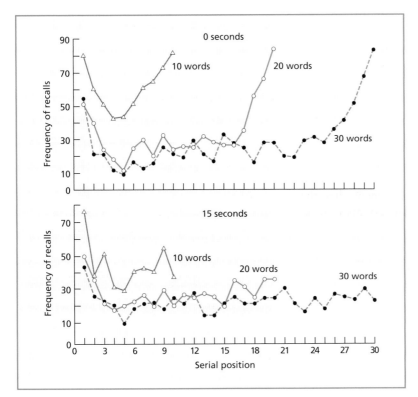

Figure 2.3 Serial position curves for lists of 10, 20, or 30 words recalled immediately or after a 15-second delay. Note that for each list length the last few items are very well recalled on immediate test—the recency effect—but not after the delay. From Postman and Phillips (1965). Copyright © Psychology Press.

study, Bjork and Whitten (1974) required their subjects to recall sequences of words presented under three conditions. The baseline condition involved presenting a list of words for immediate free recall. As expected, this resulted in a clear recency effect. In a second condition, the gap between presentation and recall was filled by a 20-second backward counting task, which—as expected—removed the recency effect. I̶   third, crucial condition, 20 seconds ̶   ̶ting was interposed between ̶   ̶s presented, as well as between ̶   st and recall. Under these con-̶   ̶ffect re-emerged.

̶   ̶ave also been demonstrated ̶   ntervals. In one study, for ̶   ̶ and Hitch (1977) tested ̶   ̶ rugby players to recall which tea̶   ̶d played that season; their recall show̶   clear recency effect. As not all the players had played in all the games, it proved possible to assess whether forgetting was more reflective of the amount of time elapsed, or

of the number of intervening games. Number of games proved to be the better predictor, suggesting that a simple decay hypothesis would not provide a good account of these findings. Similar **long-term recency** effects have been found in remembering parking location (Pinto & Baddeley, 1991), although—sadly—I can report that as I get older, even recency does not always prevent the need for an embarrassed wander around the grocery store parking lot.

The fact that recency effects are found across such a wide range of situations, with some cases being disrupted by a few seconds of unrelated activity such as counting whereas others persist over months, suggests that the recency effect is not limited to any single

KEY TERM

Long-term recency: A tendency for the last few items to be well recalled under conditions of long-term memory.

type of memory system but instead reflects a specific retrieval strategy that takes advantage of the fact that the most recent events are the most readily available to recall.

When was the last party you attended? Which was the party before that? And the one before? I suspect recalling your most recent party was the easiest, although it was perhaps not the best party.

The greater accessibility of the most recent experience of a given type could serve the highly important role of orienting yourself in space and time. When traveling and staying in a new hotel, how do you know where you are when you wake up? And when you leave the hotel for dinner, how do you remember your current room number and don't recall instead the number from last night or the night before that?

As in the case of the Peterson effect, the most plausible interpretation of recency seems to be in terms of retrieval. Crowder (1976) likens the task of retrieving items from a free-recall list to that of discriminating telephone posts located at regular intervals along a railway track. The nearest post will be readily distinguishable from the next, while as the posts recede into the distance, the problem of separating one from the other becomes

Crowder's (1976) analogy likened the task of retrieval from a free recall list to that of discriminating between a string of telephone posts; the further away the post is from the observer, the more difficult it becomes to distinguish it from its neighbor.

increasingly hard (Box 2.2). Both this and the Peterson effect can be seen in terms of a

Box 2.2 Recency

TIME FROM PRESENTATION OF THE FIRST ITEM (P_1) IN SECONDS

	Delay (sec) at R_2		Discrimination Ratio
	P_1	P_2	$(P_1 : P_2)$
	22	2	11 : 1
	30	10	3 : 1
	50	30	1.67 : 1

P_1 = Presentation of item 1
P_2 = Presentation of item 2
R_2 = Recal of item 2

discrimination ratio, based on the temporal distance between the item being retrieved and its principal competitor. On immediate recall, the most recent item has a considerable advantage, but with increasing delay, discriminating the last item from the one before becomes less and less easy (Glenberg, Bradley, Stevenson, Kraus, Tkachuk, Gretz et al., 1980; Baddeley & Hitch, 1977, 1993; Brown, Neath, & Chater et al., 2007).

MODELS OF VERBAL SHORT-TERM MEMORY

By the late 1960s, the evidence seemed to be swinging firmly in the direction of abandoning the attempt to explain STM in terms of a unitary system, in favor of an explanation involving a number of interacting systems, one of which was closely identified with the extensive evidence accumulated from verbal STM. I will use one out of a range of models of verbal STM, the concept of a *phonological loop*, to tie together the rich body of research that continues to develop in this area, before going on to give a brief account of alternative theories.

The phonological loop

The concept of a **phonological loop** forms part of the multicomponent working memory model proposed by Baddeley and Hitch (1974). The phonological loop is assumed to have two subcomponents, a short-term store and an articulatory rehearsal process. The store is assumed to be limited in capacity, with items registered as memory traces, which decay within a few seconds. However, the traces can be refreshed by subvocal rehearsal, saying the items to yourself, which depends on a vocal or subvocal articulatory process.

Consider the case of digit span. Why is it limited to six or seven items? If there are few digits in the sequence, then you can say them all in less time than it takes for the first digit to fade away. As the number of items increases, total time to rehearse them all will be greater, and hence the chance of items fading before they are refreshed will increase, hence setting a limit to memory span. The loop model is able to account for the following prominent features of verbal STM:

The phonological similarity effect

A major signature of the store is the **phonological similarity effect**, Conrad's (1964) demonstration that letter span is reduced for similar sounding items. Thus, remembering a sequence of five dissimilar words (e.g. *pit, day, cow, pen, hot*) is relatively easy, whereas remembering those that are phonologically similar (e.g. *cat, map, man, cap, mad*) is much harder. Note, however, that this is not a general effect of similarity, as sequences that are similar in meaning (e.g. *huge, wide, big, long, tall*) are only slightly more difficult than dissimilar sequences (e.g. *old, wet, thin, hot, late*) (Figure 2.4).

One final point to this story is that the phonological similarity effect disappears if the lists are increased in length and participants are allowed several learning trials. Under these circumstances, similarity of meaning becomes much more important (Baddeley, 1966b). This does not mean that phonological coding is limited to STM, as without phonological LTM we could never learn to pronounce new words. It does however mean that LTM gains more from relying on meaning than on sound. We return to this point in Chapters 4 and 5.

The phonological similarity effect is assumed to occur when information is read

---

KEY TERMS

Phonological loop: Term applied by Baddeley and Hitch to the component of their model responsible for the temporary storage of speech-like information.

Phonological similarity effect: A tendency for immediate serial recall of verbal material to be reduced, when the items are similar in sound.

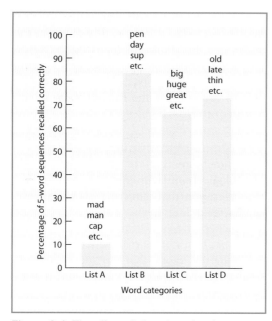

Figure 2.4 The effect of phonological and semantic similarity on immediate serial recall of five-word sequences. Phonological similarity leads to poor immediate recall whereas similarity of meaning has little effect. From Baddeley (1966a). Copyright © Psychology Press.

out from the short-term memory trace; similar items have fewer distinguishing features, and hence are likely to be confused. Auditory speech is assumed to feed directly into the phonological store. Visually presented items can also be fed into the store if they are nameable, such as digits, letters, or nameable objects, through a process of vocal or subvocal articulation, whereby you say the items to yourself.

The subvocal rehearsal system will be blocked if you are required to repeatedly say something unrelated such as the word "the," an activity known as **articulatory suppression**. Saying "the" means that you are not able to refresh the memory trace by subvocally pronouncing the remembered material. It also prevents you from subvocally naming visually presented items, such as letters, which prevents them from being registered in the phonological store. For that reason, it does not matter whether items are phonologically similar or

not, when they are presented visually and accompanied by articulatory suppression. Both similar and dissimilar items will be retained at a lower but equivalent level.

However, it is important to note that even when suppressing, people can still remember up to four or five visually presented digits. This suggests that although the phonological loop typically plays an important role in digit span, it is not its only basis. We will return to this point later. With auditory presentation, the words gain direct access to the phonological store despite articulatory suppression, and a similarity effect occurs.

The word length effect

As we saw, most people can remember sequences of five dissimilar one-syllable words relatively easily. As word length increases, performance drops from around 90% for five monosyllables to about 50% for lists of five-syllable words. As word length is increased, the time taken to speak the words also increases (Figure 2.5). This relation between recall and the rate of articulation can be summarized by the statement that people can remember about as many words as they can say in 2 seconds (Baddeley, Thomson & Buchanan, 1975).

Interpreting these findings within the phonological loop model is relatively simple. Rehearsal takes place in real time, as does trace decay, with the result that longer words, taking longer to say, allow more decay to occur. Baddeley et al. (1975) attributed the **word length effect** to forgetting during rehearsal. However, Cowan, Day, Saults, Keller, Johnson, and Flores (1992) demonstrated that word

KEY TERMS

Articulatory suppression: A technique for disrupting verbal rehearsal by requiring participants to continuously repeat a spoken item.
Word length effect: A tendency for verbal memory span to decrease when longer words are used.

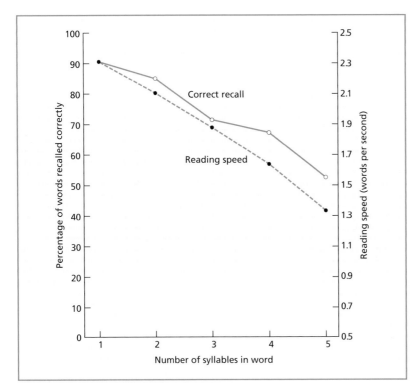

Figure 2.5 The relationship between word length, reading rate, and recall. Long words take longer to rehearse and also produce lower memory spans. From Baddeley, Thomson, and Buchanan (1975). Copyright © Elsevier. Reproduced with permission.

length also caused forgetting due to the fact that longer words take longer to recall, and Baddeley, Chincotta, Stafford, and Turk (2002) showed that both effects occur. Articulatory suppression, by requiring participants to utter an irrelevant sound, stops the process of verbal rehearsal. This abolishes the word length effect. Unlike the phonological similarity effect, this disruption occurs regardless of whether presentation is auditory or visual; if articulation is blocked, neither method of presentation will allow verbal rehearsal, and hence the word length effect is abolished (Baddeley et al., 1975).

The word length effect is extremely robust but its interpretation remains controversial. An alternative to the Baddeley et al. (1975) suggestion that the effect was based on trace decay, with longer words taking more time to rehearse and recall, is the proposal that longer words are more complex and this leads to more interference (e.g. Caplan, Rochon, & Waters, 1992). A third interpretation suggests

that long words, having more components to be remembered, are more vulnerable to fragmentation and forgetting (e.g. Neath & Nairne, 1995), although this interpretation has now been abandoned by its earlier proponents (Hulme, Neath, Stuart, Shostak, Suprenant, & Brown, 2006). However, the controversy is still far from resolved (see Mueller, Seymour, Kieras, & Meyer, 2003; Hulme et al., 2006; Baddeley, 2007; Lewandowski & Oberauer, in press, for further discussion of this complex issue).

Happily, although it is an important issue, the question of whether the greater degree of forgetting observed with long words is due to time-based trace decay, or interference from subsequent syllables is not crucial to the general concept of a phonological loop operating as part of a multicomponent working memory model. This is fortunate, as the issue of whether short-term forgetting reflects trace decay, interference, or both, has—over the last 40 years—been extremely difficult to settle.

Irrelevant sound effects

Students often claim that they work better to a background of their favorite music or radio program. Are they right? In 1976, Colle and Welsh showed that STM for sequences of visually presented digits was impaired when participants were required to ignore speech in an unfamiliar foreign language. However, digit recall was not impaired when irrelevant foreign speech was replaced by unpatterned noise. Salame and Baddeley (1982) went on to look directly at the effect of meaning by comparing the influence of irrelevant spoken words and irrelevant **nonsense syllables** on digit-sequence recall. They found that both meaningful words and nonsense produced an equivalent disruptive effect, suggesting that the meaning of the irrelevant material was unimportant. Indeed, recalling digit sequences when the irrelevant sounds themselves comprised digit names (*one, two*) caused no more disruption than when the same phonemes were presented but in a different order as nondigit words (e.g. *tun, woo*).

Both they and Colle (1980) suggested that the irrelevant speech effect might be seen as the memory equivalent to the masking of auditory speech perception by irrelevant sound. Perhaps the irrelevant spoken item gains access to the phonological store, and adds noise to the memory trace? However, white noise disrupts perception, but does not impair recall, whereas irrelevant speech does. Furthermore, in contrast to auditory masking, STM performance is not influenced by the intensity of the irrelevant sound (Colle, 1980). Even more problematic for the auditory masking analogy is the fact that the degree of disruption of STM is unrelated to the phonological similarity between the irrelevant sound and the items remembered. Irrelevant words that are similar in sound to the remembered items are no more disrupting than are dissimilar words (Jones & Macken, 1995; Le Compte & Shaibe, 1997).

But what about music? Salame and Baddeley (1989) found that music interfered with digit recall, finding that vocal music was more disruptive than instrumental. Jones and Macken (1993) observed that even pure tones will disrupt performance, provided they fluctuate in pitch. They proposed what they termed the *Changing State hypothesis*. This assumes that retention of serial order, whether in verbal or visual memory, can be disrupted by irrelevant stimuli providing that these fluctuate over time (Jones, Macken, & Murray, 1993). Jones (1993) relates the **irrelevant sound effect** to theories of auditory perception, presenting as an alternative to the phonological loop hypothesis their *Object-Oriented Episodic Record (O-OER) hypothesis*. This is discussed later.

The problem of serial order

It was clear by this time that the purely verbally specified phonological loop model had two major shortcomings. First, it had no adequate explanation of how serial order is stored. Given that the classic digit span task principally involves retaining serial order, this is clearly a major limitation. Second, the model has no clear specification of the crucial processes involved in *retrieval* from the phonological store. Both of these limitations demand a more detailed model, preferably computationally or mathematically simulated so that clear predictions can be made and tested. Fortunately, it has proved possible to convince a number of groups with the appropriate skills that this is a worthwhile enterprise.

A number of models based on the phonological loop have been developed, handling the question of serial order in somewhat different ways, agreeing on which issues are important but differing on how best to tackle them. The various models tend to agree in assuming both a phonological store,

---

KEY TERMS

Nonsense syllables: Pronounceable but meaningless consonant-vowel-consonant items designed to study learning without the complicating factor of meaning.

Irrelevant sound effect: A tendency for verbal STM to be disrupted by concurrent fluctuating sounds, including both speech and music.

Box 2.3 Methods of storing serial order

1. Chaining

    A → B → C → D

    Each item is associated with the next. Recall begins with the first item (A), which evokes the second (B).

2. Context

    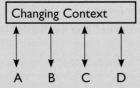

    Each item is linked to a changing context, which may be time-based. The context then acts as recall cue.

3. Primacy

    Each item presented receives activation. The first receives the most, the next a little less, and so forth. Items are recalled in order of strength. Once recalled, that item is suppressed and the next strongest chosen.

and a separate mechanism for serial order, with similarity influencing retrieval from the store. Most phonological-loop-related models reject a chaining interpretation of serial order, proposing instead that order information is carried either by some form of ongoing context (Burgess & Hitch, 1999, 2006), by links to the first item as in the *Primacy Model* of Page and Norris (1998), or links to both the first and last items (Henson, 1998). Rehearsal is assumed to involve the retrieval of items from the phonological store and their subsequent re-entry as rehearsed stimuli.

Only one of these models has so far explicitly addressed the irrelevant sound effect. Page and Norris (2003) suggest that irrelevant speech adds noise to the serial order mechanism, rather than to the phonological store, the component responsible for the effects of phonological similarity (Box 2.3). This provides an explanation of why similarity between the remembered items and the irrelevant items has no effect; they influence different parts of the system and hence do not interact.

COMPETING THEORIES OF VERBAL SHORT-TERM MEMORY

We have so far focused our discussion mainly on the explanation of short-term verbal memory offered by the phonological loop hypothesis. This approach has two advantages: it provides a coherent account of a range of very robust STM phenomena, and it does so in a way that explicitly links them to those other aspects of working memory that will be discussed in the next chapter. It is important to bear in mind, however, that other ways of explaining these data have been proposed. Some of these will be described briefly before moving on to a broader discussion of working memory, and the question of why we need a working memory.

One approach to STM is that proposed by Dylan Jones and colleagues (Jones, 1993; Jones & Macken, 1993, 1995) as the Object-Oriented Episodic Record (O-OER) theory of STM. This was developed to account for the influence on STM of irrelevant sound. It is influenced by research on auditory perception and proposes that sequences of items are represented as points on a multimodal surface; however, it assumes that both auditory and visual serial recall involve the same system operating on a common representation. Recall involves retrieving the trajectory of the points representing the sequence, rather like reading off points on a graph. Irrelevant sounds might create competing trajectories, disrupting subsequent recall (Jones, 1993).

The assumption that verbal and visual STM involve the same system has not been supported by subsequent experiments (Meiser & Klauer, 1999) and is inconsistent with evidence from neuropsychological studies in which some patients are found with impaired verbal and preserved visual STM (Shallice & Warrington, 1970; Vallar & Papagno, 2002) whereas other patients show the opposite pattern (Della Sala & Logie, 2002). Furthermore, its account of memory for serial order would appear to depend on chaining, an approach that is not well supported.

Another model that has been applied to verbal STM is James Nairne's *Feature model* (Nairne, 1988, 1990), which replaces the proposed separation between LTM and STM by proposing a single memory system in which each memory item is assumed to be represented by a set of features, which are of two basic types: *modality dependent* and *modality independent*. If you read the word

HAT, it will have both visually dependent features, such as the case in which it is printed, and visually independent features, such as its meaning. When you hear HAT, rather than read it, the independent features such as meaning will be the same but the dependent features will be acoustic rather than visual. Forgetting is assumed to depend on interference, with new items disrupting the features set up by earlier items, resulting in errors in recall.

The Feature model is represented by a computer program that can be used to make predictions as to the outcome of different experimental manipulations. By making various assumptions, it is possible to use the model to account for many of the results that have been used to support the phonological loop hypothesis. The phonological similarity effect is explained on the grounds that similar items have more common features, leading to a greater likelihood that a similar but incorrect item will be retrieved. Irrelevant sound is assumed to add noise to the memory trace of each individual item. Articulatory suppression is also assumed to add noise, and in addition to be attention demanding (Nairne, 1990). By making detailed assumptions about the exact proportion of modality-dependent and modality-independent features and the relative effect on these of articulatory suppression and irrelevant sound, the feature model is able to simulate a wide range of results (Neath & Surprenant, 2003), although very little justification is given for the very specific assumptions required by the various simulations.

The Feature model does have difficulty in accounting for a number of findings. It predicts that irrelevant sound will impair recall only when it occurs at the same time as the memory items are encoded. However, it disrupts recall even when it occurs *after* presentation of the memory items, even when rehearsal is prevented by suppression (Norris, Baddeley, & Page, 2004). The Feature model also has a problem explaining why the word-length effect disappears in mixed lists of long and short words. This has led to its abandonment by some of its proponents in favor of the next model to be described: the SIMPLE model (Hulme et al., 2006; Brown et al., 2007).

Brown et al. (2007) propose a very broad-ranging memory model that they call the SIMPLE (Scale Invariant Memory, Perception, and Learning) model, which they apply to both STM and LTM. It is basically a model of forgetting based on retrieval, with more distinctive items being more readily retrievable. It places emphasis on temporal discriminability but goes beyond earlier attempts to use this mechanism to explain recency effects in free recall by developing a detailed mathematical model. It is probably too early to evaluate SIMPLE, which appears to handle free recall well but appears to be less well suited to explaining serial recall (Lewandowski, Brown, Wright, & Nimmo, 2006; Nimmo & Lewandowski, 2006). As in the case of the Feature model, SIMPLE does not currently attempt to cover the executive aspects of working memory.

A further way of modeling serial order is to assume that order is maintained by a context signal. As mentioned earlier, one of these assumes a time-based context incorporating trace decay (Burgess & Hitch, 1999, 2006). This assumption is rejected by Farrell and Lewandowski (2002, 2003), who propose—in their SOB (Serial-Order-in-a-Box) model—that order is maintained using an event-based context signal, with forgetting based on interference between events.

It might seem strange that the apparently simple task of recalling a sequence of digits in the right order should prove so difficult to explain. However, as mentioned earlier, the problem of how a system like the brain that processes events in parallel can preserve serial order has challenged theorists since it was first raised by Karl Lashley (1951), over 50 years ago.

VISUO-SPATIAL SHORT-TERM MEMORY

Imagine you are in a well lit room that is suddenly plunged into darkness. Would you be able to find the door? If there was a box of matches on the desk in front of you, would you remember that it was there? These two questions concern two related but separable aspects of visual working memory, one concerned with spatial memory (*where?*) and the other with memory for objects (*what?*). The evidence suggests that you would be able to maintain a general heading towards the door for about 30 seconds (Thomson, 1983). Your memory for precise location within reach declines rather more rapidly (Elliot & Madalena, 1987).

Spatial short-term memory

Posner and Konick (1966) required their participants to remember where along a line a stimulus had occurred. Retention was good after an unfilled delay, but declined when digit processing was required in the interval, with the degree of forgetting increasing with the complexity of the digit task. As the intervening task was not spatial or visual in nature, the implication is that it interfered with capacity to rehearse or hold in mind the initial stimulus. A similar result was obtained by Dale (1973) using a task involving retention of the location of a black dot in a two-dimensional white field.

Object memory

Irwin and Andrews (1996) presented their participants with an array of different colored letters. After a brief delay, an asterisk appeared in the location previously occupied by one of the letters. This was a cue to recall the letter, the color, or both. Participants were just as good at reporting both letter and color as they were at reporting just one of these features. Performance was highly accurate up to four items, after which it declined with number of letters. It was of course possible that participants were relying on the phonological loop for the letter names, complicating interpretation.

This was avoided in a series of studies by Vogel, Woodman, and Luck (2001), who used as stimuli bars of varying width, orientation, and other features such as texture, making accurate verbal coding in the brief presentation phase virtually impossible. They again found a limit of four objects. Interestingly, it did not appear to matter how many features each object comprised. In one condition, for example, the array contained a total of sixteen features (four objects each with four features), but all four complex objects appeared to be encoded effectively. Vogel et al. concluded that the system was limited on the basis of the number of *objects* but that objects could vary in complexity without affecting performance (Figure 2.6). In one study, articulatory suppression was used to prevent verbal coding; this had no effect on performance, confirming their suggestion that their task does not depend on verbalization. They also found no evidence of forgetting over a brief unfilled delay.

Woodman and Luck (2004) interposed a visual search test in which the participants scanned an array looking for visually specified targets in the interval between presentation and

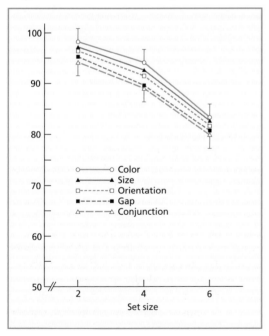

Figure 2.6 Visual recognition performance as a function of number of objects presented and number of features per object. Performance is very sensitive to number of objects but not to number of features each object comprises. Data from Vogel et al. (2001).

test of sets of colored shapes. They found that memory for spatial location was impaired by scanning, but that object memory, as reflected in memory for the color of the stimulus, was not. Oh and Kim (2004) studied the effect of memory on the *speed* of visual search, finding that the requirement to concurrently remember a set of *objects* had no impact on visual search rate, whereas a concurrent *spatial* retention task slowed down the rate at which people could search far a specified target.

It therefore appears to be the case that we can remember up to four objects, even when each comprises a number of different features, and that this does not decline over a period of a few seconds, even when interpolated activity is involved. However, memory for *spatial location* appears to be more vulnerable, and to interact with other spatial activities. It seems possible that this difference might reflect the need to maintain a *spatial framework* if a precise response must be made, a capacity that might be disrupted by other spatially related activities, including the kind of eye movements that are likely to be involved in visual search.

The visual–spatial distinction

We have made a distinction between spatial STM—remembering *where*, and object memory—remembering *what*. In practice, these two systems work together but tasks have been developed that particularly emphasize one or other of these two forms of visuo-spatial memory. A classic *spatial* task is the block tapping test in which the participant is faced with an array of nine blocks (Figure 2.7). The experimenter taps a number of blocks in sequence and the participant attempts to imitate this, with the length of sequence increasing until performance breaks down. This is known as *Corsi span*, after the Canadian neuropsychologist who invented it, and is typically around five blocks, usually about two items below digit span.

Visual span can be measured using a series of matrix patterns in which half the cells are

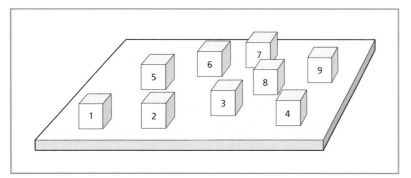

Figure 2.7 The Corsi test of visuo-spatial memory span. The experimenter taps a sequence of blocks and the participant seated opposite attempts to imitate. The numbers are there to help the experimenter.

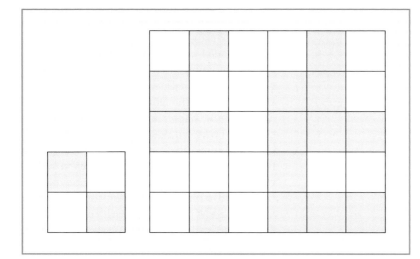

Figure 2.8 Visual pattern span. Participants are shown and then required to recall a series of matrices with half the cells filled. The test begins with a simple 2 × 2 matrix (left) and increases in size up to the 5 × 6 matrix (right). From Della Sala et al. (1999). Copyright © Elsevier. Reproduced with permission.

filled and half left blank (Figure 2.8). The participant is shown a pattern and asked to reproduce it by marking the filled cells in an empty matrix. Testing starts with a simple 2 × 2 pattern, and the number of cells in the matrix is gradually increased to a point at which performance breaks down, usually around the point at which the matrix reaches around 16 cells.

Evidence for the distinction between these two measures of spatial and visual span comes from studies in which a potentially interfering activity is inserted between presentation and test. When this involves spatial processing, such as sequentially tapping a series of keys, Corsi span is reduced; pattern span is more disrupted by a visual processing task such as viewing shapes (Della Sala, Gray, Baddeley, Allamano, & Wilson, 1999).

Visual STM is not of course limited to remembering patterns, but also involves shapes and colors. This is shown particularly clearly in a series of studies by Klauer and Zhao (2004) in which they contrast a spatial task that involves remembering the location of a white dot on a black background, and a visual task involving memory for Chinese ideographs. In each case, the stimulus is presented and followed by a 10-second retention interval, after which participants must choose which of eight test items has just been presented. During the 10-second delay, participants perform either a spatial or a visual task. In the spatial task, 12 asterisks are presented, with 11 moving randomly and the twelfth stationary; the task is to identify the stationary item. The visual interfering task involves processing a

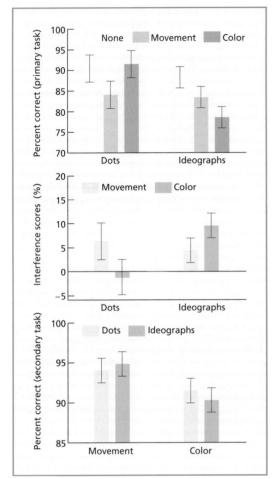

Figure 2.9 Memory for dot location and for Chinese ideographs. Only movement disrupts spatial memory, whereas pattern memory is more disrupted by intervening colors. Data from Klauer and Zhao (2004).

series of colors, seven of which are variants of one color, perhaps red, whereas one, the target, is in the blue range. As shown in Figure 2.9, the spatial location of dots was disrupted by movement but not color, whereas ideographs showed the opposite effect.

Neuropsychological approaches to the study of short-term memory

In 1966, Brenda Milner reported the case of a young man, HM, who had had the misfortune to suffer from intractable epilepsy. This can be the result of scar tissue within the brain that leads to excessive electrical activity, ending in epileptic seizures. It is often the case that surgical removal of the scar tissue greatly alleviates the seizures. HM had such an operation and his seizures were reduced, but unfortunately the operation left him densely amnesic. The reason for this was that surgical lesions had been made on both sides of the brain, in the region of the hippocampus, which we now know plays a crucial role in long-term episodic memory.

The case of HM was important practically, because it highlighted the need to take careful account of the function of the area of brain being removed and—theoretically—because of the light that it cast upon the nature of LTM. HM was impaired in his capacity to learn new material, whether visual or verbal, and to update his knowledge of the world, a classic case of the amnesic syndrome that is discussed in Chapter 11. There were aspects of memory, however, that were preserved in HM. He could remember events that had happened before his operation and he could learn certain tasks, such as those involving motor skill.

HM also had preserved digit span, suggesting that STM and LTM performance might depend on different memory systems reflecting different areas of the brain. Baddeley and Warrington (1970) therefore explored the proposed STM–LTM distinction in more detail, using a group of carefully selected patients who were densely amnesic but with otherwise normal intellectual skills, and examining their performance on a range of STM and LTM tasks. Like HM, they proved to have preserved digit span. They also showed normal performance on the Peterson task, and preserved recency in free recall, while showing a marked deficit in performance on primacy and earlier items in the free recall list. These results are discussed further in Chapter 11.

Deficits in verbal short-term memory

At the same time, Tim Shallice and Elizabeth Warrington (1970) were studying a patient with the opposite pattern of memory problems.

Patient KF had a digit span of only two items, grossly impaired Peterson task performance, and showed little recency in free recall. Other patients were subsequently identified who showed an equivalent pattern (Vallar & Shallice, 1990). These two types of patient—amnesic patients with normal performance on STM and impaired LTM, and patients with impaired STM and preserved LTM—offered what is known as a **double-dissociation**. This provides strong, although not perfect, evidence for the need to assume at least two separate systems or processes. For example, if only the amnesic patients had been studied, it could be argued that their preserved capacities such as recency and digit span simply reflected easier tasks than those that were impaired. The fact that other patients show exactly the opposite rules out this interpretation.

Shallice and Warrington's patient proved not to have a general deficit in STM, but rather a specific phonological STM deficit. Consequently, his performance was much better when his digit span was tested using visual presentation, consistent with his preserved visual memory as tested on the **Corsi block tapping** test. A similar pattern was shown by patient PV (Basso, Spinnler, Vallar, & Zanobia, 1982; Vallar & Baddeley, 1987), who developed a very pure and specific deficit in phonological STM following a stroke. Her intellect and language were otherwise unimpaired, but she had a digit span of two and failed to show either a phonological similarity or word length effect in verbal STM. As is characteristic of such patients, she showed a grossly reduced recency effect in immediate verbal free recall. She did however show normal long-term recency. This was tested using a task involving the solution of a series of anagram puzzles, followed by an unexpected request for recall. Both PV and control patients showed a clear recency effect with better recall of later solutions, even though recall was unexpected and had been followed by the need to tackle later anagrams. This pattern suggests that it is not PV's capacity to use a recency strategy that is impaired, but rather her capacity to use this to boost immediate verbal memory, which presumably relies on a phonological or verbal/lexical code.

Deficits in visuo-spatial short-term memory

Whereas some patients such as KF and PV have a deficit that is limited to verbal STM, other patients show the opposite pattern with normal verbal STM and impaired performance on either visual or spatial STM measures. One such patient, LH, had suffered a head injury in a traffic accident and was grossly impaired in his capacity to remember colors or shapes. However, he had excellent memory for spatial information such as locations and routes (Farah, Hammond, Levine, & Calvanio, 1988). Another patient, LE, suffered brain damage as a result of lupus erythematosus. She also had excellent spatial memory and was well able to drive an unfamiliar route between her home and the laboratory where her cognitive skills were tested. However, she did have impaired visual memory coupled with a grossly impaired capacity to draw from memory (Wilson, Baddeley, & Young, 1999). She was a talented sculptor, who found that she had lost her capacity to visualize. She could not remember what her earlier sculptures looked like and dramatically changed her style (Box 2.4).

Other cases occur whose visual STM is preserved, but who have impaired spatial memory. Carlesimo, Perri, Turriziani, Tomaiuolo, and Caltagirone (2001) describe patient MV, who suffered damage to the right frontal lobe following a stroke, whose visual memory

> ### KEY TERMS
>
> **Double-dissociation:** A term particularly used in neuropsychology when two patient groups show opposite patterns of deficit, e.g. normal STM and impaired LTM, versus normal LTM and impaired STM.
>
> **Corsi block tapping:** Visuo-spatial counterpart to digit span involving an array of blocks that the tester taps in a sequence and the patient attempts to copy.

Box 2.4 Patient LE

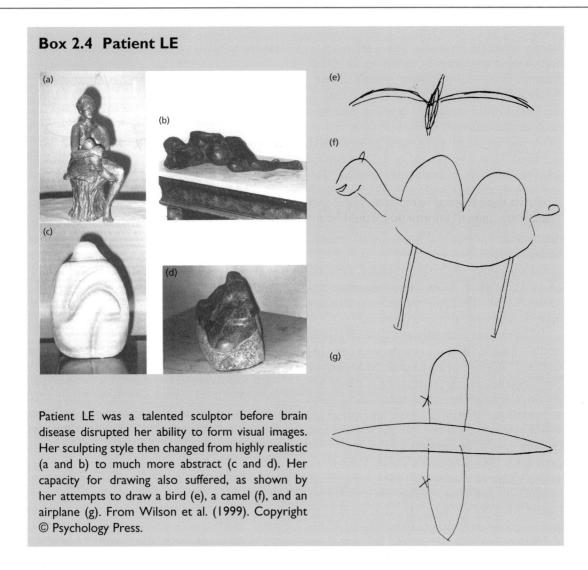

Patient LE was a talented sculptor before brain disease disrupted her ability to form visual images. Her sculpting style then changed from highly realistic (a and b) to much more abstract (c and d). Her capacity for drawing also suffered, as shown by her attempts to draw a bird (e), a camel (f), and an airplane (g). From Wilson et al. (1999). Copyright © Psychology Press.

performance was normal, but who was very impaired on the Corsi block tapping span and on a task requiring STM for imaging a path through a matrix. Luzatti, Vecchi, Agazzi, Cesa-Bianchi, and Vergani (1998) report a similar case in which progressive deterioration of the right hemisphere led to spatial memory deficits on tasks such as describing the location of landmarks in her home town, while having a good memory for colors and shapes.

You might have noticed that the deficits shown by patients with **visuo-spatial STM** problems tend to go beyond the simple storage of visual and spatial stimuli, involving more complex tasks such as creating and manipulating mental images and using these in complex tasks, such as sculpting and spatial orientation. They have, in other words, led to deficits in both STM and working memory, the topic of the next chapter.

KEY TERM

Visuo-spatial STM: Retention of visual and/or spatial information over brief periods of time.

SUMMARY

The term short-term memory (STM) refers to the storage of small amounts of information over brief periods of time. It is distinguished from working memory (WM), which is assumed to combine storage and processing and to serve as a mental workspace for performing complex tasks. The study of STM began with the digit span task used as a measure of mental capacity. Span is usually around six or seven digits, but is likely to be shorter for words and even shorter for nonsense syllables or words in a foreign language. Performance is limited by number of chunks rather than items, with different types of material being more or less chunkable.

In the late 1950s, the idea of a unitary general memory system was challenged, largely based on two experimental paradigms. The Peterson short-term forgetting effect demonstrated that small amounts of information would be forgotten within seconds if rehearsal was prevented, and was initially interpreted in terms of trace decay. It was later shown that the very first item presented showed little forgetting, suggesting an interpretation in terms of interference from prior items rather than decay. This indicates the need for a theory that incorporates retrieval.

The second influential paradigm was free recall, where the recency effect is typically lost within seconds if rehearsal is prevented, and is resistant to the many long-term memory phenomena that influenced earlier items. The existence of long-term recency suggests that it reflects a particular type of retrieval strategy that can be applied across a range of different memory systems.

Subsequent work has moved on to the study of the characteristics of various STM systems. Verbal STM has been shown to be influenced by phonological similarity and by the length of the words being retained. The phonological loop hypothesis attempts to explain this within a broader working memory framework by assuming a temporary store and an articulatory rehearsal process that can be interrupted by articulatory suppression. A number of models have been proposed to explain this overall pattern of results. Some are based on the phonological loop model, others include the Feature hypothesis, which is principally influenced by models of LTM; the Object-Oriented Episodic Record model, influenced mainly by irrelevant sound effects; and the Scale Invariant Memory, Perception, and Learning model (SIMPLE), which is strongly influenced by the need to give an account of recency.

Visual STM can be divided into visual and spatial memory. Memory for spatial location appears to show forgetting over a period of seconds, while memory for visual objects does not. We appear able to retain up to four objects, with performance declining beyond this point. Somewhat surprisingly, the number of features an object comprises does not seem to be obviously limited. Visual and spatial components have been proposed as part of the visuo-spatial sketchpad, a component of working memory that is a counterpart of the phonological loop.

Neuropsychological evidence supports the behavioral distinctions proposed. A number of cases have revealed the potential separation between verbal STM and both LTM and visual STM, with the pattern of deficits being broadly consistent with the phonological loop hypothesis.

Patients with visuo-spatial STM deficits have also been reported, some who appear to have disruption of the visual store, reflected in impaired pattern span, whereas others show impaired spatial STM as reflected in the Corsi block tapping task. The lesion sites leading to these neuropsychological deficits are broadly consistent with evidence from neuroimaging that are discussed in Chapter 3.

FURTHER READING

- **Logie, R. H.** (1995). *Visuo-spatial working memory*. Hove, UK: Psychology Press. An account of visual STM from a multicomponent working memory perspective.

- **Luck, S. J., & Vogel, E. K.** (1997). The capacity of visual working memory for features and conjunctions. *Nature, 390*, 279–281. An important paper that forms a link between the study of visual attention and visual STM.

- **Melton, A. W.** (1963). Implications of short-term memory for a general theory of memory. *Journal of Verbal Learning and Verbal Behavior, 2*, 1–21. A classic paper presenting an interpretation of STM in terms of stimulus–response interference theory.

- **Vallar, G.** (2006). Memory systems: The case of phonological short-term memory. A festschrift for *Cognitive Neuropsychology*. *Cognitive Neuropsychology, 23*, 135–155. An explanation and account of phonological loop from the viewpoint of neuropsychology.

- **Waugh, N. C., & Norman, D. A.** (1965). Primary memory. *Psychological Review, 72*, 89–104. Another classic paper presenting an information-processing alternative to interference theory.

CHAPTER 3

WORKING MEMORY

Alan Baddeley

How are you at mental arithmetic? Could you multiply 27 × 3? Try it.
Different people use different methods; in my own case, I multiplied the 7 by 3 resulting in 21, then held the 1 in mind and carried the two, before then going on to multiply 2 × 3, and so forth, interleaving the retrieval of numerical facts, with holding and manipulating the temporary totals. I had, in short, to use working memory, simultaneously holding and processing information. This active use of memory is the focus of the present chapter.

The idea that short-term memory (STM) serves as a working memory was proposed by Atkinson and Shiffrin (1968), who devised the model briefly described in Chapter 1. Because it had a great deal in common with many similar models that were popular at the time, it became known as the *modal model*.

As Figure 3.1 illustrates, the modal model assumes that information comes in from the environment and is processed first by a parallel series of brief temporary sensory memory systems, including the iconic and echoic memory processes discussed in Chapter 1. From here, information flows into the *short-term store*, which forms a crucial part of the system, not only feeding information into and out of the *long-term store*, but also acting as a *working memory*, responsible for selecting and operating strategies, for rehearsal,

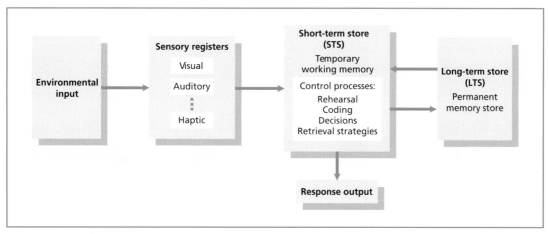

Figure 3.1 The flow of information through the memory systems as conceived by Atkinson and Shiffrin's modal model. Copyright © 1971 Scientific American. Reproduced with permission.

and generally serving as a global workspace. Atkinson and Shiffrin (1968) created a mathematical simulation of their model, concentrating on the processes involved in the rote rehearsal of verbal items and on the role of rehearsal in the transfer of information from the short-term to the long-term store. For a while, the modal model seemed to offer a neat solution to the question of how information is manipulated and stored. Before long, however, problems began to appear.

One problem concerned the assumption that simply holding items in the short-term store would guarantee learning. This view was challenged by Craik and Lockhart (1972), who proposed instead the principle of **levels of processing**, which maintains that learning depends on the way in which material is processed, rather than time in short-term storage. This important theory is discussed in Chapter 5.

The Atkinson and Shiffrin model also had difficulty in accounting for some of the neuropsychological evidence. You may recall that Shallice and Warrington (1970) described a patient who appeared to have a grossly defective short-term store. According to the modal model, the short-term store plays a crucial role in transferring information into and out of long-term memory (LTM). This STM deficit should therefore lead to greatly impaired long-term learning in such patients. Furthermore, if the short-term store acts as a general working memory, these patients should suffer severed disruption of such complex cognitive activities as reasoning and comprehension. This was not the case. One patient with grossly impaired STM was a very efficient secretary, another ran a shop and a raised family, and a third was a taxi driver (Vallar & Shallice, 1990). In short, they showed no signs of suffering from a general working-memory deficit.

Within a very few years, the concept of STM had moved from simplicity to complexity. A wide range of new experimental techniques had been invented, but none of them mapped in a simple straightforward way onto any

of the original theories proposed to account for the wide range of studies of STM. At this point, many investigators abandoned the field in favor of the study of LTM, opting instead to work on the exciting new developments in the study of levels of processing and of semantic memory.

At just the point that problems with modal model were becoming evident, Graham Hitch and I were beginning our first research grant in which we had undertaken to look at the relationship between STM and LTM. Rather than attempt to find a way through the thicket of experimental techniques and theories that characterized both fields, we opted to ask a very simple question, namely, if the system or systems underpinning STM have a function, what might it be? If, as was generally assumed, it acted as a working memory, then blocking it should interfere with both long-term learning and complex cognitive activities such as reasoning and comprehending. Not having access to patients with this specific STM deficit, we attempted to simulate such patients using our undergraduate students, a process that happily did not require physical removal of the relevant part of their brain, but did involve keeping it busy while at the same time requiring participants to reason, comprehend, and learn (Baddeley & Hitch, 1974).

Virtually all theories agreed that if verbal STM was characterized by any single task, that task was digit span, with longer sequences of digits occupying more of the capacity of the underlying short-term storage system. We therefore combined digit span with the simultaneous performance of a range of other tasks such as reasoning, learning, and comprehension, which were assumed to depend on this limited-capacity

KEY TERM

Levels of processing: The theory proposed by Craik and Lockhart that asserts that items that are more deeply processed will be better remembered.

system. Participants were given a sequence of digits that they were continually required to rehearse out loud at the same time as they were performing other cognitive tasks. By varying the number of digits being held, it should be possible to vary the demand on this limited-capacity system. If it did indeed reflect a working memory responsible for reasoning and other tasks, then the longer the sequence, the greater the digit load and the greater the interference should be.

One experiment involved presenting a simple reasoning task in which students had to verify a statement about the order of two letters. The task is shown in Box 3.1. Try it yourself.

Somewhat to our surprise, people were able to do this, even when holding simultaneously and repeating sequences of up to eight digits, beyond memory span for many of those tested. As Figure 3.2 shows, average time to verify the sentences increased systematically with digit load, but not overwhelmingly so. The total time taken with eight digits was about 50% more than base-line. Perhaps more remarkably, the error rate remained constant at around 5%, regardless of concurrent digit load.

What are the implications of these results for the view that the short-term store serves

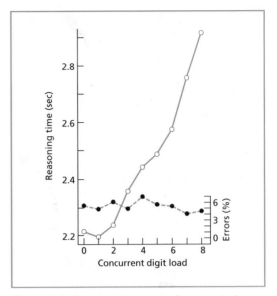

Figure 3.2 Speed and accuracy of grammatical reasoning as a function of concurrent digit load. From Baddeley (1986). Copyright © Oxford University Press. Reproduced with permission.

as a working memory? The error rate suggests that performance can go ahead quite effectively regardless of concurrent digit load, whereas the processing time data suggest that there is *some* involvement, although not of overwhelming magnitude. Results from studies of learning and comprehension gave broadly equivalent results (Baddeley & Hitch, 1974), supporting some kind of working memory hypothesis, but not one that depended entirely on the memory system underpinning digit span.

We therefore proposed a somewhat more complex model, which we called *working memory*, a term invented but not further elaborated by Miller, Galanter, and Pribram (1960). The emphasis on "working" aimed to dissociate it from earlier models of STM, which were primarily concerned with storage, and to emphasize its functional role as a system that underpins complex cognitive activities, a system that supports our capacity for mental work and coherent thought (Baddeley & Hitch, 1974).

Box 3.1 Examples from the grammatical reasoning test used by Baddeley and Hitch (1974).

		True	False
A follows B	B → A		
B precedes A	A → B		
B is followed by A	B → A		
A is preceded by B	B → A		
A is not preceded by B	A → B		
B does not follow A	A → B		

Answers: T, F, T, T, T, F.

THE MULTICOMPONENT MODEL

The model we proposed had three components (Figure 3.3); one of these, the **phonological loop**, is assumed to be specialized for holding sequences of acoustic or speech-based items. A second subsystem, the **visuo-spatial sketchpad** performs a similar function for visually and/or spatially encoded items and arrays. The whole system is controlled by the *central executive*, an attentionally limited system that selects and manipulates material in the subsystems, serving as a controller that runs the whole show. One way of gaining a feeling for the concept is to try the following: Think of your current house or apartment, and work out how many windows it has. Then move on to the next paragraph.

How many windows? How did you reach that number? You probably formed some sort of visual image of your house; this relies on the sketchpad. You presumably then counted the windows verbally using the phonological loop. Finally, throughout this process there was a need for your central executive to select and run the strategy. These three components of working memory will be considered in turn, beginning with the phonological loop, which—as mentioned previously—could be regarded as a model of verbal STM embedded within a more general theory of working memory.

The phonological loop

As we saw in Chapter 2, the phonological loop is basically a model of verbal STM. It accounts for a wide and rich range of findings using a simple model that assumes a temporary store and a verbal rehearsal process. It is not free of critics, but has proved fruitful for over 30 years without—so far—being replaced by a widely accepted better model. But how does it fit into the broader context of working memory? What is it for?

What use is the phonological loop?

On the evidence presented, the phonological loop simply increases span by two or three items on the rather artificial task of repeating back numbers. So what, if any, is its evolutionary significance? Has evolution thoughtfully prepared us for the invention of the telephone? And if not, is the loop anything more than "A pimple on the anatomy of cognitive psychology," as suggested by one critic?

In an attempt to answer this question, two Italian colleagues, Giuseppe Vallar and Costanza Papagno, and I began to study a patient—PV—who had a very pure phonological loop deficit. Her digit span was two items but her intelligence, LTM, and short-term visual memory were excellent. She spoke fluently and her general language skills seemed normal. PV ran a shop, successfully raised a

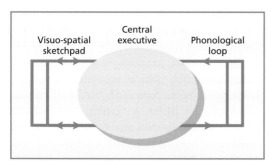

Figure 3.3 The initial Baddeley and Hitch working memory model. The double arrows are intended to represent parallel transfer of information to and from the sketchpad, and the single arrows the serial rehearsal process within the phonological loop. Based on Baddeley and Hitch (1974).

KEY TERMS

Phonological loop: Term applied by Baddeley and Hitch to the component of their model responsible for the temporary storage of speech-like information.

Visuo-spatial sketchpad: A component of the Baddeley and Hitch model that is assumed to be responsible for the temporary maintenance of visual and spatial information.

family, and seemed to have few problems in her everyday life. Did she have any areas of major difficulty? If she did, this would give us a clue as to what function was served by her defective phonological loop.

We began with the hypothesis that the loop might have evolved to assist language comprehension (Vallar & Baddeley, 1987). PV did have some problems, but only with a particular type of long sentence, where it is necessary to hold on to the first few words until the end of the sentence in order to understand it. This was not enough to create problems for PV in everyday life, and it is hard to see evolution favoring the development of a special subsystem to facilitate long-winded communication.

A second hypothesis was that the phonological loop system has evolved to help us learn language. People who have acquired a phonological loop deficit when adult, as is the case for PV, would experience few difficulties because they would already have mastered their native language. However, if they were required to learn a new language, they might have problems. We investigated this by requiring PV to learn to associate each of eight Russian words with their equivalent in Italian, PV's native language (Baddeley, Papagno, & Vallar, 1988). With spoken presentation, after ten trials, all of the control participants had learned all eight Russian words, whereas PV had not learned one (Figure 3.4). Could it simply be that she was amnesic? This was not the case, as when the task involved learning to associate two unrelated native language words such as *castle-bread*, a task that typically relies on **semantic coding** (Baddeley & Dale, 1966), she was quite unimpaired. Our results thus lent support to the possibility that the phonological loop is involved in language acquisition.

However, while a single case can be extremely informative, it is possible that the individual might be highly atypical, and hence ultimately misleading. Given that STM-deficit patients are rare, we opted to test our hypothesis further by disrupting the phonological loop in normal participants who were attempting to learn foreign language vocabulary.

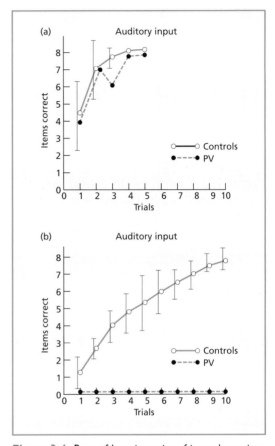

Figure 3.4 Rate of learning pairs of items by patient PV and controls. Her capacity to learn pairs of meaningful words was unimpaired (panel a), but she was not able to learn foreign language vocabulary (panel b). From Baddeley, Papagno, and Vallar (1988). Copyright © Elsevier. Reproduced with permission.

We predicted that disrupting the loop would cause particular problems in learning foreign vocabulary, just as in the case of PV. In one study, articulatory suppression was used (Papagno, Valentine, & Baddeley, 1991). When participants were required continually to repeat an irrelevant sound during learning, this proved

---

KEY TERM

Semantic coding: Processing an item in terms of its meaning, hence relating it to other information in long-term memory.

to disrupt foreign language learning, assumed to rely on the phonological loop, but had little effect on learning pairs of native language words. In another study, Papagno and Vallar (1992) varied either the phonological similarity or the length of the foreign words to be learnt, manipulating two factors known to influence the phonological loop. When the responses were foreign words, then similarity and length impaired performance to a much more substantial extent than occurred when both words were in the native language of the participants. The conclusions drawn from PV of the importance of the loop for learning new word forms therefore appeared to be supported. However, they still were confined to adults acquiring a second language. The system would clearly be more important if it also influenced the acquisition by children of their native tongue.

Susan Gathercole and I investigated this question by testing a group of children with a specific language impairment (Gathercole & Baddeley, 1990). These children were 8 years old, had normal nonverbal intelligence, but had the language development of 6-year-olds. Could this reflect a phonological loop deficit? When given a battery of memory tests, they proved to be particularly impaired in their capacity to repeat back unfamiliar pseudo words. Note that this task not only requires participants to hear the nonwords, but also to hold them in memory for long enough to repeat them. On the basis of this, we developed the **nonword repetition test** in which pseudo words of increasing length are heard and must be repeated (e.g. *ballop*, *woogalamic*, *versatra-tional*). We tested language-impaired children, other children of the same age with normal language development, and a group of 6-year-olds who were matched for level of language development with the language-impaired group but who, being younger, had a lower level of nonverbal performance. The results are shown in Figure 3.5, from which it is clear that the language-disordered 8-year-old children perform more poorly even than the 6-year-olds. In fact, they were equivalent

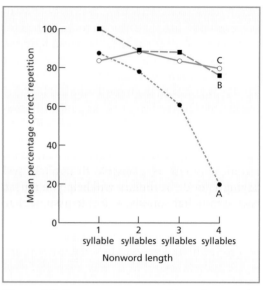

Figure 3.5 Percent correct repetition of nonwords by children with a specific language impairment (A), children of the same age (B), and children matched for language level (C). Adapted from Gathercole and Baddeley (1990).

to 4-year-olds in their nonword repetition capacity. Could their poor nonword repetition performance be related to their delayed language development? Is level of vocabulary related to nonword repetition performance in normal children too?

In an attempt to investigate this, a cohort of children between the ages of 4 and 5 years who were just starting school in Cambridge, England, were tested using the nonword repetition test, together with a test of nonverbal intelligence and a measure of vocabulary. This involved presenting four pictures and pronouncing the name of one of them; the child's task was to point to the appropriate picture. As the test proceeded, the words became less and less common. Testing ended when performance broke down

KEY TERM

Nonword repetition test: A test whereby participants hear and attempt to repeat back nonwords that gradually increase in length.

because the child no longer knew the words. Performance on these three tests was then correlated to see to what extent vocabulary was related to intelligence and to nonword repetition. The results are shown in Table 3.1, from which it is clear there was a substantial correlation between the capacity to hear and echo back a word and level of vocabulary development.

Of course, correlation does not mean causation. It is just as plausible to assume that having a good vocabulary will help you repeat back unfamiliar sounds, as it is to assume that capacity for repeating unfamiliar sounds will help you acquire new vocabulary. A study of the development of vocabulary in 5- to 6-year-old children (Gathercole & Baddeley, 1989) suggested that phonological memory was indeed the crucial factor at this stage. However, as children become older they are increasingly able to use existing vocabulary to help learn new words (Baddeley, Gathercole, & Papagno, 1998). This is reflected in the fact that new words that contain letter sequences that resemble fragments of existing vocabulary (e.g. *contramponist*) are easier to repeat back than words that have a more unfamiliar letter structure (e.g. *skiticult*). However, future vocabulary is better predicted by performance on these unusual items. This is presumably because such items gain less support from existing vocabulary and hence continue to rely on the phonological loop (Gathercole, 1995). Whereas the link with vocabulary acquisition is probably the clearest evolutionary application of the phonological loop, it is likely that the loop also facilitates the acquisition of grammar, and probably also of reading (Baddeley et al., 1998). Indeed, the nonword repetition test is used widely in the diagnosis of dyslexia, although reduced phonological loop capacity is likely to represent only one of a range of variables that can impact on the complex skill of learning to read.

The phonological loop and action control

We have so far discussed the loop as a rather limited storage system that plays a relatively passive role in cognition. Miyake and Shah (1999b) suggested that this might well underestimate its importance, and this is proving to be the case. In one study, for example (Baddeley, Chincotta, & Adlam, 2001b), we were interested in the capacity to switch attention between two tasks. We used the simple task of adding or subtracting one from a series of digits, thus, given 8, the response should be 9 in one case and 7 in

Table 3.1: Relation between vocabulary scores at age 4 and other variables. There is a strong relationship with nonword repetition performance. From Gathercole and Baddeley (1989).

Measures	Correlation coefficient	Simple regression (% variance)	Stepwise regression (% variance)
Chronological age	0.218	5[a]	5[a]
Nonverbal intelligence	0.388	15[b]	13[b]
Nonword repetition	0.525	27[b]	15[b]
Sound mimicry	0.295	9[b]	0
Total	0.578	33[b]	—

[a]$P < 0.05$; [b]$P < 0.01$.

the other. Participants were given a column of additions (e.g. 5 → 6: 8 → 9: 3 → 4, etc.), or a column of subtractions (e.g. 5 → 4: 8 → 7: 3 → 2, etc.), or were required to alternate, adding to the first, subtracting from the second, adding to the third etc. (e.g. 5 → 6: 8 → 7: 3 → 4, etc.). Alternation markedly slowed down performance, particularly when participants had to "remember" to switch, rather than having plus and minus signs beside each digit. However, performance was slower when participants had to suppress articulation while performing the switching condition, suggesting that they had been relying on a subvocal set of instructions to keep their place. Similar effects have been observed and investigated further by Emerson and Miyake (2003) and by Saeki and Saito (2004).

It is notable that participants in psychological experiments very frequently appear to rely on verbal coding to help them perform the task. This was investigated by two Russian psychologists—Lev Vygotsky (1962) and Alexander Luria (1959)—who emphasized the use of verbal *self-instruction* to control behavior, studying its application to the rehabilitation of brain-damaged patients and to its development in children (Box 3.2). Sadly, Vygotsky and Luria have so far had little direct influence on recent developments in cognitive psychology. One can only hope that further investigation of the role of speech in the control of action will remedy this.

We have described the development of the phonological loop model in some detail. This is not because it is the only, or indeed the most important, component of working memory; it certainly is not, but it is the component that has been investigated most extensively and, as such, provides an example of how relatively simple experimental tasks can be used to study

Box 3.2 Alexander Luria

Alexander Luria; 1902–1977.

The Russian psychologist Alexander Romanovitch Luria developed an ingenious method for studying the influence of language on the control of action. In one experiment, he asked children of different ages to squeeze a bulb when a red light came on, but not to squeeze for a blue light. Before the age of 3, children typically press in response to both lights, even though they can report the instruction correctly, and can perform it correctly if given the instruction "press" when the red light comes on but no instruction with the blue light. A few months later, they are themselves able to make the appropriate verbal responses, but still do not perform the action. By age 5, they are able both to speak and act appropriately, only later managing to act without giving themselves a verbal cue. Luria also demonstrated that patients with frontal-lobe damage could have difficulty with this task, and could be helped through verbal self-cueing.

complex cognitive processes and their practical implications.

We move on now to the visuo-spatial sketchpad, which has been rather less extensively investigated and will be described more briefly.

IMAGERY AND THE VISUO-SPATIAL SKETCHPAD

Suppose you were asked to describe a famous building such as the Taj Mahal. How would you do it? Try.

You probably based your description on some form of visuo-spatial representation, a visual image perhaps? An observer might also have seen you using your hands as a spatial supplement to your verbal account. People vary hugely in the extent to which they report having visual imagery. In the late nineteenth century, Sir Francis Galton, a Victorian gentleman, contacted his friends and asked them to remember their breakfast table from that morning, and then describe the experience. Some reported imagery that was almost as vivid as vision, whereas others denied having any visual imagery whatsoever. Such differences in reported vividness appear to have surprisingly little relationship to how well people perform on tasks that would be expected to make heavy demands on visual imagery, such as visual recall (Di Vesta, Ingersoll, & Sunshine, 1971). Those studies that have found any differences tend, somewhat surprisingly, to observe *poorer* performance on visual memory tasks by participants reporting strong visual imagery (Heuer, Fischman, & Reisberg, 1986; Reisberg, Clayton, Heuer, & Fischman, 1986). The reason for this unexpected finding appears to be that people with vivid imagery do not have better *memories*, but use vividness as a sign of the accuracy of their recall and are more likely to misjudge a vivid but erroneous memory to be correct. This suggests that subjective reports, however convinced we are about whether we do or do not have vivid imagery, might reflect the way in which we choose to categorize and describe our subjective experiences, rather than their content or capacity (Baddeley & Andrade, 2000).

Image manipulation

Figure 3.6 shows a task studied by Shepard and Feng (1972). If the shapes depicted were made out of paper, both could be folded to create a solid, with the shaded area being the base. Your task is to imagine folding the shapes (shown on the left-hand side of Figure 3.6) and decide whether the arrows will meet head on. Try it.

Shepard and Feng found that the time it took participants to come to a solution was systematically related to the number of folds that would have been required.

Tasks like this are often used to select people for jobs, such as architect and engineer, that are likely to involve visual or spatial thinking. They also tend to be somewhat better performed by men than by women, who are likely to use a more

How would you describe the Taj Mahal? Would vivid, visual imagery be the basis of your description?

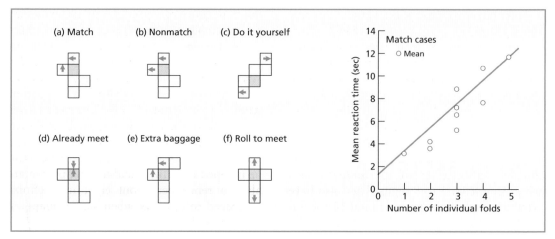

Figure 3.6 Left: Examples of six types of paper folding problems used by Shepard and Feng (1972). Your task is to decide what would happen if the shapes were folded and made into a cube. Would the arrows meet? Right: Average time to decide whether the arrows on the cubes would match as a function of number of imaginary folds necessary to reach that decision. The circles represent each of 10 different types of problem. Data from Shepard and Feng (1972).

analytic and piecemeal approach (Linn & Petersen, 1985). A subsequent study by Hsi, Linn, and Bell (1997) found that female University of California Berkeley engineering students were less good at performing a spatial manipulation test and were also likely to do less well on a difficult graphics course for which 25% of students obtained either a D or failed grade. Shi et al. spoke to experienced engineers about the strategies of spatial manipulation they used and, on the basis of this, produced a one-day intensive course on spatial manipulation strategies. This was highly successful in improving performance to a point at which the gender differences disappeared and virtually no failures occurred.

A number of studies have tried to study spatial manipulation within the laboratory. Finke and Slayton (1988) developed the following task:

First, form an image of the capital letter J. Then imagine capital D. Now rotate the D through 90 degrees to the left and place it on top of the J. What does it look like?

The answer is an umbrella. Pearson, Logie, and Gilhooly (1999) tried to analyze in more detail the processes involved. They gave their participants four, six, or eight symbols (e.g. square, triangle, circle, etc.), requiring them to use them to create an object that they should then name, and afterwards draw. If they had failed to produce an object after 2 minutes, participants were required simply to recall the memorized symbols. The role of the visuo-spatial sketchpad and the phonological loop in the task was studied by means of concurrent tasks, using either articulatory suppression to disrupt the loop, or tapping a series of spatial locations to disrupt the sketchpad. Pearson et al. found that spatial tapping disrupted the capacity to create novel objects, suggesting that this aspect depends on the sketchpad, but had no effect on the capacity to remember what shapes were involved. However, the latter was disrupted by articulatory suppression, suggesting that the names of the shapes to be manipulated were held in the phonological loop.

The study by Pearson et al. is a good example of the way in which the visuo-spatial sketchpad and phonological loop can work together to enhance performance. A very striking example of this comes from a study using a group of Japanese experts in mental calculation who are very skilled at using the traditional calculating aid, the abacus, which involves manipulating beads within a framework. Hatano and Osawa (1983a, 1983b) studied calculators who were able to dispense with the actual abacus, relying instead on imagining the abacus. Experts can mentally add and subtract up to 15 numbers, each comprising from 5 to 9 digits. They also have extremely high digit spans, around 16 for forward and 14 for backward recall. However, their enhanced span was limited to digits. Their span for other verbal material, such as consonants, for which the abacus imagery could not be used, was no better than that of a control group. As would be expected if the experts were relying on visuo-spatial imagery, their digit span was markedly disrupted by a concurrent spatial task, unlike control participants, whose performance was more disrupted by articulatory suppression.

Just as spatial activity can disrupt imagery, so imagery can interfere with spatial processing. A striking example of this occurred when I was visiting the US. I was listening to an American football game between UCLA and Stanford and forming a clear image of the game while driving along the San Diego freeway. I suddenly realized that the car was weaving from lane to lane. I switched to music and survived and on returning to Britain decided to study the effect under slightly less risky conditions. One of the imagery tasks used is shown in Figure 3.7. A sequence of sentences is heard and must be repeated. When the sentences can be mapped onto the visual matrix, people are able to remember about eight instructions, compared to only six when spatial mapping is not feasible.

Unfortunately, my department did not own a driving simulator for use as the spatial task, so instead I used a pursuit rotor, an ancient piece of equipment in which the participant is required to perform a tracking task, keeping a stylus in contact with a moving spot of light. When performing this task, the imagery advantage enjoyed by the spatially imageable sentences disappears (Baddeley, Grant, Wight, & Thomson, 1973). The interference proved to be spatial in nature rather than visual, since performance was disrupted by the task of tracking the *location* of an *auditory* sound source while blindfolded, but not by making

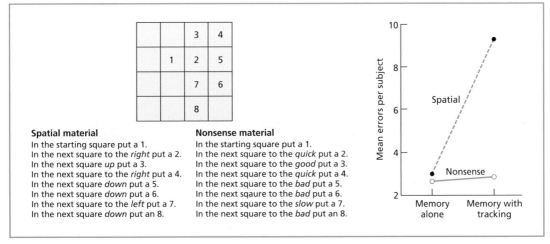

Figure 3.7 Left: Examples of the material developed by Brooks and used to study the visuo-spatial sketchpad. Participants must repeat the sentences from memory but can use the matrix to help them. Data from Brooks (1967). Right: The influence on recall of the Brooks sentences of a concurrent visuo-spatial tracking task. Data from Baddeley et al. (1973).

a *visual* but nonspatial brightness judgment (Baddeley & Lieberman, 1980).

Whereas this particular task appears to depend on spatial imagery, more purely visual imagery can also help in verbal recall. A powerful way of learning to associate pairs of words is to combine them into an interactive image; for example, to associate *violin* and *banana*, one might imagine a concert violinist using a large banana as a bow. Such object-based imagery tends to be disrupted by presentation of irrelevant pictures or colors, which participants are instructed to ignore (Logie, 1995). Indeed, under appropriate conditions, even a flickering dot pattern can disrupt the use of visual imagery (Quinn & McConnell, 1996a, 1996b).

Working memory and imagery

Virtually all the experimental work described so far focuses on the performance of tasks that are presumed to depend on visuo-spatial processing. However, investigators such as Shepard and Kosslyn avoid making any claims about how this relates to our subjective experience. A series of experiments by Jackie Andrade and myself tried to tackle this contentious problem, testing the hypothesis that visual imagery reflects the operation of the sketchpad, and auditory imagery the phonological loop (Baddeley & Andrade, 2000). We asked participants to form and judge the vividness of visual or auditory images. Participants were tested under baseline conditions, or under either articulatory suppression, which was predicted to make auditory imagery seem less vivid, or with a concurrent spatial tapping task known to disrupt visuo-spatial imagery. When the images were of novel material that had just been presented, comprising sequences of tones or arrays of shapes, our predictions worked well, with auditory imagery appearing less vivid under articulatory suppression, and visual imagery under spatial tapping. However, when the images were drawn from LTM, for instance of a local market, or the sound of the ex-British Prime Minister Margaret Thatcher's voice, there was evidence for only minimal involvement of the loop and sketchpad. We concluded that a vivid image is one that has the potential for retrieving sensory detail; when the detail depends on STM, the loop and sketchpad will set the limit to such information, and hence of the rated vividness of the image. When the image is based on LTM, however, the role of the loop and sketchpad is much less important. When I form an image of my local market, for example, I "see" a particular flower stall, a stallholder, and an array of flowers. This almost certainly represents a construction based on the accumulated experience of the stall over many years, rather than a detailed representation

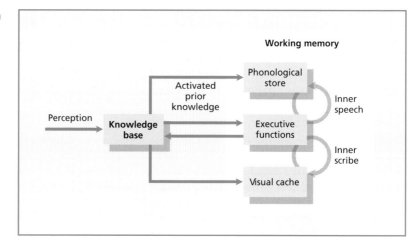

Figure 3.8 Logie's version of the multicomponent working memory model in which the visual cache is the counterpoint to the phonological store, and the inner scribe is an active rehearsal process that is the visuo-spatial counterpoint of subvocal speech. From Logie and van der Meulen (in press), based on Logie (1995).

of a particular display. Our evidence suggests however that this representation does not depend very crucially on the sketchpad, so where is it held? We shall return to this point when we discuss the fourth component of working memory, the **episodic buffer**.

Logie (1995) has proposed a structure for the visuo-spatial sketchpad that is somewhat analogous to that of the phonological loop, namely a passive store that he terms the **visual cache**, and an active spatial rehearsal process, the *inner scribe* (Figure 3.8). He proposes that the system provides a visuo-spatial workspace for performing complex tasks, but somewhat more controversially argues that it is always fed by LTM.

THE CENTRAL EXECUTIVE

Working memory is assumed to be directed by the central executive, an attentional controller rather than a memory system. Its main mode of operation is assumed to be that proposed by Norman and Shallice (1986), who assumed two modes of control, one of which is automatic and based on existing habits whereas the other depends on an attentionally limited executive. Driving a car would be an example of the first type of semi-automatic control. The activities involved can be relatively complex, so that potential conflicts can occur, for example between continuing to drive and slowing down in response to a traffic signal, or another driver entering the road. There are assumed to be well-learned procedures for resolving such conflicts automatically. Because such behavior is based largely on well learned habits, it requires little attention. Have you ever had the somewhat worrying experience of arriving at your driving destination with no recollection of how you got there? Were you conscious during the trip? You almost certainly were, but thinking about other matters and leaving the routine decisions to your conflict-resolution system.

However, when automatic conflict resolution is not possible, or when a novel situation arises, for example, a road is closed for repairs, then a second system is called into action, the **supervisory attentional system (SAS)**. This is able to intervene, either in favor of one or other of the competing options or else to activate strategies for seeking alternative solutions. It is the SAS component that is assumed to be crucial to the central executive.

Donald Norman and Tim Shallice had somewhat different purposes in jointly producing their model. On the one hand, Norman was interested in slips of action, whereby a lapse of attention produces unforeseen consequences. These are sometimes trivial, as when you set off on a Saturday morning to drive to the grocery store and find yourself taking your regular route to work instead. On other occasions, such slips of attention can have tragic consequences, as when pilot error can lead to a plane crash. Both of these reflect situations in which the SAS fails to operate when it should.

Shallice, on the other hand, was principally interested in patients with frontal lobe damage, who appear to have problems of *attentional control*. This is sometimes reflected in perseveration, repetitively performing the same act or making the same mistake repeatedly. Patient RR, for example (Baddeley & Wilson, 1988), was asked during an occupational therapy session to measure and cut a series of lengths of tape. He persistently grasped the tape at the wrong

> ### KEY TERMS
>
> **Episodic buffer:** A component of the Baddeley and Hitch working memory model, which assumes a multidimensional code, allowing the various subcomponents of working memory to interact with long-term memory.
>
> **Visual cache:** A component of Logie's model of visual working memory. It forms a counterpart to the phonological store and is maintained by the inner scribe, a counterpart to phonological rehearsal.
>
> **Supervisory attentional system (SAS):** A component of the model proposed by Norman and Shallice to account for the attentional control of action.

point, leaving very short tape lengths. When this was pointed out, he crossly responded "I know I'm getting it wrong!" but was unable to break out of the incorrect action sequence.

On other occasions, the same patient might continually fail to *focus* attention, simply responding to whatever environmental cues are present. This sometimes leads to what is known as *utilization behavior*, in which the patient uninhibitedly makes use of whatever is around, drinking the tester's cup of tea for example, or on one occasion picking up a hypodermic syringe and attempting to inject the examining doctor. In the absence of control from the SAS, the patient simply responds to any cues or opportunities afforded by the environment. The frontal lobes are assumed to be the part of the brain necessary for adequate operation of the SAS, with damage potentially leading to failures in the attentional control of action, particularly when the damage is extensive and extends to both the right and left frontal lobes.

Another function of the frontal lobes is to *monitor* behavior, checking that it is appropriate. Failure to do this can lead to bizarre behavior or **confabulation**. Patient RR, for example, woke up in bed on one occasion and demanded from his wife, "Why do you keep telling people we are married?", "But we are" she said, "we have three kids," going on to produce the wedding photographs. "That chap looks like me but it's not because I am not married," the patient replied. An hour or so later he appeared to have forgotten the incident and strongly denied it (Baddeley & Wilson, 1986).

A major function of the central executive is that of attentional focus, the capacity to direct attention to the task in hand. Consider a complex task like playing chess. What is the role of working memory? One approach is to use concurrent tasks to disrupt each of the subcomponents of working memory. Holding (1989) showed that counting backwards disrupted the capacity of players to remember a chess position, concluding that verbal coding was important. However, counting backwards also demands executive processing. Robbins, Anderson, Barker, Bradley, Fearneyhough,

According to Robbins et al. (1996), selecting good chess moves requires use of the central executive and the visuo-spatial sketchpad, but not of the phonological loop.

Henson et al. (1996) therefore compared the effects on the recall of chess positions of articulatory suppression, spatial tapping, and an attentionally demanding task known as random generation, in which participants try to produce a stream of numbers, making the sequence as random as possible. We tested both highly expert and relatively inexperienced players. The two groups differed greatly in overall performance, but all showed the same interference pattern. Articulatory suppression had no influence, suggesting that the phonological loop was not involved, whereas the visuo-spatial task did impair performance but not as much as random generation. We found the same result when the task was changed from remembering the chess positions to choosing the best next move, indicating an important role for both the sketchpad and central executive in planning as well as remembering a chess position.

Another attentional capacity that is attributed to the central executive is that of dividing attention between two or more

KEY TERM

Confabulation: Recollection of something that did not happen.

tasks, for example chatting to a passenger while driving. On the whole, this seems to proceed reasonably safely. If the traffic situation becomes complex, the driver can cease speaking and the passenger is likely to see why, and postpone the conversation. This is not the case with a cell phone conversation, however, during which there might also be a much more serious attempt to convey complex information or discuss an important business matter. As we saw in the section on the sketchpad, if spatial information is involved, this is likely to interfere with steering control. Even more important, however, is the effect of concurrent telephoning on the capacity to make sensible driving decisions. Brown, Tickner,

and Simmonds (1969) had their participants drive a route marked out on an airfield that involved going through gaps of varying width between polystyrene blocks. A concurrent verbal reasoning task did not impair the drivers' skill in steering through such gaps, but it seriously disrupted their judgment with the result that they tended to attempt gaps that were narrower than the car. The danger in telephoning while driving does not principally result from what the driver's hands are doing but from what the brain is neglecting to do (Box 3.3).

Studies of patients with Alzheimer's disease suggest that they find dividing their attention across tasks particularly hard. One study (Baddeley, Bressi, Della Sala, Logie, & Spinnler,

Box 3.3 Inattention when driving causes accidents

A naturalistic study that videoed drivers and the road ahead for a total of 2 million miles of driving time recorded 82 crashes, with 80% implicating driver inattention during the

previous 3 seconds (National Highway Safety Administration, 2006). Cell (mobile) phone use is a potent source of such inattention, with accidents being four times more frequent when a cell phone is in use, regardless of whether it is hand held (Redelmeier & Tibshirani, 1997).

A laboratory study by Strayer and Johnston (2001) showed that drivers who were using cell phones were substantially more likely to miss a red light (panel a) and were significantly slower at applying the brakes (panel b), regardless of whether or not the phone was hand held. From Strayer and Johnston (2001). Copyright © Blackwell Publishing. Reproduced with permission.

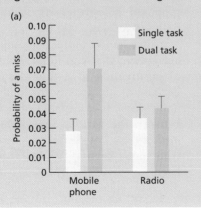
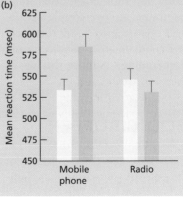

1991a) compared the capacity to combine activities across three groups: Alzheimer patients and elderly and young control participants. Two tasks were used, a tracking task and a digit span task. The experiment began by ensuring that the three groups were performing at the same level. This involved establishing digit span and tracking skill for each participant, and resulted in the use of somewhat shorter digit sequences and slower target speeds in the patients and elderly controls. At this point, we required all groups to perform both tasks at the same time. We found that the normal elderly and young groups showed a similar modest drop in performance under combined conditions, whereas the Alzheimer patients showed a marked deficit. Subsequent research showed that this was not a result of simply increasing the cognitive load as our patients showed a clear dual-task deficit even when the two tasks were made very simple. Furthermore, this differential deficit did not occur with single tasks—even when they were made more difficult, patients and controls responded in a very similar way (Logie, Cocchini, Della Sala, & Baddeley, 2004). A practical implication of this finding is that such patients might be able to follow a conversation with one person quite well, but lose track when more people take part (Alberoni, Baddeley, Della Sala, Logie, & Spinnler, 1992).

It has been suggested that the central executive is required if attention has to be switched between two or more tasks (Baddeley, 1996). However, the idea that switching might always be the function of a single attentional system appears to be an oversimplification, with some aspect of switching being relatively automatic whereas others are almost certainly attentionally demanding (Allport, Styles & Hsieh, 1994; Monsell, 2005).

THE EPISODIC BUFFER

A major problem with the three-component model of working memory was that of explaining how it was linked to LTM. Memory span for words in a sentence is about fifteen compared to a span of five or six for unrelated words (Brener, 1940). However, it is not clear how this can be accounted for within the three-component model. Fifteen words are substantially more than the capacity of the phonological loop, and enhanced recall of sentences is not limited to those that can readily be turned into visual imagery. At a broader level, it is of course unsurprising that this is the case. The order of words within a sentence is constrained by the rules of grammar and by the overall meaning of the sentence, both allowing the chunking process described in Chapter 2 to increase span, and in both cases depending on LTM. However, this then raises the question of exactly how working memory is able to take advantage of long-term knowledge: How do working memory and LTM interact?

This was by no means the only problem for the three-component model. Digit span itself presents a challenge. Given that we can typically remember seven or more digits, and two or three of these come from the loop, where are the other items stored? If in visual STM, how is this combined with phonological STM? Finally, as we noted in the Baddeley and Andrade study of the vividness of imagery described in Chapter 2, those images that are based on LTM such as that of a familiar market scene do not appear to depend at all heavily on the visuo-spatial and phonological subsystems. So where is the information for such complex images held while the judgment of vividness is made? In an attempt to provide an answer to these questions, I proposed a fourth component, the episodic buffer (Baddeley, 2000).

The episodic buffer is assumed to be a storage system that can hold about four chunks of information in a multidimensional code. Because of its capacity for holding a range of dimensions, it is capable of acting as a link between the various subsystems of working memory, also of connecting these subsystems with input from LTM and from perception. Each of these information sources uses a different code, but these can be combined within the multidimensional buffer.

I also proposed that information was retrieved from the episodic buffer through conscious awareness. This linked the working memory model with an influential view as to the function of consciousness. Baars (1997, 2002) suggests that conscious awareness serves the function of pulling together separate streams of information from the various senses and **binding** them into perceived objects and scenes. He links this to the proposal that consciousness serves as a mental workspace that assists in performing complex cognitive activities, in short, a working memory. He uses the metaphor of a theater, in which consciousness is represented by the stage on which an ongoing play is played by actors, who are seen as analogous to the various interactive cognitive processes.

In its initial form (Baddeley, 2000), the episodic buffer was assumed to be an active system, entirely controlled by the central executive. It was assumed to be capable of binding together previously unrelated concepts, to create new combinations, for example, combining the concepts of ice hockey and elephants, to imagine an ice-hockey-playing elephant. This novel representation can be manipulated in working memory, allowing one to answer questions such as what position the elephant should play. It could, for instance, do some crunching tackles, but might it be even more useful in goal?

At a more routine level, it was suggested that executive processes were necessary to bind the words in a sentence into meaningful chunks, or indeed to bind perceptual features such as shapes and colors into perceived objects. If this was the case, then one would expect that disrupting the executive with a demanding concurrent task would interfere with binding. More recent evidence suggests that this is probably not the case. A demanding concurrent task impairs STM for shapes and colors but does not disrupt the capacity to bind this information into colored objects (Allen, Baddeley, & Hitch, 2006). Similarly, disrupting the executive impairs immediate memory for both unrelated word lists and sentences, but does not reduce the capacity to bind or chunk the words into sentences (Allen & Baddeley, 2008).

If this preliminary evidence is sustained, it would suggest a change in the model of consciousness proposed from the theater analogy in which the episodic buffer is the centre of an *active* binding process to a more passive system: A screen on which information from a range of sources is displayed, with the active process of combination proceeding off-screen.

The concept of an episodic buffer is still at a very early stage of development, but has already proved useful in a number of ways. At a theoretical level, it bridges the gap between the multicomponent Baddeley and Hitch (1974) model with its emphasis on storage, and more attentionally focused models such as that of Cowan (1999, 2005). In doing so, it has emphasized the important question of how working memory and LTM interact, and more specifically has stimulated research on the issue of how different sources of information are bound together. This has led to further links between the multicomponent model and studies concerned with visual attention and memory (Luck & Vogel, 1997; Vogel, Woodman, & Luck, 2001), and with the classic issues of language comprehension (Daneman & Carpenter, 1980; Kintsch & van Dyck, 1977).

The current model of working memory is shown in Figure 3.9. This is essentially an elaboration of the original three-part model, with two major changes. One of these reflects the assumed link to LTM from the phonological and visuo-spatial subsystems, one allowing the acquisition of language, and the other performing a similar function for visual and spatial information. This is much less investigated than is the language link, but is assumed to be involved in acquiring visual and spatial knowledge of the

KEY TERM

Binding: Term used to refer to the linking of features into objects (e.g. color red, shape square, into a red square), or of events into coherent episodes.

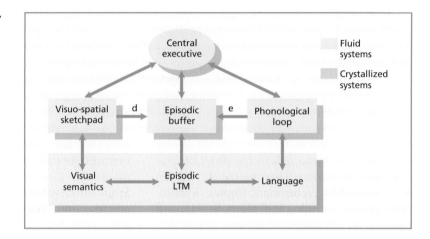

Figure 3.9 The Baddeley (2000) version of the multicomponent working memory. Links to long-term memory have been specified and a new component, the episodic buffer, added.

world, for example learning the shape and color of a banana, or the layout of a city.

The second major change is the inclusion of the episodic buffer. In the original version of the buffer (Baddeley, 2000) it was accessed only through the central executive. However, the evidence just described on binding visual and verbal information into chunks suggests that information can access the buffer directly from the visuo-spatial and phonological subsystems and from LTM (arrows d and e). Finally, an even more recent attempt to account for the way in which emotion influences working memory also assigns a major role to the episodic buffer (Baddeley, 2007).

However, although the multicomponent model has thrived in the 30 years since it was proposed, it is by no means the only model of working memory. Indeed, a great deal of research on working memory, particularly in North America, has used a very different approach, less influenced by studies of STM and data from neuropsychological patients and strongly influenced by methods based on individual differences between normal participants.

INDIVIDUAL DIFFERENCES IN WORKING MEMORY

This approach to working memory was sparked by a study by Daneman and Carpenter (1980),

who were interested in the possible role of working memory in language comprehension. They took as the defining feature of working memory, the need for the simultaneous storage and processing of information, and then set out to develop a task that would measure this. They proved remarkably successful. The task they produced appears to be a very simple one. Participants are required to read a series of sentences and subsequently recall the last word of each. Try it for yourself:

A sailor returned from a long voyage having acquired a parrot as a pet.

It was a terribly cold winter with many violent storms.

The play was an enormous success and ran for many years.

What were the three last words?

They were *pet, storms, years.* Span is typically between two and five sentences.

Daneman and Carpenter (1980) showed that their working memory span task was able to predict the prose comprehension capacity of their student participants, a result that has been replicated many times. Daneman and Merikle (1996) review 74 studies showing broadly similar results. A total of 38 studies looked at working memory span and global comprehension, finding an average correlation of .41; another 36 studies using more specific language processing measures found an average correlation of .52. In both cases, correlations were higher than those obtained for verbal STM tasks (.28 and .40, respectively).

Working memory span has also proved able to predict a wide range of other capacities. High-span participants are better at prose composition (Benton, Kraft, Glover, & Plake, 1984), obeying complex instructions (Engle, Carullo, & Collins, 1991), and taking notes (Kiewra & Benton, 1988). The capacity to predict performance extends beyond language tests to performance on a course concerning logic gates (Kyllonen & Stephens, 1990), and on a 40-hour long course on the PASCAL programming language (Shute, 1991). A study by Kyllonen and Christal (1990) compared performance on a series of working memory tasks with a battery of reasoning ability measures taken from standard IQ tests, finding a very high correlation. The principal difference was that the IQ tests appeared to depend somewhat more on prior experience, and the working memory measures somewhat more on speed. Engle, Tuholski, Laughlin, and Conway (1999) obtained a similar result finding a high correlation between working memory and fluid intelligence.

Variants of the working span task are already being applied to practical problems. They form an important component of a battery of tests developed by Susan Gathercole and Susan Pickering based on the multicomponent working memory model, which they have applied to detecting and predicting learning problems in school-age children (Gathercole & Pickering, 2000a). Their test battery has separate measures of phonological loop and sketchpad performance based on tasks involving verbal or visuo-spatial STM, together with what they term *complex span* tasks—visual and verbal processing tests that, like the Daneman and Carpenter task, involve simultaneously storing

and manipulating information and hence tap the central executive.

Analysis of the performance of school-age children is broadly consistent with predictions from the multicomponent model, allowing the separate components of working memory to be estimated and related to academic performance. Children who have been identified as having special educational needs perform poorly overall on the working memory battery (Gathercole, Pickering, Knight, & Stegmann, 2004b). Scores on specific subtests are also informative, with delayed reading and arithmetic being associated with poor performance on both phonological STM and complex span tasks in 7- to 8-year-old children (Gathercole & Pickering, 2000b), whereas complex span continues to predict maths and science scores at the age of 14 (Gathercole, Lamont, & Alloway, 2006).

What are children with poor working memory performance like? Gathercole's group decided to sit in on classes and observe how these children differed from their classmates. Children with low working-memory scores were typically described by their teachers as "dreamy" or inattentive; not disruptive, but failing to follow instructions and to do the right thing at the right time. Gathercole et al. noted, however, that the instructions were often quite complex, for example "Put your reading cards back in the envelope, your pencils back in the box, and then sit on the carpet in the corner." The child would begin the task and then apparently lose track. The children themselves reported that they forgot. However, this memory problem was not something that the teacher typically realized.

It later became clear that a good number of these children were diagnosed with ADHD (attention deficit hyperactivity disorder), which, as its name suggests, has two potentially separable components of which one—attention deficit—might well be linked to working memory performance. This is being investigated by Gathercole's group, which has developed a program to enable teachers to identify children with problems based on

Gathercole et al. found that children with low working memory scores were typically described by their teachers as "dreamy" or inattentive; however ADHD may well be responsible as it is linked to working memory performance.
© Royalty-Free/Corbis.

working-memory limitations and to modify their teaching accordingly (Gathercole & Alloway, 2008).

THEORIES OF WORKING MEMORY

Given the predictive power of complex span measures, there is great interest in understanding why they are successful. Attempts to develop a theory of working memory based on individual differences typically involve breaking working-memory performance down into a number of more basic components, devising tasks that aim to tap these components, and then examining the extent to which each of these is able to predict performance on tests of reasoning, intelligence, or academic performance. Part of this process of analysis involves studying the extent to which particular tasks are related to each other, in ways that might suggest the nature of the underlying structure of the memory and processing systems involved.

Happily, there tends to be broad agreement, with most analyses stressing the importance of an attentionally based control system, analogous to the central executive

within the multicomponent working memory model. This tends to be strongly involved in complex tasks, with a smaller contribution from two or more components that appear to be responsible for the simple storage of verbal and visuo-spatial material, respectively (Engle et al., 1999; Miyake, Friedman, Rettinger, Shah, & Hegarty, 2001; Gathercole, Pickering, Ambridge, & Wearing, 2004a). Again, this broadly resembles the structure proposed by the Baddeley and Hitch model. Most theories of working memory focus on the executive component, often simply attributing the STM functions to relatively unspecified "activation of LTM," although the use of active verbal rehearsal is typically accepted as a source of temporary storage.

Although most theories derived from the study of individual differences have proved to be broadly compatible with the multicomponent model, this resemblance is not always obvious. Nelson Cowan's influential approach to working memory is a good example of a conflict that is more apparent than real (Baddeley, 2001, 2007; Cowan, 2001, 2005).

Cowan's embedded processes theory

Cowan described working memory as "cognitive processes that retain information in an unusually accessible state" (Cowan, 1999 p. 62). For Cowan, working memory depends on activation that takes place within LTM, and is controlled by attentional processes (Figure 3.10). Activation is temporary and decays unless maintained either through active verbal rehearsal or continued attention.

Activated memory is multidimensional, in that way resembling my own development of the concept of an episodic buffer, the main difference being that I assume that items are downloaded from LTM and represented within the episodic buffer, whereas Cowan suggests that the "addresses to locations in LTM are held." It is not clear at this point how one would distinguish between these two views. The main consequence is a differential

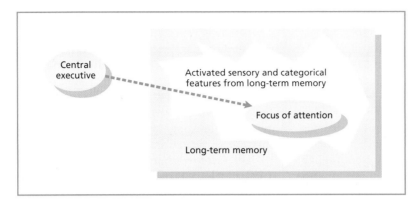

Figure 3.10 Cowan's embedded-processes model of working memory. A central executive controls focus of attention, which acts on recently activated features from long-term memory. The focus can hold approximately four objects in mind at the same time. Adapted from Cowan (1988).

emphasis, with Cowan being particularly concerned with working memory *capacity* where he argues strongly for a capacity of four chunks (Cowan, 2005), rather than the seven originally proposed by Miller (1956). This influence reflects Cowan's interest in attention, and in the development of memory during childhood rather than in the more peripheral aspects of working memory and the neuropsychological evidence that have featured prominently in my own approach. The importance of a verbal subsystem is certainly not denied by Cowan, who has in fact done important work on phonological STM (e.g. Cowan, 1992; Cowan et al., 1992), although his theory is less concerned with its detailed modeling.

Engle's inhibitory control theory

One of the most active and innovative groups using the individual differences approach to working memory is that associated with Randy Engle and colleagues. Whereas much of the work using the working-memory span measure has been limited to observing correlations between span and various cognitive capacities, Engle has consistently focused on the theoretical issue of understanding what capacities and processes underpin such associations.

Turner and Engle (1989), for example, demonstrated that the predictive capacity of complex span was not limited to measures based on sentence processing. They developed the *operation span* measure in which each

to-be-remembered word is followed by arithmetic operations; for example, *Apple*, 7 + 2 – 1 = ? *House*, 5 – 1 + 6 = ? and so on; the words are then recalled. This measure correlates highly with the initial-sentence span task and is also is a good predictor of cognitive performance.

Engle (1996) proposes that performance on a complex span task is made difficult by the need to protect the memory of the presented items from *proactive interference (PI)*, the tendency for earlier items to compete at retrieval with the items to be recalled. Evidence for this comes from a range of sources and is typically based on a procedure whereby a complex span task is given to a large group of students, with those performing particularly well or particularly badly then being chosen for further investigation. Then, rather than looking for an overall correlation across participants, Engle tests for differences between these two extreme groups in their capacity to perform various other tasks.

In one study, participants were required to remember three successive free recall lists, each comprising one word from each of ten semantic categories, for example one animal, one color, one country. As expected, use of the same categories but different instances across successive trials led to poorer recall of later lists. As predicted (Kane & Engle, 2000), this interference effect proved to be reliably greater in low working-memory span participants. Performance on the first list did not differ, suggesting that resistance to interference rather than learning capacity was the crucial factor.

Engle suggests that the capacity to resist interference is not limited to memory. In one study Conway, Cowan, and Bunting (2001) required participants to repeat a stream of digits presented to one ear and ignore messages presented to the other. Unexpectedly, the person's name was included in the unintended stream. When subsequently questioned, the low span participants were much more likely to have detected their names, even though instructed to ignore that source, presumably because they were less able to shut out the irrelevant material, as predicted by the **inhibition** theory (Conway et al., 2001).

These and other studies do indeed suggest that there is a genuine and important link between complex span and capacity to resist interference, although it is entirely plausible to assume that both reflect some kind of more general executive capacity that plays an equally important role in other cognitive functions. However, the nature of inhibition is itself open to question. A study by Friedman and Miyake (2004) found evidence for two types of inhibition, one reflecting a capacity to inhibit a powerful response tendency, such as moving your eyes to fixate a visual target, and the other a quite separate inhibition effect, reflecting interference within memory. Both were modestly related to the Daneman and Carpenter reading span measure: For prepotent response inhibition the correlation was .23, whereas resistance to inhibition in memory correlated .33.

The time-based resource-sharing model

Whereas Engle and colleagues focus on the importance of interference with the remembered words, an alternative possibility is that complex span reflects the capacity to prevent the decay of the memory trace through rehearsal. This does not necessarily mean subvocal rehearsal, but simply "keeping in mind" the items, perhaps by intermittently focusing attention on the fading trace. Evidence for such rehearsal comes from the

observation that short-term forgetting in the Peterson task is present when the delay following the three consonants to be remembered is filled by a demanding backward counting task, but not when simple articulatory suppression is required (Baddeley, Lewis, & Vallar, 1984a). This suggests that participants can maintain the items in some way without needing to continue to verbalize them.

The **resource-sharing** hypothesis was been developed by a French group involving Pierre Barrouillet and Valerie Camos, who replaced the arithmetic task used in Turner and Engle's (1989) operation span task with a simple letter-reading task that was, however, strictly paced. Thus, participants were required to remember words while concurrently processing letters coming rapidly one after the other. This apparently simple task correlated even more highly with measures of reading and arithmetic than did conventional complex span measures (Lépine, Barrouillet, & Camos, 2005). Barrouillet et al. (2004) explained this, and other related findings, by arguing that more complex tasks allow brief gaps in which rehearsal might occur, whereas their more rigidly controlled simple task minimizes such rehearsal.

A related theory is the **task-switching** hypothesis proposed by Towse and Hitch (1995; Towse, Hitch, & Hutton, 2000), who also assume a trace decay interpretation with participants switching

KEY TERMS

Inhibition: A general term applied to mechanisms that suppress other activities. The term can be applied to a precise physiological mechanism or to a more general phenomenon, as in proactive and retroactive inhibition, whereby memory for an item is impaired by competition from earlier or later items.
Resource sharing: Use of limited attentional capacity to maintain two or more simultaneous activities.
Task switching: A process whereby a limited capacity system maintains activity on two or more tasks by switching between them.

attention between maintaining the trace and performing the secondary task.

In conclusion, although there is no doubt that complex span is a very powerful predictor of a wide range of cognitive performance, we still do not fully understand why. Given the importance of this issue, it continues to be an area of great research activity.

Long-term working memory

Ericsson and Kintsch (1995) proposed a theory of **long-term working memory**. This refers to the use of LTM to assist in temporary storage. It includes the use of long-term knowledge to assist prose recall but was also strongly influenced by Ericsson's interest in the performance of people who have a specific expertise in remembering. In one study, Chase and Ericsson (1982) repeatedly tested the digit span of an individual over many days of practice, finding that his span grew and grew, eventually reaching a span of around 80 digits. On questioning him, they discovered he had developed a special mnemonic technique. He was an enthusiastic runner and had developed a system of coding the number sequences in terms of running times for particular distances and levels of performance; for example, *a very fast time for the 800 meters*. Another example came from the expert memory of a waiter who used a particular structure to memorize the orders of his customers (Ericsson & Polson, 1988). The use of the visual image of an abacus by the expert calculators discussed earlier would be another example of long-term working memory. It does not, therefore, represent an overall theory of memory but rather a particular use of LTM, which is discussed further in Chapter 16 on improving your memory.

THE NEUROSCIENCE OF WORKING MEMORY

This chapter has focused on the psychology of working memory based almost entirely on behavioral methods of study. However, an enormous amount of work has been concerned with investigating the anatomical and neurophysiological basis of working memory. Initially, this approach relied principally on the type of neuropsychological evidence; more recently, two further methods have become prominent: single-cell recording in monkeys, and neuroimaging studies based on normal human participants.

Single-cell recording approaches to working memory

Single-cell recording involves placing electrodes in individual cells within the brain of an awake monkey and then recording the cells' activity as a function of a range of presented stimuli. The method was pioneered by Hubel and Weisel (1979), who were awarded the Nobel prize for their work on the analysis of visual processing using single-cell recording. This method was extended to the study of memory by Fuster (1954) and by Patricia Goldman-Rakic (1988), who carried out a series of classic studies in which monkeys were taught to fixate a central point on a screen, maintaining their gaze while a peripheral light stimulus was presented in one of several locations. If they maintained fixation until a recall signal, and then moved their eyes to the appropriate location, they received a reward. Funahashi, Bruce, and Goldman-Rakic (1989) detected cells within the frontal lobe of the monkey that were active during this retention period. If activity continued until the recall signal, a correct response was typically made, whereas discontinued activity was followed by forgetting. This led some commentators to identify the particular area

---

> **KEY TERM**
>
> **Long-term working memory:** Concept proposed by Ericsson and Kintsch to account for the way in which long-term memory can be used as a working memory to maintain complex cognitive activity.

in the frontal lobe as *the* source of working memory. However, later work has identified cells behaving in a similar way in other parts of the brain (Goldman-Rakic, 1996), suggesting that the frontal areas were part of a more general system, as would indeed be predicted by a multicomponent model of working memory.

A behavioral version of this task has been developed for use with human participants, with schizophrenic patients being found to be impaired (Park & Holzman, 1992). This has caused some excitement, because of the potential link between an important disease and a very specific neurophysiologically related measure. However, although this certainly does indicate a deficit in working memory in schizophrenic patients, the effect is not particularly dramatic and other deficits, such as those in episodic LTM, are probably more important from a practical viewpoint (McKenna, Ornstein, & Baddeley, 2002). However, it seems likely that single-unit recording methods of studying memory will continue to provide an important link between psychological and neurobiological approaches to memory.

Neuroimaging working memory

A closer and more extensive link between psychological and neurobiological approaches to memory is provided by a rapidly growing body of work applying the various techniques of brain imaging described in Chapter 1 to the study of working memory. The initial studies used positron emission topography (PET), which you might recall involves introducing a radioactive substance into the bloodstream and using this to monitor the amount of activity occurring in different brain regions. Two groups were particularly active in applying this method to the study of working memory. In London, Paulesu, Frith, and Frackowiak (1993) carried out a study that was based on the phonological loop hypothesis. They identified two separate regions, one in the area between the parietal and temporal lobes of the left hemisphere, which appeared to be

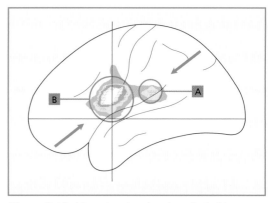

Figure 3.11 Neuroimaging the phonological loop. A study using positron emission tomography identified area A with phonological storage and area B with the articulatory rehearsal process. Redrawn from Paulesu et al. (1993).

responsible for phonological storage, and a second more frontally based region known as Broca's area, known to be involved in speech production but that appeared to be linked to subvocal rehearsal (Figure 3.11).

The second group, led by John Jonides and Edward Smith at the University of Michigan, has been particularly active in using neuroimaging to investigate working memory, carrying out a sustained series of carefully designed and theoretically targeted experiments (Smith & Jonides, 1997). The first direct comparison of visual and verbal working memory was provided by Smith, Jonides, and Koeppe (1996). In their verbal memory task, participants were shown four letters, followed by a probe letter. Participants had to decide whether the probe letter had been contained in the previous set of four. A baseline control involved presenting both the stimulus and the probe simultaneously: everything was the same except for the need to remember. If the amount of brain activation in this baseline condition is subtracted from the activation involved when memory is also required, then the difference in blood flow should reflect the additional demand made by the need to remember, over and above that involved in perceiving and processing the experimental stimuli. Like Paulesu et al., Smith and colleagues found that

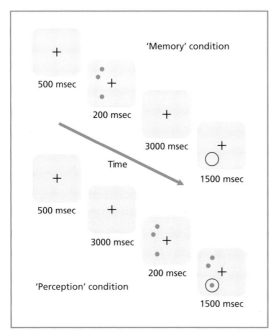

Figure 3.12 Schematic drawing of the events on each trial of the spatial memory and spatial perception tasks used by Smith et al. (1996). Copyright © Oxford University Press. Reproduced with permission.

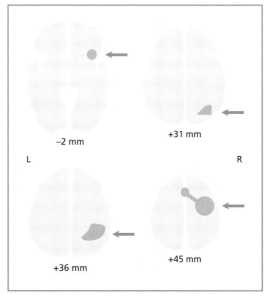

Figure 3.13 Illustration depicting PET images of the four areas activated in the visuo-spatial working memory study. Based on Smith et al. (1996).

verbal STM activated two separate areas in the left hemisphere.

In the case of visuo-spatial memory, participants were shown an array of three dots, followed after a delay by a circle (Figure 3.12). They had to decide whether this coincided with the location of one of the dots. Again, a baseline was established in which the dots and circle were presented at the same time. As indicated in Figure 3.13, visual memory resulted in activation in a series of areas in the right hemisphere (Smith et al., 1996).

Further studies (reviewed by Smith & Jonides, 1997) observed a distinction between **spatial working memory** as described above, and memory for an *object or pattern*, such as an abstract shape. Spatial memory activates more dorsal or upper regions of the brain whereas **object memory** tends to be more concentrated on lower or ventral areas (Figure 3.14). It is notable that research on visual processing in nonhuman primates (Mishkin, Ungerleider, & Macko, 1983), has identified two separable

visual processing streams, with the dorsal stream being concerned with spatial location (*where*), and the ventral processing stream with shape and object coding (*what*).

You might recall that the concept of a central executive was strongly influenced by evidence from patients with frontal lobe damage. It is therefore unsurprising that neuroimaging evidence suggests that executive processes tend to rely heavily on frontal areas. One method of investigating this is through the N-back task, in which the participant sees a sequence of items and is required to press a button whenever a repeat occurs. The easiest condition is when the requirement is to

KEY TERMS

Spatial working memory: System involved in temporarily retaining information regarding spatial location.
Object memory: System that temporarily retains information concerning visual features such as color and shape.

Figure 3.14 Combined data from studies involving short-term memory from visual objects (pink) or spatial location (blue). The distinction is mainly between the ventral locations for object memory, and dorsal for locations. Based on Smith and Jonides (1999).

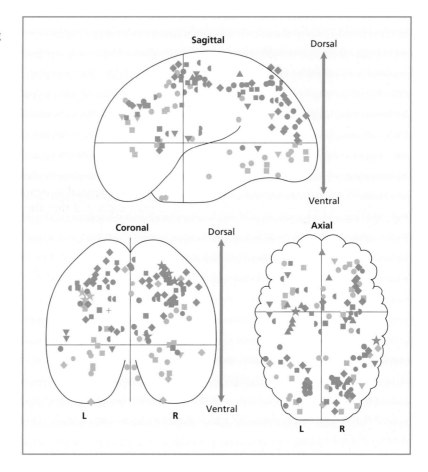

detect immediate repeats, (e.g. 1, 7, 9, 6, 6), as minimal memory is involved. The task can be made a little harder by requiring a match between the presented item and the item presented one back (e.g. 7, 9, 6, 2, 6 where the participant should respond to the second 6). The task can be made more and more difficult by increasing the lag, as it is necessary to hold an increasingly long sequence while inhibiting each item once it is too far back. The task has a further advantage: It can be used in a broadly equivalent form to study either verbal or nonverbal visuo-spatial memory. For both the verbal and visuo-spatial N-back tasks, frontal activation occurs and increases systematically with the executive load as determined by the number of items back that need to be monitored and hence demand made on the central

executive (Braver, Cohen, Nystrom, Jonides, Smith, & Noll, 1997; Owen, McMillan, Laird, & Bullmore 2005).

However, although there is no doubt that the frontal lobes play a crucial role in executive processing, there is much less agreement on the extent to which specific executive capacities are located in particular frontal areas. Some investigators have suggested the possibility of quite detailed mapping of separable executive processes (e.g. Shallice, 2002) whereas others point to the lack of consistency across studies at anything other than the broadest level (Duncan & Owen, 2000). It seems likely that settling this controversy will depend on the development of better methods at both the behavioral and neuroimaging level.

SUMMARY

The Atkinson and Shiffrin modal model, although proposed as a model of working memory, was principally based on verbal STM. It encountered problems both regarding its assumption of the transfer of information to LTM through simple rehearsal, and because of its difficulty in explaining why patients with grossly affected STM did not have general working memory problems.

Baddeley and Hitch proposed a multicomponent model of working memory comprising an attentional controller, the central executive, and two subsystems. One of these, the phonological loop, holds and manipulates speech-based information, while the visuo-spatial sketchpad performs a similar function for visual and spatial information.

Study of patient PV's very limited digit span suggested that the phonological loop might have evolved to facilitate the acquisition of language. Disrupting the loop impairs the learning of a second language. The capacity to hear and repeat back a nonword, which is assumed to depend on the phonological loop, is impaired in children with specific language problems, and provides a good predictor of level of vocabulary development in healthy young children.

The visuo-spatial sketchpad is necessary for the use of imagery both to store visuo-spatial information and also to use it to solve problems. Logie has presented a model of the sketchpad that by analogy with the phonological loop contains a store, the visual cache, and a system for spatial manipulation, the inner scribe.

Control of action by the central executive is assumed to operate along the lines initially proposed by Norman and Shallice. This involves a combination of semi-automatic control, based on existing schemas and habits, coupled with a capacity for intervention by the supervisory attentional system (SAS). The central executive is assumed to be analogous to the SAS and to be capable of both focusing and dividing attention, and to be defective in patients with frontal lobe damage.

More recently, an additional component—the episodic buffer—was proposed. This involves a multidimensional code that allows the various components of working memory to interact and to link with both perception and LTM.

Individual differences in working memory have been studied extensively using a range of measures, all based on the need to combine the storage and manipulation of information. Such measures have proved extremely successful in predicting performance across a wide range of cognitive tasks.

Theoretical interpretations of working memory are broadly consistent with the multicomponent model, but concentrate mainly on explaining the nature of the executive component. Influential theories include Cowan's embedded processes approach, strongly influenced by his interest in attention, whereas Engle and colleagues suggest that the capacity to inhibit disruptive information is crucial. A number of other groups stress the need to control the limited attentional resources as a crucial factor. This is currently a very lively area.

Neurobiological evidence has played an important role in the study of working memory. This was based initially on the study of the single neuropsychological cases, together with the study of single-cell recording in monkeys performing working memory tasks. More recently, there has been considerable research on working memory using neuroimaging techniques, producing results that are broadly consistent with both the data from patients, and the multicomponent model.

FURTHER READING

- **Andrade, J.** (2001). *Working memory in perspective*. Hove, UK: Psychology Press. A discussion of the strengths and limitations of the Baddeley and Hitch multicomponent model of working memory by a group of younger investigators working in the area.

- **Atkinson, R. C., & Shiffrin, R. M.** (1971). The control of short-term memory. *Scientific American*, *225*, 82–90. A good summary of the modal model for the general scientific reader.

- **Cowan, N.** (2005). *Working memory capacity*. Hove, UK: Psychology Press. A recent overview of Cowan's approach to working memory. It proposes that the capacity of working memory is four chunks, rather than Miller's magic number seven.

- **Engle, R. W., Cantor, J., & Carullo, J. J.** (1992). Individual differences in working memory and comprehension: A test of four hypotheses. *Journal of Experimental Psychology: Learning, Memory, and Cognition*, *18*, 972–992. Discusses a range of hypotheses about working memory and the methods for evaluating them.

- **Fletcher, P. C., & Henson, R. N. A.** (2001). Frontal lobes and human memory: Insights from functional neuroimaging. *Brain*, *124*, 849–881. Discussion of the role played by the frontal lobes in memory from a neurological and psychological viewpoint.

- **Logie, R. H.** (2003). Spatial and visual working memory: A mental workspace. *Psychology of Learning and Motivation*, *42*, 37–78. An overview of the visuo-spatial aspects of working memory by one of the leading investigators in the field.

CHAPTER 4

LEARNING

Alan Baddeley

Why are you reading this chapter? I assume that at one level or another you hope to learn something, although perhaps only enough to get through your next test! If you are a student, then you have probably spent a large part of your life learning. Such a lengthy period of learning is not evolution's usual solution to survival in a complex world. Many very successful species, such as ants, crocodiles, viruses, and butterflies, come into the world preprogrammed with the equipment to survive. Humans, however, are a species that can only survive by learning. Without it, we would have no language, no complex tools, no transport systems, and little in the way of society. So what do we know about learning?

As the next few chapters will illustrate, we know a good deal; we know there are different kinds of learning leading to different kinds of memory. We know that forgetting depends on the capacity to retrieve what we have learned. And we know that this in turn depends on how we learned it. In short, the various stages of learning and memory are interrelated and, ideally, should be discussed together. However, that would result in a single, huge, and complex chapter. Instead, we have opted for a series of interlinked chapters moving from learning, through episodic memory to retrieval and forgetting, attempting to remind you of the important links by cross-chapter references.

Philosophers have considered the nature of learning and remembering for over 2000 years, without coming to an agreed understanding, so when in the 1880s, a young German philosopher, Herman Ebbinghaus, proposed an experimental study of memory, he was being extremely bold. Ebbinghaus devoted 2 or 3 years to this ambitious enterprise before moving on to study other topics such as intelligence and color vision. However, in that brief period he laid the foundations of a new science of learning and memory, a science that is particularly relevant to rapidly changing societies like our own, in which people need to learn far more than did earlier generations.

Ebbinghaus decided that the only way to tackle the complex subject of human memory was to simplify the problem. He tested only one person—himself—and as he wished to study the learning of new information and to minimize any effects of previous knowledge, he invented some entirely new material to be learned. This material consisted of **nonsense syllables**: word-like consonant–vowel–consonant sequences, such as WUX, CAZ, BIJ, and ZOL, which could be pronounced but had no meaning. He taught himself sequences of such words by reciting them aloud at a rapid rate, and carefully scored the number of recitations required to learn each list, or to relearn it after a delay had caused him to forget it.

KEY TERM

Nonsense syllables: Pronounceable but meaningless consonant–vowel–consonant items designed to study learning without the complicating factor of meaning.

During his learning, he carefully avoided using any associations with real words, and he always tested himself at the same time of day under carefully controlled conditions, discontinuing the tests whenever "too great changes in the outer or inner life occurred." Despite, or perhaps because of, his use of this rather unpromising material, Ebbinghaus was able to demonstrate to the world that memory can be investigated scientifically, and in the short period of 2 years, he was able to show some of the fundamental characteristics of human memory.

If you want to assess any system for storing information, three basic questions must be answered: How rapidly can information be fed into the system? How much information can be stored? How rapidly is information lost? In the case of human memory, the storage capacity is clearly enormous, so Ebbinghaus concentrated on assessing the rate of input and, as we shall see later, of forgetting.

RATE OF LEARNING

Consider the rate at which information can be registered in memory. If you spend twice as much time learning, do you remember twice as much information? Or is there perhaps a law of diminishing returns, with each additional learning episode putting a little less information into storage? Or perhaps the relationship is the other way round: The more information you have acquired, the easier and quicker it is to add new information, rather like a rolling snowball picking up more snow with each successive revolution? Ebbinghaus investigated this problem very simply, by creating a number of lists each containing 16 meaningless syllables. On a given day, he would select a fresh list (one he had not learned before) and recite it at a rate of 2.5 syllables per second for 8, 16, 24, 32, 42, 53, or 64 repetitions. Twenty-four hours later, he would find out how much of the list he had remembered by seeing how many additional trials he needed to relearn the list by heart. To get some idea of

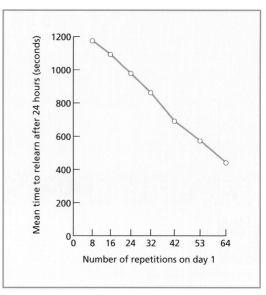

Figure 4.1 Influence of number of learning trials on retention after a 24-hour delay. From Ebbinghaus (1885).

what his experiment was like, try reading the following list of nonsense syllables as rapidly as you can for two successive trials:

JIH, BAZ, FUB, YOX, SUJ, XIR, DAX, LEQ, VUM, PIQ, KEL, WAB, TUV, ZOF, GEK, HIW

The results of this very tedious exercise are shown in the graph in Figure 4.1. The relationship between the number of learning trials on day 1 and the amount retained on day 2 is a straight line, signifying that the process of learning shows neither diminishing returns nor the snowball effect, but obeys the simple rule that the amount learned depends on time spent learning: If you double the learning time, you double the amount of information stored. In short, as far as learning is concerned, you get what you pay for.

This simple relationship has been explored extensively in the 100 years since it was discovered by Ebbinghaus and is known as the **total time hypothesis.**

It would, of course, be unwise to base such a sweeping conclusion on a single

The basic concept that, as far as learning is concerned, you get what you pay for, is known as the total time hypothesis. If you spend twice as long revising for an exam, you will store twice as much information, and will be twice as prepared for the exam!

study, even by someone as august as Herman Ebbinghaus, but there is ample further evidence. For example, do you want to become a more skilled writer? If so, the answer is to practice. A study by Astin (1993) found that the best predictor of self-reported skill in writing was number of writing skills classes taken, with amount of feedback provided by the instructor being the second best predictor. One might reasonably argue that this result is based on self-assessment, which is likely to be an unreliable measure. However, a similar conclusion was obtained by Johnstone, Ashbaugh, and Warfield (2002), who observed a steady increase in writing skill over a sequence of courses as assessed by others. This is further illustrated in the case of professional writers such as Norman Mailer (2003), who reported that he learnt to write by writing, estimating that he must have written more than half a million words before he came to his famous novel *The naked and the dead*.

Ericsson, Krampe, and Tesch-Römer (1993) emphasized the importance of practice across a number of skills, including chess, typing, and music. In relation to the last, they suggest that the very best violinists have accumulated more than 10,000 hours of solitary practice

compared to 7500 for lesser experts, 5000 for the least accomplished experts, and around 1500 hours for the committed amateur.

The generalization that "you get what you pay for" is therefore a reasonable rule of thumb for learning, but within this broad framework there are good buys and bad ones, bargains and items that are not worth the asking price. Despite the general relationship between practice and the amount retained, there are ways in which one can get better value for time spent. The rest of this chapter is concerned with ways of beating the total time hypothesis.

DISTRIBUTED PRACTICE

If you examine the Ebbinghaus learning graph closely, bearing in mind the amount of time spent in practice on day 1, you will notice that total time for learning is not in fact constant, as time spent on day 1 gives a disproportionate saving on relearning the next day. For example, 64 trials on day 1 take about 7.5 minutes; a similar time is needed to learn the list completely on day 2, making a total of 15 minutes. However, if only 8 trials are given on day 1 (about 1 minute), then it takes nearly 20 minutes to learn the list on day 2. Dividing practice fairly evenly over the 2 days, therefore, results in more efficient learning than cramming most of the practice into the second day. This is an instance of a very widespread phenomenon, known as the **distributed practice** effect. What this means is that it is better to distribute your learning

KEY TERM

Total time hypothesis: The proposal that amount learned is a simple function of the amount of time spent on the learning task.
Distributed practice: Breaking practice up into a number of shorter sessions; in contrast to massed practice, which comprises fewer, long, learning sessions.

trials sparsely across a period of time than to mass them together in a single block of learning. As far as learning is concerned, "little and often" is an excellent precept.

A good example of this arose a few years ago when my colleagues and I were asked to advise the British Post Office on a program that aimed to teach a very large number of mailmen (know as postmen in Britain) to type. Postal coding was being introduced and this required the mail sorters to type the postal code using a keyboard resembling that of a typewriter. The Post Office had the option of either taking postmen off their regular jobs and giving them intensive keyboard training, or of combining the training with their regular jobs by giving them a little practice each day. There were four feasible schedules: An intensive schedule of two 2-hour sessions per day, intermediate schedules involving either one 2-hour or two 1-hour sessions per day, or a more gradual approach involving a single 1-hour session of typing per day. We therefore assigned postmen at random to one of the four groups and began the training.

Figure 4.2 shows the rate at which the four groups acquired typing skill. The time it took to learn the keyboard and the subsequent rate of improvement were both strongly affected by the particular training schedule used. The postmen who trained for only 1 hour a day learned the keyboard in fewer hours of training and improved their performance more rapidly than those who trained for 2 hours a day; and they in turn learned more rapidly than those who trained for 4 hours per day. Indeed, the 1-hour-per-day group learned as much in 55 hours as the 4-hours-per-day group learned in 80. They also appeared to continue to improve at a faster rate and, when tested after several months without further practice, they proved to have retained their skill better than the 4-hours-per-day group (Baddeley & Longman, 1978).

This result did not stem from fatigue or discontent on the part of the 4-hours-per-day group. Indeed, when questioned afterwards, the 1-hour-per-day postmen were the least contented with their training schedule because, when measured in terms of the number of days required to acquire typing skill, they appeared to be progressing less rapidly than their 4-hours-per-day colleagues. In drawing practical conclusions, of course, this should be borne in mind; 4 hours per day might be a relatively inefficient way of learning to type when measured on an hourly basis, but it did mean that the group reached in 4 weeks the standard it took the 1-hour-a-day group 11 weeks to achieve. Distributed practice is more efficient, but it might not always be practical or convenient.

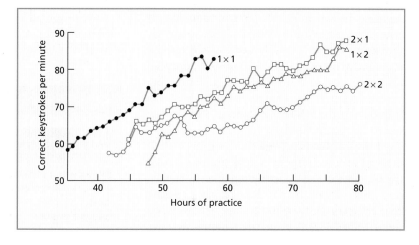

Figure 4.2 Rate of learning a typing skill for a range of training schedules: I × I equals one session of I hour per day, 2 × I equals two such sessions, I × 2 is one session of 2 hours and 2 × 2 two 2-hour sessions. From Baddeley and Longman (1978). Copyright © 1978 Taylor & Francis. Reproduced by permission (http://www.tandf.co.uk/journals).

In recent years there has been a good deal of interest in a method originally proposed by Tom Landauer and Robert Bjork (1978) that involves what might be called the microdistribution of practice. Suppose you are trying to learn French vocabulary and have the following list of words to master:

- stable = *l'écurie*
- horse = *le cheval*
- grass = *l'herbe*
- church = *l'église*
- castle = *le château*
- cat = *le chat*
- table = *la table*
- bird = *l'oiseau*

If you are presented with a single item on two occasions, do you remember it better if it is presented and tested in rapid succession, or is recall better if the two presentations and test are spaced further apart? Fortunately, the answer is clear; spaced presentation enhances memory. On that basis alone, one should go through the whole vocabulary list before testing by re-presenting the first item, as that will maximize the space between two successive presentations. Unfortunately, however, life is not so simple, as it is also the case that if you succeed in remembering an item for yourself, this strengthens the memory more than if you have the item provided for you; this is known as the *generation effect*. The implications of this are exactly the opposite to the distribution of practice effect. The sooner an item is tested, the greater the probability that you will be able to recall it, and hence the greater the probability that learning will be strengthened.

EXPANDING RETRIEVAL

The solution to this dilemma is to use a flexible strategy in which a new item is tested initially after a short delay, ensuring that it is still recallable. Then, as the item becomes better learned, the practice–test interval is gradually extended, the aim being to test each item at

TABLE 4.1: Expanding retrieval—an example based on learning French vocabulary.

Teacher	Learner
stable = *l'écurie*	
stable?	*l'écurie*
horse = *le cheval*	
horse?	*le cheval*
stable?	*l'écurie*
horse?	*le cheval*
grass = *l'herbe*	
grass?	*l'herbe*
stable?	*l'écurie*
horse?	*le cheval*
grass?	*l'herbe*
church = *l'église*	
church?	*l'église*
grass?	*l'herbe*
church?	*l'église*
stable?	*l'écurie*
grass?	*l'herbe*
horse?	*le cheval*

the longest interval at which it can reliably be recalled. Hence, a learning sequence for the list of French words just given might be as shown in Table 4.1: If the learner fails an item in the vocabulary list, it should be presented after a shorter delay; whenever the learner is correct, the delay should be increased.

In creating their new mnemonic method, known as **expanding retrieval**, Landauer and Bjork (1978) combined two basic principles

KEY TERM

Expanding retrieval: A learning schedule whereby items are initially tested after a short delay, with pretest delay gradually increasing across subsequent trials.

derived from the laboratory study of verbal memory. The first is the distribution of practice effect and the second is the generation effect; items that you yourself have generated successfully are remembered best. In recent years, a number of studies have explored these underlying principles in more detail, part of a very welcome current concern to apply the results of the memory laboratory to learning in the classroom. Pashler, Rohrer, Cepeda, and Carpenter (2007) studied the spacing effect across a range of different materials, including the acquisition of foreign language vocabulary, learning to solve mathematical problems, acquiring obscure facts, learning the definition of uncommon words, and learning from maps. They found that spacing is beneficial for all of these materials.

How far apart should spacings be? This proves to depend on the length of the delay between learning and testing, with the optimum interval between learning episodes being between 10 and 20% of test delay. Hence, for testing after 10 days there should be a delay of 1 or 2 days between trials, whereas for a 6-month test delay, a 20-day interval between learning trials is best. In general, longer inter-trial delays are preferable to short. It should be noted, however, that it is important for participants to receive feedback as to the correct answers, having made their response, although it proves not to be crucial whether the feedback is immediate or somewhat delayed (Pashler et al., 2007).

As in the case of the postmen learning to type, later studies have confirmed that spaced practice leads to less forgetting. In one study, Pashler et al. (2007) gave their students one sequence of ten mathematical problems, or two sets of five presented 2 weeks apart. When tested after 1 week, the two groups were equivalent, but after 4 weeks there was a clear advantage to spaced learning.

THE IMPORTANCE OF TESTING

A second crucial feature of the Landauer and Bjork method is the importance of testing one's

memory. Pashler et al. found that giving a test trial with feedback was more effective than giving an extra learning trial. The importance of retrieval for learning was shown particularly clearly in an elegant study by Karpicke and Roediger (2008). They studied foreign language vocabulary learning across four conditions. The first involved the standard procedure of repeatedly presenting and testing a list of 40 Swahili–English word pairs (e.g. mashua–boat). A second adopted the procedure of dropping a pair once it had been learned, a procedure often recommended in study guides as it allows the learner to concentrate on the unlearned items. A third condition ceased testing learned pairs but continued to present them. The final condition did the opposite: learned pairs were not presented but continued to be tested. Recall was then tested a week later. Which conditions do you think led to best recall?

The results are shown in Figure 4.3. We should first note that the rate of learning in week 1 was identical across conditions. Retention was not. The two conditions that had continued *testing* learned pairs both recalled 80%; the two conditions in which testing was abandoned when pairs were learned were equally poor, at around 30% recall. Repeated presentation without test had had no effect at all. Remember this next time you are revising for a test!

The importance of the generation effect—producing the answer from memory rather than being given it—was also stressed by Metcalf and Kornell (2007), who tested foreign language vocabulary learning, for example learning that the French word for *house* is *maison*. At test, they found that even a brief delay between testing with the English item (*house*) and being given the answer (*maison*) was enough to induce an attempt at retrieval that was much more helpful to long-term learning than presenting the English and foreign words at the same time.

Does it matter how knowledge is tested? Marsh, Roediger, Bjork, and Bjork (2007) found that a multiple-choice test enhanced subsequent long-term recall. However, McDaniel, Roediger, and McDermott (2007) observed that

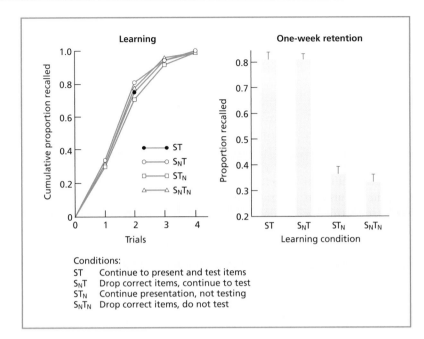

Figure 4.3 The importance of testing for later remembering. The pattern of learning and test trials had no effect on rate of learning, but the presence of tests had a major effect on what was remembered 1 week later. From Karpicke and Roediger (2008). Copyright © 1980 AAAS. Reprinted with permission.

short-answer tests were more effective than multiple-choice in enhancing subsequent recall.

THE IMPORTANCE OF FEEDBACK

One danger of encouraging learners to generate answers is that they can produce errors, which, in the absence of explicit feedback, might then persist. Kay (1955) required his students to learn a prose passage and then recall it once a week for several weeks. He found that although the passage was repeated every week, errors made at the beginning tended to persist. Fortunately, this does not appear to be the case if direct feedback is given. In one study, Pashler et al. (2007) encouraged various levels of guessing on a multiple-choice task involving obscure facts such as:

The weight of what land animal is equal to the weight of a blue whale's tongue?

a.   Bengal tiger
b.   Grizzly bear

c.   Wolverine
d.   African elephant
    (The answer is d.)

Pashler et al. found no difference between groups instructed not to guess, those required to guess but given immediate feedback, and those for whom the feedback was delayed. It is, however, perhaps worth noting at this point that an encouragement to guess is not helpful for amnesic patients, presumably because they are not able to remember the feedback (Baddeley & Wilson, 1994). Unlike healthy young participants, they benefit more from learning procedures that try to avoid errors (see Chapter 11).

Expanding retrieval is a rare example of a completely new learning technique resulting from verbal learning research. It prompted Ulrich Neisser, normally rather skeptical about the achievements of modern memory research, to produce the following limerick:

You can get a good deal from rehearsal

If it just has the proper dispersal.

You would just be an ass,

To do it en masse:

Your remembering would turn out much worsal.

MOTIVATION TO LEARN

An important factor that has not been mentioned so far is motivation. This might seem strange in the light of most studies of animal learning, in which motivation is regarded as of paramount importance. This is probably because rewarding or punishing the animal is the only way the experimenter can be sure that the animal will attend to the experimental conditions and exhibit what it has learned. Fortunately, experimental human subjects are in general rather more cooperative. Most subjects in memory experiments want to do well, to please the experimenter or to convince themselves that they have good memories, or perhaps because it is simply more interesting to attempt to do well than to display a complete lack of interest. Provided participants give their full attention to a task, level of motivation is not usually an important factor.

A Swedish professor, Lars-Goren Nilsson (1987), found his students very reluctant to accept this view, so he set up the following experiment to prove his point. He had groups of students learn lists of words under various conditions. In one condition no pressure was put on the students to do well; they were simply told that they were taking part in an experiment on memory. In a second condition, the students were not given motivating instructions during learning, but at the time of recall were told that a substantial cash prize would be given to the person who recalled the greatest number of words. Students in a third group were told about the cash prize before they began learning. The learning performance of the three groups did not differ. A subsequent experiment included social competition as a means of increasing motivation and produced exactly the same result: no effect of motivation level on learning.

Does this mean that motivation is quite irrelevant to learning? As any schoolteacher will tell you, this is certainly not the case. The effect of motivation is indirect, however: It will determine both the amount of time and the degree of attention devoted to the material to be learned, and this in turn will affect the amount of learning. Hence, if I were to ask you to learn a list of words comprising ten animal names and ten flower names, and I were to offer you a coin for each animal name recalled and a banknote for each flower, there is little doubt that you would remember more flowers than animals. The reason would be that you would simply spend more time on the flowers, producing a result that would be equivalent to my presenting the flowers for a longer time. In a classroom situation, motivation is likely to affect learning because it affects the amount of attention children give to the material they are being taught. If they are interested, they will pay attention; if they are bored, they are likely to think about other things.

REPETITION AND LEARNING

Some theories of learning have suggested that all that is required is repetition of the material to be learned. Such a view would probably have appealed both to Ebbinghaus and to Victorian educators, with their emphasis on learning by heart. However, a number of experiments have recently suggested that simple repetition, with no attempt by the learner to organize the material, might not lead to learning. Think of a penny in your pocket. Can you remember exactly what is on each side? Try it! Figure 4.4 shows the results of a study by Rubin and Kontis (1983), who asked their participants to recall the features of four American coins. The coins are shown on the left of the figure, and the most commonly recalled version of each coin is shown on the right.

A colleague, Debra Bekerian, and I were able to explore the importance of

Figure 4.4 The results of a study by Rubin and Kontis (1983) recording the features that most US students thought appeared on each of four coins. Column (a) shows the actual features and column (b) the most frequent responses. From Rubin and Kontis (1983). Copyright © The Psychonomic Society. Reproduced with permission.

repetition in connection with a major advertising campaign (Bekerian & Baddeley, 1980). A number of years ago, a new international agreement among European radio stations made it necessary for the BBC to reassign some of the British wavelengths. To acquaint the public with this fact, and to familiarize them with the changes, the BBC embarked on an extensive advertising campaign. Over a period of 2 months, radio programs were regularly interrupted by detailed information about the new wavelengths, supplemented by slogans and complex jingles.

We decided to test the effectiveness of the campaign by questioning about 50 members of our panel of people who volunteered to come along to the Applied Psychology Unit in Cambridge to take part in experiments on functions such as memory, visual perception, and hearing. In this instance, most of our volunteers were Cambridge housewives. At that time, it was common for mothers to stay at home when their children were young. We asked them how much time they spent listening to each radio channel and, on the basis of this and information provided by the BBC about the frequency of announcements, we estimated that most of them had heard the announcements about the new wavelengths well over a thousand times. We asked them to recall the new wavelengths both by writing down the numerical frequencies and by marking a visual display resembling a radio dial.

How much had our subjects learned? The BBC had been successful in conveying the fact that the change was about to occur, as virtually every participant was aware of it. There was also considerable knowledge about the exact date of the change, with 84% reporting it correctly. However, memory for details of the new wavelengths was appalling. Only 25%, on average, even attempted to give the numerical frequencies, and although more people were prepared to attempt to represent them by marking the dial display, most of these attempts were little better than would be expected on the basis of pure guessing. Furthermore, knowledge of the old frequencies was little better. People probably relied on visual cues on the radio dial to tune in to their favorite programs. So why was the date of changeover so well remembered? Presumably because our participants *did* regularly use dates.

Fortunately, in addition to the radio advertising campaign, the BBC also circulated every household by mail with information about the new wavelengths, and included adhesive stickers with the letters. When we conducted a follow-up survey shortly after the changeover, we found that it was these stickers that had saved the day for most people. Seventy percent of our follow-up group had indeed had difficulty learning the new wavelengths, but for the most part they coped successfully by waiting until the changeover had taken place, then hunting for the new wavelengths and marking them with the stickers that the BBC had sensibly provided.

What conclusions can we draw from this? One is that such saturation advertising is not particularly suitable for conveying complex information. If one simply wants people to remember "Botto washes whitest," telling them so a thousand times will cause the message to be retained, although not necessarily believed. In the case of complex information that does not map onto one's existing way of thinking, however, the total effect appears to be minimal learning and maximum frustration.

Change blindness

Although it might be somewhat surprising that so little was learned about pennies and radio wavelengths despite so many presentations, one could argue that this is because we were testing fine detail of no real interest to the learner. You don't need to check your pennies to make sure they are genuine, and our radio listeners simply did not use wavelength information. Somewhat more surprising, perhaps, are instances of what has become known as **change blindness**, whereby some prominent feature of the visual environment is dramatically changed, without the perceiver apparently noticing.

Figure 4.5 Change blindness: the original scenes are on the left; the images on the right are the altered versions that participants were required to judge. From Rosielle and Scaggs (2008). Copyright © Psychology Press and reproduced with permission of the author.

In one study, for example, the experimenter stopped a passer-by and asked for directions. During the conversation, it was arranged that a pair of men carrying a board passed between the two conversants, allowing the experimenter to be surreptitiously replaced by another quite different experimenter. People rarely appeared to detect this (Rensink, O'Regan, & Clark, 1997; Simons & Levin, 1998).

Could this perhaps reflect a failure to take notice of the appearance of the questioner, or of the fragility of visual STM? These possibilities were ruled out in a study by Rosielle and Scaggs (2008), who asked students to identify what was wrong with a picture of a familiar location on college campus. These were quite dramatic, for example removing the library from the scene (Figure 4.5). Ninety-seven percent of participants rated the scene as familiar, but only 20% detected the change. Despite frequent experiences, our LTM for complex scenes appears to be much less detailed than one might imagine.

IMPLICIT LEARNING

You might recall that in Chapter 1 we distinguished between *declarative* memory, in which we explicitly remember the information retrieved, and *nondeclarative* or implicit memory, in which the evidence of learning comes from a change in behavior. When riding a bicycle, for example, we do not need explicitly to remember what to do; we simply get on the bike and pedal away. The learning of motor skills is just one of a wide range of tasks that can be acquired implicitly. They can be divided into three broad categories: classical conditioning, priming in which an existing representation such as a word is activated, and procedural learning, of which motor skills are one example. These will be described in turn.

Classical conditioning

In 1902, a young American psychologist, E. B. Twitmyer reported work on the knee-jerk reflex

Russian psychologist Ivan Pavlov, a dog, and his staff, photographed circa 1925–1936. © Bettmann/Corbis.

in which a bell sounded after which a lead hammer struck the subject's knee causing an involuntary twitch. He noted that on one occasion the bell rang but the hammer was not delivered; nevertheless the reflex occurred, something that the participant reported as involuntary. Twitmyer (1902) pursued this line of research and reported it at a meeting of the American Psychological Association some 2 years later. However, his enthusiasm for the topic was not shared by the chairman of his session, Professor William James of Harvard, who cut short the discussion to avoid delaying lunch.

At about the same time, an eminent Russian physiologist, Professor I. P. Pavlov, who was shortly to receive the Nobel Prize for his work on digestion, made a similar observation. He was working on the salivatory reflex using dogs and noted that the dogs began to salivate when they heard the experimenter arrive. He pursued this insight and became even more famous than he already was (Pavlov, 1927).

As every basic textbook describes, Pavlov found that when a bell was presented at the same time as meat powder, after a while the bell alone would evoke salivation, reflecting the basic feature of classical conditioning—that pairing a neutral stimulus, the bell, with a reflex response,

KEY TERM

Change blindness: Failure to detect even quite dramatic changes in a scene, given a brief delay.

salivation, leads to learning. Pavlov also noted that if the bell was sounded repeatedly without food powder, salivation would reduce and gradually cease. He termed this the *extinction* of the conditioned response.

What would one expect if the bell followed the meat powder? Would backward conditioning occur? Although some evidence of backward or trace conditioning has been reported, the effect is very weak.

Given that sounding the bell alone leads to extinction of the conditioned response, what is the effect of sounding the bell alone for many times *before* introducing the association with food powder? This impairs the capacity to condition the salivating response; a phenomenon known as **latent inhibition**. Presenting the bell alone, whether before or after the food, breaks the clear link between bell and food.

One area that has taken advantage of classical conditioning is advertising, in which it is common practice to attempt to improve the public's evaluation of a product by associating it with a pleasant and attractive surround experience. Although there is little research on advertising in the memory literature, a relevant study was carried out a few years ago by Stewart, Shimp, and Engle (1987), who presented participants with a slide picture of a "new" brand of toothpaste in a green and yellow tube, labeled "Brand L Toothpaste." The toothpaste was presented with three other fictitious commodities, "Brand R Cola," "Brand M Laundry Detergent," and "Brand J Soap," which were paired with neutral pictures whereas the toothpaste was always followed by one of four particularly pleasant slides, sunset over an island, for example, or sky and clouds seen through the masts of a yacht. Different groups experienced the items from 1 to 20 times, and were then asked which products they would probably buy. As the graph in Figure 4.6 shows, the toothpaste was rated as more likely to be bought than the other three items, with likelihood of purchase increasing as the number of exposures increased.

The investigators went on to test two more detailed predictions from the conditioning

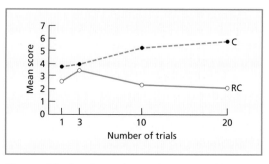

Figure 4.6 Conditioned attitude to a novel brand of toothpaste as a function of the number of conditioning trials. Participants rated the likelihood that they would choose the positively conditioned brand over the randomly associated control brand. C, conditioning; RC, random control. Data from Stewart et al. (1987).

laboratory. The first of these was that presenting the toothpaste for many trials under neutral conditions would reduce the effect of pairing it with the pleasant slides later, the latent inhibition effect. This is indeed what happened. A third study presented the pleasant slides immediately *before* the toothpaste, setting the scene for backward conditioning, which is known to be much weaker than forward conditioning. As predicted, the level of acquired pleasantness was much less, suggesting that conditioning might indeed provide a suitable model for this aspect of advertising.

Whereas Stewart et al. (1987) explicitly tried to associate a product with a positive feeling, another conditioning phenomenon suggests that even this is not strictly necessary. Simply increasing our exposure to a novel stimulus will increase its rated pleasantness, the **mere exposure effect** (see Bornstein, 1989, for a review). The effect occurs even

KEY TERMS

Latent inhibition: Classical conditioning phenomenon whereby multiple prior presentations of a neutral stimulus will interfere with its involvement in subsequent conditioning.
Mere exposure effect: A tendency for a neutral stimulus to acquire positive value with repeated exposure.

with such unpromising materials as irregular polygons presented so briefly that participants are not aware, and resulting in no subsequent recognition (Kunst-Wilson & Zajonc, 1980). Perfect and Askew (1994) investigated the mere exposure effect in an advertising context. They presented their participants with 25, full-page, color magazine advertisements. Half the participants were instructed to remember the adverts and half were not. They were then shown the 25 together with 25 new adverts and asked to rate them on the extent to which each was eye-catching, distinctive, appealing, and memorable, after which they were asked to judge which they had seen before. Participants instructed to remember recognized around 60% of the adverts they had seen compared to only 11% for the noninstructed incidental group. However, both groups rated the advertisements they had seen as more appealing and memorable, an effect that was equivalent for the two groups. It seems to be the case, therefore, that although simple repetition is not a very good way of learning about detail, it does—perhaps unfortunately—influence our emotional evaluation.

Priming

Priming is said to occur if presenting an item influences its subsequent perception or processing. For example, you might be required to read out a list of words and then, in an apparently separate experiment, to perceive words presented very briefly. Those words that you had read would be more likely to be detected than new words, even though you might not be able to remember the old words. Priming occurs across the whole range of senses, leading Schacter (1992) to categorize perceptual priming as forming a coherent memory system, on the grounds that similar principles apply to all modalities.

Priming is also found in verbal memory, and offers one way in which even densely amnesic patients can demonstrate apparently normal memory. This was discovered by Warrington and Weiskrantz (1968), who presented amnesic patients and controls with a list of words, which were then tested. When a standard recognition procedure was used, with participants required to identify those words that they had seen previously, amnesic patients performed very badly. However, they performed normally when tested using a priming procedure. This involved visually degraded versions of each word, with the instruction to "guess" what the word might be.

Related methods of using priming to demonstrate implicit memory for words include **stem completion** and word **fragment completion**. Stem completion tests implicit memory by presenting the first few letters and inviting the patient to "provide" a word that would fit (e.g. present *STAMP* and test with *ST– – –*). Note that if the patient is asked to "guess" an appropriate word, this is an implicit task, whereas given exactly the same situation and asked to "remember" the word makes it an explicit test. Graf, Squire, and Mandler (1984) tested amnesic and control participants by presenting a list of words and testing retention by free recall, cued recall in which they were asked to remember the word, and by stem completion. Their patients did very badly on free recall, were clearly impaired on cued recall but showed no deficit when tested by stem completion.

A crucial feature of priming is that it is often, although not always, dependent on reinstating the physical conditions under which encoding occurred. Graf and Mandler (1984) visually presented a list of words, such as *STAMP*, instructing subjects to process them either semantically, or in terms of their visual appearance. Retention was then tested

KEY TERMS

Stem completion: A task whereby retention of a word is tested by presenting the first few letters.

Fragment completion: A technique whereby memory for a word is tested by deleting alternate letters and asking participants to produce the word.

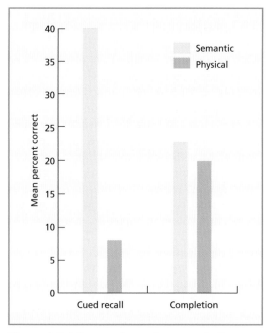

Figure 4.7 Influence of encoding semantically or physically on explicit cued recall versus implicit stem completion. Based on Graf and Mandler (1984) Experiment 3.

either by stem completion or by means of an associated semantic cue (e.g. *Letter*). There was a major advantage to semantic coding under the explicit cued recall condition, as would be expected, as semantic coding is, in general, a good method of explicit learning, as we will see in Chapter 5. However, no semantic advantage was found when performance was tested implicitly using the word fragment completion test (Figure 4.7).

A related measure of implicit memory is known as fragment completion. In this task, a previously presented word such as *elephant* is tested by giving the word with half the letters omitted e.g. – *l* – *p* – *a* – *t* and asking what word would fit that fragment. Both of these methods show preserved learning in amnesic patients (see Chapter 11). Using the fragment completion task with normal subjects, Tulving, Schacter, and Stark (1982) studied the durability of explicit and implicit verbal learning. When tested after only an hour, the request to recall the words led to better performance

than fragment completion; but after a week's delay, the pattern reversed, with little decrement in fragment completion but substantial forgetting for recall.

We have so far limited discussion of priming to verbal memory. However, as Warrington and Weiskrantz (1970) showed, priming also operates for the retention of line drawings of objects. When memory is tested by recognition, amnesic patients are severely impaired, but when the task is to identify a fragmented version of the original drawing, they show normal implicit memory. Schacter, Cooper, and Delaney (1990) showed a similar effect for two-dimensional drawings of three-dimensional objects, an effect that was absent when the drawings had represented "impossible objects" that in fact could not be represented in three dimensions, and hence that presumably did not result in a coherent and primeable representation on the brain.

Finally, whereas most priming studies have operated at a perceptual level, equivalent effects can be obtained at a deeper level. Srinivas and Roediger (1990) required participants to process lists of words that included animal names such as *rat* and *hyena*. This was followed by an apparently unrelated task involving generating as many words as possible in 60 seconds from a series of semantic categories. Items that had been encountered earlier were more likely to be generated.

Procedural learning

Some years ago, I took a course on learning to sail. It began with theory, explaining the relationship between the direction of the wind, the set of the sails, and the control of the rudder. Trying to bear these three factors in mind while handling the small boat as it keeled over in one direction or another proved far from simple, and after a while I just gave up worrying and did what seemed to work. The boat mysteriously began to behave, as did other boats on subsequent occasions. Somehow, the brain seemed to be solving problems that were beyond the reach of the conscious mind. This, of course, is not uncommon in the performance of skills. When a fielder runs to catch a cricket ball or a baseball, it is necessary to solve some complex equations to ensure that the ball and the hands reach the same place at the same time, equations that the fielder almost certainly could not solve consciously. That is not to say that performance cannot sometimes be improved by conscious strategy; for example, by giving advice as to what height to attempt to intercept the falling ball. Such strategies can, however, be limited in their value, and can on occasion be counter productive.

This was demonstrated in an intriguing experiment by Masters (1992), who was interested in the response to stress known as "choking," in which a skilled sportsman such as a golfer appears to lose that skill under pressure, going into the last round of a tournament several shots ahead, having played brilliantly, only to make a series of simple putting mistakes and lose the tournament. Masters studied this by devising a simple putting task in which participants had to knock a golf ball into a hole. A total of 400 training trials was given. Half the participants performed a demanding attentional task during learning and half did not. The crucial test occurred over the last 100 trials, which operated normally or under a stress condition. Stress was induced by telling participants that they were about to be judged by a golf professional of considerable distinction. He would decide whether participants received an increased prize or lost virtually all the money they had so far earned. The so-called professional (in fact a stooge) was clad in a golf sweater and coughed occasionally, before disappearing behind a screen. Unbeknown to the subject he actually left the room, leaving behind a tape recording of occasional coughs to convince the participants they were being watched. The results of this study are shown in Figure 4.8. It is clear that, whereas learning is somewhat impaired by the demanding concurrent task, this condition was much

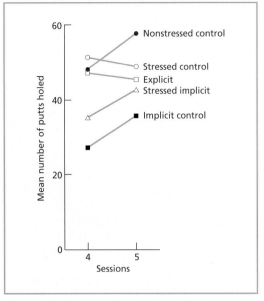

Figure 4.8 Mean number of putting shots holed as a function of skill acquisition phase (sessions 1–4) and a test phase (session 5) in the study by Masters (1992). Implicit learning led to lower performance but was more resistant to the effects of stress at test.

more resistant to stress. When questioned afterwards, it proved to be the case that the group given the concurrent task during learning was much less likely to have evolved explicit conscious strategies (less than one per person) than the control group (typically more than three).

Learning artificial grammars

One important form of learning that appears to be acquired implicitly is the grammar of our native language, which, as linguists have pointed out, tends to be lawful but complex, and appears to be acquired by native speakers with no formal grammatical instruction. A feature of grammars is that they are *generative*, that is that the items of the language can be combined and recombined in a virtually infinite number of ways, without producing ungrammatical sequences. The study of this phenomenon led to the development of a number of so-called artificial grammars, involving sequences of letters that allow certain combinations to

Figure 4.9 A finite state grammar of the type used by Reber to study implicit learning. Three examples of grammatically permissible sequences are given.

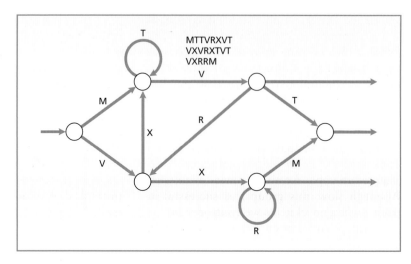

occur while others are illegal. Figure 4.9 shows one such grammar in which each node represents a letter and each arrow leads to a permissible subsequent letter, including the possibility of repetition for some, but not all, letters. Reber (1967) showed that people were able to learn such grammars, as shown by a capacity to decide at a better-than-chance level whether a completely new letter sequence was "grammatically" correct (e.g. TTVRX) or was not (e.g. TTXRV). However, successful learners were unable to say how they performed this task. Even more surprisingly, Reber (1967) showed that, having learned one grammar, participants could transfer their skill to a second grammar in which the grammatical structure was equivalent but the letters different, suggesting that they had learned rules rather than letters.

It remains open to question, however, just what is being learned in this situation. Perruchet and Pacteau (1990) point out that, given that performance on such grammar-learning tasks is typically far from perfect, much of it could be based on learning to recognize particular pairs or triplets of letters as familiar, and hence potentially grammatically acceptable. Whereas the fact that learning could transfer to other letters might seem to rule this out, Brooks and Vokey (1991) point out that similarity might operate at a number of levels other than that

of the specific letters. For example, given the sequence "ABBBXA and YXXXKY," similarities exist in three ways, the existence of a triple letter, its location in the sequence, and the fact that the sequence begins and ends with the same letter.

It is, of course, questionable as to whether one can generalize from simple artificial grammars to natural grammars and, if so, whether it is better to learn the grammar of a foreign language by explicitly learning grammatical rules—as is usually the case—or more implicitly by the **immersion method** of attempting to learn in a context in which only the second language is spoken.

It is difficult to run controlled experiments on the immersion method, but studies have been performed on teaching grammar by rule or example. Ellis (1993, 1994) compared three methods of teaching Welsh grammar. One simply involved presenting instances of the relevant grammatical forms in a random sequence, with each instance followed by

KEY TERM

Immersion method: A strategy for foreign language teaching whereby the learner is placed in an environment where only the foreign language is used.

its English translation. Participants rapidly learned to provide the relevant English translation for each instance, but showed no capacity to generalize to other material, either by stating rules or judging grammaticality. A second group was taught the relevant rules. Members of this group showed good explicit grammatical knowledge but again had difficulty in generalizing to other material. A third group was given explicit rules and then required to apply them to a range of material. Although slow, this group *was* successful in coping when novel items were introduced.

These results, and others (Scott, 1989; 1990), might seem to suggest that learning a language by the immersion method is not possible. However, this is clearly not the case, as this is how we learn our native language. The conditions of learning are, however, very different, both in the number of hours of exposure and in the age at which we acquire the language.

Complex system control

As the world becomes more complex, jobs that used to depend on basic manual and perceptual skills are increasingly being replaced by automatic processes. However, these processes themselves might need control, possibly involving situations in which automation is not yet adequate, as for example in the case of the job of an air traffic controller. There has therefore been considerable interest in understanding how such complex control tasks are learned. Berry and Broadbent (1984) developed a computer game that involved controlling a simulated sugar factory, with the need to maintain efficiency by optimizing input of raw material, its storage, and processing and controlling product output, all simultaneously. After 60 trials, participants had achieved a level of up to 80% of optimal performance. However, as in the case of sailing or grammar learning, most subjects were not clear quite what they did or why, and there was no correlation between the amount of explicit knowledge reported and level of performance.

Of course, one possibility is that the apparent lack of explicit knowledge might simply reflect the difficulty of reporting in words a strategy that was not itself verbal. A number of attempts to tackle this issue have used a method known as "teach back," in which the learner is asked to instruct a naive participant how to perform the task. Stanley, Mathews, Buss, and Kotler-Cope (1989) used this method in a study extending to 570 trials, and found some evidence for the capacity to transmit information, but only after many, many learning trials.

LEARNING AND CONSCIOUSNESS

There is no doubt that a great deal of our learning is implicit, in the sense that we can learn skills without being able to reflect and report on precisely what we know. That does not, of course, mean that consciousness is not necessary for learning. Addressing this issue requires

Although there have been claims that we can learn during sleep, these claims are not readily substantiated. There is, however, evidence that sleep may indeed help consolidate what we have already learned.

consideration of a definition of consciousness. For present purposes, I suggest we use as our basis what Damasio (1994) refers to as *core consciousness*. By core consciousness, Damasio means the dimension that ranges from being fully awake and alert, to deep sleep and indeed coma. Learning clearly tends to be better when one is awake than asleep, or indeed half asleep, but is any learning possible in the absence of normal consciousness? There have, over the years, been claims that one can learn in one's sleep, a tempting proposition for the student with a busy social life, but—alas—this is not supported by the available evidence (see Druchman & Bjork, 1994, for a review). There is, however, evidence that sleep might help consolidate what we have already learned (see pp. 258–259).

An issue of considerable recent concern stems from reports of patients undergoing surgery under general anesthesia who were conscious during the operation. This is both possible and alarming. A general anesthetic typically contains three components: an analgesic to dull the pain, an anesthetic to cause loss of consciousness, and a muscle relaxant, which, although helpful to the surgeon, means that even if you *can* experience the surgery, you are not able to indicate that fact.

A whole research area has sprung up around this issue, with the evidence currently suggesting that such unfortunate episodes of explicit recall of surgery probably reflect periods of relatively light anesthesia. Electrophysical techniques have now been developed for measuring depth of anesthesia and validated using cognitive measures in healthy volunteers (e.g. Andrade, Munglani, Jones, & Baddeley, 1994). Given an adequate level of anesthesia, there is little evidence for explicit recall, but implicit measures such as priming suggest that some learning can occur under anesthesia (Andrade, 2005; Deeprose & Andrade, 2006). Does that therefore mean that learning can occur without consciousness? This would probably be an unwise conclusion, given that consciousness is not all or none, but it does suggest that conscious awareness might be less important for implicit than for explicit learning.

EXPLAINING IMPLICIT MEMORY

We have discussed implicit and explicit memory as though they were two separate but broadly equivalent classes of learning. This view has led to a number of attempts to come up with a coherent explanation of this dichotomy (Roediger & McDermott, 1993; Neath & Surprenant, 2003). Such attempts, however, assume that the various types of learning described as implicit form a coherent category. An alternative, and I myself think more plausible, view, is that what these various demonstrations of implicit learning have in common is the *absence* of the involvement of episodic learning, a specific system that is geared to "gluing together" events that we experience at the same time.

Implicit memory is in short a category defined by exclusion. The fact that a number of instances *lack* a given feature is not a very solid basis for seeking a common explanation for them. Insects, birds, reptiles, and crustaceans all have in common the fact that they are not mammals; this does mean that we would expect them to be similar in any fundamental way. Perceptual priming, classical conditioning, motor skill learning, and grammar acquisition can all be characterized as *not* requiring episodic memory. However, the fact that they involve widely different perceptual processing and learning systems, and tend to depend on different areas of the brain, suggests that it is unlikely that they will form a coherent group reflecting a single common learning mechanism.

LEARNING AND THE BRAIN

In 1949, the great Canadian psychologist Donald Hebb produced a speculation about the biological basis of learning that continues to be influential. He proposed that long-term learning is based on **cell assemblies**. These occur when two or more nerve cells are excited at the

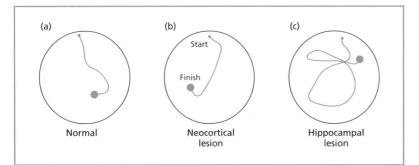

Figure 4.10 Typical swimming paths shown by rats within a Morris water maze. Normal rats (a) rapidly acquire a direct path, as do rats with cortical lesions (b), whereas hippocampal lesions result in a failure to learn (c). Data from Morris et al. (1982).

same time. This involves the synapse—the gap between two separate neurons—being repeatedly activated, whereupon the chemistry of the synapse changes, leading to a strengthened connection. This is often summarized by the phrase "neurons that fire together wire together." Hebb (1949) contrasts the long-term development of all assemblies with a short-term memory process based on temporary electrical activity within existing cell assemblies. Hebb's proposal that long-term learning is based on the development and growth of further synaptic connections has continued to be influential, both through its influence on the search for the neurobiological basis of learning and also for its influence on computer-based simulations of learning.

In the 1960s, a neurophysiological mechanism that appeared to perform in the way Hebb proposed was identified. Bliss and Lomo (1973) found that repeated electrical stimulation of an axonal pathway led to a long-term increase in the size of potentials generated by the neurons beyond the synapse, a process they termed **long-term potentiation (LTP)**. They found that LTP was particularly strongly represented in the hippocampus and surrounding regions, an area that research on animals and on brain-damaged patients suggests is intimately concerned with long-term memory (see Chapter 11).

Evidence for the importance of the hippocampus in learning and of long-term potentiation (LTP) comes from a series of studies using the Morris water maze. This involves a circular tank filled with milky water that obscures the location of a platform located just

below the surface. A rat placed in the tank will swim around until it finds the platform and then pull itself up. As shown in Figure 4.10(a) and (b), in later trials the rat can locate the platform much more rapidly. This is not the case for rats with lesions to the hippocampus, which, as Figure 4.10(c) demonstrates, show little evidence of learning. In a second series of studies, instead of being lesioned the rats were administered a substance known as AP5, which has been shown to block the induction of LTP in the hippocampus. This impaired spatial learning; the degree of impairment increases with the size of dose of AP5 (Morris, Garrud, Rawlings, & O'Keefe 1982; Morris, Davis & Butcher, 1990).

Further evidence for the possible role of LTP came from studies demonstrating that drugs that enhance synaptic transmission also tend to enhance learning (Staubli et al., 1994). LTP is also found in other parts of the brain, including the amygdala, which is closely associated with fear-based learning. Drugs that block LTP have also been shown to reduce such learning (LeDoux, 1998).

KEY TERMS

Cell assembly: A concept proposed by Hebb to account for the physiological basis of long-term learning, which is assumed to involve the establishment of links between the cells forming the assembly.
Long-term potentiation (LTP): A process whereby synaptic transmission becomes more effective following a cell's recent activation.

A great deal is known about the complex relationship between neurotransmitters and learning, with one form of glutamate, N-methyl-D-aspartate (NMDA) playing an important role in LTP (Abel & Lattal, 2001). In addition to analysis at the neurochemical level, it is now becoming increasingly clear that genetic factors play an important role. (See Kandel, 2006, for a detailed review of this area by one of its pioneers, who has recently become a Nobel laureate.)

However, although it is widely accepted that NMDA receptors are *necessary* for the synaptic change that is assumed to underpin learning, it is less certain that they are *sufficient* to induce learning, or whether other psychological processes, such as attention for example, mediated by other brain mechanisms might also be necessary (Martin, Ungerleider, & Haxby, 2000; Shors & Matzel, 1997).

Underlying much of the work just described is the concept of **consolidation**, a process whereby a temporary memory trace becomes established. The term can be used in two ways, one meaning refers to changes at a molecular level, as discussed here, the other applies to a process at a systems level whereby information in one part of the brain is modulated or transferred to another part. This is covered in Chapter 5. Much of the evidence for consolidation comes from attempts to interfere with one or more of these processes, using either electrical brain stimulation or a drug, after which the experimental animal no longer shows evidence of learning. However, this does not necessarily mean that the trace has been damaged, simply that it is not retrievable at the time of testing.

A classic example comes from early studies that taught rats that stepping down from a block led to paw shock, something that animals learn rapidly and refuse to step down. However, when learning is followed by an equivalent of electroconvulsive therapy (ECT) in humans, they appeared to lose the memory, and readily step down. Initially, it was suggested that this demonstrated the failure of the memory trace to consolidate. However, it was subsequently discovered that the memory

trace had not in fact been destroyed, as giving the animal a foot shock acted as a "reminder" that effectively reinstated the learning. The trace had not been abolished, simply made more difficult to retrieve (Miller & Matzel, 2000).

A second source of difficulties for the classic concept of consolidation came from the observation by Nader, Schafe, and LeDoux (2000) of a phenomenon they termed "reconsolidation." This reflects the fact that memory traces become vulnerable to disruption whenever they are recalled. This raises the question of why something that is already consolidated should become disruptable. This, and related data, is beginning to cast doubt on the original concept of consolidation. Alternatives are beginning to be proposed. Nadel and Moscovitch (1997, 1998), for example, have put forward their *multiple-trace theory*, in which each retrieval sets up new traces involving both semantic and episodic memory (Nadel, 2007).

IMPLICIT LEARNING IN THE BRAIN

Conditioning

One of the reasons for rejecting the idea that all types of implicit learning and memory reflect a single system is the evidence that different neural structures are involved in different types of learning. This is shown particularly clearly in the case of classical conditioning. Studies based on animals suggested an important role for the amygdala, an almond-shaped structure within the brain that has repeatedly been found to be involved in emotion and fear conditioning (LeDoux, 1998). Evidence for the importance of the **amygdala** in human

---

KEY TERMS

Consolidation: The time-dependent process by which a new trace is gradually woven into the fabric of memory and by which its components and their interconnections are cemented together.

conditioning comes from a study by Bechara, Tranel, Damasio, Adolphs, Rockland, and Damasio (1995), who describe a conditioning study involving a healthy control group and three very different patients. One had bilateral damage to the amygdala; a second had bilateral damage to the **hippocampus**, which is known to be important for episodic memory; and a third had bilateral damage to both structures. In one study, a series of different colored slides were presented, with one color—blue—being followed by a blast from a loud horn. This aversive stimulus leads to an increase in skin conductants, a measure of anxiety that became conditioned as a response to the blue slide but not to slides of other colors. After the experiment, each of the three patients and the control group were asked what colored slides they had seen, and whether one was associated with the loud horn.

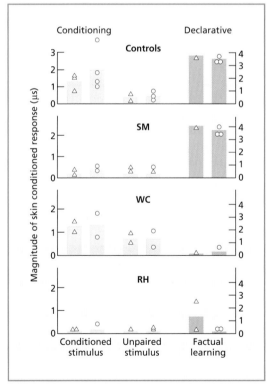

Figure 4.11 Control data and performance of three contrasted patients (SM, WC, and RH) studied by Bechara et al. (1995). Copyright © 1995 AAAS. Reprinted with permission.

The results are shown in Figure 4.11. The patient with bilateral amygdala damage (SM) failed to condition, but was able to remember the colors and identify the blue slide as associated with the horn. In short, he had explicit episodic memory but did not condition. The second patient, a classic amnesic case with hippocampal damage but intact amygdala (WC), showed clear evidence of conditioning but was unable to describe the slides. The third patient with damage to both the hippocampus and the amygdala (RH) showed no conditioning and no evidence of recollection. The control participants showed both conditioning and episodic memory for the slides.

Further evidence for the crucial role of the amygdala comes from a range of neuroimaging studies (Büchel & Dolan, 2000). In one study, Büchel, Morris, Dolan, and Friston (1998) used faces as stimuli, associating one with a loud aversive tone. They observed conditioning in a system involving the amygdala, the cingulate cortex, and in motor-related regions that they identify with a "readiness to escape" response. A further study by Morris, Ohman, and Dolan (1998) demonstrated that conditioning was possible even when faces were masked to a point at which participants failed to report them. Interestingly, activation was principally in the right amygdala when the stimulus was masked, whereas it was principally left in the unmasked condition.

Priming
Schott, Henson, Richardson-Klavehn, Becker, Thoma, Heinze, and Düzel (2005) used fMRI to investigate the implicit and explicit

KEY TERM

Amygdala: An area of the brain close to the hippocampus that is involved in emotional processing.
Hippocampus: Brain structure in the medial temporal lobe that is important for long-term memory formation.

components of the stem completion task. They began by presenting participants with 160 words, with the instruction to count the number of syllables in each. Participants were then tested by being presented with 240 stems comprising the initial letters of each of the 160 old words, together with 80 new words. In the first experiment, participants were given an explicit memory instruction to try to remember the words, but that if they could not recall, then to produce the first that came to mind. A second study was equivalent except that no mention of memory was made, participants were simply asked to produce the first word that came to mind. Explicit memory in the first condition was associated with *increased* blood flow in both left and right parietal and temporal lobes and in the left frontal region. By contrast, priming in the absence of memory was associated with *decreases* in blood flow in the left fusiform gyrus and in both frontal and occipital regions. This reduction in blood flow presumably reflected the easier processing of the primed words.

Procedural learning

Of the many forms of procedural learning, one that has been studied extensively is the serial reaction time task. In a typical version, participants would have four keys, each associated with a light, and would be required to press the relevant key as rapidly as possible when the lights came on. This would then activate the next light and so on. The sequence would initially be random, but would then switch to a sequence containing regularities such that some sequential patterns were more frequent than others. With practice, performance on these sequences improves. The sequence is then switched back to random, whereupon participants who have shown a learning effect slow down, as their learning is no longer relevant. Learning on this task also occurs in amnesic patients. The implicit nature of learning is also shown by the fact that when normal participants are simultaneously performing a demanding task that is sufficient to make them unaware of the regularities, learning still occurs (Nissen & Bullemer, 1987; Nissen, Knopman, & Schacter, 1987).

Hazeltine, Grafton, and Ivry (1997) carried out a neuroimaging study using this task in which the implicit condition involved a demanding concurrent tone-counting task. This was then repeated with eight random and eight quasi-random blocks under single task conditions. Neuroimaging data indicated that when learning was implicit because of dual-task conditions, learning-related changes were found in the *left* motor and supplementary motor cortex, whereas a shift to the *right* hemisphere occurred under the single-task conditions, with the right prefrontal cortex, premotor cortex, and the right temporal lobe involved, as in a previous study (Grafton, Hazeltine, & Ivry, 1995).

SUMMARY

The capacity to learn is crucial for the development of both the individual and society. Scientific study of learning began in 1885 with the work of Ebbinghaus, who demonstrated the possibility of studying learning by experimentation. Using nonsense syllables, he showed that learning occurs in a linear fashion, and that learning is enhanced when practice is distributed, rather than massed. However, learning benefits from successful retrieval, hence testing is important for learning. Test trials can result in better learning than further learning trials, provided feedback is available to discourage repeated errors. The expanding retrieval method combines distributed practice with learning from retrieval to create an effective learning procedure, with important practical implications.

Intention to learn and motivation are not in themselves essential, but are important in focusing the learner's attention on the task in hand.

Simple repetition is typically not the best method of learning, which is more likely to be enhanced by elaborative processing, which links the new material to what is already known. However, rote repetition might be helpful for certain tasks, such as learning to pronounce the words in a foreign language.

Many kinds of learning are implicit, and are demonstrated by performance rather than through conscious recall. Types of implicit learning include classical conditioning, perceptual priming, and procedural learning such as is involved in acquiring motor skills. Quite complex and subtle learning can occur, as in the case of the implicit acquisition of the rules of grammar and in our capacity gradually to improve in the control of complex systems without apparently being consciously aware of the underlying rules. Finally, whereas explicit learning depends on conscious awareness, evidence seems to suggest that this is less central to implicit learning.

Although there are attempts to offer a unitary explanation for all types of implicit learning, it seems more likely that they form a negative category: What they appear to have in common is an absence of the need to rely on episodic memory. Neuroimaging research reinforces this conclusion, suggesting the involvement of a range of different mechanisms that operate anatomically separable systems.

Hebb proposed that all long-term learning depends on the development of cell assemblies, based on persisting changes of the cellular level. This in turn is thought to depend on a process of consolidation involving glutamate receptors, and being potentially disruptable. Cellular consolidation is assumed to result subsequently in consolidation at the systems level, involving the transfer of information from the hippocampus to cortical areas.

FURTHER READING

- **Hartley, J.** (1998). *Learning and studying*. London: Routledge. A discussion of the implications of what we know about learning for the way in which we should study.

- **Hill, W. F.** (2002). *Learning* (7th edn). Boston: Allyn & Bacon. A text providing a broad overview of the psychology of learning.

- **Kandel, E. R.** (2006). *In search of memory: The emergence of a new science of mind*. New York: Norton. A scientific autobiography from the Nobel Prize laureate. It covers the neurobiological basis of memory in a very clear and accessible way.

- **Schacter, D. L.** (1994). Priming and multiple memory systems: Perceptual mechanisms of implicit memory. In D. L. Schacter & E. Tulving (Eds.), *Memory systems 1994* (pp. 233–268). Cambridge, MA: MIT Press. Schacter makes the case for regarding a range of perceptual priming phenomena as components of a coherent system.

- **Squire, L. R.** (1993). The organization of declarative and non-declarative memory. In T. Ono, L. R. Squire, M. E. Raichle, D. I. Perrett, and M. Fukuda (Eds). *Brain mechanisms of perception and memory: From neuron to behavior* (pp. 219–227). New York: Oxford University Press. An account of Squire's views on the structure of long-term memory.

CHAPTER 5

EPISODIC MEMORY: ORGANIZING AND REMEMBERING

Alan Baddeley

Where were you at 8.00 p.m. yesterday evening? What is your earliest memory? When did you last see the sea? All these questions demand a special kind of memory, one that allows you to access specific memories located at a particular point in time: they require *episodic memory*. You will recall from Chapter 1 that this term was devised by Endel Tulving to emphasize the difference between the recollection of specific events and *semantic* memory, generalized knowledge of the world. It is episodic memory that allows what Tulving calls "mental time travel," allowing us to travel back and "relive" earlier episodes, and to use this capacity to travel forward and anticipate future events. You might remember meeting a friend yesterday evening and agreeing to play tennis tomorrow afternoon for instance, and will "travel forward in time" to plan your day accordingly.

The crucial feature of episodic memory is the capacity to remember specific events. For this, you need some kind of mental filing system that will allow you to distinguish that event from similar events on other occasions. This in turn needs three things. The first is a system that allows you to encode that particular experience in a way that will distinguish it from others. Second, it requires a method of storing that event in a durable form, and finally it requires a method of searching the system and retrieving that particular memory. The present chapter is concerned with the first of these processes, the way in which organization is used to "catalog" our experiences so as to make them accessible when we need to remember them.

Although the defining feature of episodic memory is the capacity to recollect specific events, such events might then accumulate and consolidate to form the basis of semantic memory, our knowledge of the world. Although the precise relationship between episodic and semantic memory remains controversial (e.g. Tulving, 2002; Squire, 2004), impaired episodic memory in amnesic patients is generally associated with impaired knowledge acquisition. Martin Conway and colleagues studied the learning and retention of material from a psychology course. After a short delay, much of the information was recalled as episodes, for example, the experience of being told about rats swimming through milky water in the Morris study of the role of the hippocampus in learning. When tested several months later, however, this information had become separated from recollection of the learning event and had become incorporated into the semantic memory, at least of the more successful students (Conway et al., 1992). In that sense, the chapter that follows is as much about learning as is the previous chapter.

The psychology of memory has been, and continues to be, influenced by two rather different traditions. The first of these is the Ebbinghaus tradition, whereby the study of human memory is made possible by focusing on clearly specified experiments with tightly constrained goals. The danger of this approach is that it could lead us to focus on narrow problems that tell us little about how memory works in the world outside the laboratory.

The second tradition attempts to tackle the study of memory in all its complexity, accepting that our capacity to control any single study will inevitably be limited, but trusting in the belief that multiple studies will allow clear conclusions to be drawn. This more naturalistic approach was pioneered by Frederic Bartlett, a British philosopher turned experimental psychologist who had wide interests in anthropology and social psychology. Bartlett (1932) argued that, in attempting to control the experimental situation, Ebbinghaus had simply thrown out the most important and interesting aspects of human memory. Bartlett deliberately chose to study the recall of complex material, such as drawings and folk tales from unfamiliar cultures. Rather than study the gradual accumulation of information over successive learning trials, he preferred to use the errors that his participants made as a clue to the way in which they were encoding and storing the material. His methods of study were much more informal than those used by Ebbinghaus, often including several recalls by the same participant over periods of days or even longer. In a typical study, Bartlett (1932) would present his Cambridge University students with North American Indian folk tales such as:

The war of the ghosts

One night two young men from Egulac went down to the river to hunt seals, and while they were there it became foggy and calm. Then they hear war-cries, and they thought: "Maybe this is a war-party." They escaped to the shore, and hid behind a log. Now

canoes came up, and they heard the noise of paddles, and saw one canoe coming up to them. There were five men in the canoe, and they said: "What do you think? We wish to take you along. We are going up the river to make war on the people."

One of the young men said: "I have no arrows."

"Arrows are in the canoe," they said.

"I will not go along. I might be killed. My relatives do not know where I have gone. But you," he said, turning to the other, "may go with them."

So one of the young men went, but the other returned home. And the warriors went up the river to a town on the other side of Kalama.

The people came down to the water, and they began to fight, and many were killed. But presently the young man heard one of the warriors say: "Quick, let us go home: that Indian has been hit."

Now he thought: "Oh, they are ghosts."

He did not feel sick, but they said he had been shot.

So the canoes went back to Egulac, and the young man went ashore to his house, and made a fire. And he told everybody and said: "Behold I accompanied the ghosts, and we went to fight. Many of our fellows were killed, and many of those who attacked us were killed. They said I was hit, and I did not feel sick."

He told it all, and then he came quiet. When the sun rose he fell down. Something black came out of his mouth. His face became contorted. The people jumped up and cried. He was dead.

Now close the book and try to recall the story as accurately as you can. What Bartlett (1932) found was that the remembered story was always shorter, more coherent, and tended to fit in more closely with the participant's own viewpoint than the original story.

A central feature of Bartlett's approach was to stress the participant's *effort after meaning*; exactly the opposite of Ebbinghaus's explicit attempt to avoid meaning. Rather than being a simple recipient of information, participants were actively striving after meaning, trying to capture the essence of the material presented. Indeed, one of Bartlett's students, Bronislav Gomulicki (1956), observed that the recall protocols provided by people attempting to remember one of Bartlett's stories were indistinguishable by independent judges from the attempts of others to summarize, with the story present.

A second feature of Bartlett's theory was his postulation of the concept of a *schema*, a long-term structured representation of knowledge that was used by the rememberer to make sense of new material and subsequently store and recall it. This concept of schema has subsequently proved to be highly influential and will be discussed further in Chapter 6, which is concerned with semantic memory. Bartlett emphasized the role of social and cultural influences on the development of schemas, which in turn determine the way in which material is encoded, stored, and subsequently recalled. These tendencies were especially great with a story like *The war of the ghosts*, in which several features were incompatible with European expectations (or those of Americans unfamiliar with the North American Indian culture). Hence, the supernatural aspect of the story was often omitted. In addition, features of the story that were puzzling to the readers were rationalized by distorting them to fit their expectations. Hence "something black came out of his mouth" became "foamed at the mouth."

Bartlett (1932) interpreted his findings by arguing that the systematic errors and distortions produced in the participants' recalls were due to the intrusion of their schematic knowledge. However, it is possible to criticize Bartlett's experimental approach. The instructions he gave to his participants were rather vague and he hardly ever carried out any statistical tests on his data! More worryingly, many of the recall distortions he observed were due to deliberate guessing rather than genuine problems in memory. This was demonstrated by Gauld and Stephenson (1967), who found that clear instructions emphasizing the need for accurate recall eliminated almost half of the errors obtained using Bartlett's vague instructions.

Despite these problems with Bartlett's procedures, there is convincing support for his major findings from well-controlled studies. For example, consider a study by Sulin and Dooling (1974). They set out to test Bartlett's theory, including his assumption that systematic, schema-driven errors will be greater at a long retention interval than after a short delay because schematic information lasts longer in memory than information in the text. Sulin

In Sulin and Dooling's (1974) study, participants used their schematic knowledge of Hitler to incorrectly organize the information about the story they had been told. The study revealed how schematic organization can lead to errors in long-term memory and recall. © Bettmann/Corbis.

and Dooling presented some participants with a story about Gerald Martin: "Gerald Martin strove to undermine the existing government to satisfy his political ambitions … He became a ruthless, uncontrollable dictator. The ultimate effect of his rule was the downfall of his country" (Sulin & Dooling, 1974, p. 256). Other participants were given the same story but the main actor was called Adolf Hitler. Those participants told the story was about Adolf Hitler were much more likely than the other participants to believe incorrectly they had read the sentence, "He hated the Jews particularly and so persecuted them." Their schematic knowledge about Hitler distorted their recollections of what they had read at a long retention interval (1 week) but not at a short one (5 minutes).

A more controlled way of studying memory bias than story recall is by using ambiguous stimuli and providing disambiguating labels. The classic study here is again a very old one. Carmichael, Hogan, and Walter (1932) presented the visual stimuli shown on the left of Figure 5.1 for subsequent recall. Each item was sufficiently ambiguous as to fit two different verbal labels, for example a beehive or a hat. When participants were later asked to draw the stimuli from memory, their drawings were strongly influenced by the label they had been given. It is tempting to think of this again as a bias in the way in which the material was perceived and stored. However, a subsequent study by Prentice (1954) suggested otherwise. The encoding conditions were the same as for the Carmichael et al. study, but retrieval load was minimized by using recognition rather than recall. The label effect disappeared under these circumstances, suggesting that the bias occurred at retrieval rather than encoding; the appropriate information was stored but the difficult task of recalling by drawing led to an undue influence of the verbal labels. We shall return to the topic of bias and memory in Chapter 14 on eyewitness testimony.

Before moving on from the role of verbal labeling, we should note that it can be helpful. This was shown by Bower, Karlin, and Dueck (1975) in a study in which people were asked to recall apparently meaningless patterns or "droodles" such as shown in Figure 5.2. Free recall of these patterns was very poor. However, recall was greatly improved when each droodle was accompanied by an interpretative label. Bower et al. conclude that "memory is aided whenever contextual cues arouse appropriate schemata."

Figure 5.1 Examples of the ambiguous items used by Carmichael et al. (1932). Copyright © American Psychological Association. Reproduced with permission.

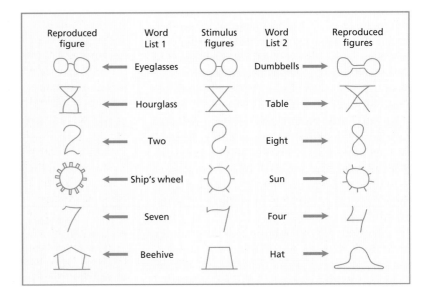

Reproduced figure	Word List 1	Stimulus figures	Word List 2	Reproduced figures
	← Eyeglasses		Dumbbells →	
	← Hourglass		Table →	
	← Two		Eight →	
	← Ship's wheel		Sun →	
	← Seven		Four →	
	← Beehive		Hat →	

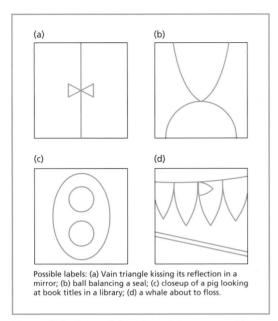

Possible labels: (a) Vain triangle kissing its reflection in a mirror; (b) ball balancing a seal; (c) closeup of a pig looking at book titles in a library; (d) a whale about to floss.

Figure 5.2 A set of droodles of the type used by Bower et al. (1975). Subsequent recall was greatly enhanced when the droodles were accompanied by their titles. What titles would you suggest? Possible answers are given below the figure.

MEANING AND MEMORY

Bartlett's principal criticism of Ebbinghaus was that his attempt to separate memory from meaning meant that he was studying simple repetition habits, which had very little relevance to the way in which our memories work in everyday life. In fact, by the time Bartlett was making his criticism of Ebbinghaus's approach, it was already clear that, whereas Ebbinghaus himself might have succeeded in excluding meaning from his learning strategy, this was not the case for the less determined students who subsequently participated in verbal learning experiments. In 1928, Glaze had his students rate the extent to which each possible consonant–vowel–consonant suggested one or more real words; some suggested several words, for example, the syllable *CAS* might suggest *castle*, *cast*, and *casino*, whereas a syllable such as *ZIJ* is far harder to link with meaningful existing words. There is clear evidence that

syllables rated as more meaningful are easier to recall (Jung, 1968).

So does that mean that people are explicitly relying on words to remember the syllables? The rate at which Ebbinghaus recited these syllables made that unlikely, and even at the subsequent slower standard rate of 2 seconds per syllable, forming and using associations is very difficult for all except the most meaningful syllables. It seemed more likely that Bartlett's suggestion that this task involves developing "repetition habits" might be closer to the mark, with those syllables that follow most closely the structure of English being the easiest to acquire, an effect that we have already noted for immediate memory. This indeed proved to be the case (Underwood & Schulz, 1960; Baddeley, 1964).

By the 1960s, the use of nonsense syllables in verbal learning studies was dying out and being replaced by studies using word lists, for which meaning was clearly highly important. The dominant tradition in verbal learning was still that of stimulus–response associationism, with interest focusing on the influence of pre-existing associations between words on ease of list learning. Underpinning this approach was the view that memory could be explained purely in terms of associations or links between words. When prior interword associations were strong, such as *bread–butter*, learning would be easier then when they were more remote such as *castle–tower*.

Up to this point, investigators into verbal learning had tended to rely largely on such standard tasks as serial recall, in which items are recalled in the order presented, and paired-associate learning in which participants were required to learn word pairs, (e.g. *dog–bishop*), so that when given the first item the stimulus (*dog*) they must produce the response (*bishop*). By the 1950s, however, experimenters were increasingly using the less constrained task of free recall, in which participants are asked to produce as many words from the list as they can remember, in any order. Using this method, Deese (1959) showed that lists that were highly associated were easier to recall than lists with few interword associations, and Jenkins and Russell (1952) noted that when a number of associated words, such as *thread*, *needle*, and *mend*, were included in a mixed list, even though they were presented separately, they tended to be recalled as a cluster.

One of the most surprising developments at this time was the recognition of the importance of visual imagery. The verbal learning tradition was still not one that welcomed the idea of subjects indulging in anything as non-observable as visual imagery. However, there was overwhelming evidence that a rating of the extent to which a word evoked an image was a very powerful predictor of how well it would be remembered. The person who made this discovery was Allen Paivio, a muscular Canadian of Finnish descent who had had the further distinction of being Mr Canada. Paivio placated the more traditionalist verbal learners by pointing out that he was merely predicting one form of behavior, remembering word lists, on the basis of another behavior, the rating responses of his participants. The fact that the rating instruction relied on introspection, the extent to which a given word evoked a subjectively experienced image, could then be conveniently ignored.

I suggest you try a free recall experiment for yourself. Take a sheet of paper and a pen. Then read out the following list of words (List A), at a steady rate of about 2 seconds per word. Then close your eyes and recite the alphabet to get rid of the recency effect before writing down as many words as you can in any order.

List A:
virtue, history, silence, life, hope, value, mathematics, dissent, idea

How many did you remember? Now try the next list (List B) using exactly the same procedure.

List B:
church, beggar, carpet, arm, hat, teapot, dragon, cannon, apple

You probably found the second list easier. As you might have noticed, the second list

Dual-coding hypothesis is a process whereby words can be encoded in terms of both their visual appearance and their verbal meaning to create interacting images and improve the likelihood of successful retrieval—a crocodile biting a football, for example.

comprises words that are more concrete and more imageable than the first. Paivio studied the effect of imageability extensively, explaining his findings in terms of the **dual-coding hypothesis**, whereby words that were imageable, such as the name of concrete objects (e.g. *crocodile*), could be encoded in terms of both their visual appearance and their verbal meaning. For example, a visual image of a crocodile could be generated and linked to one or more other imageable words from the list. If football had also occurred, you might image the crocodile biting a football. Creating interacting images tends to be much harder for abstract words such as *hope* and *theory*. There are therefore two routes to retrieval for imageable words rather than one—visual and verbal—so if one route is lost the other might still survive and allow recall (Paivio, 1969, 1971).

Before we move on, try one more list, reading it out and then recalling in just the same way as lists A and B.

List C:
large, grey, elephants, terrified, by, roaring, flames, trampled, tiny, defenseless, rabbits.

KEY TERM

Dual-coding hypothesis: Highly imageable words are easy to learn because they can be encoded both visually and verbally.

How many did you get that time? I suspect rather more than for lists A or B for an obvious reason. Unlike A and B, list C comprised a meaningful, if slightly odd, sentence.

LEARNING AND PREDICTABILITY

What is the crucial difference between sentences and unrelated word strings? One obvious difference stems from the fact that strong relationships exist between the words in a sentence but not between the words in a list. Language is redundant in the sense that successive words are not equally probable; adjectives tend to come before nouns and pronouns are generally followed by verbs. The meaning of the topic being written or spoken about also constrains the selection of words. All of these are reflected in the tendency for each word in a sentence to be predictable on the basis of surrounding words. Hence, if I were to ask you to play a guessing game in which I presented parts of sentences and asked you to guess the next word, you would do reasonably well.

Even within meaningful text, quite marked differences occur in the degree of redundancy or predictability. One way of measuring this is the Cloze technique. People are presented with a passage from which every fifth word has been deleted. Their task is to guess the missing words. Try it yourself on the following two passages. The first is from a children's storybook, the second from a classic novel.

The sly young fox—to eat the little—hen for his dinner.—made all sorts of—to catch her. He—many times to—her. But she was—clever little hen. Not—of the sly fox's—worked. He grew quite—trying to catch the—red hen. One day—sly young fox said—his mother, "Today I—catch the little red—. I have made the—plan of all." He—up a bag and—it over his back. "—shall put the little—hen in this bag,"—said to his mother. (Extract from *The sly fox* by Vera Southgate.)

In the first place,—had by that time, —the benefit of his—education: continual hard work,—soon and concluded late,—extinguished any curiosity he—possessed in pursuit of—, and any love for—or learning. His childhood's—of superiority, instilled into—by the favors of—Mr Earnshaw, was faded—. He struggled long to—up an equality with—in her studies, and—with a poignant though silent—: but he yielded completely;—there was no prevailing—him to take a—in the way of—upward, when he found—must, necessarily, sink beneath—former level. (Extract from *Wuthering heights* by Emily Bronte.)

The missing words from the first passage were *wanted, red, he, plans, tried, catch, a, one, plans, thin, little, the, to, will, hen, best, picked, slung, I, red, he.* From the second passage the words omitted were *he, lost, early, begun, had, once, knowledge, books, sense, him, old, away, keep, Catherine, yielded, regret, and, on, step, moving, he, his.* Most people find the children's text more predictable and fill in considerably more words. Redundancy as measured by the Cloze technique is a reasonably good predictor of both the judged readability of text and of its memorability. The more redundant and predictable a piece of prose, the easier it is to recall (Rubenstein & Aborn, 1958).

LEVELS OF PROCESSING

All the previous examples could be regarded as reflecting the influence of meaning, extending from the richness with which individual items can be encoded through to passages varying in their predictability. But why does meaning facilitate long-term learning?

One possibility is that storage in STM relies on a phonological code, whereas LTM is semantically based. This is an unsatisfactory explanation for two reasons. First, it is clear that we *can* demonstrate long-term learning for phonological information, otherwise how would we ever learn the sound of words in the language? Furthermore, simply saying that LTM uses a semantic code does not explain why a semantic code is helpful.

An answer to this puzzle was offered by Craik and Lockhart (1972) with their *Levels of Processing* hypothesis. This moves away from the idea of memory stores that have particular codes, emphasizing instead that the way in which material is manipulated determines its durability in LTM. They propose that information is taken in by the organism and processed to varying depths. In the case of a printed word for example, its visual characteristics would be processed first, followed by the spoken sound of the word, and then its meaning.

Craik and Tulving (1975) carried out a series of experiments in which words were presented visually and participants asked to make three different types of judgment. One involved shallow visual processing (Is this word in upper or lower case? *TABLE*), one was phonological (Does this word rhyme with dog? *Log*), and the deepest required semantic processing (Does the word *field* fit into this sentence? The horse lived in a —). Having performed these various operators on the words, participants were unexpectedly confronted with a list of words and asked which ones they had just been shown. Half of the words were new and half had been processed in one of the three ways, involving case, rhyme, or semantic judgment. Craik and Tulving found that, the greater the **depth of processing** had been, the better the subsequent memory. As Figure 5.3 shows, this was a clear effect and was particularly marked for questions to which the answer was "yes."

This demonstration of better recognition following deeper processing was, of course, exactly as predicted by the levels of processing hypothesis, but why were "yes" responses better recalled than "no"? Craik and Tulving suggest that this is because, for positive items, the word to be recalled was integrated more closely with the encoding question, particularly in the semantic condition. If a sentence

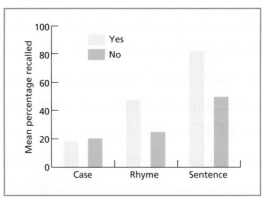

Figure 5.3 Effects of type of encoding task on subsequent word recognition. Based on Craik and Tulving (1975).

made sense when linked with the target words, as in "The horse lived in a field," remembering the sentence would help remind you of the target, perhaps an image of a horse in a field. This source of help would not be so readily available for a negative item such as "Does the word *fork* fit into 'The horse lived in a —'?"

Could it be the case that semantic judgments lead to better recall simply because they take longer, in line with the total time hypothesis? In their initial experiments, it was certainly the case that deeper processing took longer. In a later experiment, Craik and Tulving slowed down the two more superficial processing tasks by making them more difficult, for example by replacing the decision as to whether the word was in upper or lower case with the requirement to count the number of vowels in the target word. They found no evidence that slower processing led to enhanced recognition.

The general principle that deeper and more elaborate processing leads to better memory has been supported by many other studies. Hyde and Jenkins (1973), for example,

KEY TERM

Depth of processing: The proposal by Craik and Lockhart that the more deeply an item is processed, the better will be its retention.

carried out an extensive series of experiments studying no fewer than 22 different encoding tasks and finding general support for a major influence of processing level on memory. This Levels of Processing effect is found for both recall and recognition, regardless of whether participants do or do not expect a later memory test. During the 1970s, many similar studies provided substantial support for Craik and Lockhart's proposals. Indeed, as a basic generalization or rule of thumb, the principle that deeper and more elaborate processing leads to better retention is arguably our most useful generalization about human memory. The effect is robust, reliable, and as we will see, very useful for anyone wanting to maximize their learning capacity. It has not, however, escaped criticism, at both a theoretical and practical level.

THE LIMITS OF LEVELS

One problem acknowledged by Craik and Tulving (1975) is that of measuring *depth of processing*. As we saw earlier, simply using processing time as a measure does not work, as a slow but superficial processing task, such as counting the number of vowels in a word, leads to longer processing but not to better recall. Indeed, the whole concept of processing depth has come under criticism, with increasing evidence suggesting that many different features of a stimulus might be processed at the same time, rather than in the strict serial order assumed, of vision-then-phonology-then-semantics. It is indeed unlikely that when a participant decides whether *dog* rhymes with *log*, he or she is totally unaware of the meaning, although the attention paid to that aspect of the word is likely to be much less than in the semantic processing case. Consequently, in the 30 years following Craik and Lockhart's important paper, levels of processing has come to be seen as an extremely valuable rule of thumb, but has not itself generated great further theoretical development.

TRANSFER-APPROPRIATE PROCESSING

A second set of problems concerns situations in which deeper processing does not always lead to better performance. Students might do poorly on retrieving information during exams not because they fail to study but because they study the incorrect type of knowledge. Consider this thought experiment. Suppose you don't know how to ride a bicycle. You approach an expert on bicycle riding, who has written a 200-page book detailing all the rules and facts that one needs to know, describing even the most minute adjustments in posture. Being an excellent student, you spend weeks memorizing everything. If you were given a test on the book, you would score 100%. Then you get on the bicycle and what happens? You crash within seconds, unable to keep balanced. You don't really know what is important about riding bicycles. You have excellent factual knowledge, but no skill.

This illustrates a broad principle known as **transfer-appropriate processing**. This principle states that for a test to reveal prior learning, the processing requirements of the test should match the processing conditions at encoding. This principle has been invoked to explain the powerful phenomenon of depth of processing. As mentioned earlier, people are quite poor at later recalling words about which they have made visual or phonological judgments, but are very good at remembering words about which they made a meaning-based judgment. This might partially reflect a bias in the way items are tested. In particular, during recall tests, people might be used to remembering the meanings of words they just encountered, and so

> **KEY TERM**
>
> **Transfer-appropriate processing (TAP):** Proposal that retention is best when the mode of encoding and mode of retrieval are the same.

the test implicitly places emphasis on meaning. To illustrate this point, Morris, Bransford, and Franks (1977) examined whether retention was determined by what people do while encoding, or was instead determined by how well the processing requirements of the test matched encoding. Morris and colleagues asked participants to make either a phonological or semantic judgment about each item in a word list.

As is commonly the case in experiments on levels of processing, participants were not warned they would have to recall. This feature, known as **incidental learning**, has the advantage that participants are not tempted to use other learning strategies over and above performing that is induced by the experimenter. The deep condition involved semantic processing, for example "Does the word that follows fit the gap in the sentence? "The—ran into the lamp-post: *car*," whereas the shallow condition involved a judgment of rhyme such as "Does it rhyme with fighter? *writer*." Memory was then tested by one of two recognition tests; the first was a standard condition in which the words were presented (e.g. *car*, *writer*), mixed in with an equal number of nonpresented words (e.g. *fish*, *lawyer*). The second type of test involved presenting a series of words and asking if an item had been presented that rhymed with that word (e.g. *bar*, *lighter*).

Morris et al. found that deeper processing led to much better performance under the standard recognition conditions, just as Craik and Tulving (1975) had shown. However, the opposite occurred with rhyme recognition: The shallower rhyme-based encoding task led to better performance.

A subsequent study by Fisher and Craik (1977) broadly replicated this result, but emphasized that there *was*, overall, a clear advantage to deeper processing. However, both sets of authors agree that it only makes sense to talk about the efficiency of a learning method in the context of the way in which memory is subsequently tested, an issue that will be explored further in Chapter 8 concerned with recognition memory.

WHY IS DEEPER CODING BETTER?

As Fisher and Craik (1977) point out, although it is not always the case, deeper processing does tend to convey an advantage under a wide range of conditions. Why should that be? Craik and Tulving (1975) suggest that semantic coding is advantageous because it allows a richer and more elaborate code, which in turn becomes more readily retrievable. They describe an experiment that supports this view. Their participants are required to judge whether a given word will or will not fit into a sentence. The sentences can be either relatively simple, such as "She dropped her *pen*" or more complex, for example: "The little old man hobbled across the castle courtyard and dropped his *pen* in the well." Memory was then tested by giving the sentence frame, and requiring the underlined word to be recalled. There was a very clear advantage to words embedded in the semantically richer sentences. This advantage was also found with unprompted free recall, but was much weaker (Craik & Tulving, 1975).

The idea that elaboration helps recall extends back at least to William James (1890), who suggested that of two men with equivalent mental capacity:

The one who THINKS over his experiences most, and weaves them into systematic relations with each other will be the one with the best memory ... All improvement of the memory lies in the line of elaborating the associates. (James, 1890, p. 662)

The idea that deeper processing involves elaboration fits in neatly with a distinction

---

KEY TERM

Incidental learning: Learning situation in which the learner is unaware that a test will occur.

made by Craik and Lockhart (1972) between two kinds of rehearsal. One of these, **maintenance rehearsal** involves continuing to process an item at the *same* level; the rote rehearsal of a telephone number by saying it to oneself would be a good example of maintenance rehearsal. They contrast maintenance rehearsal with **elaborative rehearsal**, which involves linking the material being rehearsed to other material in memory, both within the set of items being learned and beyond, just as James proposes. Craik and Lockhart suggest that only elaborative rehearsal enhances delayed long-term learning.

Evidence for this view comes from an ingenious study by Glenberg, Smith, and Green (1977), who presented their participants with numbers that were to be remembered over a delay. During the delay, participants were required to read out words, a task that they were led to believe was used simply to stop them rehearsing the numbers. Some words occurred only once during this delay-filling activity, others many times. Having recalled the numbers, people were then asked unexpectedly to recall as many of the words as they could. A nine-fold increase in number of repetitions led to only 1.5% increase in recall, although it did have a more substantial effect on recognition, with recognition probability increasing from 0.65 to 0.74. It seems likely that the slight increase in familiarity based on the recent repetition is enough to boost recognition, but that this does provide a sufficiently powerful cue to allow the original words to be evoked.

So does maintenance rehearsal never help long-term recall? Once again, it depends on the task. Mechanic (1964) required his participants to articulate each of a series of nonsense syllables either once, or as often as possible in the time available. One group was warned of a subsequent recall test, while the second group was told that the purpose of the study was to measure their speed of articulation. Mechanic's results are shown in Figure 5.4. Repeated articulation led to enhanced recall, regardless of whether recall was expected or

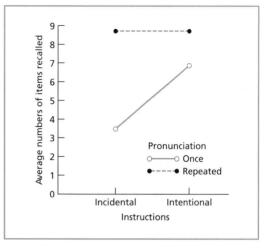

Figure 5.4 Average number of nonsense syllables recalled as a function of learning instruction and number of repetitions. Under these conditions, rote repetition enhances learning. Data from Mechanic (1964).

not, whereas participants from whom a single repetition was required did very poorly in the incidental learning condition. Presumably, knowing that recall would be required encouraged additional processing in the **intentional learning** group, whereas the requirement to articulate repeatedly rapidly discouraged further processing in either group.

So what is the difference between the results of Glenberg et al. (1977), who found virtually no advantage to repetition, and those of Mechanic, who found that repetition helped recall? A crucial issue concerns the question of exactly what the participants are learning. In the case of Mechanic's study, the syllables are unfamiliar and do not form natural existing chunks. Repeating them is likely to boost

KEY TERMS

Maintenance rehearsal: A process of rehearsal whereby items are "kept in mind" but not processed more deeply.
Elaborative rehearsal: Process whereby items are not simply kept in mind, but are processed either more deeply or more elaborately.
Intentional learning: Learning when the learner knows that there will be a test of retention.

their representation in phonological LTM. In Glenberg's study, there is no need to learn the words, as they are already in the vocabulary of the participants. The memory task in this case is to recall which particular word had just been presented, something that, as we shall see, typically depends on meaningful links *between* the words. This is likely to be helped by the rich array of semantic features that is typical of words but not of nonsense syllables.

ORGANIZATION AND LEARNING

Why does semantic coding help?

One reason why deeper processing is generally good for learning is that it emphasizes the use of a semantic code, which is potentially much richer than a code representing the sound or printed appearance of a word. But why should this help? To answer this question we need to think about the task that faces a participant in a typical levels of processing experiment, which is to view or hear a sequence of words and then try to reproduce as many as possible. The words are not, strictly speaking, being learned, as they will already be in the learner's vocabulary. The problem is to make available those words that have been presented, and no others.

One way to do this is to bind the separate words into chunks and to recall the chunks. A study by Tulving (1962) suggests that this is exactly what people do. He repeatedly presented participants with a list of words, changing their order on each trial and asking participants to recall as many as possible. Despite the fact that the order of the words was scrambled every time, Tulving noted that as people gradually learned the list, they tended to produce words in clusters or chunks that came out in the same order trial after trial. Learning consisted of building bigger and bigger chunks, a process that Tulving referred to as **subjective organization**.

What sort of factors encourage such chunking? As you might expect, such organization tends to reflect semantic variables. Read through the list below three times and then see how many you can recall.

THREAD, PIN, EYE, SEWING, SHARP, POINT, PRICK, THIMBLE, HAYSTACK, THORN, HURT, INJECTION, SYRINGE, CLOTH, KNITTING

You probably did rather well. Why?

The list was easy to recall because all the items were strongly related. They were, in fact, all *associates* of a single key word, NEEDLE. We shall return to this effect, which was originally developed by James Deese (1959), in Chapter 8 on retrieval.

Recall is also helped if the items can be chunked in terms of their semantic *categories*. Tulving and Pearlstone (1966) tested recall of lists containing groups of one, two, or four words per semantic category for example; try the following:

pink, green, blue, purple, apple, cherry, lemon, plum, lion, zebra, cow, rabbit

How may did you recall? Now try the next set:

cabbage, table, river, shirt, gun, square, iron, dentist, sparrow, mountain, hand, granite

How many that time?

Participants given sets of four items from the same category did better; they tended to recall items in category-based chunks, although sometimes omitting some categories completely. This was not because these items were entirely forgotten, as when participants in either group were then given the category names; many new words from omitted categories were then recalled.

KEY TERM

Subjective organization: A strategy whereby a learner attempts to organize unstructured material so as to enhance learning.

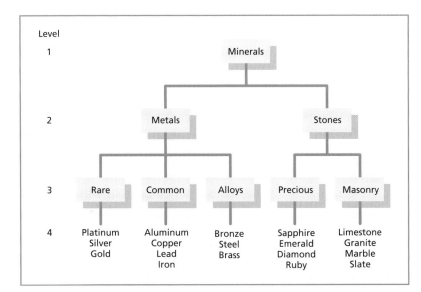

Figure 5.5 The "minerals" conceptual hierarchy used by Bower et al. (1969). Recall is much higher than when the same words were presented in scrambled order.

A particularly effective way of organizing material is through a hierarchical structure such as that shown in Figure 5.5. Bower, Clark, Lesgold, and Winzenz (1969) presented this material either in the form of a logically structured hierarchy or with the items in scrambled order. Participants given the hierarchical condition averaged 65% correct compared with only 19% when the same words were scrambled. Of course, it is not always possible to organize material in terms of a hierarchy. Fortunately, as Broadbent, Cooper, and Broadbent (1978) demonstrated, considerable benefit can also be obtained by structuring material in a matrix such as that shown in Table 5.1.

The examples we have provided so far rely on material that is artificially designed to fit into generally accepted semantic categories. It is often the case, however, that the material we must remember is not formally organized in this way. Does that mean that organization is not relevant? Certainly not, as we saw from Tulving's (1962) subjective organization study; when asked to learn an apparently meaningless jumble of unrelated words, people will begin to make links that form them into meaningful chunks. Indeed, given the semantic richness of language and the ingenuity of learners, it is virtually impossible to produce

Table 5.1: Data from Broadbent et al. (1978).

	Mammals	**Birds**
Farmyard	Cow	Chicken
	Sheep	Turkey
	Pig	Duck
	Goat	Goose
Pets	Dog	Budgerigar
	Cat	Canary
	Hamster	Parrot
	Guinea-pig	Macaw

a string of words that do not suggest at least some possible clusters.

There are, however, some techniques that are more effective than others. One of these is to try to link the various words into a coherent story. This has the advantage that it not only creates chunks, but it also links the chunks together, making it less likely that any will be left out. For example given a list such as:

church, apple, beggar, carpet, arm, hat, hand, teapot, dragon, cannon

A participant might create a story such as the following "He came out of the *church* and gave an *apple* to a *beggar* sitting on a *carpet*. With his withered *arm* he clutched a *hat* and held his *hand* out for money, which he put in a *teapot* decorated by a *dragon* being shot at by a *cannon*."

Although it might be very effective, creating such stories is quite demanding and it can prove very difficult to form semantic links, particularly with rapid presentation of unrelated words (Campoy & Baddeley, 2008). There is also a danger of recalling words that were included to make a good story but which were not in the original, as in the case of "money," included in the above example to help make a plausible story. A more flexible method is that based on visual imagery, in which items are linked by imagining them interacting in some way. The interaction need not be plausible, so one can, for example, imagine a *swan* riding a *motorbike* if one wished to link those two words. Imagery mnemonics have formed an important part of the craft of memory since classical times. They are discussed in more detail as part of Chapter 16, which is concerned with improving your memory.

Intention to learn

Given that you are attending to material in an active and interested way, does it matter whether or not you are *trying* to learn it? Somewhat surprisingly, the answer appears to be "No." What is important is what you *do* with the material, not what your purpose is. This was demonstrated very neatly in a study by Mandler (1967), which involved memory for a list of relatively unrelated words. Participants were presented with a pack of cards, with a word on each. One group was told to commit the words to memory, a second group was asked to sort the words into categories comprising items that had something in common, while a third group was given this instruction together with a warning that recall would then be required. Finally, a fourth group was simply asked to arrange the words in columns. Subsequent recall showed that the group asked to organize the words on

the basis of their meaning, with no mention of later recall, did just as well as participants instructed to learn, or indeed to organize *and* learn. All three groups remembered more than the other incidental learning group, who had simply arranged the words in columns.

As we saw earlier, the levels of processing effect does not depend on whether participants *know* that recall will be required, performance depends only on what processing task is performed (Hyde & Jenkins, 1973). These results have clear implications for how you should study. The important thing is not the desire to remember, but the way in which you *process* the material. If you think about its meaning, relate it to what you already know, and consider its wider implications, you have a much better chance of learning than if you simply read and note the major points.

MEMORY AND THE BRAIN

As mentioned in Chapter 4, a great deal of research has been carried out on the role of the brain in learning, using animals to study both the processes involved at the cellular level and the brain systems involved. Whereas most of this probably also applies to much human learning, it is less clear as to whether it applies to episodic memory, the capacity to recollect specific events. Indeed, if one uses Tulving's strict definition in terms of the capacity to "re-experience" the past, this assumes a level of conscious awareness that seems unlikely to occur in many of the organisms such as the giant sea snail *Aplysia*, on which much of the work on the neural basis of learning has been developed. As Box 5.1 shows, if one uses a more behavioral definition of episodic memory, in terms of the capacity to demonstrate memory for the *what*, *where*, and *when* of an event, then this can certainly be shown in certain types of bird, such as the scrub jay, which collects and hides food for later use.

In the case of episodic memory, however, we are on firmer ground in using

5

Box 5.1 Is episodic memory uniquely human?

It all depends. Using Tulving's definition, in terms of the experience of mental time travel it would be very difficult to establish that an animal had this particular experience. Defined behaviorally, however, as the capacity to combine memory for *what*, *where*, and *when*, there is evidence for this ability in scrub jays, birds that hide food (*what*) and subsequently remember *where* it was hidden. An ingenious experiment by Clayton and Dickinson (1999) indicates that the birds also remember the *time* at which the food was hidden. Clayton and Dickinson allowed their birds to hide two types of food—mealworms, which were most preferred but that deteriorate over time, and less attractive but more durable peanuts. Depending on the delay between hiding and the opportunity to retrieve the food, birds prefer mealworms after a short delay, but peanuts when the delay is longer.

In this photo, one of Nicky Clayton's female Western scrub jays, Sweetie Pie, is caching worms. Photograph by Dean Alexis and Ian Cannell of the University of Cambridge. Reproduced with permission.

evidence from neuropsychological patients. In Chapter 1, I mentioned the classic case of HM who became densely amnesic following surgery to the temporal lobes and hippocampus on both the left and right side (Milner, 1966). Evidence from a range of patients who have developed a deficit in episodic LTM following brain damage suggests the importance of a system sometimes known as the Papez circuit, which links the hippocampus and frontal lobes (Tranel & Damasio, 2002). There is no doubt that the hippocampus plays an important role in both learning and memory, but the nature of this role is still not clear.

Doubts began to arise in studies of hippocampal damage in animals. The hippocampus lies deep within the animal's brain, making it difficult to lesion without damaging surrounding areas. However, as surgical techniques have improved this has become possible, leading to the claim that something akin to recognition memory is possible even when the hippocampus is severely damaged, provided that certain areas feeding into the hippocampus, known as the *rhinal* and *perirhinal cortex* are intact. This evidence is reviewed by Aggleton and Brown (1999), who also surveyed the human neuropsychological literature. They identified a number of cases in which otherwise dense amnesia appeared to be accompanied by well preserved recognition memory. They suggest that although the hippocampus is important, other surrounding areas are equally important, particularly in the case of recognition, a view that is by no means universally accepted (Manns & Squire, 1999; Squire, 2004).

Further support for the Aggleton and Brown position came from the discovery of a new type of amnesic patient by Farenah Vargha-Khadem and colleagues. Vargha-Khadem, Gadian, Watkins, Connelly, Van Paesschen, and Mishkin (1997) report the case of three young people who became amnesic at an early age and who show a highly atypical pattern of amnesia. The clearest of these cases is a young man, Jon, who suffered from anoxia at the time of birth, which resulted in a severe memory problem as he entered childhood. He is now in his early 20s and on standard memory tests is clearly amnesic, sufficiently so as to make it difficult, although not impossible, to live independently. Neuroimaging studies indicate that Jon has damage that appears to be limited to the hippocampus, which is abnormal in structure and only half the size that would be expected. Despite this, Jon has developed above average intelligence and has an excellent semantic memory. This seems to clash with the widely held assumption that semantic memory depends on episodic memory, which in turn relies on the hippocampus. This issue is discussed in more detail in Chapter 11 on amnesia.

Jon's case is controversial, not in terms of the evidence, which is very strong, but in its interpretation. There are certainly other cases of deeply amnesic patients whose recognition memory is *not* preserved, despite having damage that appears to be limited to the hippocampus (Manns & Squire, 1999). This might occur because these patients have further damage that has not been detected. Another possibility is that the difference might be due to Jon's very

early acquisition of the hippocampal damage. This could have allowed his brain to adapt, resulting in an atypical brain from which it would be dangerous to generalize. No doubt time, and the emergence of further cases, will resolve this issue.

Episodic memory and the healthy brain

As mentioned in Chapter 1, one method of studying the operation of the brain is by using electrodes on the scalp to record the electrical activity of the brain using the electroencephalogram (EEG). A given stimulus is presented and the resulting event-related potential (ERP) measures the time course of the relevant electrical activity, which is thought to reflect the synchronous firing of neurons within the cortex. The resulting activity is collected and averaged over a number of trials in each of the relevant conditions. This results in a pattern of activity that has a number of peaks and troughs occurring at particular times, which can be used both to distinguish between different processes, and by combining information across a range of studies, interpreting what these processes might indicate (Rugg, 2002). Although this method does not allow very precise anatomical localization, it is very sensitive to changes over time, and hence is very appropriate for studying processes that occur rapidly.

A common criticism of neuroimaging research is that it has often simply confirmed what we already knew from lesion studies. A possible exception to this is the **HERA (Hemispheric Encoding and Retrieval Asymmetry) hypothesis** proposed by Tulving,

KEY TERM

HERA (Hemispheric Encoding and Retrieval Asymmetry) hypothesis: Tulving's proposal that the encoding of episodic memories involves the left frontal lobe whereas their retrieval depends on right frontal areas.

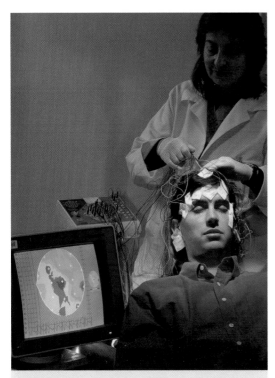

EEG tests record the electrical activity of the brain via small electrodes attached to the scalp. A stimulus is presented, and the resulting event-related potential (ERP) measures the time course of the relevant electrical activity. © Richard T. Nowitz/Corbis.

Kapur, Craik, Moscovitch, and Houle (1994). This resulted from a study in which brain activity was observed during the episodic learning and retrieval of word lists. Verbal encoding was found to strongly activate the left hemisphere frontal regions, whereas episodic retrieval activated the right frontal area. This was surprising, given that earlier lesion studies did not appear to have suggested such a distinction. Subsequent research has supported the idea that the left hemisphere is strongly involved in the encoding of verbal material (Butler, Zacks, & Henderson 1999), with deep, semantically elaborated encoding leading to a greater degree of left frontal activation then shallow encoding (Gabrieli, Cohen, & Corkin, 1998). It is notable, however, that most of the studies supporting

the HERA hypothesis used verbal material; when nonverbal stimuli such as unfamiliar faces were used, the *right* prefrontal area became important during encoding (Wagner, Schacter, Rotte, Koutstaal, Maril, Dale et al., 1998).

An example of the importance of the right frontal region for visual encoding comes from a study by Brewer, Zhao, Desmond, Glover, and Gabrieli (1998), who used a method known as event-related fMRI, whereby separate scans can be taken for each designated event. This allows the experimenter to study the encoding of each stimulus separately. It is then possible to separate-out those items that were remembered from those forgotten, and go back to study the brain activation associated with successfully learning. Brewer et al. presented a total of 48 photographs of scenes, which participants were required to categorize as indoor or outdoor. This was subsequently followed by an unexpected memory test in which the old scenes were mixed with new one and participants required to categorize each as to whether they thought it was old or new. If judged old, the participants were asked whether they could "remember" the experience of observing that scene, a clear example of episodic memory, or if they just felt that they "knew" that they had seen it. Of the studied pictures, 25% were "remembered," 27% were judged as familiar, and 48% forgotten. A number of brain areas were then identified for which activation was higher when that particular picture had been "remembered." As Figure 5.6 illustrates, one of these areas was the hippocampus. Those scenes subsequently judged to be familiar, and those forgotten, were similar in that they had failed to activate this brain area during the encoding phase.

A broadly similar study was applied to memory for words by Wagner et al. (1998), again using an event-related fMRI approach. A sequence of words was presented, with participants required to make a semantic judgment on each—deciding whether the word was concrete or abstract. The pattern of brain

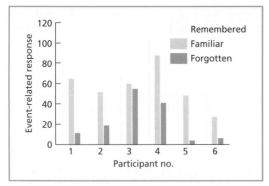

Figure 5.6 Activation in the area of the hippocampus as a function of whether an item was subsequently remembered, judged familiar, or forgotten. High activation is associated with good recall. Data from Brewer et al. (1998).

activation evoked by these word presentations was recorded separately for later analysis. Following this process, participants were presented with a mix of new and old words and were required to respond to each, saying whether they had seen it before or not, together with their level of confidence.

As expected, many areas of the brain were linked with the complex task of seeing and processing words. However, three areas were correlated with a successful remembering of a word with high confidence. These were in the left frontal region and in the areas surrounding the left and right hippocampus, just as in the study by Brewer et al.

We have discussed areas of activation associated with memory, but presumably these must result in actual physical changes that persist over time. There is indeed evidence at a microscopic level for the growth of new connections within the brain (DeZeeuw, 2007). Evidence at a more macro level is provided by an ingenious study of London taxi drivers. Before becoming a licensed London cabbie, it is necessary to acquire "the knowledge," which involves the detailed mastery of all the London streets and major buildings, with the capacity to go from one to the other by the shortest route. This takes several years to acquire, and presumably is further developed over time spent as a cabbie.

Maguire et al.'s (2006) study found that London taxi drivers had greater gray matter volume in the mid-posterior area of the hippocampi, and less in the anterior, as compared to the bus drivers.

Maguire, Vargha-Khadem, and Mishkin (2001) used structural MRI to map out the physical characteristics of the brains of very experienced taxi drivers. They found that the posterior region of the hippocampus was larger than in novice drivers, whereas other areas of the hippocampus were smaller, suggesting that the years of expert navigation had led to a physical modification of their brain. In a related study, Maguire et al. (2001) used PET to monitor the brain activity of the cabbies while they were performing a task simulating driving through London. When required to use their geographical knowledge, the right hippocampus was activated; this was not the case when they were simply following a sequence of arrows.

Hartley, Maguire, Spiers, and Burgess (2003) compared the activation associated with following a novel path from a map with that of simply completing a well-worn route, finding that the hippocampus was strongly involved in working out the novel route whereas other areas were active when the route was familiar. One could argue, of course, that London taxi drivers are an atypical group in a number of ways. Theirs is a potentially stressful occupation involving heavy traffic, cramped conditions, and air pollution. To control for this, Maguire, Woollett, and Spiers (2006) studied a group of London bus drivers with similar amounts of London driving experience, comparing them with taxi drivers. Once again, they found that taxi drivers had greater gray matter volume in the mid-posterior area of the hippocampi, and less in the anterior, than the bus drivers. Furthermore, the longer the experience

of taxi driving, the greater the difference. On cognitive testing, the taxi drivers were better at recognizing which of the series of landmarks was from London and which was not, and at judging the distance as the crow flies between selected London landmarks. Both were then tested on a task involving new learning. This required first copying a complex figure and then, after a delay, reproducing it from memory. On this new learning task, the cabbies were significantly worse than the bus drivers. It appears, therefore, that the extensive experience of the taxi drivers had built up a very complex and effective spatial representation of London, but that this had come at the expense of a reduction in the capacity for new visuo-spatial learning.

SUMMARY

Episodic memory refers to our capacity to recollect specific experiences, and to use this for "mental time travel." It depends on the capacity to encode and then retrieve specific events, something that is greatly helped if material is meaningful and well organized. Bartlett, who was influential in breaking away from the Ebbinghaus rote learning tradition, studied memory for complex material such as folk tales from other cultures. He emphasized effort after meaning, and the role of schemas, mental structures that help us organize our world knowledge.

Research on the role of meaning carried out within the traditional verbal learning tradition concentrated first on associations between words, later extending to the importance for memory of the "imageability" of words. Paivio proposed that imageability helps because of dual coding, the hypothesis that "imageable" words are well remembered because they can be encoded both visually and verbally.

Craik and Lockhart proposed the Levels of Processing hypothesis, that is, that deeper processing leads to better memory. This received broad experimental support and remains an important rule of thumb. However, problems arose in measuring depth of processing and from the need to specify the nature of both encoding and retrieval. This led to the concept of transfer-appropriate processing. Deeper coding is still generally better because it typically leads to richer and more elaborate processing, which in turn increases the number of potential routes to retrieval.

Effective methods of organizing material include hierarchies, matrices, and the linking of concepts into coherent stories. Intention to learn is helpful only if it leads to the use of good learning strategies.

The hippocampus plays an important role in episodic memory, although the relative roles of the hippocampus and surrounding anatomical regions are not fully understood. Neuroimaging has confirmed the role of the hippocampus, together with that of the frontal lobes during encoding. The role of the left and right frontal lobes in retrieval probably depends in part on whether the material learned is verbal or visuo-spatial.

Finally, evidence is beginning to accumulate for physical changes occurring in the adult brain as a result of learning. This is illustrated by the case of London taxi drivers, whose many years of acquiring spatial knowledge has resulted in a change in their hippocampal structure.

FURTHER READING

- Bower, G. H. (1970). Organization factors in memory. *Cognitive Psychology*, *1*, 18–46. A good example of research into the role of organization in learning and remembering

- Bransford, J. D., Franks, J. J., Morris, C. D., & Stein, B. S. (1979). Some general constraints on learning in memory research. In L. S. Cermak & F. I. M. Craik (Eds.), *Levels of processing in human memory* (pp. 331–354). Hillsdale, NJ: Lawrence Erlbaum Associates. Criticizes the concept of levels of processing, and proposes replacing it with transfer-appropriate-processing.

- Craik, F. I. M., & Lockhart, R. S. (1972). Levels of processing. A framework for memory research. *Journal of Verbal Learning & Verbal Behavior*, *11*, 671–684. The classic paper that first proposed the concept of levels of processing.

- Neisser, U. (1982). *Memory observed: Remembering in natural contexts*. New York: Freeman. A collection of readings illustrating the breadth and richness of information on memory when considered in its natural context. It formed part of Neisser's attempt to persuade his colleagues to extend their research beyond the laboratory.

- Roediger, H. L. III, Weldon, M. S., & Challis, B. H. (1989). Explaining dissociations between implicit and explicit measures of retention: A processing account. In H. L. Roediger, III, & F. I. M. Craik (Eds.), *Varieties of memory and consciousness: Essays in honor of Endel Tulving*. Hillsdale, NJ: Lawrence Erlbaum Associates. Describes the various ways in which implicit and explicit measures of memory differ, and offers a possible explanation.

CHAPTER 6

SEMANTIC MEMORY AND STORED KNOWLEDGE

Michael W. Eysenck

What is the capital of France? How many months are there in a year? Who is the current President of the United States? Do rats have wings? What is the chemical formula for water? Is *umplitude* an English word? What does a seismologist do? Is New York south of Washington, D.C.? What is the typical sequence of events when having a meal in a restaurant?

I am sure you found all those questions relatively easy to answer, and that you answered them rapidly. It would not be difficult to fill the whole of this book with such questions—we all possess an enormous store of general knowledge that we take for granted. The division of memory that stores all of this information is generally referred to as *semantic memory*.

All of us have an extensive semantic memory. If you were to stop the first woman you saw and test her vocabulary, you would probably discover that she knew the meaning of anywhere between 20,000 and 100,000 words. She might also know a foreign language. She would certainly know a great deal (in geographical terms) about her own neighborhood and about the wider world. She functions well in her environment because she has learned to drive a car, use a cell phone, use credit cards, and so on. She also has a great deal of specialist knowledge acquired in connection with work, hobbies, and pastimes. In addition, she has the usual interesting but nonvital mental baggage, much of it media-related, that most of us carry around in our heads—facts and images to do with politics and sport, movies and music, TV programs, and advertising.

There is considerable overlap in the knowledge each of us has stored in semantic memory (e.g. basic vocabulary; general knowledge of the world). However, it is also obvious that there are large individual differences in the contents of semantic memory. As you would expect, we generally have more information in semantic memory than most people in those areas of particular interest and importance to us (e.g. work-related knowledge). For example, expert chess players have a huge amount of information related to chess in long-term memory (see Chapter 3). Simon and Gilmartin (1973) estimated that master chess players have between 10,000 and 100,000 groups of pieces (chunks) stored in long-term memory. Each chunk contains information about a given pattern of chess pieces on the board, and these chunks help players to relate a present game position to their knowledge of previous chess games and situations.

SEMANTIC MEMORY VS. EPISODIC MEMORY

I have briefly discussed some of the key features of semantic memory. It is important to distinguish between semantic memory (general knowledge about the world) and *episodic memory* (memory for events occurring at a specific time in a specific place), despite the fact that there are important similarities between the two memory types. Suppose you remember meeting your friend yesterday afternoon at Starbuck's. That clearly involves episodic memory, because you are remembering an event at a given time in a given place. However, semantic memory is also involved— some of what you remember involves your general knowledge about coffee shops, what coffee tastes like, and so on.

There are important differences between the subjective experiences associated with episodic and semantic memory. According to Wheeler, Stuss, and Tulving (1997, p. 333), the main distinguishing characteristic of episodic memory is, "Its dependence on a special kind of awareness that all healthy human adults can identify. It is the type of awareness experienced when one thinks back to a specific moment in one's personal past and consciously recollects some prior episode or state as it was previously experienced." In the case of you meeting your friend in Starbuck's yesterday, perhaps you can remember feeling happy to be seeing your friend, that the skinny latte tasted really good, and that it was sunny so you sat at your favorite table outside.

By contrast, retrieval of information from semantic memory lacks this sense of conscious recollection of the past. Semantic memory also differs from episodic memory in that, "It is a mental thesaurus, organized knowledge a person possesses about words and other verbal symbols, their meanings and referents, about relations among them, and about rules, formulas, and algorithms [rules for solving problems] for the manipulation of these symbols, concepts, and relations" (Tulving, 1972, p. 386). In the words of Wheeler et al., it involves "knowing awareness" rather than the "self-knowing" associated with episodic memory.

It could be argued that these differences in subjective experience don't prove that semantic memory is really different from episodic memory. Accordingly, we will move on to a consideration of some of the most important research findings that provide stronger evidence concerning the relationship between semantic and episodic memory.

Findings

Let us assume for a moment that the differences between semantic and episodic memory are fairly trivial. That would mean that what is true of one type of memory would generally be true of the other type of memory. Evidence that doesn't fit the above assumption was reported by Spiers, Maguire, and Burgess (2001), in their review of 147 cases of amnesia. They found that there was impairment of episodic memory in all cases, whereas many of the patients had only modest problems with semantic memory. Thus, the impact of brain damage was much greater on episodic than on semantic memory, suggesting that the two types of memory are distinctly different from each other.

Relevant findings were reported by Vargha-Khadem, Gadian, Watkins, Connelly, Van Paesschen, and Mishkin (1997; this evidence is also discussed in Chapter 11). They studied two patients (Jon and Beth) who had suffered brain damage at an early age before they had had the chance to develop semantic memories; Beth suffered brain damage at birth, and Jon did so at the age of four. Both of them had extremely poor episodic memory for the day's activities, television programs, and telephone conversations. In spite of this, they developed reasonably good semantic memory. They attended ordinary schools, and their levels of speech and language development, literacy, and factual knowledge (e.g. vocabulary) were within the normal range.

So far, we have been considering anterograde amnesia, which refers to an impaired ability to remember information acquired after the onset of amnesia. What about retrograde amnesia (impaired retention of information acquired *before* the onset of amnesia)? Tulving (2002, p. 13) discussed the case of a

The 2002 film *The bourne identity* portrays retrograde amnesia, an impaired ability to remember information acquired prior to the onset of amnesia. © Getty Images.

patient, KC, whose retrograde amnesia was dramatically worse for episodic memory than for semantic memory: "He cannot recollect any personally experienced events …, whereas his semantic knowledge acquired before the critical accident is still reasonably intact. His knowledge of mathematics, history, geography, and other 'school subjects', as well as his general knowledge of the world is not greatly different from others at his educational level." Once again, these findings suggest that there are important differences between semantic and episodic memory.

There are many other patients who show more retrograde amnesia for episodic memory than for semantic memory, but also many who show the opposite pattern (see Kapur, 1999, for a review). For example, Yasuda, Watanabe, and Ono (1997) studied an amnesic patient who had very poor ability to remember public events, cultural items, historical figures, and some items of vocabulary from the time before the amnesia started. However, she was reasonably good at remembering personal experiences from episodic memory dating back to the pre-amnesia period.

What can we conclude from studies of retrograde amnesia? The different patterns of impairment from patient to patient suggest

(but don't prove) that episodic and semantic memory are different types of memory.

We will consider a final type of evidence indicating that semantic and episodic memory are separate. This evidence is based on the use of brain imaging while healthy participants perform various memory tasks. The basic rationale is as follows: If semantic and episodic memory are genuinely different, then we might expect that the brain areas activated during learning and retrieval would differ depending on whether any given task involved semantic or episodic memory. Wheeler et al. (1997) reviewed 20 studies focusing on learning or encoding, and reported that the left prefrontal cortex was more active during episodic than semantic encoding in 18 of them. There were also differences at the time of retrieval. Wheeler et al. considered 26 brain-imaging studies and found that the right prefrontal cortex was more active during episodic memory retrieval than during semantic memory retrieval in 25 of them.

STORING SIMPLE CONCEPTS

What information is stored in semantic memory? Much of it consists of concepts of various kinds, and we will consider how these concepts are stored. Before you read this section, test yourself on the questions in Box 6.1 on the next page.

Elizabeth Loftus and her colleagues have carried out various experiments exploring the task of coming up with particular words, given a category and a first letter as cues (Loftus & Suppes, 1972). She found that giving the category first and the initial letter afterwards (e.g. *fruit – p*) led to faster responses than giving the initial letter before the category (e.g. *p – fruit*). This suggests that it is easier to activate the category *fruit* in preparation for searching for the appropriate initial letter than all words

Box 6.1 Storing concepts

Answer the following questions, noting how long it takes you to answer each one:

Set A	Set B
1 Fruit starting with p	1 Fruit ending with h
2 Animal starting with d	2 Animal ending with w
3 Metal starting with i	3 Metal ending with r
4 Bird starting with b	4 Bird ending with n
5 Country starting with F	5 Country ending with y
6 Boy's name starting with H	6 Boy's name ending with d
7 Girl's name starting with M	7 Girl's name ending with n
8 Flower starting with s	8 Flower ending with t
Total time taken = ...	Total time taken = ...

I imagine that you took much less time to complete all the answers to Set A than to Set B. What does this mean? At the simplest level, it means that the initial letter is a much more effective cue than the last letter when you are trying to retrieve at the level of basic-level categories. This in turn tells us something about the way in which the names of such categories are stored, as there is no logical reason why the above should be the case. For example, it would be entirely possible to devise a computer program in which words could be retrieved equally rapidly regardless of whether the first, last, second, fourth, or any other letter were provided as a cue.

starting with, say, *p*. This is probably because the category *fruit* is reasonably coherent and manageable, whereas words starting with *p* represent far too large and diffuse a category to be useful. Evidence of this comes from a study in which the category was *type of psychologist* and the initial letter that of the psychologist's surname. Hence a typical question might be, "Give me a developmental psychologist whose name begins with P" (Piaget) versus "Initial letter P – a developmental psychologist." Students who were just beginning to specialize in psychology showed no difference between the two orders of presentation, whereas those who had already specialized were faster when the category was provided first. Presumably, they had already developed categories such as "developmental psychologist," whereas the novices simply searched all "psychologists," not having sufficiently developed their categories to operate otherwise.

How are concepts organized in semantic memory?

Numerous simple questions about semantic memory can be answered very rapidly by most people. For example, we can decide in about one second that a sparrow is a bird, and it takes the same length of time to think of the name of a fruit starting with *p*. This great efficiency suggests that semantic memory is highly organized or structured.

Hierarchical network model

The first systematic model of semantic memory was put forward by Allan Collins and Ross Quillian (1969). Their key assumption was that semantic memory is organized into a series of hierarchical networks. Part of one such network is shown in Figure 6.1. The major concepts (e.g. animal, bird, canary) are represented as nodes, and there are properties

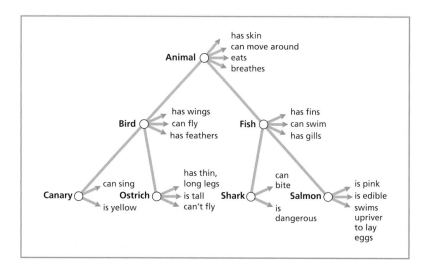

Figure 6.1 Collins and Quillian's (1969) hierarchical network.

or features (e.g. has wings, is yellow) associated with each concept. You might wonder why the property "can fly" is stored with the bird concept rather than with the canary concept: after all, one of the characteristics of canaries is that they can fly. According to Collins and Quillian, it would waste space in semantic memory to have information about being able to fly stored with every bird name. If those properties that are possessed by nearly all birds (e.g. can fly, has wings) are stored only at the bird node or concept, this satisfies the notion of cognitive economy. The underlying principle is that property information is stored as high up the hierarchy as possible to minimize the amount of information that needs to be stored in semantic memory. In other words, organization within semantic memory is based on a principle of cognitive economy.

Collins and Quillian (1969) tested their model by using a task on which participants had to decide as rapidly as possible whether sentences were true or false. To get a feeling for their task, answer the questions in Box 6.2. These aren't the specific sentences used by Collins and Quillian, they were devised by Alan Baddeley and Neil Thomson to look at the effects of various stressors on accessing semantic memory. You might not be too surprised to learn that alcohol slows down the rate at which such sentences can be verified.

According to the model of Collins and Quillian (1969), it should be possible to decide very rapidly that the sentence, "A canary is yellow," is true because the concept (i.e. "canary") and the property (i.e. "is yellow") are stored together at the same level of the hierarchy. By contrast, the sentence, "A canary can fly," should take longer because the concept and the property are separated by one level in the hierarchy. The sentence, "A canary has skin," should take even longer because there are two levels separating the concept and the property. As predicted, the time taken to respond to true sentences became progressively slower as the separation between the subject of the sentence and the property became greater.

The model is on the right lines in its claim that we often use semantic memory successfully by *inferring* the right answer. For example, the information that Leonardo da Vinci had knees is not stored directly in our semantic memory. However, we do know that Leonardo da Vinci was a human being, and that humans beings have knees, and we can confidently infer that Leonardo da Vinci had knees. This is exactly the kind of inferential process proposed by Collins and Quillian (1969).

In spite of its successes, the model suffers from various problems. As you might have noticed, a sentence such as, "A canary is yellow," differs from, "A canary has skin," not

Box 6.2 Decide as rapidly as possible whether each sentence is true ("Yes") or false ("No")

	Yes	No		Yes	No
Pork chops can be bought in shops	...	...	Antarctica tends the sick	...	...
Jamaica is edible	...	...	Beefsteaks are people	...	...
Oranges drill teeth	...	...	Chairs are furniture	...	...
California is a state of America	...	...	Priests wear clothes	...	...
London is a place	...	...	Flies carry disease	...	...
Potatoes move around searching for food	...	...	Mayors are elected representatives	...	...
Drills are scientists	...	...	Asia has high mountains	...	...
Aunts are relatives	...	...	Paris is a living creature	...	...
Spaghetti is a dish	...	...	Rattlesnakes move around searching for food	...	...
Corporals can be bought in shops	...	...	Bees treat the mentally ill	...	...
Beer is a liquid	...	...	Knives are manufactured goods	...	...
Gin is sold by butchers	...	...	Trout have fins	...	...
Fish and chips are an alcoholic drink	...	...	Squirrels are fish	...	...
Peas are edible	...	...	Lions are four-legged animals	...	...
			Sharks have wheels	...	...

only in the hierarchical distance between the concept and its property, but also in familiarity. Indeed, it is a fair bet that you have never encountered the sentence, "A canary has skin," in your life before! Conrad (1972) decided to see whether hierarchical distance or familiarity was more important in determining time to determine whether sentences are true or false. What she found was bad news for Collins and Quillian's model—when familiarity was controlled, hierarchical distance between the subject and the property had little effect on verification time.

There is another limitation with the approach of Collins and Quillian (1969). Consider the following statements: "A canary is a bird" and "A penguin is a bird." According to their theory, both statements should take the same length of time to verify, because both involve moving from *canary* or *penguin* to the level above, namely, *bird*. In fact, however, it takes longer to decide that a penguin is a bird than that a canary is a bird. Why is that the case? The members of most categories

vary considerably in terms of how typical or representative they are of the category to which they belong. For example, Rosch and Mervis (1975) found that oranges, apples, bananas, and peaches were rated as much more typical fruits than were olives, tomatoes, coconuts, and dates. Rips, Shoben, and Smith (1973) found that verification times were faster for more typical or representative members of a category than for relatively atypical members. For obvious reasons, this is known as the **typicality gradient**.

More typical members of a category possess more of the characteristics associated with that category than do less typical ones. Rosch (1973) showed this in a study in which she produced a series of sentences containing

KEY TERM

Typicality gradient: The ordering of the members of a category in terms of their typicality ratings.

The typicality effect determines that it will take longer to decide that a penguin is a bird than that a canary is a bird. A penguin is an example of a relatively atypical member of the category to which it belongs, whereas the canary—being the more representative member—can be verified more quickly.

the word "bird." Sample sentences were as follows: "Birds eat worms"; "I hear a bird singing"; "I watched a bird fly over the house"; and "The bird was perching on the twig." Now try replacing the word *bird* in each sentence in turn with *robin*, *eagle*, *ostrich*, and *penguin*. It will be obvious that whereas *robin* fits all the sentences, *eagle*, *ostrich*, and *penguin* fit progressively less well. Thus, penguins and ostriches are less typical birds than eagles, which in turn are less typical than robins.

What does this tell us about the structure of semantic memory? It strongly implies that Collins and Quillian (1969) were mistaken in assuming that the concepts we use belong to rigidly defined categories. It is much more realistic to assume that categories are loosely determined. This point was made by the philosopher Ludwig Wittgenstein (1958) using the category *games*. What are the defining characteristics of a game? What, for example, do baseball, poker, tennis, and chess have in common? It is very hard (or even impossible!) to think of a single set of features shared by all games. Wittgenstein suggested that members of the category *games* (and many other categories for that matter) are like members of a family having certain characteristics that they tend to share. Some members of the family might share several characteristics, whereas others might share only one or two, and often not the same one or two.

Some of the most convincing evidence that many concepts in semantic memory are fuzzy rather than neat and tidy was reported by McCloskey and Glucksberg (1978). They gave 30 people tricky questions such as, "Is a stroke a disease?" and "Is a pumpkin a fruit?" They found that 16 said a stroke is a disease, but 14 said it was not. A pumpkin was regarded as a fruit by 16 participants but not as a fruit by the remainder. More surprisingly, when McCloskey and Glucksberg tested the same participants a month later, 11 of them had changed their minds about "stroke" being a disease, and eight had altered their opinion about "pumpkin" being a fruit!

Spreading activation model

Collins and Loftus (1975) put forward a spreading activation theory designed to sort out the problems with the Collins and Quillian (1969) theory. Their starting point was that the notion of logically organized hierarchies was too inflexible. Instead, it is preferable to assume that semantic memory is organized on the basis of semantic relatedness or semantic distance. Semantic relatedness can be measured by asking people to decide how closely related pairs of words are. Alternatively, people can be asked to list as many members as they can of a particular category. Those members produced most often are regarded as most closely related to the category.

You can see part of the organization of semantic memory assumed by Collins and Loftus (1975) in Figure 6.2. An important feature is that the length of the links between two concepts indicates the degree of semantic relatedness between them. Thus, for example, *red* is more closely related to *orange* than it is to *sunsets*.

According to spreading activation theory, whenever a person sees, hears, or thinks about a concept, the appropriate node in semantic memory is activated. This activation then spreads most strongly to other concepts that are closely related semantically, and more weakly to those more distant semantically. For example, activation would pass strongly and rapidly from "robin" to "bird" in the sentence,

"A robin is a bird," because "robin" and "bird" are closely related semantically. However, it would pass more weakly and slowly from "penguin" to "bird" in the sentence, "A penguin is a bird." As a result, the model predicts the typicality effect.

Other predictions of the spreading activation model have been tested experimentally. For example, Meyer and Schvaneveldt (1976) carried out an experiment in which participants had to decide as rapidly as possible whether a string of letters formed a word. In the key condition, a given word (e.g. "butter") was immediately preceded by a semantically related word (e.g. "bread") or by an unrelated word (e.g. "nurse"). According to the model, activation should have spread

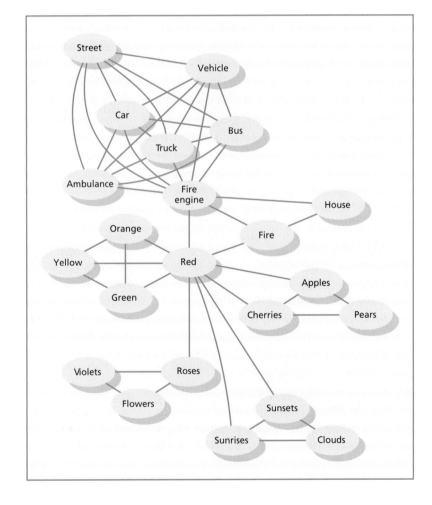

Figure 6.2 Example of a spreading activation semantic network. From Collins and Loftus (1975). Copyright © American Psychological Association. Reproduced with permission.

from the first word to the second only when they were semantically related and this activation should have made it easier to identify the second word. Thus, "butter" should have been identified as a word faster when preceded by "bread" than by "nurse." Indeed, there was a facilitation (or semantic priming) effect for semantically related words.

McNamara (1992) used the same basic approach as Meyer and Schvaneveldt (1976). Suppose the first word was "red." This was sometimes followed by a word one link away (e.g. "roses"), and sometimes by a word two links away (e.g. "flowers"). More activation should spread from the activated word to those one link away than those two links away, and so the facilitation effect should have been greater in the former case. This is precisely what McNamara (1992) found.

More support for the model comes from an interesting study by Schacter, Reiman, Curran, Yun, Bandy, McDermott, & Roediger (1996), who used the Deese–Roediger–McDermott paradigm (e.g. Roediger & McDermott, 1995), which is also discussed in Chapter 12. Participants were presented with word lists that had been constructed in a particular way. An initial word (e.g. "doctor") was selected, and then several words closely associated with it (e.g. "nurse," "sick," "hospital," "patient") were selected. All of these words (with the crucial exception of the initial word) were presented for learning, followed by a test of recognition memory.

What happened when the word not presented on the list (e.g. "doctor") was presented on the recognition test? According to the model, the missing word should be highly activated because it is so closely related to all of the list words. Schacter et al. compared brain activation when participants falsely recognized the missing word and when they correctly recognized words that had been on the list. The pattern and intensity of brain activation were very similar in both cases, indicating that there was substantial activation of the missing word as predicted by the model. This has been found in several studies including the one by Schacter et al.

The spreading activation model has generally proved more successful than the hierarchical network model at accounting for the various findings. An important reason is that it is a much more flexible approach. However, flexibility carried with it some disadvantages as well. It means that the model typically doesn't make very precise predictions, which makes it somewhat difficult to assess its overall adequacy.

ORGANIZATION OF SEMANTIC MEMORY IN THE BRAIN

We have seen that behavioral experiments can tell us much about the organization of semantic memory. However, our semantic memories are stored in the brain, and we can increase our understanding of semantic memory by focusing more directly on the brain itself. The most obvious assumption is that everything we know about any given object or concept is stored in *one* location in the brain. For example, I know several facts about my cat Lulu— she has gray fur, a small head, is very friendly, chases birds, has a hearty appetite, likes to play, purrs loudly, and so on. It seems natural to assume that all this information is stored very close together within the brain perhaps in a "Lulu node." Thus, it could be the case that semantic memories are organized in the brain at the level of whole objects. Some theorists have gone further, and argued that most of the information we possess about all living things is stored in one part of the brain, whereas most of the information about nonliving things is stored in another part.

To anticipate a little, there is increasing evidence that semantic memories are probably *not* stored in the ways described so far. An increasingly popular viewpoint is that different kinds of information about a given object are stored in different locations in the brain. Thus, for example, visual information about Lulu might be stored in a different place from auditory information about her (e.g. her loud purr) and from information about what she does (e.g. likes to play). This is often referred to as a feature-based approach. More generally, feature-based theories often assume that the visual features of most or all objects are stored in a particular brain area, with other features of objects being stored in a different brain area.

One of the ways we could try to decide between the above two approaches is by using brain imaging. In essence, if all the information I possess about Lulu is stored in one place, then the same brain area should be most activated whenever I am asked a question about any of her features. If each of Lulu's features is stored in a different place, then the brain area that is most activated will depend very much on *which* feature is asked about. Of course, the same is true of any other object as well.

Much of the research we will be considering involved brain-damaged patients. What is the basic rationale behind studying brain-damaged patients to understand semantic memory in healthy individuals? The major assumption is that the pattern of impairment shown by such patients can provide useful information concerning the ways in which our knowledge of concepts is organized within the brain. Suppose a particular patient was very good at identifying pictures of nonliving things (e.g. table, cake) but was very poor at identifying pictures of living things (e.g. horse, penguin). It would be tempting to conclude that everything we know about living things is stored in one part of the brain and everything we know about nonliving things is stored in a different part of the brain. In other words, the patient's pattern of impairment occurs because he/she has suffered brain damage to that region of the brain in which knowledge about living things is stored. Alas, we will soon see that reality is more complex than the above simple example might lead you to expect!

Findings

Many brain-damaged patients have problems only with certain semantic categories. Such patients are said to suffer from category-specific deficits. For example, Warrington and Shallice (1984) studied a patient (JBR), who had much greater problems in identifying pictures of living than of nonliving things, having success rates of 6% and 90%, respectively. He showed the same pattern when asked to define words. He defined *briefcase* as "a small case used by students to carry papers," but produced very impoverished definitions of plants and living things. For example, his definition of *daffodil* was "plant" and *ostrich* he simply described as "unusual."

The most common pattern shown by patients with category-specific deficits is that their recognition performance (identifying objects from pictures) is worse on living than on nonliving things. How can this be explained? People generally have more familiarity with nonliving than with living things (e.g. foreign animals) (Cree & McRae, 2003) and this might make it more difficult to identify living things. However, that is clearly not the whole story. For example, Caramazza and Shelton (1998) matched animate and inanimate items for frequency and familiarity. Their patient (EW) was much worse at naming animate objects than inanimate ones regardless of whether they were high in familiarity (54% vs. 94%, respectively) or low in familiarity (28% vs. 81%).

The general pattern of greater impairment for living than for nonliving things is much more common than the opposite pattern, i.e. worse recognition of nonliving than of living things. In total, more than 100 patients with a category-specific deficit for living but not for nonliving things have been discovered, plus more than 25 with the opposite impairment (Martin & Caramazza, 2003).

A substantial majority of patients with a category-specific deficit are more impaired in recognizing living than nonliving things. However, about 20% of patients with a category-specific deficit show the opposite pattern, i.e. greater impairment in recognizing nonliving things. Why are there these two patterns of impairment? This issue was addressed by Gainotti (2000), who reviewed evidence obtained from 44 patients. Of the 38 patients having a selective impairment for knowledge of living things, nearly all of them had damage to the anterior, medial, and inferior parts of the temporal lobes. By contrast, the six patients having a selective impairment for knowledge of man-made objects had damage in fronto-parietal areas extending further back in the brain than the areas damaged in the other group.

The above findings indicate that different kinds of semantic information about concepts are stored in different parts of the brain. However, we need to be wary when interpreting the findings. They do *not* necessarily indicate that concepts referring to living things are stored in one part of the brain with concepts referring to man-made objects being stored in another part. Alternative (and perhaps preferable) ways of interpreting the findings are discussed shortly.

Theoretical perspectives

How can we make sense of the various findings? One of the most influential approaches was proposed by Farah and McClelland (1991) in their sensory–functional theory. The three key assumptions of this theory are as follows:

1. Living things are distinguished from each other mainly on the basis of their visual or perceptual properties (i.e. what they look like).
2. Nonliving things are distinguished from each other mainly on the basis of their functional properties (i.e. what they are used for).
3. There are three times as many visual units within the semantic system as there are functional units.

How did Farah and McClelland (1991) obtain support for assumption 3 above? They examined the descriptors of living and nonliving things in a dictionary. Three times more of the descriptors were classified as visual than as functional. The ratio of visual to functional descriptors was much greater for living objects

than for nonliving ones (7.7 : 1 vs. 1.4 : 1, respectively).

Farah and McClelland (1991) tested their sensory–functional theory by constructing a computational model based on its assumptions. When they caused structural damage to their computational model by deactivating some of the semantic units, damage to the visual units impaired performance much more on object recognition of living than of nonliving things. By contrast, damage to the functional units had less effect. It impaired object recognition only for nonliving things. Thus, the theory can in principle account for the finding that most brain-damaged patients have greater impairment of object recognition for living than for nonlivings things. It can also account for the finding that some brain-damaged patients show the opposite pattern.

Support for sensory–functional theory was reported by Sitnikova, West, Kuperberg, and Holcomb (2006). Participants viewed pictures of animals and tools, and the experimenters measured the pattern of brain activity occurring after each picture was presented. Sitnikova et al. were especially interested in a waveform in the brain that occurs 400 ms after stimulus presentation and reflects detailed processing of meaning. Previous research had indicated that this waveform is strong in fronto-central and anterior–inferior regions when the visual features of objects are being processed. By contrast, brain areas further back in the brain in occipital, posterior–temporal, and posterior–parietal regions are associated with processing of functional properties of objects. According to sensory–functional theory, this waveform at 400 ms should be stronger in the former regions when animals are presented rather than tools, but stronger in the latter regions when tools rather than animals are presented. This predicted pattern of results was obtained by Sitnikova et al.

According to sensory–functional theory, information about objects in semantic memory is organized in terms of the distinction between sensory or visual properties and functional ones rather than that between living and nonliving. It follows from this assumption that most patients apparently suffering from category-specific deficits actually have brain damage to areas containing primarily visual or functional information about concepts—thus the entire notion of category-specific deficits might be misleading!

Lee, Graham, Simons, Hodges, Owen, and Patterson (2002) reported some support for sensory–functional theory in a brain-imaging study. Participants retrieved perceptual or nonperceptual information about living or nonliving concepts when presented with the names of the concepts. Processing of perceptual information from both living and nonliving concepts was associated with activation of left posterior inferior temporal lobe regions. By contrast, processing of nonperceptual information (e.g. functional attributes) was associated with activation of middle temporal lobe regions. Comparisons between living and nonliving concepts indicated that the *same* brain regions were activated for both types of concept. Thus, what determined which areas of the brain were activated was whether perceptual or nonperceptual information was being processed rather than whether the relevant object was living or nonliving. These findings are consistent with sensory–functional theory and with feature-based theories in general.

Similar findings were reported more recently by Marques, Canessa, Siri, Catricala, and Cappa (2008) also using brain-imaging techniques. Participants were presented with statements about the features (e.g. form, color, size, motion) of living and nonliving objects, and the patterns of brain activity were assessed while they decided whether the statements were true or false. What they found was clear-cut and largely agreed with the findings of Lee et al. (2002): "The results … highlighted that feature type rather than concept domain [i.e. living vs. nonliving] is the main organizational factor of the brain representation of conceptual knowledge" (Marques et al., 2008, p. 95).

One of the limitations of sensory-functional theory is that many properties of living things (e.g. *carnivore*, *lives in the desert*) don't seem

to be sensory or functional. Cree and McRae (2003) claimed that it isn't possible to understand the various complex patterns of impairment of concept knowledge by thinking in terms of only *two* properties: functional and sensory. Cree and McRae argued that both of these general properties should be subdivided. For example, Farah and McClelland defined an object's functional feature as "what it does or what it is used for," whereas Cree and McRae distinguished between entity behaviors (what a thing does) and functional information (what humans use it for.) We can also divide sensory properties into visual (including color), auditory, taste, and tactile ones. For example, there are similarities among fruits, vegetables, and foods because sensory features associated with taste are important to all three categories.

Cree and McRae (2003) identified *seven* different patterns of category-specific deficits occurring as a consequence of brain damage (Table 6.1). They pointed out that no previous theory can account for all (or even) most of these patterns. However, their multiple-feature approach can do so. When brain damage reduces stored knowledge for one or more properties of objects, semantic memory for all categories relying strongly on those properties is impaired.

According to Cree and McRae's (2003) multiple-property approach, the brain is organized so that any given type of property (e.g. color, motion) is stored in a particular region of the brain. There is reasonable evidence supporting that viewpoint. Martin and Chao (2001) reviewed brain-imaging findings indicating that category knowledge about color, motion, and shape is processed in different regions of the brain, typically in areas close to those associated with processing those kinds of information in visual perception.

The multiple-property approach is very promising for several reasons. First, it is based on a recognition that most concepts consist of several properties, and that these properties determine similarities and differences among categories. Second, the approach provides a reasonable account of several different

Table 6.1: Cree and McRae's (2003) explanation of why brain-damaged patients show various patterns of deficit in their knowledge of different categories. From Smith and Kosslyn (2007). Copyright © Pearson Education, Inc. Reproduced with permission.

Deficit pattern	Shared properties
1. Multiple categories consisting of living creatures	Visual motion, visual parts, color
2. Multiple categories of nonliving things	Function, visual parts
3. Fruits and vegetables	Color, function, taste, smell
4. Fruits and vegetables with living creatures	Color
5. Fruits and vegetables with nonliving things	Function
6. Inanimate foods with living things (especially fruits and vegetables)	Function, taste, smell
7. Musical instruments with living things	Sound, color

patterns of deficits in category knowledge observed in brain-damaged patients. Third, it is consistent with brain-imaging findings suggesting that different object properties are stored in different parts of the brain (Martin & Chao, 2001).

In sum, common sense would suggest that all the information we possess about any given concept or object would be stored in a specific location in the brain. That appears *not* to be the case. What is most likely is that the various kinds of information we have about an object (e.g. what humans use it for, what it does, its visual properties, its taste) are distributed in different brain areas. In ways that remain mysterious, we somehow manage to integrate all of these kinds of information rapidly and automatically when we think about any given concept.

LEARNING NEW CONCEPTS

So far, we have been concerned solely with how existing knowledge is stored and accessed but have said very little about the crucial issue of how new concepts are formed and then used appropriately in new situations. As this is an issue that lies at the heart of all education, it is obviously a very important one (although

Evidence indicates that there is often little transference or generalization of what is learned in school into different contexts unless the new situation closely resembles that in which the original learning occurred.

it is poorly understood). More specifically, educationalists hope that what students learn at school or university will transfer or generalize to different situations encountered subsequently. Much of the evidence indicates that there is often disappointingly little transfer unless the new situation closely resembles the original one in which learning occurred. For example, Bassock and Holyoak (1989) found that students who learned to solve physics problems involving velocity and distance were unable to transfer the method they had learned to solve arithmetic progression problems that were conceptually very similar. Students assumed that what they had learned was specific to the context of physics problems, and so they did not realize its applicability to another context. By contrast, students who initially learned how to solve the arithmetic progression problems *did* transfer that knowledge to the physics problems. In this case, students previously possessed much general knowledge about arithmetic and so were familiar with the notion that such knowledge can be applied in various contexts.

Barnett and Ceci (2002) reviewed research on transfer. They reported that transfer or generalization of learning from the learning situation to the transfer situation was reduced when the learning and transfer contexts differed in any of the six following ways: (1) knowledge domain; (2) physical context (learning environment); (3) temporal context (long delay between learning and context); (4) functional context (different purpose of learned behavior); (5) social context (one individual-based learning situation and one social-based learning situation); and (6) modality (e.g. visual presentation in one situation and auditory presentation in the other).

How can we produce generalization?

Suppose that learners who are asked to acquire certain knowledge are assigned randomly to two conditions: A and B. The learners in condition A acquire the knowledge more rapidly than those in condition B. Does this mean that they are in better shape than those in condition B to transfer their knowledge to a different situation? It seems reasonable to assume that the answer is "Yes!", but very often that is not the correct answer. As Schmidt and Bjork (1992) pointed out, learning that occurs rapidly is often rather superficial and specific to the original learning context. Apparently paradoxically, learning that is slower might also be deeper so that it transfers better to other situations.

Evidence consistent with the viewpoint of Schmidt and Bjork (1992) was reported by

Mannes and Kintsch (1987). They asked their participants to study a passage of text so that they would remember it. For one group, the text was preceded by an outline that had the same organization as the text. For a second group, the text was preceded by an outline having a different organization from the text. Superficial learning as assessed by ability to recall the original text was better in the first group than in the second group. However, participants in the second group did better when asked to solve creative problem-solving tasks that required a deep understanding of the text. The efforts that participants in the second group made to relate the outline to the text reduced their ability to recall the text but increased their understanding of it. This increased understanding meant that they were better placed than participants in the first group to generalize or transfer their knowledge to the creative problems.

A promising line of investigation into concept learning (and ways of trying to ensure that it generalizes) was developed by John Bransford and his colleagues at Vanderbilt University in Tennessee. This research is described in detail in Bransford's (1979) book *Human cognition*. However, some of the flavor of his approach is given by the following example taken from the doctoral dissertation of one of his students, K. E. Nitsch.

Of central interest to Nitsch was the issue of how to ensure that concepts that are learned will transfer to situations other than those used during learning. In one of his experiments, he manipulated the range of examples used in learning the new concepts CRINCH and MINGE—this was high in the varied context condition and low in the consistent context condition (Box 6.3).

The participants in both groups mastered the meanings of CRINCH and MINGE to the point where they could apply them accurately. After that, they moved on to an entirely new set of instances selected from social contexts different from those previously experienced. For participants in Group 1, the correct application rate of the concepts dropped from

Box 6.3 Learning new concepts

Group 1: Varied context

CRINCH: To make someone angry by performing an inappropriate act, originally used by waitresses.

Usage: When a man does not remove his hat on entering a church; when a spectator at a public event blocks the view of those behind; when someone flicks ash over a beautifully polished table; when diners complain about slow waitress service.

MINGE: To gang up on a person or thing; originally used by cowboys and cowhands.

Usage: When a band of dissatisfied sailors threaten their captain with mutiny; when an audience boos a mediocre act on stage; when someone is helpless to defend himself against attack; when a group of cowboys join forces against a rustler.

Group 2: Consistent context

CRINCH: To make someone angry by performing an inappropriate act; originally used by waitresses.

Usage: When a diner fails to leave a tip; when diners argue about the prices on the menu; when a diner deliberately spills ketchup; when diners complain about slow or inefficient service.

MINGE: To gang up on a person or thing; originally used by cowboys and cowhands.

Usage: When three or more riders decide to converge on a single animal; when three or more work together to brand an animal; when three or more encircle a wolf or other marauder to prevent its escape; when three or more join forces against a rustler.

91% in the old context to 84% in the new context. This drop was much less than for Group 2 participants, whose correct application fell from 89% to 67%. Thus, if we want to teach concepts that will generalize to new settings, it is important to expose the learner to a wide range of examples. Unfortunately, there is a price to be paid for this approach. Nitsch's consistent- or single-context group found it relatively easy to learn the new concepts within four trials, but the varied-context group had much more difficulty and required additional training.

Nitsch then decided to try to find a form of training that produced the benefits of varied training while at the same time avoiding the problems created by being presented with too wide a range of examples. Accordingly, he used a hybrid-context group that was trained with examples drawn from the original context in which each concept was said to have originated followed by three trials with varied contexts. This group was compared against a single-context group (trained entirely on examples drawn from the original context) and a varied-context group (trained on examples drawn from several different contexts). All three groups were then tested on their ability to apply each concept to new social situations.

What did Nitsch find? First, as in the previous study, all groups performed at a level of around 90% correct when tested with the original context. Second, again as in the previous study, participants in the same-context group had more difficulty applying the concepts in new situations than did those in the varied-context group (69% vs. 82%, respectively). The new finding was that the hybrid-context group performed even better than the varied-context group (91% correct). Third, the hybrid-training group needed no more initial training than the same-context group. The conclusion is clear: It is easier to acquire new concepts if the range of examples learned is limited, but if we want the information to generalize it is important to give fairly broad experience in the training situation itself.

Most professional training courses are designed to be consistent with the above conclusion. Medical students start by learning in somewhat oversimplified fashion how the body works. Then they learn about the effects of various diseases on normal function. During their clinical training, they are exposed to a range of illnesses within each of a number of hospital departments. Within any given department, the number of possible illnesses will be constrained so that the students will not need to be too worried about neurological factors while they are attached to a consultant gastroenterologist or about skin diseases during their familiarization with obstetrics. As junior doctors, they have to confront a much wider range of illnesses, and with much less direct supervision. By the time they emerge as fully qualified doctors, they have enough experience to allow them (hopefully!) to bridge the gap between textbook examples of disease and diseases in real people. Real people are seldom textbook cases of anything.

SCHEMAS

Our discussion so far in this chapter might have created the false impression that nearly all the information contained in semantic memory is in the form of simple concepts. In fact, much of the knowledge stored in semantic memory consists of larger structures of information. One of the main reasons for assuming that there is far more to semantic memory was expressed clearly by Kintsch (1980, p. 612): "Semantic memory as a static structure independent of context and specific use just won't do." Knowing the meanings of numerous words and concepts is undoubtedly of great usefulness to us. However, such knowledge on its own would be totally insufficient to allow us to interact successfully and flexibly with the world around us.

What additional kinds of information and knowledge are stored in semantic memory? An extremely influential early answer to that question was provided by Sir Frederic Bartlett

(1932), who argued strongly for the importance of what he called schemata (schemas in American English)—a *schema* is a well-integrated chunk of knowledge about the world, events, people, or actions (see Chapter 5). One of Bartlett's key insights was that what we remember is influenced very much by the schematic knowledge we already possess.

The schemas stored in semantic memory include what are often referred to as *scripts* and *frames*. **Scripts** deal with knowledge about events and consequences of events (Schank & Abelson, 1977). By contrast, **frames** are knowledge structures referring to some aspect of the world (e.g. building) containing fixed structural information (e.g. has floors and walls) and slots for variable information (e.g. material or materials from which the building is constructed).

Bower, Black, and Turner (1979) considered in detail the kinds of information typically found in scripts. They asked people to list 20 actions or events that usually occur when eating at a restaurant. In spite of the varied restaurant experiences of their participants, there was much agreement on the actions associated with the restaurant script. At least 73% of the participants mentioned sitting down, looking at the menu, ordering, eating, paying the bill, and leaving. In addition, at least 48% included entering the restaurant, giving the reservation name, ordering drinks, discussing the menu, talking, eating a salad or soup, ordering dessert, eating dessert, and leaving a tip.

Schematic knowledge (including that contained in scripts and frames) is useful for three main reasons. First, schemas allow us to form *expectations*. In a restaurant, for example, we expect to be shown to a table, to be

KEY TERMS

Script: a type of schema relating to the typical sequences of events in various common situations (e.g. going to a restaurant).
Frame: A type of schema in which information about objects and their properties is stored.

given a menu by the waiter or waitress, to order food and drink, and so on. If any one of these expectations is violated, we usually take appropriate action. For example, if no menu is forthcoming, we try to catch the eye of the waiter or waitress. Schemas (including scripts) help to make the world a more predictable place than would otherwise be the case, because our expectations are generally confirmed. Sometimes events that do not match our schema-based expectations are well remembered because they are distinctive. For example, we have excellent memory for unexpected events such as a waiter spilling soup in a customer's lap (Bower et al., 1979) or a lecturer smoking a cigarette (Neuschatz, Lampinen, Preston, Hawkins, & Toglia, 2002).

Second, schemas play an important role in reading and listening because they allow us to fill in the gaps in what we read or hear and so enhance our understanding. More specifically, they provide the basis for us to draw inferences as we read or listen.

The study by Bransford and Johnson (1972; Box 6.4) shows very clearly how useful schemas can be in allowing us to make sense of what we read. Thankfully, however, you probably don't have to read many texts as difficult to make sense of as their one about washing clothes.

It would be easy (but mistaken) to conclude that schematic knowledge is only useful when you are confronted by texts that are almost incomprehensible in the absence of such knowledge. In fact, we actually use schematic knowledge all the time to enhance our understanding of virtually everything we read or hear. Consider the following story taken from Rumelhart and Ortony (1977):

1. Mary heard the ice-cream van coming.
2. She remembered the pocket money.
3. She rushed into the house.

You probably made various assumptions or inferences while reading the story: Mary wanted to buy some ice-cream; buying ice-cream costs money; Mary had some pocket money in the house; and Mary had only a limited amount of time to get hold of some money before the ice-cream van arrived. Note that none of these assumptions is explicitly stated

Box 6.4 When it is difficult to understand a text

Bransford and Johnson (1972) argued that people wouldn't understand a passage properly if it were written in such a way that it was hard to work out the underlying schema or theme. They used a passage, the first part of which is given below. Put yourself in the position of participants in their study, and see whether you can understand it:

The procedure is quite simple. First, you arrange items into different groups. Of course, one pile may be sufficient depending on how much there is to do. If you have to go somewhere else due to lack of facilities that is the next step; otherwise, you are pretty well set. It is important not to overdo things. That is, it is better to do too few things at once than too many. In the short run this may not seem important

but complications can easily arise. (Bransford & Johnson, 1972, p. 722)

Did you work out what the passage was all about? Participants reading the passage in the absence of a title rated it as incomprehensible and recalled an average of only 2.8 different ideas ("idea units") from it. In contrast, those supplied beforehand with the title "Washing clothes" found it easy to understand and recalled 5.8 idea units on average. Relevant schematic knowledge (i.e. the title providing the theme of the passage) had a beneficial effect on recall because it helped comprehension of the passage rather than because the title acted as a useful retrieval cue. We know this because participants receiving the title *after* hearing the passage but *before* recall recalled only 2.6 idea units on average.

Although we are generally unaware of drawing inferences whilst reading or listening to a story, there is convincing evidence that this happens nearly all the time. © Roy McMahon/Corbis.

in the three sentences, and that it is our schematic knowledge that allows us to fill in the gaps in the story. We are generally not aware of drawing inferences while we are reading or listening to a story, but there is convincing evidence that this happens nearly all the time.

Third, schematic knowledge can assist us when we perceive visual scenes. For example, Palmer (1975) presented a scene (e.g. a kitchen) in pictorial form, followed by the very brief presentation of the picture of an object. This object was either appropriate to the context (e.g. loaf) or inappropriate (e.g. mailbox). There was also a further condition in which no contextual scene was presented initially. The probability of identifying the object correctly was greatest when it was appropriate to the context, and so the activation of schematic knowledge facilitated visual perception. Performance was worst when the context was inappropriate, because the schematic knowledge that was activated was unrelated to the object subsequently presented.

Errors and distortions

So far, we have seen that our schematic knowledge is generally very useful. It makes

the world a more predictable place, it enhances our understanding of what we read and hear, and it can facilitate visual perception of the world around us. However, there are costs that must sometimes be paid when making use of schematic knowledge.

Bartlett (1932) was the first psychologist to demonstrate this when he presented his Cambridge University students with North American Indian folk tales such as *The war of the ghosts*, which they had to read and then later recall. *The war of the ghosts* is reproduced in Chapter 5 (p. 94) and seems very strange to those of us who are unfamiliar with very different cultures. What Bartlett found was that the remembered story was always shorter, more coherent, and tended to fit in more closely with the participant's own viewpoint than the original story. This was especially the case with a story like *The war of the ghosts*, in which several features are incompatible with the expectations of those not familiar with North-American Indian culture. Such individuals tended to omit the supernatural aspect and to rationalize puzzling features of the story by changing them to fit their own expectations.

Bartlett (1932) interpreted his findings by arguing that the systematic errors and distortions produced in the participants' recalls were due to the intrusion of their schematic knowledge. However, Bartlett's experimental approach can be criticized. The instructions he gave to his participants were rather vague and he hardly ever carried out any statistical tests on his data! More worryingly, many of the recall distortions he observed were due to deliberate guessing rather than genuine problems in memory. This was shown by Gauld and Stephenson (1967), who found that clear instructions emphasizing the need for accurate recall eliminated almost half of the errors obtained using Bartlett's vague instructions.

In spite of these problems, there is convincing support for Bartlett's major findings from well-controlled studies. For example, consider the study by Sulin and Dooling (1974), which is also described in Chapter 5 (pp. 95–96) and in which the participants' schematic knowledge about Hitler distorted recollections of what they had read at a long retention interval (1 week) but not at a short one (5 minutes); see also the study by Brewer and Treyens (1981) (Box 6.5).

Schemas also play a role in determining what people remember when presented with information about controversial issues. What tends to happen is that people remember information consistent with their own views better

Box 6.5 Schemas in everyday life: Brewer and Treyens (1981)

Brewer and Treyens (1981) pointed out that much of the information that we remember during the course of our everyday lives is acquired incidentally rather than deliberately. For example, you might remember the shapes and colors of the covers of many of your books, but it is unlikely that you deliberately set out to learn and remember this information. Accordingly, Brewer and Treyens decided to see whether people would show schema-driven memory errors in incidental memory. They also decided to use a naturalistic learning situation rather than asking their participants to read artificially constructed texts.

Brewer and Treyens (1981) asked participants to spend a very short period of time (about 35 seconds) in a room designed to look like a graduate student's office before the experiment proper took place (Figure 6.3). The room contained a mixture of schema-consistent objects you would expect to find in a graduate student's office (e.g. desk, calendar, eraser, pencils) and schema-inconsistent objects (e.g. a skull, a toy top). Some schema-consistent objects (e.g. books) were omitted.

After the participants had left this room and gone to another room, they were unexpectedly tested on their memory for the objects in the first room. Many of the participants initially provided written free recall of all the objects they could remember, followed by a recognition memory test including words referring to objects, some of which had been present in the room and some of which had not.

What did Brewer and Treyens (1981) find? First, participants recalled more objects that were schema consistent than those that were schema inconsistent, and this was the case

Figure 6.3 The "graduate student's" room used by Brewer and Treyens (1981) in their experiment. Copyright © 1981 Elsevier. Photo reproduced with kind permission of Professor Brewer.

both for objects that were present and those that weren't. Second, there was an interesting finding based on objects that were not present in the room but were "recognized" with high confidence—these objects were nearly all ones that were highly schema-consistent (e.g. books, filing cabinet). This is clear evidence for schemas leading to errors in memory. Third, most participants recognized many more objects than they recalled. Brewer and Treyens wondered *which* objects recognized with high confidence by the participants were most likely to have been recalled. The answer was objects very consistent with the room schema (e.g. typewriter), suggesting that the schema was used as a retrieval mechanism to facilitate recall.

than inconsistent information—this is known as consistency bias. According to Wiley (2005), the schematic knowledge possessed by people who know relatively little about a controversial issue will mostly be consistent with their own views. It is easier for them to add schema-consistent information to that knowledge base than it is to add schema-inconsistent information. Consistency bias is the consequence. Suppose, however, that we presented information that was consistent and inconsistent with their views to people who already possessed considerable schematic knowledge about the issue in question. They should find it equally easy to remember information favoring and opposed to their own views, because there would be schematic support for both types of information. Precisely this finding was reported by Wiley (2005).

Evaluation
Schema theories have proved generally successful. Of particular importance, they have identified some of the main reasons why our memories are sometimes distorted.

However, there are various limitations with schema-based theories. First, they tend to be rather vague. The evidence strongly suggests that we possess schemas, but their precise scope and nature remain unclear.

Second, the theories have little to say about the factors determining *when* people use schematic knowledge to draw inferences. Consider an experiment by Murray and Burke (2003). Participants with high, moderate, and low reading skill were presented with predictive inferences (e.g. inferring *break* when presented with a sentence such as "The angry husband threw the fragile vase against the wall"). All three groups showed some evidence of drawing these predictive inferences, presumably by making use of their relevant schematic knowledge. However, only participants with high reading skill drew these inferences rapidly and automatically, indicating that some people find it easier than others to access schematic knowledge.

Third, our memory representations are often richer and more complex than is implied

by schema theories. For example, consider restaurant scripts. It might be true that we have a basic restaurant script. However, we also know that you don't sit down before ordering your food at fast-food restaurants, expensive restaurants are most likely to have wine waiters, you need to book at some restaurants but not others, and so on. Most schema-based theories have not focused on these complexities.

Fourth, while schema theory can account for many of our recall errors, it seems to predict that we should make more errors than is actually the case—we seem to be better at discriminating between schema-based and text-based information than is assumed by the theory.

Disorders of concept and schema-based memory
I have argued that we can distinguish between at least two major types of information in semantic memory. First, there are relatively abstract concepts generally corresponding to individual words. Second, there are broader and more flexible organizational structures based on schemas and scripts. If that assumption is correct, we might expect some brain-damaged patients to have greater problems with accessing concept-based information than schema- or script-based information. There should also be others who find it more difficult to use schema or script information than information about specific concepts. As we will see, there is some support for these predictions.

What brain-damaged patients have special problems with accessing concept-based information? Many are patients with *semantic dementia*. This condition involves severe problems in accessing the meanings of words and objects but good executive functioning in the early stages of deterioration. Note, however, that the precise symptoms exhibited by patients with semantic dementia vary from one patient to another. Funnell (1996) found that EP, a patient with semantic dementia, retained reasonable access to script knowledge. For example, when she was involved in arranging the next research appointment, she went to the kitchen and collected her calendar and a ballpoint pen. EP also used a needle correctly when given a button to sew on to a shirt. However, her performance was extremely poor when tested on the meanings of common objects (e.g. ballpoint pen, needle, scissors). On one task, each object was presented with two additional objects, one of which was functionally associated with the use of the target objects (e.g. the ballpoint pen was presented with a pad of writing paper and a small printed book). She performed at chance level when instructed to select the functionally associated object.

Similar findings with another semantic dementia patient, KE, were reported by Snowden, Griffiths, and Neary (1994). KE found it difficult to identify and use her own objects when they moved to an unusual location in her home. However, she showed evidence of script memory by carrying out everyday tasks appropriately and by using objects (e.g. clothes pegs) correctly when they were in their usual location (e.g. her own peg-bag).

Which brain-damaged patients have greater problems with accessing script-related information than the meanings of concepts? Scripts typically have a goal-directed quality (e.g. you use a script to achieve the goal of having an enjoyable restaurant meal), and it is generally assumed that executive functioning within the prefrontal cortex is very useful in constructing and implementing goals. Some patients with damage to the prefrontal cortex seem to have particular problems with scripts. For example, Sirigu, Zalla, Pillon, Grafman, Agid, & Dubois (1995) asked patients with prefrontal damage to generate and evaluate various types of scripts (routine events, nonroutine events, and novel events). These patients produced as many events as patients with posterior lesions and healthy controls, and retrieved the relevant actions as rapidly as members of the other two groups. These findings suggested that the prefrontal patients had as much stored information about actions

relevant to various events as the other patients and healthy controls. However, the prefrontal patients made many mistakes in *ordering* actions within a script and at deciding which actions were of most importance to the achievement of any given event. Thus, they had particular problems with script-based knowledge requiring *assembling* the actions within a script in the optimal sequence.

Cosentino, Chute, Libon, Moore, and Grossman (2006) studied patients with fronto-temporal dementia (including damage to the prefrontal cortex) who showed attentional deficits and poor executive functioning. These patients, as well as those with semantic dementia and healthy controls, were presented with various scripts. Some of these scripts contained sequencing errors (e.g. dropping fish in a bucket occurring *before* casting the fishing line) whereas others contained semantic or meaning errors (e.g. placing a flower on the hook in a story about fishing). Patients with semantic dementia and healthy controls both detected as many sequencing errors as semantic ones (Figure 6.4). By contrast, the temporo-frontal patients with poor executive functioning failed to detect almost twice as

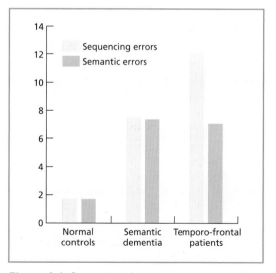

Figure 6.4 Semantic and sequencing errors made by patients with semantic dementia, temporo-frontal patients, and normal controls. Data from Cosentino et al. (2006).

many sequencing errors as semantic ones. Thus, these patients had relatively intact semantic knowledge of concepts combined with fairly severe impairment of script-based knowledge.

What conclusions can we draw from research on concept-based and schema-based impairments in brain-damaged patients? On the assumption that conceptual knowledge and schematic knowledge are stored in separate brain regions, we might expect to find some patients having a greater impairment of conceptual than of schematic knowledge and others showing the opposite pattern. The available evidence provides some support for this prediction and thus for the assumption upon which it is based. However, this is a complex area of research and so any conclusions that are drawn need to be somewhat tentative.

SUMMARY

There is an important distinction between semantic memory and episodic memory. The former (but not the latter) involves conscious recollection of the past. The extent of anterograde and retrograde amnesia for episodic and semantic memories often differs considerably, suggesting that the two types of memory are distinctly different. Brain imaging indicates that somewhat different brain areas are activated during learning depending on whether the task involves episodic or semantic memory, and the same is true during retrieval.

According to the hierarchical network model, semantic memory is organized into numerous hierarchical networks. It is assumed that information about the properties of objects is stored as high up the hierarchy as possible to maximize cognitive economy. The model's assumption that the concepts we use belong to rigidly defined categories is wrong.

According to the spreading activation model, activation of a given concept causes activation to spread most strongly to other concepts that are closely related semantically. The model explains the typicality effect and the effects of semantic priming. However, the model's flexibility makes it hard to test properly.

Attempts have been made to understand the organization of semantic memory by studying brain-damaged patients with category-specific deficits. Such patients often have much greater problems in identifying living than nonliving things, but many exhibit more complex problems. According to sensory–functional theory, visual properties of objects are stored in different regions of the brain from their functional properties. The further assumption that visual properties are especially important with living things and functional properties with nonliving things explains many findings. Cree and McRae (2003) expanded this theory into a more complex multiple-property approach in which sensory and functional properties were subdivided to produce several additional properties. This approach provides a more adequate account of the findings from brain-damaged patients than does sensory–functional theory.

When people learn new concepts of kinds of information, they often find it difficult to apply what has been learned to situations differing from the one used during learning. Nitsch found that an effective way of ensuring that knowledge about concepts generalizes to new situations is to make sure that concept learning occurs in various different contexts.

Schematic knowledge is useful because it allows us to form appropriate expectations and to draw inferences to fill in the gaps in the information presented to us. However, schematic knowledge causes distortions in memory when what we read or hear is inconsistent with that knowledge. The distinction between schemas/scripts and concepts corresponding to individual words has received support from studies on brain-damaged patients—some patients have greater problems with schema/script information than with concept-based information, whereas other patients exhibit the opposite pattern.

FURTHER READING

- Brewer, W. F. (2000). Bartlett, functionalism, and modern schema theories. *Journal of Mind and Behavior*, *21*, 37–44. The author examines in an illuminating way the similarities and differences between Bartlett's theoretical approach and those of more contemporary schema theorists.

- Cree, G. S., & McRae, K. (2003). Analyzing the factors underlying the structure and computation of the meaning of chipmunk, cherry, chisel, cheese, and cello (and many other such concrete nouns). *Journal of Experimental Psychology: General*, *132*, 163–201. The authors put forward an important new theoretical framework for understanding how concepts are stored in the brain.

- Hart, J., & Kraut, M. (2007). *Neural basis of semantic memory*. Cambridge: Cambridge University Press. The relationship between semantic memory and the brain is discussed in all its complexity in an authoritative way in this book.

- Murphy, G. L. (2002). *The big book of concepts*. Cambridge, MA: MIT Press. This book provides a well-written and comprehensive account of theory and research on concepts.

CHAPTER 7

AUTOBIOGRAPHICAL MEMORY

Alan Baddeley

C an you remember your first school? The names of your teachers? Your friends? An incident, pleasant or unpleasant?

To answer these questions, you need **autobiographical memory**. Autobiographical memory refers to the memories that we hold regarding ourselves and our relations with the world around us. Is it important? Certainly. But is it a separate kind of memory? Yes and no. No, given that it almost certainly depends on the episodic and semantic memory systems we have already discussed. Yes, because the role that it plays in our lives differs in interesting and important ways from other functions of memory. Remembering facts about ourselves, such as our name, when we went to school, and where we live, is autobiographical but forms a personal aspect of semantic memory. Remembering coming to work today is also autobiographical but involves recollecting an episodic experience. The fact that autobiographical memory involves both of these inevitably means that it is complex, and much that constitutes this chapter is descriptive rather than theory driven. This is meant not as a criticism but as an account of the relatively early stage of development of our understanding of this intriguing area.

We will begin by discussing the function of autobiographical memory and why it is important, leading on to the thorny question

Recalling the names of our school friends requires autobiographical memory, which in turn depends upon both episodic and semantic memory.

of how to study it. The problem here is that, unlike most of the research we have discussed so far, the experimenter has no control over the learning situation, which makes it difficult to analyze the processes involved in either the acquisition or forgetting of autobiographical memories.

KEY TERM

Autobiographical memory: Memory across the lifespan for both specific events and self-related information.

WHY DO WE NEED AUTOBIOGRAPHICAL MEMORY?

Williams, Conway, and Cohen (2008) propose four functions of autobiographical memory. These include *directive* functions, for example what happened the last time you tried to change a car tire, and a more *social* function. Sharing autobiographical memories can be a very pleasant and socially supportive activity (Neisser, 1988). In my own case, hearing my sons reminisce about childhood family holidays is an example. Conversely, when autobiographical memory is disrupted by amnesia or dementia, this can be one factor that impairs relationships (Robinson & Swanson, 1990), leading to the feeling that "This is not the person I married." Autobiographical memories can also play an important role in creating and maintaining our *self-representation*, hence the value of reminiscence therapy (Woods, Spector, Orrell, & Davies, 2005), a process described in Chapter 13 whereby elderly patients with memory problems are encouraged to build up a set of reminders of their earlier life based on photographs and personal mementos—items that bring back memories of their younger days. Finally, autobiographical recollection can be used to help us cope with adversity. One of the problems of depression is that patients find it difficult to recollect positive life experiences when depressed, whereas negative recollections are more readily available, a retrieval effect known as **mood-congruent memory**.

However, although these functions might be plausible, they are largely speculative. In an attempt to obtain empirical evidence on this matter, Hyman and Faries (1992) questioned people about memories they frequently talked about, and the situations in which they were discussed. There were very few reports of autobiographical memory being used directively to solve problems, with the sharing of experience and passing on of advice being more common. In a subsequent study they used cue words,

finding a distinction between memories that were used internally for self-related functions and those used in interacting with others, but again little evidence of directive use of autobiographical memory.

Bluck, Alea, Habermas, and Rubin (2005) devised the Thinking About Life Experiences (TALE) questionnaire, specifying particular situations and then categorizing the resulting reports as directive, self-related, nurturing existing social relationships, or developing new social relationships. The factor analysis of the results found considerable overlap between the directive function, the self-related function, and those related to nurturing and developing relationships. Hence, although it remains plausible that autobiographical memory has a number of different functions, it is doubtful that they are clearly separable into different categories in actual practice.

One weakness with the research described so far is the problem of adequate methodology. The studies assume, for example, that participants are aware of the function of their autobiographical memories and can remember their autobiographical memories and the situations that evoked them in sufficient detail to categorize them. In an area as complex as autobiographical memory, there is clearly a need for the development of a range of methods of study. This is discussed next.

METHODS OF STUDY

One method of tackling this problem is to use diaries in which participants record events,

---

KEY TERM

Mood-congruent memory: Bias in the recall of memories such that negative mood makes negative memories more readily available than positive, and vice versa. Unlike mood dependency, it does not affect the recall of neutral memories.

and subsequently try to remember them. This is a useful approach but one that places great demands on the participants. A second approach is to probe memory, for example asking for a memory associated with a cue word such as *river*, then analyze the nature of the responses. A third method is to ask for memories associated with either a specific time period, or a major public event such as the 9/11 attack on New York. Finally, as in the case of semantic and episodic memory, we can learn a good deal from what happens when autobiographical memory breaks down, as the result either of brain damage or emotional stress. Each of these approaches is discussed in turn.

Diaries

One problem in studying autobiographical memory is that of knowing what was initially experienced, and one solution to this is to record events in a diary that allows later memories to be objectively checked. Linton (1975) used this method to study her own autobiographical memory. She kept a diary for over 5 years, recording 2 events per day, each being briefly described and written on an index card. She tested herself each month by randomly picking out two index cards and deciding whether she could remember the order in which incidents occurred and the date. Because she chose cards at random and then replaced them, she would sometimes test herself on the same incident on several occasions. As Figure 7.1 shows, she observed a powerful effect: The more often an event was probed, the better it was retained. This provided further evidence for the value of spaced retrieval on long-term learning as discussed in Chapter 4 (see p. 74).

A classic diary study was carried out by the Dutch psychologist Willem Wagenaar (1986), who kept a diary for over 6 years, on each day recording two events, together with

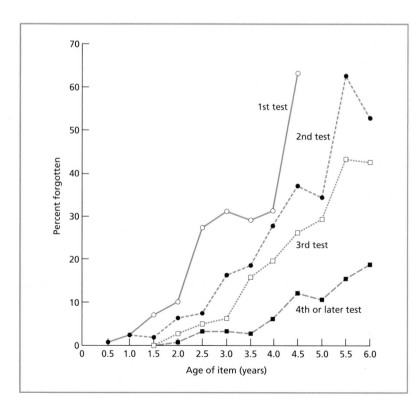

Figure 7.1 Probability of forgetting an autobiographical diary item as a function of elapsed time and number of prior tests. From Linton (1975). Copyright W.H. Freeman. Reproduced with permission.

four features or cues to that event. As shown in Figure 7.2, he recorded *who* was involved, *what* the event was, *where* it occurred, and *when*. He also rated the incident for its saliency and whether it was something that happened frequently or was rather unusual, in addition to recording the degree of emotional involvement and whether this was pleasant or unpleasant. He recorded a total of 2400 incidents. He then tested his memory by selecting an incident at random and cueing himself with one, two, or three retrieval cues, randomizing the order in which the *who*, *what*, *where*, and *when* cues were presented. Figure 7.3 shows the mean percentage of questions answered correctly as a function of number of cues. Wagenaar found that the *who*, *what*, and *where* cues tended to be equally good at evoking a memory, whereas the *when* cue, which simply provided the date, was much less efficient. This is perhaps not surprising. Can you remember where you were on 19 July last year? Neither can I.

Wagenaar reports that he found the task to be surprisingly difficult and unpleasant, but that given sufficient cues he could recollect most of the incidents eventually. In a number of cases, he could not remember anything, despite all his recorded cues. However, in those cases where another person was involved, they would typically be able to evoke a recollection, which could be verified by his providing additional information. Does that then mean

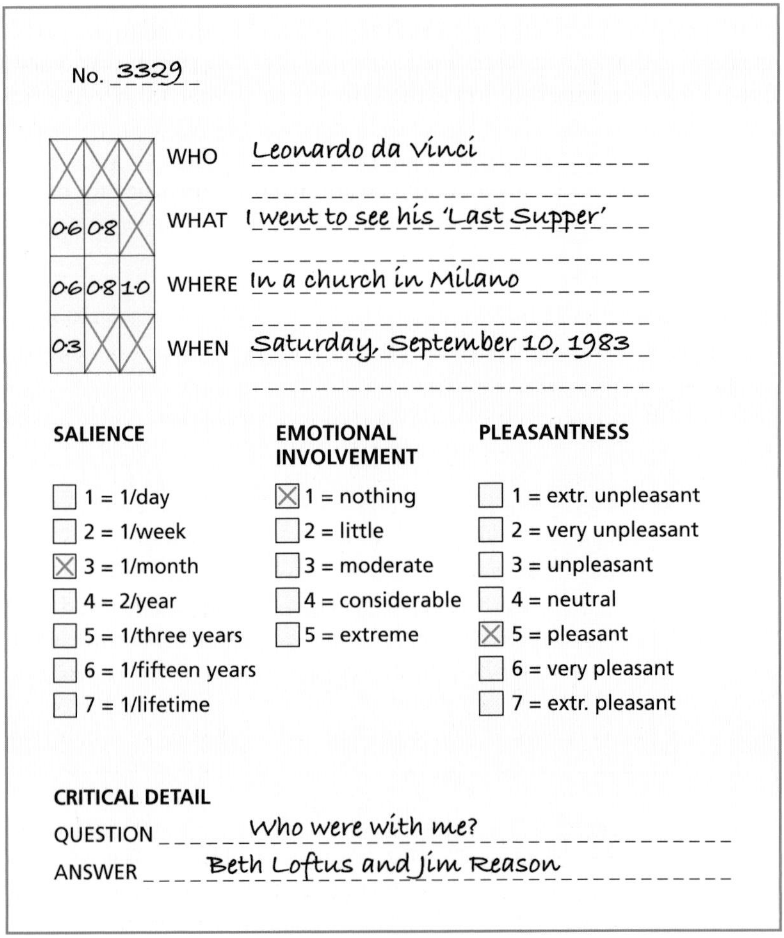

No. 3329

WHO Leonardo da Vinci

06 08 — WHAT I went to see his 'Last Supper'

06 08 10 — WHERE In a church in Milano

03 — WHEN Saturday, September 10, 1983

SALIENCE
- [ ] 1 = 1/day
- [ ] 2 = 1/week
- [x] 3 = 1/month
- [ ] 4 = 2/year
- [ ] 5 = 1/three years
- [ ] 6 = 1/fifteen years
- [ ] 7 = 1/lifetime

EMOTIONAL INVOLVEMENT
- [x] 1 = nothing
- [ ] 2 = little
- [ ] 3 = moderate
- [ ] 4 = considerable
- [ ] 5 = extreme

PLEASANTNESS
- [ ] 1 = extr. unpleasant
- [ ] 2 = very unpleasant
- [ ] 3 = unpleasant
- [ ] 4 = neutral
- [x] 5 = pleasant
- [ ] 6 = very pleasant
- [ ] 7 = extr. pleasant

CRITICAL DETAIL

QUESTION Who were with me?

ANSWER Beth Loftus and Jim Reason

Figure 7.2 An example of a recorded event from Wagenaar's diary study (1986). Copyright © Elsevier. Reproduced with permission.

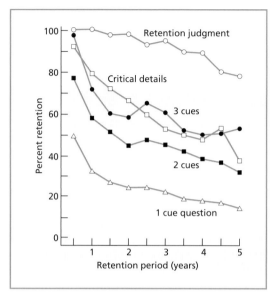

Figure 7.3 Recall of autobiographical incidents as a function of time, given one, two, or three retrieval cues. From Wagenaar (1986). Copyright © Elsevier. Reproduced with permission.

that we never forget anything? Almost certainly not. Wagenaar selected events that were most likely to be highly memorable; the process of selection would in itself involve retrieval, and in effect a rehearsal, while the process of deciding on his *who*, *where*, *what*, and *when* cues would involve a relatively deep level of processing (Craik & Lockhart, 1972). This degree of selection and implicit rehearsal is a problem for diary studies, because they result in memories that are atypically well encoded.

Brewer (1988) tried to avoid the biased selection problem in a study that sampled events at random. His ten participants were each given a beeper and a tape recorder. The beeper went off at random intervals, at which point participants were to say what they were doing, where, what the significance of their activity was, its goal-directedness, and their emotional state. The incidents were tested at delays ranging from 0 to 46 days, using one or other of their ratings as a cue. A total of 414 events were recorded, of which 26% were correctly recalled, 28% were wrong, and 46% evoked a blank. It is likely that, given more

cues, more would be recalled but it seems unlikely that all of the 74% failed memories would be recollected by any means.

A more detailed analysis of the nature of the items recalled was made by Conway, Collins, Gathercole, and Anderson (1996) in a study involving two participants who kept diaries over a period of months, recording both events and thoughts. These were then mixed with plausibly invented alternatives and recognition was required. This was followed by a categorization as to whether the item was "remembered," accompanied by a feeling of recollecting the initial experience, or simply "known." True events were more likely to evoke a remember response than foils, with events being twice as likely to evoke recollection as entries than were thoughts.

In conclusion, diary studies have been useful in giving some idea of the richness of autobiographical memory, and of the relative importance of different types of event and experience. They do, however, suffer from problems of sampling bias in the events recorded, together with a tendency for the encoding process itself to result in the enhanced learning of the events selected. Finally, the method requires considerable perseverance from the diarists, who are therefore likely to be a small and atypical sample of the general population.

The memory probe method

An alternative to the diary method is that of cued recall, a method first used by Galton (1879). It was subsequently revived by Crovitz and Shiffman (1974), who gave their participants a word and asked them to recollect an autobiographical memory associated with that word. For example, given the cue word *horse*, this might evoke a memory of the first time you rode a horse. The method has also been adapted to probe for memories from a given time period such as childhood, or of a particular type of incident, for example a happy memory. Despite its simplicity and relative lack of control, this method has been used widely, and productively.

A prominent feature of probed autobiographical memories is their distribution across the lifespan. When left free to recall memories from any period in their life, all healthy participants, whether young or old, tend to recall few autobiographical memories from the first 5 years of life, termed **infantile amnesia** (see Chapter 12, p. 280). They also tend to produce plenty of memories from the most recent period. Those over the age of 40, however, also show a marked increase of memories from the period between the ages of 15 and 30, the so-called **reminiscence bump** (Rubin, Wetzler, & Nebes, 1986). A cross-cultural study illustrated in Figure 7.4 shows a similar pattern across participants from China, Japan, Bangladesh, England, and the US (Conway, Wang, Hanyu, & Haque, 2005). However, there are cultural differences in the average date for the first memory, which occurs at an average age of 3.8 for US and 5.4 for Chinese participants (Wang, 2006a, 2006b). This might reflect differences in the way that mothers talk to their children, with the US interaction tending to be more elaborate, emotionally oriented, and focused on the past than occurs in Chinese culture (Leichtman, Wang, & Pillemer, 2003). This might also account for a tendency for US recollections of early memories to be longer, more elaborate, and more emotionally toned and self-focused than occurs with Chinese

KEY TERMS

Infantile amnesia: Tendency for people to have few autobiographical memories from below the age of five.
Reminiscence bump: A tendency in participants over 40 to show a high rate of recollecting personal experiences from their late teens and 20s.

respondents, whose recollections tend to be briefer and to have a stronger collective than individual emphasis (Wang, 2001).

There have been a number of attempts to explain the pattern of autobiographical memories across the lifespan. It probably reflects both a recency effect (see Chapter 2, p. 25) and at least two other processes, one accounting for infantile amnesia (the lack of memories from the first 1 or 2 years of life) and the other concerned with the high rate of recalling episodes from the teens and 20s. A number of interpretations of infantile amnesia have been proposed. These include Freudian repression, the late development of the hippocampus, and the undeveloped nature during infancy of a coherent *self*, something that is gradually built up on the basis of memories and experiences. The intriguing topic of infantile amnesia is discussed in Chapter 12.

Most interpretations of the reminiscence bump tend to focus on the fact that this is a

Figure 7.4 Lifespan retrieval curves for participants from five countries. From Conway et al. (2005). Copyright © 2005 SAGE Publications. Reprinted by permission.

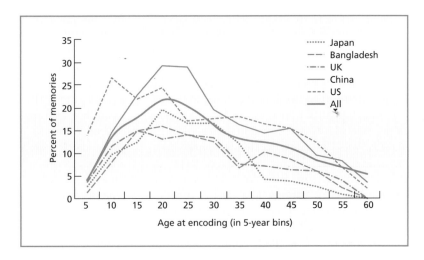

The reminiscence bump describes a period when many important life events, such as falling in love, getting married, and having children, tend to happen.

KEY TERM

Life narrative: A coherent and integrated account of one's life that is claimed to form the basis of autobiographical memory.

period when many important things in our lives tend to happen. Berntsen and Rubin (2004) asked their participants to rate a number of important life events, finding that the average age for first falling in love was 16 years, college memories tended to be a rather later 22 years, marriage at an average age of 27, and children at 28. All fell within the period of the bump, making this an important period within what is sometimes known as the **life narrative**. This represents a coherent account that we create for ourselves as we progress through life—the story of who we are and how we got to this point in our life. Events that influence this are

likely to be important to us, to be more likely to be retrieved, and to be more deeply encoded. Furthermore, such events as beginning college, making new friends, and falling in love are all likely to be relatively emotionally intense, a factor that increases the accessibility of memories (Dolcos, LaBur, & Cabeza, 2005), particularly when these are positive and occur in young adulthood (Berntsen & Rubin, 2002).

Glück and Bluck (2007) further elaborate the life narrative hypothesis. They collected a total of 3541 life events from 659 participants aged between 50 and 90 years. Participants were asked to rate the memories on their emotional *valence*, on a negative to positive scale, their *personal* importance, and the extent to which the remember felt that they had *control* over events. A reminiscence bump was found, but only for positive events over which participants felt that they had a high degree of control, a result that they interpret as consistent with the importance of autobiographical memory in creating a positive life narrative (Figure 7.5).

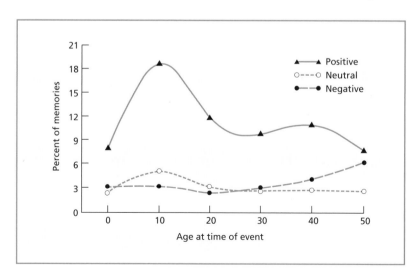

Figure 7.5 Distribution of involuntary memories for participants who were over 40 years old. Only positive memories show the reminiscence bump. From Glück and Bluck (2007). Copyright © The Psychonomic Society. Reproduced with permission.

An intriguing exception to the observation of a reminiscence bump in a person's early 20s occurs when memories are cued by smell. Despite an initial report by Rubin, Groth, and Goldsmith (1984) of equivalence across verbal, visual, and olfactory cues, Chu and Downes (2002) found that memories evoked by smell peaked at an earlier age (6–10 years) than the typical verbally cued reminiscence bump. Willander and Larsson (2006) replicated this using a sample of 93 volunteers ranging in age from 65 to 80 years. They cued with items that could not only be represented as a word, but also as a picture or a smell (e.g. *violet*, *tobacco*, *soap*, *whiskey*). Like Chu and Downes, they found a distinct tendency for smells to evoke memories that are rated by their participants as earlier than visually or verbally cued events. How could we explain this? Are odor-induced memories more emotional? No, Larsen et al. found that the visual cues gave rise to more emotional memories. Perhaps odor cues are less easily rehearsed and hence become less tied to our developing life narrative?

It is, of course, the case that the probe studies described all depend to some extent on the accuracy with which participants can date events. As we saw from Wagenaar's diary study, memory for dating of an incident was the weakest of all the cues. This also presents a practical problem for the many practically oriented survey studies that are retrospective in nature, requiring respondents to remember, for example, when they last went to the doctor. A study by Means, Mingay, Nigam, and Zarrow (1988) asked patients who had made at least four medical visits in the last year to recall and report them, subsequently checking against the doctor's records. Performance was poor, particularly for visits that had clustered (25% correct versus 60% for more isolated occasions). People tend to date events indirectly, either by recollecting incidental features such as the weather, "the trees were bare," or by linking it to some other event that can itself be dated, such as holiday in Paris or the eruption of Mount St Helens (Baddeley, Lewis, &

Nimmo-Smith, 1978; Loftus & Marburger, 1983). These, in turn, are likely to be located within the broader context of a life narrative.

A THEORY OF AUTOBIOGRAPHICAL MEMORY

The systematic study of autobiographical memory began more recently than most other aspects of episodic memory and, as a result, much of what has been described could be regarded as operating at a level of natural history. That is not intended as a criticism. Good natural history leads to soundly based theory that in turn should result in the creation and testing of specific hypotheses. One attempt to develop an overall theory of autobiographical memory is that proposed by Martin Conway (2005).

Conway defines autobiographical memory as a system that retains knowledge concerning the *experienced self*, the "me." It is always addressed by the content of the memory but does not always produce recollective experience, hence you might know that you had a trip to Paris last year, but only recollect the episodic detail later, or indeed not at all. Such recollective experiences occur when autobiographical knowledge, our personal semantic memory, retains access to associated episodic memories, for example when the knowledge that you went to Paris connects with a specific recollection, such as seeing the Eiffel Tower in the rain.

Such autobiographical memories are transitory and are constructed dynamically on the basis of the **autobiographical knowledge base**. The knowledge base itself ranges from

KEY TERM

Autobiographical knowledge base: Facts about ourselves and our past that form the basis for autobiographical memory.

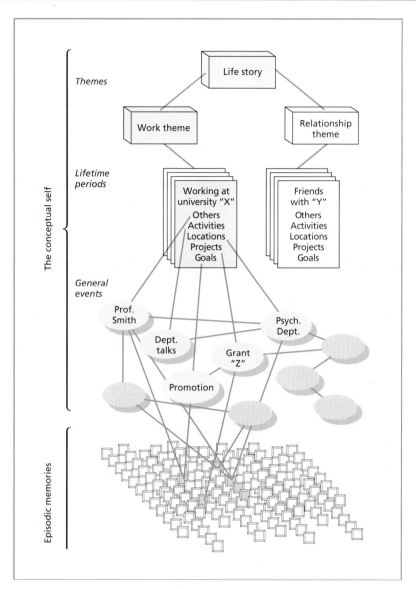

Figure 7.6 The knowledge structures within autobiographical memory, as proposed by Conway (2005). Copyright © Elsevier. Reproduced with permission.

very broad-brush representations of lifetime periods to sensory–perceptual episodes, which are rapidly lost. Finally, the whole system depends on the interaction between the knowledge base and the *working self*. The working self is assumed to play a similar role in autobiographical memory to that played by working memory in cognition more generally (Conway & Pleydell-Pearce, 2000). These broad ideas were developed by Conway (2005) into a more detailed account

of the way in which the self interacts with memory (Figure 7.6).

The **working self** comprises a complex set of active goals and self-images. For example,

---

KEY TERM

Working self: A concept proposed by Conway to account for the way in which autobiographical knowledge is accumulated and used.

I have the active goal of describing Conway's ideas and am doing so by dictating this while walking along a country road with the sun on my face. The working self modulates access to long-term memory, and is itself influenced by LTM. To write this, I need to access my knowledge of Martin Conway's views. The working self comprises both conceptual self-knowledge—my occupation, my family background, and my professional aims—which in turn are socially constructed on the basis of my family background, the influence of peers, school, myths, and other factors that make up the complex representation of myself.

To summarize, the working self is a way of encoding information about *what is*, *what has been*, and *what can be*. To be effective, however, it needs to be both coherent and to correspond reasonably closely with outside reality. When this link is lost, problems occur, which might—in extreme cases—lead to confabulation or delusion. Conway and Tacchi (1996), for example, describe a patient suffering frontal-lobe damage following a road traffic accident who had comforting but totally false memories of the support provided by his family.

The autobiographical knowledge base has a broadly hierarchical structure, with an *overall life story* being linked to a number of broad themes, work and personal relationships for example. These in turn split up into different time periods; for example, *When I was an undergraduate*; *My first job*; *My hopes for the future*. These comprise a number of general "events," which can include individuals and institutions as well as activities, for example, *The psychology department*; *Professor Smith*; *Departmental talks*; *Promotion*. These are still conceptualized at a relatively abstract level but can lead to specific episodic memories; for example, my interview with Professor Smith on applying for a job, or the last departmental research talk I heard. These in turn might have been stored at a more fundamental level containing more detailed sensory–perceptual information; for example, the room where the interview was held, the weather outside, or

Professor Smith's tone of voice in offering me the job. In recollecting an event, it is this essentially arbitrary sensory detail that typically convinces us that we have a genuine memory rather than a confabulation (Johnson, Foley, Suengas, & Raye, 1988). Such detail is often visual in character, which is one reason why vivid visual flashbacks are so convincing and so disturbing.

Following Tulving (1989), Conway refers to the process of recollecting such detail and recognizing it as familiar as being based on **autonoetic consciousness**, the capacity to reflect on our thoughts. This ability to reflect on our memories is of course essential in deciding whether a recollection is an accurate record of our past or confabulation. Accessing such detailed knowledge tends to be relatively slow, typically taking several seconds, whereas access to semantic memory is often performed almost immediately (Haque & Conway, 2001). As we saw earlier, patients with frontal-lobe damage can have difficulty both in accessing autobiographical memories and also, once accessed, in evaluating them, or perhaps more precisely in the failure to evaluate.

Conway's theory provides a useful framework that pulls together what we know about autobiographical memory, which in turn is likely to lead to further more theoretically oriented questions. For example, how might we test the assumption that the autobiographical database is divided in the way proposed by Conway (2005)? A further challenge is offered by the need to explain the increasingly rich evidence accumulating from situations in which autobiographical memory might appear to be atypical, either because it appears to be unusually detailed or because it is impaired or

KEY TERM

Autonoetic consciousness: A term proposed by Tulving for self-awareness, allowing the rememberer to reflect on the contents of episodic memory.

distorted by stress or disease. A range of such instances is described next.

Flashbulb memories

Do you remember where you were when you first hear of the 9/11 attack on the World Trade Center? Unlike humdrum events such as routine visits to the doctor, certain occasions appear to give rise to remarkably clear detailed and persistent memories. Brown and Kulik (1977) asked people to recall how and when they had first heard of the assassination of President Kennedy. They found a degree of vividness and detail that was surprising, leading them to propose a new kind of memory system, which they termed **flashbulb memory**. They argued for a separate process that, given appropriate conditions, leads a special mechanism resulting in a qualitatively different memory record. They termed this process the "now print" mechanism, whereby extreme emotion was assumed to lead to an almost photographic representation of the event and its physical context. In subsequent years, this has proved to be an extremely popular area of study. It now seems that whenever a disaster occurs, a cognitive psychologist somewhere will be devising a questionnaire to establish whether flashbulb memories have occurred, and to try to answer some of the questions raised by Brown and Kulik's claim.

There is no doubt that people do report very vivid recollections of the point at which they remember hearing about major disasters. It is also the case that the probability of report of a flashbulb memory depends on the degree to which the remember was likely to be affected by the event. Black people were more likely to have flashbulb memory concerning the deaths of Martin Luther King and Malcolm X than were white participants (McCloskey, Wible, & Cohen, 1988), and Danes who reported an involvement with the Danish resistance movement were more likely to have a flashbulb experience, and be able to report on the weather, time of day, and day of the week for the invasion and liberation of Denmark than those who were less directly involved (Berntsen & Thomsen, 2005).

But do we need to assume a special mechanism to account for these results? The Brown and Kulik conclusions have been challenged on two fronts. First is the question of whether flashbulb memories are as accurate as they seem, and second whether one needs a special mechanism to explain them. In a study based on the Challenger space disaster, Neisser and Harsch (1992) compared the recall of the experience of learning about the event, testing people after 1 day and retesting after 2½ years, finding a substantial drop in accuracy. For example, after 1 day, 21% reported first hearing about the disaster on TV, whereas after 2½ years this had increased to 45%. Similarly, Schmoick, Buffalo, and Squire (2000) reported considerable forgetting of the experience of hearing the result of the OJ Simpson trial over a period of 32 months.

Flashbulb memories are vividly clear and persistent memories. What were you doing when you heard about the World Trade Center attacks on September 11th 2001? © Sean Adair/ Reuters/Corbis.

KEY TERM

Flashbulb memory: Term applied to the detailed and apparently highly accurate memory of a dramatic experience.

A further problem is the question of what should be the baseline against which one judges whether a memory is unusually accurate or vivid. Rubin and Kozin (1984) report that memories of high-school graduation or an early emotional experience can be just as clear and vivid.

Davidson, Cook, and Glisky (2006) contrasted memory for the 9/11 World Trade Center attack with everyday memories, finding that after a year there was a correlation of .77 between the initial and subsequent recollection for the 9/11 incident, indicating very good retention, compared with a correlation of only .33 for more everyday memories. By contrast, however, Talarico and Rubin (2003) found the same degree of loss of detail of 9/11 for flashbulb and everyday memories, although participants *believed* that their memory of 9/11 was clearer. The crucial difference between these two studies might be that, whereas Talarico and Rubin's participants themselves produced and recorded their everyday events, and hence generated their own retrieval cues, in the Davidson et al. study the experimenters chose the events to be recalled. Cueing an exceptional event in an unambiguous way is much easier for the experimenter than providing an adequate cue for an everyday event in someone else's life.

However, although there is doubt as to whether the degree of recall is quite as impressive as suggested by Brown and Kulik, there is no doubt that people do have vivid autobiographical memories of flashbulb incidents. In terms of interpretation, however, the problem is that there are a number of reasons why this might be. First of all, such incidents are highly distinctive, with little danger of their being confused with other events, which is not the case for most everyday memories. Second, we tend to talk about such events and watch them repeatedly on TV, in effect, rehearsing them. Third, they tend to be important events that potentially change some aspect of our lives and surroundings; and fourth, they tend to give rise to emotions.

Given that all of these are likely to enhance memory in one way or another, do we need an additional quite separate theory? Perhaps not. And if not, is it worthwhile attempting to untangle these various contributions that operate under conditions that are by their very nature hard to control? But no doubt such studies will continue, if only because the phenomenon is dramatic and intriguing. My own inclination, however, is to attempt to understand the possible contributions independently, perhaps subsequently attempting to bring them to bear on the phenomenon of flashbulb memory. One such potential contributor concerns the effect of social and emotional factors on autobiographical memory.

Social and emotional factors

As we saw in Chapter 5, we tend to construct our memories rather than simply calling them up like a book being chosen from a library. Consequently, memory in general, and autobiographical memory in particular, is likely to be influenced by our hopes and needs. This is illustrated very clearly in a classic study by Neisser (1981) of the testimony of John Dean, one of the Watergate conspirators, whose testimony against President Nixon was so detailed that the press labeled him "the man with the tape-recorder memory." In this case, however, there was a real tape recording against which his memory could be compared. Dean's memory proved to be very accurate in terms of broad gist, but there was a persistent tendency for his account to exaggerate his own role and significance.

A tendency to place ourselves center-stage probably plays a part our memories of most of us, perhaps because it helps us maintain our self-esteem. We are not lacking in ways of defending ourselves against challenges to our self-esteem. We readily accept praise but tend to be skeptical of criticism (Wyer & Frey, 1983; Kunda, 1990), often attributing criticism to prejudice on the part of the critic (Crocker & Major, 1989). We are inclined to take credit for success when it occurs but deny responsibility for failure (Zuckerman, 1979). If this stratagem fails, we are rather good at

When testifying to the Watergate Committee in June 1973, John Dean's recall of specific events consistently exaggerated his own role and significance. © Bettmann/Corbis.

selectively forgetting failure and remembering success and praise (Crary, 1966). Although this tendency to preserve our self-esteem can seem pathological, there is evidence to suggest that it serves a useful function. As noted in our discussion of mood-congruent memory, there is a tendency for depressed mood to bias recollection, leading to the differential recall of negative memories from one's past. This process of rumination tends to become self-perpetuating, hence deepening the depression. Perhaps as a defense against this process, there is a tendency for depressed patients to retrieve much less rich and detailed—and hence perhaps less distressing—autobiographical memories.

This tendency for depressed patients to have much less rich and detailed autobiographical memories is one result of their preoccupation with negative thoughts (Healy & Williams, 1999; Dalgleish, Spinks, Yiend, & Kuyken, 2001). This was first reported by people who had recently attempted suicide. When asked to generate an autobiographical memory in response to cue words, depressed patients would respond with a very general response. Hence given the cue *angry*, they might respond "When I've had a row," whereas control participants are more specific, for example "With my supervisor last Monday." This tendency is reversed when depression is successfully treated (Williams, Watts, MacLeod, & Mathews, 1997).

A good experimental example of the tendency to preserve self-esteem is provided by Conway (1990), who asked his students prior to an exam to report their expected grades, the importance of such grades, their hours of study, how well they had prepared, and how valid the test would be. Two weeks after results were announced, he asked each student the same set of questions. For those who got better results than expected, the amount of work reported was the same but the importance of the result was increased. Those who had underperformed reported doing less work, resulting in the claim by the students that the grade was less important and less valid.

Of course, the levels of emotion involved in exam results, although significant, are not massive. It is difficult and ethically dubious to carry out experiments involving extreme emotions, but occasionally the opportunity arises for studying such emotions in a naturalistic context. Wagenaar and Groeneweg (1990) were able to do so in connection with the trial of John Demanjuk who, in the early 1980s, was accused of being a particularly brutal concentration camp guard, known as Ivan the Terrible, during the Second World War. In this connection, they were able to reinterview victims who had first testified some 40 years before. Most witnesses claimed to recognize Demanjuk as Ivan the Terrible, with 74% of his victims and 58% of those who had not suffered directly claiming recognition, a high rate given the amount of elapsed time. Two separate subgroups had seen Demanjuk on television. In both groups, 80% reported recognition, indicating an important potential source of eyewitness error when accused persons are shown in the media.

In general, the unprompted information that the camp survivors produced was accurate when compared to earlier accounts. Twelve of the thirteen who spontaneously mentioned whether Jews were housed in tents or barracks were accurate, whereas only fourteen out of twenty-five who did not volunteer this information were correct. Somewhat surprisingly, even quite dramatic events such as being beaten up or witnessing another prisoner being mur- dered, often appeared to have been forgotten, although there was no clear evidence that such very negative emotional memories were harder to recall than more neutral information.

Recovered memories

Why are dramatic events sometimes so poorly remembered? Freud (1904) proposed that we tend to repress memories associated with negative emotions, so could this be an example of Freudian repression?

A major component of Freudian theory is that the ego defends itself from anxiety by repression, the active holding back of potentially threatening memories. As a general theory of forgetting, it has received little support but has been influential in certain clinical situations. One of the most controversial of these con- cerns child abuse, where a number of therapists assert that, first of all, abuse as a child can lead to a range of subsequent adult psychological and emotional problems that result directly from repression of memory of the abuse. They furthermore suggest that uncovering this hypo- thetical trauma will lead to a cure, a case argued strongly in a book entitled *The courage to heal* (Bass & Davis, 1988). This book suggests that, for example, "if you are unable to remember any specific instance … but still have a feeling that something abusive happened to you, it probably did" (Bass & Davis, 1988, p. 21), and "so far no-one we talked to thought she might have been abused and thereafter discovered that she hadn't been … if you think you are abused and your life shows symptoms, then you were" (p. 22). The "symptoms" referred to include low self- esteem, suicidal or self-destructive thoughts, depression, and sexual dysfunction, symptoms that—sadly—are not rare. Consequently, there have been many cases, in the US in particular, of therapists "uncovering" abuse that might or might not have occurred, with potentially cata- strophic implications for family relationships.

On occasion, such "recovered" memories can be quite bizarre. At a time when rumors of satanic ritualistic abuse were common, Paul Ingram, who held a high position in the local

Sheriff's office was arrested for child abuse in Olympia, Washington. After many hours of questioning he finally admitted he had abused his daughter and that he was also a member of a satanic cult. The prosecution brought in a Professor of Sociology from the University of California Berkeley—Richard Ofshe—to further investigate the situation. To test the truth of the confessions, Ofshe invented an incident in which he said that two of the children of the accused, a son and daugh- ter, had been forced to have sex in front of him. Initially he reported no memory of this incident, but subsequently thought he could recall vague pictures of such a scene. Having then prayed for the scene to be revealed to him, he wrote a detailed, three-page account. Meanwhile, his son was questioned and reported on his dreams that:

Son: "I've had dreams of little people … short people coming and walking on me … walking on my bed."
Psychologist: "What you saw was real."
Son: "Well this is a different dream. Every time a train came by, a whistle would blow, I would wake up but I couldn't move … I couldn't move my arms."
Psychologist: "You were being restrained?"
Son: "Right, and there was someone on top of me."
Psychologist: "These things happened to you. It's real, not an illusion."

Before long, the son remembered "being held down by witches" and joining his father in abuse (Loftus, 1993). The term **false memory syndrome** has been coined to describe this phenomenon.

KEY TERM

False memory syndrome: Term applied to cases, particularly of child abuse, in which the rememberer becomes convinced of an event that did not happen.

False memory syndrome

This idea of *false memory syndrome* led to massive polarization of opinion; again, principally in the US. Some therapists reject the concept of a false memory syndrome as simply a mechanism for defending pedophile parents (Dallam, 2001). However, many psychologists are appalled at the potential for therapists to ruin lives by manipulating suggestible patients, driven by an unsupported theory (see Loftus, 1993, for a more detailed discussion on this point). This has resulted in an explosion of research concerned with false memory: how it can be generated, and avoided.

There is no doubt that people can be induced into believing that events have happened, particularly if they are susceptible, as in the case of children. Bruck, Ceci, Francoeur, and Barr (1995) questioned children at varying periods of time after a medical examination. A crucial question concerned whether the doctor had looked in the child's ear, which had not been the case. When leading questions such as, "He looked in your ear didn't he?" were used a significant number of a positive response occurred, increasing as time elapsed. In another study, adults were encouraged to believe that they had been lost in a shopping mall as a child, or had knocked over a bowl of punch at a wedding (Loftus, 1993; Loftus & Pickrell, 1995). In a review of such studies, Wade and Garry (2005) report that whereas most people are able to resist such suggestions, an average of 37% of participants succumb to such persuasion, and in addition might come up with quite detailed and vivid memories. Given that patients with psychological problems such as depression or an eating disorder are likely to be desperate to find a cure, and that a number of therapists clearly believe that the route to this is through unearthing childhood abuse, there is no doubt that the potential for creating false memories is present.

However, no-one denies that childhood abuse occurs, or that it will not be forgotten to at least some extent. Loftus (1994) accepts that in cases of undoubted abuse, 19% of victims report some forgetting, whereas Brown,

Scheflin, and Whitfield (1999), evaluating some 68 cases, report that almost all showed some forgetting. We will return to the question of stress and amnesia, but for present purposes it is perhaps sufficient to note that memory is potentially malleable, particularly in states of high suggestibility such as it is reasonable to expect in the therapist–patient relationship. Consequently, reports of "recovered memory" should be treated with considerable caution. This is particularly the case as, given that even if such abuse has occurred, it is by no means clear that making the patient aware of it will enhance recovery.

Post-traumatic stress disorder

The term **post-traumatic stress disorder (PTSD)** applies to the symptoms that can follow from situations of extreme stress such as rape, near drowning, or a horrific traffic accident. PTSD often involves "flashbacks," extremely vivid memories of the scene of the initial terror. This might be accompanied by nightmares and a more general state of anxiety (Foa, Rothbaum, Riggs, & Murdock, 1991). Whereas there is often a life-threatening aspect to the experience generating the flashback, this is not essential. As a student, I worked for a time as a hospital porter. We occasionally had to wheel bodies to the morgue, not something I found easy to adapt to, although the body was covered by a device known locally as the "tureen." Then, on one trip, I had to pass through the autopsy room and suddenly caught sight of the body of naked woman ripped open. The image kept coming back at apparently random moments, and I can still "see it" some 50 years later, although happily with considerably less vividness. My own experience was relatively

KEY TERM

Post-traumatic stress disorder (PTSD): Emotional disorder whereby a dramatic and stressful event such as rape results in persistent anxiety, often accompanied by vivid flashback memories of the event.

mild and certainly not directly threatening. How much worse must it be continually to re-experience a rape, or being surrounded by people being burned in a fire, or drowning in a shipping disaster (Cardena & Spiegel, 1993, Foa & Rothbaum, 1998)?

Do flashbacks represent a different kind of memory? Brewin (2001) suggests a distinction between *verbally accessible memory*, which links with the normal memory system, and *situationally accessible memory*, which is highly detailed when it occurs as a flashback but cannot be called to mind intentionally. It is certainly the case that considerable memory for detail can occur in the context of amnesia for other aspects of the situation. Harvey and Bryant (2000) describe a patient who was a passenger involved in a road traffic accident and who has vivid flashback memories of the car they hit, its color, the floral hat worn by one of its occupants, and a soft toy in the rear window, but who could recall nothing after that point. He was a skilled professional driver and felt considerable guilt at not having called out to warn the driver. Eventually, it was demonstrated to him that his perception of the time available was illusory, and that he had absolutely no possibility of influencing the accident. He subsequently recovered from his PTSD, but never went back to driving as a professional.

The precise mechanism underlying memory disturbance in PTSD remains uncertain. One possibility is that it is based on classical conditioning, with the environmental stimuli associated with the horrific moment being powerfully associated with the feeling of terror. As a result, incidental stimuli or thoughts can act as a conditional stimulus that can trigger off the emotional response, bringing back the associated memory. Indeed, some treatments of PTSD use this model, encouraging extinction of the fear response. The response is cued by having the patient imagine the scene under safe conditions controlled by the therapist, leading gradually to the extinction of the fear response (Rothbaum & Davis, 2003). Sometimes, virtual reality techniques are used,

for example having a pilot who has developed PTSD under combat conditions fly a simulated helicopter sortie over "virtual Vietnam."

In many cases, such treatment leads to a reduction of the symptoms. However, this is not always the case. Furthermore, it is of course the case that, given an equivalent level of stress, not everyone develops PTSD, and those who do sometimes recover spontaneously. Figure 7.7 shows the approximate proportion of people responding in each of these ways following exposure to a traumatic event such as a terrorist attack or the death of a spouse (Bonanno, 2005). What makes the difference?

The answer to this question might lie in the response of the autonomic nervous system (ANS) to stress. In a threatening situation, the amygdala signals the ANS to release adrenalin and cortisol, stress hormones that alert the organism for flight or fight. When the danger passes, the brain normally signals the adrenal glands to stop producing stress hormones, gradually bringing the body back to normal. It is suggested that in PTSD patients, this corrective process is reduced, leading to a more prolonged period of stress. There is some

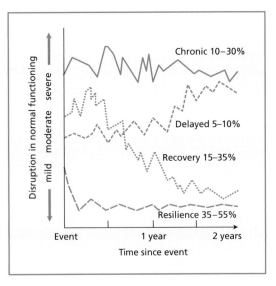

Figure 7.7 Patterns of recovery function following post-traumatic stress disorder (PTSD), with the approximate percentage of patients following each pattern. Data from Bonanno (2005).

evidence that treatment with propranolol, which aids this recovery process, might reduce the likelihood of PTSD (Pitman, Sanders, Zusman, Healy, Cheema, Lasko et al., 2002; Vaiva, Ducrocq, Jezequel, Averland, Levestal, Brunet, & Marmar, 2003). This does not lead to forgetting of the traumatic event but it does reduce the emotional impact of the associated memories.

There is also some evidence that patients with PTSD might have a somewhat smaller hippocampal volume than those without. This raises the question of whether the stress has had a direct causal impact on the size of the hippocampus, or whether a small hippocampus has made the patient more vulnerable. Animal studies have suggested that prolonged stress can disrupt the operation of the hippocampus, possibly even leading to a neuronal death (Sapolsky, 1996; McEwen, 1999). A recent ingenious study by Gilbertson, Shenton, Ciszewski, Kasai, Lasko, Orr, and Pitman (2002) tackled this problem by studying Vietnam veterans who had developed PTSD, and who had a twin who had not experienced Vietnam. Both PTSD veterans and their unexposed twins had smaller hippocampi than veterans who had experienced stress in Vietnam without developing PTSD and their unexposed twins. It appears to be the case, therefore, that a reduced hippocampus makes one more vulnerable to PTSD, presumably because of the problem in recovering from the huge surge in adrenalin associated with extreme stress.

Involuntary memories

Do the flashbacks that occur in PTSD represent a different kind of memory? They are clearly atypical in their negativity and emotional intensity, but do they imply a different mechanism from normal recall? A recent study by Berntsen and Rubin (2008) suggests that this might not be the case.

This study begins with an analysis of PTSD in a sample of 118 Danes who were tourists in Thailand or Sri Lanka at the time of the Tsunami catastrophe in December 2004. About half had experienced or witnessed danger to life and had experienced intense fear, helplessness, or horror. Some 40% of respondents reported recurrent memories, with the likelihood of this increasing for those who were close to the threatening wave. As expected, the frequency of the recurrent memories tended to coincide with the point of maximum emotional impact, with those directly threatened by the wave having recurrent memories of escaping, whereas those who had heard about the tragedy rather than directly witnessing it, tending to have recurrent memories of searching for loved ones or of the possible worst-case scenario. Broadly speaking, the pattern of recurrent memories was characteristic of those found in PTSD cases more generally.

A standard clinical interpretation of such involuntary memories is in terms of what Neisser (1967) refers to as the **reappearance hypothesis**, which implies that "the same memory image, or other cognitive unit, can disappear and reappear over and over again." An example is that of a man who kept seeing headlights coming towards him because he had seen the same thing shortly before a car crash in which he was involved (Ehlers, Hackmann, & Michael, 2004). Note that this type of memory, if it occurs, differs greatly from the reconstructive view of memory that is associated with normal remembering.

Berntsen and Rubin (2008) noted that the evidence for the unchanging nature of such memories is based only on clinical report, and proposed to investigate the extent to which intrusive memories in PTSD follow the same course as intrusive memories more generally. They proposed that such memories will also occur in the general population, and will follow

> ### KEY TERM
>
> **Reappearance hypothesis:** The view that under certain circumstances, such as flashbulb memory and PTSD, memories can be created that later reappear in exactly the same form.

the same pattern as is found in autobiographical memory more generally. More specifically, they proposed that such memories are more accessible for a number of reasons, including that they are: (1) more recent (Rubin & Wenzel, 1996); (2) more arousing (McGaugh, 2003); (3) more likely to occur for positive events (Walker, Skowronski, & Thompson, 2003); and (4) likely to show the reminiscence bump, at least in older participants.

Berntsen and Rubin (2008) began with a telephone survey of 1504 Danes aged between 18 and 96, asking each about the frequency of recurrent memories and recurrent dreams. As Figure 7.8 shows, such memories are frequent, and decline somewhat with age. Recurrent dreams are less frequent and show a modest correlation with recurrent memories.

As panel (b) in Figure 7.8 shows, as we get older, we tend to have more positive recurrent memories, which are also more intense. Panel (c) of Figure 7.8 shows that recent recurrent memories are more likely, whereas panel (d), which is based on respondents over the age of 40, indicates that such positive recurrent memories are likely to come from late childhood and adolescence, namely that they show a characteristic reminiscence bump.

A final study was concerned with the extent to which recurrent memories were identical across repetitions. Berntsen and Rubin (2008) carried out a diary study in which nine participants nominated their most traumatic experience when filling in a PTSD questionnaire, after which they kept an involuntary memory diary for the next few weeks.

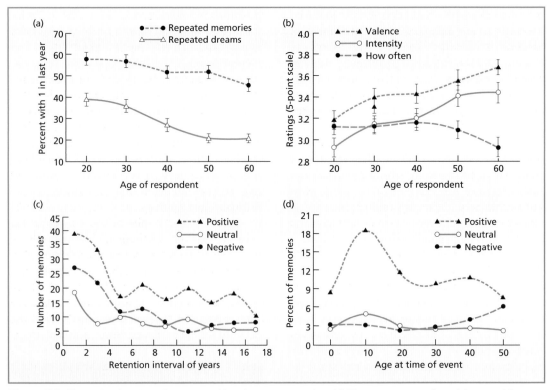

Figure 7.8 Retention functions for repeated involuntary memories. (a) The percentage of participants with a repeated memory or dream in the last year as a function of the age of the participant. (b) The mean ratings of valence, intensity, and frequency as a function of the age of the participant. (c) The retention function for positive, neutral, and negative repeated involuntary memories for all participants. (d) The distribution of positive, neutral, and negative repeated involuntary memories from age 0 to 50 for those participants who were 40 years old or older. From Berntsen and Rubin (2008). Copyright © The Psychonomic Society. Reproduced with permission.

Each participant recorded from two to seven recurrent memories of the traumatic incident. Eight of the nine cases showed no evidence of exact repetition of either time or of the precise features of the incident. Berntsen and Rubin conclude that the flashbacks that are observed in PTSD do not comprise a special type of memory but have the same characteristics as recurrent memories in the normal course of life, and that both reflect the same basic principles as are found across all types of autobiographical memory.

PSYCHOGENIC AMNESIA

Fugue

The term "fugue" refers to a sudden loss of autobiographical memory, usually accompanied by wandering. Stories based on this condition seem to attract makers of films and writers of novels, presumably because of its dramatic nature. It typically lasts a few hours or days and on recovery leaves the patient amnesic for the fugue period (Kihlstrom & Schacter, 2000). Schacter, Wang, Tulving, and Freedman (1982), for example, described the case of a young man who, when attending his grandfather's funeral became amnesic for all but recent events, together with a few islands of happy memories from the past. His memory subsequently recovered while watching a funeral on TV.

The main characteristics of fugue states are that: (1) they are typically preceded by stress, for example an accusation of embezzlement (Kopelman, Green, Guinan, Lewis, & Stanhope, 1994), and are more common in wartime (Sargant & Slater, 1941); (2) depressed mood is common; (3) there is often a history of transient organically based amnesia; and (4) it is often difficult to discount the possibility of ulterior motive. For example, Kopelman (1987) describes a somewhat extreme case who had experienced some ten to twelve prior fugue episodes, was depressed, had attempted suicide, and who claimed amnesia for a road

traffic accident that occurred while he was driving disqualified, uninsured, and drunk. Potential ulterior motives are usually rather more subtle than this but do need to be taken into account.

As might be expected, the symptoms of psychogenic amnesia are somewhat varied. General semantic knowledge and intelligence are normally well preserved and there might be islands of autobiographical memory. New learning, for example of word lists, is typically severely impaired. Attempts to cue memory directly tend to be unsuccessful. The use of amytal or hypnosis to access forgotten memories is typically not effective, but if the patient is intentionally simulating amnesia then the use of drugs or hypnosis could allow the patient to "recover" without loss of face (Kopelman, 2002b).

Psychogenic focal retrograde amnesia

As discussed in Chapter 13, brain damage that results in anterograde amnesia is often accompanied by retrograde amnesia; that is, loss of access to memories that were acquired before the trauma. However, there are cases of densely amnesic patients, such as HM and KJ, who show good memory for their life before the onset of amnesia. The opposite pattern, in which very substantial retrograde amnesia is reported in the absence of anterograde amnesia, is rare, although a few cases have been reported. Such patients cannot explicitly remember their past but can apparently learn about their earlier life when told by others, and then remember what they have been taught about themselves. Such cases are scientifically very interesting, although there are almost always doubts as to whether such cases might or might not be complicated by social and emotional factors.

A rather dramatic case is reported by Della Sala, Freschi, and Lucchelli (1996), concerning a 33-year-old man who fell down the stairs at his parents-in-law's house. He showed an initial loss of personal identity, together with a prolonged loss of autobiographical memory, claiming he could not recognize his wife, friends, or relatives, although he did succeed in remembering his computer codes. Subsequently, he showed a decreasing interest in his wife and joined an "unusual role-playing group" that excluded his wife. He began collecting sado-masochistic porn and entered into a homosexual relationship that led to divorce. Della Sala et al. comment on a possibility of a "functional" amnesia. Most such cases are much less extreme, the pattern of symptoms complex and their interpretation difficult. It is important not to assume a given pattern of symptoms is "psychogenic," simply because it does not fit our preconceptions.

Situation-specific amnesia

A dramatic example of the type of amnesia that could readily be dismissed as malingering occurs in cases of violent crime and murder, with approximately 30% of perpetrators claiming to be amnesic for the incident (Kopelman, 2002b; Pyszora, Barker, & Kopelman, 2003). Amnesia is most common in association with extreme emotion, for example in crimes of passion, with the probability of amnesia increasing with the violence of the offence (Yuille & Cutshall, 1986). It is also more likely when alcohol is a factor, possibly because of "blackout" effects, which might reflect a failure of memory consolidation, or retrieval-based or state dependency. What you encode when drunk is best recalled when drunk (Goodwin, Powell, Bremer, Hoine, & Stern, 1969). Yuille and Cutshall (1986) report that some 33% of cases recover the relevant memory during a 3-year follow-up, with a further 26% showing partial recovery, suggesting that in these cases at least, the problem is one of retrieval rather than consolidation.

Are such instances genuine cases of amnesia, or simply evidence of malingering? Schacter (1986) inclines to the latter view that psychogenic amnesia often reflects an intentional strategy. A much earlier study by Hopwood and Snell (1933), who studied a 100 such cases in Broadmoor, the high-security psychiatric prison in the UK, concluded that some 78% were genuine, 14% faked, and 8% doubtful. But how would one reach this conclusion with any degree of certainty? Clearly, only with great difficulty.

There are, however, a number of features that suggest that violence-related amnesia is a genuine phenomenon rather than a form of malingering. First of all, it might occur with prisoners who have spontaneously reported their crime to the police and make no attempt to evade capture. Second, amnesia is not accepted as a mitigating factor in UK law, or in many other countries, so there would be no practical advantage. Third, a similar pattern occurs in the case of victims or eyewitnesses of violent crime who have no reason to dissimulate (Kuehn, 1974). Finally, there does seem to be a consistency across accounts with comments like "so horrifying … that I just can't remember anything" or "it seems to be forming a picture and then … my head hurts and it gets all jumbled up again" (O'Connell, 1960).

Multiple person disorder

The idea that one person could contain two or more very different personalities was popularized by Robert Louis Stevenson's book *Dr Jekyll and Mr Hyde*. This disorder is described by Kihlstrom and Schacter (2000) as "the crown jewel … of the functional amnesias," generating over 2000 papers, two-thirds of them in the decade before their review. And yet Kopelman (2002b), a London neuropsychologist and psychiatrist, describes the disorder as rare. The reason is that, like crown jewels in general, it is not distributed evenly around the world. Indeed, Merskey (1992) suggests that it simply reflects a fashion for certain symptoms, encouraged in patients by "reinforcing behavior" from psychologists, psychiatrists, and the outside world.

Such "fashions" in psychiatric symptoms do seem to occur. A good example is of that classic hysterical symptom *glove anesthesia*,

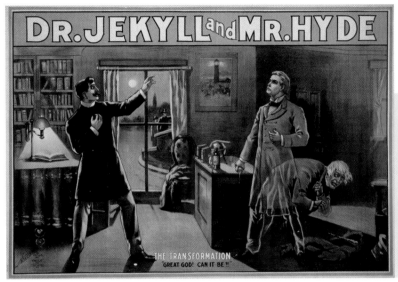

The concept that one person could contain two or more very different personalities was popularized by Robert Louis Stevenson's book *Dr Jekyll and Mr Hyde*. There have been dozens of major stage and film adaptations, and countless references in popular culture. Image courtesy of the Library of Congress.

when the patient reports a pattern of lack of feeling in the hand that involves the whole of the hand up to the wrist, something that is anatomically very unlikely, given the pattern of innervation of the hand. This symptom was relatively widespread in the early years of the twentieth century, but seems to be very rare now. Another example is catatonia, a rigid immoveable posture that once was common in schizophrenic patients but is now rarely if ever seen.

The different multiple personalities displayed by a patient might or might not be mutually aware. A study by Nissen, Ross, Willingham, MacKenzie, and Schacter (1988), of a woman with 22 personalities found 8 of them to be mutually amnesic. In those personalities that are mutually amnesic it is possible to demonstrate common implicit memory, for example by presenting words to one personality and requiring stem completion from another (Eich, Macauley, Loewenstein & Dihle, 1997), whereas explicit recall across personalities might be absent.

It is not clear what produces multiple person disorder and why it differs from one culture to another. One possibility suggested by Kopelman (2002b) is that patients might be trying out a new mode of life. But if so, you might have expected Nissen et al's (1988) patient to have found something suitable before needing 22 attempts.

ORGANICALLY BASED DEFICITS IN AUTOBIOGRAPHICAL MEMORY

Whereas psychogenic amnesia can often have an organic component, other sources of loss of autobiographical memory are very clearly the result of brain damage of a particular kind (see Chapter 11). Organically based amnesia differs from psychogenic amnesia in that a sense of personal identity is rarely lost, whereas problems in orientation in time and place are very common. This can result in persistent questioning, with the same questions asked again and again, a symptom that can be extremely tedious for the carer. Although autobiographical memory is a relatively recent area of investigation, neuroimaging studies are already revealing its anatomical basis.

AUTOBIOGRAPHICAL MEMORY AND THE BRAIN

Neuropsychological studies

The semantic episodic distinction

Organically based retrograde amnesia typically leads to a loss of both episodic memories of specific incidents, and of more semantic autobiographical knowledge such as the names of school teachers. However, although retrograde amnesia typically affects both aspects of autobiographical memory, this is not always the case. De Renzi et al. (1987) describe an Italian woman who could remember virtually no public events—neither the war, which she had lived through, nor the assassination of the Italian Prime Minister. Nor could she recognize photographs of famous people from that period, although she could remember incidents of her personal life extremely well. The only public event that she seemed to remember was the wedding in England of Prince Charles to Lady Diana Spencer, who she described as a scheming girl just like the one that married her own son. Other studies have reported the opposite pattern. Dalla Barba, Cipolotti, and Denes (1990) describe a patient with Korsakoff syndrome and a severe episodic memory deficit who was good at recalling famous people and events but could not remember aspects of personal autobiography.

Confabulation

Confabulation occurs when the autobiographical information is false but not intentionally misleading. A distinction can be made between spontaneous and provoked confabulation. Provoked confabulation can occur as a result of an amnesic patient's attempt to fill in a gap in knowledge, so as to avoid embarrassment. In one sense this is not too different from normal behavior, when we might produce a reasonably accurate account but include detail beyond what we can really remember, perhaps to make a better story. Spontaneous confabulation tends to be much more florid, is less common, and tends to be linked to frontal lobe damage.

Consider, for example, patient RR, who had extensive bilateral damage to his frontal lobes following a driving accident (Baddeley & Wilson, 1988). When asked about the accident, he happily provided a detailed account that involved his getting out of his car and carrying out a polite but extremely repetitive conversation with the driver of the lorry that had hit him, with each apologizing to the other multiple times. He had in fact been unconscious for a lengthy period following the accident and could almost certainly not remember it. He was no longer capable of driving and gave a totally implausible account of how he had subsequently driven himself to the rehabilitation center, giving a lift to a fellow patient he rather ungallantly described as "a fat piece." Confabulation can also result in action. On one occasion, RR was found heading along the road outside the center pushing a fellow patient in a wheelchair to show his friend a sewage farm he was working on as an engineer. He had in fact worked on such a project, but it was many years ago and a good distance away.

Confabulation is typically found in patients with a dysexecutive syndrome resulting from damage to the frontal lobe, which probably interferes with autobiographical memory in two ways. First, such patients have difficulty in setting up appropriate retrieval cues. The previously described patient RR, for example, was very poor at generating items from semantic categories. Given the category *animals*, for example, he produced *dog ... animals ... there must be thousands of them! ... Did I say dog?* However, given appropriate retrieval cues, *an Australian animal that hops*, for example, he readily came up with the right answer.

A second problem is that of evaluating the outcome of a memory search, with the result that information that would clearly be implausible to most normal or indeed most brain-damaged people is accepted and elaborated by dysexecutive patients. RR responded in an autobiographical memory study to the cue word *letter*. He described sending a letter to an aunt recounting the death of his brother Martin. When he was reminded that Martin visited him regularly, he accepted this, explaining that his mother had had a later son, also called Martin (Baddeley & Wilson, 1986).

Delusions

Delusions are patently false beliefs about the patient and the world. They can be highly elaborated and very persistent. In this respect, they differ from confabulation, which tends to be temporary in nature and often lacks coherence. Whereas confabulations tend to be associated with front-lobe damage, delusions tend to occur more frequently in schizophrenia, in which the organic underpinning is much less clear-cut, with no evidence that deluded patients are any less executively competent than patients without such delusions (Baddeley, Thornton, Chua, & McKenna, 1996).

Delusions can appear to be fantastic in nature. For example, one patient believed that angels were removing his internal organs. When asked why he believed this rather than that he was merely feeling ill, he referred to what the angels said, implicating auditory hallucinations, which often occur in patients with schizophrenia (Baddeley et al., 1996). Delusions can be highly elaborated, involving beings from other planets, and are often paranoid in nature, with patients believing that their mind is being controlled from outside, by the government or foreign powers (Frith, 1992). Other delusions are more positive in tone, patients regarding themselves as secretly related to the royal family, or in some cases as being a reincarnation of Jesus Christ. One such patient complained to me that someone else on his ward was claiming to be Jesus and, when asked how he interpreted this, happily replied that the other chap was obviously wrong.

Delusions appear to be ways of explaining extraordinary experiences; for example, voices telling you to do things; feelings of threat or of grandeur; or that your actions are controlled by others. Such feelings are inconsistent with one's normal experience and lead some patients to create a modified version of the world in which their bizarre experiences do make sense. Delusions of persecution can be frightening, but delusions can, on occasion, also be somewhat comforting, as in the case of a young man who simultaneously believed himself to be a Russian chess grandmaster and a famous rock guitarist. When asked how this was possible, given that he did not speak Russian or play the guitar, he replied that neither of these skills was possible in his present state, but when in his Russian state he could speak Russian fluently, and play the guitar when in musician mode (Baddeley et al., 1996).

The anatomical basis of autobiographical memory

Greenberg and Rubin (2003) note that patients with damage to the areas involved in visualization tend to have poor autobiographical memory, suggesting—as others have—that visual imagery might play an important role. Conway, Pleydell-Pearce, Whitecross, and Sharpe (2003) used EEG to study the cortical activation associated with the task of reading a cue word, evoking a related autobiographical memory, holding it, and then reporting the memory. They found that the early stages involved left prefrontal cortex, presumably reflecting the executive processes involved in evoking the memory, followed by activation that spread back to the occipital and temporal lobes, consistent with an important role for visual imagery, a pattern that was broadly similar to that subsequently found by Addis, Moscovitch, Crawley, and McAndrews (2004).

Although not as extensively investigated as episodic memory more generally, an increasing number of neuroimaging studies are focusing on autobiographical memory. A recent overview combines data from 24 different studies (Svoboda, McKinnon, & Levine, 2006) and concludes that the evidence supports a distinction between episodic and semantic aspects of autobiographical memory, together with a

---

KEY TERM

Delusions: False beliefs, often found in schizophrenic patients, that seem well founded to the patient but implausible to a neutral observer.

tendency for the presence of emotion to shift the balance of activation across the right and left hemispheres.

In one study, Cabeza, Prince, Daselaar, Greenberg, Budde, Dolcos, et al. (2004) had their student participants take photographs at specified locations on the Duke University campus. These were then mixed in with photographs taken by other undergraduates, and presented in an event-related fMRI study. Both types of photograph activated a common episodic memory network that involved the medial temporal and prefrontal regions. In addition, the self-generated photographs activated areas of the medial prefrontal cortex that were known to be associated with self-referential processing, as well as areas associated with recollection (hippocampus) and visuo-spatial memory (visual and parahippocampal regions).

It might be argued that the autobiographical significance of your own versus someone else's photograph of a familiar scene could be somewhat minimal. Another study (Greenberg, Rice, Cooper, Cabeza, Rubin, & LaBar (2005) used a more conventional technique in which participants first generated cue words for 50 of their own autobiographical memories, recording their subjective responses to each. An fMRI study then presented each of the cue words, requiring the participants to press a button when they retrieved the relevant memory. This condition was contrasted with a semantic retrieval task in which participants were asked to give an appropriate response to a series of category names (e.g. the cue *animal* might evoke *elephant*). Autobiographical retrieval led to more activation of the amygdala, which is related to emotion; the hippocampus, related to episodic memory; and the right inferior frontal gyrus, linked to self-related processing. The semantic retrieval condition led to more prolonged activation of the left frontal region (Figure 7.9).

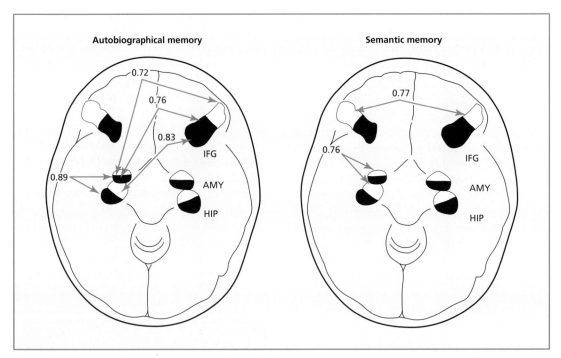

Figure 7.9 Patterns of activation during autobiographical memory and semantic memory retrieval. The numbers represent correlation between the activity in areas linked by the arrows. White and black represent separate areas of each structure. Based on Greenberg et al. (2005). AMY, amygdala; HIP, hippocampus; IFG, inferior frontal gyros.

SUMMARY

Autobiographical memory helps us create a coherent representation of ourselves and our lives. It can also be used socially as in reminiscing with old friends, and can in addition operate in problem-solving mode when we learn from specific earlier experiences.

Autobiographical memory is difficult to study because we often have no record from the time that the memories are initially encoded, and hence cannot check their accuracy. One method of avoiding this problem is through diaries, which are qualitatively rich but tend to be selective both in terms of the events selected and in terms of those prepared to keep a diary. An alternative is the probe method, whereby autobiographical memories are evoked either by presenting a cue word or by asking for memories from a specified life period.

For people over the age of 40, the temporal distribution of recalled events typically shows a peak extending from late teens to early 30s, the reminiscence bump. This is generally attributed to the fact that this is an important period in building up a life narrative, a coherent story about who we are and where we come from.

Theories of autobiographical memory are beginning to develop but much of the field is still concerned with individual phenomena such as flashbulb memories, the apparently very precise and rich memories that we appear to retain regarding striking events such as hearing of the death of President John F Kennedy. Like flashbulb memory, post-traumatic stress disorder (PTSD), appears to offer another case in which a highly emotional event appears to lead to a very specific and detailed memory. There is controversy as to whether either flashbulb memories or flashbacks in PTSD represent a special type of memory or are explicable using the same processes as are assumed in normal autobiographical memory.

Another area of considerable controversy concerns the concept of false memory syndrome. This has resulted from cases in which therapists claim to have uncovered forgotten memories of child abuse in their patients. Sometimes these are clearly false and can be quite bizarre. This has encouraged an extensive research effort to study ways in which false memories can be implanted, either intentionally or otherwise.

Psychogenic amnesia occurs when strong negative emotion disrupts retrieval from autobiographical memory. It is contrasted with deficits in autobiographical memory resulting from organic causes, which might interact with social and emotional factors to produce confabulations and delusions.

We conclude with a brief review of the way in which neuroimaging techniques are contributing to an understanding of the neurological and neuroanatomical basis of autobiographical memory.

FURTHER READING

• Conway, M. A., Pleydell-Pearce, C. W., Whitecross, S., & Sharpe, H. (2002). Brain imaging autobiographical memory. *The Psychology of Learning and Motivation, 41,* 229–263. A review of some of the contributions made by neuroimaging to the study of autobiographical memory.

- **Gardiner, M.** (2006). The memory wars, parts two and three. *Skeptical Enquirer*, *30*, 246–250. Discusses the controversies surrounding reports of memories of abuse recovered during therapy, and evaluates the evidence and the resulting controversies.

- **Neisser, U.** (1981). John Dean's memory: A case study. *Cognition*, *9*, 1–22. A classic study of autobiographical memory in which it proved possible to compare the recollection of a series of important events by the participants in the Watergate affair, in which Dean's conversations with President Nixon were recorded, and hence could subsequently be checked.

- **Rubin, D. C.** (1996). *Remembering our past: Studies in autobiographical memory*. Cambridge: Cambridge University Press. A collection of chapters describing various approaches to autobiographical memory. Edited by David Rubin, who has been one of the most active and innovative contributors to the study of autobiographical memory.

- **Williams, H. L., Conway, M. A., & Cohen, G.** (2008). Autobiographical memory. In G. Cohen and M. Conway (Eds). *Memory in the real world* (3rd edn) (pp. 21–90). Hove, UK: Psychology Press. An extensive review of research on autobiographical memory, which incorporates Conway's theoretical approach.

CHAPTER 8

RETRIEVAL

Michael C. Anderson

Imagine that it is 10.00 p.m. and you are packing for an international flight early the next morning. You need your passport, but it's nowhere to be found. Deep concern sets in.

It's midnight. Your flight is at 6.00 a.m. You drive to work, dig through drawers, and look on every shelf. *No passport.* Returning to your car, you peer under the floor-mats, rummage through the trunk, and grasp hopefully under the seats, as light rain soaks your back. You are now fully panicked.

Returning home, you march through every room, staring with the full laser beam of consciousness at every inch. You leaf through books, imagining that the passport will drop out gracefully on the floor. At 4.00 a.m., you begin dredging for memories. "When is the last time you had it? I remember putting it in this room that I'm sitting in, but I've already looked there." After concentrating intensely for 20 minutes, memory delivers nothing but fleeting images, and you're left with nothing but a powerful feeling that it's around somewhere. You decide to have one last look.

Then, in a box that you have already inspected numerous times, you lift a paper at the bottom. There it is! It all floods back— the when, how, and why. "Oh yeah... that's right, I put the passport in this box when I was cleaning my home office in preparation for guests arriving 2 months ago!" It's 5.00 a.m. You pack madly, race to the airport, and

merciful flight attendants allow you on the plane, sleepless, and shoeless because you ran from airport security screening in your two differently colored socks.

This event actually occurred to me and was, to say the least, memorable. The story illustrates a crucial point about memory. Quite often, memories are stored perfectly well but, for whatever reason, we have difficulty retrieving them. Clearly the event of putting the passport in the box was alive and well in my memory; yet, even after 20 minutes of deliberately searching my memory, the trace remained vexingly inaccessible. But the instant I saw the passport, the memory returned, in full vividness. Why couldn't I retrieve this information?

Clearly, having good memory is not just about encoding material well. One also has to be able to retrieve information. As any student knows, it is possible to study extensively, and then, on the exam, suddenly be unable to recollect the study material. In this chapter, we consider the processes of retrieval, and what factors influence retrieval success.

"ON THE TIP OF THE TONGUE"

Subjectively, perhaps the most convincing evidence that our memory contains information that we cannot access comes from the experience of being asked a question for which

The tip-of-the-tongue state is an extreme form of pause, where the word takes a noticeable time to come out—although the speaker has a distinct feeling that they know exactly what they want to say. © image100/Corbis.

we are sure we know the answer, although we cannot produce it at that precise moment; we feel we have it "on the tip of the tongue."

Some years ago two Harvard psychologists, Roger Brown and David McNeil (1966), decided to see whether this feeling was based on genuine evidence or was simply an illusion. They set up a *tip-of-the-tongue* situation by

reading out a series of definitions of relatively obscure words to their participants and asking them to name the object being defined. For example, "A musical instrument comprising a frame holding a series of tubes struck by hammers." Participants were instructed to indicate if they were in the tip-of-the-tongue state (convinced that they knew the word although they were unable to produce it). When this occurred, they were asked to guess at the number of syllables in the word and to provide any other information, such as the initial letter. They were consistently much better at providing such information than one would have expected by chance. Other studies have shown that giving the participant the initial letter, in this case "x," frequently tends to prompt the correct name, "xylophone."

The task of trying to remember the names of capital cities of countries is a good way of evoking this effect. Read rapidly through the list of countries in Box 8.1, covering up the initial letters of their capital cities. Eliminate those countries that you can immediately produce the answer for and also those for which you feel you do *not* know the answer.

Box 8.1 Tip-of-the-tongue experience

Try recalling the capital cities of each of the countries listed, first by covering up the letters to the right. When you feel you can't recall any more of them, then use the provided letter cues. Did you encounter a tip-of-the-tongue experience? Check your answers at the end of the chapter (Box 8.2).

	Country	First letter of capital city		Country	First letter of capital city
1	Norway	O	11	South Korea	S
2	Turkey	A	12	Syria	D
3	Kenya	N	13	Denmark	C
4	Uruguay	M	14	Sudan	K
5	Finland	H	15	Nicaragua	M
6	Australia	C	16	Ecuador	Q
7	Saudi Arabia	R	17	Colombia	B
8	Romania	B	18	Afghanistan	K
9	Portugal	L	19	Thailand	B
10	Bulgaria	S	20	Venezuela	C

Concentrate on the rest. Any luck? If not, see if the letter cues jog your memory. Check your answers at the end of this chapter.

In general, the feeling that you know something is often a good indication that you do—given the right prompting. In a capital city recall test similar to that just described, recall was over 50% when letters were given for the cities people thought they knew, but only 16% for those they thought they didn't. Similarly, my powerful feeling that my passport was located in my home office was, in fact, correct.

We have established, then, that our memory store contains more information than we can access at any given moment. But what determines the accessibility of this information? To address this question, we need a basic idea of how the retrieval process works.

THE RETRIEVAL PROCESS: GENERAL PRINCIPLES

To describe how retrieval works, it is helpful to introduce some terminology. During retrieval, we are usually seeking a particular memory—a particular fact, idea, or experience, often called the *target memory* or the *target trace*. Suppose, for example, I asked you to recall what you had for dinner last night. To answer, you would try to recollect the event. In this case, your memory for having dinner last night would be the target.

When we search for a target in memory, we usually have some idea of what we are looking for. In the dinner example, you knew you were searching for a dinner event that happened yesterday evening. This specification can be likened to the words one might type into the search window of an internet search engine. Without such a specification, there is nothing for your memory to work with, and so it would return nothing, just as typing nothing into a search engine will not yield websites. These snippets of information that allow you to access a memory are known as *retrieval cues*, or simply *cues*. In general, **retrieval** is a progression from one or more cues to a target memory, with the aim of making that target available to influence ongoing cognition.

But how do cues help us to retrieve target memories? Traces in memory are believed to be linked up to one another by connections that are usually called *associations* or *links*. Suppose, for example, I ask you to say the first thing that comes to mind to each of the following words: *dog*, *hot*, *up*, or *cow*. Chances are, you probably thought *cat* or *bone* for *dog*, *cold* for *hot*, *down* for *up*, and *milk* for *cow*. These ideas, like dog and cat, are strongly linked in most people's memories—that is, they are associated. Associations are structural linkages between traces that vary in strength. For example, if I asked you to name a *fruit*, you might quickly say *banana*, but a guava is also a fruit. The fact that *guava* does not come to mind so readily reflects its weaker association to *fruit*. Retrieval, then, is a progression from one or more cues to a target memory, via associative connections.

Memories can be retrieved from a variety of cues. If instead of asking you, "What did you have for dinner last night?" I had asked, "When was the last time you had peas?" you might say, "Oh, I had peas last night for dinner." You would have accessed the same memory but by means of different cues than in the former example. Many things can serve as cues; the smell of peas might remind you of last night; or the song on the radio might be the same one you played while dining on peas. Our memories are remarkably flexible; any aspect of the content of a memory can serve as a reminder that could access the experience, a property known as *content addressable* memory. We essentially have a mental "search engine," but we can search with just about any type of information.

KEY TERM

Retrieval: The process of recovering a target memory based on one or more cues, subsequently bringing that target into awareness.

The preceding ideas help us to talk about the structures involved in memory, but they do not say much about the process. How do we progress from cues to target memories, via associations? Although there are many theories, one useful idea is that retrieval occurs by a process called spreading activation. According to this idea, each memory has an internal state of its own, reflecting how "excited" or "active" it is, a state referred to as the memory's **activation level**. Activation has several important properties. The activation level varies, and determines how accessible a trace is in memory, with higher levels of activation reflecting greater accessibility. A trace's activation level increases when something related to it is perceived in the world (e.g. seeing a plate of peas will activate the idea *peas* and probably your dinner of peas), or when attention is focused directly on the trace (when I ask you to think of *peas*). This activation persists for some time, even after attention has been removed.

How does the concept of activation help us to think about retrieval? One idea is that memories automatically spread activation to other memories to which they are associated. This *spreading activation* is like "energy" flowing through connections linking traces. The amount of activation spread from the cue to an associate is larger the stronger the association, and activation is spread in parallel to all associates. If the target accumulates enough activation from the cue, it will be retrieved, even though other associates might be activated as well. So, if you saw the name *Beckham*, attention to this idea would increase its activation, which in turn would activate associates, like *football*. As a result, *football* would be retrieved. The idea that traces have activation that spreads is central to many theories of memory, and provides a useful way of thinking about how cues access memories. To refine our definition of retrieval further then, retrieval is a progression from one or more cues to a target memory, via associative connections linking them together, through a process of spreading activation.

FACTORS DETERMINING RETRIEVAL SUCCESS

Knowing that retrieval is the progression from cues to a target memory did not help when I needed to find my passport. Why does retrieval work sometimes, but not others? We consider several factors here, each demonstrating something important about the nature of retrieval (Figure 8.1).

Attention to cues

Retrieval is less effective if cues are present, but not attended, or not attended enough. Suppose, for example, that while searching for my passport I didn't see the box that contained it. If so, there is no way that the box could have cued memory. In reality, I searched the box many times, and so was clearly looking at it. Even so, I might not have fully attended to the box, being so distracted by my worries. Many theories assume that the activation given to a concept increases with attention. If so, diminishing attention might make a cue less useful and lead retrieval to fail.

One way of removing attention from cues is by giving people a secondary task to perform during retrieval. When distracted in this way, people's retrieval usually grows worse, especially if the secondary task requires them to pay attention to related materials. This point is made well in several studies by Myra Fernandes and Morris Moscovitch (2000, 2003), who asked people to recall, out loud, lists of words that had been presented to them auditorally (Figure 8.2). At the same time, participants made judgments about entirely different items appearing on a computer screen. Compared to a control condition in which people did not do

---

KEY TERM

Activation level: The variable internal state of a memory trace that contributes to its accessibility at a given point.

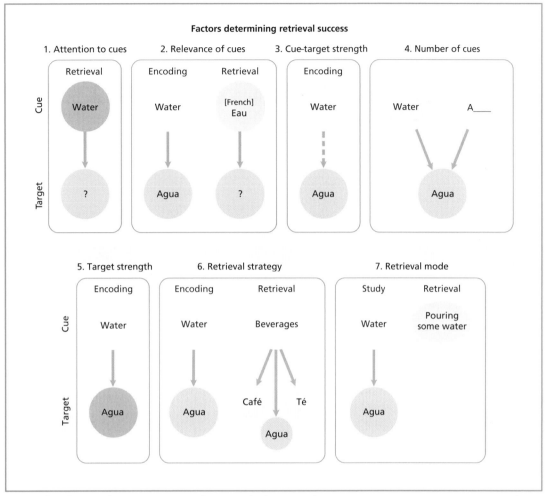

Figure 8.1 Factors determining retrieval success. In this example, assume you are attempting to retrieve the Spanish word for *water*. (1) Failing to take full advantage of the cue (*water*), due to divided attention, renders it a less effective reminder of the target (*agua*). (2) Cues explicitly studied with the target are better than cues that one has not studied with it (e.g. the French word for water, *eau*). (3) If the cue was never strongly associated with the target during encoding, the cue would be less helpful during retrieval. (4) Access to additional relevant cues, such as a letter-stem, facilitates retrieval. (5) Weak items in memory are difficult to retrieve. (6) Adopting an inefficient retrieval strategy (e.g. recalling all sorts of Spanish beverages until you stumble upon the target word) wastes time and generates distracting responses. (7) Encountering a stimulus without the intention to retrieve the target from memory reduces the probability of eliciting the target.

a secondary task, distracting people impaired retrieval by as much as 30–50%, especially when the judgment items were words as well. By contrast, making judgments about numbers or pictures produced far less interference. Such effects of dividing attention are largest when you have to generate items from memory (recall), but are also found when you simply have to recognize whether you have seen something.

Dividing attention can also reduce retrieval even when the secondary task is totally unrelated, although usually not as much. For example, when Craik, Govoni, Naveh-Benjamin, and Anderson (1996) asked people to perform a simple visuo-motor secondary

Figure 8.2 Retrieving words under divided attention conditions negatively affects retrieval success, especially with distractor tasks (e.g. semantic or phonological) that are similar to the task of interest (in this case, recalling words). Data from Fernandes and Moscovitch (2000).

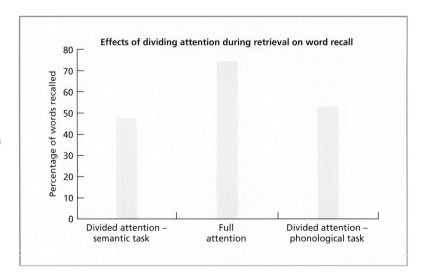

task, it reduced their recall of words presented earlier. The interfering effects of unrelated tasks grow when the task is more demanding (Rohrer & Pashler, 2003). It is worth highlighting, however, that dividing attention at retrieval is less disruptive to how much is recalled than dividing attention at encoding. This asymmetry has been taken to indicate that, under such circumstances, retrieval can quite often proceed with less attention than encoding (Baddeley, Lewis, Eldridge, & Thomson, 1984b; Craik et al., 1996). This proposal fits with the idea that once cues are presented and attended, automatic spreading activation can often bring a trace to mind. Nevertheless, if accurate and complete recall is necessary, full attention is required.

Relevance of cues

Having retrieval cues does little good if they are unrelated to the target. This might seem too obvious to mention, but we often search memory with inappropriate cues. Consider the time that I left the grocery store, and stood, trying to remember where I had parked my car. After several minutes of not recollecting anything, I realized that I had driven my neighbor's car. The moment I realized this, up popped the memory. I had essentially asked my memory the wrong question with the wrong

cue (*my car*). This type of mistake happens often. Have you ever tried to remember the location of your keys, presuming you must have placed them in one of their usual spots (e.g. a basket on the counter)? If you put your keys in an unusual spot, these retrieval cues will be fruitless.

It's tough enough finding your car in a sea of vehicles, but it's even harder to find if you're using the wrong cues. For instance, trying to remember where your sports car is wouldn't be very useful if, in fact, you drove the family sedan. © Girl Ray/Corbis.

Sometimes, cues that seem as though they ought to be effective turn out not to be effective at all. Consider the time that I intended to return a movie to the movie rental store. In the morning, standing by the breakfast table, I put the movie in my backpack. On the way home later that day, when passing the movie rental store, I looked right at the store, but failed to remember to return the movie. When I got home, however, and saw the kitchen table, I remembered, "Ahhh, I forget to return the movie!" So, why did seeing the video rental store not remind me to return the video? It ought to have been an outstanding cue! And why was the kitchen table such an effective reminder, when kitchen tables have nothing to do with movies? Actually, this pattern makes sense, if you consider what was encoded. The thing to be remembered was the intention to return the movie, which was encoded in the morning in the kitchen, with the table present. Indeed, the movie was lying on the table, and so was associated to it. By contrast, the video rental store was absent during encoding, and so was not associated with the video. Thus, when the video rental store became available later as a cue, there was no association that could spread activation to the intention to return the video.

The foregoing example illustrates a well-established idea known as the **encoding specificity principle**. This principle states that for a cue to be useful, it needs to be present at encoding, and encoded with the desired trace. In fact, cues that are specifically encoded with a target are more powerful even if, on the face of it, they might seem less good than other cues that have a pre-existing relationship with the target. In one experiment demonstrating this principle, Tulving and Osler (1968) presented participants with target words for later recall; each target was accompanied by a cue that had a weak association with the word to be retained. An example might be the word *chair* accompanied by the cue word *glue* (e.g. participants might see *glue–chair*). After encoding, participants were asked to recall the targets, either unaided or prompted by the cue with

which each was paired. Cue words substantially increased recall of the targets, illustrating the power of cues to facilitate recall. But not all cues should be equally good, according to Tulving. For instance, although *table* is a valid associate of *chair*, it will not be as effective a cue as *glue* because *table* was not presented during encoding. Tulving and Thomson (1973) went on to show that this encoding specificity effect is powerful.

There are other ways of showing the same effect. For example, if I give you a sentence such as "The man tuned the piano," but give another person the sentence "The man lifted the piano," then the cue *something heavy* is likely to be a very poor retrieval cue for you, but a good one for your colleague (Barclay, Bransford, Franks, McCarrell, & Nitsch, 1974). Thus, we remember what we experience and we access our memory by using a fragment of that experience as a key to the whole. So, even though a video rental store really seems like it *ought* to be a great cue for remembering to return the video, it is far less effective than the kitchen table because only the latter was encoded with the intention.

Cue–target associative strength

Retrieval can fail if cues are relevant but weak. As discussed previously, associations vary in strength, and it is this strength that determines the rate at which activation spreads between a cue and a target. Hence, if an association between a cue and a target is poor, retrieval failure might occur. Anyone who has ever memorized vocabulary words in a foreign language knows that associating new words to their native language equivalents can be difficult; it is possible to have stored the foreign word (e.g. be able to recognize it as

---

KEY TERM

Encoding specificity principle: The more similar the cues available at retrieval are to the conditions present at encoding, the more effective the cues will be.

one that you have seen) and nevertheless be unable to retrieve the right meaning. Similarly, associating a new person's face to their name frequently fails, even when we recognize the person's face, and the name, if it is given to us. Thus, retrieval success depends on how associated the cues are to the target, which depends on the time and attention we spend encoding the association. Perhaps one reason why the box did not remind me of storing the passport is that in hurrying to neaten my home for guests, I did not devote enough attention to the passport's location.

Number of cues

Retrieval often improves when more relevant cues are added. Consider the exercise you did on the "tip of the tongue." If you had initially tried to recall the meanings of the words and failed, but felt that you knew the right answer, getting the letter as an additional hint probably brought the meaning to mind. Similarly, the cardboard box by itself was insufficient to cue my memory of the passport, but when I saw the passport lying at the bottom of it, I recalled this event instantly. Importantly, the passport by itself would not have cued this memory. Suppose that I had been assisted by someone who found the passport while I was in another room. If the other person showed me the passport, I would not have suddenly remembered storing it in the box. I would have said, "Where did you find it?" It was the *combination* of the passport and the box that elicited the memory. It makes sense that adding cues helps. Assuming that the person attends to both cues, both will become activated. This activation will spread to the target; because there are two sources of activation, the target should grow active quickly, and be more easily retrieved.

There is evidence that adding cues does not simply cause additive improvements, however, but can sometimes be superadditive. Research on *dual cuing* suggests that having two cues is often far more beneficial than you would expect than if you simply added the probability of retrieving the target from each cue separately. Consider an example based on research by Rubin and Wallace (1989),

who examined how providing both semantic and rhyme cues affected the likelihood of generating particular responses from memory. If we asked you to name a *mythical being*, you might mention *unicorn* or *boogie monster* or any number of other such creatures. If we asked you to name a word that rhymes with *post*, you might say *host* or *most*, or any of the numerous words that rhyme. But if we instead asked you to name a mythical being that rhymes with *post*, you would be quite likely to say *ghost*. Rubin and Wallace showed that the probability of generating a particular item like ghost in response to either cue alone could be quite low (e.g. 14% for a semantic category, 19% for a rhyme cue by itself), but was dramatically higher with the two in combination (97% for both semantic and rhyme cues together). This might be one reason why it is so useful to encode information elaboratively, as discussed in Chapter 5 on encoding. Elaboration associates the material to many cues that might be used during later retrieval.

Strength of the target memory

If a memory is weakly encoded, even a good cue might be insufficient to trigger retrieval. In the framework described earlier, if the target has low activation, the lower starting point should make it more difficult for a cue to activate that item, even given a relevant cue. For example, words vary greatly in their frequency of usage in a language, with some words being very high frequency, such as *dog*, and others being known, but rarely used, such as *helmet*. Higher-frequency words are better recalled. One interpretation is that higher-frequency words are more strongly represented, owing to their repeated exposure. Similarly, how well people will recall a set of singly presented words or pictures varies with the amount of time given to encode those items, reflecting greater success at encoding.

Retrieval strategy

Retrieval can be influenced by the strategy one adopts. For example, after studying a word list, I might (if I were naive) try to recall the words by working through the alphabet and retrieving items associated with each letter. If materials are organized at encoding, going through that organization at retrieval would be an ideal strategy, as discussed in Chapter 5 on organization. In addition, which order to recall a group of items is also a strategy choice; should I start at the beginning, or go in reverse order? In the case of retrieving my passport location, I tried many strategies for retrieving, such as remembering the last time I had the passport, and recalling all my recent trips.

One nice illustration of the impact of retrieval strategy comes from a clever study by Richard Anderson and James Pritchert (1978). Their participants read a story about boys skipping school, hiding out in the home of one of the boys. The story described objects contained in the home and participants were asked, during reading, to adopt the perspective of either a burglar or a homebuyer. On a later test, both groups recalled a similar amount, although the items recalled were biased towards things relevant to their respective perspectives. Interestingly, however, participants received a second recall attempt, adopting either the same perspective, or an alternative one. Unsurprisingly, participants adopting the same perspective recalled the same items again; intriguingly, however, those adopting a different perspective (e.g. the perspective of a burglar, after having initially encoded and retrieved as a homebuyer), recalled significantly more items relevant to that new perspective. Thus, retrieval improved because of a mere change in retrieval strategy. This study highlights how we might often—unbeknownst to us—adopt a viewpoint when recalling the past. This perspective provides a schematic structure that guides retrieval, constraining our recall to things relevant to the schema. To maximize recall, one might try to recall from different perspectives. We return to this idea in our discussion of the cognitive interview method in Chapter 14.

Retrieval mode

During my passport mishap, I looked at the box containing the passport many times. I even searched the box, but it never reminded me of storing the passport. Although the box might have been weakly associated to the passport, another possibility exists: perhaps I was in the wrong frame of mind when looking at the box. It's true that I focused attention on the box while searching it. But perhaps I was so fixated on searching it that this got in the way of memory. If I had tried to remember that event while looking at the box it might have proven to be an effective cue.

It is worth considering that many of the stimuli in our daily lives have associations to the past, but we aren't bombarded by memories every waking second. You put on your shoes this morning, but you probably didn't remember when you bought them, even though your shoes are a perfectly good cue for that event, and even though you could probably remember that event if you wanted to. Although we are often spontaneously reminded of experiences without intending to retrieve them, it is perhaps more surprising that we are not always being reminded, given the abundance of cues around us. It seems, then, that in some cases we have to be in the right frame of mind or **retrieval mode** to recollect our past (Tulving, 1983).

According to research on retrieval mode, for retrieval to be effective it is necessary to adopt a cognitive set that ensures that stimuli will be processed as probes of episodic memory. A nice illustration was recently reported by Herron and Wilding (2006), who measured brain electrical activity during retrieval. Participants encoded lists of words that appeared on either the left or right side of a screen. Later, they were presented with these words mixed in with new ones, and were asked to do one of two tasks on each. On episodic trials, they had to judge whether the word was one they had seen earlier and, if so, what side of the screen it had appeared on; on semantic trials,

---

KEY TERM

Retrieval mode: The cognitive set, or frame of mind, that orients a person towards the act of retrieval, ensuring that stimuli are interpreted as retrieval cues.

they had to judge whether the word referred to an object capable of moving on its own (e.g. *buzzard*)—a judgment that did not require recalling what they had just seen. Importantly, each word was preceded for 4 seconds by a cue telling people which judgment they had to perform on the upcoming word. By recording brain activity over the 4 seconds when participants were getting ready to make their judgment, they could see whether there was a distinctive neural pattern linked to getting ready for retrieval. Herron and Wilding found relatively greater positive electrical brain activity over the right frontal cortex—an area involved in attentional control—when people were preparing to retrieve than when they were preparing to make a semantic judgment. Moreover, they found that when people did several episodic judgments consecutively, their judgment accuracy and speed improved with each trial, consistent with the idea that it takes time to "get into the swing" of retrieval. Thus, retrieval benefits from getting into the right mental configuration, a task accomplished by the right prefrontal cortex.

CONTEXT CUES

Although we have been discussing cues generically, it is worth highlighting one variety of cue that is quite important: **context cues**. *Context* refers to the circumstances under which a stimulus has been encoded. For example, you would probably agree that general knowledge of the word *pomegranate* differs from the particular memory of seeing a pomegranate at the local market, or from having seen the word *pomegranate* on this page. The latter cases concern particular occasions or *episodic memories*, which are distinguishable by the place and time they took place. The *spatio-temporal or environmental context* of the grocery store event includes the setting of your local market on Tuesday, for example.

Memory retrieval is often influenced by context, sometimes intentionally, other times not. When we intentionally retrieve the past,

"Have you taken out the trash?" The chances are that you have, on many occasions in your lifetime, but it is doubtful that this is what you are being asked! It is vital, therefore, to specify spatio-temporal context if you wish to retrieve a specific event (and avert a wrathful response!). © H. Armstrong Roberts/Corbis.

it is necessary to specify the part of the past we wish to recollect. If your room-mate asks whether you took out the trash, she is not asking you to recollect any event from your past in which you took out the trash. If you did not constrain retrieval to the context of the previous day, you might recollect some previous occasion and falsely say you took it out. The result: one annoyed room-mate. Thus, one of the cues you must include during retrieval is the spatio-temporal context of the event you are hoping to recollect.

KEY TERM

Context cues: Retrieval cues that specify aspects of the conditions under which a desired target was encoded, including (for example) the location and time of the event.

The concept of context is not limited to spatio-temporal context but also includes other aspects of the circumstances. The *mood context* of an event refers to the emotional state that a person was in when the event took place, whereas the *physiological context* refers to the pharmacological/physical state that one was in (e.g. under the influence of a certain drug, or alcohol). One can also distinguish *cognitive context*, which can mean a particular collection of concepts that one has thought about in the temporal vicinity of the event. In our later section on context-dependent memory, we will discuss how all of these types of context can constrain what we retrieve of our past, even when we are not aware of it. Context cues also play a role in defining the types of retrieval tasks often used to study memory.

RETRIEVAL TASKS

Each day, life leaves its boot-prints in our mental clay, and these imprints influence us in many ways. Sometimes, we are deliberate users of memory, trying consciously to recollect what happened in times past. Other times, we might not intend to be influenced by memory, but are, without being aware of it. Psychologists have devised numerous methods for testing retrieval that get at these circumstances. These tests reflect various circumstances in daily life, and differences in memory across test types have taught us important lessons about the structures and processes of memory.

Direct memory tests
Tests that ask people to retrieve their past are known as **direct or explicit memory tests** (Schacter, 1987; Richardson-Klavehn & Bjork, 1988). Because they ask people to recall particular experiences, these tests require context as a cue. Direct tests vary in the number of cues given, the amount to be retrieved, and in the involvement of retrieval strategies. *Free recall* relies on context the most heavily because people must retrieve an entire set of studied

items without overt cues, freely—that is, any order. For example, if you studied 25 words and then tried to recall them in any order, you would be performing free recall. Free recall mimics situations in daily life in which we must produce a lot of information in no particular order. Recalling who was at a party last night, recalling the items on a grocery list that you left at home, and even answering the question, "What did you do today?" are all cases of free recall. Free recall also necessitates the use of strategies for generating the answers in some order. Thus, this test is sensitive to one's skills at organizing information at encoding, and selecting strategies at retrieval.

By contrast, cued recall provides additional cues, and very often focuses on particular items in memory. In laboratory studies, this might include providing an associate of a previously studied word or an initial letter as a cue. Cued recall tests are intended to mimic situations when we are recalling a particular item or experience in response to a cue. Recalling who drove you to the party last night, or which grocery store you went to today are examples of cued recall. Cued recall requires context as a cue, but context is supplemented with specific information that focuses search. Cued recall is often easier than free recall and doesn't rely as heavily on retrieval strategies to recall items.

Recognition tests are usually the easiest type of direct test because they simply require a decision: Did you encounter this stimulus on this occasion? If, after asking you to study a set of 25 pictures or words, I presented you with those 25 items intermixed with 25 new ones, and asked you to indicate, for each, whether you had seen it in the original list, I would be giving you a recognition test. Recognition tests pop up all the time. One especially critical

KEY TERM

Direct/explicit memory tests: Any of a variety of memory assessments that overtly prompt participants to retrieve past events.

example that we discuss in Chapter 14 (on eyewitness testimony) is when eyewitnesses are asked if anyone in a lineup was the person they saw committing a crime. Recognition tests can be accomplished in two ways: one that relies heavily on context, another that relies on it less. We will return to this in depth in a later section on recognition.

Indirect memory tests

In a famous legal case, *Bright Tunes Music* v. *Harrisongs Music*, George Harrison of the Beatles was sued for borrowing substantial portions of the song *He's so fine* by the Chiffons and using them in his song *My sweet lord*. Harrison lost his case, even though he insisted that he did not consciously copy the song.

As another example, as a child, Helen Keller was accused of plagiarism due to her story *The frost king*, which bore a remarkable resemblance to Martin Canby's *The frost fairies*, a fairy tale that had been read to her when she was very young. Here again, Keller did not have any awareness of what she was doing, and the experience was traumatic for her. There are many apparent cases of such *cryptomnesia*, in which a person believes they are creating something new such as a piece of artwork, but is recalling a similar work they have encountered. Can memories influence us unconsciously?

In fact, we are frequently influenced by our experiences, without being aware of it. Suppose, for example, you find an anagram puzzle in your newspaper. As you are trying to solve the anagram for "pomegranate," you might well find that the solution comes very easily if you had just read about pomegranates earlier in the day. Your performance on a task (anagram solving) has benefited from the experience even though you were not trying to recall the past. Many demonstrations show that such influences are possible. These examples illustrate what is known as an indirect memory test, which is taken as a measure of *implicit memory* (Schacter, 1987; Richardson-Klavehn & Bjork, 1988).

Indirect tests measure the influence of experience without asking the person to recall the past. These measures have a "sneaky" quality to them, in that they try to eliminate, from the participants' viewpoint, any scent that they are memorizing, or, on the test, retrieving things. In a typical implicit memory experiment, participants might first encode a list of words. For each word, people might make a simple judgment, such as whether the object denoted by the word refers to a living thing—a task chosen to not arouse suspicions that memory might be tested. Afterwards, the participants would perform a task involving some of the old words, mixed with new words. The test usually asks the person to perform some task that can be done without recalling any particular experience. Many indirect tests are possible, and there is usually a "cover story" about why the experimenter is interested in the task. In a lexical decision task, participants would receive words and nonwords (e.g. *glork*) and for each would decide as quickly as possible whether the letter string presented was a legal English word. In a perceptual identification task, participants receive briefly presented words (e.g. 30 milliseconds), covered by a visual mask (e.g. a row of Xs) to make them difficult to see. Their task is simply to say the word they saw. On word fragment completion tests (e.g. p–m–gr–n–t–) or word stem completion tests (po——), people would list the first word that comes to mind that fits the letters.

In each of the foregoing tests (Table 8.1), people are better at doing the task for previously viewed words than for the new words, even when they are unaware of the connection to the prior phase: They make lexical decisions faster, identify difficult-to-see words more accurately, or generate word fragment completions more frequently. Similar tests exist for other stimuli classes, such as for pictures and sounds. Performance consistently shows characteristics that differ from those observed on explicit tests. For example, the benefit is often sensitive to the perceptual match between encoding and test stimuli. For instance, changing perceptual

TABLE 8.1: Typical types of direct and indirect retrieval tasks used in the laboratory to study explicit and implicit memory.

Test category	Test type	Example retrieval instructions
Free recall	Direct/explicit	"Recall studied items in any order."
Cued recall	Direct/explicit	"What word did you study together with *leap*?"
Forced-choice recognition	Direct/explicit	"Which did you study: *ballet* or *monk*?"
Yes/No recognition	Direct/explicit	"Did you study *ballet*?"
Lexical decision	Indirect/implicit	"Is *ballet* a word? Is *mokn* a word?"
Word fragment completion	Indirect/implicit	"Fill in the missing letters to form a word: *b–l–e–*."
Word stem completion	Indirect/implicit	"Fill in the missing letters with anything that fits: *bal* ——
Conceptual fluency	Indirect/implicit	"Name all the dance types you can."

modalities between study and test (from hearing words at encoding, to a visual test) can reduce the benefits observed. Although many of these tests focus on perceptual qualities of the stimulus (i.e. are perceptually driven), some indirect tests measure the influence of experience on conceptual tasks, and are known as conceptually driven indirect tests. For example, if I gave you semantic categories and asked you to generate as many members of each as possible—a measure known as conceptual fluency—you would be more likely to list *buzzard* in the *birds* category than you would be if you had not read this chapter today.

How do indirect and direct tests differ? They do not necessarily differ in the core mechanisms described in the beginning of this chapter. For example, indirect tests provide cues that initiate a retrieval process that accesses a remnant of experience, perhaps through spreading activation. They do differ, however, in that indirect tests do not require recall of the past, and so context is not used intentionally as a cue. Rather, only the directly presented cues such as the letters of the word, or the fragments of the picture, are used consciously. Despite the absence of contextual cuing, recent experience with the stimulus improves performance, a phenomenon known as **repetition priming** (see Ochsner, Chiu, & Yp, 1998, for a review).

Repetition priming is widely accepted as a case in which past experience influences us unconsciously. This implicit influence does not mean that the memory traces accessed by indirect tests are identical to those that underlie episodic memory. In fact, explicit memory is supported by additional contextual representations in the hippocampus. Thus indirect tests differ both in the absence of contextual cuing, and in the content and neural locus of the traces that they access.

Of course, it is natural to wonder whether this influence is truly unconscious. Perhaps people realize they are being tested on the earlier material and just recall things intentionally. Indeed, not everyone is fooled. Nevertheless, even when people profess no awareness of the connection, benefits occur. Indeed, amnesic patients, who are unable to recollect much about an experience after just a few moments, show perfectly normal performance on indirect tests. This fact—that explicit memory is impaired in amnesia, but implicit memory is intact—is the foundation of a fundamental

KEY TERM

Repetition priming: Enhanced processing of a stimulus arising from recent encounters with that stimulus, a form of implicit memory.

revision in how psychologists think about memory: that memory is composed of multiple distinct systems (Squire, 1992b; see Gabrieli, 1998 for a review). Indirect tests illustrate how the boot-prints of experience can influence us without our knowing it. All of this ought to leave us more sympathetic to George Harrison and Helen Keller.

THE IMPORTANCE OF INCIDENTAL CONTEXT IN EPISODIC MEMORY RETRIEVAL

When people retrieve the past, they use context to focus retrieval on the desired place and time. But can we be influenced by context unintentionally? Suppose that you experienced an event in one environment or mood, and later wish to retrieve that experience when in a different environment or mood. How will memory compare to a situation in which one is in the same location or mood at retrieval that was present at encoding? As it turns out, the match of the current context to the one we are retrieving matters, a phenomenon known as **context-dependent memory**. Several types of context-dependent memory exist, including environmental, mood, and state-dependent memory.

Environmental context-dependent memory

One evening, I was sitting in my home office when I decided that I could really go for a cup of tea. After walking downstairs, I found myself in the kitchen wondering why I was there. I knew that I had come downstairs for something, and that that something was in the kitchen, but I couldn't remember what it was. So I went upstairs to my home office and it popped into my head: I wanted tea. Why did retrieval fail and then succeed? It seems likely that returning to the original environment reinstates the spatial context in

which the event was originally encoded, aiding retrieval.

Context-dependent memory effects do in fact occur. Some years ago, Duncan Godden and Alan Baddeley explored this phenomenon in connection with an applied problem, namely that of training deep-sea divers (Godden & Baddeley, 1975). Earlier experiments of Baddeley's on the effect of cold on divers had suggested quite incidentally that the underwater environment might induce strong context dependency. This suggestion was supported by the observations of a friend who was in charge of a team of divers attempting to watch the behavior of fish about to enter, or escape from, trawl nets. Initially, he relied on debriefing his divers when they surfaced, only to find that they had apparently forgotten most of the fishy behavior they had seen. Eventually, he had to send his divers down with underwater tape recorders so that they could give a running commentary on the fishes' activities. Intrigued by this, Godden and Baddeley set up an experiment in which divers listened to 40 unrelated words either on the beach or under about 10 feet of water. After the 40 words had been heard, the divers were tested either in the same environment or in the alternative one. The results, shown in Figure 8.3, were very clear: Material learned underwater was best recalled underwater, and material learned on land was best recalled on land. Similar findings have been observed with a variety of other changes in physical context, including changes in room, and with many types of stimuli, including pictures, words, and faces.

Smith and Vela (2001) reviewed research on context-dependent memory and drew several important conclusions. One broad principle that characterizes when people

KEY TERM

Context-dependent memory: The finding that memory benefits when the spatio-temporal, mood, physiological, or cognitive context at retrieval matches that present at encoding.

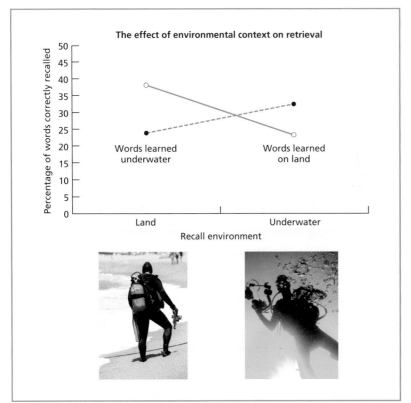

Figure 8.3 Words learned and tested in the same environment (i.e. data points falling within the top half of the graph) are better recalled than those items for which the environmental context varied between study and test (i.e. bottom half of the graph). Data from Godden and Baddeley (1975).

show sensitivity to environmental context is that people need to pay some attention to the physical environment during encoding. A more inward focus of attention during encoding reduces or eliminates incidental context effects. Context-dependent memory effects also grow in size as the delay between encoding and retrieval increases, which might account for why returning to a childhood home one has not visited in a long time creates the feeling of being "flooded" with memories one has not thought about in years. Finally, and, quite usefully, the mere mental reinstatement of context greatly reduces context-dependent memory effects. Hence, if one is trying to retrieve an experience or fact encoded in a vastly different context, it is often beneficial to imagine the elements of the physical environment such as the objects that were present, layout, and other details.

State-dependent memory

Context-dependent memory effects also occur when the learner's internal environment is changed by means of drugs such as alcohol, an effect known as state dependency. Goodwin and colleagues (1969) cite clinical evidence of this. Heavy drinkers who hide alcohol or money when drunk are unable to remember where it is hidden once they are sober; when they become drunk again, they remember. Goodwin studied this effect using a whole range of tests and found, in general, that what is learned when drunk is best recalled when drunk. Similar results have been shown with a range of other drugs, for example with nitrous oxide, sometimes used to anesthetize patients, marijuana (Eich, 1980), and even caffeine. In a review, Eich (1980) convincingly showed that state dependency is observed only when memory is tested by recall; it disappears when recognition testing is used. It appears that the participant's internal state helps to access the memory, but that when access is made easy by presenting an item for recognition, search is unnecessary.

State-dependent memory effects also occur from a variety of changes in physiological state that occur naturally. One interesting example comes from a study by Christopher Miles and Elinor Hardman (1998), who examined whether aerobic exercise might produce state-dependent memory. They had participants learn a list of auditorally presented words, either while they were resting comfortably on an exercise bicycle or while they were pedaling the bike quickly enough to raise their heart rate to 120–150 beats per minute. Then, after rest, they asked their participants to free-recall the words when at rest or when bicycling, as before. Strikingly, people who got to recall the words in the same cardiovascular state—whether at rest both times or exercising both times—recalled the words 20% better than did people who shifted their state between encoding and recall. Thus, aspects of our physiological state are encoded incidentally as part of the episodic experience, and re-creation of that state at retrieval helps memory. Students who read course material while on their stairmaster or exercise bicycle should take note of this, as should athletes who need to remember the lessons about performance learned off the field, while on the field.

Mood-congruent and mood-dependent memory

When depressed people are asked to recall autobiographical memories, they tend to recall unhappy incidents; the more depressed the individual, the more rapidly the unpleasant experience is recalled. Of course, this might simply be because depressives indeed lead less pleasant lives, explaining why they are depressed. One study avoided this problem by selecting patients whose level of depression fluctuated systematically throughout the day, as sometimes occurs in depression (Clark &

Teasdale, 1982). During sad times of the day, these individuals were consistently less likely to produce happy memories than at other times. Similar results have also been obtained with normal participants, using a procedure known as the Velten technique. A happy or sad mood is induced by encouraging participants to ponder sets of sad or happy statements (Velten, 1968). While sad, participants were slower at evoking positive memories (Teasdale & Fogarty, 1979).

The preceding findings provide evidence of **mood-congruent memory** (Blaney, 1986). This term refers to the greater ease in recalling events that have an emotional tone that matches the current mood of the person. Thus, it is easier to recall happy memories in a happy mood, and sad memories when in a sad mood. Indeed, the fact that people in a depressed mood have difficulty retrieving pleasant memories might be part of the problem of depression. If a person is depressed, he or she will be likely to recall unpleasant incidents from the past, further deepening the depression. Cognitive approaches to the treatment of depression involve helping the person to access less depressing memories and revalue the more positive aspects of their lives. Moreover, given the biases in retrieval evident in mood congruent memory, one would do well not to make hasty decisions in a powerful mood state. If you are upset with someone, chances are that all you will remember about them are unpleasant experiences, even if many positive memories might otherwise be available for retrieval.

Although mood-congruent memory is an interesting phenomenon, it is not a demonstration of incidental context-dependent memory because the main thing determining recall probability is the match of the mood context

---

KEY TERM

Mood-congruent memory: Bias in the recall of memories such that negative mood makes negative memories more readily available than positive, and vice versa. Unlike mood dependency, it does not affect the recall of neutral memories.

Mood-congruent memory refers to the enhanced ease in recalling events that have an emotional tone similar to our current mood. If we're feeling happy and content, we are more likely to recall pleasant memories; when depressed we are likely to retrieve unpleasant ones.

being retrieved to the current mood. As such, it is not that mood state at encoding is being incidentally attached to otherwise neutral events, and acting as incidental context. To establish such **mood-dependent memory**, one needs to show that the ease with which a memory is recalled depends on the match in mood states between encoding and retrieval, not merely on the congruency of what is recalled with the retrieval mood state. In one demonstration of this, Eric Eich, Dawn Macaulay, and Lee Ryan (1994) found evidence of mood dependent memory when they asked people to generate events from their past in response to cues (e.g. *ship*, *street*). They induced participants to be in either a pleasant (P) or unpleasant (U) mood at encoding, and then again at retrieval, which took place 2 days later. Mood was induced by having participants listen to either merry or melancholy music, while entertaining elating or depressing thoughts. Once the relevant mood was established (as rated by the participant), encoding or, 2 days later, retrieval, commenced. They found that free recall of the events generated 2 days earlier was better when the mood state at test matched that at encoding, irrespective of whether the event recalled was itself positive neutral, or negative in tone.

Cognitive context-dependent memory

One's internal context also includes the particular ideas, thoughts, and concepts that have occupied our attention during encoding and retrieval. It seems safe to speculate, for example, that during Picasso's Blue Period, blue was very much on his mind. Can the general cognitive context in which one encodes an experience influence our ability to retrieve that information later? One example of the influence of cognitive context is the tendency for language context to influence what memories one retrieves most easily.

In a nice illustration by Viorica Marian and Ulric Neisser (2000), a group of Russian–English bilinguals were asked to tell stories about their lives in response to word prompts. The participants were told that half of the session would be conducted in English and the other half in Russian. Within each segment, only one of the languages was spoken, and participants received cue words in that same language in response to which they were to generate a memory from any time in their lives. Interestingly, when the interview was conducted in Russian, participants generated Russian memories (i.e. memories they had experienced in a Russian speaking context) to 64% of the those cues, whereas when the interview was conducted in English, they only generated Russian memories to 35% of the cues. The opposite pattern occurred for English memories.

Marian and Neisser argue that linguistic context acts like other forms of incidental context. They suggest that bilinguals may have two language modes, in which memories take place and are stored. When that mode is

KEY TERM

Mood-dependent memory: A form of context dependent effect whereby what is learnt in a given mood, whether positive, negative, or neutral, is best recalled in that mood.

recreated, by conversing in a given language, their incidental cognitive context favors retrieval of memories acquired in that mode. Other studies have replicated this pattern, and have extended it to memory for academic material, and even general semantic knowledge. For example, Marian and Fausey (2006) found that bilinguals were better at remembering information (e.g. about chemistry, history, etc.) when tested in the same language in which the material was studied.

It is fascinating to think that whole segments of your life—both personal memories and general knowledge—might be rendered less accessible by the language you currently speak—a fact, if true, that must affect the sizeable portion of the planet that is bilingual. Given this, students who pursue studies in foreign countries have challenges not faced by their native language colleagues—challenges that extend beyond mastering a new language. The challenges they face provide an illustration of the influence of incidental context on the experiences that lie within our mental grasp.

Reconstructive memory

So far, we have characterized retrieval as bringing to mind an intact memory. Retrieval is sometimes more involved when we are retrieving something on the fringe of accessibility, however. We might be able to recall aspects of the experience but be forced to "figure out" other aspects. The term **reconstructive memory** refers to this active and inferential aspect of retrieval. Some of the flavor of reconstructive memory is given by the following account, which Alan Baddeley produced a few days after the experience had taken place.

November, 1978

On the train platform I notice a familiar face and I decide to see if I can remember who he is. Two associations occur, the name Sebastian *and something to do with children.* Sebastian *seems to me to be a useful cue, but all it calls up is an association with teddy bears through Evelyn Waugh's* Brideshead revisited. *I also*

sense there are some associations with a darkish room with books, but nothing clear enough to suggest any useful further search.

A little later, for no apparent reason, babysitting pops up and I recall that we were both members of a mutual babysitting group, that his name is indeed Sebastian, although I cannot remember his second name, and that he lives in a road whose location I am quite clear about, and in a house that I can visualize easily. A clear image of his sitting-room appears, together with the fact that it contains finely printed books, and that he is by profession a printer. I remember noticing that he has a printing press in one room. I have no doubt that I have identified him.

Two days later, it occurs to me that I still have not remembered his surname or the name of the street in which he lives. I have no clues about his name, but know that he lives in either Oxford Road or Windsor Road. I have a colleague who lives in the one that Sebastian does not live in. If I have to guess, I would say that he lives in Oxford Road, and that my colleague lives in Windsor Road. I try again to remember his surname. Sebastian… Nothing. And then for no obvious reason Carter *appears. It feels right, although not overwhelmingly so. Then the association* Penny Carter *appears as his wife's name. I am sure that this is correct, reinforcing my belief that his name is Sebastian Carter.*

I go to the telephone directory. After this effort I had better be right. Carter *is indeed in Oxford Road. I ring and ask him, "Was he on the 14.36 train to Liverpool Street on Tuesday?" He was.*

This experience illustrates several important points. First, there certainly is an automatic retrieval process whereby information "pops up" for no obvious reason. The name *Sebastian* and

---

KEY TERM

Reconstructive memory: An active and inferential process of retrieval whereby gaps in memory are filled in based on prior experience, logic, and goals.

the association with babysitting were examples. Second, when the appropriate information does not spring to mind, we seem to take the fragments and use them like a detective might use a clue. In the case of the clue *Sebastian*, associations were followed up, each of which could be rejected. By contrast, the vague association with children produced *babysitting* and then a clear image of the Carters' house. This in turn produced other information, including the fact that Sebastian Carter is a printer and a visual image of a printing press in his house.

Reconstruction is often driven by background knowledge that suggests plausible inferences. Such inferences might even lead us to believe we are remembering something when we are not. In one nice study, Dooling and Christiaansen (1977) gave participants the following passage to read and study:

Carol Harris's need for professional help
Carol Harris was a problem child from birth. She was wild, stubborn, and violent. By the time Carol turned eight, she was still unmanageable. Her parents were very concerned about her mental health. There was no good institution for her problem in her state. Her parents finally decided to take some action. They hired a private teacher for Carol.

The participants were tested 1 week later. Just before the test, half of the participants were told that the story about Carol Harris was really about Helen Keller; the other half was told nothing. Interestingly, the participants told that the story was about Helen Keller were far more likely to claim that they recognized seeing sentences like, "She was deaf, dumb, and blind," when they had not seen them. Presumably, hearing about Helen Keller just before the test activated knowledge they had about her, leading them to believe they remembered something that they did not experience. Here we have a clear example of reconstructive inference influencing what people think they remember. Such errors grow more likely as time goes by, because the original memory grows less accessible (Spiro, 1977).

In Dooling and Christiaansen's (1977) study participants claimed that they had seen sentences describing Helen Keller as "deaf, dumb, and blind," when in reality they had not. This is an example of reconstructive inference influencing what people think they remember. Photo of Helen Keller courtesy of the Library of Congress.

Although reconstructive processes often lead to errors in recollection, they are in fact quite useful, and often result in us recalling correct information and making plausible inferences about what must have happened. Nevertheless, when veridical recall is essential (e.g. eyewitness memory), reconstructive errors can have grave consequences. A person who witnesses a fight and later unintentionally misrecollects who started the fight based on stereotype-based reconstructive memory is a serious danger to the accused.

RECOGNITION MEMORY

Thus far, we have focused on free and cued recall as models of retrieval. Very often, however, we use our memories not to generate things but to make a decision about whether we have encountered a stimulus. We might scan a list of phone numbers in the hopes of picking out the one we wish to dial; we might see a person on the street and wonder whether we have met them before; or we might be called on to identify the perpetrator of a crime in a police lineup. This situation, known as **recognition memory**, warrants a special discussion because different processes are engaged. Unlike recall, recognition presents the intact stimulus, and hence requires a judgment: did you see this stimulus in a certain context? A number of consequences follow from this that pertain to the measurement of recognition, and to the way that people solve the task.

First, recognition tests fundamentally require a discrimination between stimuli that a person experienced in a particular context and things that they didn't. Because the person must discriminate "old" from "new," a test is only meaningful if it includes both old *and* new items, forcing the rememberer to show his/her skill at making good discriminations. These non-studied items are called distractors, lures, or sometimes foils, and are akin to the other members of the lineup who the police think are innocent. In laboratory research, distractors are sometimes presented together with the old item, and the person must choose one of the items, which is known as a *forced-choice recognition test*. Other tests present one item at a time, and ask people to make a yes or no decision to each, with old and new items intermixed; this is known as a *yes/no recognition test*. Distractors on such tests provide valuable information about how much a person's recognition judgment can be trusted.

How do we take people's responses to distractors into account? In measuring recognition for a set of material, a single error does not make someone's retention bad. People with a good memory sometimes make mistakes. If so, how do we take the number of mistaken identifications into account? Should somebody with 10% mistaken recognitions be judged as having deficient retention? If

so, then is the memory of a person with 10% mistaken recognitions necessarily less good than a person with 5%? What about someone who correctly identifies 85% of the old items but has 10% mistaken identifications? Is that person's memory worse than that of someone who recognizes 40% of the old items, but has only 5% mistaken identifications?

To make matters worse, we need to consider people's tendencies for guessing when making a recognition judgment. Sometimes an incorrect judgment of "Yes" to a new item does not reflect a sincere belief in having seen the item (unlike our hypothetical eyewitness), but rather the person's uncertainty together with a need to make a decision. For the same reason, some of the "Yes" responses to old items will reflect guessing. Indeed, in police lineups, the social situation puts pressure on witnesses to identify somebody, leading some people to guess, based on who seems familiar. To see how much influence guessing can have, imagine two participants given a recognition task. Person A is told that there will be both old and new items on the test, but that there will be no penalty for incorrectly circling new items; Person B is told that incorrect responses to new items will be harshly penalized. The latter person will surely be more conservative than the former, greatly reducing their tendency to respond "Yes" to new items, and also their "Yes" responses to old items about which they are somewhat unsure. Clearly, guessing is an issue, and the rate of guessing can vary, depending on people's biases.

This discussion raises a general issue in measuring recognition memory: distinguishing memory from decision making. Some means of estimating the amount of information in memory is essential, and this method must

KEY TERM

Recognition memory: A person's ability to correctly decide whether they have encountered a stimulus previously in a particular context.

separate out judgment biases. To devise such a method, however, requires a theory of the memory processes that enter in a recognition judgment. We discuss such an approach next.

Signal detection theory as a model of recognition memory

One approach to understanding recognition builds on the concepts developed in **signal detection theory**, which evolved from research on auditory perception (Green & Swets, 1966). In a typical auditory detection experiment, people listen for a faint tone presented in a background of white noise, and are instructed to press a button if they detect a tone. Depending on how faint the tone is, people will not be perfect, and so four types of event occur. A tone might be presented and the person might correctly claim that he/she heard it; this is known as a *hit*. Sometimes, a tone is presented that is not detected; this is a *miss*. Perhaps a tone is not presented but the person mistakenly claims to have heard it, this is a *false alarm*. Finally, people quite often claim not to have heard a tone when the tone was not presented; this called a *correct rejection*.

A similar situation exists on a yes/no recognition test. On a recognition test, a participants must decide whether they sense "familiarity" in the stimulus. Deciding if a stimulus seems familiar enough to classify as "old" is like deciding whether there is enough auditory evidence to claim you heard a tone. As with auditory detection, four outcomes are possible. If the item was studied and the person correctly classifies it as "old," it is a hit; if it is old, but misclassified as "new," it is a miss. If the item is new and the person misclassifies it as "old," it is a false alarm; and if the person correctly judges it as "new," it is a correct rejection.

Signal detection theory provides a useful way of thinking about recognition that comes with tools necessary to distinguish true memory and guessing. Signal detection theory proposes that memory traces have *strength values* (see the discussion of activation level above, p. 170) that reflect their activation in

memory, which dictate how familiar they seem. Traces are thought to vary in their familiarity, depending on how much attention the item received at encoding or how many times it was repeated. Importantly, the theory assumes that new items will have familiarity as well, although usually less than items that have been studied. Their familiarity might arise if the new items have been seen frequently outside the experiment, or, instead, if they are similar to studied items. In terms of the police lineup example, a person might seem powerfully familiar to a witness because the witness saw them before (just not at the crime), or because they look a lot like the actual perpetrator.

But how do these ideas help? One key idea is that the familiarity of a set of items is normally distributed, and that the studied and new items each have their own distributions. These distributions are likely to vary in the average level of familiarity. In most cases, the average familiarity for studied (old) items will be higher than the average for new items due to the recent exposure of old items; although, as illustrated in Figure 8.4, these distributions might overlap. This overlap arises because some old items might have been encoded poorly, and so will not have received much of a boost in memory strength, whereas some new items might seem especially familiar. For some participants, these distributions could be

KEY TERM

Signal detection theory: A model of recognition memory that posits that memory targets (signals) and lures (noise) on a recognition test posses an attribute known as strength or familiarity, which occurs in a graded fashion, with previously encountered items generally possessing more strength that novel items. The process of recognition involves ascertaining a given test item's strength and then deciding whether it exceeds a criterion level of strength, above which items are considered to be previously encountered. Signal detection theory provides analytic tools that separate true memory from judgment biases in recognition.

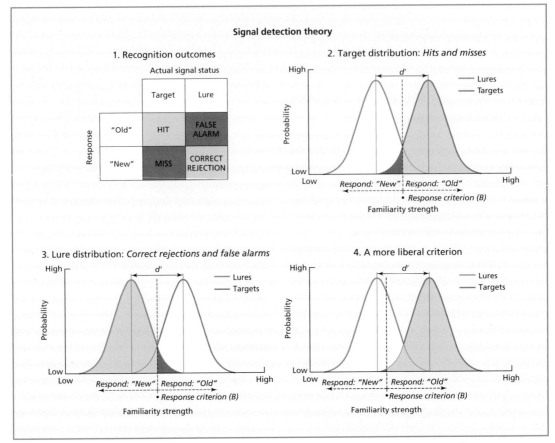

Figure 8.4 (1) Recognition outcomes, jointly based on item (signal) status and the participant's response. (2) Familiarity distributions for targets and lures. Hits are in green; misses in red. (3) Correct rejections (green) and false alarms (red). (4) Shifting the response criterion leftward increases hits and false alarms.

very close, with only a minimal difference in average familiarity across the old and new distributions. For others, the distributions might be very far apart, and even nonoverlapping, if they studied the list quite well. Increasing study time, or the number of repetitions of each studied item would also push the old distribution farther away from new items, increasing overall familiarity.

Importantly, how well a person can discriminate studied from new items depends on the difference in the average familiarity between their old and new distributions. In other words, a participant's ability to discriminate two sets of items can be measured by the distance between the averages of the old and

new distributions, as shown in Figure 8.4. In the language of signal detection theory, this distance is known as d' ("d prime").

But how does a recognition judgment take place? To address this issue, the theory proposes that people choose a criterion level of familiarity, above which they will judge a test item as old and below which they will judge an item as new. The bottom-right panel of Figure 8.4 illustrates one positioning of the criterion on the familiarity continuum. Notice that by placing the criterion in this location, some old items will fall below the criterion for "oldness," and so will be classified as misses. Old items that fall above the criterion, however, will be "hits." Similarly, some new items will have familiarity that exceeds the criterion, leading people to classify them incorrectly as old; these are false alarms. New items falling below the criterion will be classified as correct rejections. Thus, our four outcomes (hit, miss, false alarm, correct rejection) can be understood, given their familiarity, relative to the criterion and status (old or new).

The idea that people set a criterion for judging "oldness" helps to define what a judgment bias is. To see this, notice what would happen if the criterion is "loosened" by shifting it farther to the left on the familiarity continuum, allowing less familiar items to be classified as "old." This would ensure that the vast majority of old items will be hits, and there will be very few misses. Unfortunately, this would also increase the proportion of new items judged as old, and so will increase the false alarm rate. When the criterion is made strict (shifted to the right), a complementary thing happens: People will be unlikely to commit a false alarm, but will suffer increased misses. These two ways of shifting the criterion describe what happens when a person adopts either a liberal or conservative guessing strategy, respectively. By placing the criterion between the means of the two distributions, the person would be unbiased. The familiarity value at which a person places their criterion is referred to as β (beta), and estimates the tendency to guess.

Given this analysis, signal detection theory provides mathematical tools for estimating a person's ability to discriminate old from new items and their guessing strategies. By computing a person's hit rate (proportion of old items judged old) and their false alarm rate (proportion of new items judged old), one can compute d' and β and so disentangle these factors. More importantly, signal detection theory provides a conceptualization of how recognition judgments take place. The idea that memories lie on a continuum of strength, and that people use this internal "sense" of familiarity to judge their experience with an item has proved to be an extremely useful theory.

Certain phenomena appear challenging, however, for signal detection theory to explain.

For example, on free recall tests, words used frequently in a language are better recalled than are words used infrequently. This advantage makes sense considering that high-frequency words, by virtue of repetition, are likely to be represented more strongly in memory than are low-frequency words and therefore should be easier to encode (Hall, 1954; Sumby, 1963). If item strength underlies this effect, high-frequency words should also be better recognized according to signal detection theory. In fact, the opposite occurs: low-frequency words are better recognized than high-frequency words, a phenomenon known as the *word frequency effect* in recognition memory (e.g. Gorman, 1961; Kinsbourne & George, 1974; Glanzer & Bowles, 1976). The word frequency effect thus suggests that some factor other than item strength must contribute to recognition memory. For these and other reasons, many theorists believe that another process contributes to recognition—a process that is much more akin to recall. We discuss this view next.

Dual-process accounts of recognition memory

Seeking technical advice one afternoon, I made my way to the Media Services Office where a pleasant woman greeted me, all smiles. Responding in kind, I extended my hand, introducing myself saying, "Hi, I'm Mike Anderson from the Psychology department, and I was wondering if there was someone here who might help me with my website." She looked at me blankly, paused, and said, "I know who you are." She did look exceedingly familiar, but I wasn't sure where from. She said, "You really don't remember, do you?" I had to admit that I couldn't place her. She explained that we had gone on a date several years earlier—a date lasting *6 hours*. The date took place in an entirely different city (where she used to live) several hours from where we currently were. The moment she revealed this, I remembered the whole context, and recognized her completely, offering embarrassed apologies. Good friends now, she will never let me forget this event.

This story illustrates something that has happened to most of us—the experience of *knowing* somebody (or some thing), without having the ability to *remember* where from. The experience illustrates an important point: One can have a very high degree of familiarity for a stimulus, but still feel as though recognition is incomplete. It seems as though recognition judgments can be made in one of two ways: You can make a judgment based on how familiar a stimulus seems, a process known as **familiarity-based recognition**; alternatively, you can recognize something by recalling the particulars of the experience, a process known as **recollection**. According to **dual-process theories of recognition**, both of these processes contribute to recognition (Atkinson & Juola, 1974; Mandler, 1980; Jacoby & Dallas, 1981; Aggleton & Brown, 1999; Yonelinas, 1999). The familiarity process is characterized as fast and automatic, yielding, as output, a perception of the memory's strength, without the recall of particulars. It is well characterized by signal detection theory. The recollection process, by contrast, is slow, and more attention demanding, much more like the recall processes emphasized in the earlier part of this chapter—cued recall, to be precise. It involves generating information about the context of experiencing the stimulus.

A number of methods have been developed to isolate the contributions of recollection and familiarity. One method, known as the **remember/know procedure** (Tulving, 1985), asks people to make judgments on the test about why they feel they recognize the item. In particular, people are asked to report whether they recognize each item on the basis of *remembering* (i.e. consciously recollecting the particulars of the study event), or *knowing* (i.e. judging that the item seems very familiar, in the absence of memory for the details of the event). "Remember" responses are taken to measure recollection, whereas "know" responses are taken to measure familiarity-based recognition (Yonelinas, 2002; see also

Gardiner, Ramponi, & Richardson-Klavehn, 2000). Other methods rely instead on people's ability to prove that they can recollect the details of the conditions under which they encountered an item. For instance, in the **process dissociation procedure** (Jacoby, 1991) participants might study a visually presented list of words, followed by a second list of auditorily presented items. On the later recognition test, one group of participants is told to say "Yes" for each test item they remember encountering in *either* the seen or the heard list (the inclusion condition). A different group is asked to say "Yes" *only* to items from the list they heard (i.e. the exclusion condition). In the inclusion condition, people's correct recognition of visually presented items (from the first list) should mix items they recognize based on familiarity, and items they recognize based

KEY TERMS

Familiarity-based recognition: A fast, automatic recognition process based on the perception of a memory's strength. Proponents of dual process models consider familiarity to be independent of the contextual information characteristic of recollection.

Recollection: The slower, more attention-demanding component of recognition memory in dual process models, which involves retrieval of contextual information about the memory.

Dual-process theories of recognition: A class of recognition models that assumes that recognition memory judgments can be based on two independent forms of retrieval process: recollection and familiarity.

Remember/know procedure: A procedure used on recognition memory tests to separate the influences of familiarity and recollection on recognition performance. For each test item, participants report whether it is recognized because the person can recollect contextual details of seeing the item (classified as a "remember" response) or because the item seems familiar, in the absence of specific recollections (classified as a "know" response).

Process dissociation procedure (PDP): A technique for parceling out the contributions of recollection and familiarity within a recognition task.

on recollection. To measure how much of a person's performance is due to the recollection process, we need a way to "subtract out" familiarity. Thus, we need an estimate of familiarity, in the absence of recollection. Cleverly, this can be estimated from people's errors in the exclusion condition. That is, when people are specifically asked to say "Yes" to an item only if they heard it in the second list, then if they accidentally say "Yes" to an item that had been visually presented, it must imply that the item is familiar but that people can't remember for sure where the item is from, and so could not be recollecting it. So, recollection can be estimated by simply subtracting these erroneous errors from the overall recognition rate of items from List 1 in the inclusion condition. These methods can thus be used to isolate the contributions of recollection and familiarity.

In a review of research using these and other methods to measure familiarity and recollection, Andrew Yonelinas (Yonelinas, 2002) identified several generalizations that support the distinction between these processes. First, estimates of whether someone can recollect a stimulus appear to be far more sensitive to disruption by distraction. If your attention is divided during an experience, you are less likely later to have the ability to recollect it, but the stimuli involved in the experience might remain familiar. Similarly, distraction during the recognition test itself is consistently more disruptive to recollection than it is to judgments of familiarity. These findings support the claim that recollection is a controlled, attention-demanding process. Consistent with this view, groups with diminished attention, such as older adults and patients with damage to the prefrontal cortex, often show deficits in recollection, but an intact sense of familiarity for recently seen stimuli. Information about how familiar a stimulus seems is also retrieved much more quickly than information necessary for recollection, consistent with the view that familiarity judgments reflect an automatic process. These findings strongly support the view that two qualitatively distinct retrieval processes underlie recognition.

SOURCE MONITORING

We have talked about retrieval as re-activating a trace based on cues. We often have need, however, to identify the source of what we retrieve. We have already discussed the need to recall the context of an event. Did we take our pills today or yesterday, and did I park here today, or last week? But this is only one case of the broader need to distinguish the sources of one's recollections. Did I hear this story from Susan or Maria? Did I learn this fact from the *National Enquirer* or *Consumer Reports?* Did I *see* the person perform this action or did somebody *tell* me about it? The processes of examining the origins of what we retrieve and deciding whether it is from a particular source is known as **source monitoring** (Johnson, Hashtroudi, & Lindsay, 1993).

Unfortunately, people are not always careful in monitoring where their recollections come from, and so make mistakes. Such mistakes sometimes occur when people let their guard down, as in casual conversations, in which it might not seem important to be sure of the source. For example, you may recall that Maria told you something, when Susan did, and get Maria into trouble. Grandparents may misremember which grandchild is interested in which hobby, or whether they have told you their most recent favorite joke, or someone else. Such misattribution of the source of your recollections is referred to as a source misattribution error.

How do people monitor the sources of their memories? To evaluate source, contextual details need to be recollected so that people

KEY TERM

Source monitoring: The process of examining the contextual origins of a memory in order to determine whether it was encoded from a particular source.

can ascertain a memory's origins. According to Marcia Johnson and colleagues, this occurs by exploiting regularities in the information we receive from different sources. For example, if we need to decide whether we learned a fact by hearing it or reading it, we would evaluate the auditory detail and visual detail in the trace. An abundance of auditory detail would allow us to conclude that we heard it, whereas the converse would be true for visual detail. In deciding whether something we have recalled was a real experience or was imagined, the relative prevalence of perceptual detail as opposed to memory for cognitive operations (e.g. as would be involved in generating an image) would guide our decision about the memory's "realness." Of course, people make mistakes. When someone is induced to form a mental image of a word, he/she is more likely later to mistakenly claim he/she saw a picture of the object (Henkel, Franklin, & Johnson, 2000). This reflects an unintended consequence of relying on the above strategies, with people mistaking imagined details for perceptual experience. Breakdowns in source monitoring may be partially responsible for delusions in which people cannot distinguish their imaginings from true occurrences. We return to a discussion of source misattribution errors in Chapter 10 in our discussion of motivated forgetting, and in Chapter 14, on eyewitness testimony.

SUMMARY

Our long-term memories are capable of storing huge amounts of information, making effective retrieval a priority. As we all know, however, retrieval sometimes fails even given effective encoding. To understand how this happens requires that we understand how retrieval takes place. Retrieval begins with one or more cues that spread activation across associations to traces stored in memory. This process breaks down when the cues are inappropriate or are only weakly associated to the target, when the target was poorly learned, when we cannot devote adequate attention to retrieval, when we do not have enough cues, and even when we are in the wrong "frame of mind" for retrieving. Retrieval success is also influenced—often without our realizing it—by elements of the incidental context at retrieval, and their match to those present at encoding, including environmental, state, mood, and cognitive context. Of course, retrieval strategy can also influence performance, especially when large amounts of information need to be recalled.

Although people tend to think of retrieval as intentionally recalling the past, retrieval takes many forms. Direct tests explicitly measure retention of episodes, and make use of spatio-temporal context as a cue. Context cues are especially important in direct tests such as free recall, but also are needed during cued recall and recognition. By contrast, indirect tests measure the influence of the past with tasks that do not make reference to remembering. Context is not intentionally used as a cue, allowing indirect tests to provide a measure of implicit memory. Implicit memory phenomena such as repetition priming provide evidence for the unconscious influence of experience on behavior, and can be fully intact in amnesic patients. Repetition priming reflects the after-effects of processing in cortical structures outside of the hippocampus, arising from recent encounters with a stimulus. Explicit memory reflects the contribution of additional brain structures, such as the hippocampus, to the storage and retrieval of contextual information.

Recognition memory is thought to involve not one but two retrieval processes. We can recognize having seen a stimulus when it seems familiar to us, an assessment that occurs quickly and automatically. This process is well characterized by a signal detection model, which provides a way of separating true memory from guessing biases. We can also recognize a stimulus by recollecting the occurrence of encountering it before, a process thought to be more attention demanding, slower, and qualitatively distinct from the assessment of familiarity.

Quite often, retrieval involves not merely activating traces but reconstruction through plausible inferences based on background knowledge. Even when active reconstruction is unnecessary, people often make inferences about what they have retrieved, to decide how to use that information. People routinely infer the source of what they remember, for example, to ascertain whether the trace is the one they sought, is trustworthy, and, is in fact, a memory or something imagined. Such attributions involve considering the attributes of the trace recalled, in relation to what would be expected to be stored in memory, given a source. Source misattribution errors reflect one way in which retrieval can break down through an error of commission, rather than omission.

Retrieval failures of the sort experienced by me at the outset of this chapter can clearly arise from a variety of sources. It is important to understand the circumstances under which retrieval fails so that we can understand how retrieval works. When retrieval fails, it raises the question of whether information is truly there, or has been forgotten. In our next chapter, we turn to the subject of forgetting.

FURTHER READING

- **Gabrieli, J. D. E.** (1998). Cognitive neuroscience of human memory. *Annual Review of Psychology*, 49, 87–115.

- **Roediger, H. L., & Guynn, M. J.** (1996). Retrieval processes. In E. L. Bjork and R. A. Bjork (Eds.) *Memory* (Vol. 10, pp. 197–236). San Diego: Academic Press.

- **Yonelinas, A. P.** (2002). The nature of recollection and familiarity: A review of 30 years of research. *Journal of Memory and Language*, 46, 441–517.

Box 8.2 (Answers to Box 8.1)

	Country	First letter of capital city		Country	First letter of capital city
1	Norway	Oslo	11	South Korea	Seoul
2	Turkey	Ankara	12	Syria	Damascus
3	Kenya	Nairobi	13	Denmark	Copenhagen
4	Uruguay	Montevideo	14	Sudan	Khartoum
5	Finland	Helsinki	15	Nicaragua	Managua
6	Australia	Canberra	16	Ecuador	Quito
7	Saudi Arabia	Riyadh	17	Colombia	Bogata
8	Romania	Bucharest	18	Afghanistan	Kabul
9	Portugal	Lisbon	19	Thailand	Bangkok
10	Bulgaria	Sofia	20	Venezuela	Caracus

CHAPTER 9

INCIDENTAL FORGETTING

Michael C. Anderson

O ver the Christmas holiday, my sister asked, "Do you remember when you knocked over the Christmas tree?" I said, "What are you talking about? I never did that!" Puzzled, my sister said, "Yes you did, don't you remember?" My brother added, "Yes, you were hurrying to squeeze behind the tree so you could take a picture of Aunt Dottie and Uncle Jim as they came up the driveway when you knocked the tree over." Indignant, I said, "What … what are you talking about … you must be mixing me up with someone else." My father insisted, "No, you definitely knocked the tree over. It was a big mess, and we made fun of you for it." He added that he remembered me feeling bad about ruining the tree, even though everyone said it was okay. They simply couldn't believe that I had forgotten this.

Reluctantly, I accepted that this event must have happened. I struggled to recall details and couldn't come up with anything. I said, "When did this happen? When I was a kid?" My sister replied, "No, it was about 3 or 4 years ago when we were in New York." I was shocked. I called my other brother and he confirmed every detail and was able to recall the year it had occurred. In fact, I remembered that Christmas in New York and my mother's new camera (which I was using), but I simply could not remember this event. After many months and repeated searching, I still could not bring any trace of the experience to mind.

Before you start wondering whether I'm amnesic, consider how much of *your* life *you* remember. Take a break from reading and try

From life's embarrassing mishaps, to the mundane details of our daily life, many of our memories are forgotten. How and why are certain memories lost while others remain vivid for a lifetime?
© Lambert/Archive Photos.

an exercise. Get out a sheet of paper and list everything that you did from the time you got up until the time you went to bed yesterday, including details about who you saw, and any conversations or thoughts. Chances are, you did pretty well and came up with a lot of detail. Perhaps you left out one or two minor things that you would recall if reminded. Next, do the same thing for the day that occurred *1 week* earlier. You can probably still recall a lot, but with much more effort, and you most likely feel that you are forgetting more. Finally, try the same thing, but for a day that occurred exactly *1 year* prior to yesterday. Try very hard. Most likely, after significant effort, you probably didn't recall much except perhaps some broad outlines that you are probably only guessing at, and only then after much reconstruction. The same uncomfortable fact is true for the majority of the days in your life, except for truly special events and the recent past.

In fact, consider this: *this very moment* that you are consciously experiencing, will, if your history serves as any guide, join the rest of those lost experiences. One cannot help but wonder how it is possible for something that is the full focus of your consciousness right now to ultimately be so completely lost. Is this the fate of all experience? When you are 80, will you only remember 1% of your life in any detail? Are all of your memories there, and just inaccessible?

The function of memory is never more conspicuous and astonishing than when it fails us. In this chapter, we consider the mechanisms that underlie forgetting. One might wonder why forgetting should be treated in a separate chapter from retrieval, in which we discussed why retrieval fails us. Indeed, retrieval failure *is* a form of forgetting. Forgetting is worthy of being distinguished, however, because of the potential for distinct forgetting processes that contribute to retrieval failure. Moreover, an emphasis on forgetting leads one to focus on changes in retrievability over time. What factors produce those changes? What would life be like if we never forgot?

In addressing these questions, research on memory has focused on both **incidental forgetting** and **motivated forgetting**. Incidental forgetting occurs without the intention to forget; motivated forgetting occurs when people engage processes or behaviors that intentionally diminish accessibility for some purpose. It is likely that to explain the full range of experiences that people have with forgetting, theories of both types of forgetting are needed. We discuss incidental forgetting here, and motivated forgetting in the next chapter.

A REMARKABLE MEMORY

What would it be like to remember every thing that ever occurred to you? Although no such person has yet been found, there are people with astounding memory. Recently, Elizabeth Parker, Larry Cahill, and James McGaugh (2006) reported the fascinating case of AJ, a 41-year-old woman who had a breathtaking capacity to remember her past. AJ remembers every single day of her life since her teens in extraordinary detail. Mention any date over several decades and she finds herself back on that day, reliving events and feelings as though they happened yesterday. She can tell you what day of the week it was, events that took place on all surrounding days, and intricate details about her thoughts, feelings, and public events, all of which can be verified by personal diaries she has kept over 30 years. AJ reports that these memories are vivid, like a running movie, and full of emotion. Her remembering feels automatic, and not under conscious control, a claim supported by the fact that her recollections occur immediately, with no struggle.

One might think that having such a remarkable memory would be wonderful. But it's not all good. When unpleasant things happen, AJ wishes she could forget, and the constant bombardment by reminders is distracting and sometimes troubling. In AJ's words:

My memory has ruled my life ... It is like my sixth sense ... There is no effort to it ...

KEY TERMS

Incidental forgetting: Memory failures occurring without the intention to forget.
Motivated forgetting: A broad term encompassing intentional forgetting as well as forgetting triggered by motivations, but lacking conscious intention.

I want to know why I remember everything. I think about the past all the time … It's like a running movie that never stops. It's like a split screen. I'll be talking to someone and seeing something else … Like we're sitting here talking and I'm talking to you and in my head I'm thinking about something that happened to me in December 1982, December 17th, 1982, it was a Friday, I started to work at Gs [a store] … I only have to experience something one time and I can be totally scarred by it … I can't let go of things because of my memory … Happy memories hold my head together … I treasure these memories, good and bad … I can't let go of things because of my memory, it's part of me … When I think of these things, it is kind of soothing … I knew a long time ago, I had an exceptional memory … I don't think I would never want to have this but it's a burden.

Parker et al. (2006) have termed AJ's condition *hyperthymestic syndrome*, from the Greek word *thymesis*, meaning remembering. In short, AJ has uncontrollable remembering. Clearly, AJ's experience of life is very different from ours and illustrates a cost she pays for her perfect memory: she can remember the good times but at the cost of suffering the persistence of bad times. Would you choose AJ's memory over your own? Perhaps forgetting is not all bad. Later in this chapter, we will discuss the possibility that forgetting serves a useful function.

THE FUNDAMENTAL FACT OF FORGETTING

Clearly, AJ's experience is atypical, as most of us forget the events of our days. How are we to understand forgetting? A good place to begin discussing this phenomenon is to acknowledge a fundamental fact: for most people (and organisms), *forgetting increases as time progresses*. Although this surely comes as no surprise, you might not have considered the nature of the relationship between memory and time. If you had to guess, would you say that people forget at a constant rate? To address this question, one simply needs to measure how likely forgetting is as a memory grows older. Once again, the classic study was conducted by Hermann Ebbinghaus (1913), using himself as the participant and nonsense syllables as the material to be learned. Ebbinghaus learned 169 separate lists of 13 nonsense syllables then relearned each list after an interval ranging from 21 minutes to 31 days. He always found that some forgetting had occurred and used the amount of time required to learn the list again as a measure of how much had been forgotten. He found a clear relationship between time and retention.

You will recall from Chapter 3 that the relationship between learning and remembering was more or less linear, with the long-term memory store behaving rather like a bath being filled by a tap running at a constant rate. But how about forgetting? Is it simply like pulling the plug out of the bath, causing information to be lost at a constant rate, or is the relationship less straightforward? The results obtained by Ebbinghaus are shown in Figure 9.1. This graph represents a quantitative relationship between memory and time, referred to as a **forgetting curve**, or sometimes a **retention function**. As you can see, Ebbinghaus's forgetting was extremely rapid at first, but it gradually slowed down over time; the rate of forgetting he exhibited was more logarithmic than linear. As with Ebbinghaus's other work, this result

KEY TERM

Forgetting curve/retention function: The logarithmic decline in memory retention as a function of time elapsed, first described by Ebbinghaus.

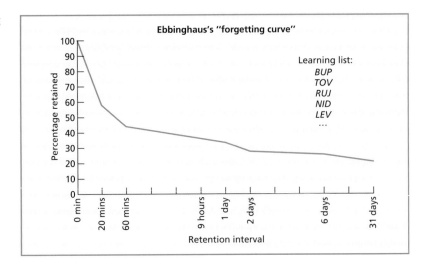

Figure 9.1 The forgetting curve that Ebbinghaus (1913) obtained when he plotted the results of one of his forgetting experiments. His finding, that information loss is very rapid at first and then levels off, holds true for many types of learned materials. Data from Ebbinghaus (1913).

has stood the test of time and applies across a wide range of learning conditions.

Most studies on the rate of forgetting have, like Ebbinghaus's, concerned themselves with highly constrained materials such as lists of nonsense syllables or unrelated words. Is this representative of what happens to personal memories? What happens when more realistic material is recalled over longer intervals? Answering this presents a major problem. Consider the question posed earlier about what you were doing one year ago. If you were to give an answer, how would I know whether you were correct? It is extremely unlikely that the necessary information remains available. One solution is to question respondents about events that were sufficiently noteworthy to attract the attention of most people at the time they happened. This strategy was followed by Meeter, Murre, and Janssen (2005), who selected headlines in both newspapers and television broadcasts for each day over a 4-year period. They amassed over 1000 questions about distinct and dateable events, of which each participant would answer a randomly chosen 40. Cleverly, these investigators used the internet to attract participants, allowing them to test the memory for over 14,000 participants from widely different age groups from countries across the world. They

tested their respondents' memory for these events by both recall and recognition.

The results obtained by Meeter et al. (2005) show that substantial forgetting of public events does occur, with participants' recall for the events dropping from 60 to 30% in just a single year. The forgetting curves showed a steep initial decline, followed by a slowed rate of forgetting at longer delays, especially when recall was tested, much like that observed with nonsense syllables by Ebbinghaus over a century ago. They also found that people performed much more poorly when their recall was tested, recalling only 31% of the answers correctly over the years, compared to 52% correct when they simply had to recognize the right answer from among options. These findings lend confidence to the basic conclusions about forgetting from laboratory studies.

The forgetting curves we have discussed so far have been concerned mainly with memory for distinct events, which are relatively poorly learned. What of information that has been more thoroughly and deliberately learned? Light was thrown on this by an intriguing study by Bahrick, Bahrick, and Wittlinger (1975), who traced 392 American high-school graduates and tested their memory for the names and portraits of classmates. Their study showed that the ability to both

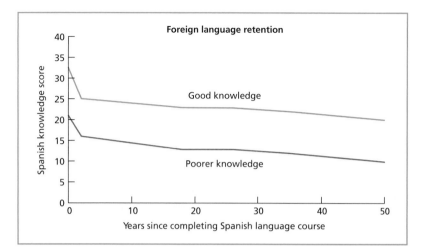

Figure 9.2 People who learned Spanish in college showed rapid forgetting over the first 3 or 4 years, followed by remarkably little forgetting over the next 30 years (Bahrick, 1984). Those who had a good knowledge (upper line, in blue) continued to have a clear advantage, even 50 years later. Data from Bahrick (1984).

recognize a face or a name from among a set of unfamiliar faces or names and to match up names with faces, remained remarkably high for over 30 years. In contrast, the ability to *recall* a name in response to a person's picture showed more extensive forgetting, just as was found in the previously discussed study of memory for major news events.

Harry Bahrick is a Professor at Ohio Wesleyan University, which—in common with many American colleges—has an annual reunion for alumni. Bahrick has made ingenious use of this tradition to study the retention by alumni of a range of material: from the geography of the town where the university is located to the vocabulary of foreign languages learned at college. Figure 9.2 shows the effect of delay on memory for a foreign language (Spanish, in this case). The most striking feature of the graph is the way in which forgetting levels out after about 2 years, with little further loss up to the longest delay, virtually 50 years later. It is as if forgetting occurs only up to a certain point, beyond which memory traces appear frozen. Using an analogy to the permanently frozen ground in Polar regions, known as permafrost, Bahrick (1984) has suggested the term *permastore* for this stable language learning performance. The second point to note is that the overall retention is determined by the level of initial learning, at least as far

as learning a foreign language is concerned. Thus, for well-learned materials, it seems, the forgetting curve might flatten out after an initial period of forgetting, and show little additional forgetting over long periods.

ON THE NATURE OF FORGETTING

The discussion of forgetting functions raises an issue concerning what counts as "forgetting." The studies by Meeter et al. and by Bahrick found much greater forgetting when recall was tested, compared to recognition. In fact, this is a robust pattern: *Recognition is generally easier than recall.* A reasonable conclusion to draw from this fact is that recognition tests reveal that more often resides in memory than is measured by recall. If so, is it truly fair to characterize failures to recall information evident in these forgetting functions as actual forgetting, when many of those unrecalled traces reside in memory? Shouldn't we reserve the term *forgetting* to refer to the permanent loss of traces? This issue highlights a distinction aptly named by Endel Tulving—the distinction between a memory's availability in the cognitive system (whether it is in storage or not), and its accessibility (whether one can access a memory, given that it is stored): the **accessibility/availability distinction**. Should we count inaccessibility as forgetting, or only unavailability?

Unfortunately, reserving *forgetting* to refer only to memories made unavailable renders it impossible to ever measure forgetting. The reason is that determining whether a memory has been permanently lost is quite a bit trickier than one might suspect. What will be our evidence of unavailability? Failed recall? Clearly not, as the foregoing results establish. Failed recognition? Again, recognition can fail, even when it can be proved that a trace is in memory, given the proper reinstatement of context. Although an experience might seem lost forever, perhaps the right cue has just not come along. As discussed in Chapter 8, it took the sight of the passport in the box to pry loose my memory for storing it there. It is thus quite difficult to distinguish inaccessibility from unavailability. Moreover, when memories transition from being recallable to only being recognizable, this might, in principle, be due to weakening of the trace. Permanent loss might not be all or none, but might happen in a graded fashion. For these reasons, and because reduced accessibility is a memory failure, inaccessibility is considered forgetting.

FACTORS THAT DISCOURAGE FORGETTING

The studies by Harry Bahrick illustrate how forgetting, although perhaps inevitable for many memories, might be slowed for some types of knowledge. Which factors discourage forgetting? One obvious point is that if you learn something well to begin with, forgetting is less likely, or at least it takes much longer. But are there some ways of strengthening a memory that increase resistance to forgetting more than others? What memories will you have when you are 80?

The apparent flattening-out of the forgetting curve over time demonstrates that memories are not equally vulnerable to forgetting at all points in their history. Another way of describing the relationship of time and memory is in terms of *Jost's Law*, named after a nineteenth-century psychologist, which states that if two memories are equally strong at a given time, then the older of the two will be more durable and forgotten less rapidly. It is as if two opposing forces are at work to determine retention over time; the mechanisms of forgetting, but also some process that makes surviving memories grow tougher with age. Indeed, it is widely believed that new traces are initially vulnerable to disruption until they are gradually stamped into memory. The time-dependent process by which a new trace is gradually woven into the fabric of memory and by which its components and their interconnections are cemented together is known as *consolidation*. At least two types of consolidation have been proposed. According to research on *synaptic consolidation*, the imprint of experience takes time to solidify because it requires structural changes in the synaptic connections between neurons. These modifications rely on biological processes that may take hours to days to complete (Dudai, 2004). Until those structural changes occur, the memory is vulnerable. Research also implicates a process known as *systemic consolidation*, which holds that the hippocampus is initially required for memory storage and retrieval but that its contribution diminishes over time until the cortex is capable of retrieving the memory on its own (Squire, 1992c; Dudai, 2004). As is discussed further in Chapter 11, the hippocampus is thought to accomplish this by recurrently reactivating the

KEY TERM

Accessibility/availability distinction: Accessibility refers to the ease with which a stored memory can be retrieved at a given point in time. Availability refers to the distinction indicating whether a trace is or is not stored in memory.

brain areas involved in the initial experience (e.g. the areas involved in hearing the sounds, seeing the sights, essentially "replaying" the memory) until these areas are interlinked in a way that could recreate the original memory. Until the memory becomes independent of the hippocampus, it is vulnerable to disruption. Estimates of the duration of systemic consolidation vary, with some evidence suggesting that it might take years in humans. So, it seems that a process exists that strengthens memories over time, retarding their forgetting, and that this process involves recurring retrieval of some sort.

Interestingly, intentionally retrieving an experience also has an especially potent effect on the rate at which a memory is forgotten. This fact was illustrated compellingly by Marigold Linton (1975), using herself as a participant. Every day for 5 years, she noted in her diary two events that had occurred. At predetermined intervals she would randomly select events from her diary and judge whether she could recall them. Given the fact that she was sampling in this way any given event could crop up many times. She was therefore able to analyze her results to find out what effect earlier recalls had on the later memorability of the event. Her results are shown in Figure 9.3;

the items that were not retested showed dramatic forgetting over a 4-year period (65% forgotten). Even a single test was enough to reduce forgetting, whereas items tested on four other occasions showed an impressively low probability of forgetting after 4 years (only 12% forgotten). So, it seems that personal memories, if retrieved periodically, grow resistant to forgetting, in much the same way as did the cases of permastore for well-learned material reported by Bahrick and colleagues. Other examples of the memory-enhancing power of retrieval are discussed in Chapter 16 on improving your memory.

Although retrieval enhances retention, we must be cautious about what is being retrieved. People are tempted to assume that if they are recalling something that happened 20 years ago, that they are recalling a 20-year-old memory. This might be true if we have not recalled the memory in the interim. However, if we have retrieved the memory at all, perhaps we are retrieving a memory of what we have retrieved previously. The event of retrieving something is itself a memory, with its own context, and particulars. The more often that we retrieve an experience, the more of these retrieval events will exist in memory. As long as the information retrieved each time is accurate and complete, this process will enhance recall. If recollections are incomplete or inaccurate due to reconstructive inferences, what we remember may not be what originally happened.

It appears, then, that retrieval might play a very special role in determining which elements of experience will be preserved throughout our lives. Each time that we get together and reminisce with friends or family, we are implicitly selecting which memories to more firmly establish. And for those of us who keep a diary, reviewing the day's events and retrieving them not only provides an objective record of their occurrence but might also increase the longevity of those memories, especially if they are reviewed from time to time. Retrieval clearly has a special effect on retention. Later on, I will discuss research demonstrating that, ironically,

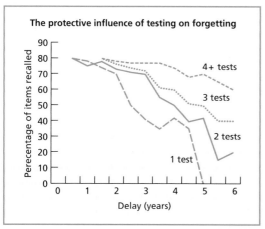

Figure 9.3 The probability of remembering something depends on the number of times it has been retrieved or called to mind. Recalling an event reduces the rate of forgetting. Data from Linton (1975).

retrieval also plays a powerful and complementary role in determining what we forget.

FACTORS THAT ENCOURAGE INCIDENTAL FORGETTING

Knowing that retrieval retards forgetting is useful, but why does forgetting occur in the first place? What factors contribute to retention loss? Experimental psychologists have traditionally emphasized incidental forgetting, stressing the involvement of passive processes that occur as a by-product of changes in the world or the person. For example, forgetting has been attributed to decay, contextual shifts, and to **interference**. This passive view fits the general feeling most of us have that we are the unwilling victims of memory loss. This perspective often fits reality: we do forget things unintentionally, even when they are important. Here, we consider several of the most important factors.

Passage of time as a cause of forgetting

The most obvious way of describing the forgetting curve is that memory gets worse as time goes by. Perhaps the cause is that simple: memory traces grow weaker with time. Memories may simply fade, rather like a notice that is exposed to sun and rain gradually fades until it becomes illegible. The idea that memories get weaker over time is known as **trace decay**. Many investigators favor the view that trace decay partially determines the loss of information from verbal and visual working memory (e.g. Broadbent, 1958; Baddeley, 1986; Cowan, 1988; Page & Norris, 1998; Towse, Hitch, & Hutton, 2000; Gold, Murray, Sekuler, Bennett, & Sekuler, 2005), although this approach has its critics (Nairne, 2002). Decay also plays a role in how theorists think about repetition priming and familiarity, with some proposing that these effects decay quickly (e.g. Eichenbaum, 1994; McKone, 1998; Yonelinas & Levy, 2002). Many

proposals about trace decay have in common the idea that activation decays gradually, even if the item remains stored. For example, recent exposure to the word *helmet* might activate a pre-existing concept. Although activation might fade, the concept remains.

There is another sense of decay, however, in which a memory's structural elements degrade, not just activation levels. Thus, associations between features or the features themselves might deteriorate. Does this happen? This issue is related to the age-old question of whether memories are stored permanently and merely grow inaccessible. On one level, the answer seems obvious: memories are not permanent and decay must exist. We cannot disregard that we are biological beings. Our memories survive in tissue that continually changes, with neurons dying and connections weakening or being modified. We know, for instance, that a time-dependent process degrades the synaptic connections between neurons that support a recently learned behavior in *Aplysia* (a sea slug), with a corresponding degradation in the learned behavior (Bailey & Chen, 1989). It is not far-fetched to believe that a similar degradation occurs in humans, perhaps underlying time-dependent decay. If neurons die, and connections degrade, the survival of memories over long stretches of time in fact seems the greater mystery.

Although decay seems inevitable, experimental psychologists are rightly skeptical about behavioral evidence for it. The reason is that demonstrating decay behaviorally is exceptionally difficult. Proving that decay exists requires a demonstration that forgetting grows over time, in the absence of other activities such as the storage of new experiences or rehearsal. Rehearsal of the memory in question must

KEY TERMS

Interference: The phenomenon in which the retrieval of a memory can be disrupted by the presence of related traces in memory.
Trace decay: The gradual weakening of memories resulting from the mere passage of time.

be controlled because, as discussed earlier, retrieval strengthens memories, which would undercut efforts to see decay. As we will later discuss, storing new experiences after a trace has been encoded must be controlled because new memories introduce interference that might disrupt recall. When these constraints are considered, the person would essentially need to be kept in a mental vacuum, devoid of rehearsal, thoughts, or experiences that might contaminate the state of memory and complicate the interpretation of forgetting. To make matters worse, even if forgetting occurred in the absence of interference, it remains unclear whether the trace has become unavailable, or is merely inaccessible. Thus, it might be impossible to establish evidence for decay behaviorally, even if it does exist.

Correlates of time that cause forgetting

For the foregoing reasons, experimental psychologists have favored the view that time is merely correlated with some other factor that causes forgetting. Two possibilities have been examined. First, as time goes by, the incidental context within which we operate gradually shifts, perhaps impairing retrieval of older memories. Second, over time, people store many new similar experiences that might interfere with retrieving a particular trace. Although these factors do not disprove decay, they provide alternative explanations for the forgetting curve that do not rely on this process.

Contextual fluctuation

As discussed in Chapter 8, retrieval hinges on the number and quality of cues available during recall. When irrelevant cues are used, retrieval can fail. Retrieval can fail when a cue that was previously relevant changes over time. For instance, family members change in appearance, making them match less well the original cue associated to a memory. Moreover, when incidental context at retrieval does not match the one present at encoding, forgetting is more likely. One explanation of the forgetting curve then, is that as time progresses, changes in

context become greater, on average because the world changes and we change. With time, we encounter new stimuli, people, and situations, and we have new thoughts and emotions. As such, one's incidental context will be most similar to the one that we were in a short while ago, and grow less similar over time. The idea that **contextual fluctuation** contributes to forgetting has been advocated in numerous models of memory (e.g. Mensink & Raaijmakers, 1988).

Changes in context may partially explain the striking phenomenon of *infantile amnesia*, which is discussed further in Chapter 12. Infantile amnesia refers to the difficulty most people have in remembering the first several years of their lives. One hypothesis is that the incidental contexts of young children are so vastly different from that of adults that childhood memories simply cannot be retrieved. Young infants have not developed language, for example, and so lack the conceptual and linguistic ambiance in which we exist as adults. Children also surely experience things differently from the adults that they become, with things seeming relatively larger at younger ages. So, infantile amnesia may rest in part on changes in environmental, cognitive, and perhaps emotional context.

Interference

Over time, experiences accumulate. Like the clutter of papers on your desk, adding new memories affects how easily we find things already stored. When memories are similar, this problem should be even worse, like having many similarly labeled papers on a desk. The idea that storing similar traces impedes retrieval is known as *interference*. Interference is likely

> **KEY TERM**
>
> **Contextual fluctuation:** The gradual drift in incidental context over time, such that distant memories deviate from the current context more so than newer memories, thereby diminishing the former's potency as a retrieval cue for older memories.

to be a serious issue when you consider that people are, by their nature, creatures of habit. People enjoy their routines, be they reading the newspaper in the morning, parking in the same spot each day, or getting their morning coffee at the same time. Sticking to routines, however, makes life less memorable. We remember what we had for dinner last night, but not 2 weeks ago. Such forgetting doesn't simply reflect the passage of time. We can easily remember experiences for a long time if they are unique: Having dinner at the neighbors' house a year ago is far more memorable than having dinner at our own house 3 months ago. It is the presence of other traces in memory that compromises retrieval. Because the number of similar traces will increase over time, interference provides a straightforward account of the forgetting curve. The emphasis on interference as a source of forgetting has a long history (Müller & Pilzecker, 1900) and was a preoccupation of research on memory for the nearly three-quarters of a century (see Postman, 1971; Crowder, 1976; Anderson & Neely, 1996, for reviews).

How does adding similar experiences into memory hurt us? To understand this, it is helpful to step back and discuss a fundamental discovery about what likely underlies interference. Early in the history of memory research, investigators identified a central feature in common to most situations associated with interference: Interference arises whenever the cue used to access a target (Figure 9.4, top left) becomes associated to additional memories. The

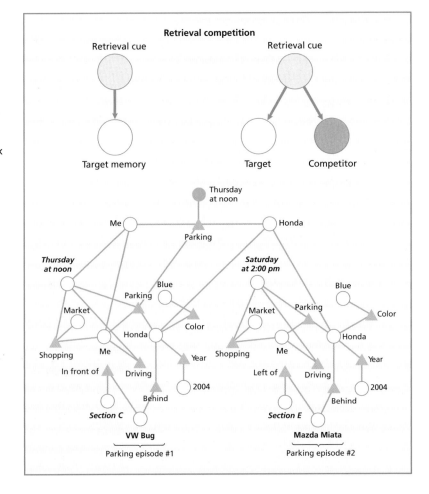

Figure 9.4 Top left: A retrieval cue associated to a single target item. Top right: A retrieval cue becomes associated to a competitor interfering with recall of the target. Bottom: A more complex example of interference, with multiple, shared retrieval cues and complex memories with many features. From Anderson and Neely (1996). Copyright © Academic Press. Reproduced with permission from Elsevier.

canonical interference situation is illustrated in the top right panel of Figure 9.4 in its most general form, with a single cue linked to many associates. By this view, progressing from a cue to a target depends not only on how strongly that cue is associated to the target but also on whether the cue is related to other items. Why does attaching more memories to a cue make retrieving a particular target difficult? Although theories vary about the particulars, most agree that when a cue is linked to multiple items, those items compete with the target for access to awareness, an idea known as the **competition assumption** (Anderson, Bjork, & Bjork, 1994). Essentially, a cue activates all of its associates to some degree, and they "fight" one another. As such, any associates other than the target memory are called *competitors*. In general, any negative effect on memory arising from having competitors is called interference. Interference increases with the number of competitors a target has. This idea is supported by the tendency for recall to decrease with the number of to-be-remembered items paired with the same cue, a generalization known as the **cue-overload principle** (e.g. Watkins, 1978). In essence, as a cue becomes attached to too many things, its capacity to access any one trace is compromised.

How do these ideas explain why storing similar memories causes interference? Consider an example in which you are recalling where you parked your car in a shopping mall you visit frequently. While parking, you will have encoded aspects of your parking experience into a memory. Other parking memories similar to this one will also contain characteristics of the target, including the fact that you drove a car, the type of car you drove (e.g. a 2004 blue Honda) and, perhaps, your goal of shopping. If important elements of the target (e.g. the concepts of yourself, of parking, and of your Honda) serve as the cues to your car's location, other memories sharing those features will be evoked as well. Figure 9.4, bottom, illustrates this by showing how the situation illustrated with one cue may

be scaled up to the many cues available in this example (e.g. "Me," "Parking," and "Honda"). Thus, competition for a shared cue is a useful way of viewing interference between similar traces.

The notion of competition among items that share retrieval cues is very general. For instance, items in memory need not be episodes to compete. Indeed, even retrieving the meaning of a word can involve retrieval interference. To convince yourself of this, try the following demonstration, illustrated in Table 9.1. Each of the words listed in this table has entirely distinct verb and noun meanings, with the verb meaning being the less common. For each word, try to generate an associate of its verb meaning. For instance, for the word *duck*, you would generate a word like *crouch*, signifying that you thought of the verb meaning. Do this for each word as quickly as possible.

For native speakers of English, this task is perplexingly difficult because they instantly retrieve the noun meaning of the word, and must work to get past that dominant association. If this happened to you, you experienced competition from the noun meaning during the retrieval of the verb.

Interference phenomena

A number of qualitatively distinct situations produce interference. For instance, the storage of new experiences can interfere with retrieving older ones, but older memories can also impede retrieval of newer ones. In this section, we review some of the most important interference phenomena and key results that

> ### KEY TERMS
>
> **Competition assumption:** The theoretical proposition that the memories associated to a shared retrieval cue automatically impede one another's retrieval when the cue is presented.
> **Cue-overload principle:** The observed tendency for recall success to decrease as the number of to-be-remembered items associated to a cue increases.

Table 9.1: Interference effects

	Cue	Related verb
E.g.	*Duck*	*Crouch*
1	*Loaf*	
2	*Post*	
3	*Court*	
4	*Root*	
5	*Sock*	
6	*Shed*	
7	*Fence*	
8	*Lobby*	
9	*Stump*	
10	*Fawn*	
11	*Lodge*	
12	*Sign*	
13	*Bark*	
14	*Pine*	
15	*Bowl*	
16	*Prune*	
17	*Duck*	
18	*Rail*	
19	*Sink*	
20	*Ring*	

Adapted from Johnson and Anderson (2004).

have been discovered. It is important to bear in mind that although the particulars of these situations vary, the underlying mechanisms that produce forgetting may in fact be similar. In the section to follow, we consider candidate mechanisms.

Retroactive interference

At the beginning of this chapter, you were asked to list all of the things you did yesterday, the same day last week, and the same day last year. If you did this exercise, you undoubtedly confronted the uncomfortable fact that you remember little of what has happened in your life. Why? As we have discussed, the difficulty might be due to several sources, including decay and contextual fluctuation. But there is an excellent chance that a lot of that forgetting comes about due to **retroactive interference**. Retroactive interference refers to forgetting caused by encoding new traces into memory in between the initial encoding of the target and when it is tested. Essentially, some process associated with storing newer experiences impairs the ability to recall ones farther back in time. With every new trip to McDonald's, every morning ride on the bus, and every day you spend seated in front of a computer screen at work, previous McDonald's trips, morning rides, and days at work grow farther from your mental grasp.

The methods used to study retroactive interference have tended to focus on simple materials that conform closely to the canonical interference situation described earlier. This phenomenon is often studied using the classic retroactive interference design illustrated in the left half of Figure 9.5. In the experimental condition, people study a first list of pairs (upper box), and then a second list. Very often the pairs in the first list (e.g. *dog–sky*) have their cue words repeated in the second list, but are paired with a new response word (e.g. *dog–rock*) that people have to learn in place of the older one. After the second list is learned, people are usually tested by giving them the first word of each pair and asking them to recall the response from the first list (e.g. *dog–?*). In the control condition, people also study a first list, but engage in irrelevant filler activity in the interval, during which people in the experimental condition study

KEY TERM

Retroactive interference: The tendency for more recently acquired information to impede retrieval of similar older memories.

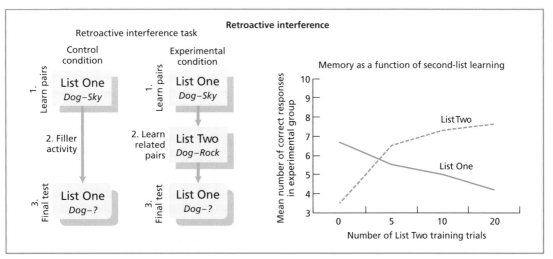

Figure 9.5 Left: A retroactive interference task in which participants learn two lists of word pairs, in series. A control group skips second-list learning. Right: Final cued-recall results (for both lists) by list-two training trials. Memory for list two increases with practice, while list one declines with list-two practice. Data from Barnes and Underwood (1959).

the second list. Thus, these two conditions allow us to ask the crucial question: "What is the effect of learning new information (i.e. list two) on the ability to remember information that was previously studied (i.e. list one), relative to a situation in which no additional information was learned at all (i.e. control condition)?"

The general findings are that: (1) introducing a highly related second list impairs the ability to recall items from the first list, compared to the control; and (2) increased training on second-list items continues to harm retention of first-list items further, as training progresses. This is especially true when the lists one and two share a common cue word (e.g. *dog*, as in the previous example); in fact, there is often little retroactive interference when the pairs on the two lists are unrelated. Thus, not every type of intervening experience impairs memory—the experience needs to be similar. A typical example of retroactive interference is illustrated in the right half of Figure 9.5, which is taken from a classic study by Barnes and Underwood (1959). Notice that as people were given increasing amounts of training on the second list of pairs, their memory for those pairs gets better, whereas their retention

of first-list pairs grows quite a bit worse. We know that this increased forgetting is not due to the mere passage of time, because in the control condition the same amount of time has gone by in between learning the pairs and the final test. Thus, learning something new can impair memory substantially.

But are the lessons from artificial laboratory materials applicable to memory for personal experiences? It would be helpful if it could be shown that something like retroactive interference occurs with realistic memories. Such studies exist and generally confirm the importance of retroactive interference. In one study by Hitch and Baddeley, rugby players were asked to recall the names of the teams they had played earlier in the season (Baddeley & Hitch, 1977). Figure 9.6 shows the probability of their recalling the name of the last team played, the team before that, and so forth. It proved to be the case that most players had missed some games, either due to injury or other commitments, so that for one player the game before last might have taken place a week ago and for another it might have been 2 weeks or even a month before. It was therefore possible to ascertain whether forgetting depended on elapsed time or on the number of

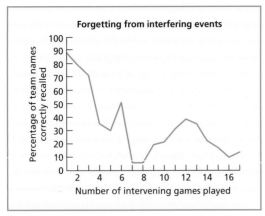

Figure 9.6 This graph, showing rugby players' memory for the names of teams recently played, demonstrates the tendency for recent events to interfere with memory of similar events from the past. Data from Baddeley and Hitch (1977).

intervening games. The result was clear. Time was relatively unimportant, whereas the number of intervening games was critical, indicating that forgetting was due to interference rather than trace decay. Apparently, their memory of having played a whole rugby game could be made less accessible simply because they have played many rugby games since then.

Proactive interference

One afternoon, I walked up to the top of an exceptionally steep street outside the psychology department to discover, to my horror, that my car had been stolen. After a moment's reflection, I realized that I had not parked my car there this *afternoon*, but rather this *morning*. This afternoon, I had parked my car on an entirely different, preposterously steep hill one street over. I was the unhappy victim of *proactive interference*, or the tendency for older memories to interfere with the retrieval of more recent experiences and knowledge. Most of us are acquainted with the irritation of proactive interference. It occurs, for example, when we fail to recall our new password because our old one intrudes during recall, refusing to be ignored or abandoned simply because it is out of date. Or, if we are seriously unlucky, we might call our current

partner by our previous partner's name in an absent-minded moment. In each case, well-encoded events or facts rear their ugly head and disrupt retrieval of something more recent.

Although we have emphasized how retroactive interference affects long-term retention, proactive interference plays a powerful role in determining the rate of forgetting. This was demonstrated dramatically by Benton Underwood. Underwood (1957) was interested in explaining why participants who had learned a list of nonsense syllables should show so much forgetting after 24 hours. It occurred to Underwood that proactive interference was a real possibility. The reason was that almost all work on human learning at the time was done in a few laboratories, all of which used undergraduate participants. If you happened to be a student in one of these departments, you were likely to be required to participate for many hours in verbal learning studies. Underwood thought that it might be interference from the many *previous* lists of nonsense syllables that caused forgetting. Fortunately, it was possible to find out how many previous lists each participant had learned in other experiments and to plot the amount of forgetting in a 24-hour period as a function of this prior experience. In fact, naive students, who had no previous experience remembered 80% of the list items after 24 hours, whereas students with 20 or more prior learning trials on different lists remembered fewer than 20% 24 hours later. Proactive interference had a giant effect on retention, largely determining the rate at which students forgot the material after an extended delay.

Experiments examining proactive interference have often used an experimental design that is highly related to the retroactive interference design described earlier. The proactive interference paradigm (Figure 9.7) resembles the retroactive interference design, except that: (1) it tests people's memory for the list-two responses rather than the list-one responses; and (2) in the control condition, the rest period (or performance of irrelevant activity) replaces list-one learning rather than list-two learning.

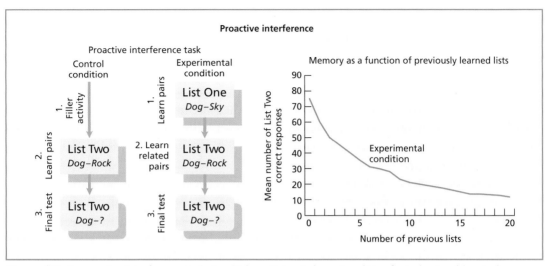

Figure 9.7 A proactive interference task, in which participants learn two lists of word pairs. A control group skips first-list learning. Right: A meta-analysis of final test cued-recall data following a 24-hour delay, given varying numbers of preceding lists. List-two memory decreases as the number of prior lists increases. Adapted from Underwood (1957).

Thus, this design allows us to explore how previously acquired knowledge (i.e. list one) might impair our ability to recollect new information (i.e. list two), relative to a situation in which the previous knowledge had not been learned (control, list two). Studies using the proactive interference procedure have demonstrated that people are more likely to forget items from a list when a prior list has been studied. The amount of proactive interference is greatest when the two lists share a common cue. Proactive interference effects are most severe when recall is tested rather than recognition.

Part-set cuing impairment

Recent exposure to one or more competitors exacerbates the problems we have in retrieving a target memory. For example, most of us have forgotten the name of someone and have been offered assistance by a well-meaning friend who supplies guesses about the name we are seeking. Unless the friend is lucky and guesses correctly, it often feels as though his or her suggestions make matters worse. Sometimes recall fails until a much later point when, unencumbered by the clutter of incorrect guesses,

your mind yields the delinquent name. If you have had this happen, you have had firsthand experience with the phenomenon of **part-set cuing impairment**.

Part-set cuing impairment refers to the tendency for target recall to be impaired by the provision of retrieval cues drawn from the same set (e.g. category) of items in memory (Mueller & Brown, 1977). The basic finding was discovered by Slamecka (1968), who had people study lists composed of words from several semantic categories (e.g. *trees*, *birds*). On the final test, some people were given some of the members from each category as cues to help them recall the remainder; others were given no such cues. Of concern was people's recall of the remaining noncue items in the experimental condition relative to recall for those items when no cues were given.

KEY TERM

Part-set cuing impairment: When presenting part of a set of items (e.g. a category, a mental list of movies you want to rent) hinders your ability to recall the remaining items in the set.

Have you ever walked into a store, only to forget about your intended purchase? Blame part-set cueing, the tendency for the presence of some items as retrieval cues (like the CDs on display in the storefront) to impair one's ability to retrieve other items within the same set (the desired CD).

Slamecka expected that the cues would help recall for the noncue items. To his surprise, when recall was scored for the noncue items, people receiving cues performed worse than those who received no cues! This has become known as part-set cuing impairment because providing part of the set (in this case, part of the category) as cues impaired recall of the remaining items. Part-set cuing might be one reason why every musical CD that we make a "mental note" to purchase the next time we are at the store seems to disappear from our minds the moment we enter and peruse items displayed on the shelves.

The idea that supplying hints might impair memory is both surprising and ironic. In retrospect, however, it makes good sense, given the situation of interference described at the outset. Presumably, a set of items is defined by some common cue (e.g. *fruit* or *birds*), to which many items are associated. If presenting some items from the set strengthens their associations to the cue, perhaps stronger items provide greater competition during the retrieval of noncue items, impairing their recall. The idea that cues add more competition is consistent with the finding that as more members of the set are provided as cues, the worse memory becomes for the remainder (see Nickerson, 1984, for a review).

If people's instinct to be helpful and provide cues sometimes harms memory, what would happen if a group of people got together and tried to collaboratively remember things that they had all experienced or learned? Would one person's recounting prompt others to remember more than they would have, or might it cause part-set cuing impairment? Recent work indicates that when people get together to remember material that they each learned, they remember less when recalling the information as a group than they do when each person recalls information separately and their results combined into a common score. This phenomenon, known as **collaborative inhibition** can arise from the mechanisms that produce part-set cuing inhibition (Weldon & Bellinger, 1997). If group members are generating lots of items while you are listening, the interference this causes can disrupt your retrieval. Thus, research on part-set cuing might help to explain the effects of group effort on generating a diversity of new ideas and recollections.

Retrieval-induced forgetting

An ironic feature of human memory is that the very act of remembering causes forgetting. It's not that remembering harms memory for the retrieved experience. Rather, retrieval can harm recall of other memories or facts related to the retrieved item. Anderson et al. (1994) referred to this phenomenon as **retrieval-induced forgetting**.

KEY TERMS

Collaborative inhibition: A phenomenon in which a group of individuals remembers significantly less material collectively than does the combined performance of each group member individually when recalling alone.
Retrieval-induced forgetting (RIF): The tendency for the retrieval of some target items from long-term memory to impair the later ability to recall other items related to those targets.

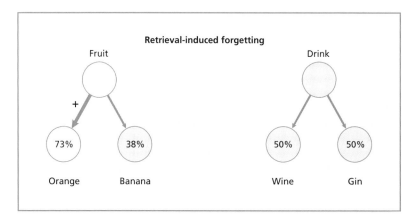

Figure 9.8 In this example, participants perform retrieval practice on *orange* but not *banana* or any members from the *drink* category (baseline). The final test scores indicate that, relative to baseline, practice facilitates recall of the practiced items, whereas unpracticed items from practiced categories suffer retrieval-induced forgetting. Adapted from Anderson (2003).

The phenomenon of retrieval-induced forgetting is usually studied with a procedure known as the **retrieval practice paradigm** (Anderson et al., 1994), which is illustrated in Figure 9.8. In this procedure, people first study simple verbal categories, like *fruits, drinks,* and *trees* for a later memory test. Following this, people are asked to repeatedly recall some of the examples that they just studied, from some of the categories. For example, participants might receive the cues *fruit-or—* for the retrieval of the item *orange.* Following retrieval practice, a test is given in which people are asked to recall all examples that they remember seeing from every category. Clearly, on this final test, people will recall the examples that they practiced quite well. More interesting, however, is how well they recall the remaining unpracticed examples (e.g. *fruit–banana*), compared to unpracticed items from baseline categories that are also studied, but none of whose examples receive retrieval practice (e.g. *drinks–scotch*). Strikingly, as can be seen in Figure 9.8, retrieval practice enhances recall of practiced items (e.g. *fruit–orange*), but it impairs related items (e.g. *fruit–banana*). So, it seems that the very act of remembering can cause forgetting.

If retrieval causes forgetting, students might have reason to be concerned about how they study for exams. Consider the plight of students who have limited time to prepare. You must prioritize your time, and the issue arises as to what to pass over.

Research on retrieval-induced forgetting suggests that selectively reviewing facts impairs nonreviewed material, particularly related material. Neil Macrae and Malcolm MacLeod (1999) tested this idea by giving students facts like those they might learn in a classroom. Participants studied ten geography facts about each of two fictitious islands (*Tok* and *Bilu*; e.g. *The official language of Tok is French* or *Bilu's only major export is copper*). Students then performed retrieval practice. For one island, they practiced retrieving five of its ten facts. A final test followed, cued by the name of each island. Macrae and MacLeod found that practice facilitated the later recall of practiced facts (70%) over baseline facts about the unpracticed island (38%), but at the cost of impairing retention of related but unpracticed facts (23%). Similar effects have been demonstrated with complex textual materials when the test involved either short-answer or essay tests, although not on multiple-choice exams (Carroll, Campbell-Ratcliffe, Murnane, & Perfect, 2007). So, one must be careful about what one leaves out whilst studying, because omitting material will hasten its forgetting.

Selective retrieval occurs often in daily life. One situation of concern arises when members

KEY TERM

Retrieval practice paradigm: A procedure used to study retrieval-induced forgetting.

of law enforcement, detectives, and lawyers interview a witness after a crime. Answering interrogators, of course, requires retrieval. John Shaw, a psychologist who had once been a Los Angeles public defender, thought that such questioning might harm witnesses' memories for nonquestioned material, an intuition based on experiences with some of his own clients. To examine this possibility, Shaw, Bjork, and Handal (1995) told a group of participants to imagine that they had attended a party and that, on leaving, they noticed that their wallet was missing. Participants then watched slides of a student's apartment and paid attention to the details contained therein so that they might assist the police in an investigation. The slides contained a number of household items plus two categories of critical items (i.e. college sweatshirts and schoolbooks). Participants were then given structured questions about some of the objects (e.g. sweatshirts) during the *interrogation phase*. Consistent with Shaw's experience, they found that interrogating people about some stolen items impaired their memory for related items. So, retrieval-induced forgetting could have significant implications for how witnesses should be questioned.

If retrieval impairs memory, then simply discussing an experience with someone might alter whether people will remember what was omitted. Conroy and Salmon (2006) examined

Retrieval-induced forgetting suggests that selectively reviewing facts impairs non-reviewed material. What implications could this have for the questioning procedures used, for example, in a court of law? © Tim Pannell/Corbis.

this idea by having young children participate in a staged event at school called *Visiting the pirate*, during which the children engaged in a number of activities across a variety of scenes. For example, in the *Becoming a pirate* scene, the children were asked to hoist a sale, bang a drum, put on pirate clothes, greet a pirate, and put their name in the pirate's book; whereas in the *Winning the key* scene, they might have fed a bird, looked through a telescope, steered the pirate ship, and done a dance. On the next 3 days, the children discussed the event with another experimenter, who asked them questions about only some parts, such as, "Tell me about the animal that you fed." On the final day, the children recalled the nondiscussed elements less well than did a control group of children who engaged in no discussion at all. Conroy and Salmon speculated that children's memory of their growing up years will be shaped by the way in which parents and family members reminisce, with nondiscussed aspects growing appreciably less accessible over time.

If discussions with other people about a shared past can lead one to forget what is not discussed, then forgetting can, in a sense, be contagious. A friend who has forgotten some parts of an experience will leave the forgotten parts out while reminiscing about it. Might selective remembering on the part of one person cause forgetting of the non-discussed material in others? Alexandru Cuc, Jonathan Koppel, and William Hirst (2007) looked at this possibility in recent work on socially-shared retrieval-induced forgetting. One study replicated the experiment of Anderson et al. (1994; discussed earlier) with a twist: they had two people, seated side by side, studying the same pairs. In the retrieval practice phase, however, one participant performed retrieval practice whereas the other sat silently and observed, monitoring their partner's recollections for accuracy. Both then took the final test. As expected, the participant who performed retrieval practice showed retrieval-induced forgetting. Surprisingly, however, the silent observer also showed this effect. Cuc and colleagues observed the same effect when they used stories as materials; they even observed it when people were allowed to discuss the stories freely with one another: The nondiscussed elements of the story for one person were more likely to be forgotten by the other. It seems that when we are amongst others discussing past events, we spontaneously recall those events along with the person doing the recounting, and, in doing so, subject ourselves to retrieval-induced forgetting for whatever the speaker remains silent about. If this is so, then retrieval-induced forgetting might be one mechanism by which a society's collective memory of an event comes to be more uniform over time. It might also provide a means of political manipulation, when silences about certain facts or events are deliberate, and mass media is used to trumpet certain elements of the past. As Cuc and colleagues remark, "Silence is not always golden."

Retrieval thus appears to be a powerful force that shapes memory, for the better and for the worse. As discussed earlier, Marigold Linton's observations indicate that retrieval greatly enhances the longevity of a memory, but the current results show that, when retrieval is incomplete, the benefits might be offset by the forgetting of other things. To understand the importance of this finding, one need only consider how pervasive this basic process is in our daily cognitive experience. That is, any cognitive act that makes reference to traces stored in memory, which is likely to be all processes, employs retrieval. If retrieval is a source of forgetting, then accessing what we already know might contribute to forgetting, independent of the encoding of new experience. The role of retrieval in causing forgetting has led to a new perspective on why the situation of interference is associated with forgetting (Figure 9.9). We discuss this perspective shortly.

Interference mechanisms

As the preceding discussion illustrates, many "interference" situations impair retention. Although these phenomena describe *when* forgetting will arise, they do not say *how* forgetting occurs—that is, they do not specify the mechanisms. Why does presenting cues impair recall? Why does retrieval-induced forgetting occur? Why does introducing new learning impair retention of previously acquired material? First, we consider classical mechanisms proposed to explain interference, and show how they can be extended to explain phenomena like part-set cuing and retrieval-induced forgetting. Then we consider a more recent view in which inhibitory processes associated with retrieval cause forgetting.

Associative blocking

Once, while recalling the British term for what Americans call a "Christmas ornament," I persistently recalled "Christmas balls" (what

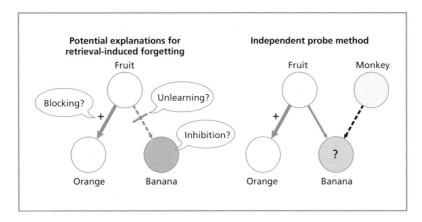

Figure 9.9 Left: Practiced items could block target recall during the final test, producing retrieval-induced forgetting. Alternatively, the connection between cue and target could have been unlearned during retrieval practice. Inhibition involves a reduction in the target memory's activation, itself. Right: Only inhibition correctly predicts that forgetting generalizes to independent cues.

Belgians call Christmas ornaments), instead of "Christmas baubles." "Christmas balls" kept intruding until I gave up. In essence, "Christmas balls" blocked "Christmas baubles." After drifting off to other activities, the right answer "popped" to mind. Perhaps something like this tip-of-the-tongue experience might explain interference. For instance, in retroactive interference, people might forget first-list responses because the cue used to access them now elicits the second-list responses. In part-set cuing, presenting exemplar cues might strengthen their association to the category, leading them to intrude when people try to retrieve noncue exemplars. In each case, a cue elicits a stronger competitor, leading us to perseverate helplessly on something that we know to be incorrect. The idea that such a process explains interference was proposed by McGeoch in his (1942) *response competition theory*, modern versions of which are known as **associative blocking** (see Anderson et al., 1994).

The core assumption of the blocking hypothesis is the idea that memories compete for access to awareness when their shared cue is provided. The degree of interference should increase as the cue grows more strongly associated to the competitor, exhibiting what Anderson et al. (1994) refer to as *strength-dependent competition*. But how does a stronger competitor impair recall? Consider an example from retrieval-induced forgetting, in which you are trying to recall *banana* after having practiced *fruit–orange*. According to the blocking theory, the cues on the final test (e.g. *fruit*) to recall *banana* lead the person to accidentally retrieve the stronger practiced item, *orange*. Once accidentally retrieved, *orange* will achieve greater prominence, having been practiced again, making it even more likely to be accidentally retrieved. And so the cycle would continue, because, with each accidental retrieval, the wrong answer grows stronger. Eventually, people might simply give up. So, according to the blocking theory, people forget unpracticed exemplars of practiced categories

because associations to the practiced memories dominate retrieval. Blocking can also explain the cue-overload principle: The more memories associated to a cue, the more likely it should be to accidentally retrieve a wrong answer, setting the blocking process in motion. If so, the reason you can't remember your dinner 4 months ago is because retrieval calls to mind recent dinners to such an extent that you give up.

Associative unlearning

Suppose that your acquaintance describes a conversation at a party several years ago. You might recall, in good detail, elements of the party, including your friend's attendance, various conversations, as well as several amusing events. However, you might forget discussing a topic with your friend, despite your friend's most confident confirmations—even when you clearly recollect discussing the topic. Subjectively, it seems as though your memory has become fragmented, impairing your judgment about how elements of the experience go together. This apparent fragmentation can reflect damage to the associations between elements of that event caused by storing subsequent experiences. Perhaps such damage underlies my inability to recollect knocking over the Christmas tree.

Research on the **unlearning** hypothesis of retroactive interference (Melton & Irwin,

---

KEY TERMS

Associative blocking: A theoretical process hypothesized to explain interference effects during retrieval, according to which a cue fails to elicit a target trace because it repeatedly elicits a stronger competitor, leading people to abandon efforts to retrieve the target.

Unlearning: The proposition that the associative bond linking a stimulus to a memory trace will be weakened when the trace is retrieved in error when a different trace is sought.

1940) is relevant to these ideas. According to the hypothesis, the association between a stimulus and a trace will be weakened whenever that trace is retrieved inappropriately. In effect, the bond between the cue and the target gets "punished." For example, suppose that you try to retrieve the new password to your e-mail account. According to the unlearning view, if you recall your old password and realize the mistake, the association between the cue password and the original password will get weakened, decreasing the chances that it will pop up again in the future. If the old password is punished often enough, the association might grow so weak that it will no longer activate that trace; the stimulus will be decoupled from the response. This view can explain retrieval-induced forgetting if we assume that, during retrieval practice, competing items intrude and are punished. It explains retroactive interference in the same way. So, whereas blocking attributes forgetting to very strong competitors, unlearning says that associations into the target are too weak.

The unlearning and blocking hypotheses are not incompatible. In fact, according to the classical two-factor model of retroactive interference (Melton & Irwin, 1940), both mechanisms are needed. It is worth emphasizing, however, that proof of unlearning is difficult to establish, for the same reasons that it is difficult to prove that memories are permanently forgotten, as discussed earlier in this chapter. Also, although blocking explains why forgetting appears to grow in magnitude as competitors are strengthened, there are reasons to doubt whether strengthening a competitor, by itself, produces forgetting, as will be illustrated shortly. For these reasons, an alternative view has arisen that attributes the forgetting arising from interference to inhibitory processes.

Inhibition as a cause of forgetting

The preceding discussion raises an important point: Sometimes it is maladaptive for a trace to be accessible. Retrieving a target can be disrupted by highly accessible competitors and people need a way to limit this distraction. Although unlearning is one way to accomplish this, another is to inhibit the offending trace. Consider an analogy. Suppose that you normally wear a watch, but one day the wristband breaks and you can't wear it. If someone then asks you what time it is, you might look at your wrist reflexively, even when you know the watch is absent. This might happen several times before you learn to look at the clock instead. Clearly, what is normally a useful and overlearned habit has, for the time being, become an inappropriate response that must be shut down so that an alternative but more appropriate response can be given. Humans and other organisms have the ability to terminate responses, either so that an alternative can be given or so that all responding can be stopped. Stopping is thought to be accomplished by a mechanism that inhibits the response. Inhibition reduces the activity level of the response, ceasing its production in a manner analogous to how inhibiting a neuron would reduce its influence on other neurons.

The same demands confronted in shutting down interfering responses occur for internal actions, such as retrieval. As discussed in the section on proactive interference, if somebody asks for our telephone number, we might automatically remember our old number even though we have switched phones. Recalling the new number requires that we stop retrieval of the old one, which can be accomplished by inhibition. If the old number is inhibited, however, it will grow harder to recall, even if it remains available. In the context of retrieval-induced forgetting, *banana* might become activated and intrude during the retrieval of *fruit–or—*. To facilitate the retrieval of *orange*, perhaps *banana* is inhibited, with persisting inhibition making it harder to retrieve that item. *Banana*, like the habit of looking at one's wrist, might be inhibited to support the current goals. Are inhibitory processes engaged during retrieval?

One area of research that has examined the role of inhibition during retrieval is retrieval-induced forgetting (Levy & Anderson, 2002). Inhibition makes several predictions about retrieval-induced forgetting that are not made by either the blocking or unlearning theories. According to inhibition, performing retrieval practice on *fruit–orange* impairs the recall of *banana* because *banana*, as the competing memory (like looking at the wristwatch), is inhibited by activation-reducing mechanisms. If *banana* is truly inhibited, one might imagine that *banana* would be harder to recall generally, whether one tests it with *fruit* as a cue, or, say, another unrelated associate, such as *monkey–b—*. In other words, inhibition predicts that retrieval-induced forgetting should generalize to new cues, thus exhibiting *cue independence*. By contrast, both blocking and unlearning attribute forgetting to problems with the associations linking *fruit* to either *banana* or *orange*. Hence, according to these theories, retrieval-induced forgetting should be cue dependent. That is, as long as you switch to another cue, like *monkey*, which circumvents the stronger association from *fruit* to *orange* and the potentially weaker association from *fruit* to *banana*, no impairment should be found for *banana*. Cue-independent forgetting has been observed many times (Anderson & Spellman, 1995; see Anderson, 2003, for a review), indicating that inhibition does play a role in causing retrieval-induced forgetting.

According to the inhibition hypothesis, the need to overcome interference during retrieval triggers inhibition. If so, then active retrieval on practiced items should be necessary to induce forgetting of competitors. For example, simply replacing retrieval practice trials (e.g. *fruit–or—*) with a chance to re-study *fruit–orange* multiple times should eliminate later forgetting of competitors like *banana*. Forgetting should disappear because giving people *fruit–orange* to study eliminates any struggle to retrieve *orange*, and thus any need to resolve interference from *banana*. This retrieval-specificity property is a consistent feature of retrieval-induced forgetting (see Anderson, 2003). Thus, even though both retrieval practice and extra study exposures strengthen memory for the practiced items to the same degree, only retrieval practice impairs retention of the unpracticed competitors. There appears to be something special about the need to reach into memory and retrieve something that induces forgetting, consistent with the idea that inhibition is involved. This finding doesn't favor the blocking hypothesis, however, which predicts that strengthening practiced shapes should impair recall of competitors, regardless of whether strengthening is accomplished by retrieval or study.

If inhibitory processes overcome interference from competitors, the amount of retrieval-induced forgetting should depend on the degree of interference during retrieval practice. If the other associates of a cue don't cause interference, inhibition should be unnecessary. In an early demonstration of this, Anderson et al. (1994) varied whether competing items were high-frequency examples of their respective categories (e.g. *fruit–banana*) or low-frequency examples (e.g. *fruit–guava*). Intuitively, one might imagine that a high-frequency example like *banana* would be resistant to forgetting, whereas a low-frequency item might be vulnerable. The analogy to the wristwatch example, however, suggests that the opposite could be true. It is precisely because one reflexively checks one's wrist when the watch is not there that one must inhibit that response to prevent it from occurring. If so, then high-frequency examples, like *fruit–banana* might be prime targets for inhibition because they come to mind so readily, whereas low-frequency exemplars might not need to be inhibited. This is exactly what Anderson and colleagues found. This property is known as *interference dependence*, or the tendency for retrieval-induced forgetting to be triggered by interference from a competing item.

One important feature of retrieval-induced forgetting that speaks against blocking theories is that the amount of forgetting appears unrelated to how strong the practiced associations become as a result of practice. Research on retrieval specificity, for example, shows that it is possible to greatly strengthen practiced items through repeated study, without impairing unpracticed competitors. If strengthening practiced items were enough to cause forgetting, one should have observed forgetting under these circumstances. Indeed, strengthening a competitor may not be necessary at all to trigger retrieval-induced forgetting. In a recent study, Benjamin Storm, Elizabeth Bjork, Robert Bjork, and John Nestojko (2006) had the clever idea to see whether it was merely the retrieval attempt that created retrieval-induced forgetting. Participants in this retrieval practice paradigm were, for some categories, given retrieval practice cues that were impossible to complete. So, for example, they might have received the cue *fruit–lu—* to complete during retrieval practice, even though no fruit begins with *lu*. Strikingly, even though people could not complete any of these retrieval practice tests, they showed as much retrieval-induced forgetting for the remaining unpracticed exemplars as they did for categories in which retrieval practice trials could be completed. So the struggle to extract a trace from memory, in the face of interference is the important trigger for retrieval-induced forgetting, not the strengthening of the practiced items. This property is referred to as *strength independence*.

Taken together, the properties of cue independence, retrieval specificity, interference dependence, and strength independence converge to support a role of inhibition as a source of forgetting (Table 9.2). If so, it suggests that many of our experiences with forgetting might arise from the need to control interference. It is precisely because we are distracted by momentarily irrelevant information in our memories—those unintended looks at our "mental wristwatch"—that we engage inhibition to refocus on what we hope to retrieve from memory. On the one hand, it might seem ironic that the mechanisms

Table 9.2: Properties of retrieval-induced forgetting

Property of retrieval-induced forgetting	Description
Cue independence	The tendency for forgetting caused by inhibition to generalize to novel test cues on the independent probe test (e.g. *monkey–b—* for *banana*, which was originally studied with the cue *fruit*)
Retrieval specificity	Active retrieval from long-term memory is necessary to induce forgetting of related information. For example, having to retrieve *orange*, given *fruit–or—* generates retrieval-induced forgetting of unpracticed competitors (e.g. *banana*), whereas simply studying the intact pairing (*fruit–orange*) does not
Strength independence	The degree to which competitors are strengthened by retrieval practice is unrelated to the size of the retrieval-induced forgetting deficit. Thus, strengthening an item by presenting the intact pairing (*fruit–orange*) does not induce retrieval-induced forgetting, whereas engaging in an impossible retrieval attempt (e.g. *fruit–lu—*) still results in forgetting of unpracticed competitors
Interference dependence	Interference by competitors during retrieval of targets is necessary for retrieval-induced forgetting of those competitors to occur. Therefore, high-frequency competitors (e.g. *fruit–banana*), which pose greater competition than low-frequency competitors (e.g. *fruit–guava*) are more likely to be inhibited than vice versa

we use to direct retrieval are the ones that ultimately contribute to forgetting. On the other hand, as Robert Bjork suggests, such forgetting might be adaptive because it helps to reduce interference from information that might no longer be as relevant as it once was (Bjork, 1989). If information remains in memory and can be revived (e.g. by re-exposure), forgetting may be very functional.

A FUNCTIONAL VIEW OF INCIDENTAL FORGETTING

Experimental psychologists have traditionally focused on passive mechanisms of forgetting, including trace decay, contextual fluctuation, the use of inappropriate retrieval cues, and interference processes such as blocking. The presumption has been that people are the passive victims of forgetting, with memory loss arising from factors that simply happen to us, such as random changes in the environment, and the addition of traces into memory. Although such processes contribute to forgetting, research on inhibition suggests a different outlook. According to the inhibitory control view, much of the forgetting that we experience arises from the need to control the retrieval process in the face of competition. It is the process by which we combat interference—inhibition of competing traces—that precipitates forgetting, not the mere presence of other traces in memory. By this view, reducing the accessibility of competing traces is adaptive because it facilitates retrieval, but also because it makes subsequent retrievals of the same information easier, reducing future competition. These observations highlight that inhibitory processes can be quite adaptive. This functional view conceptualizes forgetting as a positive outcome, and highlights how a properly functioning memory system must be as good at forgetting as it is at remembering (Bjork, 1988; Anderson & Spellman, 1995; Anderson, 2003; Bjork, Bjork, & Macleod, 2006). Thus, rather than being victims of forces beyond our control, many cases of forgetting might be tied to the very mechanisms that enable the effective control of cognition.

SUMMARY

Whether we like it or not, the vast majority of life's experiences are forgotten. What mechanisms underlie forgetting? To address these questions, we must first understand the characteristics of forgetting, including the scope of the problem and what constitutes forgetting. The fundamental fact is that forgetting increases as time goes by. Research on the forgetting curve reveals that the rate of forgetting is precipitous at first, but then tapers off gradually, following a logarithmic form. Many types of material follow this pattern, although the rate of forgetting varies depending on the nature of the test, and how well learned material is. Recall is more difficult than recognition, with the latter revealing evidence of retention not observed with recall. Forgetting is dramatically reduced for well-learned facts and experiences, especially when materials are repeatedly retrieved.

Experimental psychologists distinguish between the accessibility of an item and its availability, with loss of availability referring to the elimination of an item from storage. Both deficits in accessibility and availability are considered forgetting. It is difficult ever to establish that a trace has been permanently lost, however, as it is always possible to suppose that the right retrieval cues have not been found. Thus, although permanent forgetting might exist, and might even be likely when one considers the biological system on which memory rests, it remains difficult to establish a case for this possibility through behavioral evidence alone.

To understand the fundamental fact that forgetting increases over time, several approaches have been offered. The most straightforward approach proposes that memories get weaker over time. Although decay is likely to be a biological reality and some evidence exists in non-humans, establishing a case for decay at the behavioral level is difficult because one has to control for the influence of other known forgetting factors, and establish that memories have been permanently lost. A different approach is to suppose that it is not time, *per se*, that causes forgetting, but some factor correlated with time, such as contextual fluctuation or interference. Both of these theories can accommodate the basic features of the forgetting curve, while also explaining mysteriously long-lived memories that would be difficult to explain if decay were the primary cause of forgetting.

The idea that similar memories interfere with one another during retrieval has occupied a central position in theories of forgetting. The fundamental situation of interference arises when a retrieval cue becomes associated with multiple traces. When a cue is presented for the retrieval of a target, the other associates of that cue compete with the target for access to awareness. The more competitors that are attached to a cue, the worse recall of any one item becomes, a generalization known as the cue overload principle.

Many interference phenomena have been discovered. For example, previously encoded traces can disrupt retrieval of recently learned ones, a finding known as proactive interference. Conversely, recently encoded traces can impede the retrieval of older memories, known as retroactive interference. Both proactive and retroactive interference are believed to contribute to the increase in forgetting over time, insofar as time is correlated with the storage of similar traces. In part-set cuing impairment, presenting some material as cues for the retrieval of other related memories impairs retention, showing that even after traces have been stored, recent exposure to some impairs recall of others. Research also indicates that retrieval impairs retention of related traces, known as retrieval-induced forgetting.

The mechanisms that underlie interference have long been a subject of research. Blocking theories attribute interference to the tendency for stronger traces persistently to intrude during retrieval of weaker ones, leading the person to abandon search. Unlearning theories propose that interference causes destructive changes to the associations that underlie a trace, as a result of learning mechanisms that punish inappropriate retrievals. Inhibition theories propose that forgetting arises, in part, from the suppression of interfering traces by inhibitory mechanisms that resolve competition. Research using the retrieval induced forgetting paradigm has provided specific evidence favoring the inhibitory view. This research suggests that some of the forgetting we experience arises as an adaptive consequence of controlling the retrieval process. This view highlights, more broadly, the notion that forgetting may sometimes be desirable. As the case of AJ illustrates, having a perfect memory can be a burden. We take up this topic further in Chapter 10 on motivated forgetting.

FURTHER READING

- **Anderson, M. C., & Neely, J. H.** (1996). Interference and inhibition in memory retrieval. In E. L. Bjork & R. A. Bjork (Eds.), *Memory: Handbook of perception and cognition* (2nd edn). (pp. 237–313). San Diego: Academic Press.

- **Levy, B. J., & Anderson, M. C.** (2002). Inhibitory processes and the control of memory retrieval. *Trends in Cognitive Sciences*, 6, 299–305.

- **Smith, S. M., & Vela, E.** (2001). Environmental context-dependent memory: A review and meta-analysis. *Psychonomic Bulletin and Review*, *8(2)*, 203–220.

CHAPTER 10

MOTIVATED FORGETTING

Michael C. Anderson

P eople usually think of forgetting as something bad. It is to lose our cherished past, to forget friends' names, and to neglect our responsibilities. But as AJ's remarkable memory illustrates (see Chapter 9, pp. 192–193), forgetting might be more desirable than we think. AJ often yearns to forget, so that she can avoid continually reliving the events and emotions of terrible times. She has difficulty "letting go" and "getting past" things that most of us get over quickly. These sentiments reveal that, more often than we realize, forgetting is exactly what we need to do. Sometimes we confront reminders of experiences that sadden us, as when after the death of a loved one or when, after a broken relationship, objects and places evoke memories of the lost person. Other times, reminders trigger memories that make us angry, anxious, ashamed, or afraid; a face might remind us of an argument that we hope to get past; an envelope might bring to mind a very unpleasant task we are avoiding; or an image of the World Trade Center in a movie might elicit upsetting memories of 11 September. In the popular film, *Eternal sunshine of the spotless mind*, the main character, Joel, suffers so badly from memories of his lost love, Clementine, he seeks out a memory deletion clinic, to have all memories of her removed from his brain. Unfortunately, although we might at times yearn for them, no such clinics exist, and we cannot avoid life's tendency to insert memories we wish were not there.

Jim Carrey's character, Joel, in Michel Gondry's film *Eternal sunshine of the spotless mind*, hires a service to permanently erase painful memories of his ex-girlfriend from his mind. While such technology is science fiction, our desire and ability to control our memory is very much a reality. © Steve Sands/New York Newswire/Corbis.

People do not take this situation lying down, however. They do something about it. When we confront reminders to unwanted memories, a familiar reaction often occurs—a flash of experience and feeling followed rapidly by an attempt to exclude the memory from awareness. Unlike in most other situations, retrieval is unwanted and must be shut down. Suppressing retrieval shuts out the intrusive memories, restoring control over the direction of thought and our emotional well-being. Indeed, for veterans, witnesses of terrorism, and countless people experiencing personal traumas, the day-to-day reality of the need to control intrusive memories is all too clear. Any serious and general treatment of forgetting therefore needs to consider the motivated involvement of individuals as conspirators in their own memory failures. Is my failure to remember knocking over the Christmas tree (see Chapter 9, p. 191) simply an accident of normal forgetting? Is the fact that you "forgot" to do that unpleasant task, *yet again*, truly an innocent mistake? In this chapter, we consider what is known about how people forget things that they would prefer not to remember.

LIFE IS GOOD, OR MEMORY MAKES IT SO

With surprising consistency, people across the world, of all ages, ethnicities, and income levels report being generally happy with their lives. This feeling of well-being is widespread, and often defies people's objective circumstances. It is found in people with physical or mental disabilities, and in people with low incomes (Diener & Diener, 1996; Lykken & Tellegen, 1996). Research suggests that memory contributes to this perceived well-being. Our assessment of how we are doing in life relies on what we remember. For example, people show a strong **positivity bias** in what they remember over the long-term. In an early illustration of this bias, Waldfogel (1948) gave participants 85 minutes to generate as many memories as they could recall from the first 8 years of their lives. Of these memories, people rated 50% as pleasant, 30% as unpleasant, and 20% as neutral, suggesting that, for whatever reason, positive memories were simply more accessible. A similar finding occurs when, instead of asking people to generate memories intentionally, you ask them to note memories that "spontaneously" pop into mind over a longer period. Of the involuntary reminders reported in a study by Bernsten (Bernsten, 1996), 49% were pleasant, 32% neutral, and 19% unpleasant. This positivity bias increases as we get older and grow to focus

more on emotional goals and on maintaining a sense of well-being. Why do such effects occur? Are memories of positive events more frequent because those types of events are more common, or might people's motivations have something to do with it?

Susan Charles, Mara Mather, and Laura Carstensen (2003) conducted a simple and compelling study suggesting that our memory biases are no accident. They asked younger and older adults to view 32 scenes. The scenes included a mixture of pleasant, neutral, and rather unpleasant images. After a 15-minute delay, participants recalled as many of the pictures as they could. As illustrated in Figure 10.1, pictures with emotional content were recalled better, in general, than were neutral pictures, and older adults recalled fewer pictures than did younger adults. Importantly, however, as participants got older, their memories became progressively more biased in favor of positive scenes over negative ones, even though all scenes were viewed for the same amount of time: Whereas young participants recalled positive and negative scenes with equal frequency, older adults recalled nearly twice as many positive as negative scenes. A subsequent test revealed that older adults could recognize the positive and negative scenes equally well, indicating that they both made it into memory. For some reason, however, negative events were not recalled as well. Similar age-related emotional biases have been observed with words and faces (Leigland, Schulz, & Janowsky, 2004). In a review of research on aging and positivity effects, Mather and Carstensen (2005) build a compelling case that, as we get older and life grows short, people focus more on maintaining a sense of well-being, and less on

KEY TERM

Positivity bias: The tendency, increasing over the lifespan, to recall more pleasant memories than either neutral or unpleasant ones.

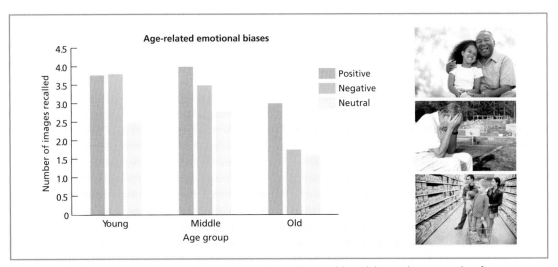

Figure 10.1 Although memory overall tends to decline with age, older adults tend to remember fewer negative memories relative to positive ones, demonstrating an age-related positivity bias. From Charles, Mather, and Carstensen (2003). Copyright © American Psychological Association. Reproduced with permission. Right: Examples of the types of positive, negative, and neutral images that were used in the study.

goals concerning knowledge and the future. As a result, people grow skilled in **emotion regulation**, which includes, in part, controlling what we remember. How could this possibly happen? What processes contribute to motivated forgetting?

TERMINOLOGY IN RESEARCH ON MOTIVATED FORGETTING

It is important to clarify certain terms and distinctions that will arise in our discussion of how motives alter our memories. Perhaps the most well known term relating to motivated forgetting is **repression**, popularized by Sigmund Freud through his psychoanalytic theory. In Freud's framework, repression refers to a psychological defense mechanism that banishes unwanted memories, ideas, and feelings into the unconscious to reduce conflict and psychic pain. It is one in an arsenal of defensive processes that includes rationalization, projection, and many others. Although

Freud used repression in a number of ways, he offered the following simple definition: "The essence of repression lies simply in the function of rejecting and keeping something out of consciousness" (Freud, 1917, p. 147).

Within this framework, repressed contents were not eliminated from the mind, but were excluded from conscious awareness. They could still influence behavior unconsciously, manifesting themselves in our dreams, preferences, choice of topics we discuss, and even our emotional reactions. Moreover, repressed contents were not guaranteed to remain

> **KEY TERMS**
>
> **Emotion regulation:** Goal-driven monitoring, evaluating, altering, and gating one's emotional reactions and memories about emotional experiences.
> **Repression:** In psychoanalytic theory, a psychological defense mechanism that banishes unwanted memories, ideas, and feelings into the unconscious in an effort to reduce conflict and psychic pain. Theoretically, repression can either be conscious or nonconscious.

unconscious but were thought to pop up again on later occasions, a phenomenon Freud referred to as the *return of the repressed* (e.g. Freud, 1900, 1917).

A distinction is sometimes drawn between *repression* and *suppression*, with the former being an unconscious process and the latter being conscious and intentional. By this view, repression refers to an automatic, defensive process by which a memory is excluded from consciousness without a person ever being aware of its presence. Suppression, on the other hand, refers to intentional, goal-directed exclusion of ideas or memories from awareness. Although the modern psychoanalytic tradition maintains this distinction, Mathew Erdelyi (2006) has shown that the distinction was introduced by Anna Freud, Sigmund Freud's daughter. Erdelyi argues that Freud used the terms interchangeably, and that the distinction distorts his theoretical viewpoint. In this chapter, the term repression can refer to either sense, but when the term suppression is used, we intend to refer specifically to the voluntary sense of the word.

Several other terms often arise that are not linked to Freudian theory, including intentional forgetting and motivated forgetting. *Intentional forgetting* refers to forgetting arising from processes initiated by a conscious goal to forget. It includes conscious strategies to forget, such as suppression and intentional context shifts. Although we discuss intentional forgetting, this term does not capture those cases when forgetting is nonaccidental, but not consciously intended. The broader term *motivated forgetting* encompasses these potential cases. For example, if every time you see someone associated to an unpleasant event your mind steers towards topics unrelated to that event, this motivated bias might induce forgetting without being generated by an intention to forget. Nevertheless, this type of forgetting would clearly be motivated.

Motivated forgetting encompasses the term **psychogenic amnesia**, which means any forgetting that is psychological in origin, and not attributed to biological damage or dysfunction—forgetting that is psychological in genesis. Although psychogenic amnesia and motivated forgetting might be treated synonymously, psychogenic amnesia is generally used for cases of profound and surprising forgetting of major chunks of one's life, or to profound forgetting of a particular event that ought to be remembered. The term is theoretically and mechanistically neutral in that it does not presume Freud's theoretical framework, nor does it say how forgetting is accomplished, merely that the source is psychological rather than biological. Motivated forgetting includes these cases, but it also includes more ordinary, day-to-day examples in which people forget unpleasant things in a way that would not call for clinical evaluation.

FACTORS THAT PREDICT MOTIVATED FORGETTING

Theoretically, controlling unwanted experiences can be accomplished by manipulating any stage of memory. The simplest way to avoid remembering unpleasant events is to limit encoding. You might literally look away from a stimulus, or focus instead on only its pleasant aspects; or, if you are unfortunate enough to have looked at something unpleasant, you might cease elaborative thoughts. If an unwanted experience is encoded, you might avoid reminders to prevent retrieval; or, if reminders are inescapable, you might endeavor to stop retrieval. In all of these examples, mechanisms involved in "normal forgetting" are engaged in service of your emotional goals. Research on motivated forgetting has addressed all of these factors, which we discuss next.

KEY TERM

Psychogenic amnesia: Profound and surprising episodes of forgetting the events of one's life, arising from psychological factors, rather than biological damage or dysfunction.

Instructions to forget

Have you ever told someone to "Forget about it?" Does saying that make a difference? When you recommend this, you presumably have reason to believe that the person can do it. We often have good reason to put things out of mind, even when they are not emotionally significant. Consider Bjork's (1970) example of a short-order cook who, during a typical morning breakfast shift, must process dozens of similar orders. Having completed an order such as, "Scramble two eggs, crisp bacon, and an English muffin," the cook's performance can only suffer if prior orders have not been forgotten. Similarly, we have all experienced times when, after completing a demanding activity, such as an examination, we must "let go" of the information so that our minds can shift to new endeavors. When we return to the "dropped" material, we are often surprised that the knowledge once readily available now eludes us. These examples suggest that forgetting can sometimes be initiated to reduce the tendency for proactive interference to impede our concentration. This idea is often studied with the **directed forgetting** procedure (Bjork, 1970, 1989; see MacLeod, 1998, for a review), in which participants are overtly instructed to forget recently encoded materials.

Directed forgetting: Basic findings

There are two variants of the directed forgetting procedure, each of which involves different forgetting processes. In *item-method directed forgetting*, a participant receives a series of items to remember, one at a time. After each item, an instruction appears, indicating that the participants should either continue to remember it or to forget it, because they will no longer be held responsible for it. After the list ends, participants are given a test of *all* of the to-be-remembered and to-be forgotten words. Interestingly, recall for to-be-forgotten words is often substantially impaired, relative to to-be-remembered items. For example, Basden and Basden (1996) observed worse recall for to-be-forgotten than for to-be-remembered items

regardless of whether the items presented were pictures (78% versus 36% for remember and forget items, respectively), words (72% versus 46%), or words for which participants were asked to construct imagery (85% versus 42%).

Informatively, directed forgetting effects observed with the item method also occur on recognition tests (Basden, Basden, & Gargano, 1993). For these reasons, most theorists believe that item method directed forgetting effects reflect deficits in episodic encoding. If you were a participant in such a procedure, you would, in all likelihood, "hang on" to a word by phonological rehearsal, for example, until you knew whether it was to be remembered or to be forgotten. The *remember instruction* would trigger elaborate semantic encoding, whereas the *forget instruction* would give you permission to simply release the word from rehearsal. This finding illustrates one way in which people exercise control over what they permit into memory—by regulating whether a stimulus is granted elaborative processing. Mather and Carstensen's (2005) participants might have employed some version of this strategy, though their encoding was apparently deep enough to support subsequent recognition.

The *list-method directed forgetting* procedure presents the instruction to forget only after half of the list (often 10 to 20 items) has been studied, and usually as a surprise. Typically, deception is employed, in which the experimenter tells the participant that the list they just studied was for "practice," and that the real list is about to be presented. At other times, the experimenter might pretend that the participant had received the wrong list, which they should "forget about." Following this instruction, a second list is presented. A final test is then given, quite often for both lists, but

KEY TERM

Directed forgetting: The tendency for an instruction to forget recently experienced items to induce memory impairment for those items.

sometimes only for the first list. Participants are asked to disregard the earlier instruction to forget, and to remember as much as they can. Performance in this *forget group* is contrasted with a *remember group*, which follows the same procedure except that the instruction after the first list simply reminds people that they should continue remembering the first list. Two findings are observed consistently: First, when participants believe that they can forget the first list, they often do much better at recalling the second list on the final test, compared to the remember group. In other words, the proactive interference one finds from the first list often disappears when people believe that they can forget that list, providing a clear *benefit* of an instruction to forget. Second, "forget" instructions impair people's recall of items from the first list, compared to performance in the remember condition, reflecting a *cost* of a forget instruction. An illustration of the different varieties of directed forgetting is provided in Figure 10.2; a classic example of directed forgetting taken from a study by Geiselman, Bjork, and Fishman (1983) appears in Figure 10.3.

List-method directed forgetting effects exhibit interesting properties that distinguish them from effects observed with the item method. First, it is unlikely that participants use shallow encoding to forget first-list items. Participants do not receive any hint that they will have to forget anything until the entire first list has been studied, and so they have no motive to not encode effectively. Thus, list-method directed forgetting more likely

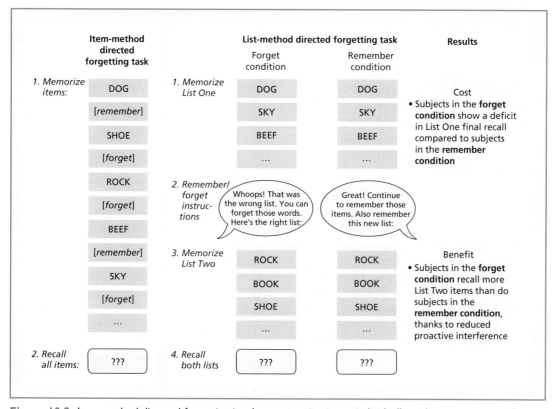

Figure 10.2 Item-method directed forgetting involves presenting items individually with an instruction, after each, to remember or forget. List-method directed forgetting presents many items before some participants receive an instruction to forget it and learn a second list. Memory is impaired for the first list in the forget condition; second-list performance is augmented.

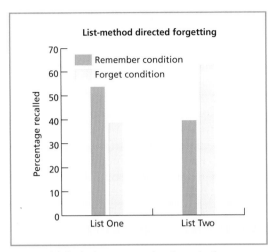

Figure 10.3 A classic example of results from a list-method directed forgetting experiment. Note that, relative to the remember condition, recall of List One is decremented in the forget condition, whereas List-Two recall is superior, thereby illustrating the cost and benefit of the instruction to forget. Data from Geiselman, Bjork, and Fishman (1983).

reflects a retrieval deficit. Consistent with this idea, list-method directed forgetting effects usually disappear when recognition is tested. Second, unlike in the item-method (Basden & Basden, 1996) items in the list method reveal their presence on implicit memory tests. Indeed, to-be-forgotten items can sometimes exert a greater influence on behavior when memory is tested implicitly. For example, Bjork and Bjork (2003) found that when some to-be-forgotten names were included on a later (apparently unrelated) *fame judgment test* presenting a set of famous and nonfamous names, to-be-forgotten (nonfamous) names were judged as more famous than were to-be-remembered (nonfamous) names in the remember condition. Presumably, participants had forgotten where they knew the name from, due to directed forgetting, and misattributed its familiarity to fame. This finding illustrates how Freud might not have been far off when he claimed that intentionally forgotten materials influence behavior outside of people's awareness.

List-method directed forgetting illustrates how, when people no longer wish to remember events, they can intentionally reduce their

accessibility. Can such processes be engaged to forget more realistic personal experiences with emotional content? Susan Joslyn and Mark Oakes took a novel approach to this issue. They asked students to record in a diary two unique events that happened to them each day over a 5-day period (Joslyn & Oakes, 2005). Participants wrote a brief narrative and a title summarizing each experience, and they also rated the events for emotional valence and intensity. For example, one student recorded this event, entitled *Crow chase*:

A few friends and I were walking through campus when we suddenly saw a crow running around on the ground following a squirrel. It was so funny! We stood and watched them for a few minutes, exchanging funny squirrel stories and other animal stories. (Joslyn & Oakes, 2005, p. 4)

After the first week of recording, students turned in their diaries. The forget group was told that the events recorded on the first 5 days would be used for a different study and that they should forget them, so that they could focus on events from the second week, which they would have to remember. The remember group was told that they would have to remember the events from the first week, as well as the ones from the upcoming week. Over the next 5-day period, the students then recorded a new set of events. After the second week ended, participants turned in their diaries and were then asked to remember all of the events they had recorded during both weeks. Joslyn and Oaks found that participants instructed to forget had poorer memory for events from the first week than did participants instructed to remember. This pattern was even observed for a group of "practice memories" that participants recorded in their first week that neither group believed they would have to recall. Interestingly, impairment was even found with negative and positive mood events. Related findings were observed by Amanda Barnier and colleagues (Barnier, Conway, Mayoh, &

Speyer, 2007) for personal memories learned outside of the experiment.

Mechanisms underlying list-method directed forgetting

Two leading theories can explain list-method directed forgetting. According to the **retrieval inhibition hypothesis,** an instruction to forget the first list inhibits list-one items, impairing recall. This inhibition does not, however, do permanent damage, and memories remain available. Inhibition merely limits retrieval by reducing activation of unwanted items. This view explains why intentionally forgotten items are difficult to recall, but can be recognized if we assume that re-presentation of forgotten items restores their activation levels. By contrast, according to the **context shift hypothesis** (Sahakyan & Kelley, 2002), instructions to forget mentally separate the to-be-forgotten items from the second list. If a person's mental context changes between the first and the second lists and if the second list context remains active during the final test, to-be-forgotten items should be recalled more poorly because the new context is a poor retrieval cue for them, similar to the notion of cognitive context discussed in Chapter 8.

To test the context shift hypothesis, Sahakyan and Kelley varied the mental context in between two lists of words. Might such a context shift produce the pattern observed in directed forgetting? In their context shift condition, participants encoded a first list of words and then performed a simple task designed to shift their "frame of mind." Participants were asked to imagine, for 1 minute, what their life would be like if they were invisible. The reasoning was that by performing such a bizarre task, participants would enter into studying the second list in a different mental context than was present while they were studying the first list (perhaps one in which they thought the experimenters were crazy). If the context shift hypothesis is correct, this simple manipulation should impair people's memory for the first list, even in the absence of any instruction to forget it. This in fact occurred: Participants given this context shift task showed much poorer retention of the first list on a later test. These findings suggest that part of the directed forgetting effect may arise from a shift in mental context induced by the intention to forget. This hypothesis is not inconsistent with retrieval inhibition, however, if mental context shifts are accomplished by inhibiting the unwanted context instead of individual items (Anderson, 2003). In either case, the deficit induced by instructions to forget (in laboratory studies) is produced by diminished access to the context in which forgotten events were encoded.

Research on directed forgetting establishes that people have some ability to forget intentionally. One method is to deprive experiences of elaborative encoding (item-method directed forgetting), increasing the chances that those memories will be forgotten quickly. The consequence of this method is a generalized deficit in recall or recognition, including diminished influence of the experience on indirect tests. Alternatively, unwanted memories can be rendered less accessible by a process that impairs access to the context to which the to-be-forgotten memories are associated. The to-be-forgotten items can continue to influence participants on indirect tests, suggesting that even in the absence of awareness, intentionally forgotten items might make their

---

KEY TERMS

Retrieval inhibition hypothesis: A proposed mechanism underlying list-method directed forgetting suggesting that first-list items are temporarily inhibited in response to the instruction to forget and can be reactivated by subsequent presentations of the to-be-forgotten items.

Context shift hypothesis: An alternative explanation for list-method directed forgetting, positing that forget instructions separate first-list items into a distinct context, which unless reinstated during the final test will make the later context a relatively ineffectual retrieval cue.

presence known. Both item and list-method directed forgetting can impair neutral as well as emotionally negative materials.

Motivated context shifts and changes in stimulus environment

The preceding discussion illustrates how simply changing one's mental context (e.g. intentionally shifting to a new line of thought) can diminish access to past events. If changing mental context can induce forgetting, perhaps changing other elements of incidental context might work as well. People know this intuitively. For example, when something traumatic happens in one context, people avoid returning to that context to prevent from being reminded. If the location is a home or a town of residence, people will often change homes or towns to get over the unpleasant incident. When the unwanted memory concerns a person, people often avoid exposure to that person. If people cannot remove themselves from an environment, they will sometimes seek to change the environment itself. For example, in the aftermath of the fatal shootings at Columbine High School in Colorado, families of the victims lobbied to have the school library at which the shootings took place torn down and replaced with an entirely different structure, removing reminders to the horrible events.

Motivated context shifts are likely to occur when it is too late to minimize encoding. To limit awareness of the memory, people avoid reminders. The avoidance of cues, especially shifts in environmental context, might facilitate normal forgetting processes in several ways. First, by avoiding reminders, the person deprives a memory of retrievals that ordinarily strengthen and preserve it (Erdelyi, 2006). Essentially, retrieval practice is prevented. Preventing reactivation of the trace should encourage decay processes, if they exist. Second, by changing environmental context, the incidental context within which one operates should mismatch the one in which the event took place, hindering retrieval. If the new context allows a person to recover, mood

Sometimes people are so motivated to control their memories that they alter the physical environment to remove retrieval cues. Such was the case at Columbine high school in Colorado. Following the shootings, families of the victims lobbied to demolish and rebuild the library where the incident took place. © Najlah Feanny/Corbis.

context will change, making spontaneous retrieval of the event less likely.

Intentional retrieval suppression

Sometimes we cannot avoid reminders to unpleasant events. When this happens, we only have two choices: be reminded or stop retrieval. To see how people might stop retrieval, consider the following example. Suppose that you have an argument with a significant other. The next time you see them, chances are you will be reminded of the argument, recreating the upset feelings. If you are motivated to "get past" the argument, and sustain a good feeling about the person, you might put the memory out of mind, especially if the argument was not of great consequence. You might find this difficult at first, requiring concentration to redirect your thoughts and emotions to more constructive ends. With repeated encounters, however, the remindings often grow less frequent. After much time, you might be unable to recollect the argument. Such forgetting is not a bad thing. Healthy relationships require at least some "forgive and forget." Without this, people dwell on small transgressions, never forgetting any upset or wrongdoing. AJ wishes that she could forget, because unpleasant memories trouble her long past the time when others would have succeeded in banishing them from mind. People often confront reminders to difficult memories that can make them sad, angry, anxious, or ashamed, and they quickly adjust their thoughts.

How do people suppress retrieval? To shed light on these issues, Collin Green and I considered an analogy between how people control unwanted memories and how they control action. We noted that unwanted memories have an "intrusive" quality, seeming to "leap" to awareness in response to reminders, despite our intention to avoid them. This reflexive quality seems similar to reflexive actions. Importantly, we clearly have the ability to stop physical actions. Consider a time that I knocked a potted plant off my kitchen windowsill. As my hand darted to catch the falling object, I realized that the plant was a cactus. Mere centimeters from it, I stopped myself from catching the cactus. The plant dropped, and was ruined, but I was relieved to have avoided being pierced with little

People reflexively try to catch a falling object. But in certain situations (if the object is a cactus, for example), this prepotent motor response would be painfully inappropriate. We are fortunate to have the ability to stop ourselves in mid-action. Can we also stop ourselves from retrieving memories? © Tim Flach.

needles. This illustrates the need to override a reflexive response to a stimulus. Without the capacity to override reflexive responses, we could not adapt behavior to changes in our goals or circumstances. If we can stop reflexive actions, perhaps we have the machinery to stop retrieval. Indeed, controlling retrieval may build on these mechanisms of behavioral control to achieve **cognitive control**.

Retrieval suppression: Basic findings

How do we control reflexive actions? As discussed in Chapter 9, suppressing action can be accomplished by inhibition. Might suppressing retrieval be accomplished in the same way? To look at this, Collin Green and I (Anderson & Green, 2001) developed a procedure modeled after the go/no-go task, which is used to measure people's ability to stop motor responses. In a typical go/no-go task, people press a button as quickly as possible whenever they see a letter appear on a computer screen, *except* when the letter is an X, for which they are to withhold their response. The tendency to withhold the response measures inhibitory control over action (e.g. how well a person could avoid catching the cactus). To see whether people's attempts to stop retrieval might engage inhibitory control, we adapted this procedure to create the **think/no-think paradigm**.

The think/no-think procedure is intended to mimic those times in life when we stumble upon a reminder to a memory we would prefer not to think about, and try to keep it out of mind. In the simplest version, people study a set of cue-target pairs (e.g. *ordeal–roach*), and

KEY TERMS

Cognitive control: The ability to flexibly control thoughts in accordance with our goals, including our ability to stop unwanted thoughts from rising to consciousness.
Think/no-think (TNT) paradigm: A procedure designed to study the ability to volitionally suppress retrieval of a memory when confronted with reminders.

are then trained to recall the second word (e.g. *roach*) whenever they encounter the first word as a reminder (e.g. *ordeal*). By training pairs in this way, we hoped that the left-hand word would serve as a powerful reminder. In the next step, participants enter the think/no-think phase, which requires them to exert control over retrieval. Most of the trials require the person to recall the response whenever they see the reminder but, for certain reminders (colored in red), participants are admonished to avoid retrieval. So, for example, upon seeing the word *ordeal*, participants are asked to stare directly at this reminder, but nevertheless willfully prevent the associated memory from entering consciousness. It is emphasized that it is insufficient to avoid *saying* the response, and that preventing the memory from entering awareness is crucial. Can people recruit inhibitory control to prevent an unwanted memory from intruding into consciousness? If so, this procedure might capture the essence of repression, which, as Freud said, "Lies simply in the function of rejecting and keeping something out of consciousness" (Freud, 1917, p. 147).

Of course, we cannot observe people's conscious awareness, so it is difficult to know whether someone prevents a memory from entering consciousness. Instead, the think/no-think procedure measures the after-effects of stopping retrieval. If inhibition persists, perhaps stopping retrieval repeatedly might cause forgetting, much like how the memory of the argument grows less accessible with repeated encounters with your friend. To measure this behavioral footprint of suppression, participants receive the studied cues (*ordeal*) on a final test and are asked to recall the target memory (*roach*) for every one.

As Figure 10.4 reveals, there is a sizable difference in people's ability to recall "Think" and "No-Think" items on the final test. This difference, known as the *total memory control effect* (Anderson & Levy, in press; Levy & Anderson, 2008), illustrates how a person's intention to control retrieval alters retention. Exactly how intention influences performance is not clear from this effect alone, however.

Including a third set of pairs that are studied initially, but that do not appear during the think/no-think phase (i.e. baseline items), allows us to measure the positive control effect, and the negative control effect.

The *positive control effect* can be seen in Figure 10.4 as the enhanced memory for "think" items above baseline recall, and is caused by intentional retrieval. This effect confirms that when people are inclined to be reminded, cues enhance memory. The *negative control effect* can be seen in the memory deficit for "no-think" items below baseline recall, and this is due to participants intentionally shutting down retrieval. Thus, when people avoid reminders, presenting cues triggers inhibitory processes that impair memory. The negative control effect is counterintuitive. Most people would expect that repeatedly encountering reminders would improve memory, but clearly this outcome depends on people's disposition as to whether they wish to be reminded. As can be seen in Figure 10.4, the negative control effect for no-think items is also seen when people are tested with a novel test cue, showing that impairment is cue-independent. As discussed in Chapter 9, this suggests that the item was inhibited.

Brain mechanisms underlying retrieval suppression

Might people really control intrusive memories in the same way they control overt action? Evidence for this possibility comes from neuroimaging studies assessing whether similar brain systems are involved in stopping retrieval and stopping action. For instance, with John Gabrieli, Kevin Ochsner, Brice Kuhl, and colleagues, I conducted a functional MRI study contrasting brain activity during no-think and think trials (Anderson, Ochsner, Cooper, Robertson, Gabrieli, Glover, et al., 2004). If suppressing retrieval engages mechanisms also involved in motor stopping, more activation should be found in those regions during no-think trials, in which stopping is required, than during think trials. Consistent with this hypothesis, suppressing retrieval

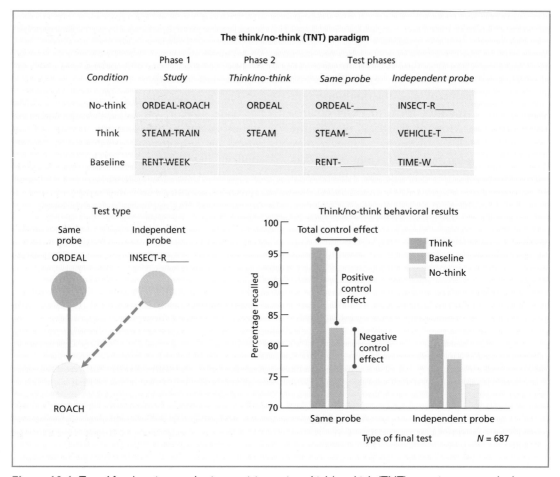

Figure 10.4 Top: After learning word pairs, participants in a think/no-think (TNT) experiment are asked to either think or not think about an item's associate. Participants' memory for all items is then assessed. Lower left: A depiction of the two types of final tests. Lower right: Results of a TNT meta-analysis by test type.

recruited a network of brain regions including left and right lateral prefrontal cortex, and anterior cingulate cortex. This network overlaps strongly with that involved with motor inhibition, even though no motor responses were required. The lateral prefrontal cortex plays an especially critical role in stopping reflexive motor action (e.g. Aron, Fletcher, Bullmore, Sahakian, & Robbins, 2003). In fact, stimulation of this brain region during a "go" motor response induces monkeys to stop their movement (Sasaki, Gemba, & Tsujimoto, 1989). This overlap confirms the idea that stopping unwanted actions and memories engages a common inhibitory process.

But how might our memories be controlled? The answer lies in the brain region that appears to be targeted by control: the hippocampus. The hippocampus is essential for forming episodic memories (Squire, 1992c), and increased hippocampal activation has been linked in prior neuroimaging studies to a person's subjective experience of consciously recollecting an event. Suppressing an unwanted reminder requires that people stop memory retrieval so as to prevent conscious recollection. If people seek to prevent conscious recollection, then perhaps retrieval suppression might reduce hippocampal activity. Indeed, Anderson et al. (2004) found reduced hippocampal

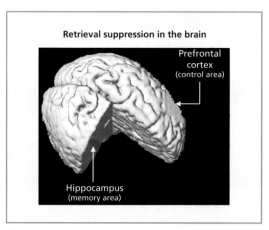

Retrieval suppression in the brain

Prefrontal cortex
(control area)

Hippocampus
(memory area)

Figure 10.5 A rendering of the neuroimaging results of Anderson et al. (2004). The lateral prefrontal cortex (depicted in green) is recruited during no-think trials to suppress neural activity in the hippocampus (in red), thereby preventing unwanted memories from coming to mind.

activity when participants suppressed retrieval, indicating that people can intentionally regulate hippocampal activation to disengage recollection (Figure 10.5). Thus, depending on whether people wish to be reminded by a cue, they are able to control hippocampal activation, influencing later retention.

Can such mechanisms be effective for more complex emotional memories? Recent studies indicate that suppressing retrieval of negative memories causes as great or greater inhibition, relative to suppressing either neutral traces (Depue, Banich, & Curran, 2006; Depue, Curran, & Banich, 2007) or positive traces (Joormann, Hertel, Brozovich, & Gotlib, 2005). Effective suppression has even been observed when people suppress aversive scenes. In two studies by Brendan Depue, Marie Banich, and Tim Curran (2006, 2007), participants learned to pair certain unfamiliar faces with unpleasant scenes. For example, one face might have served as the reminder for a scene of a bad accident and another might have been paired with a badly deformed infant. Depue and colleagues found that presenting the face reminders and asking people to suppress retrieval impaired later recall of the aversive pictures, replicating

negative control effects observed with word pairs. Depue et al. (2007) also replicated the activation of the lateral prefrontal cortex and the reduced hippocampal activity during "no-think" trials. Thus, inhibitory control appears effective at suppressing more naturalistic memories, suggesting it may be a fruitful model for how people regulate awareness of unpleasant memories.

It appears that when people want to not "catch their mental cacti" and avoid an unwelcome reminding, they engage systems that are also necessary for motor stopping. The difference between motor and memory control appears to be the area of the brain influenced by control; with motor inhibition, motor areas are modulated by lateral prefrontal cortex, but with memory inhibition, people instead "close down memory lane" by down-regulating activation in the hippocampus (Anderson & Weaver, in press).

Extreme emotional distress

Perhaps amongst the most striking and unusual form of motivated forgetting arises in *psychogenic amnesia*. Consider the dramatic case of AMN, a 23-year-old insurance worker (Markowitsch, Kessler, Van Der Ven, Weber-Luxenburger, Albers, & Heiss, 1998). AMN discovered a small fire in his basement and left the house to call for help. He did not inhale smoke, and he smashed the cellar door and immediately ran out of the house. That evening, he appeared dazed and frightened, and the next morning, when he awoke, he no longer knew what his profession was or where he lived. After 3 weeks, he entered the hospital. On examination, it became clear that his memories extended only until the age of 17. He barely recognized his partner, whom he had known for 3 years, and did not recognize his friends or co-workers. After 3 weeks of therapy, he reported one of his earliest memories as a child: at the age of 4, he saw a car crash, which set another car in flames; he was then witness to the driver's screams and his death in the flames, with his head pressed against the window. Since that time, fire had been AMN's worst fear. Despite this, AMN showed normal psychological and physical development and, throughout his life, showed no evidence of psychological illness. A full examination revealed no obvious evidence of brain damage, although greatly reduced metabolism was discovered in memory-related areas. Eight months later, at the time of the report, AMN's deficits in personal memory remained.

Cases like this illustrate several characteristics of psychogenic amnesia. First, psychogenic amnesia is triggered by severe psychological stressors. For AMN, a particular event makes contact with a trauma and triggers a massive reaction. The stressful event can cause a profound loss of personal memories, often despite a lack of observable neurobiological causes. In striking contrast, memory for public events and general knowledge is often intact. Unlike in AMN's case, amnesia can be *global*, in that it affects the entirety of a person's history. Indeed, in a form of psychogenic amnesia known as **psychogenic fugue** state (Hunter, 1968), people forget their entire history, including who they are. In such cases, people are often found wandering, not knowing where to go or what to do. Triggering events include such things as severe marital discord, bereavement, financial problems, or criminal offense. A history of depression and also head injury make a person more vulnerable to fugue states, when coupled with acute stress and trauma. Fugue typically lasts a few hours or a few days and, when the person recovers, they remember their identity and history once again. However, they often have persisting amnesia for what took place during the fugue.

Functional amnesia can also be situation specific, with the person experiencing severe memory loss for a particular trauma. Committing homicide; experiencing or committing a violent crime such as rape or torture; experiencing combat violence; attempting suicide; and being in automobile accidents and natural disasters have all induced cases of situation-specific amnesia (Arrigo & Pezdek,

Members of the military, like many nonuniformed individuals, suffer unimaginable traumas all too often. Such events have the potential to spark psychogenic amnesia, in which memories for the trauma become inaccessible. © David Turnley/Corbis.

1997; Kopelman, 2002a). As Kopelman (2002a) notes, however, care must be exercised in interpreting cases of psychogenic amnesia when there are compelling motives to feign memory deficits for legal or financial reasons. However, although some fraction of psychogenic amnesia cases can be explained in this fashion, it is generally acknowledged that true cases are not uncommon. Both global and situation-specific amnesia are often distinguished from the organic amnesic syndrome (discussed in Chapter 11) in that the capacity to store new memories and experiences remains intact.

Given the dramatic nature of memory loss in such cases, there is usually a concerted effort to help the person recover their identity and history. Deliberate attempts to remind the person of his/her past and identity rarely work, however. Memories can sometimes be recovered spontaneously when particular cues are encountered (Abeles & Schilder, 1935; Schacter, Wang, Tulving, & Freedman, 1982).

KEY TERM

Psychogenic fugue: A form of psychogenic amnesia typically lasting a few hours or days following a severe trauma, in which afflicted individuals forget their entire life history, including who they are.

For example, Kopelman (1995) reported a patient who spontaneously recalled, on seeing the name of an author on the spine of a book, that he had a friend who was dying of cancer who shared that name. Although some patients appear to recover spontaneously or with supportive therapy, Kritchevsky, Chang, and Squire (2004) found that only two of the ten patients they studied recovered fully, even 14 months after onset. Clearly, the conditions under which memories can be recovered need to be more fully understood.

FACTORS THAT PREDICT MEMORY RECOVERY

As the preceding discussion highlights, people can be motivated to forget at one time but then wish to recall forgotten memories later. Although the need for recovery is dire in psychogenic amnesia, it is also an important goal in less dramatic instances of forgetting. At some point, you need to face that unpleasant task that you keep suppressing; to do so, you need to extract it from memory when making your to-do list. Or you might encounter people who remember some embarrassing event that occurred to you that you simply cannot recall (like knocking over a Christmas tree) and, in your astonishment, might seek to release it from the dungeons to which it has been banished. Perhaps you are undergoing therapy and need to discuss past experiences. In this section, we consider factors that predict when motivated recovery can occur.

Passage of time

The passage of time is, of course, associated with forgetting. In some cases, however, memory paradoxically improves with delay even when no effort to retrieve is made. The classic demonstration comes from Ivan Pavlov, in his studies of classical conditioning. Pavlov found that when a classically conditioned salivary response was extinguished, the response gained in strength again after 20 minutes (Pavlov, 1927). Pavlov referred to this finding as **spontaneous recovery**. Spontaneous recovery is a robust phenomenon (Rescorla, 2004), including in research on conditioned emotional responding. After a conditioned response has been extinguished, spontaneous recovery increases with time, although conditioned responses do not generally return to full strength. Moreover, with repeated recovery/extinction cycles, the conditioned response recovers less each time. Spontaneous recovery illustrates that some types of memory, when seemingly forgotten, can once again return unbidden.

Similar findings have been observed for declarative memory. The idea that memory might improve over time originated in research on retroactive interference and was premised on an analogy between retroactive interference and extinction in conditioning (Underwood, 1948). In particular, according to the unlearning hypothesis discussed in Chapter 9, whenever a "response" is retrieved by accident, the association between the cue and the mistaken response is punished via a process akin to extinction. If so, retroactive interference should dissipate. Consistent with this hypothesis, Underwood (1948) found significant retroactive interference at short delays but performance on the first list improved at longer delays. Spontaneous recovery has been observed in a large number of retroactive interference studies since that time (see Brown, 1976, and Wheeler, 1995, for reviews).

Mark Wheeler (1995) reported several nice illustrations of spontaneous recovery in episodic memory. In one study, Wheeler presented students with twelve pictures, giving them three opportunities to study the items.

KEY TERM

Spontaneous recovery: The term arising from the classical conditioning literature given to the reemergence of a previously extinguished conditioned response after a delay; similarly, forgotten declarative memories have been observed to recover over time.

The students were then told that the list had been for practice, and that the real lists would begin. They then received two additional lists of twelve pictures, with a free-recall test occurring after each. After the third list was presented, students were given a free-recall test for the pictures studied on the first list either immediately, or after about 30 minutes. As can be seen in Figure 10.6, recall from the first list suffered significant retroactive interference from learning two intervening lists, compared to a control group who performed irrelevant distractor activities instead of learning second and third lists. Notice, however, that after about 30 minutes, free recall of the first-list pictures actually gets better. Wheeler demonstrated the same effect with lists of categorized words, and also with word pairs, showing that recovery is general. Although most studies of

spontaneous recovery have examined intervals up to 30 minutes, some have found recovery after several days. The stronger memories are, the more likely they will be to exhibit recovery (Postman, Stark, & Henschel, 1969).

Why does episodic memory improve over time when the overwhelming majority of research indicates the opposite relationship? One feature shared by spontaneous recovery in both classical conditioning and episodic memory is the explicit rejection of particular responses that had previously been relevant. As discussed earlier, the need to stop unwanted responses is one of the main conditions thought to engage inhibition. If retroactive interference reflects the persisting effects of inhibition, perhaps forgotten items recover because inhibition is gradually released. Thus, the factor that differentiates when memory

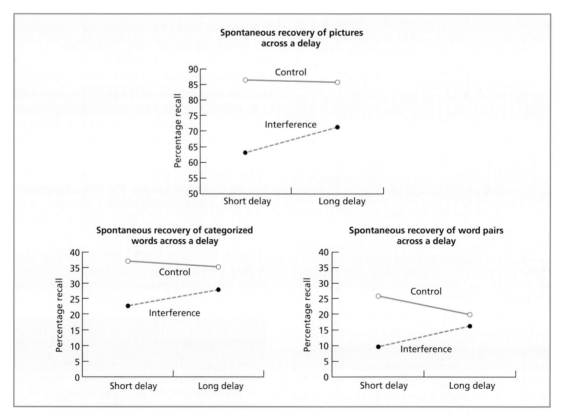

Figure 10.6 A series of experiments conducted by Wheeler (1995) demonstrating that the retroactive interference produced by intervening lists of pictures, words, or word pairs observed at short delays is diminished after a longer delay. Note that memory for items in the interference condition improves with delay in each case. From Wheeler (1995). Copyright © American Psychological Association. Reproduced with permission.

will improve and when it will decline may be the involvement of inhibition. Consistent with this, Malcolm MacLeod and Neil Macrae (2001) found that retrieval-induced forgetting was significantly reduced after a 24-hour delay, suggesting that in some cases inhibition might dissipate over time. Given the tendency for emotionally unpleasant experiences to come back and haunt us, even after frequent suppression, spontaneous recovery seems likely to be a force behind the reappearance of forgotten traces.

Repeated retrieval attempts

After a long struggle trying to recall an experience, is it worth continuing to search even when your intuition tells you that there is nothing to be recalled? Doesn't that feeling mean that the event has been lost forever? Perhaps not. Consider my experience trying to remember the location of my passport (described at the start of Chapter 8). After strenuous effort, I had no recollection whatsoever of storing this item, and felt that I would never remember. Yet the moment I found it, I instantly recalled placing it in that location, showing that the memory was there. On the contrary, my efforts to remember knocking over the Christmas tree discussed in the last chapter have proven fruitless, despite prolonged recall attempts, stretching over months. When you fail to recall numerous times, doesn't it mean that the memory will not be recovered?

Interestingly, the answer to this question often is "no." Repeated retrieval attempts typically increase the amount recalled, even when the person feels that he/she cannot recall more. This phenomenon was first discovered by Ballard (1913), who asked young schoolchildren to memorize poetry. Over successive recalls, Ballard found that the children would often recall new lines of poetry that they had failed to recall previously. Ballard referred to this phenomenon as **reminiscence**, which he defined as, "the remembering again of the forgotten without relearning" or "a gradual process of improvement in the capacity to revive past experiences" (Ballard, 1913). Ballard noted that even when the overall number of

lines of poetry did not increase across retrievals, students often included newly recalled lines in later attempts not present in earlier ones. Overall recall sometimes didn't improve, however, because the benefits of recalling new lines were countered by students' failures to recall lines previously recalled. Nevertheless, often the amount of reminiscence exceeded this intertest forgetting, yielding improvement overall. When overall recall improves through repeated testing (when reminiscence exceeds inter-test forgetting), a person has exhibited **hypermnesia**, a term introduced by Mathew Erdelyi to contrast this with the amnesia normally arising from the passage of time.

Although neglected for decades, Mathew Erdelyi and colleagues revived interest in this phenomenon in a series of striking demonstrations. In an amusing example, Erdelyi tricked a psychology PhD student, Jeff Kleinbard, into becoming a participant in a week-long study of hypermnesia. The student was interested in pursuing research on hypermnesia. To help him get a feel for the phenomenon, Erdelyi had Kleinbard join participants in a testing session. Participants studied 40 line drawings of objects. Participants then spent 5 minutes recalling as many of the pictures as possible (by writing the name of the object) on a blank sheet with 40 lines. If they could not recall all 40 items, the students were required to make educated guesses about what the remaining unrecalled pictures might be. This testing procedure continued for 5 recall attempts. When Kleinbard went to Erdelyi's office to score his recall, Erdelyi challenged him to continue his recall efforts over an entire week—a challenge that Kleinbard accepted. Each day, Kleinbard filled out recall sheets as many times as he

> ### KEY TERMS
>
> **Reminiscence:** The remembering again of the forgotten, without learning or a gradual process of improvement in the capacity to revive past experiences.
> **Hypermnesia:** The improvement in recall performance arising from repeated testing sessions on the same material.

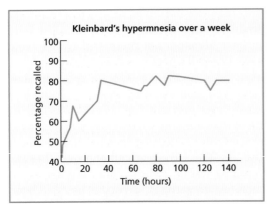

Figure 10.7 The recall data of an unwitting participant in an investigation of hypermnesia. Repeated retrieval attempts over a period of about a week led to a striking improvement in the percentage of pictures recalled. Data from Erdelyi and Kleinbard (1978).

cared to. When done, he inserted each sheet into an envelope and did not review them again. As can be seen in Figure 10.7, Kleinbard's total recall improved dramatically over the testing days, starting at 48% on the first day and rising to 80% by the final day. Indeed, when one considers his cumulative recall (i.e. giving him credit for each item recalled at any point up until and including a given test), Kleinbard's recall went from 48% to 90%. This occurred despite the fact that, on the first day, Kleinbard had tried his hardest to recall as many items as possible. Thus, Erdelyi and Kleinbard had essentially reversed Ebbinghaus's forgetting curve, by which memory gets progressively worse over time.

How might hypermnesia come about? Kleinbard stated that one of the most important factors was by visualization and reconstruction. In his own words:

By far, the most interesting subjective experience was getting a general "visual feeling" in my mind for a particular shape such as a length or roundness. I remember seeing a vague, oblong shape in my mind from which I was able to extract such items as gun, broom, and baseball bat; from an oval shape—football and pineapple; from an inverted cup

form—bell, funnel, and bottle (the bottle in the stimulus resembled a bell-jar); from a rectangular box—table and book. Just before many of these recoveries, I often experienced what might best be described as a "tip-of-the-eye" phenomenon, in which I was certain a particular item was on the verge of recovery but which would take its time before suddenly coalescing into an image in consciousness.
(Erdelyi & Kleinbard, 1978, p. 280)

Erdelyi and Kleinbard (1978) found the same pattern with a group of six additional participants, three of whom studied pictures and three of whom studied words. Participants who studied words, however, showed more modest hypermnesia than those who studied pictures, suggesting that imagery plays an important role in determining whether traces can be unearthed with repeated recall. Indeed, several participants noted "tip-of-the-eye" experiences much like that of Kleinbard.

Hypermnesia is a robust phenomenon, and can be observed in simple laboratory sessions lasting less than an hour (Payne, 1987). Hypermnesia is largest on free recall tests, but has been found on cued recall and recognition tests. The effect has been found with both verbal and visual materials, although effects are consistently larger with imageable materials. Of course, hypermnesia increases with increasing numbers of recall tests, and several investigations indicate that this effect does not simply reflect increases in time *per se*, as giving a single long test often does not yield as much benefit as many repeated tests. Nor does hypermnesia seem to reflect participants guessing more loosely as time goes on, because the frequency of false recalls often does not go up with repeated testing.

But can hypermnesia be found with complex, realistic memories? In one interesting illustration, Susan Bluck, Linda Levine, and Tracy Laulhere (1999) studied memory for a public event that many people had witnessed, and for which objective verification of details was possible: the televised reading of the verdict in the OJ Simpson murder trial. The reading of the verdict took place at 10.04 a.m. on 2 October 1995 in Los Angeles. The 14.5-minute proceeding was televised by a single courtroom camera shared by all television networks. Eight months after the verdict had been televised, Bluck et al. recruited people who viewed the coverage and asked them to remember as much as they could, including details that occurred before, during, and after the reading of the verdict. Participants were interviewed three times in a row to obtain their complete recollection of every detail. Within each interview, participants were prompted several times with requests for further details, making sure that they had recalled everything they could. Significant hypermnesia occurred, with the number of verifiable details remembered increasing from 27% to 52% across the three attempts.

But can hypermnesia occur for memories that people have deliberately tried to forget? On the one hand, the motivation to not remember might engage processes that have a special impact, making memories difficult to recall. Moreover, the same motivational factors that led to the memories being forgotten might also come into play during retrieval, undermining recovery. On the other hand, if someone decides to remember something he/she had previously tried to forget, might the change in disposition undo avoidant tendencies, and render forgotten material subject to hypermnesia? I might initially have been motivated to not think about knocking over the Christmas tree, but my motivations certainly changed years later. Although research examining hypermnesia for intentionally forgotten memories is rare, several studies using the directed-forgetting procedure demonstrate that hypermnesia does occur for intentionally forgotten items (Goernert & Wolfe, 1997; Goernert, 2005).

It is natural to worry whether repeated retrievals might introduce persisting errors that come to be attributed to actual experience. In a nice illustration, Linda Henkel (2004) showed participants slides that contained either line drawings with their names (e.g. an image of a lollipop, plus the word *lollipop*), or simply the names with no picture. For each slide, participants were asked to think of functions of the object, and when a drawing was absent, to try to visualize a typical example. Participants then received three recall tests. Participants exhibited robust hypermnesia, but also showed an increase in source misattribution errors. With each test, participants grew more likely to falsely claim that they had seen an image of an object that they had only imagined. This tendency was especially likely when participants had seen physically or conceptually similar objects on the list. However, the overall rate of erroneous recalls is often surprisingly low, compared to accurate recall, in studies examining repeated recall of emotional eyewitness events (Bornstein, Liebel, & Scarberry, 1998) or autobiographical memory (Bluck et al., 1999).

Cue reinstatement

After putting unwanted memories out of mind, we sometimes stumble upon reminders. Walking around a corner, you might see a car matching the model your former partner used to drive. Rummaging through a box, you might find a gift from a loved one who has died. Veterans of Iraq who see someone make a sudden movement alongside the road while driving might be transported back to the roadside bomb attack they experienced. Unintended reminders illustrate the power of cues to reinstate unwanted memories. Cues have the same power, of course, when one reverses course, and intends to remember something that one previously wished to forget.

Steven Smith and Sarah Moynan (2008) compellingly demonstrated how people might come to forget and then later recover experiences, given the right cues. Very often one needs to confront reminders of unpleasant experiences on a recurring basis. One way of handling this might be to think about or discuss only some aspects of the experience while avoiding the unpleasant parts, perhaps rendering the nondiscussed elements less accessible. To simulate this, Smith and Moynan presented people with a categorized word list. The 21 categories included things such as *furniture*, *fruit*, *drinks*, but also emotional categories like *disease*, *death*, and *gross*. Following encoding, the experimental group made judgments about the examples from 18 of the 21 categories, three times each, encouraging selective reprocessing of parts of the list. In the control group, the same time was spent on irrelevant tasks. Participants were then asked to recall all of the category names, including ones that were left out of the intervening phase. As can be seen in the top portion of Figure 10.8, participants exhibited truly remarkable forgetting of the three category names omitted from the intervening phase. Importantly, this occurred even when categories involved emotional items such as curse words or words concerning death. In some cases, recall of the avoided categories was 70% lower than the control group, despite comparable delays and demands on attention in the intervening phase. Clearly, biasing attention to certain elements of an experience can induce dramatic rates of forgetting.

What happened to the forgotten items? Participants in the experimental condition clearly had difficulty recalling the omitted categories. If asked, they might feel as though they could not recall any more. Smith and Moynan (2008) showed that this was not true, however. After participants tried to recall the categories, they were given the category names, in turn, and asked to recall the examples. As can be seen in bottom of Figure 10.8, once the category names were given, the control and experimental participants recalled exactly the same number of items per category, and recalled these at a very high rate. Thus, retention of the items was preserved, once the right cue appeared. Indeed, of the 10 "death" words experimental participants had encountered, they recalled nearly 60% (an amount identical to that recalled by the control group) when cued with the category, even though moments earlier only 10% of the participants

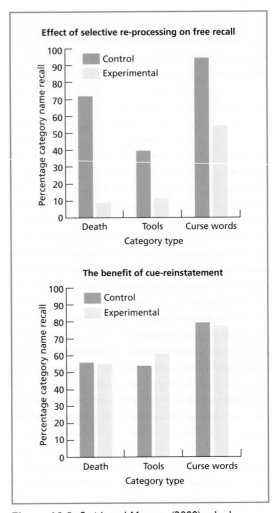

Figure 10.8 Smith and Moynan (2008) asked participants to selectively review a subset of categorized word lists. Top: The free-recall test revealed forgetting for nonreviewed categories. Bottom: Exemplars from categories participants failed to generate during free recall could often still be retrieved using category cues. From Smith and Moynan (2008). Copyright © Blackwell Publishing. Reproduced with permission.

could even recall seeing death words on the list (compared with 70% of the participants in the control condition). This illustrates that unpleasant experiences can sometimes be forgotten, given the right motivated biases in reminiscing about the event, and later recovered, given the right reminders.

But can cues really help recover memories that were intentionally forgotten? In one example, Goernert and Larson (1994) found that directed forgetting could be "released" by simply presenting a subset of the items participants studied on the first list as cues. Without any cues, participants showed a directed forgetting effect, with those people instructed to remember recalling 44% of the first list words, and those instructed to forget recalling only 21%. If participants were given either four or eight cues, their first list recall increased to 29% and 31%, respectively. Of course, the potency of cueing is also shown when people receive to-be-forgotten items on a recognition test, in which directed forgetting effects are not usually observed (with the list-method). Seeing the item itself is a potent reminder, much like seeing a videotape of an experience we have tried to forget would prove an alarmingly effective cue.

Reinstating context can also help to recover memories intentionally forgotten. For example, Sahakyan and Kelley (2002) showed that reinstating mental context can undo the effects of instructions to forget in the list-method directed forgetting procedure. Participants were exposed to an unusual context just prior to encoding the first list of words: the presentation of the theme from the Star Wars® soundtrack. Later, on the final test, Sahakyan and Kelley asked participants to reinstate the mental context that they had been in upon entering the room, including anything that they could remember about how they felt or what they thought. Would reinstating the incidental context bring back intentionally forgotten material? When the context was not reinstated, participants showed a 22% deficit in the forget condition compared to the remember condition. The context-reinstatement group, however, showed only an 8% directed forgetting effect. These findings demonstrate that motivated forgetting processes often reduce the accessibility of unwanted memories, but do not alter their availability in storage. Often, these memories remain, awaiting a time when they are sought and when the right cues are available. One question that arises is whether experiences can reside in memory, untouched and inaccessible, and be reinstated after a long delay, given the right cues. Next, we consider an important societal issue on which our understanding of these processes bear, and illustrate recovery in real life.

RECOVERED MEMORIES OF TRAUMA: INSTANCES OF MOTIVATED FORGETTING?

Most people have heard stories in which a person claims to have recovered a memory of a deeply unpleasant event, after years of being unaware of it. Sometimes famous cases receive media attention because they have led to legal charges of childhood sexual abuse against priests or parents. At other times, fictionalized cases appear on television or film, with a recovered memory as a plot device. Some people hear about recovered memories through friends or family who have had such experiences. As a memory instructor for many years, I have been approached by many students claiming to have recovered memories of abuse (several times a year). The idea that people can repress disturbing experiences is a central tenet of psychoanalytic theory. Indeed, many therapists would say that they routinely see repression and recovery in their clients. Can an unpleasant experience be forgotten and then recovered years later?

There are excellent reasons to be cautious in interpreting such reports. Retrieval is imperfect. When people have difficulty remembering, they might engage in reconstruction and inference that adds things to memory that might not have taken place. Moreover, people often confuse the sources of their memories, frequently failing to distinguish things that they have imagined, heard about, read, dreamt, or seen in a movie with things that truly happened. The dangers of such possibilities grow when people participate in therapies that have, as their objective, the goal of uncovering repressed memories. The use of hypnosis, guided imagery, and other suggestive techniques can create an environment in which it is difficult to discern fact from fiction. The cost of a memory error might be the accusation of a family member of childhood abuse when none has occurred.

The possibility of false memories, and concern over their consequences, does not, however, imply that recovered memories are untrue. One should place equal emphasis on the possibility that such experiences might reflect true events, and that failure to acknowledge this will have consequences for the victim and others who could suffer abuse at the hands of the perpetrator. In this section, we consider whether recovered memories are real and, if so, how often, how people have sought to establish these facts, and the possible mechanisms by which such experiences might come about. We begin by describing several case reports in which the memory recovery experience came about in different ways.

Cases of recovered memories

The following are real recovered memory cases, although the names have been changed. In Case 1, a person recovers a memory gradually, in suggestive therapy. Case 2 recounts a woman who abruptly remembered an abuse memory, outside of therapy, when confronted with powerful reminders. Case 3 is the story of a woman who recovered a series of deeply unpleasant events outside of therapy, and who, as a result, sought therapy.

Case 1

As reported by Geraerts (2006), Elizabeth Janssen became very depressed. Her marriage was falling apart and she even quit her job for a while. Elizabeth and Carl went to a marriage counselor to solve their problems. After several sessions, the therapist referred them to a colleague because she could not figure out why they stopped caring for each other and why their sex life was unsatisfactory. Elizabeth and Carl then started individual therapy with this psychiatrist. Almost immediately, Elizabeth was diagnosed with a major depressive disorder. She was told that she had to uncover her repressed memories of early childhood

abuse, as this was the underlying cause of her disorder.

At first, Elizabeth vehemently denied having been abused, and certainly not by her beloved father, as her psychiatrist insinuated. Her psychiatrist insisted that a childhood trauma must have happened to her; he had seen the same symptoms in so many patients. He started using guided imagery, instructing Elizabeth to imagine scenes of the supposed abuse even though Elizabeth continued to deny, although less fervently, that she had such memories. Because no abuse memories were surfacing, Elizabeth was given books about child abuse survivors to read; she was told that if something felt uncomfortable while reading these books, this would indicate that similar things happened to her. To help Elizabeth remember the abuse, hypnosis was used. After 2 months of intense therapy, Elizabeth gradually recovered vivid images of being abused. She said that she could see herself lying in bed as her father came into her room at night. While she was very anxious, he performed terrible and painful sexual acts on her. "Yes, even penetration." These traumatic events allegedly continued until she went to boarding school at age twelve. Meanwhile, Elizabeth's husband Carl had been in therapy with the same psychiatrist. He was told that he also suffered from depression. After several weeks, Carl had recovered being sexually abused by several priests at boarding school.

When asked how she had felt after recovering these abuse memories, Elizabeth said that she had never felt such a relief. It turned out that not she, but her father, was responsible for her depression. She broke off all contact with her parents. Contact with her sister and brother also became infrequent because they did not believe her story.

Case 2

Another report by Geraerts (2006) describes Mary de Vries, who had been working in the hospital as a pediatric nurse. She had a happy marriage and a 3-year-old daughter. She had been very happy that, after several years of trying, she had finally become pregnant. However, the birth of her daughter, Lynn, elicited serious problems. When Mary came home with Lynn from the hospital, she felt uncomfortable when her husband was taking care of their baby. She almost never left him alone with their daughter; she always wanted to be there when he was washing her or changing her nappies. She really could not stand the thought of her husband doing something bad to Lynn. Her mistrust resulted in heavy arguments between the couple. Mary did not even know why she mistrusted him.

Almost at the same time, her mother fell ill. Her mother had been living alone on the coast since her second husband, Mary's stepfather, had left her. Mary reassured her mother and told her that she would come over for a couple of days with her baby and would help her with the housekeeping. While she was cleaning, she entered her former bedroom. Mary said that she suddenly had a complete recollective experience in which "a whole series of pictures were running through my head." The cascade of memories horrified, shocked, overwhelmed, surprised, and baffled her at the same time. Suddenly she remembered vulgar events that occurred in that room. She remembered that her stepfather had approached her several times while she was playing there. He had fondled her genitals several times. Mary just could not talk with her mother about these horrible memories. A few days later, when Mary got home, she called her sister. Mary told her what had happened at their mother's place. First, her sister said nothing. After a couple of minutes, she told Mary that she had always vividly remembered that she had been molested by their stepfather as well.

Case 3
Herman and Schatzow (1987) report the following case, which subsequently appeared in *Science News* (Bower, 1993). After losing more than 100 pounds in a hospital weight-reduction program she had entered to battle severe obesity, Claudia experienced flashbacks of sexual abuse committed by her older brother. She joined a therapy group for incest survivors, and memories of abuse flooded back. Claudia told group members that from the time she was 4 years old to her brother's enlistment in the Army 3 years later, he had regularly handcuffed her, burned her with cigarettes, and forced her to submit to a variety of sexual acts. Claudia's brother had died in combat in Vietnam more than 15 years before her horrifying memories surfaced. Yet Claudia's parents had left his room and his belongings untouched since then. Returning home from the hospital, Claudia searched the room. Inside a closet she found a large pornography collection, handcuffs, and a diary in which her brother had extensively planned and recorded what he called sexual "experiments" with his sister.

What do we make of such cases?
The previous cases make several important points. First, memories can be recovered in many ways. In some cases, memories are recovered gradually, through active search and reconstruction, sometimes targeted at remembering abuse the person is not sure ever occurred. In other cases, the experience comes to mind spontaneously, without active search. Memories are sometimes recovered outside of therapy, triggered by a compelling need to explain some powerful reaction or feeling. Indeed, of the 634 cases of recovered memories reported by a sample of 108 British clinical psychologists in study by Andrews, Brewin, Ochera, Morton, Bekerian, Davies, et al. (1999), 32% reported recovering their memories prior to therapy of any kind.

These cases also illustrate that corroboration is sometimes lacking. In Case 1, no evidence was produced to prove that the abuse had occurred, other than the conviction of the therapist and, eventually, of the patient. Nobody else in the person's family believed the story, nor did the patient herself prior to the insistence of the therapist. It is common for corroboration to be lacking, as the hypothetical event is usually thought to have taken place years earlier, outside the view of anyone other than the accuser, who, at the time of the event, is usually a child. In such cases, it is impossible to know whether corroboration is missing because the event is not real or because care was taken to conceal it. Corroboration has often been possible, however, as illustrated in the latter cases. Indeed, there any many cases of individuals recovering memories that have been objectively corroborated. These cases provide compelling proof of the phenomenon of recovery: It is possible to forget an emotionally significant event over many years and later recover it.

The cases also highlight a serious concern about reports of recovered memories. Case 1 illustrates that some reports come through therapeutic techniques that are overly suggestive. Elizabeth Janssen had no predisposition to believe that her father had abused her but her therapist was very insistent about it. In fact, the therapist appears eager to apply repression of abuse as a diagnosis. Despite her protests, Janssen was made to repeatedly imagine and try to remember abuse she did not believe occurred, in some cases under hypnosis. Only after all this did Janssen come to believe in the event. Although such repeated retrievals might have revealed real memories, as suggested by work on hypermnesia, it also seems possible that Janssen could no longer distinguish her previous imaginings from true memories, as suggested by the Henkel (2004) work discussed earlier. When a therapist has a conviction of a memory's reality, and a client starts to feel as though he/she is remembering (even if the remembering is of previous imaginings), it can become difficult to discount the possibility that the memory is real. Thus, some cases of recovered memories might be false memories unwittingly encouraged by therapists who intend to help the patient.

Differing origins of recovered memory experiences

The preceding discussion suggests that memories recovered under differing circumstances might be produced by different processes. On the one hand, memories recovered through suggestive therapy might be more likely to reflect suggestions by the therapist rather than true recovery. On the other hand, memories recovered spontaneously, outside of therapy or in therapy, without suggestion, might be more likely to be genuine. These memories could have been forgotten by any of the mechanisms outlined in this chapter. If so, corroboration should be more likely for memories recovered spontaneously than for memories recovered through suggestive therapy.

Recently, Elke Geraerts, Jonathan Schooler, Harald Merckelbach, and colleagues (2007) sought to corroborate abuse memories of people who have always remembered their abuse, and people who have recovered it. After filling out a questionnaire about their memory of the abuse, participants were queried about sources of corroboration. Independent raters, blind to the group in which a participant fell, used this information to seek evidence that would corroborate the event. A memory was considered corroborated if: (1) another individual reported learning about the abuse within a week after it happened; (2) another individual reported having been abused by the same perpetrator; or (3) the perpetrator admitted to committing the abuse. Strikingly, memories recovered spontaneously, outside of therapy, were corroborated at a rate (37%) that was comparable to that observed for people with continuously accessible memories (45%). Memories recovered through suggestive therapy, however, could never be corroborated (0%). Although this lack of corroboration does not imply that those recovered memories are false, the lack of evidence does not permit confidence in their reality, and recommends caution in interpretation. More generally, these findings suggest that not all recovered memories are the same, and that discontinuous memory does not make an experience any less real than something a person has always remembered.

The foregoing findings suggest that recovered memories can originate in different ways for people who recollect the abuse spontaneously, and for those who recall it through suggestive therapy. Geraerts and colleagues hypothesized that memories recalled through suggestive therapy might be the product of suggestion, a possibility consistent with the lack of corroboration. People recalling memories spontaneously, by contrast, might genuinely have forgotten the experience, and later remembered it. Alternatively, the spontaneously recovered group might have recalled the event, but have forgotten that they have recalled it before. The latter possibility is suggested by a case reported by Jonathan Schooler (Schooler, Ambadar, & Bendiksen, 1997), in which a woman "recovered" a memory of childhood abuse for "the first time," only to be informed by her spouse that they had discussed the event at length years earlier. Might people who have spontaneous recovery experiences simply be forgetting prior occasions of thinking about it?

To explore these possibilities, Geraerts, Arnold, Lindsay, Merckelbach, Jelicic, and Hauer (2006) first investigated whether people reporting recovered memories had a tendency to underestimate prior remembering. They invited people with recovered or continuous memories to write down a memory from their childhood for each of 25 titles. The titles described common things that happen to children like *being home alone* or *going to the dentist*. For some of these titles, participants were asked to concentrate on emotionally negative aspects of the event (e.g. for *being home alone* this might be the feeling of being frightened), but for others, the positive aspects (e.g. for the home alone title, this might be getting to do whatever you want). Everyone returned 2 months later and generated the same memories, yet again. There was one switch, however: Sometimes people retrieved the events in the same emotional frame as before, but for other titles, they were asked to retrieve the event in the opposite emotional frame. So, for example, if they had recalled *being home alone* in a positive light during the first visit, they recalled the same event again, but focused on the negative aspects. When this second visit was complete, people returned to the laboratory for a third and final time 2 months later. They recalled all of the events

yet again, but this time they recalled each one in the same emotional frame in which they had recalled it during the first visit. Critically, after recalling each memory, people were asked to remember whether they had recalled that same memory during the second (i.e. middle) visit. Interestingly, when the emotional framing on the final visit differed from the one on the second visit, people were quite like to forget having remembered the event during that second visit, compared to when the emotional framing remained the same. Thus, shifting the way that people thought about the same memory (whether positively or negatively) from one occasion to the next made them forget thinking about the memory before. Importantly, this tendency was much greater for people reporting recovered memories than it was for people reporting continuous memories, or people without any history of abuse (Figure 10.9).

So it seems that one reason why people might have a recovered memory experience is that they simply forget having remembered the event before. They might forget prior cases of remembering if, for example, the mental context present when they are having their recovery experience differs from the mental context on prior occasions in which they thought of the event. By this view, it is not that people have forgotten the event for all those years, it is that they simply can't remember having remembered, perhaps due to context-dependent memory.

If this process underlies authentic reports of recovered memories, then perhaps people who spontaneously recover their memories of childhood abuse would be more likely to show pronounced underestimation of prior remembering than would participants who recovered their memories through suggestive therapy. By contrast, if people who recover their memories through suggestive therapy are especially prone to suggestion, perhaps they might show an exaggerated tendency towards false-memory formation. To examine these possibilities, Geraerts and colleagues (in press) tested people with spontaneously recovered memories, people with memories

Figure 10.9 The ability to recall prior remembrances is diminished if the retrieval perspective differed between them (other-framing condition). Geraerts et al. (2006) found that this tendency is greatest in individuals who previously reported recovered memories of abuse, distinguishing them from abuse victims who reported continuous memories of their trauma and controls. Data from Geraerts et al. (2006).

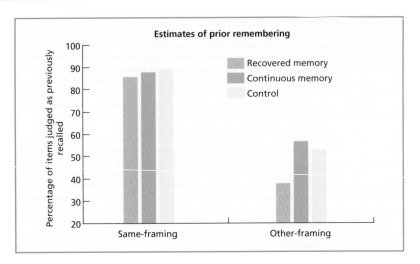

recovered through suggestive therapy, and people with continuously available memories on the preceding task. Strikingly, only participants who had recovered their memories spontaneously showed exaggerated forgetting of prior remembering; patients who recovered their memories in suggestive therapy or people with continuous memories showed no such pattern. When tested on a simple laboratory task designed to estimate susceptibility to the formation of false memories, however, only people who recovered their memories in suggestive therapy showed exaggerated false-memory formation; neither the spontaneously recovered memory group nor people with continuous access to their memories showed such a pattern. These findings lend force to the idea that memories recovered in suggestive therapy and recovered spontaneously have fundamentally different origins.

The discussion thus far does not explain why some people might show greater susceptibility to forgetting prior to remembering. One possibility is that people with authentic abuse experiences might engage some of the motivated-forgetting processes discussed earlier to limit intrusive remindings of the unwanted experience. So, for example, they might learn to engage inhibitory control to suppress intrusive thoughts. If so, perhaps the reason why these people cannot remember their prior incidences of remembering is that these memories have

been disrupted by the same processes at work in retrieval-induced forgetting or the think/no-think procedure discussed earlier. This hypothesis has received some support (Geraerts et al., 2007). People with spontaneously recovered memories are better at suppressing thoughts of unpleasant experiences than are people with memories recovered through suggestive therapy, or people with continuously accessible memories. Thus, people might learn to habitually suppress remindings of those events, causing them to forget their prior thoughts.

If the thought-suppression hypothesis is correct, does this present an alternative to the idea that memories can be repressed, and later recovered? It depends. On the one hand, if a memory must be consistently inaccessible over many years for it to count as repression, this research suggests a different mechanism. On the other hand, Freud emphasized the *return of the repressed* and the idea that repression needed to be actively maintained. If repression requires continual reinstatement, then suppressing intrusive remindings over the span of many years simply reflects reinstatement. Further work is required to establish the mental and biological mechanisms that account for these, and other cases of motivated forgetting. It is clear, however, that what we remember is not random, and aligns with our motivations and goals of emotional regulation.

SUMMARY

When we try to understand why we remember what we do, we cannot disregard our motivations. We often have compelling reasons for limiting retrieval of certain experiences. Sometimes, those reasons relate to functional goals, like concentration or ensuring that we access only current knowledge; at other times, they concern the regulation of emotions. People don't like to feel sad, anxious, afraid, ashamed, or embarrassed. Yet we sometimes confront reminders to memories that make us feel these feelings. When the world calls to mind such memories, people regulate their feelings by intentionally controlling memory. If such experiences are forgotten, it aids our long-term objective of maintaining a positive emotional state. The results of these ongoing efforts can be seen in people's remarkable capacity for selective remembering.

Experimental psychology has revealed a number of factors related to motivated forgetting. Surprisingly, simply telling someone to forget something often works. In some cases, this reflects a motivated failure to deeply encode a stimulus; in other cases, forgetting instructions disrupt retrieval access. Such processes might result either from the engagement of inhibitory control to suppress the preceding events, shifts in mental context, or both. People can also achieve motivated forgetting by intentionally shifting or modifying their physical context, depriving themselves of reminders. When reminders cannot be avoided, people engage inhibitory control to suppress retrieval itself, an action that impairs memory for the suppressed event. Retrieval suppression is supported by the lateral prefrontal cortex, and works in part by reducing activation in the hippocampus. Unwanted memory retrievals can also be stopped by generating diversionary thoughts, which can add interference that blocks later spontaneous retrievals of the unwanted memory, engage retrieval induced forgetting, or both. Most of these processes have been demonstrated with complex emotional materials, suggesting that they might be sufficient to account for how people regulate memory of naturally occurring events.

Sometimes, people might want to remember memories they previously wished to forget. Several factors predict when and how recovery is possible. The mere passage of time, even in the absence of efforts to retrieve, can increase the accessibility of a memory. Spontaneous recovery often occurs when memory has initially been actively dampened by inhibitory control, such as with extinction and retroactive interference. Memories can also be recovered through repeated efforts to recall. Strikingly, even when people try and fail to recall a memory repeatedly, and they are sure that they cannot recall it, later attempts might succeed. Hypermnesia and reminiscence can, at times, yield dramatic reversals of the Ebbinghaus forgetting curve. Memories can be reinstated given the availability of suitable cues. Even when memories seem impossible to recall, reinstatement of physical or mental context, or presentation of particular reminders, can, in some cases, restore a memory with little loss in information. Most of these recovery processes have been demonstrated with complex and emotional events.

Many of the motivated forgetting and motivated recovery processes discussed here could have a hand in producing recovered memory experiences. A recovered memory experience occurs when a person recollects an especially unpleasant event that is believed to have been inaccessible over many years. Such experiences have been reported for all manner of emotional events, including memory for wartime experiences, physical violence, and childhood sexual abuse. The debate about recovered memories of childhood sexual abuse has received attention, in part, because of concern over the possibility that some recovered memory experiences may be false. False recovered memories might arise, for example, when people participate in prolonged periods of recollecting an abuse event, guided by highly suggestive memory recovery techniques. False memories of abuse have indeed been induced by such procedures, underlining the role of suggestion and source memory failures in shaping what people believe has happened to them. On the other hand, many recovered memories of sexual abuse have proven to be real events that can be corroborated by physical evidence and even a confession of the perpetrator. This raises the issue of when and how often recovered memories may be real, and how such experiences come about.

Memories of childhood abuse recovered in suggestive therapy are not as easy to corroborate as memories recovered spontaneously, outside of therapy. Although lack of corroboration does not indicate that a recovered memory is false, some evidence suggests that people recovering memories under such circumstances are more suggestible. This raises the possibility that some of these recovery events might not reflect real abuse, but rather the unwitting result of suggestive therapeutic techniques. Memories recovered spontaneously, however, appear to be corroborated to the same degree as continuously accessible memories, suggesting that many of these experiences reflect real abuse. People recovering memories under these circumstances exhibit a pronounced tendency to forget their prior experiences of remembering, and also show special skill at suppressing thoughts about anxious memories. These findings suggest that some recovered memory experiences arise because people forget prior reminders of the event, perhaps through some of the motivated-forgetting processes discussed above, especially inhibition.

Research on motivated forgetting and its biological underpinnings is receiving increased attention in psychology and neuroscience due, in part, to the obvious practical problem of understanding how people control unwanted memories of past traumatic experiences. Research in this area will help to clarify how people's motivations and emotions, and our efforts to deliberately control how we feel, influence what elements we retain of our past.

FURTHER READING

- Bjork, R. A. (1989). Retrieval inhibition as an adaptive mechanism in human memory. In H. L. Roediger & F. I. Craik (Eds.), *Varieties of memory and consciousness: Essays in honour of Endel Tulving* (pp. 309–330). Hillsdale, NJ: Lawrence Erlbaum Associates.

- Cheit, R. E. (Director). *Recovered memory archive*. Online. Available: www.RecoveredMemory.org

- Erdelyi, M. H. (2006). The unified theory of repression. *Behavioral and Brain Sciences*, 29(5), 499–551.

- Loftus, E. F., & Davis, D. (2006). Recovered memories. *Annual Review of Clinical Psychology*, 2, 469–498.

- MacLeod, C. M. (1998). Directed forgetting. In J. M. Golding & C. M. MacLeod (Eds.), *Intentional forgetting: Interdisciplinary approaches* (pp. 197–218). Mahwah, NJ: Lawrence Erlbaum Associates.

CHAPTER 11

AMNESIA

Alan Baddeley

We all have memory lapses, some more embarrassing than others. On one occasion, I agreed to appear on a live radio phone-in program, the *Jimmy Mack Show* from Glasgow. As I lived in Cambridge at the time, it was agreed that I would participate from the local radio station. That morning I was reading the newspaper before checking my diary and setting off for work, when I glanced at the TV and radio section, prompting the awful realization that I should at that moment be telling the world about the wonders of memory. I leapt on my bike and arrived just before the end of the program, sheepishly muttering about the terrible traffic in Cambridge, to be asked by the host if I could give the listeners a few hints on how to improve their memory!

So we all have bad memories, but what is it like to have a genuine memory problem—not the devastatingly dense amnesia experienced by Clive Wearing and described in Chapter 1, but the much more common level of memory deficit that accompanies many conditions including stroke, Alzheimer's disease, and traumatic brain injury? A very good account of the problems associated with memory deficit is given by Malcolm Meltzer, a clinical psychologist who experienced memory problems following a heart attack that led to anoxia (Meltzer, 1983).

Meltzer emerged from a 6-week coma knowing who he was and recognizing his family, but thinking he was 33 years old whereas in fact he was 44. On returning home, he could not remember where things were kept and, unlike a pure amnesic patient, also had problems in remembering skills such as how to set an alarm clock, when bills should be paid, where was a good place to go for a vacation, and how one might get there. He also had problems with his working memory:

*Organization of thinking was hampered …
I had trouble keeping the facts in mind,
which made it difficult to organize them …
comparing things along a number of variables
is difficult to do when you cannot retain the
variables.* (Meltzer, 1983, p. 4)

Meltzer found it hard work to watch films or TV because of the difficulty in remembering the plot or, in the case of sports, which team was which and which was ahead. He tended to find spatial orientation difficult and even walks in a familiar neighborhood were liable to result in his getting lost. A particular problem was the impact of his amnesia on his capacity to interact with people:

*Having conversations could become a
trial. Often in talking with people I was
acquainted with, I had trouble remembering
their names or whether they were married, or
what our relationship had been in the past.
I worried about asking where someone's
wife is and finding out that I had been at her
funeral two years before.*

Often if I didn't have a chance to say immediately what came to mind, it would be forgotten and the conversation would move to another topic. Then there was little for me to talk about. I couldn't remember much about current events or things I read in the paper or saw on TV. Even juicy tit-bits of gossip might be forgotten. So in order to have something to say, I tended to talk about myself and my "condition." My conversation became rather boring. (Meltzer, 1983)

Eventually, with considerable perseverance, Meltzer recovered sufficiently to return to work, and of course to write a paper, providing for carers and therapists a very clear insight into the problems that result from memory deficit.

STUDYING AMNESIA

Unlike much research in cognitive psychology, the study of amnesia depends critically on clinical psychologists who are interacting with patients for practical and professional reasons. The clinical priorities vary from one center to another, with investigators from different backgrounds tending to emphasize different approaches. In the case of the Montreal Neurological Institute, as Brenda Milner's (1966) study of HM the classic case of impaired episodic LTM described in Chapter 2 demonstrates, there was a need for the neuropsychologist to identify the function of different brain areas so as to guide the neurosurgeon and minimize any unwanted side effects. Milner's approach therefore tended to stress anatomical localization, and be less concerned with the development of theory in cognitive psychology.

A second important pioneer in this area was Elizabeth Warrington, who works at the National Hospital for Nervous Diseases in London. This is the principal UK center for neurology, and often receives patients who show an unusual pattern of symptoms, presenting a challenge to diagnosis. Elizabeth was interested in linking the nature and location of their brain dysfunction with the development of a better functional understanding of the cognitive deficits shown by patients, and in this connection often chose to collaborate with mainstream cognitive psychologists.

A similar collaboration occurred in a third main research group concerned with amnesia, located at The Boston Veterans Administration Hospital, where a clinical neuropsychologist, Nelson Butters, worked with a cognitive psychologist, Laird Cermak. A major problem confronting the hospital was that of treating service personnel who had developed alcoholism, which in many cases resulted in Korsakoff syndrome, the principal source of amnesic patients for this group. Korsakoff syndrome is an alcohol-related problem in metabolizing the vitamin thiamine, which in turn leads to brain damage in areas such as the hippocampus and diencephalon, which are essential for episodic memory.

The difference between the practical demands facing these three groups can lead to apparent scientific discrepancies, potentially resulting in controversy. In fact, all three approaches are necessary but serve different functions. From the viewpoint of a cognitive psychologist, the most informative studies are those in which the deficit concerned is theoretically important and pure, regardless of whether it results from surgery, a stroke, or alcoholism. From a neurosurgical viewpoint, however, the link between function and anatomy is the crucial issue, with the anatomical localization of the patient's brain lesions being more important than the implications of the deficit for understanding normal cognitive function. Finally, if one wishes to understand a particular disease, be it Korsakoff syndrome, Alzheimer's disease, or schizophrenia, then it is essential to study patients with that disease, even though the nature, the purity, and extent of both their anatomical and cognitive deficits are likely to vary from one patient to the next. Of course, it is possible to select patients with relatively pure cognitive deficits, but symptom complexity is an important feature of the disease, and hence should be studied rather than avoided. These additional complicating features can, however, potentially give rise to controversy when, for example, a disease-based study is used to draw strong theoretical conclusions, as we shall see below.

TERMINOLOGY

A crucial distinction is that between **anterograde amnesia** and **retrograde amnesia**. Anterograde amnesia refers to a problem in encoding, storing, or retrieving information that can be used in the *future*, hence the prefix *antero*. By contrast, retrograde amnesia refers to loss of access to events that happened in the *past*, typically before the onset of the disease. The densely amnesic patient HM, described in Chapter 2, is a classic case of anterograde amnesia because his capacity for new learning was greatly restricted but his ability to recall events from before his operation was relatively well preserved. In this respect, he can be contrasted with Boswell, a patient who was also densely amnesic and unable to acquire new episodic information, but who also was unable to retrieve factual knowledge from the past (Damasio, Eslinger, Damasio, Van Hoesen, &

KEY TERMS

Anterograde amnesia: A problem in encoding, storing, or retrieving information that can be used in the future.
Retrograde amnesia: A problem accessing events that happened in the past.
Post-traumatic amnesia (PTA): Patients have difficulty forming new memories. Often follows a severe concussive head injury and tends to improve with time.
Transient global amnesia (TGA): Apparently normal individuals suddenly develop severe problems in forming and retrieving new memories. The cause is unknown and the condition tends to resolve relatively rapidly.

Cornell, 1985), and hence who suffered from both anterograde and retrograde amnesia. You might recall that Clive Wearing, who was described in Chapter 1, similarly showed dense anterograde amnesia together with retrograde amnesia reflected in his very patchy access to earlier memories.

Other types of amnesia include **post-traumatic amnesia (PTA)**, a state that often follows a severe concussive head injury. A patient in PTA has difficulty forming new memories, a condition that tends to improve gradually over time (Levin & Hanten, 2002). Finally, **transient global amnesia (TGA)**, is

The 2001 film *Memento* chronicles the story of Leonard, an ex-insurance investigator who can no longer build new memories, as he attempts to find the perpetrator of a violent attack that caused his post-traumatic anterograde amnesia and left his wife dead. The attack is the last event he can recall. © Corbis Sygma.

a condition in which an apparently normal individual suddenly develops severe problems in forming and retrieving new memories, a state that fortunately tends to resolve relatively rapidly. The cause of TGA, and indeed, the question of whether it has one or many causes, is still unclear (Goldenberg, 2002).

ANTEROGRADE AMNESIA

The amnesic syndrome

A classic case of the amnesic syndrome would have preserved intellect and language coupled with a dense impairment in the capacity for episodic learning, whether tested visually or verbally, and whether by recall or recognition. Whereas memory disruption might result from almost anything that interferes with the normal functioning of the brain, the pure but dense amnesia that constitutes the classic amnesic syndrome tends to be associated with a more limited range of different causes. These include bilateral damage to the temporal lobes and hippocampus, **alcoholic Korsakoff syndrome**, prolonged anoxia, and encephalitis resulting from brain infection. Any of these is likely to result in cognitive deficits that extend beyond amnesia, but all can on occasion result in a dense but pure deficit of episodic memory.

Elizabeth Warrington and I studied a group of patients varying in their etiology or source of disease but all having preserved intellect and grossly impaired episodic memory (Baddeley & Warrington, 1970). They were all densely amnesic, showing greatly impaired capacity for learning verbal or visual material, whether tested by recall or recognition. They had, however, preserved digit span and showed a normal recency effect in a task involving the free recall of 10 unrelated words, although performance on earlier items was markedly impaired (Figure 11.1).

Our patients also performed normally on the Brown–Peterson short-term forgetting task, not only in terms of their rate of forgetting but also in the point at which forgetting leveled off,

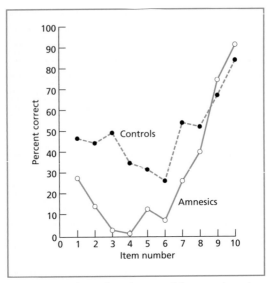

Figure 11.1 Immediate free recall in amnesic and control patients. Amnesic patients show preserved recency and impaired recall of earlier items. From Baddeley and Warrington (1970). Copyright © Elsevier. Reproduced with permission.

well above baseline. This led to controversy, as Cermak, Butters, and Moreines (1974), testing a group of amnesic Korsakoff patients in Boston, observed impaired Peterson performance. They also found that their patients failed to show the normal release from proactive interference (see Chapter 2, p. 23) when the words to be remembered in the Peterson task were changed from one semantic category to another, for example from animals to flowers (Cermak & Moreines, 1976), whereas our patients showed the normal pattern, with performance improving dramatically on the first trial with the new category. The failure to find release in the Boston patients was attributed by Cermak

> **KEY TERM**
>
> **Alcoholic Korsakoff syndrome:** Patients have difficulty learning new information, although events from the past are recalled. There is a tendency to invent material to fill memory blanks. Most common cause is alcoholism, especially when this has resulted in a deficiency of vitamin B1.

and Butters to an absence of deep semantic coding, thus providing what appeared to be a neat explanation of amnesia in terms of the Craik and Lockhart levels of processing hypothesis (see Chapter 5, p. 99). They made a number of suggestions regarding possible methodological differences between our study and theirs that might explain the discrepancy between our results.

The issue was finally resolved when Cermak (1976) tested SS, a patient with a very pure amnesia resulting from a brain infection, who behaved like the London amnesic patients. Careful further investigation indicated that the Boston Korsakoff patients had a less pure memory deficit than was at first supposed. As is often—although not always—the case, the patients with Korsakoff syndrome showed subtle signs of damage to the frontal lobes resulting in impaired executive function. The Peterson task involves maintaining a memory representation at the same time as performing the demanding interpolated task of counting backwards. As such, it involves working memory and not simply verbal STM, and hence is sensitive to frontal lobe damage.

What can amnesic patients learn?

Despite their problem with new episodic learning, it has been known for many years that there are certain things that pure amnesic patients are able to learn. A classic anecdote from the Swiss neuropsychiatrist Claparède (1911) concerns an informal experiment he carried out on one occasion on the ward round in his clinic. Each day he would visit and shake hands with his patients. On one occasion, he secreted a pin in his hand when shaking hands with an amnesic woman. Next day she refused to shake hands but could not remember why. This is, of course, an instance of classical conditioning in which the handshake is associated with pain. Subsequent studies, under more controlled conditions, have shown that amnesic patients show normal classical conditioning. In one study (described in Chapter 4; see p. 79), a light was followed by a puff of air to the eye causing an automatic blink response (Warrington & Weiskrantz, 1978; Gabrieli, McGlinchey-Berroth, Carrillo, Gluck, Cermak, & Disterhoft, 1995). After a number of paired presentations of light and air puff, the light alone was able to evoke a blink, an instance of classical avoidance conditioning. However, confronted with the equipment and asked what it did, patients were quite unable to remember.

Priming

As noted in Chapter 4, Warrington and Weiskrantz (1968) found that, although their amnesic patients were grossly impaired in their capacity for recalling or recognizing items from a list of words or pictures, they performed as well as controls when asked to identify a visually degraded version of the relevant words or pictures. A similar result was obtained by Graf, Squire, and Mandler (1984), when they compared amnesic and control patients on two tasks. One was implicit and involved stem completion, a task in which a list of words (e.g. *METAL*) is presented and then tested by providing the initial letters (e.g. *ME – – –*) and asking participants to "guess" a word that would fit. The second task, cued recall, also involved presenting the word stem, but this time asking participants to *remember* what word had been presented. There was a clear difference between the two groups when given the explicit *remember* instruction, but not with the implicit stem completion task.

Skills

Corkin (1968) observed that HM showed normal performance on a task involving tracing a star observed through a mirror, a task that is initially frustratingly difficult but to which you rapidly adapt. Brooks and Baddeley (1976) tested amnesic patients on a pursuit rotor task in which you have to keep a stylus in contact with a moving target. Both patients and controls showed a similar rate of improvement with practice. As Figure 11.2 shows, novel perceptual tasks such as reading words

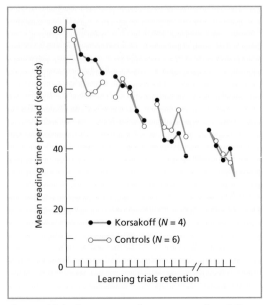

Figure 11.2 Acquisition of a mirror-reading skill across three daily sessions, and retention 3 months later. The amnesic Korsakoff patients learned and retained the skill as well as controls. Data from Cohen and Squire (1980).

printing in mirror-transformed script can also be learned by amnesic patients as readily as control participants (Cohen & Squire, 1980).

Controlling complex systems

Another form of implicit learning involves highly complex skills such as these involved in learning an artificial grammar or controlling a complex system simulating the operation of a sugar-producing factory (see Chapter 4, p. 85). Amnesic patients have been shown to be quite able to learn such skills (see Squire, Knowlton & Musen, 1993, for a review).

Hedonic adaptation

Johnson, Kim, and Risse (1985) were interested in the phenomenon whereby an unfamiliar experience, such as hearing a Korean melody for the first time, is often judged negatively, but then, with repeated presentations leads to increasingly positive judgments (see p. 81). They observed this effect in their amnesic patients, who nevertheless denied ever having heard such a melody before.

THEORIES OF AMNESIA

Although there is considerable agreement as to the phenomena associated with the amnesic syndrome, there is much less agreement on how to interpret them. One suggestion is that amnesic patients lack the capacity to consolidate memory traces (Milner, 1968, Squire & Alvarez, 1995; Cahill, Haier, & Alkire, 1996). This is essentially a physiological interpretation, although it clearly has implications for performance at the psychological level. A number of such explanations have been proposed at a more cognitive level, including:

Levels of processing

As noted earlier in this chapter, Cermak and colleagues, noting that their Korsakoff patients apparently failed to take advantage of semantic coding in a release from a proactive interference paradigm suggested that a failure to encode deeply might lie at the root of their memory problem. Cermak and Moreines (1976) attempted to test this hypothesis in a levels of processing study and found that their patients showed little advantage from the deep processing condition. However, a subsequent study indicated that this was due to a floor effect. The patients had shown so little learning in any condition that no differences could be detected. When the task was made easier, patients showed the standard levels of processing effect (Cermak, & Reale, 1978).

In a further investigation of this issue, Meudell, Mayes, and Neary (1980) used cartoons as their stimulus material. In the shallow encoding condition, participants looked for minor differences between two very similar drawings. In a second condition, they were asked to memorize the cartoons for later test, whereas in the deepest condition they were asked to describe the cartoons and rate them for humor. The patients with alcoholic Korsakoff syndrome performed more poorly overall, but as Figure 11.3 shows had retained a normal sense of humor and showed just as clear a depth-of-processing advantage as did controls.

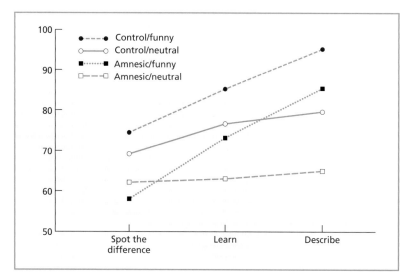

Figure 11.3 Effect of encoding instructions on subsequent recognition of humorous or neutral cartoons by amnesic patients and controls. Both groups are helped by humor and by deeper encoding instructions Adapted from Meudell et al. (1980).

Faster forgetting?

There are at least two versions of the consolidation hypothesis. The first assumes that long-term traces are simply not established. The second proposes that they are set up, but decay rapidly. This latter hypothesis would predict that amnesic patients would forget at a faster rate. A variant of this hypothesis is the proposal that one subgroup of amnesics— patients with damage to the hippocampus— forget faster than those with damage to other temporal lobe structures (Squire, 1981). In fact, given that the initial level of learning is equated, there is no evidence to suggest faster forgetting in either subgroup of amnesic patients (Huppert & Piercy, 1978a; Kopelman, 1985). Somewhat surprisingly, although any condition that compromises brain function is liable to lead to impaired learning, very few of these result in faster forgetting, once material has been acquired.

Retrieval

Warrington and Weiskrantz (1970) initially interpreted their puzzling results in terms of retrieval, arguing that the word-fragment cues that were so effective at test helped performance by ruling out potentially interfering responses. However, they subsequently rejected this interpretation on the grounds that other predicted effects did not occur (Warrington & Weiskrantz, 1978).

Contextual processing

An essential quality of episodic memory is that it allows individual specific memories to be retrieved. An influential theory as to what makes this possible proposes that individual episodes are linked to the specific time and place of the experience. This provides a way of specifying that experience, and subsequently retrieving that particular memory rather than others occurring at a different time or place. Loss of the capacity to link experiences to their spatial and temporal context would therefore grossly disrupt subsequent recollection. In a study using rats, Winocur and Mills (1970) observed that animals with hippocampal lesions were particularly bad at making use of environmental context in a spatial learning task, suggesting to Winocur (1978) that a failure to associate memories with context may also apply to human amnesic patients.

Evidence for a deficit in contextual memory came from an ingenious study by Huppert and Piercy (1978a, 1978b). They took advantage of the fact that people are very good at recognizing pictures that they have previously been shown, demonstrating first that the performance of amnesic and control patients can be roughly equated by giving the patients longer to encode the pictures than the controls. Their study involved presenting pictures either once or twice on each of 2 successive days. After the second day's presentation, participants were shown a sequence of pictures and asked to say whether they had seen each picture. If they recognized a picture they were then to decide on which day that picture had been shown.

The crucial comparison concerned the pictures that had been seen twice on day 1. Huppert and Piercy found that amnesic patients were more likely to say that items presented twice on day 1 had in fact been presented on day 2, presumably because the degree of familiarity was greater. The controls showed exactly the opposite pattern, being more accurate in assigning items to day 1 if they had been presented twice. Two presentations meant two chances of linking that picture to the day 1 context. In the absence of the link to context provided by episodic memory, the amnesic patients had to rely on a general feeling of familiarity. This did not allow them to distinguish between greater familiarity resulting from two presentations, and that resulting from a recent experience.

Schacter, Harbluk, and McLachlan (1984) showed a similar effect, using as their material the answers to Trivial Pursuit questions such as "What was Bob Hope's favorite food?", again finding that amnesic patients are bad at recalling *when* information is acquired tending to confuse recency with degree of familiarity. The term *source amnesia* has been applied to this characteristic difficulty that amnesic patients experience in recollecting the source of a given memory.

Amnesia: a modal model

In an attempt to pull together the overall pattern of data, I proposed what I termed a modal model of amnesia, a simple interpretation of the amnesic syndrome that appeared to capture

In Huppert and Piercy's (1978a; b) study, amnesic patients were more likely to say that pictures presented twice on day 1 had in fact been presented on day 2 demonstrating a deficit in contextual memory. © BSIP, MENDIL / Science Photo Library.

most if not all of the evidence (Baddeley, 1998). This accepted a deliberately unspecified version of the consolidation hypothesis, whereby learning in episodic memory involved associating items with their context using some form of "mnemonic glue." This clearly nontechnical term was deliberately selected so as to indicate that it was *not* based on any sophisticated neurobiological evidence but simply accepted that a neurobiological interpretation of some form seemed necessary. This does not rule out a contextual hypothesis, as it could be argued that the essence of episodic memory is the capacity to "glue" experiences to a specific context, thus providing a contextual tag that allows individual experiences to be retrieved.

This simplified model of amnesia assumed that recall and recognition involved the same underlying storage processes, although they placed different constraints on subsequent retrieval. It assumed that semantic memory represented the residue of many episodes. Over time, the capacity to retrieve individual experiences might have been lost through forgetting, but it was assumed that those features that were shared by repeated episodes could be retrievable through a separate mechanism. Although this modal model seemed to give a plausible account of the classic amnesic syndrome, it was not clear how to test it and I myself ceased to work on amnesia.

Some years later, however, I was asked to talk about amnesia at a retirement symposium for Elizabeth Warrington. Because of our earlier work together, I agreed. I had not subsequently published anything on my speculative modal model of amnesia and thought it would be a good opportunity to obtain feedback from an expert audience. Despite absent-mindedly leaving my slides on the train en route, the talk seemed to go reasonably well. Then, shortly after the meeting, I was invited by Faraneh Vargha-Khadem, from the Institute of Child Health in London, to visit and test a patient, Jon, an experience that convinced me that my modal model of amnesia might well be wrong, or at any rate far too simple.

Developmental amnesia

Jon has the misfortune to have been born prematurely and had to spend his early days in an incubator. He suffered breathing problems resulting in anoxia, and substantial damage to his hippocampus. Somewhat unusually, this appears to be the limit of the damage to his brain. It was however, severe, with his hippocampus being less than half the normal size, and somewhat atypical in its structure.

At about the age of 5, Jon's parents began to suspect that he had memory problems, and this proved to be the case. However, despite having a degree of amnesia that made it difficult for him to cope independently, Jon has developed above average intelligence and good semantic memory skills. Furthermore, although his recall memory is clearly impaired, his recognition performance tends to be within the normal range. Figure 11.4 shows the performance of Jon and two matched control participants on the Doors and People Test (Baddeley, Vargha-Khadem, & Mishkin, 2001c). This test was developed to provide a separate measure for visual and verbal recall and recognition, allowing each of these components to be assessed separately and then combined to give overall visual scores, overall verbal scores, and combined

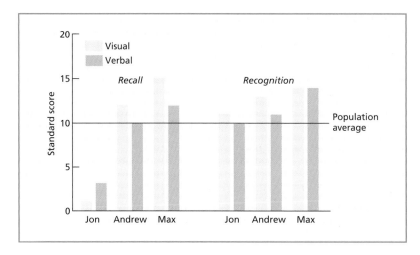

Figure 11.4 Performance on the Doors and People test of visual and verbal recall by Jon, a developmental amnesic patient, and two controls. Jon is impaired on recall but not recognition. From Baddeley et al. (2001). Copyright © 2001 MIT Press. Reproduced with permission.

recall versus recognition. A similar level of preserved performance was found on a wide range of other tests of recognition, confirming earlier observations on Jon and a number of other similar patients by Vargha-Khadem, Gadian, and Mishkin (2001), although subsequent studies suggest that Jon's recognition performance might not be completely normal (Gardiner, Brandt, Vargha-Khadem, Baddeley, & Mishkin, 2006).

Jon presents a number of problems for the proposed modal model of amnesia. First, if episodic memory is impaired how can semantic memory develop? Second, although the link between memory and intelligence is not clearly specified by the modal model, one might expect crystallized intelligence, based on prior learning, to be impaired, resulting, for example, in reduced vocabulary. This is not the case. Subsequent research suggests, however, that although Jon's knowledge of the world is excellent, it might take him longer than controls to acquire new facts (Gardiner, Brandt, Baddeley, Vargha-Khadem, & Mishkin, in press). Third, if recall and recognition involve essentially the same storage process, why, in Jon's case, can recognition be so well preserved and recall so impaired?

A hint as to the answer to this question comes from the previously described distinction between *remembering* based on the capacity to recollect a learning episode, to travel backwards in time to re-experience it, in Tulving's terminology, and the capacity to *know* that one has previously encountered an item, in the absence of recollective experience (see Chapter 1, p. 11). We attempted to assess Jon's capacity to "remember," but had considerable difficulty teaching him the distinction between remembering and knowing. Eventually, he declared that he understood the distinction and we went ahead. Jon used the remember-and-know categories about as often as controls. However, when control participants made a remember judgment they could describe their recollection, for example *The word "dog" reminded me of my granny's dachshund*. Jon did not. He reported that he

tried to form a visual image of the cards on which the words had been presented, and if his image of the word was clear and bright then he categorized this as remembering. In short, he appeared to be using a strength rather than a recollective criterion.

Further evidence on this point came from an evoked electrophysiological response study that studied the electrical response of Jon's brain when attempting to recognize words that had previously been presented, and categorize them as "remembered" or "known." This study took advantage of the fact that "remember" judgments are accompanied by a specific activation pattern that differs from that evoked by "know" responses. Jon proved to lack the remember component (Düzel, Vargha-Khadem, Heinze, & Mishkin, 2001). Finally, Maguire, Vargha-Khadem, and Mishkin (2001) succeeded in finding a few memories from Jon's life that seemed to evoke the crucial episodic experience of reliving an event. When such memories were evoked in a brain-imaging study, he finally showed the standard "remember" pattern of brain activation, indicating that he does have the capacity to recollect but has great difficulty in laying down the memory traces on which such recollective experiences are based.

To summarize, it appears to be the case that Jon can learn, in the sense of building up familiarity, but that he is very impaired in his capacity to recollect. The fact that he has none-the-less acquired a rich semantic memory and above-average intelligence presents a clear challenge to theory and to earlier assumptions regarding the role of the hippocampus.

There is no doubt that Jon is far from typical as an amnesic patient. More specifically, Squire and colleagues have presented data from groups of amnesic patients who appear to have lesions limited to the hippocampus, and who behave in the standard way, with no evidence of preserved recognition memory (Reed & Squire, 1997; Manns & Squire, 1999). Why the difference? One possibility is that Jon acquired his hippocampal damage at a very early age whereas most amnesic patients become amnesic as adults. Given the greater potential plasticity of the young brain, it is possible that Jon's brain might have developed in such a way that the preserved tissue can supplement his damaged hippocampus. If this is the case, then one should find an association between the likelihood of finding a pattern such as that shown by Jon and the age of onset of the patient's amnesia. Testing this is not simple, as although similar cases to Jon are now being identified more widely, they tend not to have such a precisely limited area of neurological damage, or such a specific pattern of cognitive impairment. This issue is currently being pursued by Vargha-Khadem and colleagues, but the outcome is still unclear.

A second possibility is that the pattern of deficits shown by Jon reflects the specificity of the area of the damage within his brain, being limited to the hippocampus, whereas the surrounding regions comprising the *perirhinal* and *entorhinal* cortices appear to have been entirely spared. There is no doubt that some of the earlier claims for the importance of the hippocampus stem in part from associated deficits. In animal lesion studies, it is very difficult to lesion the hippocampus without influencing these areas, and in brain-damaged patients the damage is very rarely both extensive and confined to the hippocampus. In the case of the patients reported by Squire and colleagues (Reed & Squire, 1997; Manns & Squire, 1999), it is also possible that areas beyond the hippocampus might be compromised, in ways that are not readily detectable.

Aggleton and Brown (1999) proposed, prior to the study of Jon's memory, that whereas the hippocampus is important for episodic memory, familiarity-based recognition judgments might be based on the perirhinal regions that are preserved in Jon. They cite a number of cases from the literature with preserved recognition in the presence of clearly impaired recall, a pattern subsequently recorded by Mayes, Holdstock, Isaac, Hunkin, and Roberts (2002) in an adult-onset case in whom the sparing of recognition memory appeared to be associated with a lesion limited to the hippocampus.

So, does Jon really present a challenge to a simple modal model of amnesia, as I initially concluded? Or does he reflect the danger of drawing overgeneral conclusions from developmental cases? No doubt, as more cases appear and as our methods of assessing the extent of anatomical damage improve, this issue will in due course be resolved, as too will the role of episodic memory in the development of the semantic system.

RETROGRADE AMNESIA

Whereas anterograde amnesia refers to the incapacity to lay down new memories, retrograde amnesia refers to the impaired capacity to retrieve old memories. The two often go together, but are not highly correlated (Shimamura & Squire, 1991; Greene & Hodges, 1996; Kapur, 1999). For example, two patients studied by Baddeley and Wilson (1986) both had dense but pure amnesias with high and well-preserved intelligence, but one appeared to have excellent retrograde memory and could, for example, talk in great detail about his wartime experiences, whereas the other had at best only a hazy memory of his past. He knew he had been in the Navy and gone to university but could not remember in what order; he knew he had previously broken his arm, but could not recall how.

A few cases have been reported with the opposite pattern (Kapur, 1999). There is, however, often a possibility that the patient might be consciously or unconsciously avoiding recall of the period preceding the traumatic incident for emotional reasons (see Chapter 7 for further discussion).

Assessment of retrograde amnesia

Measuring the degree of retrograde amnesia presents one problem that is not shared with anterograde amnesia, namely that the tester typically does not have control over the learning of the material to be recalled, as learning might have occurred many years before. The first attempt to quantify degree of retrograde amnesia was made by Sanders and Warrington (1971), who presented their patients with photographs of people who were famous for a limited period at different points in time, finding that their amnesic patients typically performed more poorly on this task than the controls. They also observed that earlier memories were better preserved, so-called *Ribot's law*. This asserts that older memories are more durable than those acquired more recently (Ribot, 1882).

A number of similar scales have subsequently been developed using a range of material, including news events, winners of classic horse races, and TV shows that aired for a single season (e.g. Squire, Haist, & Shimamura, 1989). This general method suffers from two practical problems. First, the degree of knowledge of news events or races is likely to vary substantially across patients; second, scales of this sort are, of course, continually aging, as the recent events become progressively more remote, hence requiring a continuous process of revising and revalidating.

An alternative method is to probe the patient's memory of their earlier life by requesting autobiographical recollections, which can then if necessary be checked through a spouse or carer (see Chapter 7). Galton (1879) developed a cue word technique whereby a word is presented, for example, *mountain*, after which the participant is asked to recollect a personal event concerning a mountain, and then date the memory in time. Try it yourself, with the word *river*. What did you find?

In my own case, I recollected being in a rowing boat on a river, holding on to the bank and finding the boat drifting further and further out. Curiously, I can't remember whether I eventually fell in. I was about 16 at the time.

This probe method was further developed by Crovitz and Shiffman (1974) and used to study retrograde amnesia by Zola-Morgan, Cohen, and Squire (1983). Unfortunately, it is a somewhat laborious process; people with normal memory tend to produce large amounts of material, which must then be transcribed

and evaluated, whereas amnesic patients who are principally of interest tend to produce much less.

In an attempt to reduce these methodological problems, Kopelman, Wilson, and Baddeley (1990) developed the Autobiographical Memory Interview (AMI), which involved asking people to remember specific information selected from a range of time periods. Some were remote, for example the name of their first school, others intermediate, such as their first job, whereas others probed more recent events, such as where the patient spent last Christmas. These were essentially factual questions that could be regarded as probing a form of **personal semantic memory**. In addition, for each life period, participants were asked to recollect a *specific* personal event. An example from childhood might be winning a race at school. These episodic recollections were then rated in terms of amount and specificity of information retrieved.

The test was validated using both healthy people and a range of patients and was found to be sensitive and reliable. Even patients with Korsakoff syndrome, who are commonly believed to be inclined to confabulate, produced either accurate recall, as validated by relatives, or simply said they could not remember (Kopelman et al., 1990). This and related scales have been used increasingly widely in line with the increased interest in autobiographical memory and its disorders (see Chapter 7). Retrograde amnesia generally leads to impairment in autobiographical memory on both the personal and the semantic scales. However, cases who show differential impairment do occur, some with personal memories intact (De Renzi, Liotti, & Nichelli, 1987) and others showing the opposite pattern (Hodges & McCarthy, 1993). This issue is discussed in more detail in Chapter 7 in terms of its implication for theories of autobiographical memory.

KEY TERM

Personal semantic memory: Factual knowledge about one's own past.

Kopelman et al.'s (1990) Autobiographical Memory Interview (AMI) measured the extent of retrograde amnesia by asking people to remember specific information selected from a range of time periods, and to recall a temporally specific personal event, such as winning a race. © H. Armstrong Roberts/Corbis.

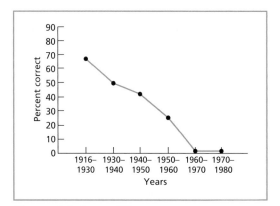

Figure 11.5 Patient PZ's retrograde amnesia gradient for information from his published autobiography. The earlier the information the better it is recalled. From Butters and Cermak (1986). Copyright © Cambridge University Press. Reproduced with permission.

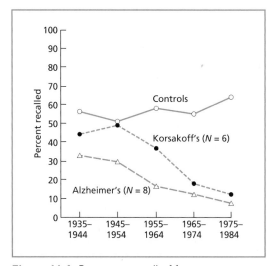

Figure 11.6 Percentage recall of famous news events as a function of when they occurred. Data from Kopelman (1989).

Temporal retrograde amnesia gradients

When it occurs, retrograde amnesia tends to follow a somewhat different pattern across different patient groups. Patients with alcoholic Korsakoff syndrome show a steep decline in recent memories compared with patients who are alcoholic but without memory deficits (Zola-Morgan et al., 1983). A particularly interesting case is that of PZ, a distinguished experimental psychologist who had completed his memoirs shortly before succumbing to Korsakoff syndrome. Because of this, it was possible to identify events and facts that it was clear that he knew just prior to the onset of amnesia. As Figure 11.5 shows, he did indeed show a very striking loss of memory for people he had remembered well enough to describe in

his autobiography, written shortly before the onset of amnesia.

Kopelman (1989) compared the rate of decline in memory between two amnesic groups: patients with Korsakoff syndrome and patients suffering from Alzheimer's disease, and controls who were selected to be matched for age. As Figure 11.6 shows, the decline in memory for new events from different periods was much steeper in the Korsakoff patients. It is not clear why this should be the case. One might argue that the long periods of drinking by the Korsakoff patients might have resulted in fewer experiences worth remembering. However, it seems equally likely that the gradual onset of Alzheimer's disease would have had a similar effect. It seems more likely that the discrepancy reflects differences in the causes of the two amnesias at a neurobiological level.

Explanations of retrograde amnesia

There have been fewer studies of retrograde than anterograde amnesia, and less extensive theoretical analysis. This has begun to change in recent years with a number of models proposed, often accompanied by computer simulations to check that they are indeed able to predict the results claimed. Three of these models—those of Alvarez and Squire (1994); McClelland, McNaughton, and O'Reilly (1995); and Murre (1996)—differ in detail, but all assume that the hippocampus and surrounding regions play a crucial role in memory consolidation. Unlike the consolidation assumed to operate at the cellular and subcellular levels described in Chapter 4 (see p. 88), the explanation in this case refers to **system consolidation**, the process whereby information is consolidated within the brain by a process of transfer from one anatomically based system to another. These two types of consolidation are not, of course, mutually exclusive, although failure to consolidate at a cellular level will presumably interfere with any subsequent system consolidation.

The above three models differ in detail but all assume that the hippocampus and associated regions act as an intermediary, detecting and storing novel information at a relatively rapid rate, then holding it while it is gradually transferred to more cortical areas. Unlike hippocampal storage, which is relatively rapid but temporary, links within the cortex are assumed to take longer to set up, but are more durable. This consolidation process continues to progress within the neocortex after traces have been lost from the hippocampus, with the result that memory traces that have been in the brain for many years will be particularly robust, thus accounting for Ribot's law, the greater durability of early memory traces.

An alternative model is offered by the Multiple Trace Hypothesis, proposed by Nadel and Moscovitch (1997, 1998). They argue for the role of the hippocampus in retrieval, as well as encoding. They accept a version of the model just described, which they refer to as the "standard model" but assume that the process of long-term consolidation sets up recorded traces of experience within the hippocampal complex, rather than the neocortex. They assume that this will lead to multiple hippocampal replicas of earlier experiences. The temporal gradient in retrograde amnesia is assumed to result from partial damage to the hippocampus removing some of the available traces. Older traces, being more numerous, will be more likely to survive. However, complete damage to the hippocampus should lead to total retrograde amnesia. The question of whether this or one of the more standard models gives the better account of retrograde amnesia remains an open question (Sara, 2007).

In recent years, there has been an increasing interest in the general process responsible for memory consolidation. A study in which rats became familiar with a novel environment enabled Wilson and McNaughton (1994) to identify and monitor *place cells*, individual cells within the hippocampus that become activated when the rat approaches a particular part of the learned environment. They noted that during slow-wave sleep, the deepest sleep

KEY TERM

System consolidation: Process of gradual reorganization of the regions of the brain that support memory. Information is consolidated within the brain by a process of transfer from one anatomically based system to another.

level, such place cells were reactivated, as if some process of transfer or consolidation was taking place. More recently, the neural activity generated by daytime singing in birds has been found also to occur during sleep (Dave & Margoliash, 2000).

Studies in humans suggest that sleep deprivation can interfere with the process of consolidation. In one study, Stickgold, LaTanya, and Hobson (2000) showed first of all that a visual discrimination task led to maximum improvement several days after training, despite an absence of further practice. However, this impairment was not shown by a group who were deprived of a night's sleep immediately after learning. Evidence for the importance of sleep in word learning comes from a series of studies by Gaskell and Dumay (2003). They describe a technique whereby it is possible to detect whether a new word has been fully registered in the mental lexicon by the extent to which it is capable of interfering with the processing of existing words. They taught their participants word-like new items, e.g. *cathedruke*, establishing that it was in episodic memory by recall, and then testing the extent to which they slow down the processing of a close existing word such as *cathedral*. Recall is excellent immediately after learning but the new word does not interfere with the old. When tested after a night's sleep, clear interference is found, an effect that lasts for many months. It appears, therefore, that sleep is necessary for a new item to be consolidated into a person's verbal lexicon.

The tasks considered so far are implicit. However, a similar pattern of results was found by Gais, Albouy, Boly, Dang-Vu, Darsaud, Desseilles, et al. (2007) in a study involving presenting participants with 90 pairs of concrete nouns (e.g. *rabbit – chair*) and instructing them to form an image incorporating the two. Some 30 minutes later they were asked to recall as many pairs as possible, and then were kept awake for the next 24 hours. Forty-eight hours later, after two nights of full sleep, recall was again tested. A second group was treated in exactly the same

way except that these participants were sleep deprived on the second night after having slept following their initial recall. Neuroimaging using fMRI during the 48-hour delayed recall test showed a different pattern across the two groups, with the group that had slept immediately after learning showing greater activation in the hippocampus and evidence of active links between the hippocampus and the medial prefrontal cortex, suggesting that these areas had benefited most from sleep-based consolidation.

The study of memory disorders resulting from damage to clearly specified areas of the brain has proved enormously useful in developing our theories of memory and our knowledge of brain function. Of great practical significance, however, are those conditions for which a serious memory deficit is a prominent but not inevitable symptom, and where the association between the deficit and its anatomical localization is often unclear. From the patient's viewpoint, however, regardless of its origin, a memory deficit can be a crippling affliction. It is therefore important to study memory performance in diseases of this type, and to try to develop methods of helping patients to cope with the associated memory problems. One such disease will be described next, namely traumatic brain injury; a second—Alzheimer's disease—is discussed in Chapter 13, which is concerned with aging.

TRAUMATIC BRAIN INJURY

Traumatic brain injury (TBI) occurs when the head receives a sharp blow, for example as a result of a fall, or is subject to a sudden

---

KEY TERM

Traumatic brain injury (TBI): Caused by a blow or jolt to the head, or by a penetrating head injury. Normal brain function is disrupted. Severity ranges from "mild" (brief change in mental status or consciousness) to "severe" (extended period of unconsciousness or amnesia after the injury).

acceleration or deceleration as in a car crash. The brain swirls around, resulting in damage from the bony protuberances within the skull, and from the twisting and shearing of fibers within the brain.

A few years ago I was waiting in a line of cars to leave a side road near a sea-coast resort when suddenly a blue figure arced in the air to the horror and consternation of onlookers. It was a motorcyclist hit by a car turning into the side road, resulting no doubt in one more serious head injury. Such injuries happen mainly to young men, and in the UK over 95% will survive with varying degrees of handicap. A major feature of this is difficulty in concentrating and remembering.

What sort of memory problems might our unfortunate motorcyclist expect? First of all, if the brain injury was severe, he might be expected to be in a coma, sometimes for many weeks. Indeed in the most serious cases the patient may be left in what is known as a *persistent vegetative state* in which physical functions continue to perform but mental functions do not. This in turn leads to the terrible ethical problem as to how long one should artificially maintain life in such a case. Fortunately, in most cases there will be a gradual recovery, often so gradual that it can be missed by the medical support staff. To optimize this process of monitoring, Shiel, Wilson, McLellan, and Watson (2000) developed a scale entitled the Wessex Head Injury Matrix Scale (WHIM), which picks up the tiny changes that occur in behavior as the brain slowly recovers from major trauma.

On recovering consciousness, the patient is likely to move into a state of *post-traumatic amnesia* (PTA), in which attention can be disturbed and the capacity for new learning grossly impaired. Once again, it is important to be able to monitor this gradual recovery, and to do so a number of scales have been devised (Levin & Hanten, 2002). A study by High, Levin, and Gary (1990) monitored the progress through PTA of 84 patients whose traumatic brain injury was sufficient to lead to coma. They typically first recovered

personal knowledge, who they were; followed by *place*, where they were; and finally *temporal orientation*. The estimated date was typically displaced backwards, especially in more severe cases, where there could be an error of up to 5 years. As the patients recovered, the degree of error reduced, reflecting a shrinkage of retrograde amnesia.

Length of time in PTA can vary considerably, and provides a rough, although not infallible, guide to level of probable recover (Levin, O'Donnell, & Grossman 1979). Having recovered from PTA, the patient is likely to be left with a degree of retrograde amnesia. This might initially be quite extensive, but will shrink over time, as in the classic case described below.

A green-keeper, aged 22, was thrown from his motorcycle in August 1933. There was a bruise in the left frontal region and slight bleeding from the left ear but no fracture was seen on X-ray examination. A week after the accident he was able to converse sensibly and the nursing staff considered that he had fully recovered consciousness. When questioned, however, he said that the date was February 1922, and that he was a school boy. He had no recollection of 5 years spent in Australia and 2 years in the UK working on a golf course. Two weeks after the injury he remembered the 5 years spent in Australia and remembered returning to the UK; the past 2 years were, however, a complete blank as far as his memory was concerned. Three weeks after the injury, he returned to the village where he had been working for 2 years. Everything looked strange and he had no recollection of ever having been there before. He lost his way on more than one occasion. Still feeling a stranger to the district he returned to work; he was able to do his work satisfactorily but had difficulty in remembering what he had actually done during the day. About 10 weeks after the accident the events of the past 2 years were gradually recollected and finally he was able to remember everything up to within a few minutes of the accident. (Russell, 1959, pp. 69–70)

The shrinkage in degree of retrograde amnesia is variable and typically less dramatic than that shown by our Australian green-keeper. The dense period of continuing amnesia immediately preceding the TBI is, however, very characteristic. Is the problem one of registering the experience in the first place, or consolidation of the memory trace? Light is thrown on this issue by a study by Yarnell and Lynch (1970) of American football players who have been "dinged." As they were led off, the investigator asked the name of the play that had led to the collision (e.g. Pop 22). Typically, the player could remember it immediately, but not when questioned later. Although other interpretations are possible, this certainly is consistent with a lack of early neural consolidation of the memory trace.

In Yarnell and Lynch's (1970) study of American football players the player could generally recall the name of the play that had led to the collision immediately, but not when questioned later.

There has, in recent years, been a growing interest in the long-term effects of playing high-contact games like American football and rugby league football. Gina Geffen, a neuropsychologist in Adelaide, Australia, was asked to examine an Australian-rules football player who had sustained a head injury. To obtain a comparison group, she tested a number of his colleagues using a test of speed of the semantic processing developed by Baddeley, Emslie, and Nimmo-Smith (1992). This involves the patient in reading a series of brief sentences that are either obviously true or obviously false. Typical positive sentences are *Nuns have religious beliefs* and *Shoes are sold in pairs.* Negative sentences are created by recombining positive instances, as in *Shoes have religious beliefs* and *Nuns are sold in pairs.* Go to Box 6.2 in Chapter 6 to try the test yourself.

Geffen found that not only her patient but also his team-mates in this extremely vigorous sport were somewhat impaired on this sensitive speed test of semantic processing (Hinton-Bayre, Geffen, & McFarland, 1997). Others have found similar results in other high-contact sports players, and regular testing has now become an important feature within American football. This residual deficit is of course much less severe than that found in PTA, and in American college football players appears to resolve within a few days (McCrea, Guskiewicz, Marshall, Barr, & Randolph, 2003).

What happens when patients recover from the temporary condition of PTA? Unfortunately, persistent problems of episodic memory tend to remain. Oddy, Coughlan, Tyerman, and Jenkins (1985) questioned patients and their carers some 7 years after a moderate or severe head injury. They found that 53% of the patients reported memory problems; this rose to 79% if one used the report of the carer as an index of impaired memory. Such a result raises three questions: Why do the two estimates differ? Which of them is more accurate? And how do they relate to actual performance on objective memory tests?

A probable answer to all three was provided by Sunderland, Harris, and Baddeley (1983).

We studied mild to moderate head-injured patients, some a few months and others a few years after their injury. Objective performance was measured using a number of tests that were known to be sensitive to TBI, including paired-associate learning, word and face recognition, performance on the previously described semantic processing test, and a test involving immediate and delayed recall of a short prose paragraph. In addition, patients and carers were both asked to complete a questionnaire regarding their memory problems, and in addition to keep a regular diary in which memory lapses were recorded.

As expected, both recent and more remote TBI groups performed more poorly than a control group on the various tests of memory and attention. This effect was equivalent across the two groups, regardless of whether the TBI was recent or more remote, suggesting that unfortunately the memory deficit tends to persist. The subjective measures also showed a difference between the ratings for patients and control participants. The central interest, however, was the relationship between the objective memory measures and memory complaints. This tended to be low for all except the prose passage recall, with correlations being particularly low for self-report by patients, and lower for questionnaires than diaries. We suggested that this was because the questionnaire measure itself depended on remembering, and that the patients simply tended to forget that they had forgotten. It is also the case that amnesic patients can be unaware of their memory deficit, even though it is very obvious to all around them. One densely amnesic patient I tested frequently expressed surprise at her continued failure to recall throughout a test session, remarking at frequent intervals that "I pride myself on my memory." Such lack of insight can make rehabilitation difficult, but fortunately does not occur in all amnesic patients.

The lack of correlation between most of the objective memory measures and reported lapses is worrying, given that such measures play an important role in assessing, advising,

and helping the patient. However, this problem was already being tackled by Barbara Wilson, a clinical neuropsychologist working at Rivermead Rehabilitation Centre in Oxford.

Wilson came from a background of treating learning-disabled people using behavioral methods initially influenced by BF Skinner's approach to learning based on operant conditioning. This involves a very pragmatic approach based on closely monitoring the patient and systematically rewarding the relevant behavior. Wilson decided to develop a measure based on the capacity of patients to perform a range of practical memory tasks that were selected as being those on which she and carers had observed that patients were most likely to suffer memory problems in their everyday life. The resulting Rivermead Behavioural Memory Test (RBMT) comprised the tasks shown in Table 11.1.

We validated the RBMT using a large sample of patients who had suffered brain damage, from a range of different causes, correlating performance with reports of memory lapses by therapists who kept a record over many hours of treatment (Wilson, Cockburn, Baddeley, & Hiorns, 1989b). The correlations proved to be high and, as expected, the test proved superior to more standard measures of memory performance in predicting such everyday lapses.

Of course, the acid test for a measure that hopes to predict everyday function must depend on a correlation with performance in everyday life. Wilson (1991) was able to achieve this by following-up a total of 43 patients with severe memory disorders, all of whom she had tested some 5–10 years before. She took as her measure of coping the extent to which patients were able to live an independent life. The results are shown in Figure 11.7, together with the equivalent prediction based on a standard clinical assessment, the Wechsler Memory Scale (WMS). As can be seen, the RBMT does an excellent job, the two exceptions being cases that were not in fact amnesic, one having a phonological STM deficit and the other being a rare case of retrograde amnesia in the absence of anterograde. The WMS

TABLE 11.1: The components of the Rivermead Behavioural Memory Test (RBMT). The items were chosen to probe performance on aspects of everyday memory that were potentially problematic for patients.

The Rivermead Behavioural Memory Test	
1	Remembering a new name—first name.
2	Remembering a new name—second name.
3	Remembering a belonging.
4	Remembering an appointment.
5	Picture recognition.
6	Newspaper story—immediate and delayed recall.
7	Face recognition.
8	Remembering a new route—immediate recall.
9	Remembering a new route—delayed recall.
10	Remembering to deliver a message.
11	Orientation.
12	Date.

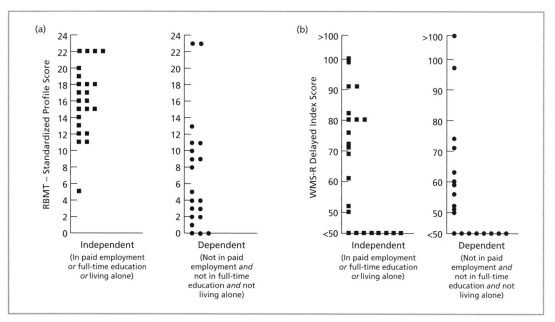

Figure 11.7 (a) Performance on the Rivermead Behavioural Memory Test (RBMT) and capacity to live independently. A follow-up of patients with memory problems. (b) Performance on the Wechsler Memory Scale—revised on the independent and dependent group. From Wilson (1991). Copyright © 1991 Psychology Press.

fairs rather less well. That does not, of course, indicate that it is a poor test; it is highly sensitive to memory impairment but was not designed to predict everyday problems. Both types of test are needed, together with theoretically based measures that can analyze the nature of the memory deficits observed more precisely than either of these, and potentially, by identifying the patient's strengths and weaknesses, facilitate subsequent treatment.

SUMMARY

The study of amnesia is driven by important clinical problems, and both benefits from, and enriches, theories of normal memory function. It is a very good example of the way in which theory and practice can fruitfully interact. This is shown in the classic amnesic syndrome in which a patient may have a gross deficit in episodic memory, but be otherwise cognitively unimpaired, with clear implications for the nature of long-term memory.

The amnesic syndrome typically involves damage to a circuit linking the temporal lobes, frontal lobes, and hippocampus. This can result from a number of diseases, including alcoholic Korsakoff syndrome, bilateral brain lesion, anoxia, or brain infection. Although the amnesia can be pure, in most cases the deficit will be accompanied by other cognitive problems.

It is important to distinguish between anterograde amnesia, reflecting the difficulty in acquiring new information, and retrograde amnesia, loss of access to memories from before the amnesic episode. Pure anterograde amnesia involves a substantial deficit in the acquisition of new memories, whether based on visual or verbal material, and whether tested by recall or recognition. In the amnesic syndrome, working memory is typically well preserved, as is access to semantic memory, although the capacity to add new information to semantic memory is typically defective. Implicit memory is also preserved, as measured by studies of priming, procedural learning, or classical conditioning. Rate of forgetting is typically unimpaired.

Early theories of amnesia in terms of levels of processing or proactive interference have now been superseded by variants of a contextual learning interpretation, which might reflect impaired consolidation. Most theories accept a role for the hippocampus, but surrounding areas are almost certainly also important. There is currently controversy as to whether the hippocampus is necessary for recognition memory, but general agreement that it plays a role in the subjective feeling of "remembering" that is sometimes regarded as essential to episodic memory.

Retrograde amnesia refers to the failure to access earlier memories. Methods of assessment include questionnaires requiring the recall or recognition of public events from different time periods, cueing autobiographical memories by Galton's single word probe method, and more structured autobiographical memory interviews.

These typically show a gradient of impairment, with earlier memories being better preserved, so-called Ribot's law. Theories of retrograde amnesia typically involve some version of the concept of consolidation, whereby information is transferred from the hippocampus to the cortex. Recent research suggests that sleep may play an important role in such transfer.

An important practical source of memory problems is that of traumatic brain injury (TBI), in which a blow or sudden acceleration or deceleration from a car crash causes disruption of brain tissue. A severe TBI will initially lead to coma, followed by a period of post-traumatic amnesia (PTA), a confused state in which new learning is impaired. PTA typically resolves gradually to leave a milder but more permanent memory deficit.

Rehabilitation of such patients requires adequate assessment. Tests of everyday memory play an important role in identifying problems and helping patients. Tests that are sensitive to memory deficit in general may be less good at predicting everyday memory problems. Specific tests of everyday memory have now been devised that successfully predict the severity of such difficulties, potentially important for rehabilitation. As such they provide a valuable addition to existing tests that focus on the issue of exactly what cognitive capacities have been impaired.

FURTHER READING

- **Baddeley, A. D., Kopelman, M. D., & Wilson, B. A.** (Eds.) (2002). *The handbook of memory disorders* (2nd edn). Chichester, UK: Wiley. A good source of evidence on specific types of memory disorder. It contains chapters on various types of memory deficit, and on ways of helping patients cope with memory problems.

- **Baxendale, S.** (2004). Memories aren't made of this: Amnesia at the movies. *British Medical Journal*, *329*, 1480–1483. An amusing analysis of the way in which amnesia is portrayed in movies, and a discussion of the implications of this for the public perception of memory and its deficits.

- **Parkin, A. J.** (Ed.) (1997). *Case studies in the neuropsychology of memory*. Hove, UK: Psychology Press. Accounts of individual patients that give a feeling for the way in which different forms of memory disorder influence the lives of patients.

- **Parkin, A. J., & Leng, N. R. C.** (1993). *Neuropsychology of the amnesic syndrome*. Hove, UK: Psychology Press. Although now somewhat dated, this presents a very clear account of the amnesic syndrome.

- **Wearing, D.** (2005). *Forever today*. New York: Doubleday. Deborah's Wearing's account of the devastating amnesia suffered by her husband, Clive, casting light on the human cost of severe memory disorder.

CHAPTER 12

MEMORY IN CHILDHOOD

Michael W. Eysenck

Think back to the days of your early childhood. What is the earliest memory that you can bring to mind? What age were you at the time? What else can you remember from that period? Perhaps you remember only a single isolated incident.

Don't worry if you find it difficult to think of any very early memories. Most people remember very little (if anything) of what occurred before the age of 2 or 3. For example, Rubin (2000) combined data from numerous studies in which adults reported autobiographical memories (memories of specific events that had happened to them in the past). Of those memories based on events occurring before the age of 11, only 1% occurred before the age of 3. More generally, systematic studies of autobiographical memory suggest a dearth of memories before the age of about 5 years. This phenomenon is known as *infantile amnesia* (alternatively, childhood amnesia), and is also discussed in Chapter 7.

Although the existence of infantile amnesia has been known about for a very long time, it remains fairly difficult to study. One problem is that it is not easy to assess the accuracy of adults' claimed memories of early childhood given that several decades might have passed since the events allegedly occurred. One way forward is to focus on significant events that can be precisely dated and verified by a third party. The birth of a brother or sister falls into this category, and has been investigated in several studies. In one study (Sheingold & Tenney, 1982), college students and children aged 4, 6, 8, and 12 were asked to recall the birth of a brother or sister that occurred when they were aged between 3 and 11 years. They were asked questions such as, "Who took care of you while your mother was in hospital?", "Did the baby receive presents?", "Did you receive presents?" The mothers were asked the same questions. There was surprisingly little

In Sheingold and Tenney's (1982) study, children who had been under 3 when their brother or sister was born remembered virtually nothing, providing strong evidence for infantile amnesia. Children older than 3 at the time had surprisingly strong memories for the event.

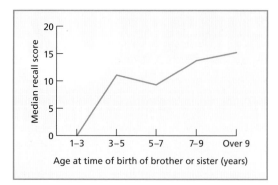

Figure 12.1 When college students were asked to recall the birth of a sibling, they remembered virtually nothing if the event had occurred before they were 3 years old: an example of infantile amnesia (Sheingold & Tenney, 1982).

forgetting regardless of the length of time that had elapsed since the event among participants who had been at least 3 years old at the time (Figure 12.1). However, children who had been under 3 when their brother or sister was born remembered virtually nothing, thus providing strong evidence for infantile amnesia.

Another issue is deciding whether adults' reported memories of early childhood are genuine recollections or are based on knowledge obtained from others (e.g. parents). In a study by Crawley and Eacott (2006), adults recalled events from their childhood. Memories that the adults believed to be genuine recollections differed in several ways from memories that were based on second-hand knowledge. For example, the former memories were more pictorial and less verbal than the latter ones, they involved more feelings, and they were more complete. Thus, most of those childhood memories that adults regard as genuine recollections may well actually be genuine.

A key feature of infantile amnesia is that it involves *adults* failing to recall autobiographical memories of their early life. If we are to understand what is involved in infantile amnesia, we need to start by considering the development of autobiographical memory during the early years of childhood. In other words, we will be focusing on what infants and older children can remember days, weeks,

or months after learning. This is important—if it turns out that young children cannot form autobiographical memories in the first place then there is no mystery about their failure in adulthood to remember the events of their early childhood.

Before we focus on infants' autobiographical memory, we will consider other forms of memory in infants and young children. This will not only provide a more complete picture of what infants can and cannot remember, but will also allow us to see whether infants have particular problems in forming and/or retrieving autobiographical memories.

MEMORY IN INFANTS

It is easier said than done to assess the memory abilities of infants. The most serious problem is that infants' language abilities are either virtually nonexistent or very limited in scope. As a result, experimenters cannot use verbal instructions to tell infants what they are to learn. In addition, tests of memory (unlike with studies on older children and adults) typically require infants to produce certain motor responses in view of their inability to report verbally what they have learned. Even when memory is assessed by motor responses, the limited motor skills possessed by infants under the age of 12 months means that there are real constraints on the kinds of memory tasks that are suitable. Finally, the necessary reliance on nonverbal memory responses when testing infants means that it is very difficult (or impossible) to assess the extent to which they are consciously aware of what they remember. As we will see, ingenious experimenters have surmounted all of these problems.

As was discussed earlier in the book (Chapter 1), there is an important theoretical distinction between *explicit or declarative memory* on the one hand and *implicit or non-declarative memory* on the other. It is generally assumed that the former type of memory is associated with conscious recollection whereas the latter type is not. However, we cannot assess the presence of conscious recollection in infants. How, then, can we decide whether infants' memories on any given task involve declarative or implicit memory? According to Richmond and Nelson (2007), there are two major criteria that we can use:

1. *Amnesia filter*: We know from research with adults suffering from amnesia (see Chapter 11) that they have severely deficient declarative or explicit memory but essentially intact implicit or procedural memory. Thus, amnesics' ability or inability to perform well on a task often indicates the type of memory on which it depends.
2. *Parameter filter*: Research on healthy adults has indicated that performance on declarative memory tasks is generally much more affected than that on implicit memory tasks by changes in study time, retention interval, and changes in context between learning and test.

Issues relating to the development of declarative or explicit memory and of implicit memory are discussed very thoroughly by Rovee-Collier, Hayne, and Colombo (2001).

For now, we will focus mainly on the development of declarative memory. Later in the chapter, we consider implicit memory and the reasons why implicit memory develops fully at a younger age than declarative memory. There has been a marked change in thinking about declarative memory. As Bauer (2004, p. 347) pointed out, "Historically, infants and very young children were thought incapable of explicit memory." More recently, numerous studies have reported clear evidence of declarative or explicit memory in infants at younger ages than were previously thought possible.

Findings

Important research on infant memory was carried out by Carolyn Rovee-Collier and her colleagues (Rovee-Collier, 1989) (Box 12.1).

Box 12.1 The mobile conjugate reinforcement paradigm (Rovee-Collier, 1989)

Rovee-Collier (1989) argued that it is important when assessing learning in babies to use situations that interest and motivate them, otherwise there is a danger of underestimating how much they can learn and remember. She achieved this by suspending a mobile over the baby's crib and attaching it to the baby's foot via a ribbon (Figure 12.2); when the baby kicked, the mobile moved. Young babies seem to enjoy this, because they rapidly learn to kick when the mobile is present.

The task used by Rovee-Collier involves three distinct phases. First, there is a baseline phase, during which the ribbon attached to the infant's foot is also attached to the side of the crib but not to the mobile. Second, there is the learning phase, during which the ribbon attached to the infant's foot is also attached

(continued overleaf)

Figure 12.2 An infant in Rovee-Collier's causal contingency paradigm (left) during baseline, when kicking cannot activate the mobile and (right) during acquisition, when the ankle ribbon is attached to the mobile. From Rovee Collier, Sullivan, Enright, Lucas, and Fagen (1980). Copyright © 1980 AAAS. Reprinted with permission.

Box 12.1 (continued)

to the mobile. During this phase, the infant learns that his/her kicking (a response) causes the mobile to move (the reward or reinforcement). Finally, there is the test phase. In this phase, the ribbon attached to the infant's foot is once again attached to the side of the crib and not to the mobile. Memory is shown when the infant's rate of kicking in the test phase is greater than in the baseline phase. The strength of the infant's memory can be assessed by varying the length of time between the learning and test phases.

What Rovee-Collier (1989) found when the time between learning and test ranged from 1 to 14 days is shown in Figure 12.3. Two- and 3-month-old babies showed evidence of retention. However, the level of performance in 2-month-olds dropped to a level comparable to the initial baseline of kicking after 2 days, whereas the 3-month-olds still showed a reliable effect after a week.

Rovee-Collier (1989) also considered the effect of presenting a reminder. This consisted of a moving mobile (controlled by the experimenter) that was presented to the infants some time before being tested. This reminder resulted in memory returning virtually to its initial level even when testing took place after a delay of 2 weeks. More strikingly, the reminder was sufficient to reactivate a significant amount of kicking at a delay of 1 month.

The learning observed by Rovee-Collier (1989) was quite specific. Babies trained on a mobile consisting of yellow blocks, for example, didn't respond to a mobile consisting of metal butterflies. However, infants who were trained on various mobiles did show generalization in that they kicked in response to a novel mobile.

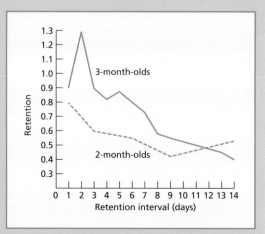

Figure 12.3 Even 2-month-old babies show evidence of "remembering" the experience of finding a mobile moves when they kick. In 3-month-olds the effect is very clear (Rovee-Collier, 1989).

In essence, these findings suggest that the babies acquired something similar to a concept. Another feature of their learning was that it was context sensitive. For example, if an infant was tested in the bedroom or the kitchen rather than the test crib, no kicking response was observed. In similar fashion, there were fewer kicking responses if the decor of the crib was changed.

How do we know that performance on the mobile conjugate reinforcement task involves declarative memory? Rovee-Collier (1997) reviewed evidence indicating that infants' performance on this task is determined by several factors, such as participant age, retention interval, and contextual change. All of these factors are more important in declarative memory than in implicit memory.

The task she devised is known as the mobile conjugate reinforcement paradigm. It involves operant conditioning, because the infant receives reward or reinforcement when he/she makes the appropriate response.

One of the limitations of the mobile conjugate reinforcement paradigm is that it is only suitable for use with infants up to the age of about 7 months. However, Hartshorn and Rovee-Collier (1997) introduced a similar task that is suitable for older infants. On this task, infants learn to press a lever to make a miniature train move around a track. The infants show declarative memory by continuing to press the lever even when this doesn't make the train move.

In the years since the development of the mobile conjugate reinforcement and train tasks, infants' memory has been studied using numerous different tasks (see Hayne, 2004, for a review). Of particular importance is the deferred imitation task (see Bauer, 2004, for a review). What happens in *deferred imitation* is that the experimenter uses objects to produce an action sequence (e.g. using a mallet to hit a metal plate), which the infant then tries to imitate at a later time. Before discussing the relevant research, note that the famous Swiss developmental psychologist, Jean Piaget (1896–1980), believed that infants could show deferred imitation only towards the end of their second year of life.

Andrew Meltzoff was the first researcher to use deferred imitation as a mechanism to study memory in infants. Meltzoff (1985) made use of a dumb-bell consisting of two wooden blocks connected by plastic tubing. Three groups of 14-month-old infants were exposed to one of the following conditions: (1) observing the experimenter pull the toy apart (imitation condition); (2) observing the experimenter move the toy in a circle (control condition); and (3) giving the toy to the infant (baseline condition). Twenty-four hours later, all the infants were given the toy. Of those in the imitation condition, 45% immediately pulled it apart, compared to an average of only 7.5% in the other two conditions. Thus, the infants in the first condition showed clear evidence of deferred imitation. Performance was even better in 24-month-olds, 70% of whom showed deferred imitation. In subsequent research (Collie & Hayne, 1999), some evidence of deferred imitation was found in 6-month-old infants. On average, these infants remembered an average of one out of five observed actions over a period of 24 hours.

Older infants show impressive performance on deferred imitation tasks. For example, about 60% of 16-month-olds exposed to an action sequence produced the actions in the right order after a 12-month delay (Bauer, Wenner, Dropik, & Wewerka, 2000).

Deferred imitation involves declarative or explicit memory. Part of the evidence supporting that statement comes from research on adult amnesic patients. Amnesic patients have severely impaired declarative memory. If successful performance on the deferred imitation task requires declarative memory, then adult amnesic patients should show little evidence of deferred imitation. That is precisely what has been found (McDonough, Mandler, McKee, & Squire, 1995). Bauer, Wenner, and Kroupina (2002) obtained evidence of deferred imitation in infants who hadn't acquired language. Several months later, these infants were able to talk about events associated with their performance of the deferred imitation task. This suggests that their memories of the task were stored in a form accessible to language. It is generally assumed that only declarative memories are accessible to language.

What is the youngest age at which newborns show evidence of memory? There is amazing (and somewhat controversial) evidence that the answer is almost from the moment of birth. DeCasper and Fifer (1980) used a procedure in which high-amplitude sucking on a nipple activated a tape recording of the infant's own mother or another infant's mother. Newborns less than 3 days old demonstrate a clear preference for their own mother's voice via their sucking behavior. Querleu, Lefebvre, Renard, Titran, Morillion, and Crepin (1984) obtained similar findings when testing newborns only 2 hours after birth!

Principles of memory development

Hayne (2004) argued that the available evidence is consistent with four principles of infant memory development. First, older infants typically encode or store information faster than younger ones. For example, consider the amount of learning time that is needed to produce good performance on the deferred imitation task discussed earlier at a retention interval of 24 hours. The evidence suggests that 6-month-olds need about twice as much exposure to the to-be-imitated actions as do 12- and 18-month-olds (see review by Hayne, 2004).

Second, older infants remember information for longer retention intervals than younger ones. Relevant evidence here comes from the mobile conjugate reinforcement paradigm and the associated train task, both of which were discussed earlier. Declarative memory on these tasks in their standard forms has been shown to last for only 2 weeks in 6-month-olds but for about 12 weeks in 18-month-olds (see Hayne, 2004).

Third, older infants make use of a greater variety of retrieval cues than do younger ones. For example, consider the following study by Hayne, Boniface, and Barr (2000) using the deferred imitation task. Infants aged 6, 12, and 18 months all showed deferred imitation when the same stimulus object was used for the demonstration and the subsequent test. When the object was changed, however, this prevented deferred imitation in infants of 6 and 12 months, but had no effect on deferred imitation performance in 18-month-olds. In other words, older children can use their memories in a much more *flexible* way than younger ones.

Fourth, forgotten memories can be retrieved when a reminder is presented. For example, Rovee-Collier, Sullivan, Enright, Lucas, and Fagen (1980) gave 3-month-olds training on the mobile conjugate reinforcement task. They were then tested 14 days later to assess their declarative memory. Some of the infants received a reminder in the form of a 3-minute exposure to the mobile being moved by the experimenter 24 hours before testing. The infants who hadn't received a reminder showed substantial forgetting on the test. In contrast, the infants who had had a reminder showed as much memory on the test as did other infants tested only 1 day after training.

Cognitive neuroscience

We have seen that declarative memory in infants develops very rapidly over the first 2 years or so of life. Why is this the case? Many factors are involved. Infants show evidence of cognitive development in many ways (e.g. increased attention, acquisition of language, increasing knowledge), and these developing cognitive abilities undoubtedly contribute to the aged-related improvements in declarative memory. According to cognitive neuroscientists, however, there is another important factor, namely, the development of the brain. Among the issues addressed by cognitive neuroscientists is that of the difference in the development of declarative memory and implicit memory in infants. There is some evidence that implicit memory in the form of simple conditioning can be seen in newborn infants (DeCasper & Fifer, 1980).

The original cognitive neuroscience theory was put forward by Schacter and Moscovitch (1984), who argued that implicit memory is controlled by an early-developing memory system in the brain that might even be present at birth. By contrast, the development of declarative or explicit memory depends upon a late-developing memory system in the brain that reaches maturity between 8 and 10 months of age.

Which parts of the brain are involved in implicit and declarative memory? So far as implicit memory is concerned, there is reasonably good agreement that parts of the striatum, the cerebellum, and the brainstem are all involved in implicit learning and memory (see Richmond & Nelson, 2007, for a review). What is important here is that these brain structures are mature very early in life. This helps to explain why there is evidence of implicit memory shortly after birth.

So far as declarative memory is concerned, it depends heavily on structures in the medial temporal lobe, including the hippocampus and the parahippocampal cortex (Richmond & Nelson, 2007). Much of this brain system is formed before birth. However, the dentate gyrus within the hippocampal formation has only about 70% of the adult number of cells at birth. It continues to develop until about the end of the first year of life, and other parts of the hippocampal formation might not be fully developed until the child is between about 2 and 8 years of age (Richmond & Nelson, 2007). These late-developing parts of the hippocampal formation could help to explain why declarative memory continues to develop over the early years of life.

Other brain areas are also involved in declarative memory. For example, the prefrontal cortex is known to be involved of memories after a delay (see Bauer, 2004, for a review). The density of synapses in the prefrontal cortex increases substantially at about 8 months of age, and continues to increase until the infant is 15–24 months of age (Bauer, 2004).

Other changes within the brain are also likely to influence the development of declarative memory. For example, there is rapid myelination of axons within the central nervous system during the first year of life. This has the effects of increasing the efficiency with which electrical impulses can be transmitted. This process of myelination is important because it allows infants to process stimuli more rapidly and efficiently, and this in turn probably leads to enhanced memory for those stimuli. Webb, Long, and Nelson (2005) assessed processing speed in the brain when infants between 4 and 12 months of age were presented with their mother, a stranger, their favorite toy, and a novel toy. Visual processing occurred faster in the older infants than in the younger ones.

What are the strengths and limitations of the cognitive neuroscience approach advocated by Richmond and Nelson (2007)? As Richmond and Nelson (2007, p. 367) pointed out, "By addressing how changes in brain are related to changes in memory, we may begin to move the field beyond simply describing early development to understand the mechanisms that drive it." Another strength is that the approach offers at least a partial understanding of differences between declarative and implicit memory in infants.

The greatest limitation of the cognitive neuroscience approach is that its emphasis is on correlations or associations between rate of maturation of brain systems and rate of improvement in memory performance. It is speculative to conclude that the maturational changes in the brain are *causally* related to changes in memory performance.

DEVELOPMENTAL CHANGES IN MEMORY DURING CHILDHOOD

We have seen so far that young children show considerable advances in declarative memory over the first 2 or 3 years of life. There is overwhelming evidence that the development of declarative memory continues for many years after infancy, at least until adolescence (Siegler, 1998). In this section, we first consider explanations for the progressive improvements in declarative memory throughout childhood. After that, we briefly consider circumstances in which errors in memory actually increase as children develop! Finally, we discuss differences in the development of declarative and implicit memory.

Development of declarative memory

Why does declarative memory in children become better and better during the process of development? Siegler (1998) identified four possible answers to this question. First, the capacity of short-term memory or working memory may increase over the years. Second, children develop more memory strategies (e.g. rehearsing the to-be-remembered information) as they develop, and they also learn to use those strategies more efficiently. Third, older children possess much more knowledge than younger ones, and this makes it easier for them to learn and to remember new information. Fourth, there is **metamemory**, which is the knowledge that we possess about our own memory and how it works. Metamemory develops during the course of childhood, and it seems reasonable that children with good metamemory can use their memory systems more effectively than those lacking metamemory.

Bear in mind that the above four factors are not entirely separate from each other. All of the aspects of the memory system are connected in some way with all of the other aspects. As a result, what we will be doing is considering the memory system in children from various perspectives. We return to this issue in the summary at the end of the section.

Basic capacity

As we saw in Chapter 3, the working memory system as described by Baddeley (e.g. 1986) originally consisted of three components. There was a central executive (resembling an attentional system), a phonological loop (used for verbal rehearsal), and a visuo-spatial sketchpad that stores visual and spatial information. There is considerable evidence that the working memory system is of crucial importance for the processing and performance of numerous tasks (see Chapter 2). More recently, Baddeley (2001) has identified a fourth component (the episodic buffer) that combines information from the phonological loop, the visuo-spatial sketchpad, and long-term memory and stores it relatively briefly. In view of the general importance of the working memory system, it is of considerable interest to see whether there are developmental changes in some (or all) of its components. We will ignore the episodic buffer because there is, as yet, relatively little information concerning developmental changes in its capacity.

The most thorough investigation of developmental changes in the three original components of working memory was reported by Gathercole, Pickering, Ambridge, and Wearing (2004a), who studied boys and girls between the ages of 4 and 15 who performed a range of memory tasks relevant

to working memory. Here are examples of the tests they used to assess each component:

- *Phonological loop*: A digit recall test in which spoken random strings of digits had to be recalled in the correct order (digit span).
- *Central executive*: A backward digit recall test resembling the digit recall test except that the digits had to be recalled in reverse order.
- *Visuo-spatial sketchpad*: A visual pattern test in which participants see a two-dimensional grid consisting of filled and unfilled squares followed by recall of the pattern.

Why did Gathercole et al. (2004a) discover? First, there were progressive improvements year by year in all three components of the working memory system (Figure 12.4). It seems reasonable that much of the enhanced overall memory performance during childhood is attributable to the large increases in the capacity of these three components. Second, the structure of working memory was fairly constant across the years of childhood. This suggests that even children as young as 6 have a functioning phonological loop, visuo-spatial sketchpad, and central executive.

Content knowledge

One of the most obvious differences between older and younger children is that older ones possess considerably more knowledge of nearly all kinds. This might be of major importance to understanding the development of memory, because memory performance is generally better when the learner can relate what he/she is learning to relevant stored knowledge (see Chapter 5).

If the amount of knowledge possessed by the learner is a key determinant of memory

KEY TERM

Metamemory: Knowledge about one's own memory and an ability to regulate its functioning.

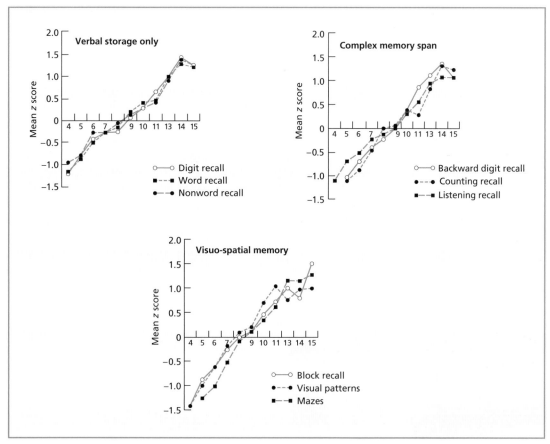

Figure 12.4 Developmental changes in verbal storage only (phonological loop), complex memory span (central executive), and visuo-spatial memory (visuo-spatial sketchpad) between the ages of 4 and 15 expressed in mean z-scores. From Gathercole et al. (2004a). Copyright © American Psychological Association. Reprinted with permission.

performance, then a well-informed child might remember some things better than an ill-informed adult. This prediction was tested by Chi (1978), who studied digit recall and reproduction of chess positions in 10-year-olds skilled at chess and adults knowing little about chess. The adults performed better than the children on digit recall. However, the children's recall of chess positions was over 50% better than that of the adults (Figure 12.5).

Schneider, Gruber, Gruber, Gold, and Opwis (1993) compared children and adults with comparable chess expertise. Both groups remembered chess positions comparably well and much better than nonexpert children and adults. Thus, memory for chess positions

depends largely on expertise and hardly at all on age.

Memory strategies
When adults try to remember information, they typically make use of various memory strategies (e.g. verbal rehearsal, mnemonics) to assist them. Not surprisingly, older children are much more likely than younger ones to use a range of memory strategies in their learning. Much of the research in this area has involved categorized list recall, and so we will focus on that task here. What typically happens is that participants are presented with a certain number of words belonging to each of a number of categories (e.g. four-footed animals, articles

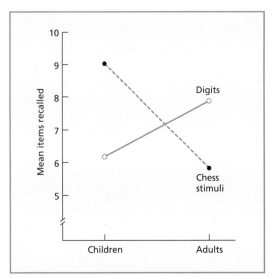

Figure 12.5 Immediate recall of chess positions and digits in children (mean age 10 years 6 months) with expert knowledge of chess and in adults with limited knowledge of chess. Adapted from Chi (1978).

Schneider, Gruber, Gruber, Gold, and Opwis (1993) discovered that memory for chess positions depends largely on expertise and hardly at all on age.

of furniture). These words are presented in random order and the list presentation is followed by free recall (recall of the list words in any order).

Most adults given the above task deal with it by using an organizational strategy in which they rehearse the words category by category. Their subsequent recall of the list is also organized strongly on a categorical basis. This organizational strategy is effective, because adults whose rehearsal and recall are strongly

organized in categories recall more than those whose rehearsal and recall are less organized (Weist, 1972).

What do children do when learning categorized lists with the items presented in random order? Schneider, Knopf, and Stefanek (2002) addressed this issue in a longitudinal study using children between the ages of 8 and 17. The children were presented with four pictures belonging to each of six categories (e.g. animals, food) and could arrange these pictures as they wished. After that, they recalled as many pictures as possible. Free recall increased steadily over time, being approximately 50% higher when the children were 17 than when they were 8. At the older ages, there was more sorting of the pictures into their categories during learning (Figure 12.6). In addition, as can also be seen in Figure 12.6, children at the older ages recalled the pictures to a greater extent category by category (this is known as clustering).

Metamemory

As children grow older, they show increasing evidence of *metamemory* or knowledge about their own memory and how it works (see Schneider, 1999, for a review). For example, Yussen and Levy (1975) found that pre-schoolers' memory span was five items less than they had predicted, whereas 9-year-olds only overestimated their memory span by one item. DeMarie and Ferron (2003) studied the memory performance of children between the ages of 5 and 11 across a wide range of memory tasks. They found clear evidence for a metamemory factor among the older children (ages 8 to 11), but there was very little indication for such a factor among the younger children (ages 5 to 8).

Does metamemory knowledge generally predict memory performance? Schneider and Pressley (1998) found in a meta-analysis of 60 studies that the correlation between metamemory and memory performance was +.41. This correlation indicates that there is a moderate tendency for children with good metamemory to have superior memory performance to

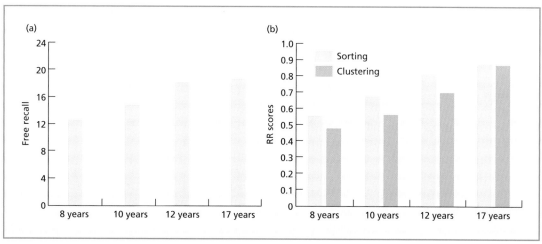

Figure 12.6 (a) Free recall and (b) sorting during learning and clustering during recall assessed by ratio of repetition (RR) at ages 8, 10, 12, and 17. From Schneider et al. (2002). Copyright © American Psychological Association. Reprinted with permission.

children with poor metamemory. Why isn't the relationship stronger? Children might not be motivated to use effective memory strategies they possess, they might feel that a good memory strategy isn't needed when a word list is short, and so on.

Summary

There are several reasons why older children generally remember much more than younger ones. The main components of the working memory system all increase in capacity during childhood, children's knowledge increases, their use of effective strategies increases, and they develop a greater awareness of their own memory system (metamemory). As was mentioned in the introduction to this section of the chapter, these factors are all interconnected.

We will look at three examples. First, consider evidence that the capacity of the phonological loop as assessed by digit span increases during childhood (Gathercole et al., 2004a). One way of increasing digit span is by adopting the strategy of grouping the digits into threes (Ryan, 1969). Second, one of the reasons why metamemory is related to memory performance is because children with a good knowledge of their own memory systems are

more likely to select appropriate learning strategies than those with poor metamemory. Third, organizational strategies (e.g. rehearsing words category by category) are increasingly used by children as they grow older. Probably one of the reasons why this happens is because their increased knowledge makes it easier for them to identify meaningful associations between words.

Verbatim and gist memory

Does declarative memory on all memory tasks improve throughout childhood? The answer is "No," and it is instructive to consider the circumstances in which declarative memory is actually more error prone as children grow up. The key research in this area is based on a theoretical approach developed by Brainerd and Reyna (2004), who argued that there are two kinds of memory trace. First, there are verbatim traces, which contain accurate and detailed information about to-be-remembered stimuli (e.g. the font in which a word is printed). Second, there are gist memory traces, which can contain a considerable amount of semantic information about to-be-remembered stimuli (e.g. associating the word "France" with information that it produces much wine and cheese). Thus, verbatim traces reflect the learner's "actual" experience, whereas gist traces reflect the learner's "understanding" of his/her experiences.

Findings

Verbatim and gist memory both improve considerably during childhood. Brainerd and Reyna (2004) focused on verbatim memory by presenting nonsense words (e.g. *cexib, zuteg*) followed by a test of recognition memory. Children of 11 had much better verbatim memory than children aged 5. Gist memory also improves during childhood, as children extract increased meaning from to-be-remembered information (see Brainerd & Reyna, 2004, for a review). For example, suppose a list is presented in which four members of each of six categories (e.g. four-footed animals; articles of furniture) are presented followed by free recall (writing down the list words in any order). Adults typically recall the list category by category, whereas children below the age of about 10 or 11 do not (Bjorklund & Jacobs, 1985).

You might be wondering what happened to the promised research showing more errors in memory with increasing age. According to Brainerd and Reyna (2004), this is most likely to occur in the following circumstances:

- The learning task leads older children to produce more gist memory traces than younger ones.

- The memory test requires verbatim recall or recognition.
- Greater gist memory increases the likelihood of false recall or recognition of information very similar in meaning to the to-be-remembered information.

The main experimental approach involves the Deese–Roediger–McDermott paradigm (e.g. Roediger & McDermott, 1995; discussed in Chapter 6, p. 121), in which word lists constructed in a particular way are presented. A common word (e.g. "doctor") is selected, and then the 15 words most closely associated with it (e.g. "nurse," "sick," "hospital," "patient") are selected. Those 15 words (but *not* the original word) are then presented, followed by a test of free recall or recognition memory. What is of key interest is the extent to which participants falsely recall or recognize the original word (e.g. "doctor"). The findings based on several experiments are shown in Figure 12.7. As you can see, false recall and false recognition both increase progressively during the years of childhood. There is an increase in semantic processing with age, and so older children are more likely than younger ones to focus on the original word (e.g. "doctor") when presented with its associates.

Additional evidence that the tendency of older children to use gist processing can increase false memory was reported by Brainerd and Mojardin (1998). Children aged

Figure 12.7 Increases in false recall and false recognition during childhood assessed by the Deese–Roediger–McDermott paradigm. From Brainerd and Reyna (2004). Copyright © 2004 Elsevier. Reproduced with permission.

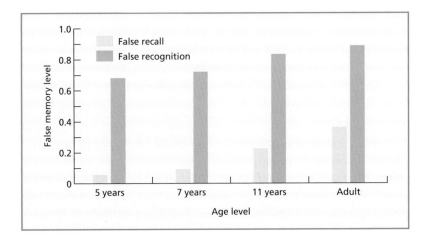

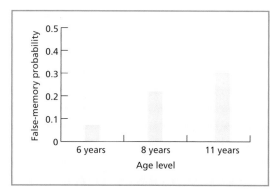

Figure 12.8 False recognition of gist-consistent sentences at 6, 8, and 11 years of age. Based on data from Brainerd and Mojardin (1998).

6, 8, and 11 listened to sets of three sentences (e.g. "The coffee is hotter than the tea," "The tea is hotter than the cocoa," "The cocoa is hotter than the soup"). On the subsequent recognition test, participants decided whether the test sentences had been presented in precisely that form initially. The key condition was one in which sentences having the same meaning as original sentences were presented (e.g. "The cocoa is cooler than the tea"). False recognition on these sentences increased steadily with age (Figure 12.8).

In sum, it is important to distinguish between verbatim and gist memory traces. The fact that older children form more gist memory traces than younger ones is generally an advantage. However, it can become a disadvantage when the memory test requires verbatim recall or recognition.

Declarative vs. implicit memory

We saw earlier in the chapter that declarative memory improves rapidly during infancy. However, it is less clear that the same is true of implicit memory. There is a marked difference in the development of these types of memory during the rest of childhood. Declarative memory becomes markedly better over the years, but there are generally very small effects of age on implicit memory. Murphy, McKone, and Slee (2003) reviewed studies on implicit memory in children. Nonsignificant effects of

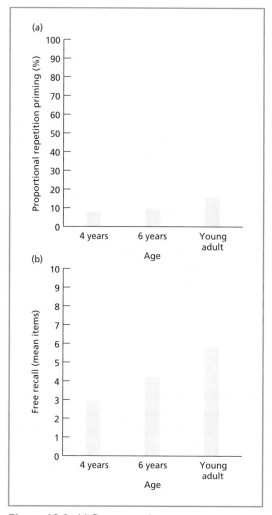

Figure 12.9 (a) Proportional repetition priming (implicit memory) and (b) free recall (explicit memory) in 4-year-olds, 6-year-olds, and young adults. Data from Russo et al. (1995).

age on memory performance were found in 15 out of 18 studies.

We can see the different effects of age on implicit and declarative memory in a study by Russo, Nichelli, Gibertoni, and Cornia (1995), who asked children to identify degraded pictures of objects, some of which had been seen before in intact form. The measure of implicit memory was based on the extent to which performance was better with objects previously seen than with those not previously seen. As can be seen in Figure 12.9, fairly similar levels of implicit memory were observed in 4-year-olds, 6-year-olds, and young adults (nonsignificant differences). By contrast, explicit memory for the pictures was highest in the adult group and lowest in the 4-year-olds.

Before we consider how to explain the different patterns of age on declarative and implicit memory, it is worth noting that changes in implicit memory with age have been reported occasionally. Consider, for example, a study by Vaidya, Huger, Howard, and Howard (2007), who presented young adults and children (aged 6 to 13) with visual arrays containing one target and eleven distracters. The task was to detect the orientation of the target (facing left or facing right) as soon as possible. Some of the visual displays were repeated whereas others were not. What was of interest was to see whether participants would be able to use information from the repeated displays to speed up their performance compared to those displays that were novel.

What did Vaidya et al. (2007) find? The young adults responded significantly faster to repeated visual displays than to novel ones, indicating that they had remembered useful information from previous presentations of each display. By contrast, the children showed no difference in response time between repeated and novel displays. Neither the adults nor the children showed any evidence of explicit or declarative memory for the repeated visual displays. As a result, Vaidya et al. concluded that there was evidence for implicit memory in young adults but not in children. It is not known precisely why there are stronger age-related effects on performance on this task than on most other implicit memory tasks. However, Vaidya et al. speculate that implicit memory on this task requires complex associative processes to integrate information from the entire visual display, and children are less able to do this.

Why are there typically no age-related changes in implicit memory in childhood? In general terms, implicit memory involves more basic processes than declarative memory, and so is less affected by children's developing cognitive skills and abilities. More specifically, the factors known to influence improvements in declarative memory during childhood (i.e. basic working memory capacities; content knowledge; memory strategies; and metamemory) are of much less importance in implicit memory.

AUTOBIOGRAPHICAL MEMORY AND INFANTILE AMNESIA

We have seen that learning can occur during the first few months of life, and that infants can display memory over relatively long periods of time. However, these studies are of very limited (or no) value in terms of shedding light on the causes of infantile amnesia. Of much more relevance are studies concerned with infants' ability to remember the events of their own lives. Perhaps infants have good memory for action sequences but very poor autobiographical memory. In fact, as we will see, infants are reasonably good at remembering events that have happened to them. That means that a failure to store autobiographical memories is probably not the primary reason for infantile amnesia.

When you consider the relevant evidence, be warned that it isn't easy to decide whether young children have "genuine" autobiographical memories. One important reason is that young children typically have very limited language abilities. That means that they are generally not very good at communicating precisely what they can remember of their lives. As a result, it is often unclear whether the child really understands that the events he/she is describing really happened to him/her.

Findings

Katherine Nelson (1988) described the intriguing single case of Emily, a child who had developed the rather convenient habit of talking to herself in her cot before she went to sleep. Her nightly monolog between the ages of 21 and 36 months was recorded and analyzed. At 21 months, she was already recalling events from 2 months before, such as the family car breaking down. Her monolog was mostly very unstructured, and generally didn't relate to particularly salient or important events such as Christmas or the birth of a baby brother. She typically talked about ordinary things such as being picked up at the babysitter's or other children quarreling at playgroup.

Many of Emily's reminiscences were from the previous day, but some went back as far as 6 months. At about 24 months, she began to construct explicit rules and generalizations (e.g. "You can't go down the basement with jamas on"; "When Emily go mormor [grandma] in the daytime ... that's what Amy do sometime") or speculations about the future ("Maybe the doctor take my jamas off"). At about 36 months of age, Emily stopped producing monologs at bedtime and the study ended. We have compelling evidence from this case study that 2-year-olds can remember specific events.

We need to be wary about generalizing from a single child (who was perhaps rather precocious) to the majority of children. However, broadly similar findings based on 10 children with an average age of 33 months were reported by Fivush, Gray, and Fromhoff (1987). Preliminary interviews with the children's parents established significant events (e.g. a trip to Disneyland, an airplane trip, trip to the zoo) that each child had experienced once or twice. After that, interviewers asked the children questions about several recent events (those occurring within the previous 3 months) and distant events (those occurring more than 3 months ago). The children responded to 59% of the recent events asked about and to 52% of the distant ones. On average, they produced 12 items of information about each kind of event, and were particularly good at remembering activities and objects rather than people or locations. These findings provide some evidence that 2-year-olds form autobiographical memories and remember them over periods of at least several months.

Peterson (2002) reviewed studies on autobiographical memory in infants. First, she considered studies in which recall of autobiographical memories was assessed within 12 months of the events in question. The findings support and extend those of Fivush et al. (1987), suggesting that 2-year-olds probably have some limited autobiographical memory for events occurring several months previously.

Second, Peterson (2002) discussed studies in which recall for events was assessed between 1 and 2 years after the event in question. In general, how much could be recalled depended very much on the child's age at the time of the event. For example, Peterson and Rideout (1998) studied young children who had been taken to a hospital emergency room for treatment of a traumatic injury. These children's memories for their injuries and hospital treatment were assessed 6 months, 1 year, and 1½ to 2 years afterwards. Recall was much worse and more error prone in children who were 1-year-olds when the injury occurred than in those who were 2-year-olds. Indeed, half of the children between 12 and 18 months of age at the time of the event could remember nothing at all about it 18 months later. What was of crucial importance in determining how much children could remember about their injury and hospitalization was whether they possessed the language skills to talk about the event at the time it happened.

Third, Peterson (2002) reviewed studies in which children's memories of events were assessed more than 4 years afterwards. The child's age at the time of the event was very important. For example, Quas, Goodman, Bidrose, Pipe, Craw, and Ablin (1999) studied children's long-term recall for a medical procedure called voiding cystourethrogram fluoroscopy (VCUG), which involves stressful and painful genital contact. None of the children who had been 2 at the time of the procedure had long-term memory of it, and only 50% of those who had been 3

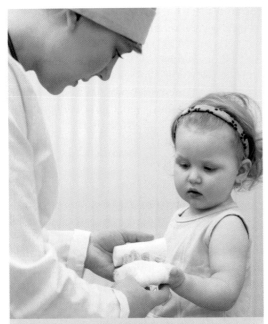

Peterson and Rideout (1998) concluded that how much children could remember about their injury and hospitalization depended on whether they possessed the language skills to talk about the event at the time it happened.

recalled the procedure several years later. By contrast, almost 70% of children who had been 4 at the time recalled the VCUG years later, as did nearly all of those who had been 5 or 6 at the time. Among those children who remembered the procedure, recall was as accurate several years afterwards as at shorter intervals.

Simcock and Hayne (2003) pointed out that memory in young children is typically assessed by means of verbal report. If young children produce limited verbal reports of events that have happened to them, we cannot readily decide whether this is due to their poor memory for the event or to their inability to express what they remember in words. In view of the limited language skills of young children, it is likely that research based only on verbal report has systematically *underestimated* what young children can remember.

The above issue was investigated by Simcock and Hayne (2003). Children between the ages of 24 and 48 months played a game with a "magic shrinking machine." Large objects [e.g. a teddy bear 28 cm tall (11 inches); a ball

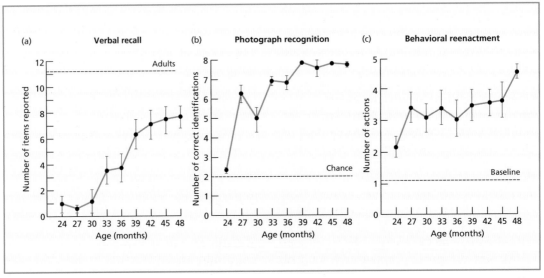

Figure 12.10 (a) Mean items reported during verbal report, (b) mean photographs identified (maximum = 8), and (c) mean target actions performed (maximum = 5) by children aged between 24 and 48 months. From Simcock and Hayne (2003). Copyright © American Psychological Association. Reproduced with permission.

17 cm (7 inches) in diameter] were placed in the machine and much smaller versions [e.g. a teddy bear 10 cm (4 inches) tall; a ball 5 cm (2 inches) in diameter] emerged from the machine, having apparently "magically" shrunk.

Twenty-four hours later, the children were given three memory tests for their experience with the magic shrinking machine. First, there was a test of verbal recall. Second, there was a nonverbal photograph recognition test in which they had to select photographs of objects that had been placed in the machine. Third, there was a test of behavioral re-enactment, in which the children were asked to show how the magic shrinking machine worked. The findings were striking, with memory performance assessed by verbal report lagging behind that shown by the other two tests (see Figure 12.10). More specifically, only children aged 33 months and above showed even reasonable verbal recall, whereas children from the age of 27 months performed well on the photograph recognition and behavioral re-enactment tasks.

How should we interpret these findings? They certainly seem to show that younger children possess much more information about their experiences than is apparent from their verbal reports. There are probably two reasons why they performed better on the photograph and behavioral re-enactment tasks than on the verbal report task. First, the former tasks placed much less reliance on language. Second, the children were presented with much more information as retrieval cues in the photograph and behavioral re-enactment tasks than in the verbal report task, and this would have made the former tasks simpler.

Conclusions

There is reasonable evidence that even 1- and 2-year-old children can recall personal events (but often only in fragmentary form) when questioned several months later. However, children under the age of 3 typically have much poorer verbal recall of even significant events (e.g. traumatic injury) when their memories are tested years afterwards. A key difference between young children who manage to recall autobiographical memories years after an event and those who do not seems to be the language skills they possessed at the time of the event. Of potential importance, studies in which there is exclusive reliance on verbal recall to assess what children can remember of past events may well minimize younger children's actual ability to remember those events.

Infantile amnesia

The most famous (or perhaps it should be notorious) account of infantile amnesia is the one provided by Sigmund Freud (1915/1957; see Chapter 10). He argued that infantile amnesia occurs through repression, with threat-related thoughts and experiences (e.g. sexual feelings towards one's parents) being consigned to the unconscious. More specifically, Freud claimed that such threatening memories are changed into more innocuous memories (he called them screen memories). This is a dramatic theory, but there is practically no evidence to support it. The most obvious problem is that it totally fails to explain why adolescents and adults cannot remember *positive* and *neutral* events from early childhood in spite of the fact that such events should not be subject to repression.

In recent years, two impressive theoretical explanations of infantile amnesia and of the ways in which autobiographical memory develops have been proposed. First, there is an approach that emphasizes the role played by the development of the cognitive self (e.g. Howe & Courage, 1997). Second, there is the social cultural approach (e.g. Fivush & Nelson, 2004) based on the assumption that social and cultural factors are of prime importance in the development of autobiographical memory. We consider these two approaches in turn.

Cognitive self

According Howe and Courage's (1997) theoretical approach, infants can only form autobiographical memories *after* they have developed a sense of self to whom events having *personal* significance can occur. There is evidence that a

In Lewis and Brooks-Gunn's (1979) study, infants recognizing their own reflection, by reaching for their own nose rather than the one in the mirror, were considered to be demonstrating a level of self-awareness.

sense of self develops towards the end of the second year of life. For example, Lewis and Brooks-Gunn (1979) carried out a study in which infants who had had a red spot applied surreptitiously to their nose were held up to a mirror. Those recognizing their own reflection and so reaching for their own nose rather than the one in the mirror were claimed to show at least some self-awareness. Practically no infants in the first year of life showed clear evidence of self-awareness, but 70% of infants between 21 and 24 months did so.

Visual self-recognition is associated with other measures of the development of the self-concept. Lewis and Ramsay (2004) assessed visual self-recognition, personal pronoun use ("I", "me"), and pretend play at different ages, arguing that children need some sense of self to pretend to be someone else. Of those children at any given age who used personal pronouns and engaged in pretend play, the great majority also showed visual self-recognition. Thus, visual self-recognition seems to be a valid measure of the development of the self.

The crucial assumption of Howe and Courage's theory is as follows:

The development of the cognitive self late in the second year of life (as indexed by visual self-recognition) provides a new framework around which memories can be organized. With this cognitive advance ..., we witness the emergence of autobiographical memory and the end of infantile amnesia. (Howe & Courage, 1997, p. 499)

The finding that the cognitive self appears shortly before the onset of autobiographical memory around or shortly after children's second birthdays (Fivush et al., 1987; Peterson, 2002) fits the theory. However, it doesn't show in any way that the former plays any role in *causing* the latter. Stronger evidence comes in a study by Howe, Courage, and Edison (2003), who, working with infants aged between 15 and 23 months, found that self-recognizers had better memory for personal events than infants who were not self-recognizers when controlling for language ability. They also followed a group of infants from the age of 15 to 23 months. Not a single child showed good performance on a memory test for personal events before achieving self-recognition.

What also needs to be explained is why it is that children aged 2 and 3 can form autobiographical memories and remember them for several months but have nearly always forgotten them by the time of adulthood. Howe and Courage (1997) argued that autobiographical memories are most likely to be remembered for very long periods of time if they are rehearsed frequently, and young children simply don't engage in much rehearsal of remembered information.

Social cultural theory

The social cultural developmental theory (e.g. Fivush & Nelson, 2004) provides another plausible account of infantile amnesia. According to this theory, language and culture both play central roles in the early development of autobiographical memory. Language is important in part because we use language to communicate our memories. Experiences occurring before children develop are difficult to express in language later on.

The parents' use of language is also very important both at the time an event is occurring and when discussing it subsequently. Nelson (1989) focused on interactions between mothers and children while they were wandering around a museum. These interactions were categorized as "freely interacting" or as "practical." The former interactional style was free wheeling and reminiscing, and involved mothers relating what was seen in the museum to previous experiences shared with their child. By contrast, the practical style involved the mother asking questions such as, "What do you think this is for?"; "What do you think this statue is made of?" When tested for memory of the experience a week later, the mothers and children who had freely interacted answered an average of 13 out of 30 questions, whereas the more practical group could answer only 5.

Fivush and Nelson (2004) argued that parents vary along a dimension of elaboration when discussing the past with their children. Some parents discuss the past in great detail when talking to their children whereas others do not. According to the theory, children whose parents have an elaborative reminiscing style will report more and fuller childhood memories. There are some important cultural differences here, because mothers from Western cultures tend to talk about the past in a more elaborated and emotional way than do mothers from Eastern cultures (Leichtman, Wang, & Pillemer, 2003).

Most of the available evidence is consistent with the social cultural developmental theory. As predicted, the mother's reminiscing style is an important factor. Children's very early ability to talk about the past was much better among those whose mothers had an elaborative reminiscing style than among those whose mothers rarely talked about the past (Harley & Reese, 1999). Perhaps the simplest explanation of that finding is that children whose mothers talk in detail about the past are being provided with good opportunities to rehearse their memories.

It has also been found that the language skills available to children at the time of an experience determine what they can recall about it subsequently. Simcock and Hayne (2002) asked 2- and 3-year-old children to describe their memories for complex play activities at periods of time up to 12 months later. The children *only* used words they had already known at the time of event. This is impressive evidence given that the children had acquired hundreds of new words during the period of time between having the experience and subsequently describing it.

Cross-cultural research reveals that adults from Eastern cultures have a later age of first autobiographical memory than adults from Western cultures (Pillemer, 1998). It has also been found that the reported memories of early childhood are much more elaborated and emotional in American children than in those from Korea or China (Han, Leichtman, & Wang, 1998). These findings are predictable on the basis of cultural differences in mothers' reminiscing style. Another possibility is that American children are more inclined to report their personal experiences than are those from Eastern cultures.

Evaluation

Three points need to be emphasized. First, the two theories just discussed should *not* be regarded as mutually exclusive. For example, it can be argued that the *onset* of autobiographical memory in infants depends on the emergence of the self, with its subsequent expression being heavily influenced by social factors, cultural factors, and infants' development of language. Second, there is reasonable research evidence that *all* of the main factors identified in the two theories are involved in the development of autobiographical memory. Third, whereas the research evidence is supportive, most of it is limited in the sense that it shows an *association* in time between, for example, the mother's reminiscing style and autobiographical memory performance in her child. The presence of an association does *not* demonstrate that the memory performance was *caused* by the reminiscing style although it is consistent with a causal explanation.

CHILDREN AS WITNESSES

Throughout this chapter, we have focused mainly on basic research designed to understand how and why children's memory abilities improve systematically throughout childhood. However, research on children's memory also has very important practical applications. For example, in legal cases children are increasingly being asked to provide reports of their experiences whether as victims or witnesses of a crime (see Chapter 14 for a discussion of eyewitness testimony in adults). In England and Wales, one reason for this is because the Home Office and Department of Health decided in 1992 that video-recorded interviews with children were admissible in criminal and family law cases.

There are two central questions to discuss. First, there is the issue of the accuracy and reliability of children's reports of alleged crimes. Second, there is the issue of what steps can be taken to maximize the accuracy of such reports. We consider the first issue in this section of the chapter, and then move on the second issue in the next section.

As we saw earlier, young children have reasonable memory for specific events, particularly when suitable cues are provided. For example, Fivush, Hudson, and Nelson (1984) investigated memories of a visit to the Jewish Museum in New York by 5-year-olds. The visit included an explanation of archeological methods and the chance to dig in a sandbox to find artifacts. Recall of this event showed considerable forgetting. However, 6 years later the children successfully recalled 87% of the original information when given appropriate cues.

The issue of how well children can remember events has become increasingly important as the extent of child physical and sexual abuse has become more fully realized. In such cases, the evidence typically depends on the testimony of one or more children. In 1983, for example, a 36-year-old woman who ran a nursery school was convicted of murder and of twelve counts of child abuse mainly on eyewitness testimony from 29 children who had attended the school.

As children are often asked to provide evidence about traumatic events, such as physical and/or sexual abuse, we need to consider whether their memory for such events is likely to be better or worse than their memory for neutral or positive events. According to Freud's repression theory (discussed in Chapter 10), children should tend to repress memory of traumatic events, which would as a consequence be more difficult to recall than nontraumatic events. By contrast, much of the memory research discussed in this book indicates that experiences that are significant and distinctive are generally better remembered than those that are insignificant and nondistinctive. As the great majority of traumatic events are both significant and distinctive, the prediction follows that traumatic memories should typically be better remembered than nontraumatic ones.

How accurately do children recall events?

Cordón, Pipe, Sayfan, Melinder, and Goodman (2004) reviewed studies on children's memory for traumatic and nontraumatic events occurring in early childhood. They concluded that the similarities between memories for the two types of event greatly outweigh the differences:

Memories of traumatic and nontraumatic experiences have much in common. In particular, the same variables that influence memory for nontraumatic events, such as age, delay, and the nature of the event, are also important determinants of memory for early childhood trauma. Age at the time of the event emerges as a crucial factor in the ability to consciously access memory for traumatic events. (Cordón et al., 2004, p. 122)

A central concern about using children to provide eyewitness testimony is that children tend to be suggestible, which can lead to systematic errors in their recall of events. In general, suggestibility is greater during the early years of childhood than the later ones (see Bruck & Ceci, 1999, for a review). Bruck and Ceci (1997) found enhanced suggestibility in 3- to 4-year-olds, but this reduced with age with 10- to 12-year-olds being no more suggestible than adults. In their study, children were read a story about a little girl called Lauren on her first day at school. Lauren eats eggs for breakfast, then has a stomachache, which she forgets about when allowed to play with another child's toy. Misleading information was introduced by asking the question, "Do you remember the story about Lauren, who had a headache because she ate her cereal too fast? Then she felt better when she got to play with her friend's game?" This is what is known as a leading question, because it carries with it an implication as to the correct answer.

The children were tested individually for their understanding of the story and then the experimenter left. Two days later, the children were again tested individually, and chose between pairs of pictures. One picture showed Lauren eating eggs and the other eating cereal; another pair portrayed Lauren with a stomachache or a headache. Memory performance was only slightly affected by age when no misleading information (i.e. the leading question) was given (Figure 12.11). By contrast, memory accuracy was much lower in younger than in older children when misleading information was given.

The research of Ceci, Baker, and Bronfenbrenner (1988) suggests that young children are more susceptible to memory bias than older ones. But how suggestible are children when questioned about emotionally loaded events relating to abuse they have observed? Thompson, Clarke-Stewart, and Lepore (1997) took a step in the direction of answering this question. Five- and six-year-olds witnessed one of two events. In the innocent event, a janitor called Chester cleaned some dolls and other toys in a playroom. In the abusive event, Chester handled the dolls roughly and in a mildly abusive way. Some children were then questioned by an accusatory interviewer, who suggested the janitor had been abusive; other children were questioned by an exonerating interviewer, who suggested the janitor was innocent. The remaining children were questioned by a neutral interviewer who avoided making suggestions. The children described what the janitor had done to their parents immediately after the interview and 2 weeks later.

Children's eyewitness memories were generally accurate when questioned by the neutral interviewer. However, the children's accounts typically conformed to the interviewer's suggestions when the interviewer was accusatory or exonerating. In other words, the janitor was reported by the children as having behaved

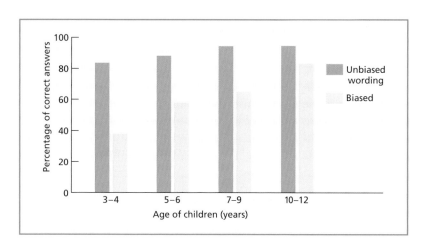

Figure 12.11 This graph shows the effects of misleading information on the memory of children of different ages. When unbiased wording is used, recall is more or less equally high across the age range, but under biased conditions younger children are more easily misled (Ceci et al., 1988).

abusively when the interviewer was accusatory, but as having behaved innocently when the interviewer was exonerating. When the children were then asked neutral questions by their parents, their descriptions of the event were generally consistent with what they had said to the interviewer.

You might think that it is not surprising that young children were influenced by the strong and blatant interviewer bias in the Thompson et al. (1997) study. However, children are fairly suggestible in many situations *not* involving strong interviewer bias. Bruck and Ceci (1997) asked preschool children on five separate occasions to describe two true events (e.g. a recent punishment) and two false events (e.g. witnessing a thief stealing food). By the third interview, nearly all of the children accepted that both the false events had actually happened. Most of the children continued to argue that the false events were true when they were questioned later by a new interviewer who had been instructed to adopt a nonsuggestive approach. The children's descriptions of the true and false events were similar in terms of the numbers of spontaneous statements and details (e.g. about conversations).

Evaluation

Why do young children produce systematically distorted reports of events when exposed to suggestive influences? Two main factors are involved (Roebers & Schneider, 2005). One factor is social compliance. Young children might yield to social pressure and a lack of social support even when their own recollection is accurate; this is especially likely when they are interviewed by someone much older than themselves. The other factor is cognitive incompetence. Young children might come to believe their own distorted memory reports because of limitations in processing, attention, or language. Evidence for this second factor comes from the findings of several studies (see Bruck & Melnyk, 2004, for a review). In these studies, children continued to produce false memories even after having been warned that

the interviewer might have been mistaken in his/her suggestions.

What can be done?

From a practical perspective, it is important to maximize the accuracy of children's eyewitness reports. Perhaps the most obvious approach is to take steps to reduce problems of social compliance by ensuring that those involved in interviewing children avoid leading questions. That is certainly desirable. However, interviewer bias can manifest itself in several ways other than through the use of leading questions. For example, an interviewer can display bias by rewarding desired answers, criticizing nondesired answers, repeating specific questions within an interview, and so on.

Garven, Wood, and Malpass (2000) explored interviewer bias in the form of the interviewer's reactions to children's answers to various questions. In their study, kindergarten children recalled details about a visitor called Paco, who came to their classroom. The children were asked misleading questions about plausible events (e.g. "Did Paco break a toy?") and about bizarre events (e.g. "Did Paco take you to a farm?"). In one group, children was praised when they answered positively to these misleading questions but criticized when they answered negatively; the other group of children received no feedback from the interviewer. The children receiving praise and criticism falsely agreed with 35% of the plausible questions and 52% of the bizarre ones, whereas those not receiving feedback agreed with only 13% of the plausible and 5% of the bizarre questions. These group differences did not just reflect social pressure at the time of interview, because the children exposed to interviewer bias continued to provide false answers to the misleading questions when interviewed subsequently by different neutral interviewers. Thus, if we are to obtain accurate information from child eyewitnesses, we must ensure that there is no interviewer bias of any kind.

Most children watch several hours of television every week, and it is possible that one reason why children's eyewitness memory is distorted is because they tend to confuse real-life and television events. For example, they might see disturbing sexual scenes on television, and then incorporate some elements of what they have seen into their answers when questioned about real-life experiences. In other words, young children might be poor at monitoring the sources of events.

The above considerations led Thierry and Spence (2002) to study the effects of source-monitoring training on the eyewitness memory of 3- and 4-year-olds. All the children initially watched as the experimenter (Mrs Science) presented live and video-taped demonstrations of science experiments. After that, all the children watched live and video puppet shows. One puppet (Billy) featured in both shows, both of which were watched by another puppet (Terry). Children in the source-monitoring training condition were given the following instructions: "Terry can never remember what Billy did in real life and what Billy only did on TV. Billy hates that. Let's show Billy that you can remember what he did for you and Terry in real life and what you and Terry only saw him doing on TV" (Thierry & Spence, 2002, p. 431). Finally, the children were questioned about events from the initial live and video-taped demonstrations featuring Mrs Science. On average, children not trained in source monitoring made five times as many errors in attributing events correctly to the live and video-taped sources as those who had been trained (twenty-six vs. five errors).

Memory for events can also be improved by putting the person back into the situation in which the event took place. For example, I spent my early years in a suburb of south London close to Crystal Palace Football Club. I have often driven along the streets I knew as a child, and this acts as an effective trigger to recall childhood events. This makes sense in terms of Tulving's (e.g. 1979) encoding specificity principle (see Chapter 8). According to this principle, we generally store away contextual information about events, and memory should be maximal when the information

available at the time of retrieval (including context) matches that in the memory trace.

Priestley, Roberts, and Pipe (1999) considered the possible beneficial effects of reinstating context on children's memory for an event. Children between 5 and 7 years of age participated in an event, "Visiting the pirate," involving becoming a real pirate, making a map, winning a key, and finding treasure. Their memory for this event was tested 6 months later. Children in the context condition were interviewed with the pirate props present, and those in the reminder condition revisited the pirate room the day before their memory was tested. These two conditions were equally effective: children in the context condition recalled an average of 19.5 items of information and those in the reminder condition recalled 20.2. Both groups performed about 40% better than a control group that had no reminder or reinstatement of context.

At least some of the information that young children store away in memory after witnessing an event is likely to be in nonverbal form. As a result, interviews with child witnesses might generally fail to access all of the relevant information they possess about events. Gross and Hayne (1999) argued that it might be possible to improve matters by asking some children to draw what they could remember about an event before asking them to provide a verbal report. The information in their verbal reports could then be compared against that provided by children who only supplied a verbal report.

In the study by Gross and Hayne (1999), 5- and 6-year-old children visited a Cadbury's chocolate factory. They were taken there by a woman wearing a purple suit and top hat and carrying a walking stick who referred to herself as "Charlie Chocolate." Children's memory for this event was tested after 1 day, 6 months, and 1 year. The findings were similar at the two shorter retention intervals, with children in the drawing condition recalling about 30% more information in their verbal reports than those who only provided verbal reports. The effects were even stronger after 1 year—the children who drew as well as providing a verbal report recalled almost twice as much information about the visit to the chocolate factory as did those in the control condition. These beneficial effects were obtained without any increase in the number of errors, thus suggesting that including drawing in memory interviews might be a very effective way of obtaining accurate and reasonably complete accounts of events.

Why was drawing so effective in enhancing the amount of information subsequently provided in verbal reports? Several factors could be involved. However, probably the most important one is that producing drawings allows children to generate their own idiosyncratic retrieval cues and this in turn enriches their verbal reports.

In sum, the good news so far as using children as witnesses is that there are several ways of increasing how much they can recall accurately about events that have happened to them. It is very important for interviewers to avoid any kind of bias (including use of leading questions). Children can be trained in source monitoring so that their recall of a crucial event does not include aspects of a different event. Two further useful approaches that can be used very generally are to reinstate the context in which the event in question happened and to provide children with the opportunity to produce drawings of the event before engaging in verbal recall of it.

SUMMARY

The distinction between declarative and implicit memory is important in understanding the development of memory in infants. Declarative memory tasks pass the amnesia filter (deficient memory performance by adult amnesics) and the parameter filter (performance much affected by retention interval and by contextual changes). Tasks such as the mobile conjugate reinforcement paradigm and deferred imitation involve declarative memory and show substantial performance improvements during the first year or so of life. There is less evidence for large improvements in implicit memory in the early years of life. The improvements in declarative memory during infancy probably depend in part on developments within the underlying brain systems (e.g. the dentate gyrus within the hippocampal formation). By contrast, the brain systems underlying implicit memory seem to be more developed at the time of birth. There are several reasons why explicit memory improves during childhood after infancy. First, all of the main components of the working memory system (central executive, phonological loop, visuo-spatial sketchpad) show increased capacity during childhood. Second, older children have more relevant knowledge. Third, older children have a greater range of memory strategies. Fourth, older children have greater metamemory or knowledge about their own memory. These four factors are interconnected. Older children can show inferior declarative memory performance to younger ones when their greater processing of gist leads them to recall or recognize information that wasn't previously presented.

Implicit memory typically does not show age-related changes during childhood. Implicit memory involves simpler processes than declarative memory, and is much less affected by working memory, relevant knowledge, memory strategies, and metamemory.

The term "infantile amnesia" refers to adults' inability to remember any childhood events before the age of 3 or 4. One explanation for infantile amnesia is that infants can only form autobiographical memories after developing a sense of self towards the end of the second year of life. Alternatively, the development of autobiographical memory might depend heavily on language and culture. This explanation receives some support from the finding that children whose parents discuss the past with them in great detail have more childhood memories than those whose parents do not.

Children are increasingly used as witnesses in court cases. Younger children tend to be more suggestible than older ones, partly because they are more likely to yield to social pressure. In addition, young children have less cognitive competence, and might come to believe their own distorted memory reports. Child eyewitnesses should not be exposed to any form of interviewer bias. Children's memory can also be improved by reinstating the context in which an event happened and by allowing them to produce drawings in addition to providing a verbal report.

FURTHER READING

- **Bauer, P. J.** (2006). *Remembering the times of our lives: Memory in infancy and beyond.* Hove, UK: Psychology Press. This book provides a comprehensive and up-to-date overview of our knowledge about the early development of memory.

- **Bruck, M., & Melnyk, L.** (2004). Individual differences in children's suggestibility: A review and synthesis. *Applied Cognitive Psychology, 18,* 947–996. This article provides a thorough analysis of changes in suggestibility and its effects on children's memory at different ages.

- **Hayne, H.** (2004). Infant memory development: Implications for childhood amnesia. *Developmental Review, 24,* 33–73. Harlene Hayne provides a thorough discussion of research on the development of memory in infants, and shows the relevance of this research for an understanding of infantile amnesia.

- **Reese, E.** (2002). A model of the origins of autobiographical memory. In J.W. Fagen & H. Hayne (Eds.), *Progress in infancy research*, Vol. 2. Mahwah, NJ: Lawrence Erlbaum Associates. Elaine Reese considers in detail the complexities involved in understanding how autobiographical memory develops, and also discusses her own theoretical approach.

- **Richmond, J., & Nelson, C. A.** (2007). Accounting for change in declarative memory: A cognitive neuroscience perspective. *Developmental Review, 27,* 349–373. This article by Jenny Richmond and Charles Nelson contains an authoritative and up-to-date account of the cognitive neuroscience approach to understanding the development of children's memory.

- **Rovee-Collier, C., Hayne, H., & Colombo, M.** (2001). *The development of implicit and explicit memory.* Amsterdam: John Benjamins. This book presents an excellent contribution to our understanding of the ways in which major memory systems develop in young children.

CHAPTER 13

MEMORY AND AGING

Alan Baddeley

We all complain about the fallibility of our memories and, as we get older, we complain more. This is what Patrick Stewart, most widely known for his role in *Star Trek*, says about learning his lines on returning to the stage in *Macbeth* and as Malvolio in *Twelfth Night* (Box 13.1).

It is difficult to compare one's own memory with that of others, and comparing it with the state of one's own memory years ago itself involves memory. There is also evidence that we become somewhat less good at reporting memory lapses as we get older (Sunderland, Watts, Baddeley, & Harris, 1986), and that complaints about memory in the elderly relate

more closely to depression than to actual memory performance (Rabbitt & Abson, 1990). We clearly need better evidence than our subjective feelings of progressive memory failure, especially given that impaired memory is the earliest and most powerful predictor of the onset of Alzheimer's disease, an increasingly serious problem with the gradual aging of the Western population. So what can you expect if you remain healthy but get older, and how will it differ from the onset of Alzheimer's?

The study of aging involves the study of change, as opposed to most of the research described so far, which assumes a system that is relatively stable, although of course one that can change as a result of learning or forgetting. There are two principal methods of studying aging, the *longitudinal* and the *cross-sectional*. In a longitudinal study, a sample of people,

---

Box 13.1 Patrick Stewart *The Observer* 29 July 2007, p. 37

With every year that passes I am more and more puzzled—and dismayed—by the mental process of learning, absorbing, internalising and finally speaking lines of dialogue. It has become the only labour in this marvellous job I love so much.

Learning lines used to be a breeze. In rep. I'd do the show, go to the pub, knock back a couple of pints, and then home and head down, into the script, knocking off an act or so before bedtime.

Not any more. Now, learning has to be planned, soberly, in advance of rehearsals and, for me, usually undertaken early in the morning.

Although our memories decline with age, frequency of complaints tends to correlate with degree of depression.

preferably selected so as to reflect the full range of the population, will be tested repeatedly, for example every 5 years, preferably over many decades (Rönnlund, Nyberg, Bäckman, & Nilsson, 2005; Rönnlund & Nilsson, 2006). The advantage of this approach is that the effects of age on the performance of each individual can be studied, subsequently allowing specified individuals, such as those developing Alzheimer's disease, to be singled out and their performance before the onset of the disease compared with that of more fortunate, healthy people. Such studies are expensive in time and funding but are already yielding crucial information about the development of a range of diseases and their genetic, physiological, and cognitive precursors.

Longitudinal designs do, however, have two major problems. The first stems from the fact that some participants will almost certainly drop out, because they move house or perhaps because they lose interest. Furthermore, people who drop out might be atypical of the rest of the sample, gradually making it less representative. There are statistical methods of attempting to correct for drop-out, but this is inevitably a complex and potentially controversial issue. A second problem concerns measures of cognition in general, and memory in particular. Even though test sessions are separated by as much as 5 years, substantial learning occurs, not just because patients learn the particular items constituting the test, but also because there are more general practice effects that can be sufficient to counteract any decrement due to aging.

This problem is avoided if one uses a cross-sectional design in which different groups of people are sampled across the age range and their performance is measured on a single occasion. The drawbacks of this approach are that one cannot, of course, relate performance to earlier data, nor can one relate performance to the future development of the individual, without at least including a later test that will be influenced by practice effects from the first test session. A further problem with this design is the so-called **cohort effect**. A **cross-sectional**

design assumes that people who are currently in their 20s and people in their 80s differ only in their age, whereas the very substantial differences in education, society, health, and nutrition between the two cohorts might well have a major influence on performance. Average scores on the Raven's Matrices intelligence test have, for example, been increasing steadily since 1940 (Flynn, 1987) in many Western societies, and the health and longevity of the general population have also steadily increased in many parts of the world.

A solution to these problems is to combine longitudinal and cross-sectional approaches by adding a new cohort of participants at each test point. In due course, comparison of these initial test groups across the years will provide a measure of any cohort effects, while comparing them with the relevant longitudinal group of that age will give a clear indication of learning effects. This approach has been used by the Betula Study carried out in Northern Sweden and named after the birch tree that predominates at those latitudes (Nilsson, Adolfsson, Bäckman, de Frias, Molander, & Nyberg, 2004). The study emphasizes memory and is beginning to show some very interesting results. One of these is that both practice effects (Figure 13.1), and cohort effects (Figure 13.2) are very substantial (Rönnlund et al., 2005).

Using a correlational approach it is possible to identify some of the causes of enhanced performance in more recent cohorts. The Rönnlund

KEY TERMS

Longitudinal design: Method of studying development or aging whereby the same participants are successively tested at different ages.

Cohort effect: The tendency for people born at different time periods to differ as a result of historic changes in diet, education, and other social factors.

Cross-sectional design: Method of studying development or aging whereby participants are sampled from different age bands and tested only once.

et al. (2005) evidence suggests an important role for nutrition, as reflected in the gradual increase over the years in average height. Years of education also appear to be associated with memory performance, independent of age. Number of children in the family, which is tentatively interpreted as reflecting the amount of attention an individual child might receive within the family, is also linked to memory performance (Figure 13.3). As each sample includes participants across the age range,

it is possible to study the way in which such variables influence the process of aging within difference cohorts. Finally, the very large numbers involved are beginning to allow genetic studies to be carried out, with the potential for identifying not only the genetic precursors to diseases, but also whether genetic links influence different aspects of memory in different ways (Nilsson, Adolfsson, Bäckman, Cruts, Nyberg, Small, & van Broeckhoven, 2006).

The Betula study, in common with most similar studies, focuses on the specific part of the lifespan involved in aging. A longitudinal study extending over the whole lifespan would, of course, take a lifetime to complete. Even so, some studies that commence with pregnancy and test at regular intervals are ongoing, although they are—for the most part—not focused on cognition and have not yet been running for a lifetime. It was therefore with great excitement that Ian Deary, an Edinburgh psychologist with an interest in intelligence, discovered that well-validated IQ tests had been given to every child in Scotland who was 11 years old in 1932 (*N* = 89,498) and that these results were still available (Deary, Whiteman, Starr, Whalley, & Fox, 2004). Through local records and press advertising, they were able to contact 550 people in the Edinburgh area who had been born in 1921

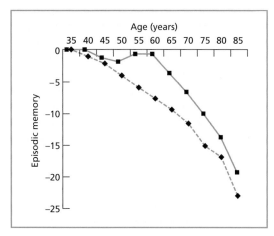

Figure 13.1 Decline in episodic memory performance between ages 35 and 85 as measured by a longitudinal (filled squares) or cross-sectional (diamonds) method. Based on Rönnlund et al. (2005).

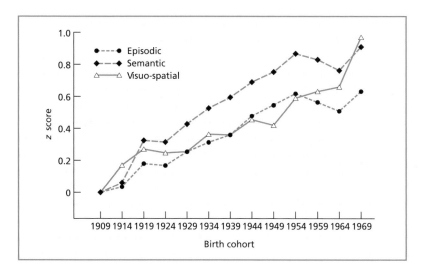

Figure 13.2 The Flynn effect for memory. Age-adjusted performance on tests of episodic memory, semantic memory, and visuo-spatial ability for individuals born at different times ranging from 1909 to 1969 show a steady increase. From Rönnlund and Nilsson (2008). Copyright © Elsevier. Reproduced with permission.

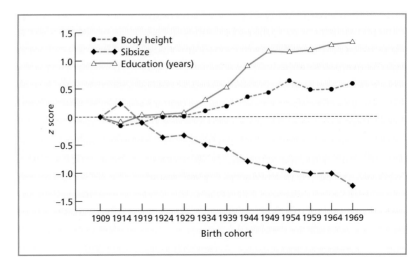

Figure 13.3 Age-adjusted height, family size, and years of education for Swedish people born between 1909 and 1969. People have become taller and better educated, while families have become smaller. From Rönnlund and Nilsson (2008). Copyright © Elsevier. Reproduced with permission.

and tested 11 years later. These volunteers were retested using the original IQ measure, together with a number of other psychological and physical measures.

People originally tested in 1932 were 80 at the time of retest and, by that point, many of the original sample had died. Deary et al. (2004) found that, for both men and women, the lowest quartile has the lowest life expectancy; differences between the remaining quartiles are small. A slight discrepancy in the general pattern occurs in the case of men during the 1940s and 1950s, which probably results from the effect of the Second World War, where certain dangerous operations such as aircrew tended to differentially select for a higher ability.

In terms of mental testing there proved to be a very high correlation between score at 11 and at age 80 ($r = .66$), although, as expected, level of performance at 80 was lower. In an attempt to identify factors that led to successful aging, IQ at 11 was correlated with a range of cognitive and physical fitness measures, namely grip strength, lung function, and time to walk to 6 meters (Deary, Whalley, Batty, & Starr, 2006). Physical fitness at 80 was predicted by IQ at 11 and was influenced by sex, social class, and the *APOE* gene, which Nilsson et al. (2006) had also found to be related to episodic and semantic memory performance in their elderly sample in the Betula study.

However, despite the growing importance of such large-scale longitudinal projects, much of the research in the field so far has relied on cross-sectional studies, typically involving the comparison of a young and an elderly sample, approximately matched for educational and socioeconomic status. We will begin by viewing the results of such studies, looking in turn at the various components of memory, then moving on to what is known about the link between the structure and functioning of the brain and aging, before concluding with a discussion of Alzheimer's disease.

WORKING MEMORY AND AGING

Short-term memory

Although both verbal and visual memory span tend to decline with age, the decline is far from dramatic, with mean digit span dropping from 6.6 items to 5.8 over the course of an adult life (Parkinson, Inman, & Dannenbaum, 1985) and spatial span using the Corsi block tapping task dropping from 5.1 to 4.7 blocks (Spinnler, Della Sala, Bandera, & Baddeley, 1988). Craik (1986) found a minimal drop in memory span for unrelated words in the elderly, a difference that increased substantially when the task was changed to one in which the words had to be recalled in alphabetic order (e.g. hear *pen dog zoo hat*, recall *dog hat pen zoo*). The crucial difference, of course, is the need to simultaneously hold and manipulate the material, in short, to use working memory.

There is broad general agreement that working memory is susceptible to the effects of age, although it is not always clear exactly which aspects are most vulnerable (Box 13.2). Whereas sentence span in which participants must process a sequence of sentences and then recall the final word does tend to be sensitive to aging, the pattern of results is less marked than one might expect. Verhaeghen, Marcoen, and Goossens (1993) review a range of studies of the effects of age on working memory span, concluding that a decrement occurs, but is rather small. May, Hasher, and Kane (1999) suggest that this decline could largely be the result of the build up of interference from earlier sequences, reflecting a problem with inhibiting irrelevant material rather than one of combining storage and processing *per se* (May et al., 1999). This is consistent with the suggestion by Hasher and Zacks (1988; Hasher, Zacks, & May, 1999) that a major cognitive effect of aging is the reduced capacity to inhibit irrelevant stimuli.

An intriguing example of the decline of the capacity to inhibit irrelevant information with age comes from a study carried out by Molander and Bäckman (1989) who tested groups of competitive miniature golf players who were matched in skill under practice conditions.

During competition however, the 50-year-old senior group showed a decline in performance in contrast to younger competitors. Under practice conditions, a heart-rate monitor indicated that younger players showed a slowing of the heart rate when making a shot, and even greater slowing during competition. In contrast, the older players showed an increase during training that was moderated during competition. Bäckman and Molander (1986) asked young and older golfers to recall specific shots made during practice and during competition. The competition had no effect on recall by the young, whereas the old recalled less accurate and more irrelevant information, suggesting a reduced capacity to shut out irrelevant stimuli.

There tends to be a decline in performance with age in many skills that involve intense concentration, including those that do not involve physical strength, such as chess, where adapting to age appears to involve a gradual

As we get older, it becomes harder at times of stress to shut out distractions, making it more likely that the older golfer will "choke" on the final putt that would have won the championship.

Box 13.2 Memory and aging

There is saying that "you are as old as you feel." But how old is that? A study by Rubin and Berntsen (2006) suggests that, from their mid forties, people begin to feel younger than their age, with the perceived age being an average of 20% younger than their actual age. Why should this be? Is it a memory effect, or just that we view the world through rose-tinted spectacles?

change in strategy. Charness (1985) studied the performance of chess players who differed in age but were matched for expertise. He found that the young players tended to scan a wide range of options, whereas the older players scanned fewer but in greater depth. This could reflect an increasing difficulty in keeping track of multiple sources of information.

There is considerable evidence to suggest that age impairs the capacity to divide attention between two sources. There is no doubt that dual-task performance is often more affected by age than performance on the two components separately (see Riby et al., 2004, for a review). The results of many such studies might, however, simply reflect the increased overall load rather than a specific deficit in the ability to coordinate two simultaneous tasks. If an elderly person has greater difficulty with each of the individual tasks, it is hardly surprising that they have even more difficulty in performing both at the same time.

To demonstrate a deficit in task combination *per se*, it is necessary to ensure that level of performance on the individual tasks is equal for the young and old groups, if necessary by making the tasks easier for the elderly. In a series of studies to be described in the section on Alzheimer's disease, digit span and a visuo-spatial tracking task were combined. Provided level of performance on the individual tasks was equated, no reliable age decrement occurred, although there was a marked effect of dementia (Spinnler et al., 1988; Baddeley et al., 2001a). Broadly speaking, however, it is probably wise to assume that working memory is progressively impaired, particularly when it involves tasks comprising either speed of processing or episodic long-term memory, which we consider next.

AGING AND LONG-TERM MEMORY

Episodic memory

There is no doubt that performance on tasks involving episodic memory declines steadily through the adult years. Although many studies have used relatively artificial material, such as the acquisition of pairs of unrelated words or the retention of geometric figures, the effects are by no means limited to such material. The Doors and People test described in Chapter 11 (p. 253) uses relatively realistic material, such as people's names and pictures of doors, and shows a decline for both recall and recognition of visual and verbal materials. A similar decline is shown in the Rivermead Behavioural Memory Test (see Chapter 11, p. 262), which was designed to mirror everyday memory situations (Wilson, Cockburn, Baddeley, & Hiorns, 1989b), and Salthouse (1991) reviews over 40 real-world activities, from actors learning lines through recall of bridge hands to memory for conversations, all of which show a decline with age.

What, then, is the nature of the episodic memory decline with age? The magnitude of the decline varies depending on nature of the memory task and the method of testing retention. Fergus Craik and his collaborators identify three factors as crucial determinants of episodic memory performance in the elderly. The first of these is the overall decline in *episodic memory per se*. This is modulated by two other variables, one being the *processing capacity* of the learner and the other concerning the level of **environmental support** provided during retrieval (Craik, 2005).

Most learning experiments involve presenting material under time constraints, and given that age tends to slow processing, then the elderly may take longer to perceive and process the material, and also to be less likely to be able to develop and utilize complex learning strategies. Craik and colleagues have explored this aspect of learning by using a secondary task to reduce the available attention in younger participants, demonstrating that

> **KEY TERM**
>
> **Environmental support:** Characteristics of a retention test that support retrieval.

under some conditions at least, performance by the young then resembles that of the elderly (Craik & Byrd, 1982).

However, the fact that both age and an attentionally demanding task impair learning does not mean that they necessarily do so by influencing the same memory process. For example, it might be that the main source of impairment in the elderly is a basic memory deficit at the neurophysiological level, possibly reflecting poorer consolidation of the memory trace, whereas the deficit shown by the young when their attention is distracted might reflect a reduction of time spent on learning because of competition from the secondary task. This was tested in a series of experiments by Naveh-Benjamin (2000) in which young and older participants were presented with pairs of words that differed in whether they were semantically associated or not (e.g. *dog – bone* versus *cat – book*). Performance was then tested by recognition. There was found to be a substantial difference between the two age groups for the unrelated items, but not for associated pairs.

The initial interpretation of these results (Naveh-Benjamin, 2000) was in terms of the attentional limitations of the elderly group. This was subsequently tested using young participants given an attentionally demanding concurrent task, with the prediction that the pattern of performance of the young would then resemble that of the elderly. This interpretation was not supported (Naveh-Benjamin, Guez, & Marom 2003a; Naveh-Benjamin, Hussain, Guez, & Bar-On, 2003b). The secondary task impaired both related and unrelated pairs to the same extent, suggesting that the difference between the young and old groups was attributable to basic learning capacity, rather than to attentional or strategic differences. Naveh-Benjamin refers to this as the **associative deficit hypothesis**.

A series of later studies has investigated the associative deficit hypothesis across a range of materials involving both words and pictures (Naveh-Benjamin et al., 2003a, 2003b), in each case replicating the relative preservation of the capacity to recognize which items had been presented together with a substantial deficit in the capacity to bind or associate unrelated word pairs. The fact that this deficit was not attributable to an attentional deficit was shown particularly clearly in a study by Naveh-Benjamin et al. (2004b) using face–name pairs. Participants were shown 40 name–face pairs for 3 seconds each and instructed to try to remember them. Three groups were tested—an elderly group and two young groups—one of which involved a demanding concurrent task that required participants to discriminate between tones and to respond as rapidly as possible. Two aspects of memory were tested. The first involved recognizing which names and faces had been presented and which were new. As the first two sets of data in Figure 13.4 show, this recognition task showed little or no effect of age, but a clear effect of the concurrent task. The second memory test involved deciding which name went with which face. As this dataset shows, there was a substantial age effect, which was reliably greater than the effect of the demanding concurrent task. The fact that the age effect was not found for recognition but is clearly present in the name–face binding condition suggests an *associative* deficit that does not appear to be explicable in attentional terms.

A striking feature of the studies by Naveh-Benjamin is the observation that the associative deficit shown by the elderly is much reduced when pairs of items are related rather than arbitrary, suggesting that there might be other situations in which the effects of aging on episodic memory may be minimized. This occurs in the case of the *self-performed task* effect. This involves a subject attempting to

---

KEY TERM

Associative deficit hypothesis: Proposal that the age deficit in memory comes from an impaired capacity to form associations between previously unrelated stimuli.

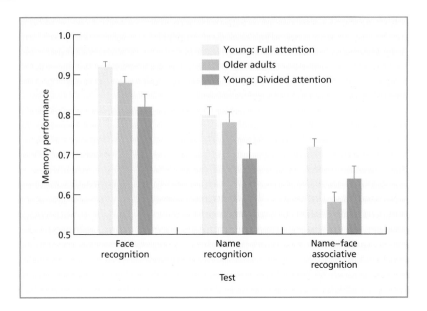

Figure 13.4 The effects of age or divided attention on recognition of individual faces or names, and recognizing a face–name association. From Naveh-Benjamin et al. (2004b). Copyright © American Psychological Association. Reprinted with permission.

remember a list of objects, each accompanied by an instruction, for example "break the matchstick" and "shake the pen," each of which has to be either passively heard or performed. Performing the act leads to substantially better subsequent free recall than simply hearing the experimenter provide the instructions, greatly reducing the age difference (Bäckman & Nilsson, 1984; Englekamp, 1998). The current view is that this procedure gains its advantage from providing an enriched level of coding involving auditory, visual, manual, and—perhaps importantly—self-related codes, with the multiple coding reducing reliance on any given feature or cue.

The third aspect of Craik's classification concerns the amount of environmental support provided at retrieval. It is in general the case that age effects show up most clearly in free recall, where there are no external cues; age decrements are somewhat less when retrieval cues are provided, and are least under recognition conditions (Craik, Byrd, & Swanson, 1987). However, although it is often the case that recognition memory can be relatively preserved in the elderly, in many such studies (as shown by the previously described studies by Naveh-Benjamin et al., 2000) this

might reflect the tendency of recall tests to involve an associative component, either explicitly, as in paired-associated learning, or implicitly, as in free recall, which is likely to depend on creating and retrieving associated chunks. As data from the Doors and People Test show, clear effects of age can be found using carefully matched recall and recognition measures. However, recognition tests typically *are* less demanding than recall, and tend to show less of a difference between younger and older groups.

Remembering and knowing

An interesting feature of the effects of age on recognition memory is that the elderly appear to be much better at recognizing that an item has occurred than in remembering the context in which it occurred (Park & Puglisi, 1985; Chalfonte & Johnson, 1996). You might recall from Chapter 8 that recognition appears to be based on two separable processes: "remembering," in which the participant recollects the learning incident and its context (for example, remembering that the word *dog* reminded you of your childhood pet) and "knowing," in which a positive identification is based on a feeling of familiarity rather than a specific recollection. Parkin and Walter (1992) presented young, middle-aged, and elderly participants with a sequence of 36 words, each printed on a flash card. Next, participants were shown the 36 old items together with 36 new items for recognition. They were required to categorize any recognized items as members of the "remember" or "know" category. There was no difference between the young and old groups in the number of words correctly identified as "known." By contrast, however, correctly "remembered" responses were greatest for the young and least for the elderly group.

This result was subsequently replicated by Rajaram (1993), who ruled out the possibility that it simply reflected a difference in level of confidence between the age groups. Hay and Jacoby (1999) applied the process dissociation method described in Chapter 8 to groups of young and old participants, finding that the old were impaired on the recollection but not on the familiarity component. Reviewing the literature on this issue, Light, Prull, LaVoie, and Healy (2000) conclude that there is strong evidence that the recollective process declines with age. Given that recollection is likely to depend on retrieving an association between the item and the context or experience of learning, this is consistent with the associative deficit hypothesis of aging and episodic long-term memory proposed by Naveh-Benjamin et al. (2003b). Whether the familiarity mechanism is entirely free from any age effect is, however, more controversial. Conclusions depend on the assumptions made in computing the familiarity measure, and in particular on whether these two mechanisms are assumed to be independent or not.

So is recognition memory spared in the elderly? The answer would seem to depend on the precise nature of the task. To the extent that recollection of the original experience is involved in the recognition decision, it clearly is not. However, if a general sense of familiarity is sufficient then recognition in the elderly is relatively well preserved.

Prospective memory

One of the most frustrating features of memory failure occurs when we plan or agree to do something and then forget to carry out that action, whether it is a relatively simple error, such as failing to pick up bread on the way home from work, or more serious, such as missing an important appointment. There is no doubt that as we get older we complain more about such everyday lapses, but are we in fact less reliable?

As we see in Chapter 15, the easiest way to study this is in a constrained laboratory situation, such as that developed by Einstein and McDaniel (1990), in which participants perform an ongoing task and are instructed to respond either after a specified time or when a specific cue occurs. Their initial study (Einstein & McDaniel, 1990) found little evidence of age effects, whereas a later investigation (Einstein, McDaniel, Richardson, Guynn, & Cunfer, 1995a, 1995b) found a decrement for time-based but not for event-based tasks; a result they interpreted on the grounds that time-based prospective memory required more self-initiated processing. However, later research suggests that both types of prospective memory tend to be impaired in the elderly.

One large-scale study involved 100 participants in each of 10 cohorts ranging from 35 to 80 years in age. The task was simply to remember to sign a form on completion of the test session. Whereas 61% of the younger 35- to 45-year-olds remembered, only 25% of 70- to 80-year-olds were successful (Mäntylä & Nilsson, 1997). Similar major declines in prospective memory have been reported by Cockburn and Smith (1991), and Maylor (1996) found that both time-based and event-based prospective memory declined with age. Some studies find a greater decline in time-based performance (Park, Hertzog, Kidder, Morrell, & Mayhorn 1997), but the opposite result was found by d'Ydewalle, Luwel, & Brunfaut (1999), suggesting that the time- versus event-based categorization might not be a particularly useful one in this context.

It is important to bear in mind that the term "prospective memory" refers to a class of situations, not necessarily mapping onto any single type of memory. To perform a prospective memory task, it is necessary to encode two things: The first is the action to be performed; the second is the time or event when that action must be retrieved. Given that the material and retrieval plan have been adequately encoded, it is then necessary to maintain this information over a delay and perform the relevant action at an appropriate time. In certain laboratory-based tasks, continuous active maintenance might be possible while performing the concurrent task, provided that participants have sufficient working memory capacity. Such continuous maintenance is much less likely, however, under many real-world situations, in which it might be necessary to maintain an intention over several days. Rehearsal could still occur, but this will presumably be intermittent involving periodic retrieval from long-term memory. In line with Craik's rule of thumb regarding memory tasks, the presence of a retrieval cue in the event-based case might be expected to enhance performance by the elderly, although the evidence suggests that this is often not sufficient to guarantee task performance.

So far, we have discussed experimental results in which prospective memory virtually always appears to be poorer in the elderly. Somewhat surprisingly, perhaps, this is not always the case in more realistic contexts. One class of prospective memory task involves instructing the participant to post a card or make a telephone call at a specific time, and under these arguably more ecologically relevant situations, older subjects often perform better than the young. For example, Rendell and Thomson (1999) tested adults in their 20s, 60s, and 80s, and found that when the tasks were embedded in their daily life, the older participants out-performed the young ones, whereas when the task was simulated in the laboratory the opposite occurred. This was replicated by Rendell and Craik (2000) using a laboratory board game called *Virtual week* to simulate everyday life more closely; again the elderly performed better than the young outside the laboratory, but poorly within.

This discrepancy between everyday life and laboratory results is usually attributed to older people being aware of the limitations of their memory and using various strategies, such as diaries and reminders, to compensate, whereas the young tend to rely more on their still-fallible memory. Rendell and Craik, however, explicitly instructed their subjects not to use external aids, and attribute the difference to the fact that their older participants lived more ordered and structured lives, making it easier to form a well-ordered plan. It could also be the case that a test of their memory was a more important feature of the lives of the elderly than it was for the younger prospective rememberers. Motivation in the real world is probably a very important variable in prospective memory. I suspect most of us forget more dental appointments than parties, and to fail to get married because one forgot to turn up would not be regarded as a very plausible excuse. Indeed, one of the reasons why forgetting appointments might be so embarrassing is because of the implication that the event, and by implication the person involved, was not regarded as very important.

Semantic memory

Unlike the steady decline in episodic memory as we grow older, semantic memory is maintained, at least as measured by vocabulary knowledge, which even continues to grow slightly with age and which hence is typically somewhat more extensive in the elderly than in the young (Giambra, Arenberg, Zonderman, & Kawas, 1995). Knowledge of historical facts also increases with age (Perlmuter, Scharff, Karsh, & Monty, 1980), although speed of access declines (Burke, MacKay, Worthley & Wade, 1991).

Vocabulary scores are sometimes regarded as providing a "hold" test, because they tend to be relatively resistant to the effects of brain damage, age, or disease, whereas speed measures tend to be highly sensitive. Both these features are measured in the SCOLP (Speed and Capacity of Language Processing) test (Baddeley, Emslie, & Nimmo-Smith, 1992). Vocabulary is tested using the spot-the-word test in which the participant must choose between pairs of items, one a word and the other a pseudo word. These range from very obvious, for example *rabbit–flotter* to more obscure pairs such as *lapidary–halitation*. Performance correlates very highly with other measures of vocabulary and is highly resistant to the effects of age, or indeed Alzheimer's disease (Baddeley, 2001).

The second component of the SCOLP involves a task based on the original semantic memory studies of Collins and Quillian (1969), who you may recall required participants to verify simple statements about the world as rapidly as possible. Sentences are either obviously true or obviously false, e.g. *snakes travel on their bellies* versus *beef steaks travel on their bellies*. Errors are uniformly low, indicating that the problem is not lack of knowledge but speed of access to that knowledge. This is highly sensitive to a range of factors, including age (Baddeley et al., 1992).

Although vocabulary is well preserved, the use of language can be constrained by age in other more subtle ways. This was shown in an ingenious study by Kemper (1990), involving a study of diaries kept over a period of 70 years by pioneers settling the American Midwest. Because the diaries were written by the same individual over a long period of time, they provide a naturalistic longitudinal study of language.

The diaries tend to show an increase in ambiguity over the years through the use of indeterminate pronouns such as "he" in "Cousins Robert and John visited us last week, despite the terrible weather. He was full of stories about the old days …". As they became older, diarists seemed to attempt to avoid this source of ambiguity by reducing the number of pronouns used. Later diaries also tended to avoid left-branching sentences such as "A roof over his head is the right of every man," which tend to place a heavier load on working memory than their right-branching equivalent "Every man has a right to a roof over his head." Despite the more constrained nature of the later diaries, independent judges tended to rate them as better written and more interesting (Kemper, Kynette, & Norman, 1992).

Implicit learning and memory

Given that implicit learning and memory involve a range of different processes, it is perhaps unsurprising that the effects of aging are not uniform. Reviewing the extensive literature, Light et al. (2000) conclude that, on balance, there is evidence for a clear but moderate age effect on priming tasks that involve response production, such as stem completion in which a list of words is presented and then tested by giving participants the first few letters of a word and asked them to produce a possible completion. They contrast this with *identification* tasks, such as deciding whether an item is a real word or not, or identifying a fragmented picture as rapidly as possible, where age effects tend to be smaller or absent.

Indeed, there are certain situations in which implicit memory effects might be stronger in the elderly. One such example is provided by the false fame effect, in which participants are first required to process a number of unfamiliar names and are then given a second list of names with the instruction to mark those that belong to people who are famous. The previously unfamiliar names that have just been processed are more likely to be erroneously judged as famous, an effect that is more pronounced in the elderly (Dywan & Jacoby, 1990). However, this is much less likely to result from the stronger implicit component in the elderly than from a weaker recollective component, resulting in a greater reliance on a sense of familiarity. In short, it reflects poorer episodic memory, a characteristic of aging that also tends to make the elderly more open to being misled by subsequent false information (Cohen & Faulkner, 1989; Schacter, Koutsaal, & Norman, 1997).

The effect of age on the acquisition of motor skills is also complex. There is no doubt that motor *performance* tends to decline as we get older, reflecting a decline in the speed of both perception and movement (Welford, 1985). This can lead to a slower rate of learning time-based tasks such as pursuit tracking, which involves keeping a stylus in contact with a moving target (Wright & Payne, 1985). However, whereas skilled *performance* certainly can be impaired, it is less clear whether, given appropriate conditions, the rate of *learning* is necessarily slower. For example, the rate of learning a sequence of motor movements or a new stimulus–response mapping might not show an age difference (Wishart & Lee, 1997). Similarly, on a task involving responding serially to four separate stimuli under self-paced conditions, young and older adults showed a comparable rate of learning (Howard & Howard, 1989), whereas Willingham and Winter (1995) found that older adults, who had never used a computer mouse before, were as adept at learning to navigate a maze on a computer as were younger participants.

So can old dogs learn new tricks? It appears to depend on the tricks. As in the case of priming, it seems likely that in tasks in which the response is obvious, and performance is measured purely in terms of improved speed, the elderly will show excellent learning, whereas tasks in which new and unobvious links must be learned are likely to create problems for the older adult. A good example of such a task was devised by Wilson, Cockburn, and Baddeley (1989a), who required patients to learn to enter the time and date into a small palm-computer. Rate of learning was extremely sensitive to episodic memory deficits. Although relatively few steps were involved, patients who had even relatively mild memory loss had great difficulty in acquiring them. Unfortunately, the rapid development of technology means that there is a constant need to learn such basic and ever-changing skills.

Use it or lose it?

There is no doubt that individual differences become more marked as people get older,

probably for a number of different reasons. One factor is certainly the general decline in health, which in turn is linked to both genetic and lifestyle differences. It appears to help if you are healthy, eat appropriately, take lots of exercise, and remain mentally active, in the sense that all of these tend to be correlated with comparative resistance to age impairment. However, a comparison of university professors and blue-collar workers in Sweden by Christensen, Henderson, Griffiths, and Levings (1997) found no difference in rate of memory decline. A study of university professors in their 30s, 50s, and 60s by Shimamura, Berry, Mangels, Rustings, and Jurica (1995) found clear evidence of a decline in reaction time and paired-associate learning, but no difference in prose recall, suggesting that meaningful material might allow the active learner to compensate for declining episodic memory. It is certainly the case that explicit memory training can help. Kliegl, Smith, and Baltes (1989) taught a visual imagery mnemonic to elderly volunteers, which resulted in their performance being better than that of untrained young participants. However, young participants gained substantially more from training than the elderly (Baltes & Kliegl, 1992).

Given that memory can be improved by training, the question arises as to whether memory-training programs should be made generally available as we get older. A number of studies have addressed this point, the most extensive being that of Ball, Berch, Helmers, Jobe, Leveck, Marsiske, et al. (2002), who divided a total of 2832 elderly participants into four groups, each of which underwent a 5- to 6-week training program. One group received memory training involving the teaching of strategies, accompanied by extensive practice on remembering words and shopping lists. A second group received training in a range of verbal reasoning tasks. A third group received speed training on visual search and divided attention tasks. Finally, a fourth group served as controls and received no explicit training.

All groups were subsequently tested on each of the three types of training material and an attempt was made to assess the impact of the training on everyday functioning. Each of the three groups improved on the skills trained, even though tested using a different format. However, no change occurred for the untrained skills, indicating that only the specific training had been effective. Unfortunately, however, there was no reliable evidence that any of the gains transferred to everyday functioning, although the authors speculate that the training might have a protective effect in slowing subsequent age-related decline. The evidence from this and other related studies seems to suggest that one can certainly teach useful memory strategies to elderly participants, and that these can generalize to novel material. In principle, this could be useful in everyday life for acquiring new information such as PIN numbers and learning new names. At present, however, the evidence for a general impact on everyday cognition is not strong.

So where do we stand on the use-it-or-lose-it question? First of all, there does appear to be solid evidence for this adage based on animal studies in which the relevant variables can be more adequately controlled. Rats raised in an enriched cage environment show

less decline in learning with age than rats that have lived in comfortable but less interesting homes (Greenough, Black, & Wallace, 1987). There is also correlational evidence to suggest a link between activity and preserved mental capacity in people (Rönnlund & Nilsson, 2008), although the direction of causation is harder to determine in the human case. Does more activity result in better memory, or does declining memory cause people to be less active? On balance, I myself would tend to favor the use-it-or-lose-it hypothesis; even if it does not protect you from cognitive decline, using it is likely to lead to a rather less boring old age.

THEORIES OF AGING

In recent years, there have been a number of attempts to account for the effects of aging on cognition in terms of one or other single factor. Probably the most influential of these macro theories has been the proposal by Salthouse (1996) that the cognitive effects of aging can all be explained by the reduced speed of processing that is a marked feature of aging. This conclusion is based on a very extensive series of correlational studies, which do indeed tend to show that the best overall prediction of overall performance in the elderly is provided by measures that depend on speed of processing, rather than processing accuracy or memory performance. There does, however, seem to be evidence that memory decline might be separable from a more general decline in cognitive function with age (Salthouse & Becker, 1998). Nonetheless, as Salthouse (1992, 1996) shows, it is possible to account for much of the influence of age on cognition in terms of a general speed factor.

One problem with such a conclusion is that it is not meaningful to talk about speed independent of the task on which it is assessed. If one combines speed across a wide range of tasks, then one could argue that one is sampling many aspects of performance, not just one. In response to this, Salthouse has focused on an

Greenough et al.'s (1987) study showed that rats who had lived in an enriched and interesting environment showed less cognitive decline than their counterparts who had lived in a more basic and less stimulating environment.

individual task, the Digit Symbol Substitution Test (DSST) taken from the Wechsler Adult Intelligence Scale (WAIS). This is indeed a good predictor of the effects of age on performance but it is far from being a pure speed test. Good performance almost certainly involves strategy and working memory as well as perceptual speed. Given that it correlates highly with measures of both verbal and nonverbal intelligence, it should, according to Parkin and Java (2000), be regarded as a measure of working memory rather than simple perceptual speed. A test based on rate of number cancellation, which might be expected to provide a purer measure of perceptual speed, proved to be a poor predictor of age decrement in their study.

Another problem with using purely correlational methods is that many physical and intellectual capacities decline together as we age, making it difficult to assign a causal role to one over and above the remainder. The method used by Salthouse and many others in the field is to look for the most powerful and robust correlation, the measure that can account for most of the statistical variance in the results. However, this depends not only on the nature and purity of the measure as described above, but also on which particular measures are selected for inclusion.

Whereas speed measures frequently do provide the highest correlations, this is not always the case. An extensive series of studies by Paul Baltes and his group in Berlin concentrated more attention on perceptual factors, finding initially that the best predictors were auditory and visual sensory thresholds, which depend on accuracy rather than speed (Baltes & Lindenberger, 1997). One might possibly argue that these would be influenced by such factors as neural transmission speed. However, Baltes and colleagues subsequently found that an even better predictor of the decline in cognition with age was grip strength, giving a whole new meaning to the term "losing one's grip"! As Lindenberger and Pötter (1998) point out, there is a danger of forgetting that correlation does not equal causation.

Perhaps the time has come to abandon the search for the single factor that underpins the decline of cognition as we get older, returning to the Ford car (or in its UK version, the Woolworths' bicycle pump) hypothesis: An optimally engineered product will aim to manufacture all its parts to the same quality, rather than waste money on overengineering some components. The result of this is that the parts all tend to last for about the same length of time before failing. Perhaps evolution is equally parsimonious?

The correlational approach is certainly not the only method of developing theories of cognitive aging. For example, Craik and colleagues, using an experimental approach, have emphasized the impact of reduced processing resources on learning and memory in the elderly, often finding that their young participants perform in a similar way to their elderly group when an attentionally demanding concurrent task reduces their available processing capacity (e.g. Craik & Byrd, 1982; Craik & Jennings, 1992). There is no doubt that attentional capacity is an important variable but, as the previously described studies by Naveh-Benjamin and colleagues indicate (Naveh-Benjamin et al., 2003a, 2003b, 2004a, 2004b), reducing the attention available to the young does not always result in performance resembling the elderly. In the case of episodic memory, the aging deficit seems rather closer to a very mild amnesia, than to a purely attentional limitation. Similarly, whereas there might be a tendency for the elderly to have difficulty in inhibiting irrelevant material, as suggested by Hasher et al. (1999), it is not clear why this should influence free recall, one of the most sensitive tests of aging. One might expect increased susceptibility to inhibition to influence short-term forgetting performance on the Peterson and Peterson (1959) task, where forgetting appears to be principally the result of proactive inhibition. However, provided initial level of performance is matched, there seems to be no difference in rate of forgetting between young and old (Parkinson et al., 1985). Hence, although age can reduce our inhibitory capacity, it seems unlikely that it is the principal cause of episodic memory decline.

A popular hypothesis over recent years has been to interpret the effects of aging in terms of the declining functions of the frontal lobes. Evidence in favor of this view has principally come from studies showing an association between the size of the aging effect and performance on tasks assumed to depend on frontal lobe function. Such tasks are varied and numerous, typically involving the executive component of working memory, and possibly also the capacity for inhibition, together with a wide range of other executive functions that are themselves still poorly understood. It is not clear how useful a general frontal hypothesis would be, at this stage. The evidence supporting the frontal aging hypothesis has recently been reviewed by Phillips and Henry (2005), who conclude that the direct evidence for a causal link between frontal-lobe atrophy and age-related cognitive decline is currently weak and that the present hypothesis relies on a simplistic interpretation of both the neuroanatomy and the neuropsychology of the frontal lobes. That does not, of course, rule out an important role for the frontal lobes in normal aging, but it does suggest that any theory that assigns a special role to the frontal lobes in aging will need to be grounded more firmly both neuropsychologically and neuroanatomically.

THE AGING BRAIN

As we grow older, our brain shrinks. This shows most clearly in the expansion of the ventricles, the channels in the brain filled by cerebral spinal fluid, which take up more space as the brain becomes smaller. While this is a good overall measure of brain size, it is not a very good measure of function, as functional change depends—crucially—on what part of the brain is shrinking. As mentioned earlier, this tends to be the frontal lobes, with the temporal and occipital lobes shrinking

more slowly. The hippocampus, crucial for memory, loses 20–30% of its neurons by the age of 80 (Squire, 1987), reflecting an initial slow decline, which subsequently accelerates, possibly as the result of disease (see Raz, 2000, for further discussion). The electrophysiological activity of the brain, as reflected in event-related potential (ERP) measures, slows steadily throughout the lifespan (Pelosi & Blumhardt, 1999), with the latency of the P300 component increasing at an average of 2 milliseconds per year, a rate of slowing that becomes more severe in dementia (Neshige, Barrett, & Shibasaki, 1988).

Studies of brain function using neuroimaging also tend to show age effects. Cabeza, Prince, Daselaar, Greenberg, Budde, Dolcos, et al. (2004), studying working memory and visual attention, observed that older subjects tended to show activation in both cerebral hemispheres on tasks that activate a single hemisphere in young participants. A comparable result was observed by Maguire and Frith (2003) in a study of autobiographical memory, with the young showing predominantly left hippocampal involvement, while the involvement of the elderly was bilateral. Reuter-Lorenz (2002) and others have attributed the broader spread of activation to an attempt by the elderly to compensate for overload in one component of the brain by utilizing other brain structures.

It is not always the case that greater activation is shown in the elderly, particularly on tasks where it may be helpful to involve relatively complex strategies. A study by Iidaka, Sadato, Yamada, Murata, Omori, and Yonekura (2001) required participants to remember pairs of related or unrelated pictures. Both young and old showed more left frontal activation for the unrelated pictures, but only the young showed additional occipito-temporal activation. This probably indicates the active use of visual imagery, as this was an area observed by Maguire, Valentine, Wilding, and Kapur (2003) to be activated when using the method of loci, a classic visual-imagery-based mnemonic strategy. This method is itself very demanding, and while consistently aiding the young, only 50% of the elderly subjects tested by Nyberg, Sandblom, Jones, Neely, Petersson, Ingvar, and Bäckman (2003) were found to benefit from using the method of loci. It appears to be the case, therefore, that older participants will attempt to compensate for cognitive decline by using additional strategies, reflected in a wider range of brain activation. However, this might no longer be possible when the task is already complex, potentially inducing reliance on a simpler strategy.

The principal contribution of studies based on neuroimaging at this point has been to identify the anatomical localization associated with different cognitive processes. An exciting new development is based on the capacity to image the distribution and operation of the neurotransmitters that play a crucial role in the neural basis of cognition. One such study concerns the link between aging and the neurotransmitter, dopamine. Post-mortem studies have indicated that as we age, dopamine levels show a loss of 5–10% per decade. This finding has been confirmed by studies using positron emission tomography (PET), whereby the density of dopamine receptors is measured using the radioactive labeling of ligands, substances that selectively bind to specific types of dopamine receptor (Antonini, Leenders, Meier, Oertel, Boesiger, & Anliker, 1993).

It is known that dopamine is implicated in many cognitive functions, and that its depletion is associated with cognitive deficits in both Parkinson's disease (Brown & Marsden, 1990) and Huntington's disease (Bäckman, Almkvist, Andersson, Nordberg, Winblad, Reineck, & Langstrom, 1997). Pharmacological studies using healthy young participants confirm the importance of dopamine. Bromocriptine, which is known to facilitate dopamine function, is found to improve spatial working memory (Luciana & Collins, 1997), whereas haloperidol, which interferes with dopamine function, has the opposite effect (Luciana & Collins, 1997; Ramaekers et al., 1999).

Bäckman et al. (2000) used PET to measure dopamine binding in volunteers across the age range. They found a substantial correlation between dopamine levels in the brain and episodic memory that accounted for some 38% of the variance in performance on word recognition, and 48% in the case of face recognition (Figure 13.5). When the effect of dopamine level was removed statistically, age had only a minimal impact on memory performance, a result that has subsequently been replicated by Erixon-Lindroth, Farde, Wahlin, Sovago, Halldin, and Backman (2005). At this early stage of the development of this line of work, it seems to show great promise, not only of developing a better understanding of how and why memory declines as we get older, but

Figure 13.5 Relationship between the levels of dopamine in two brain areas (the caudate and the putamen) and aging. From Erixon-Lindroth et al. (2005). Copyright © 2005 Elsevier. Reproduced with permission.

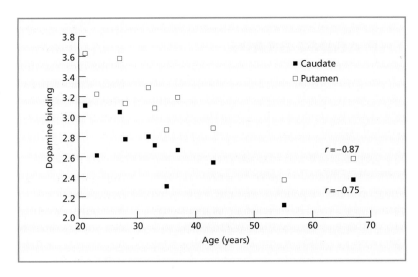

potentially also of providing pharmacological ways of easing this decline.

ALZHEIMER'S DISEASE

In 1907, Dr Alois Alzheimer first described the disease that bears his name. It is a devastating disease of the elderly. Its symptoms are varied but always include an increasingly severe deficit in episodic memory. Alzheimer's disease (AD) is the most prominent cause of senile dementia, constituting over 50% of cases of dementia. It occurs in about 10% of the population over the age of 65 with the rate increasing with age. Box 13.3 shows 10 potential signs of dementia as described in a report by the US Academy of Neurology. Because of the varied range of symptoms, the early stages of AD can be difficult to diagnose; diagnosis requires that there is a memory impairment together with at least two other deficits, which can include problems of language, action control, perception, or executive function. The disease is progressive over time and, ultimately, diagnosis depends on a

> ## Box 13.3 Warning signs of Alzheimer's disease
> The American Academy of Neurology proposed the following guidelines (Petersen et al., 2001):
>
> 1. Memory loss that affects job skills
> 2. Difficulty performing familiar tasks
> 3. Problems with language
> 4. Disorientation to time and place (getting lost)
> 5. Poor or decreased judgment
> 6. Problems with abstract thinking
> 7. Misplacing things
> 8. Changes in mood or behavior
> 9. Changes in personality
> 10. Loss of initiative
>
> It is suggested that people who show several of these should see their doctor for a thorough examination.

post-mortem examination of the brain tissue, revealing the two cardinal signs of AD: amyloid plaques and neurofibrillary tangles.

Plaques are created by faulty protein division. This results in the production of beta amyloid, which is toxic to neurons and leads to the formation of the clumps of amyloid that form the plaques. Neurofibrillary tangles occur within the neurons and are based on the microtubules that structure and nourish the cell. Abnormal proteins form, resulting in the twisting and collapse of the microtubules, and ultimately in cell death (St George-Hyslop, 2000). Both plaques and tangles can be found in the normal aging brain, but occur with considerably less density than in AD.

The disease typically develops through a series of stages (Braak & Braak, 1991) beginning in the medial temporal lobes and hippocampus, creating the initial memory problems, and then progressing to the temporal and parietal lobes and to other brain regions. However, the spread of the disease is by no means uniform and although it has been suggested that AD patients can be divided into two categories—those whose deficit is largely limited to episodic long-term memory, and those with executive working memory deficits (Becker, 1988)—a close examination of an extensive sample of well-studied patients indicates that a wider and more varied pattern of neuropsychological deficits might be observed (Baddeley, Della Sala, & Spinnler, 1991b). An extensive analysis of data from 180 patients and over a 1000 normal elderly individuals suggests that despite the potential presence of a varied range of other cognitive deficits, AD is basically characterized by a single overall feature, namely that of defective episodic memory (Salthouse & Becker, 1998).

At the level of the individual patient, the disease can develop from an initial tendency to absentmindedness and memory failure, through increasingly severe and potentially varied cognitive symptoms. These were well illustrated in a case study of the Oxford philosopher and novelist Iris Murdoch, as described by Garrard, Malony, Hodges, and Patterson (2005), who compared the sentence

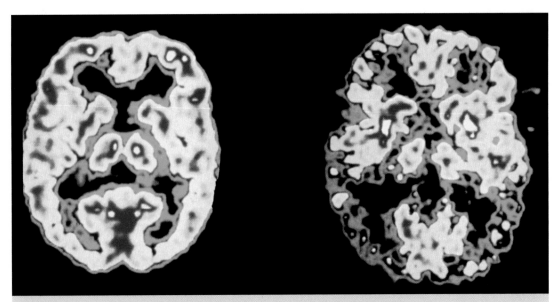

Positron Emission Tomography (PET) scans of the brain of a normal patient (left) versus an Alzheimer's disease patient. High brain activity displays as red and yellow; low activity as blue and black. The scan on the right shows reduction of both function and blood flow in both sides of the brain, a feature often seen in Alzheimer's. Alzheimer's disease is the most prominent cause of senile dementia. © Dr Robert Freidland/ Science Photo Library.

content and structure of one of Murdoch's early novels, *Flight from the enchanter*, a middle novel, *The sea*, and her final novel, *Jackson's dilemma*. They found that her last novel used considerably shorter sentences and more high-frequency words, suggesting that she was adapting to her growing language constraints. As the disease progressed, her linguistic problems increased, including word-finding difficulties, which she avoided by circumlocutions. She showed major problems in word definition, for example describing a bus as "something carried along". Her spelling deteriorated, with a word such as *cruise* being written as *crewes*, and her capacity to name pictures or to generate items from a given semantic category such as animals was increasingly impaired.

Although the decline in cognitive performance in dementia can be very worrying, social and emotional deterioration can be even more distressing, sometimes leading to the feeling of a spouse that "this is not the person I married." In the case of Iris Murdoch, she appeared

Iris Murdoch was a famous novelist who suffered from Alzheimer's disease and displayed many typical cognitive symptoms and linguistic constraints. Her life story was turned into the 2001 film *Iris*, starring Kate Winslet and Judy Dench as the younger and older Iris respectively, which went on to to win an Oscar, a Golden Globe, and a BAFTA, amongst many others. © Sophie Bassouls/Sygma/Corbis.

to maintain a very amiable disposition (Bayley, 1998), but sadly this is by no means always the case. For present purposes, however, we will limit discussion to the effects of AD on memory.

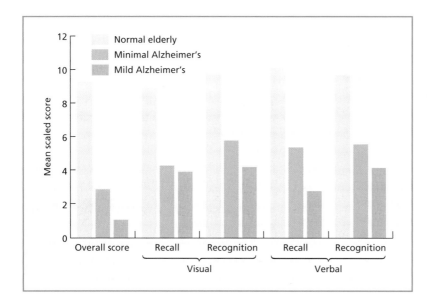

Figure 13.6 Performance on the Doors and People test of control participants, and patients at two stages of Alzheimer's disease. Patients show a progressive decline, both overall, and on the four subtests. Data from Greene et al. (1996).

Episodic memory

By the time AD has been reliably diagnosed, patients are likely to show a substantial deficit in episodic memory whether measured by recall or recognition, using verbal or visual material (Figure 13.6) or based on measures of **everyday memory** (Spinnler et al., 1988; Greene, Baddeley, & Hodges, 1996). As in the classic amnesic syndrome, the recency effect in free recall is relatively well preserved, although performance on earlier items is grossly impaired. There is evidence that as the disease progresses even recency tends to decline (Miller, 1971).

Forgetting

Despite the difficulty AD patients have in acquiring new information, once learned it appears to be forgotten no more rapidly than occurs in the normal elderly (Christensen, Kopelman, & Stanhope, 1998). Kopelman (1985) took advantage of the fact that people tend to be very good at picture recognition, taking care to vary the exposure time so as to equate the performance of normal, AD, and elderly participants when tested after 5 minutes. He then retested them after a 24-hour delay and found equivalent performance across the groups.

As noted in the case of Iris Murdoch, semantic memory declines as the disease progresses. Hodges and colleagues devised a battery for measuring semantic memory using a range of different tasks designed to ensure that any deficit observed is general, and not the result of perceptual or linguistic problems. A clear semantic deficit would be reflected in difficulties in naming pictures of objects or animals, in picking the appropriate picture given its name, in describing the characteristics of a named or pictured object, or in answering general questions such as whether an elephant has pricked up or floppy ears. In a series of studies, the Hodges group observed a steady decline in semantic memory in AD patients that was associated with degree of temporal lobe atrophy (Hodges, Patterson, & Tyler, 1994; Hodges & Patterson, 1995). The decline of semantic memory is even more precipitous in

KEY TERM

Everyday memory: Term applied to a movement within memory to extend the study of memory from the confines of the laboratory to the world outside.

semantic dementia, a disease in which episodic memory is relatively well preserved, with atrophy occurring principally in the left temporal lobe rather than the more medial focus that tends to be found in AD (Snowden, Neary, & Mann, 1996).

Implicit memory

Perhaps unsurprisingly, given that implicit learning and memory can reflect a number of different systems, the pattern of deficit in AD is somewhat complex. Heindel, Salmon, Shults, Walicke, and Butters (1989) tested patients with AD on the pursuit rotor, a task in which they were required to learn to keep a stylus in contact with a moving target. The patients performed less well initially, but improved at the same rate as an elderly control group. Similarly, Moscovitch (1982) found little impairment in the rate at which AD patients learned to read mirror-reversed words.

Fleischman, Vaidya, Lange, and Gabrieli (1997) found normal priming in a lexical decision task involving the speed of deciding whether a sequence of letters constituted a real word or not. Words that had been seen earlier led to faster responses to a similar extent for both groups. However, they found that, unlike the classic amnesic syndrome, implicit memory was not spared when tested by stem completion, in which patients were shown a word (*stamp*) and later asked to "guess" a word beginning with *st*.

Beauregard, Chertkow, Gold, and Bergman (2001) found an equivalent degree of priming on stem completion when a shallow level of processing was required, but a deficit in the AD group when deeper processing was involved. In general, patients with AD tend to show intact priming on relatively automatic tasks but reduced priming on more complex tasks, for example when recall is primed by presenting associatively related cue words (Salmon, Shimamura, Butters, & Smith, 1988; Salmon & Heindel, 1992).

Working memory in Alzheimer's disease

In general, the working memory deficit is less marked than that of episodic memory, with modest but reliable deficits in both digit span and on the Corsi block tapping test of visuo-spatial memory (Spinnler et al, 1988). Patients are able to maintain small amounts of material over an unfilled delay but, when the delay is filled with articulatory suppression, patients with AD rapidly forget, whereas normal elderly participants show a decline only when the interpolated task is intellectually demanding, such as counting backwards in threes (Morris, 1986; Morris & Baddeley, 1988). This suggests that maintenance by simple articulation remains, but that more complex forms of rehearsal are lost.

To test the executive capacity of patients with AD, Baddeley, Logie, Bressi, Della Sala, and Spinnler (1986) devised a series of tasks that combined auditory digit recall with a concurrent nonverbal task. In one study, for example, digit load was adjusted so that AD, elderly, and young participants all performed at the same level of accuracy. A similar matching occurred for a secondary tracking task in which participants had to keep a stylus in contact with a moving spot of light, with the difficulty modulated by varying the speed of movement of the spot. Having equated the two groups on the individual tasks, they were then required to perform the memory span and tracking tasks simultaneously. Young and normal elderly subjects both showed an equivalent small decrement under the combined condition, whereas the patients with AD showed a marked decline in performance. Subsequent studies showed that this deficit became more marked as the disease progressed (Baddeley et al., 2001a). The AD deficit in dual task performance was not simply due to task difficulty, as young, elder, and AD groups behaved similarly when difficulty

KEY TERMS

Semantic dementia: A progressive dementia characterized by gradual deterioration of semantic memory.
Articulatory suppression: A technique for disrupting verbal rehearsal by requiring participants to continuously repeat a spoken item.

level was varied on a single task, whereas AD patients continued to show a deficit when two very easy tasks were combined (Logie, Cocchini, Della Sala, & Baddeley, 2004).

Other aspects of attentional control have been less thoroughly studied, but the evidence available suggests that some at least are comparatively spared. For example, the capacity for sustained attention or vigilance does not appear to be particularly compromised (see Perry & Hodges, 1999, for a review).

Treatment

In an extensive review of available treatments, Doody, Stevens, Beck, Dubinsky, Kaye, and Gwyther (2001) discuss both pharmacological and behavioral attempts to alleviate AD. At that time, they identified three drugs that appeared to have some effect in slowing the course of the disease, namely *donepezil*, *rivastigmine*, and *galantamine*. These operate as inhibitors of cholinesterase, a substance that breaks down the neurotransmitter acetylcholine. Acetylcholine tends to be depleted in AD, hence the value of drugs that resist further depletion. There is a huge interest in this area within the pharmaceutical industry, given that AD is a disease that inflicts enormous cost to society on both a financial and human level. This cost is increasing as the age structure of the population changes from the historic pattern in which the young greatly out numbered the old, to one in which more and more of the population survive into old age. There is no doubt that pharmacological treatments will continue to be developed but, at present, they only appear to be able to slow the development of the disease, not to stop its progress.

In the meantime, there is considerable interest in behavioral approaches to patients with AD and their carers. During the early stages of the disease, it is possible to use methods such as errorless learning and fading cues that rely on relatively preserved procedural and implicit memory to teach skills that will stand the patient in good stead as the disease advances (Clare, Wilson, & Carter, 2000). For example, patients can be taught to use simple memory aids, such as message boards or calendars, to avoid the need constantly to ask carers the same question, which is one of the most wearing features of supporting a densely amnesic patient. A related approach is to modify the environment in simple but useful ways. Moffat (1989), for example, describes the case of a patient who was constantly mislaying his spectacles and his pipe. His frustration level was reduced by a program training him always to return his spectacles and pipe to a bright orange bag (hopefully fire proof). He would not remember where he left them, but could find them easily.

A number of programs have attempted to bring together techniques and skills aimed at helping the patient and the carer to cope with the progress of the disease. Spector, Davies, Woods, and Orrell (2000) describe a program that improved performance on the specific areas trained, and tended to reduce levels of depression, although—as in the case of the previously described programs for memory training for the elderly—this did not generalize to everyday performance.

As mentioned earlier, the purely cognitive aspects of AD are not typically the most distressing, and there is increasing interest in ways of helping patients and carers to cope with the social and emotional stresses imposed by AD. One disturbing feature of memory loss can be the problem of maintaining a sense of personal identity. This is particularly likely to be a problem for patients who need to move to a care home, and so are separated from their normal home environment and surrounded by new and unfamiliar people. A number of approaches to this problem have been developed. One is **reality orientation training (ROT)**, which involves helping patients maintain orientation in time and place, not necessarily a pleasant prospect

KEY TERM

Reality orientation training (ROT): A method of treating patients in the latter stages of dementia who have lost their orientation in time and place.

given certain realities. An occupational therapist tells the story of an elderly man admitted to a hospital based in a rather grand Victorian building. He was densely amnesic and interpreted his situation as staying in a rather splendid hotel at the seaside. The overenthusiastic therapist carefully taught him to look at the calendar to say the date and to announce the name of the hospital where he was living, which he duly did,

Reminiscence therapy helps patients to maintain a sense of personal identity by recollecting their past by constructing a personal life-story book including photographs and other mementoes. © Don Mason/Corbis.

KEY TERM

Reminiscence therapy: A method of helping dementia patients cope with their growing amnesia by using photographs and other reminders of their past life.

only to wink and say "But I know I am really at a grand hotel at the seaside!"

A rather more helpful version of ROT is provided by a technique known as **reminiscence therapy**, which helps patients to maintain a sense of personal identity by recollecting their past (Woods & McKiernan, 2005). This can involve constructing a personal life-story book, including photographs and other mementoes. This not only has the advantage of reminding patients of their earlier life, but in a group context provides links with other patients who share experience of the past. It also provides things that they can tell the therapist allowing a more natural interaction than might typically occur. However, although psychological approaches can be helpful, the best hopes for the future must lie with pharmacology.

SUMMARY

The study of aging is concerned with the study of change and can be pursued using two basic designs: longitudinal or cross-sectional. Longitudinal designs involve studying the same individuals across time, which has the important advantage of being able to follow the course of each person's aging process. Its drawbacks are that it is inevitably lengthy and is subject to the effects of learning across test sessions and of differential volunteer drop out. Cross-sectional studies are quicker but suffer from lack of data from the same individual at different ages and from cohort effects. A combination of the two, although lengthy and expensive, is the best solution.

Much current evidence on aging and memory comes from cross-sectional studies, which suggest the following:

- STM is relatively preserved (working memory is less so). Episodic memory certainly declines, the deficit is greater when additional processing is required but can benefit from environmental cues and support. The associative deficit hypothesis proposes that aging leads to a reduced capacity to form new associations, a milder form of amnesia, with capacity to "remember" more impaired in than to "know."
- Prospective memory declines when tested under laboratory conditions, but in a real-world context is well preserved, possibly as a result of better use of strategies and external cues.

The content of semantic memory continues to accumulate, as reflected in increasing vocabulary, but speed and reliability of access declines.

- Implicit memory tends to hold up reasonably well but varies with task. In the case of motor skills, performance is poorer but improves with practice at the same rate as for the young.

- A number of unitary theories of cognitive decline with age have been proposed. One influential theory attributes cognitive decline to reduced speed of processing but others have suggested increasing sensory or attentional deficit. Both these theories relied on correlational approaches, which suffer from collinearity, the tendency for many different measures to decline at the same time, making strong conclusions questionable.

- The brain tends to shrink as we get older, particularly in the frontal lobes. However, attempts to explain aging in terms of frontal lobe deficit have not so far proved fruitful. Neuroimaging suggests that older people tend to show a wider spread of neural activation, possibly resulting from an attempt to compensate for a cognitive deficit.

- Alzheimer's disease is an important and devastating burden in an aging population. It is associated with the development of amyloid plaques and neural tangles. Its most prominent feature is an episodic memory deficit, accompanied by other cognitive problems, including working memory impairment and subsequently deficits in semantic processing. Pharmacological treatments are currently at a stage where they can slow the development of the disease, but not prevent it. Psychological treatment can be helpful, with methods including errorless learning to acquire new information, and reminiscence therapy to optimize autobiographical memory.

FURTHER READING

- *American Journal of Geriatric Psychiatry*: Special Issue on "Successful aging" (2006) volume 14, issue 1. Focuses on the developing research area of how we can best adapt to the inevitable process of aging.

- Bäckman, L., Nyberg, L., Lindenberger, U., Li, S.-C., & Farde, L. (2006). The correlative triad among aging, dopamine, cognition: Current status and future prospects. *Neuroscience and Biobehavioral Reviews*, 30, 791–807. A review of the exciting developments in the neurobiology of aging. It suggests an important role for dopamine in determining the effects of age on cognition.

- Perfect, T. J., & Maylor, E. A. (2000). Rejecting the dull hypothesis: The relationship between method and theory in cognitive aging research. In T. J. Perfect & E. A. Maylor (Eds.), *Models of cognitive aging* (pp. 1–18) Oxford: Oxford University Press. A discussion and critical evaluation of attempts to provide a general theory of cognitive aging.

- Rabbitt, P. (2005). Cognitive gerontology and cognitive change in old age. Special issue of *Quarterly Journal of Experimental Psychology Section A*, Hove, UK. An overview of the cognitive psychology of aging by someone who has worked extensively using both experimental and longitudinal designs.

- Salthouse, T. A. (1996). The processing-speed theory of adult age differences in cognition. *Psychological Review*, 103, 403–428. An influential attempt to provide a unitary theory of cognitive aging in terms of processing speed.

CHAPTER 14

EYEWITNESS TESTIMONY

Michael W. Eysenck

You are a juror in a case involving serious assault. You are finding it very difficult to decide whether the defendant is indeed the person who carried out the assault. This is because nearly all the evidence that has been presented is indirect or circumstantial, and so not really very convincing. However, there *is* one piece of evidence that appears to be very direct and revealing. The person who was assaulted identified the defendant as her assailant in a lineup. When you observe this eyewitness being questioned in court, you are impressed by the fact that she seems very confident that she has correctly identified the person who attacked her so viciously. As a consequence, you and your fellow jurors all decide that the defendant is guilty of serious assault, and he is sentenced to several years in prison.

It is not all that unusual for a guilty verdict to depend heavily on eyewitness testimony. For example, thorough analysis of trials in England and Wales many years ago revealed that over 200 lineups were held in a single year. Of these, 45% led to a suspect being picked out, with 82% subsequently being convicted. Of most relevance here, there were nearly 350 cases in which eyewitness identification was the only real evidence of guilt. Even here, 74% of defendants were convicted, indicating the substantial weight given to eyewitness testimony.

Consider the following case discussed by Elizabeth Loftus (1979). On 15 May 1975, the assistant manager of a department store in Monroe, North Carolina, was forced into a car by two men, one of whom pointed a gun at him and told him to lie down in the back of the car. He got only a glimpse of the men before they pulled stocking masks over their faces. They then drove to the store and demanded that he open the safe. He convinced them he did not know the combination, so they took 35 dollars from his wallet and let him go.

The victim, Robert Hinson, could say very little about his kidnappers other than that one of them looked Hispanic and that their car was an off-white 1965 Dodge Dart. However, he also said that one of them resembled a man who had recently applied for a job in the store. On the basis of this fragmentary evidence, a composite sketch was created of one of the suspects.

Three days later the police stopped a 1965 white Plymouth Valiant and arrested the driver and passenger, Sandy and Lonnie Sawyer. Neither of them looked like the composite sketch, neither had applied for a job at the store, and both denied knowing anything about the kidnapping. At the trial, Robert Hinson positively identified the Sawyers as the men who had kidnapped him. Despite four witnesses testifying that Sandy was at home at the time of the kidnapping, and four others vouching that Lonnie was at a printing plant visiting his girlfriend, the jury found the Sawyers guilty. As they were led from the court, Lonnie cried out, "Momma, Daddy, appeal this. We didn't do it!"

The Sawyers were lucky to have the support of a determined and persevering family, a tenacious private detective, and a television producer who had become interested in the case. Their first real break came in 1976 when Robert Thomas, a prisoner at a youth center, admitted to being one of Hinson's kidnappers. Encouraged by this, the detective re-checked some of the earlier leads and discovered that Thomas had indeed applied for a job at the store shortly before the kidnapping. Furthermore, he had a friend whose mother owned a 1965 Dodge Dart. The detective went on to interview some of the jurors. Some of them admitted that the evidence had not seemed very strong, but they eventually became tired and simply went along with the majority.

The justification for a retrial seemed very strong. However, the judge decided that, despite the new evidence, too much time had elapsed. The Governor of North Carolina was petitioned for a pardon. Before the outcome was known, Thomas confessed in writing and then on camera. He subsequently recanted, but then finally withdrew his recantation. On that day, the Governor pardoned the Sawyers. They had spent 2 years in jail, had narrowly escaped sentences of 28 and 32 years, and the process of freeing them had cost their impoverished family thousands of dollars. All this misery was endured because of jurors' willingness to accept the word of the victim, who admitted that he saw his assailants only briefly. Interestingly, the jurors were much more impressed by the eyewitness testimony of the victim than that of *eight* witnesses who testified that the accused could not have been present at the crime. Clearly, there were powerful forces at work here—sympathy for the victim, outrage at the attackers, and a feeling that someone should be brought to justice. Given a plausible candidate, it is all too easy to persuade oneself that the crime is solved, especially when the victim is willing to point an accusing finger. This might seem to the jurors to provide a neat and tidy solution, but sometimes (as in the case of Sandy and Lonnie Sawyer) it produces a travesty of justice.

MAJOR FACTORS INFLUENCING EYEWITNESS ACCURACY

How reliable (or should it be unreliable?) is eyewitness testimony? This is the central question we address in this chapter. We have just discussed a case in which the victim's testimony was seriously flawed, but perhaps that is a wholly exceptional case. Unfortunately, we now know that it is not. Throughout most of the twentieth century there was generally no very satisfactory way of proving that innocent people had been found guilty on the basis of inaccurate eyewitness testimony. However, the situation changed dramatically with the introduction of DNA tests. These tests can often establish whether the person convicted of a crime was actually responsible. In the United States, approximately 200 people have been shown to be innocent by means of DNA tests, and more than 75% of these people were found guilty on the basis of mistaken eyewitness identification. During the writing of this chapter in early 2008, DNA testing led to the release of Charles Chatman, who spent nearly 27 years in prison in Dallas County, Texas. He was 20 years old when a young woman who had been raped picked him out from a lineup. As a result of her eyewitness testimony,

Eyewitness testimony has been found by psychologists to be extremely unreliable, yet judges and jurors tend to find such testimony highly believable. © image100/Corbis.

Chatman was sentenced to 99 years in prison. On his last night in prison, Chatman said to the press: "I'm bitter, I'm angry. But I'm not angry or bitter to the point where I want to hurt anyone or get revenge."

There have several other cases in Dallas in which guilty verdicts have been overturned on the basis of DNA evidence. This seems to be the case because those involved in administering the law in Dallas are more likely to store the original evidence than in most other areas. That raises the disturbing prospect that the lack of stored DNA evidence means that numerous innocent people languishing in prison have no chance of their guilty verdict being overturned.

You might assume that most judges would be knowledgeable about potential problems with eyewitness testimony, and would use their knowledge to try to ensure a fair trial. These assumptions might well not be justified. Wise and Safer (2004) asked 160 American judges to indicate their agreement or disagreement with various statements about eyewitness testimony on which psychologists have obtained relevant evidence. Worryingly, the judges on average were correct on only 55% of the items, and most believed that jurors knew less about the limitations of eyewitness testimony than they did themselves. Judges minimized the factors causing eyewitness testimony to be inaccurate. As a result, only 23% of them agreed with the following statement: "Only in exceptional circumstances should a defendant be convicted of a crime solely on the basis of eyewitness testimony."

Suspect testimony

There is considerable evidence that our powers of observation are worse than we like to think. For example, consider a study by Simons and Levin (1998) in which people walking across a college campus were asked by a stranger for directions. About 10 or 15 seconds into the discussion, two men carrying a wooden door passed between the stranger and the participants. While this was happening, the stranger was substituted with a man of different height, build, and voice wearing different clothes. If you had taken part in that study, do you think you would have realized that your conversational partner had changed? Most people answer "Yes" to that question. However, in the actual study approximately 50% of the participants failed to notice the switch! This phenomenon of failing to notice apparently obvious changes in an object is known as *change blindness*.

Direct evidence that we are often wildly optimistic about our own observational powers was reported by Levin, Drivdahl, Momen, and Beck (2002). Participants saw a number of videos involving two people having a conversation in a restaurant. In one video, the plates on their table changed from red to white, and in another a scarf worn by one of them disappeared. A third video showed a man sitting in his office and then walking into the hall to answer the telephone. When the view switches from the office to the hall, the first person has been replaced by another man wearing different clothes. These videos had previously been used by the researchers, who found that none of their participants detected any of the changes.

Levin et al. (2002) asked their participants to indicate whether they thought they would have noticed the changes if they had not been forewarned about them. The percentages claiming they would have noticed the changes were as follows: 78% for the disappearing scarf, 59% for the changed man, and 46% for the change in color of the plates. These percentage figures need to be compared against the 0% detection rates for all three changes found in research studies. Levin et al. used the term *change blindness blindness* to describe our misplaced confidence in our ability to detect visual changes. We generally think that we are processing the entire visual scene in front of us reasonably thoroughly and so are well placed to detect changes in any object. In fact, we are very much better at detecting changes in objects that we have previously looked at directly than those we haven't (Hollingworth &

Henderson, 2002). Thus, we underestimate the importance of fixating objects if we are to remember them and to detect changes in them.

The existence of change blindness is good news for those making movies. It means that we rarely spot visual changes when the same scene has been shot more than once with parts of each shot being combined in the finished version of the movie. Here are two examples: In *Grease*, while John Travolta is singing *Greased lightning*, his socks change color several times between black and white; and in *Diamonds are forever*, James Bond tilts his car on two wheels to drive through an alleyway. As he enters the alleyway, the car is balanced on its *right* wheels, but when it emerges on the other side it is miraculously on its *left* wheels!

It could be argued that an eyewitness seeing a novel and dramatic event such as a crime would be much more observant than the participants in the above studies or members of an audience relaxing at the movies. However, that is not necessarily the case. Several factors work against the eyewitness, tending to obscure and distort his/her memory. Some are obvious. The eyewitness is typically not expecting the incident in question to occur, and is often preoccupied with his/her own thoughts and plans. What he/she sees is sometimes of very short duration (e.g. when a cell phone is snatched), and criminals are usually careful to minimize their chances of being recognized (e.g. by being in disguise). As we will see, other, less obvious, factors serve to reduce the accuracy of eyewitnesses' memory.

Remembering what you expected to see

There is much evidence that our memory for events can be influenced by what we expected to see. This is notoriously the case with sporting contests—supporters of the two teams often have almost diametrically opposed memories of crucial moments in the game! For example, consider a classic study carried out by two American social psychologists, Hastorf

and Cantril (1954) on a football game between two American universities (Princeton and Dartmouth). A film of the game was shown to Dartmouth and Princeton students, and they were instructed to detect infringements of the rules. Princeton students detected more than twice as many infringements of the rules by Dartmouth than did Dartmouth students.

Expectations probably played a part in an interesting study reported by Lindholm and Christianson (1998). Swedish and immigrant students saw a videotaped simulated robbery in which the perpetrator seriously wounded a cashier with a knife. There were two versions of this robbery, with the perpetrator being Swedish (i.e. with blond hair and light skin) in one version but an immigrant (i.e. having black hair and brown skin) in the other. After watching the video, participants were shown a lineup consisting of color photographs of eight men, four of whom were Swedes and the remainder immigrants. The actual perpetrator was selected about 30% of the time,

Can you imagine elderly ladies like these committing a robbery? According to Bartlett (1932), our stereotypical schemas may influence expectations, which color our memories.

with participants performing slightly better when the perpetrator was ethnically similar to them. However, the central finding was that both immigrant and Swedish participants were about twice as likely to select an innocent immigrant as an innocent Swede. Immigrants are overrepresented in Swedish crime statistics, and this fact probably influenced participants' expectations concerning the likely ethnicity of the perpetrator of a violent crime.

Bartlett (1932) provided an explanation of *why* expectations color our memories. According to him, we possess numerous schemas or packets of knowledge stored in long-term memory, and these schemas lead us to form certain expectations (see Chapter 6). For example, Tuckey and Brewer (2003a) found that most people have the following information in their bank-robbery schema: robbers are male, they wear disguises, they wear dark clothes, they make demands for money, and they have a getaway car with a driver in it.

According to Bartlett's theory, recall involves a process of reconstruction in which all relevant information (including schema-based information) is used to reconstruct the details of an event in terms of "what must have been true." Thus, eyewitnesses' recall of a bank robbery should be systematically influenced by the information contained in their bank-robbery schema.

Tuckey and Brewer (2003a) showed eyewitnesses a video of a simulated bank robbery followed by a test of memory. As predicted by Bartlett's theory, eyewitnesses had better recall for information relevant to the bank-robbery schema than for information *irrelevant* to it (e.g. the color of the getaway car). Thus, eyewitnesses used schematic information to assist in their recall of the bank robbery.

Additional support for Bartlett's theory was reported by Tuckey and Brewer (2003b). Once again, eyewitnesses recalled the details of a simulated crime they had observed. What was of central interest was how the eyewitnesses remembered ambiguous information. For example, some eyewitnesses saw a robber's head covered by a balaclava, so that the robber's gender was ambiguous. As predicted, eyewitnesses generally interpreted the ambiguous information as being consistent with their crime schema (Figure 14.1). Thus, for example, they tended to recall the robber whose head was covered by a balaclava as being male. In other words, their recall was systematically distorted by including information from their bank-robbery schema that did *not* correspond accurately to what they had observed.

Leading questions

Perhaps the most obvious explanation for the inaccurate memories of eyewitnesses is that

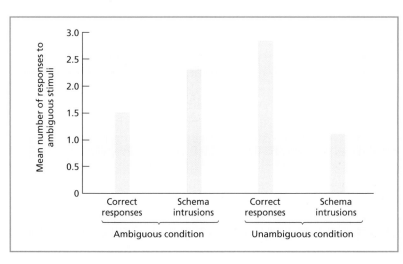

Figure 14.1 Mean correct responses and schema-consistent intrusions in the ambiguous and unambiguous conditions with cued recall. Data from Tuckey and Brewer (2003b).

they often fail to pay attention to the crime and to the criminal (or criminals). After all, the crime they observe typically occurs suddenly and unexpectedly. However, Elizabeth Loftus and John Palmer argued that what matters is *not* only what happens at the time of the crime. According to them, eyewitness memories are fragile and can—surprisingly easily—be distorted by what happens after observing the crime (e.g. the precise questions eyewitnesses are asked). In their well-known study (Loftus & Palmer, 1974), participants were shown a film of a multiple-car accident. After viewing the film, participants described what had happened, and then answered specific questions. Some were asked, "About how fast were the cars going when they hit each other?," whereas others were asked the same question but with the word "hit" replaced by "collided," "bumped," "contacted," or "smashed into."

What did Loftus and Palmer (1974) find? Speed estimates were highest (40.8 mph) when the word "smashed" was used, lower with "collided" (39.3 mph), and lower still with "bumped" (38.1 mph), "hit" (34 mph), and "contacted" (31.8 mph). One week later, all of the participants were asked, "Did you see any broken glass?" In fact, there was no broken glass in the accident. However, 32% of those who had previously been asked about speed using the verb "smashed" said they had seen broken glass. By contrast, only 14% of the participants who had been asked using the verb "hit" said they had seen broken glass. Thus, our memory for events is so fragile that it can be systematically distorted by changing one word in one question! It is likely that the precise schema that was activated varied depending on the particular verb included in the question about speed.

Loftus and Palmer's (1974) findings have been repeated many times, and it is clear that eyewitness memory is easily influenced by misleading information presented after a crime or other incident. For example, Eakin, Schreiber, and Sergent-Marshall (2003) showed participants slides of a maintenance man repairing a chair in an office and stealing some money and a calculator. Some of the eyewitnesses received misleading information presented after the slides. For example, the slides showed the maintenance man hiding the calculator under a screwdriver, whereas the subsequent information referred to a wrench. Eyewitness memory was impaired by misleading information presented after the eyewitnesses had seen the slides. More strikingly, memory was impaired even when the eyewitnesses were warned about the presence of misleading information very shortly after it had been presented.

The above findings indicate that information acquired between original learning (at the time of the event) and the subsequent memory test can disrupt performance on that test. What we have here is a clear example of *retroactive interference*, defined as disruption of memory by the learning of other material during the retention interval (see Chapter 9). Can eyewitness memory also be distorted by *proactive interference* (i.e. learning occurring *prior* to observing the critical event)? Evidence that the answer is positive was reported by Lindsay, Allen, Chan, and Dahl (2004). Participants were shown a video of a museum burglary. On the previous day, they listened to a narrative either thematically similar (a palace burglary) or thematically dissimilar (a school field-trip to a palace) to the video. Eyewitnesses made many more errors when recalling information from the video when the narrative was thematically similar than when it was thematically dissimilar. This is potentially an important finding. In the real world, eyewitnesses often have *previous experiences* of relevance to the questions they are asked about the event or crime. It is entirely possible that these experiences *might* distort some of their answers.

How does misleading postevent information distort what eyewitnesses report? According to Johnson, Hashtroudi, and Lindsay (1993), some of the inaccuracies in eyewitness recall can be understood within the source-monitoring framework. According to this framework, what happens is that a memory probe (e.g. a question) activates memory traces that overlap with it in terms of the information they contain. Any memory probe might activate memories from various sources. The individual decides on the *source* of any activated memory on the basis of the information it contains. However, there is a possibility of source misattribution, with information from the wrong event or memory being retrieved. Source misattribution is especially likely when the memories from one source resemble those from a second source.

Support for the source-monitoring framework was reported by Allen and Lindsay (1998), who presented two narrative slide shows describing two different events with different people in different settings. However, some details in the two events were rather similar (e.g. a can of Pepsi vs. a can of Coca-Cola). Participants were then asked what they remembered from the first event. There was source misattribution, with details from the second event being mistakenly recalled as if they belonged to the first event.

There are other ways in which postevent information can distort eyewitnesses' reports. One possibility is that the memories themselves are changed by this information. However, another possibility is simply that eyewitnesses are responding to social pressure (e.g. to please the experimenter). Loftus (1979) strongly supported the former possibility, arguing that the information from misleading questions permanently alters the memory representation of an incident, with the previously formed memory being "overwritten" and destroyed. She provided evidence for this viewpoint in a study in which eyewitnesses saw a pedestrian accident involving a car stopping at either a stop sign or a yield sign. Two days later, participants were asked questions about the incident, one of which biased them away from what had actually happened. More specifically, if they had seen a stop sign, the biasing question referred to a yield sign, and vice versa. Their memory of the incident was then tested by showing them pairs of slides and

asking them which sign they had seen. In the critical pair of slides, one showed a stop sign and the other a yield sign. Loftus argued that if her participants genuinely remembered the correct version but simply responded otherwise to please the experimenter, the bias could be removed by offering a high-enough pay-off for making a correct response. One group was given no reward, one was promised $1 each if they decided correctly, a third group was offered $5, and a fourth was told that the person in the experiment who scored the highest would receive $25. In spite of these incentives, between 70% and 85% of those tested selected the wrong response. This suggests (but does not prove) that the original memory trace had been altered.

Other researchers have reported some evidence that the original memory trace does survive. For example, consider a study by Bekerian and Bowers (1983). They found that the standard Loftus procedure of asking questions in a fairly unstructured way led to the same biasing effect of misleading information she had reported. However, the biasing effect disappeared when participants were questioned systematically, starting with earlier incidents and working through to later ones.

Loftus (1992) argued for a less extreme position than the one she had previously adopted. She emphasized the notion of misinformation acceptance: Eyewitnesses "accept" misleading information presented to them after an event, and subsequently regard it as forming part of their memory for that event. Accepting postevent information in this way becomes more common as the time since the event increases. It is likely that there is more than one way in which misleading postevent information causes eyewitnesses to report distorted memories of the incident they have observed.

The discovery that eyewitnesses' memory can be systematically distorted by information presented either before or after they have observed a crime or other incident is a worrying one. However, such distorting effects could be less damaging than might be imagined.

Eyewitness memory can be impaired by misleading post-event information. However, important information, such as the weapon used in a crime, is less likely to be distorted than peripheral information. © Guy Cali/Corbis.

Memory distortions are more common for peripheral or minor details (e.g. presence of broken glass) than for central details (e.g. features of the criminal) (Heath & Erickson, 1998).

The studies we have been discussing were laboratory studies and so possibly produced different results from those that might have been obtained in real-life situations. For example, Yuille and Cutshall (1986) examined the memories of eyewitnesses to a fatal shooting 5 months afterwards. In spite of the fact that the eyewitnesses had been exposed to misleading questions, all of them had highly accurate memories for what they had observed. However, this study is limited. There were only 13 participants, and they were only exposed to a relatively modest amount of misinformation.

Individual differences

Do you think the age of an eyewitness is relevant when deciding whether his/her memory for an event is likely to be accurate? If you have already read Chapter 12, then your answer should be, "Yes"! Evidence indicating that young children generally make less accurate eyewitnesses than older ones was discussed in that chapter. There is another reason why your answer should have been affirmative—as we will see, there is evidence that the eyewitness testimony of older adults is less accurate than that of young ones.

Brewer, Weber, and Semmler (2005) reviewed research on eyewitness identification in older people (in the 60- to 80-year-old range). Older people were more likely than younger adults to choose someone from a lineup, even when the culprit was not present. In addition, older people are strongly influenced by misleading suggestions. In one study (Mueller-Johnson & Ceci, 2004), older adults with an average age of 76 and young adults (average age 20) underwent relaxation techniques including body massage and aromatherapy. Several weeks later, the participants were given misleading information (e.g. that they had been massaged on parts of their body that had not been touched). The misleading information distorted the memories of the older adults much more than those of the young adults.

Dodson and Krueger (2006) showed a video to younger and older adults, who later completed a questionnaire that misleadingly referred to events not shown on the video. The older adults were more likely than the younger ones to produce false memories triggered by the misleading suggestions. Worryingly, the older adults tended to be very confident about the correctness of their false memories. By contrast, the younger adults were generally rather uncertain about the accuracy of their false memories.

Wright and Stroud (2002) considered differences between younger and older adults who tried to identify the culprits after being presented with crime videos. They found an "own age bias," with both groups being more accurate at identification when the culprit was of a similar age to themselves. Thus, older adults' generally poorer eyewitness memory is less noticeable when the culprit is an older person, perhaps because they pay more attention to the facial and other features of culprits the same age as themselves.

What can be done to enhance the memory of older adults? One of the central memory problems that older adults have is that their memories are very easily distorted by misleading or interfering information. For example, Jacoby, Bishara, Hessels, and Toth (2005) presented misleading information to younger and older adults. On a subsequent test of recall, older adults had a 43% chance of producing false memories based on the misleading information compared to only 4% for the younger adults. Two recommendations follow. First, it is even more important with older adults than with younger ones to ensure that they are not exposed to any misleading information that might distort their memory. Second, older adults often produce memories that are genuine in the sense that they are based on information or events to which they have been exposed. The specific problem is that older adults often misremember the context or circumstances in which the information was encountered. Thus, it is essential to engage in detailed questioning with older adults to decide whether remembered events actually occurred at the time of the crime or other incident.

Eyewitness confidence

Jurors tend to be influenced by how confident the eyewitness seems to be that he/she has correctly identified the culprit. This seems entirely reasonable on the face of it. However, Kassin, Tubb, Hosch, and Memon (2001) found that more than 80% of eyewitness experts agreed that an eyewitness's confidence is *not* a good predictor of his/her identification accuracy! We need to strike a balance here, because there is not always a poor relationship between eyewitness confidence and accuracy. Sporer, Penrod, Read, and Cutler (1995) combined the findings from numerous studies in which eyewitness confidence was assessed immediately after he/she had chosen a suspect from a lineup. They distinguished between choosers

(eyewitnesses making a positive identification) and nonchoosers (those not making a positive identification). There was practically no correlation or association between confidence and accuracy among nonchoosers. However, the mean correlation was +.41 among choosers, indicating that choosers' confidence predicted their accuracy to a moderate extent.

Why is eyewitness confidence often a relatively poor predictor of identification accuracy? Perfect and Hollins (1996) addressed this issue. Participants watched a film about a girl who was kidnapped and they were then given a recognition-memory test for the information in it. In addition, they were asked several general-knowledge questions. Their key finding was that participants' confidence didn't predict accuracy with questions about the film but did predict accuracy reasonably well with the general-knowledge questions. Perfect and Hollins argued that eyewitness confidence didn't predict accuracy with recall of information from the film because eyewitnesses do no know whether their ability to remember a witnessed event is better or worse than that of others. As a consequence, they have no solid basis for being low or high in confidence. By contrast, most people know whether their general knowledge compares well or badly with that of others, and this is reflected in their level of confidence.

In court cases, it is likely that the relationship between eyewitness confidence and accuracy is even less than in the laboratory. Prosecution lawyers typically coach eyewitnesses to be confident in their reporting of what they remember. In addition, eyewitnesses might be led by police officers to believe that their identification was correct (this is known as confirming feedback). Confirming feedback would also be likely to increase their confidence in what they remember.

Laboratory evidence on confirmatory feedback was reported by Bradfield, Wells, and Olson (2002). Eyewitnesses watched a 3-minute video of a young man, after which they were shown a videotaped six-person lineup and asked to identify the culprit. In the confirming feedback condition, they were told, "Good, you identified the actual suspect" regardless of whether they selected the culprit or not. In the neutral condition, eyewitnesses didn't receive any feedback. Confirming feedback increased eyewitnesses' confidence in the accuracy of their identification much more when they had been incorrect than when they had been correct. As a result, the relationship between confidence and accuracy was significantly lower in the confirming feedback condition than in the control condition.

Influence of anxiety and violence

One of the authors (Alan Baddeley) was telephoned one Sunday night by a caller announcing himself as a detective with the San Diego Police Force. He explained that he was investigating a multiple throat-slasher whose seventh victim had escaped. The woman claimed that she would be able to recognize her attacker. What, the detective asked, was the likely effect of extreme emotion on the reliability and accuracy of her testimony?

This is an important and extremely controversial issue on which the opinions of different experts vary dramatically. When 235 American lawyers were asked whether high levels of emotion would impair facial recognition, 82% of the defense lawyers argued that recognition would be impaired, compared to only 32% of prosecution attorneys. Who is right? Does extreme emotion brand the experience indelibly on the victim's memory, or does it reduce his/her capacity for recollection? We will shortly turn to a consideration of the evidence. Bear in mind, however, that laboratory studies have, for obvious reasons, not exposed participants to extremely stressful conditions; for example, not even the most zealous experimenters try to convince their participants that they are about to have their throats cut!

The typical way in which the effects of emotion on eyewitness memory are assessed is by exposing eyewitnesses to a film or staged incident in which some crucial event occurs.

KEY TERM

Weapon-focus effect: The finding that eyewitnesses pay so much attention to the attacker's weapon that that they ignore and thus cannot recall other details.

In different versions, the incident is either associated with or not associated with violence. What is generally found is that memory for a violent event is stronger than memory for the corresponding nonviolent event, but that memory for associated details is less. More specifically, violence leads eyewitnesses to show enhanced memory for what they regard as central aspects of an incident but reduced memory for peripheral aspects.

Much of the research has focused on the **weapon-focus effect**, in which the presence of a weapon causes eyewitnesses to fail to recall details about the assailant and the

Weapon focus is the phenomenon in which eyewitnesses are so distracted by the weapon used in a crime that they will fail to recall other details of the event.

environment. Loftus (1979) discussed a study in which each participant was asked to wait outside a laboratory before taking part in an experiment. In the "no weapon" condition, the participant overheard a harmless conversation about equipment failure in the experimental room, after which someone emerged holding a pen and with grease on his hands, uttered a single statement, and left. In the "weapon" condition, the participant heard a hostile interchange between two people, ending with breaking bottles, chairs crashing, and someone leaving the experimental room holding a letter opener covered with blood. Again the person uttered a single line before leaving.

All the participants in the study were subsequently given an album containing 50 photographs and asked whether or not the person who had emerged from the room was represented there. In the "no weapon" condition, participants located the correct photograph 49% of the time compared to only 33% in the "weapon" condition. This is a clear example of the weapon-focus effect. However, it seems strange in a way, because it was clearly more important for eyewitnesses to focus on the person's face when a crime had possibly been committed.

The most obvious explanation of the weapon-focus effect is that eyewitnesses tend to focus on the weapon at the expense of other aspects of the situation. Support for this explanation was reported by Loftus, Loftus, and Messo (1987), who asked participants to watch one of two sequences:

1. A person pointing a gun at a cashier and receiving some cash.
2. A person holding a check to the cashier and receiving some cash.

As expected, eyewitnesses looked more at the gun than they did at the check. As a consequence, memory for details unrelated to the gun/check was poorer in the weapon condition.

Pickel (1999) argued that there are two possible reasons for the existence of a weapon-

focus effect. First, the weapon poses a threat, and that is why eyewitnesses focus on it rather than on other aspects of the situation. Second, the weapon might attract attention because it is unexpected or unusual in most of the contexts in which it is seen by eyewitnesses. Pickel produced four videos involving a man approaching a woman while holding a handgun to evaluate these explanations:

1. Low threat; expected: gun barrel pointed at the ground; setting was a shooting range.
2. Low threat; unexpected: gun barrel pointed at the ground; setting was a baseball field.
3. High threat; expected: gun pointed at the woman who shrank back in fear; setting was a shooting range.
4. High threat; unexpected: gun pointed at the woman who shrank back in fear; setting was a baseball field.

Four groups of participants in the study by Pickel (1999) each watched one of the videos. Afterwards, the eyewitnesses were tested for their memory of the man with the gun. The findings were clear cut (Figure 14.2). Eyewitnesses' descriptions of the man were much better when the gun was seen in a setting

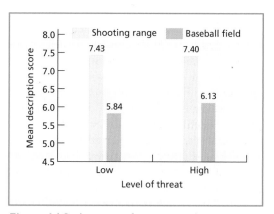

Figure 14.2 Accuracy of eyewitness descriptions of the man with the gun as a function of setting (shooting range vs. baseball field) and level of threat (low vs. high). From Pickell (1999). Reproduced with kind permission from Springer Science+Business Media.

in which guns are expected (a shooting range) than in a setting in which they are unexpected (a baseball field). However, the level of threat had no influence at all on how much eyewitnesses could remember.

We have already indicated that the emotion experienced by participants in laboratory studies is likely to be far less than that experienced by real-life victims of a violent assault. To see whether the strong laboratory evidence for weapon focus was also true of real-life crimes, Valentine, Pickering, and Darling (2003) considered the findings from over 300 real lineups. The presence of a weapon had no effect on the probability of an eyewitness identifying the suspect (but bear in mind that the suspect wasn't always the culprit!). However, Tollestrup, Turtle, and Yuille (1994) found evidence for the weapon focus effect in their analysis of police records of real-life crimes. Thus, we can tentatively conclude that there is a relatively small weapon focus effect with real-life crimes.

Weapon focus has been discussed at length. What are the general effects of stress and anxiety on eyewitness memory? Deffenbacher, Bornstein, Penrod, and McGorty (2004) carried out meta-analyses combining findings from numerous studies on the effects of anxiety and stress on eyewitness memory. In the first meta-analysis, they considered the effects of anxiety and stress on accuracy of face identification. Average correct identifications were 54% for low anxiety or stress conditions compared to 42% for high anxiety or stress conditions. Thus, heightened anxiety and stress have a definite negative impact on eyewitness identification accuracy. In the second meta-analysis, Deffenbacher et al. considered the effects of anxiety and stress on eyewitness recall of culprit details, crime scene details, and actions of central characters. The average percentage of details correctly recalled was 64% in low anxiety or stress conditions compared to 52% in high anxiety or stress conditions. This difference indicates that high anxiety or stress reduces the ability of eyewitnesses to remember details of a crime.

REMEMBERING FACES

Of all the information that eyewitnesses might or might not remember, the face of the culprit is often far and away the most important. In this section, we consider in detail the processes involved in remembering faces, and the factors that can make it hard to do so.

"I never forget a face!" One often hears people making such claims, but how justifiable are they? In view of the huge importance that accurate face recognition plays in our everyday lives, you might imagine that most people would be real experts at identifying the faces of other people. The substantial problems caused by being very poor at identifying faces can be seen most clearly in patients suffering from **prosopagnosia** or face blindness. These patients can recognize most objects reasonably well despite their enormous difficulties with faces. A young prosopagnosic Swedish woman called Cecilia Berman has described the strategies she uses to minimize social embarrassment:

Many face-blind people will greet within a second, in spite of not having had enough time to recognize someone … We have to greet everyone who might be a friend, which can be pretty much everyone we meet … Some face-blind people … become experts at pretending they knew all along who someone was when they finally learn about it … Many face-blind people go to great lengths to avoid using names … I probably use other people's names in their presence less than once a month, and always with a rush of adrenaline. (Berman, 2004, pp. 4–5)

KEY TERM

Prosopagnosia: A condition, also known as face-blindness, in which there is extremely poor face recognition combined with reasonable ability to recognize other objects.

There has been considerable controversy on the issue of whether face recognition involves different processes from object recognition (see McKone, Kanwisher, & Dunchaine, 2007, for an excellent review). The fact that most prosopagnosic patients are reasonably good at recognizing objects suggests that faces are processed differently from objects. However, the evidence is hard to interpret. Object recognition typically involves deciding what category an object belongs to (e.g. cat, dog, table). By contrast, face recognition does not involve deciding *whether* a face has been presented but rather *which* specific face it is. Perhaps prosopagnosics would have poor ability to make fine discriminations among objects (e.g. deciding which breed of dog has been presented). In fact, the evidence does not support this prediction. For example, Sergent and Signoret (1992) found that RM, who was prosopagnosic, had an excellent ability to recognize the makes, models, and years of cars. This suggests that there is something special about face processing.

Further evidence that face processing differs considerably from object processing was reviewed by McKone et al. (2007). For example, it has been found many times that the fusiform face area is much more active when faces are presented than when objects are presented. The fact that most patients with prosopagnosia have suffered damage to the fusiform face area strengthens the argument that it is of particular significance in face processing.

How well do we remember faces?

In spite of the importance of face recognition, it seems that most of us are not especially good at remembering faces. Bruce, Henderson, Greenwood, Hancock, Burton, and Miller (1999) investigated this issue. In view of the dramatic increase in the number of closed-circuit television (CCTV) cameras in the US, the UK, and elsewhere, they decided to focus on people's ability to identify someone on the basis of CCTV images. Participants were presented with a target face taken from a CCTV video, together with an array of 10 high-quality

photographs (Figure 14.3). Their task was to select the matching face or to indicate that the target face was not present in the array. Performance was disappointingly poor. When the target face was present in the array, it was selected only 65% of the time. When it was *not* present, 35% of participants nevertheless claimed that one of the faces in the array matched the target face. Allowing participants to watch a 5-second video segment of the target person as well as a photograph of their faces failed to improve identification performance.

Some factors determining whether memory for faces is good or poor were identified by Patterson and Baddeley (1977). Participants categorized photographs of unfamiliar people on the basis of various physical features (e.g. chin, nose, eyes, type of hair) or psychological dimensions such as honesty, intelligence, or liveliness. They also considered the effectiveness of disguise. They argued that although it might be easier to remember a face for its honesty or intelligence than for its nose or ears, it might well be that a broad judgment of character would be much more easily misled by disguise. It might be easier to make a person look friendlier or less intelligent than to change the shape of their face or size of their nose.

Initially, Patterson and Baddeley (1977) presented participants with photographs of amateur actors and colleagues, all photographed undisguised or wearing a beard, wig, spectacles, or any combination of them. The photographs were taken either full face or in profile. Their participants were familiarized with one photograph of each person in any one combination of disguised features. This was repeatedly presented until it was consistently recognized and the person's name given correctly. Their participants were then presented with photographs consisting of the target individuals in all possible combinations of disguise, either in full frontal view or in profile, together with a number of similarly disguised but unfamiliar people. Their task was to detect and name the target individuals.

Participants were generally better at recognizing the faces they had categorized

Figure 14.3 Example of full-face neutral target with an array used in the experiments. Readers might want to try the task of establishing whether the target is present in this array and which one it is. The studio and video images used are from the Home Office Police Information Technology Organisation. Bruce et al. (1999). Copyright © American Psychological Association. Reprinted with permission. The target is present in position 3.

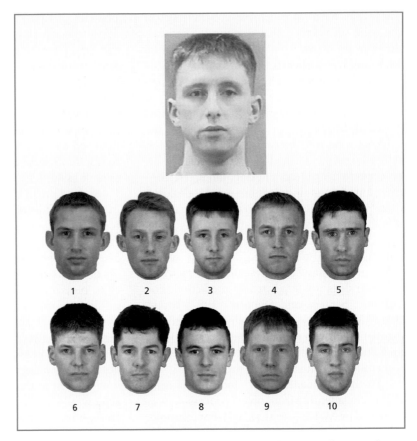

using psychological dimensions than those they had categorized using physical features. This effect was fairly small but indicated that there is no advantage in analyzing a face into its component features. The other key finding (Figure 14.4) was that the effect of disguise was very dramatic. Every time an item of disguise was added or removed the probability of recognition went down. Performance ranged from extremely good when the face was presented in its originally learned form to virtual guesswork when the maximum number of disguised features was changed.

Holistic processing

Is there something special or unusually difficult about recognizing faces compared to other objects? It has been argued (e.g. Farah, 1994) that the processing of faces differs from that of other objects in that the emphasis is much more

on holistic or global analysis. In other words, we process the *overall* structure of the face and pay little attention to the details (e.g. face, mouth, eyebrows). It is very likely that holistic or global analysis was involved in the research of Patterson and Baddeley (1977) when participants categorized faces using psychological dimensions. By contrast, object processing generally involves more detailed processing in which the parts of an object are processed in turn.

How can we test the notion that holistic processing is more important with faces than with other objects? One way is to consider how good people are at identifying faces presented inverted or upside-down. The detailed features are still easily recognized in inverted faces, but it is much more difficult to identify their overall structure correctly. As predicted, adverse effects of inversion on object recognition are much greater with faces than with nonface objects. In addition, negative effects of inversion

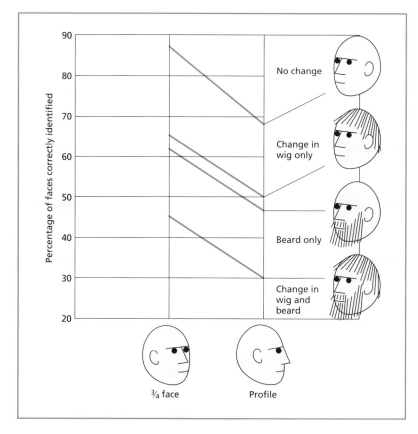

Figure 14.4 With a wig and beard, you halve your chances of being recognized as the guilty party. Faces seen in three-quarters view are much more recognizable than faces seen in profile. From Patterson and Baddeley (1977). Copyright © American Psychological Association. Reproduced with permission.

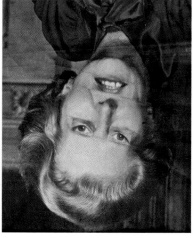

Figure 14.5 The Thatcher illusion. The figure on the left is typically seen as the same as on the right, but it isn't! From Thompson, P. (1980). Margaret Thatcher: A new illusion. *Perception, 9,* 483–484. Copyright © Pion Limited. Reproduced with permission.

with ordinary objects disappear rapidly with practice, whereas those with faces can persist for thousands of trials (see McKone, 2004, for a review). Strikingly, there is the Thatcher illusion (Figure 14.5) involving Mrs Thatcher, who was the British Prime Minister during the 1980s. This illusion occurs because we rely too much on holistic processing. When viewed as an inverted face, we do not realize that the eyes and mouth are inverted relative to the face. However, the grotesque nature of the face becomes very clear when you view it the right way up.

Unconscious transference

There is evidence that eyewitnesses might sometimes be better at remembering faces than at remembering the precise circumstances in which they saw the face. As we will see, this can have important implications. Ross, Ceci, Dunning, and Toglia (1994) carried out a study in which eyewitnesses observed an event in which a bystander was present as well as the culprit. Eyewitnesses were three times more likely to select the bystander than someone they had not seen before when they saw a lineup including the bystander but not the culprit. This effect is known as **unconscious transference**, in which a face is correctly recognized as having been that of someone seen before but incorrectly judged to be responsible for a crime. However, there was no effect when participants were informed before seeing the lineup that the bystander and the culprit were not the same person.

You might be wondering whether unconscious transference happens in real life. One real-life case occurred in Australia. A psychologist (Donald Thomson) took part in a live television discussion on the unreliability of eyewitness testimony. Some time later, he was picked up by the police, who refused to explain why they were arresting him. He assumed he was being unofficially harassed because of his strong views on eyewitness unreliability. At the police station, he was placed in a lineup. A very distraught woman identified him and Donald Thomson was then told he was being charged with rape. When he asked for details, it became clear that the rape had been committed at the same time as he had been taking part in the television discussion. He said he had a perfectly good alibi, and numerous witnesses including an official of the Australian Civil Rights Committee and an Assistant Commissioner of Police. To this, the police officer taking his statement replied: "Yes, and I suppose you've got Jesus Christ and the Queen of England, too!" It turned out that the woman had been raped while watching the program. For Thomson himself, it was an especially unpleasant way of discovering just how right he was to worry about eyewitness unreliability!

Verbal overshadowing

Suppose that you are a police officer and you have arrived at the scene of a crime that occurred only a few minutes ago. You find an eyewitness and have to decide whether to ask him/her to provide a verbal description of the culprit. It seems reasonable to assume that doing so would improve the eyewitness's subsequent ability to recognize the culprit. In fact, however, most of the evidence suggests that eyewitnesses' recognition memory for faces is actually *worse* if they have previously provided a verbal description! This phenomenon is known as *verbal overshadowing*.

Schooler and Engstler-Schooler (1990) provided the first demonstration of verbal overshadowing. Eyewitnesses watched a film of a crime. After that, some eyewitnesses provided a detailed verbal report of the criminal's appearance, whereas others did an unrelated task. Those who had provided the detailed verbal report performed worse than the other eyewitnesses on this test.

Why does verbal overshadowing occur? Clare and Lewandowsky (2004) argued that one answer is that providing a verbal report of the culprit makes eyewitnesses more reluctant to identify anyone on a subsequent lineup. As predicted, Clare and Lewandowsky found there was no verbal overshadowing effect when eyewitnesses were forced to select someone from the lineup and so could not be cautious. Excessive caution seems to be the main explanation of the verbal overshadowing effect when eyewitnesses provide a relatively *brief* verbal description of the culprit.

KEY TERM

Unconscious transference: The tendency of eyewitnesses to misidentify a familiar (but innocent) face as belonging to the person responsible for a crime.

However, when eyewitnesses are asked to provide a *detailed* verbal description, there are often various errors in that description. In such circumstances, these errors account for the verbal overshadowing effect (see Clare & Lewandowsky, 2004, for a review).

Cross-race effect

Finally, there is a controversial issue relating to eyewitnesses' ability to recognize faces. This is the *cross-race effect*, which involves more accurate recognition of same-race faces than of cross-race faces (Box 14.1).

Box 14.1 Cross-race effect

There is a considerable amount of evidence for the existence of the cross-race effect (see Shriver, Young, Hugenberg, Bernstein, & Lanter, 2008, for a review). In most studies, White participants had better recognition memory for White faces than for Black faces, and Black participants had better recognition memory for Black than for White faces. Shriver et al. discussed two hypotheses that might explain the cross-face effect. First, there is the expertise hypothesis: Most of us have had much more experience at distinguishing among same-race than cross-race faces, and so have developed expertise at same-race recognition. Second, there is the social-cognitive hypothesis: We engage in thorough facial processing of individuals with whom we identify (our ingroup) but not of individuals with whom we don't identify (outgroups). In most studies, it is simply not clear whether superior recognition memory for same-race faces than cross-race faces is due directly to race or whether it is more due to the distinction between ingroup and outgroup.

Much evidence appears to support the expertise hypothesis. Eyewitnesses who have the most familiarity and experience with members of another race tend to show a somewhat smaller cross-race effect than others (see review by Shriver et al., 2008). However, the effects of expertise or experience are small, and they also seem to be rather fragile. For example, Hugenberg, Miller, and Claypool (2007) found that the cross-race effect could be eliminated by simply instructing White participants to attend closely to the facial features distinguishing Black faces from each other.

Shriver et al. (2008) studied the cross-race effect in middle-class White students at the University of Miami. They were presented with photographs of college-aged males shown in impoverished contexts (e.g. dilapidated housing, run-down public spaces) or in wealthy contexts (e.g. large suburban homes, golf courses). On a subsequent test of recognition memory, the participants were shown photographs of faces and had to decide which ones they recognized.

What did Shriver et al. (2008) find? As can be seen in Figure 14.6, there were three main findings. First, there was the usual cross-race effect when White and Black faces had been seen in wealthy contexts. Second, there was no cross-race effect when White and Black faces had been seen in

(continued overleaf)

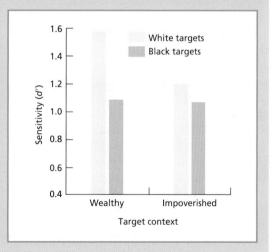

Figure 14.6 Mean recognition sensitivity as a function of target race (white vs. black) and target context (wealthy vs. impoverished). From Shriver et al. (2008). Copyright © 2008, Society for Personality and Social Psychology, Inc. Reprinted by permission of SAGE publications.

Box 14.1 (continued)

impoverished contexts. Third, the White participants recognized White faces much better when
they had been seen in wealthy contexts rather
than impoverished ones. All of these findings are
consistent with the social-cognitive hypothesis:
Middle-class White participants regarded White

faces in wealthy contexts as ingroup members,
whereas White faces in impoverished contexts
and Black faces in impoverished or wealthy context were regarded as outgroup members. As
predicted by the hypothesis, *only* ingroup faces
were well recognized.

POLICE PROCEDURES WITH EYEWITNESSES

The police obviously have no control over
the circumstances at the time of a crime. They
have to do their best to identify the culprit on
the basis of the often limited and inaccurate
memories of eyewitnesses. However, the police
do have a lot of control over the ways in
which eyewitnesses are treated. Here we will
focus on two of the most important of such
elements of control: (1) lineups; and (2) interview techniques used with eyewitnesses.

Lineups

What happens with a lineup is that the suspect is
present along with a number of nonsuspects of
broadly similar characteristics and the witness
is asked if he/she recognizes any member of the
lineup as the criminal. Of course, it is essential
that the suspect is not obviously different from
the other members of the lineup if the evidence
obtained is to be at all valid. In days gone by, it
was not unknown for this simple requirement
to be totally ignored. In one extreme case, for
example, the suspect was known to be Asian
but the lineup included only one Asian!

Suggestive evidence that the performance
of eyewitnesses is rather fallible when they try
to select the suspect from a lineup was reported
by Valentine et al. (2003). They analyzed the
findings based on 640 eyewitnesses who tried to
identify suspects in 314 real lineups organized
by the Metropolitan Police in London. Only
40% of witnesses identified the suspect, 20%
identified a nonsuspect, and the remaining
40% failed to make an identification.

What (if anything) can be done to improve
the identification performance of eyewitnesses
confronted by a lineup? One sensible
precaution (which is now in general use) is to
warn eyewitnesses that the culprit might not be
present in the lineup. This issue was explored
by Steblay (1997) in a meta-analysis based on
combining data from numerous studies carried
out under laboratory conditions. Warnings to
eyewitnesses reduced mistaken identification
rates in culprit-absent lineups by 42%,
while reducing accurate identification rates
in culprit-present lineups by only 2%. Thus,
providing a warning is clearly desirable.

Most lineups are simultaneous, meaning
that the eyewitness is presented with everyone
in the lineup at the same time. An alternative
is to have sequential lineups in which the
eyewitness sees only one person at a time.
Steblay, Dysart, Fulero, and Lindsay (2001)
considered the findings from studies in which
simultaneous and sequential lineups were
compared. Sequential lineups reduced the
chances of mistaken identification when the
culprit was absent by almost 50%. However,
sequential lineups also produced a significant reduction in accurate identification rates
when the culprit was present. What explains
these findings is that eyewitnesses adopt a
more stringent criterion for identification with
sequential than with simultaneous lineups.

Interviewing witnesses

Much of this chapter has been devoted to identifying the limitations of eyewitness memory. It
is important to recognize those limitations in
order to minimize the probability of innocent
people being wrongly convicted solely on the

basis of eyewitness testimony. However, it is also important to be constructive and to devise effective interviewing techniques so as obtain as much accurate information as possible from eyewitnesses.

Historically, the police in many countries tended to use inadequate interviewing techniques. For example, they would often ask closed-ended questions (e.g. "What color was the car?"), which mostly elicit only very limited and specific information. A preferable approach is to ask open-ended questions (e.g. "What can you tell me about the car?"). Police in the past would often interrupt eyewitnesses when they were in the middle of saying something. Such interruptions disrupt eyewitnesses' concentration and make it more difficult to retrieve relevant information. A third inadequacy in the interviewing techniques that used to be common was the tendency of police to ask questions in a predetermined order, which took no account of the answers provided by the eyewitness.

Psychologists have made several attempts over the years to produce more effective ways of eliciting information from eyewitnesses. Of particular note has been the development of the cognitive interview, which was originally devised by Geiselman, Fisher, MacKinnon, and Holland (1985). This approach is based on four general retrieval rules:

1. Mental reinstatement of the environment and any personal contact experienced during the crime.
2. Encouraging the reporting of every detail, regardless of how peripheral it might seem to the main incident.
3. Attempting to describe the incident in several different orders.
4. Attempting to report the incident from different viewpoints, including that of other participants or witnesses.

Why might we expect the cognitive interview to be effective? In short, it makes direct use of our knowledge of human memory. The first two rules above are based on the encoding specificity principle (Tulving, 1979; see Chapter 8). According to this principle, eyewitnesses will remember most when there is maximal overlap or match between the context in which the crime was witnessed and the context in which the recall attempt is made. The third and fourth rules are based on the assumption that memory traces are usually complex and contain various kinds of information (e.g. the person's mood at the time of learning). As a consequence, information about a crime can be retrieved using a number of different routes, each of which might provide information about rather different aspects of the original experience.

Fisher, Geiselman, Raymond, Jurkevich, and Warhaftig (1987) devised an enhanced cognitive interview. This includes all four rules discussed already. In addition, it makes use of the following recommendations:

Investigators should minimize distractions, induce the eyewitness to speak slowly, allow a pause between the response and next question, tailor language to suit the individual eyewitness, follow up with interpretive comment, try to reduce eyewitness anxiety, avoid judgmental and personal comments, and always review the eyewitness's description of events or people under investigation. (Roy 1991, p. 399)

How effective is the cognitive interview? The totality of the evidence indicates that it has clear advantages over traditional police interviews. Giselman et al. (1985) compared the effectiveness of three approaches when eyewitnesses were interviewed 48 hours after having watched a police training film of a violent crime. One approach was the standard Los Angeles Police interview and a second approach was the cognitive interview; the third approach involved hypnotizing eyewitnesses before asking them to recall the crime using the standard procedure. Hypnosis is highly controversial, mainly because it increases people's suggestibility and increases the amount of false information reported. Geiselman et al. found that the cognitive interview was the most effective approach—it produced slightly

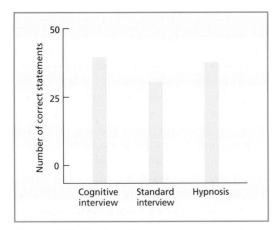

Figure 14.7 Number of correct statements using different methods of interview. Based on data in Geiselman et al. (1985).

more correct statements than hypnosis and substantially more than the standard police interview on its own (Figure 14.7).

The most thorough attempt to assess the effectiveness of the cognitive interview was reported by Kohnken, Milne, Memon, and Bull (1999), who combined the findings from over 50 studies into a meta-analysis. The cognitive interview consistently elicited more correct information than standard police interviews. Indeed, the average eyewitness given a cognitive interview produced more correct items of information than did 81% of eyewitnesses given a standard interview. However, there was a small cost in terms of reduced accuracy—the average eyewitness given a cognitive interview produced more errors than 61% of those given a standard interview. This needs to be borne in mind by police and lawyers when evaluating the evidence produced from use of cognitive interviews.

There are three final points to be made about the cognitive interview. First, it tends to be less effective at enhancing eyewitness recall when used at longer intervals of time after an incident has occurred. Accordingly, the recommendation is that eyewitnesses should be given a cognitive interview as soon as possible after the crime they have observed. Second, the cognitive interview might be of more value in increasing recall of peripheral details

than of central ones (Groeger, 1997). Third, what typically happens is that all the rules and other features of the cognitive interview are used together as a package. As a result, it is not altogether clear which aspects of the cognitive interview are most responsible for its effectiveness.

FROM LABORATORY TO COURTROOM

We have seen that psychologists have succeeded in identifying numerous reasons why jurors should be wary of accepting the reliability of eyewitness testimony. These reasons include change blindness, witnesses' prior expectations, pre- and postevent information, misplaced witness confidence, unconscious transference, verbal overshadowing, and weapon focus. This accumulating evidence led Handberg (1995) to argue in a review of legal opinion that, "Courts should admit eyewitness expert testimony to correct the misperceptions that many jurors have about the reliability of eyewitness identifications." Most psychologists accept that our knowledge of the strengths and limitations of eyewitness memory is such that it is wholly appropriate for experts on eyewitness testimony to testify

Handberg (1995) argued that many jurors have misperceptions about the reliability of eyewitness testimony and that admitting eyewitness expert testimony would help address this issue. © Royalty-free/Corbis.

in court. However, there are a few dissenting voices. For example, Ebbesen and Konecni (1997, p. 2) concluded as follows: "There is no evidence that the experts who testify would be any better at detecting witness inaccuracy than uninformed jurors … the nature of what is known about human memory is so complex that an honest presentation of this knowledge to a jury would only serve to confuse rather than improve their decision-making." In view of these differing opinions, we need to consider what conclusions can validly be drawn from the available evidence. More specifically, we will focus on the issue of ecological validity—do laboratory findings on eyewitness memory generalize to real life?

Laboratory findings are not relevant!

There are several important differences between eyewitnesses' typical experiences in the laboratory and when observing a real-life crime. First, in the overwhelming majority of laboratory studies, the event in question is observed by eyewitnesses rather than by the victim (or victims). This is quite different from real-life crimes, where evidence is much more likely to be provided by the victim than by eyewitnesses. Second, it is obviously less stressful and anxiety provoking to watch a video of a violent crime than to experience a real-life violent crime (especially from the perspective of the victim). Third, laboratory eyewitnesses generally observe the event from a *single* perspective in a passive way. By contrast, eyewitnesses to a real-life event are likely to move around and might be forced to interact with the individual or individuals committing the crime. Fourth, in laboratory experiments on face memory, participants typically have only a few seconds to study each face. With real-life crimes, however, eyewitnesses and victims have on average somewhere between 5 and 10 minutes' exposure to the criminal (Moore, Ebbesen, & Konecni, 1994). Fifth, in laboratory research, the consequences of an eyewitness making a mistaken identification

are trivial (e.g. minor disappointment at his/her poor memory). In contrast, they can literally be a matter of life or death in an American court of law.

The main way in which psychologists' knowledge of eyewitness testimony influences court cases is via the presentation of findings on eyewitness testimony by experts in the field. A central concern is that experts in eyewitness testimony (who are mostly called by the defense) will make jurors excessively skeptical about the validity of eyewitness testimony. Leippe (1995) reviewed 12 mock-juror and trial-simulation studies in which the presence versus absence of eyewitness expert testimony was compared. In 10 of the 12 studies, expert testimony significantly increased skepticism about eyewitness testimony, leading to a reduction in guilty verdicts and/or decreased belief in the evidence of eyewitnesses.

The $64,000 question is whether this increase in skepticism is a good or a bad thing. If jurors tend to believe too much in the accuracy of eyewitness testimony, it might be entirely appropriate that their skepticism should be increased. However, it would be undesirable if eyewitness expert testimony leads jurors to return not guilty verdicts even when the overall case against the defendant is strong. This issue was addressed by Leippe, Eisenstadt, Rauch, and Seib (2004), who considered the impact of expert testimony about eyewitness memory introduced towards the end of a murder-trial transcript followed by a reminder about this testimony in the judge's final instructions. The case involved a holdup at night that led to a fatal stabbing. Leippe et al. used three versions of the case in which the evidence against the defendant was very strong, moderately strong, or weak. In all three versions, the prosecution case depended in part on eyewitness testimony from a man who observed the crime from a bedroom window. In the very strong condition, DNA results indicated a 94% certainty that a blood sample taken from the defendant's jacket was that of the victim, there was clear evidence the defendant had been in a struggle (e.g. swollen eye, scraped knuckles), and the victim's wallet was found in a trash can on the block where the defendant lived.

The key findings related to the percentages of mock jurors who decided the defendant was guilty. The presence of expert testimony produced a fairly large reduction in guilty verdicts regardless of the strength of the case. Even when the overall case was very strong, expert testimony reduced guilty verdicts from 74% to 59%. It is certainly arguable that exposing mock jurors to expert testimony made them focus too much on possible inaccuracies in the eyewitness's evidence at the expense of the otherwise strong evidence against the defendant.

It is undeniable that real-life victims of a crime are generally in a much more emotional state than eyewitnesses watching a simulated crime under laboratory conditions. If (as many people believe) our memory is much better for emotionally upsetting events than for more neutral ones, then the memories of witnesses of real-life crimes should be much better than those of witnesses of simulated crimes. However, as we saw earlier in the chapter, there is evidence that high levels of anxiety and/or stress cause an impairment in eyewitness memory (Deffenbacher et al., 2004).

Other concerns about the use of eyewitness expert testimony in court cases were raised by Ebbesen and Konecni (1997). First, research findings on eyewitness memory are often inconsistent, and so there is no clear message that experts can honestly deliver. For example, Deffenbacher (1983) reviewed 21 studies concerned with the relationship between arousal and the accuracy of eyewitness memory. The findings from 10 studies suggested that high arousal *increased* eyewitness accuracy but the remaining 11 studies suggested that it *decreased* eyewitness accuracy.

Second, the accuracy of eyewitness memory depends on characteristics of eyewitnesses (e.g. their memory ability, their attention to detail, their susceptibility to stress, their age) as well as on aspects of the situation (e.g. exposure to misleading information, nature of the line-up). However, most research on eyewitness memory has focused on the situation and ignored individual differences among eyewitnesses.

Third, many of the findings obtained by researchers on eyewitness memory can be expressed in simple terms (e.g. "If the criminal has a weapon, then eyewitnesses are less likely to remember other information including the identity of the criminal"). However, the importance of any single factor (e.g. weapon focus) always depends on several other factors in the situation. For example, it seems probable that the extent of any weapon focus effect would depend greatly on the length of time involved—eyewitnesses who have several minutes to look at the criminal are likely to show less of a weapon focus effect than those who have only a few seconds. Such complexities are not studied very often and tend not to be included in eyewitness expert testimony.

Ebbesen and Konecni summarized the arguments against the value of research on eyewitness memory to the legal system as follows:

There is no direct evidence that the kinds of testimony offered by defense experts about factors that might affect eyewitness memory can improve the accuracy of jury decisions. Because the evidence is either inconsistent or insufficient in almost every area in which eyewitness experts testify and because there is no research that provides the experts, much less the jurors, with rules to use in translating the evidence to particular decisions in particular cases, we believe that eyewitness testimony is more prejudicial than probative [affording proof] and should not be allowed in court. **(Ebbesen & Konecni, 1997, p. 25)**

Laboratory findings are relevant!

In the previous section, we identified some of the more obvious differences between observers' experiences in the laboratory and in real life. What is of crucial importance is whether these differences have large and systematic effects on the accuracy of eyewitness memory. One way of obtaining relevant evidence is to compare eyewitness memory for both types of experience. Lindsay and Harvie (1988) had eyewitnesses watch an event via slide shows, video films, or live staged events. There were only small differences in accuracy of culprit identification across these three conditions, suggesting that artificial laboratory conditions don't lead to distortions in the findings obtained.

Ihlebaek, Løve, Eilertsen, and Magnussen (2003) made use of a staged robbery involving two robbers armed with handguns. In the live condition, the eyewitnesses were ordered repeatedly to "stay down." A video taken during the live condition was presented to eyewitnesses in the video condition. There were important similarities in memory in the two conditions. For example, participants in both conditions exaggerated the duration of the event, and the patterns of memory performance (i.e. what was well and poorly remembered) were similar. However, eyewitnesses in the video condition recalled more information than those in the live condition. They estimated the robbers' age, height, and weight more closely, and they also identified the robbers' weapons more accurately.

Ihlebaek et al.'s findings suggest that witnesses to real-life events are more inaccurate in their memories of those events than are those who observe the same events under laboratory conditions. This finding (if confirmed) is important. The implication is that the inaccuracies and distortions in eyewitness memory obtained under laboratory conditions provide an *underestimate* of eyewitnesses' memory deficiencies for real-life events. If so, it is legitimate to regard laboratory research as providing evidence of genuine relevance to the legal system.

Tollestrup et al. (1994) analyzed police records concerning the identifications by eyewitnesses to crimes involving fraud and robbery. What they discovered was that factors that have been found to be important in laboratory studies (e.g. exposure duration, weapon focus, retention interval) were also important in real-life crimes. Thus, for example, identification accuracy was higher when the eyewitness was exposed to the culprit for a relatively long period of time and when the interval of time between the crime and the initial questioning was short.

One of the arguments put forward in favor of the notion that eyewitness expert testimony should be presented in court cases is the assumption that jurors typically exaggerate the accuracy of eyewitnesses' memory for events they have observed. There have been several laboratory studies in which eyewitnesses observed a staged theft, provided testimony about it via cross-examination, and then tried to identify the thief from a photospread (see Leippe, 1995, for a review). Mock jurors then watched the videotaped testimony of an accurate or an inaccurate witness, and judged his/her accuracy. It is typically found that mock jurors cannot discriminate between accurate and inaccurate witnesses. More importantly in the present context, inaccurate witnesses are generally judged mistakenly to be accurate by 40–80% of the mock jurors.

Those who argue that eyewitness expert testimony should be presented in court cases often claim that most jurors are insensitive to the factors influencing the accuracy of eyewitness memory. Lindsay, Lim, Marando, and Cully (1986) used two versions of a burglary trial with mock jurors. In one version, the lighting was very good (broad daylight) and the eyewitness was exposed to the thief for more than 30 minutes. In the other version, the lighting was very poor (20 meters from a streetlight late at night) and the eyewitness saw the thief for only 5 seconds. These dramatic variations in witnessing conditions had no impact on the proportion of mock jurors reaching guilty verdicts.

The best way of reducing jurors' insensitivity to factors affecting eyewitness memory is by admitting expert testimony. Cutler, Penrod, and Dexter (1989) supplied relevant evidence in a study in which mock jurors viewed a realistic videotaped trial in which there was an armed robbery of a liquor store. The main evidence was the victim's identification of the defendant. The witnessing and identification conditions were good or poor. In the poor condition, the robber was disguised, he brandished a handgun, the identification took place 14 days after the robbery, and the lineup instructions were suggestive (the officer in charge didn't explicitly provide the witness with the option of not choosing anyone). In the good witnessing and identification condition, the robber was not disguised, his handgun was hidden throughout the robbery, the identification took place 2 days after the robbery, and the lineup instructions were not suggestive.

Cutler et al. (1989) found that the quality of the witnessing and identification conditions had a significant impact on jurors' judgments as to the accuracy of the witness's identification when they were presented with eyewitness expert testimony but had practically no effect when this expert testimony was not presented. In addition, the verdict was much more influenced by the witnessing and identification conditions when expert testimony was presented than when it was not. Thus, jurors not exposed to eyewitness expert testimony were fairly insensitive to the quality of the witnessing and identification conditions to which the eyewitness was exposed.

Another approach can be taken when trying to assess the usefulness of the knowledge of eyewitness memory obtained by psychologists in laboratory studies. What happens is that eyewitnesses view a simulated crime and their subsequent testimony about that crime is videotaped. Simulated jurors then view the videotapes and judge the witness's accuracy. After this, half of the jurors hear expert testimony based on laboratory findings concerning factors that influence eyewitness identification, whereas the other half do not. Finally, all of the jurors reach a decision. The typical finding is that jurors who have heard the expert testimony make more accurate decisions than those who have not (see Penrod & Cutler, 1995, for a review). That is fairly direct evidence for the value of laboratory studies on eyewitness testimony.

There is an important final point to be made: When eyewitness experts testify in court, they discuss only those findings from eyewitness research that are generally agreed to be well established. There could be genuine concerns if experts related these findings to the specific eyewitness involved in a court case, for example, by arguing that his/her memory is untrustworthy. In fact, however, eyewitness experts are explicitly forbidden to do this, as it is entirely up to the jurors to decide what (if any) credence they should place on the testimony of an eyewitness.

The case in favor of permitting laboratory findings obtained by eyewitness researchers to be presented in court was summarized by Leippe (1995):

The knowledge [from eyewitness research] is not perfect, and the jury decisions it influences will not perfectly serve justice without exception. Perfection has never been a reachable goal of any justice system, however. Improving the batting average of just decisions on a fair playing field is a more sensible goal, and embracing a careful eyewitness expert testimony as a judiciously applied option will help reach that goal.

It seems reasonable to conclude that the evidence obtained by eyewitness researchers is relevant and should be presented to juries. The single strongest argument in favor of this conclusion is that the findings from police records and from naturalistic research are generally very much in agreement with those obtained under typical laboratory conditions. There is also convincing evidence that most jurors can be unduly influenced by the testimony of eyewitnesses (especially confident ones), and eyewitness expert testimony can assist in making jurors properly skeptical of eyewitnesses' memories.

In spite of the value of eyewitness research, there is still much to do. We have identified many of the factors influencing eyewitness memory, but we lack a good understanding of *why* they are important and *how* they interact with each other.

SUMMARY

We generally believe that we perceive nearly everything in the visual environment in front of us. However, our frequent inability to detect changes in that environment shows that our belief is wrong. Our memories are sometimes distorted in the direction of remembering what we expected to see rather than what actually occurred. Eyewitness memories are fragile and can easily be distorted by postevent information (e.g. misleading questions) producing retroactive interference. Eyewitness memories can also be distorted by pre-event information (proactive interference). An eyewitness's confidence is often a poor predictor of the accuracy of his/her memory for an event.

Most people are not very good at remembering faces, and this is especially the case when the other person is in disguise. The processing of faces differs from that of other objects in that there is more emphasis on holistic processing and less on processing of details. Eyewitnesses are sometimes better at remembering faces than the exact situation in which they saw the face. This can lead to unconscious transference, in which eyewitnesses mistakenly identify a familiar face as belonging to the criminal. The cross-race effect probably occurs mainly because we do not process the faces of outgroup members as thoroughly as those of ingroup members.

Eyewitnesses sometimes attend so closely to the criminal's weapon that their memory for his/her features is impaired; this is known as weapon focus. However, the evidence for weapon focus is less strong with real-life crimes than with simulated laboratory ones.

We can improve the accuracy of eyewitnesses' identification performance on lineups by warning them that the culprit might not be present. Another useful strategy is to use sequential lineups rather than simultaneous ones.

Eyewitnesses remember more information about an event if questioned by means of a cognitive interview rather than by a traditional police interview. Cognitive interviews are based on the notion that memory is best when there is a close match between the context in which the crime was committed and the interview context. In addition, it is assumed that memory traces contain various kinds of information, and so information about a crime can be retrieved using various different approaches.

There are many differences between eyewitnesses' experiences when observing a crime in the laboratory and in real life. In the laboratory, the event is typically observed by eyewitnesses rather than victims, there is little or no stress involved, and eyewitnesses have only a few seconds to study the culprit. By contrast, in real life the event is generally observed by the victim, there may be extremely high levels of stress, and on average eyewitnesses and victims observe the culprit for between 5 and 10 minutes. However, the factors that have been found to influence the accuracy of eyewitness memory in the laboratory also do so with more naturalistic studies and with real-life crimes. Jurors who are informed of the findings from eyewitness research tend to be more sensitive to factors influencing eyewitness memory, and are more skeptical about the likely accuracy of what eyewitnesses claim to remember.

FURTHER READING

- Ebbesen, E. B., & Konecni, V. J. (1997). Eyewitness memory research: Probative vs. prejudicial value. *The International Digest of Human Behavior, Science, and the Law, 5,* 2–28. Potential problems with allowing eyewitness experts to testify in court are discussed in detail.

- Fisher, R. P. (1999). Probing knowledge structures. In D. Gopher & A. Koriat (Eds.), *Attention and performance XVII: Cognitive regulation of performance: Interaction of theory and application.* Cambridge, MA: MIT Press. The strengths and limitations of the cognitive interview as a technique for obtaining information from eyewitnesses are discussed in detail.

- Lindsay, R. C. L., Ross, D. F., Read, J. D., & Toglia, M. P. (2007). *The handbook of eyewitness psychology: Volume II: Memory for people.* Mahwah, NJ: Lawrence Erlbaum Associates. This book is both comprehensive and up-to-date, and contains contributions from the world's leading experts on eyewitness memory for people.

- Loftus, E. F. (2004). Memories of things unseen. *Current Directions in Psychological Science, 13,* 145–147. Some of the reasons why eyewitness testimony is fallible are considered in this article.

- Toglia, M. P., Read, J. D., Ross, D. F., & Lindsay, R. C. L. (2007). *The handbook of eyewitness psychology: Volume I: Memory for events.* Mahwah, NJ: Lawrence Erlbaum Associates. This book is an invaluable source of up-to-date information on eyewitness memory for events with contributions from leading researchers in several countries.

- Wells, G. L., & Olson, E. A. (2003). Eyewitness testimony. *Annual Review of Psychology, 54,* 277–295. This article provides a useful overview of several factors influencing the accuracy of eyewitness identification.

CHAPTER 15

PROSPECTIVE MEMORY

Michael W. Eysenck

Nearly everyone has experienced acute embarrassment on occasion when they have been introducing two people to each other and they suddenly realize that they have forgotten the name of one of them. Frustration is another emotion we can experience when forgetting occurs, as when a student sitting an examination goes blank and can't remember what he/she knows about a topic. These are failures of **retrospective memory**, which involves remembering events, words, and so on from the past typically when deliberating trying to do so.

There is an important distinction between retrospective memory and **prospective memory**. This type of memory involves remembering to carry out intended actions without being instructed to do so. Failures of prospective memory (absent-mindedness when action is required) can also be embarrassing, as when you completely forget that you had arranged to meet a friend at a coffee shop. Freud (1901, p. 157), in his usual over-the-top style, argued that the motive behind many of our missed appointments "is an unusually large amount of unavowed contempt for other people." However, failures of prospective memory are sometimes much more serious than forgetting an appointment, and can result in serious injury or death. For example, Einstein and McDaniel gave this tragic example of what can happen when prospective memory fails:

After a change in his usual routine, an adoring father forgot to turn toward the daycare center and instead drove his usual route to work at the university. Several hours later, his infant son, who had been quietly asleep in the back seat, was dead. (Einstein & McDaniel, 2005, p. 286)

Failures of prospective memory also play an important part in many aircraft accidents. For example, in the mid-1990s a DC-9 landed in Houston without the landing gear in place. The crew failed to notice that the gear wasn't down because they hadn't switched the hydraulic pumps to high. This failure in prospective memory occurred because the crew had been concentrating on coping with an unstabilized approach to the landing strip. The role played by prospective memory in fatal aircraft accidents is discussed more fully a little later in the chapter.

As Baddeley (1997) pointed out, prospective and retrospective memory differ in various ways in addition to their respective emphasis on future versus past time orientation. Retrospective memory generally involves remembering *what* we know about

---

KEY TERMS

Retrospective memory: memory for people, words, and events encountered or experienced in the past.

Prospective memory: Remembering to carry out some intended action in the absence of any explicit reminder to do so; see retrospective memory.

something and can be high in information content. By contrast, prospective memory typically focuses on *when* to do something, and has a low information content. In addition, prospective memory is of relevance to the plans or goals we form for our daily activities in a way that is not true of retrospective memory. A further difference between prospective and retrospective memory is that there are generally more external cues available in the case of retrospective memory (e.g. someone asking you a question about the past).

Marsh, Hicks, and Landau (1998) addressed the issue of how well people's prospective memories cope with everyday life. They found that people reported an average of 15 plans for the forthcoming week, of which about 25% were not completed. Most of these noncompletions were due to rescheduling and reprioritization rather than to forgetting; indeed, only 3% of the plans that had been made were forgotten.

It is often argued that stress and anxiety cause us to become absent-minded and thus to produce failures of prospective memory. The limited evidence that is available tends to support that argument. For example, Cockburn and Smith (1994) assessed prospective memory by asking participants to respond to hearing a timer by asking when they would see the experimenter again. To maximize the probability of forgetting, the experimenters made sure there was a considerable delay between the participants hearing the instructions and hearing the timer. There were significantly more failures of prospective memory among the highly anxious participants than among those less anxious.

Harris and Menzies (1999) asked their participants to generate semantic associates to 60 spoken words and to remember those words while at the same time performing a prospective memory task (placing an "x" beside items belonging to the categories of "clothing" or "body parts"). Participants who were more anxious performed worse on the prospective memory task than did those who were less anxious.

Of all the groups within society, one that might well argue that their prospective memory is the worst consists of individuals suffering from obsessive-compulsive disorder. Many patients with this disorder have so little confidence in their own prospective memories (and such an inflated sense of personal responsibility) that they repeatedly check that they have locked their front door, that the gas stove has been turned off, and so on. In spite of all this repeated checking, obsessive-compulsive patients tend to be uncertain whether they have actually performed the actions they intended to perform.

The most obvious explanation for the behavior of obsessive-compulsive patients is simply that they have a general memory deficit that includes prospective memory (Tallis, 1995). In other words, their poor prospective memory ability leads them to engage in repeated checking. Intriguingly, this does *not* seem to be correct, or at best is only a small part of what is involved. Instead of poor prospective memory making obsessionals engage in excessive checking, it is more true to argue that excessive checking leads to poor prospective

It is possible that excessive checking followed by repetition of an action leads to poor prospective memory! Obsessionals may be uncertain, for example, whether they have washed their hands today, or one of the many times in the past.

memory! How can that be so? Suppose that every day when you leave your home, you go back several times to check whether you have locked the front door. As a consequence, you would have stored away numerous memories of checking your front door, and would remember very clearly that you have checked it hundreds or thousands of times. However (and this is the central point), you might be unsure whether you have checked your front door *today* as well as numerous times in the past.

Evidence that excessive checking can lead even nonobsessional individuals to doubt whether they have carried out intended actions was reported by van den Hout and Kindt (2004). They developed an interactive computer animation in which some university students (the experimental group) were told to check repeatedly a virtual gas stove with six gas rings. On each of 22 trials, they were told which three gas rings to turn on and then turn off. The control group carried out a similar task with light bulbs, but had one final trial involving gas rings. The two groups showed the same level of accuracy when unexpectedly asked to recall which gas rings they had turned on and off on the final trial. However, the experimental group reported that their memory for what happened on that trial was less vivid and detailed than that of the control group, and they also had less confidence in their memory.

Radomsky, Gilchrist, and Dussault (2006) pointed out that van den Hout and Kindt (2004) had used a rather artificial computer-based task, and this might have influenced the findings. However, they carried out a similar study using a real kitchen stove and a real kitchen sink and obtained very similar findings to those of van den Hout and Kindt (2004). The take-home message is that repeated checking in order to be certain that a prospective memory task has been carried out can be counterproductive. Indeed, it can have the apparently paradoxical effect of *decreasing* people's confidence that the task has been performed.

ASSESSING PROSPECTIVE MEMORY

How good are your retrospective and prospective memories? You can find out by completing the questionnaire in Box 15.1 (this has been taken from Crawford, Smith, Maylor, Della Sala, & Logie, 2003).

So far we have implied that prospective memory and retrospective memory are very different from each other. However, that is an exaggeration of the true state of affairs. For example, when Crawford et al. (2003) analyzed the data from their questionnaire, they found a general memory factor as well as distinct prospective and retrospective memory factors. In the real world, remembering and forgetting often involve a mixture of prospective and retrospective memory. For example, suppose you have agreed to buy various goods at the grocery store for yourself and the friends with whom you share an apartment. Two things need to happen if you are to return to the apartment with all the necessary goods. First, you have to remember your intention of going to the store (prospective memory). Even if you remember to go to the store, you then have to remember precisely what it was you had agreed to buy (retrospective memory).

Let us return briefly to the Prospective and Retrospective Memory Questionnaire (PRMQ) in Box 15.1. To show that a questionnaire is valid (i.e. measures what it claims to be measuring) it is important to show that what people *say* on the questionnaire corresponds to their actual *behavior*. This issue was investigated by Mäntylä (2003). In his first experiment, women who claimed to have significant problems with prospective memory were compared against a control consisting of women not reporting such problems. The former group scored higher than the controls on the PRMQ, especially on items relating to prospective memory. The two groups were then given various tasks to assess their prospective and retrospective memory. For example, one

Box 15.1 The Prospective and Retrospective Memory Questionnaire (PRMQ)

1. Do you decide to do something in a few minutes' time and then forget to do it?

2. Do you fail to recognize a place you have visited before?

3. Do you fail to do something you were supposed to do a few minutes later even though it's there in front of you, like take a pill or turn off the kettle?

4. Do you forget something that you were told a few minutes before?

5. Do you forget appointments if you are not prompted by someone else or by a reminder such as a calendar or diary?

6. Do you fail to recognize a character in a radio or television show from scene to scene?

7. Do you fail to buy something you planned to buy, like a birthday card, even when you see the shop?

8. Do you fail to recall things that have happened to you in the last few days?

9. Do you repeat the same story to the same person on different occasions?

10. Do you intend to take something with you, before leaving a room or going out, but minutes later leave it behind, even though it's there in front of you?

11. Do you mislay something that you have just put down, like a magazine or glasses?

12. Do you fail to mention or give something to a visitor that you were asked to pass on?

13. Do you look at something without realizing you have seen it moments before?

14. If you tried to contact a friend or relative who was out, would you forget to try again later?

15. Do you forget what you watched on television the previous day?

16. Do you forget to tell something you had meant to mention a few minutes ago?

Retrospective memory items: 2, 4, 6, 8, 9, 11, 13, and 15

Prospective memory items: 1, 3, 5, 7, 10, 12, 14, and 16

On the basis of administering the PRMQ to 551 people, Crawford et al. (2003) reported the following statistics (approximately 68% of participants had scores within 1 standard deviation of the mean):

- Prospective memory: mean = 20.18; standard deviation = 4.91
- Retrospective memory: mean = 18.69; standard deviation = 4.98
- Total score: mean = 38.88; standard deviation = 9.15

From Crawford et al. (2003). Copyright © Psychology Press.

of the tests of prospective memory required participants to remind the experimenter to sign a paper very shortly after the experimenter had told them the session was over. As predicted, women reporting problems with prospective memory performed worse than controls on the prospective memory tasks; the two groups did not differ on the retrospective memory tasks.

In a second experiment, Mäntylä (2003) considered the relationship between scores on the PRMQ and retrospective memory assessed by word recall, face recognition, and word recall. Surprisingly, retrospective memory performance was not predicted by scores on

the retrospective memory scale of the PRMQ. This suggests that most people do not have an accurate sense of how good (or poor) their retrospective memory actually is.

WHY DO PLANE CRASHES OCCUR?

Fatal accidents involving aircraft can occur for many reasons. However, psychologists are far more interested in those accidents that are due to pilot error than those due to mechanical failures. Detailed information on the causes of 1459 fatal aircraft accidents is contained in the PlaneCrashInfo.com accident database. According to this database, 53% of all fatal accidents were due to pilot error, 7% to non-pilot human error, 20% to mechanical failure, 11% to bad weather, 8% to sabotage, and 1% to other causes.

Dismukes and Nowinski (in press) give the following concrete example of human error causing a fatal aircraft accident. At Los Angeles International airport at dusk one evening in 1991, a tower controller cleared one aircraft to position and hold on runway 24L while she cleared other aircraft to cross the other end of the runway. Unfortunately, there were various communication delays because one of the other aircraft was on the wrong radio frequency. In addition, visibility was poor because of the haze and glare. The tower controller forgot to clear the first aircraft to take off but did clear another aircraft to land on runway 24L. This aircraft crashed into the stationary plane on that runway, destroying both planes and killing 34 people. It is highly probable that the tower controller could have recalled what she had planned to do with the holding aircraft (retrospective memory) if she had been asked after the accident occurred. The problem was in forgetting to carry out that planned intention at the right time, and was thus a failure of prospective memory.

Dismukes and Nowinski (in press) carried out three studies to identify those airline flight operations that most clearly require prospective memory. In the first of these studies, they considered in detail the Boeing 737. They observed numerous flights from the cockpit jump-seat, they watched flight simulation training, and they read carefully through the written operating procedures. In the second study, they analyzed reports on the 19 major airline accidents between the years 1990 and 2001 that were attributed to crew errors. In the third study, they sampled 20% of all air carrier reports that had been submitted to the Aviation Safety Reporting System (ASRS) over a 1-year period in order to study in detail those involving memory failures.

Dismukes and Nowinski's (in press) study showed that although airline pilots have excellent knowledge and memory of all the operations needed to fly a plane, their training provides less protection against failures of prospective memory.

The most striking finding emerged from the ASRS study. Dismukes and Nowinski (in press) uncovered 75 reports in which it was possible to identify clearly the nature of the memory failure that had caused the incident or accident. In 74 cases, there was a failure of prospective memory, with only one case involving retrospective memory! Why were there practically no failures of retrospective memory? The main reason is that airline pilots receive lengthy and demanding training. As a consequence, they have excellent knowledge and memory of all the operations needed to fly a plane. Unfortunately, however, their training provides less protection against failures of prospective memory.

Dismukes and Nowinski (in press) discovered five main types of situation associated with flying an airplane in which significant demands are placed on prospective memory:

1. *Episodic tasks*: Pilots have to remember to perform later a task that is not typically performed at the time (e.g. reporting when the plane passes below 10,000 feet).
2. *Habitual tasks*: Pilots and crew need to remember to perform habitual tasks in the correct order. Note that approximately 100 actions are needed to prepare a large aircraft for departure.

3. *Atypical actions substituted for habitual ones*: Crews need to deviate from standard procedures in certain circumstances (e.g. heavy air traffic; unusual weather conditions).

4. *Interrupted tasks*: Pilots and crew have to remember to return to a task after they have been interrupted by flight attendants, mechanics, or jump-seat riders.

5. *Interleaving tasks*: Pilots and crew often have to carry out two (or more) tasks together. For example, the first officer might be re-programming the flight management system, monitoring the plane's taxiing, and handling radio communications at the same time.

Why do pilots and crew exhibit failures of prospective memory when flying aircraft? Pilots and crew typically form an explicit intention to carry out a given operation later in the sequence of operations. They then turn their attention to other tasks, relying on some prompt or cue to remind them to carry out the given operation at the appropriate time. This strategy works well under normal circumstances. However, problems can arise when there are deviations from the typical sequence of operations, as happens when atypical actions have to be substituted for habitual ones or when pilots are interrupted.

For example, when a plane is due to land shortly, the crew is generally instructed to switch radio frequencies to tower frequency and to contact the tower immediately by approach control. This instruction provides a very specific cue or prompt. However, crews are sometimes instructed by approach controllers to delay switching their radios to tower frequency until the aircraft reaches a specified distance from the airport. The ASRS data indicated that 12 out of 13 landings that occurred without tower clearance occurred when the normal prompt was missing.

Dismukes and Nowinski (in press) claimed that pilots are most likely to show failures of prospective memory when they are interrupted while carrying out a plan of action.

Why is this? They argued that interruptions often occur so rapidly and so forcefully that individuals do not think explicitly about producing a new plan or intention to deal with the changed situation. Evidence that interruptions can seriously impair prospective memory was obtained by Dodhia and Dismukes (2005). Participants answered questions arranged in blocks, each of which contained different types of questions (e.g. math, vocabulary, analogies). If an interrupting block of questions was presented before they had finished answering all the questions in a given block, they were told to return to the interrupted block after completing the interrupting block.

How successful were the participants at remembering to return to the interrupted block of questions? The findings are shown in Figure 15.1. When there was no explicit prompt to return to the interrupted block, only 48% of the participants resumed the interrupted block. Some participants were given a reminder lasting 4 seconds at the time of the interruption ("Please remember to return to the block that was just interrupted"); 65% of them resumed the interrupted block. Perhaps surprisingly, 65% of those participants who received no reminder but who spent 4 seconds staring at a blank screen immediately after being interrupted, resumed the interrupted block. There were two further conditions. In one condition, there was simply a delay of approximately 10 seconds between the end of the interrupting task and the start of the next block. In the other condition, there was a delay of the same length, but participants were given a reminder "End of interruption"). The percentages of participants resuming the interrupted task were 88% and 90%, respectively.

The above findings indicate that the provision of explicit reminders is not always very effective when people are interrupted while carrying out a task. It is important that people have a few seconds in which to formulate a new plan when an interruption changes the situation, and it is also important to have a few seconds at the end of the interruption to retrieve the intention of returning to the

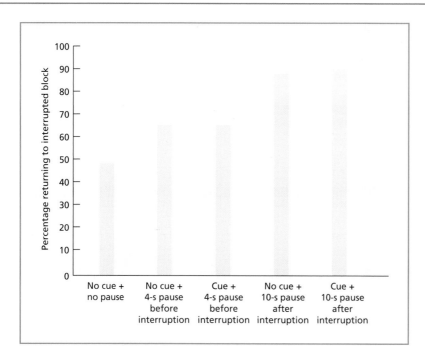

Figure 15.1 Percentage of participants returning to an interrupted task as a function of cuing and pause duration before or after interruption. Based on data in Dodhia and Dismukes (2005).

interrupted task. The implication for everyday life is as follows: when interrupted, pause for a few seconds to develop a new explicit plan that will enable you to carry out all the actions you intend to carry out.

TYPES OF PROSPECTIVE MEMORY

There are numerous prospective memory tasks, each of which has its own special features. However, we can assign most of such tasks to two categories based on the cues indicating that a given action should be performed. First, there is **event-based prospective memory**, which involves remembering to perform an action in the appropriate circumstances (e.g. passing on a message when you see someone). Second, there is **time-based prospective memory**, which involves remembering to perform a given action at a particular time (e.g. meeting your friend at Starbuck's at 4.00 p.m.).

Sellen, Lowie, Harris, and Wilkins (1997) compared time-based and event-based

prospective memory in a work environment. Participants were equipped with badges containing buttons, and were told to press their button at prespecified times (time-based task) or when they were in a prespecified place (event-based task). Prospective memory performance was better on the event-based task than on the time-based task (52% vs. 33%, respectively). This was the case even though the participants given the time-based task spent more of their time thinking about it.

How can we account for the findings of Sellen et al. (1997)? One of the key differences between the two tasks was that the intended action was more likely to be triggered by

KEY TERMS

Event-based prospective memory: A form of prospective memory in which some event (e.g. seeing a grocery store) provides the cue to perform a given action (e.g. buying some fruit).
Time-based prospective memory: A form of prospective memory in which time is the cue indicating that a given action needs to be performed.

external cues on the event-based task than on the time-based one. This greater importance for participants given the time-based task to generate their own cues might help to explain why they spent more of their time thinking about it than did those given the event-based task. It seems reasonable to assume that external cues generally act as more powerful reminders that an action needs to be performed than do internal ones. If this is the case, then we might expect that individuals should find it easier to perform event-based than time-based prospective memory tasks.

Hicks, Marsh, and Cook (2005) argued that the notion that event-based tasks are easy and time-based ones are difficult is too simple. According to them, the specificity of the prospective memory task is more important than its type (event-based vs. time-based). They tested this hypothesis in an experiment in which there was a central lexical decision task (i.e. deciding as rapidly as possible whether each letter string formed a word). There were four conditions. There were two event-based tasks, one of which was well specified (detect the words "nice" and "hit") and the other of which was poorly specified (detect animal words). There were also two time-based tasks, one of which was well specified (respond after 4 and after 8 minutes) and the other of which was poorly specified (respond after 3–5 minutes and after 7–9 minutes). The extent to which these various prospective memory tasks slowed down performance on the lexical decision task was taken as a measure of how demanding they were, which is reasonable in view of people's limited processing capacity.

What did Hicks et al. (2005) find? As can be seen in Figure 15.2, the adverse effects of event-based tasks on lexical decision times were less than those of time-based tasks. In addition, poorly specified tasks (whether event-based or time-based) disrupted lexical decision performance more than did well-specified tasks. It thus appears that more processing resources are required when an individual's intentions are poorly specified than when they are well specified.

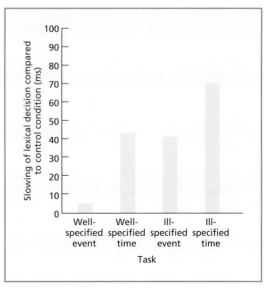

Figure 15.2 The effects of specification specificity (well-specified vs. ill-specified) and task type (event-based vs. time-based) on slowing of lexical decision time. Based on data in Hicks et al. (2005).

As well as the distinction between event-based and time-based prospective memory tasks, we can also distinguish between two types of event-based tasks: immediate-execute and delayed-execute tasks (McDaniel, Einstein, Graham, & Rall, 2004). The great majority of laboratory studies have used immediate-execute tasks in which participants are free to respond as soon as a relevant cue is detected. However, in the real world, we are often confronted by delays and interruptions that prevent us from carrying out an intended action when the relevant cue is presented. For example, we saw earlier that many airplane incidents and accidents occur when pilots are disrupted while preparing to carry out some action. Delayed-execute prospective memory tasks are ones in which circumstances prevent people from responding immediately to the cue for action.

McDaniel et al. (2004) instructed participants that a brief presentation of a red screen on their computer meant that they should press the slash key (/) as soon as they had finished their current task. On some trials, the current task was interrupted by another task, which resembles what happens all too often in the real world. Performance on the prospective memory task (pressing the slash key) was not affected by the length of the delay (between 5 and 40 seconds). However, performance was significantly worse when there was a 40-second delay involving interruption than when there was the same-length delay without interruption (79% correct responses vs. 94% correct, respectively). Thus, prospective memory performance sometimes suffers when there is a delay in execution. However, the good news is that a reminder (a small blue dot in the lower right-hand corner of the screen presented briefly after each red screen) completely eliminated the adverse effects of interruption.

AGING AND PROSPECTIVE MEMORY

Imagine an elderly person whose memory is not as good as it used to be. What do you think would be likely to be his/her main memory problems? Many people would guess that his/her most important memory problems would involve absent-mindedness and failures of prospective memory (e.g. not turning up for an appointment with the doctor; see also discussion in Chapter 13). In fact, this does *not* seem to be the case. Henry, MacLeod, Phillips, and Crawford (2004) carried out meta-analyses in which they compared the effects of aging on prospective and retrospective memory. In contrast to what common sense might suggest, they found that aging was associated more negatively with performance on free recall (a measure of retrospective memory) than with performance on tests of prospective memory.

Henry et al. (2004) carried out a further meta-analysis to compare the effects of aging on time-based and event-based prospective memory tasks. The adverse effects of aging were comparable on these two types of prospective memory. More interestingly, the effects of aging on event-based tasks were much greater when the overall processing

demands on participants were high than when they were low. For example, these demands are higher when the cue requiring participants to respond is nonspecific (e.g. any member of a large category) than when it is highly specific (e.g. a particular word). There is much evidence that older adults perform less well than younger ones on demanding tasks involving working memory (see Zacks, Hasher, & Li, 2000, for a review), and this helps to explain why they struggle to perform event-based prospective memory tasks when overall processing demands are high.

Overall processing demands are also important in time-based prospective memory, as was shown by Martin and Schumann-Hengsteler (2001) in a study on young adults (mean age 24 years) and older adults (mean age 69 years). The prospective memory task involved changing the protocol (observation) sheet every 3 minutes. The background task was the *Mastermind* game, which involves working out the colors and positions of a set of colored pins hidden from the participant's view. Three levels of complexity of the *Mastermind* task were produced by varying the number of pins and the informativeness of feedback. The prospective memory findings were striking (Figure 15.3). The performance

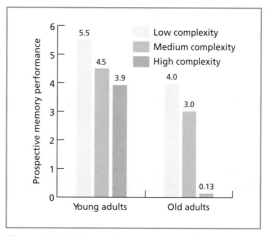

Figure 15.3 Prospective memory performance in young and older adults as a function of central task complexity. From Martin and Schumann-Hengsteler (2001). Copyright © Psychology Press.

of the older adults was greatly influenced by the processing demands of the *Mastermind* task; indeed, nearly all of them totally failed to perform the prospective memory task at all in the high-complexity condition. By contrast, there was a much smaller impact of *Mastermind* task complexity on the prospective memory performance of the younger adults.

There is a twist in this tale of aging and its effects on prospective memory. Before we become too concerned about older adults' ability to remember to carry out their intentions, we need to consider how they cope in everyday life rather than only in the laboratory. Some studies have been naturalistic, for example, assessing prospective memory by asking participants to telephone the experimenter from their home at specified times or by asking them to attend appointments. What emerges here is that older adults perform much *better* than younger ones on time-based and event-based prospective memory tasks, especially the former (see Henry et al., 2004, for a review). We don't know for sure *why* this happens. However, it seems likely that older adults devote more time to planning how they will remember to perform the tasks and suffer from fewer distractions.

What can be done to improve the prospective memory of older adults in situations in which it is poor? One effective approach involves the use of implementation intentions, which are detailed plans designed to ensure that a current goal is achieved (see Chapter 16). In a study by Chasteen, Park, and Schwarz (2001), older adults with a mean age of 71 years remembered words and pressed the zero key whenever a particular background pattern was presented. In addition, they had to perform the prospective memory task of writing down the day of the week on every sheet of paper they received during the course of the experiment. Participants in the implementation intention condition pictured themselves writing the day of the week and said out loud that they intended to write the day of the week on every sheet of paper. These participants performed the prospective memory task 57% of

the time compared to only 22% in the control condition.

THEORETICAL PERSPECTIVES

Various theorists have tried to identify the processes underlying prospective memory. One of the most influential approaches is the preparatory attentional and memory processes (PAM) theory (Smith & Bayen, 2005). According to the PAM theory, two kinds of process are always involved in successful prospective memory performance. First, there is a monitoring process, which starts when an individual forms an intention and is maintained until the required action is performed. Monitoring makes use of capacity-consuming processes such as those involved in attention. Second, there is an involvement of retrospective memory processes. These processes are needed to discriminate between prospective memory targets and nontargets and in the recollection of the intended action. In essence, retrospective memory is needed to ensure we remember *what* it is that we are supposed to be doing in the future, and the monitoring process is needed so that we perform the required action *when* the appropriate circumstances occur.

One of the main predictions from the PAM theory is that performance on a prospective memory task should be superior when participants can devote their full attentional and other resources to the task than when they cannot. There is much support for this prediction. McDaniel, Robinson-Riegler, and Einstein (1998) required participants to perform a prospective memory task under full or divided attention. In the latter condition, participants listened for three odd numbers in a row as well as performing the prospective memory task. Prospective memory performance was much better with full attention than with divided attention, indicating that attentional processes were needed on the prospective memory task (Figure 15.4). This finding is

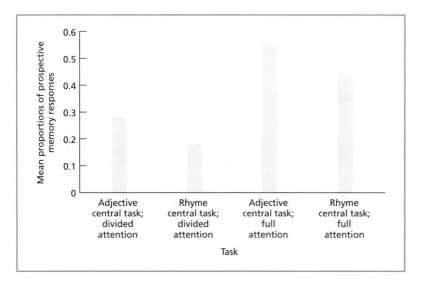

Figure 15.4 Prospective memory performance as a function of central task (generate adjectives or rhymes for list words) and attention (divided vs. full). Based on data in McDaniel et al. (1998).

consistent with everyday experience. Herrmann and Gruneberg (1993) asked people to record failures of prospective memory in their everyday lives. They were most likely to forget to do things when having a conversation or when preoccupied with some other concern.

Are prospective-memory tasks attentionally demanding even when no target stimuli requiring responses are being presented? Smith (2003) addressed this issue. The main task was lexical decision, which, as we have seen, is a task that involves deciding as rapidly as possible whether each in a series of letter strings forms a word. The prospective memory task (performed by half of the participants) involved pressing a button whenever a target word was presented. The key findings relate to performance on trials on which a target word was *not* presented. On those trials, the lexical decision was much slower for those participants performing the prospective memory task than for those not doing it (1061 ms vs. 726 ms). This finding means that a prospective memory task can utilize processing resources (and so impair performance on another task) even when no target stimuli are presented.

We can test the prediction that prospective memory tasks require the use of attentional processes by comparing individuals low and high in attentional capacity. Smith and Bayen

(2005) used a measure of working memory capacity as an approximate measure of attentional capacity to do precisely this. In their first experiment, they found that individuals with high working-memory capacity responded correctly to 88% of targets on a prospective memory task compared to only 69% for those low in working-memory capacity. In their second experiment, the primary task that had to be performed at the same time as the prospective memory task was made more difficult. This reduced performance on the prospective memory task. However, prospective memory performance was still much better among those high in working-memory capacity than those low in working-memory capacity (74% vs. 49%, respectively).

According to the PAM theory, successful prospective memory performance involves effective preparatory attentional processes and efficient retrospective memory to remember precisely what is required on the prospective-memory task. In the above experiments, Smith and Bayen (2005) found that those low and high in working-memory capacity differed in the effectiveness of their attentional processes but were comparable in retrospective memory processes.

We have seen that the PAM theory has received a reasonable measure of support.

However, the notion that we *always* use preparatory attentional processes when trying to remember to perform some action in the future seems rather implausible. After all, it often seems as if an intention to perform a predetermined action simply "pops" into our minds. Evidence supporting that viewpoint was reported by Reese and Cherry (2002) in a prospective memory study. They interrupted participants at various points during the task and asked them what they were thinking about. Only 2% of the time did they report thinking about the prospective memory task. This finding doesn't seem to fit with the notion that we maintain preparatory attentional processes constantly between the time of forming an intention to perform some action and the execution of that action. However, preparatory attentional processes might operate outside the focus of attention and so are often not readily reportable.

Einstein and McDaniel (2005) disputed the notion that successful prospective memory performance always involves active and capacity-consuming monitoring. They argued that we can sometimes perform prospective memory tasks automatically without the need for active monitoring. According to their multiprocess theory, various cognitive processes (including attentional processes) can be used to perform prospective-memory tasks. However, the detection of cues for response on a prospective-memory task will typically be automatic (and thus not involve the use of attentional processes) when at least one of the following conditions is fulfilled:

1. The cue and the to-be-performed target action are highly associated.
2. The cue is conspicuous or salient.
3. The ongoing processing on another task being performed at the same time as the prospective-memory task directs attention to the relevant aspects of the cue.

The good news for multiprocess theory is that the processing demands of a prospective-memory task do seem to depend on the three factors identified above (see Einstein & McDaniel, 2005, for a review). The bad news is that even prospective-memory tasks, which should—theoretically—be performed automatically and without monitoring, nevertheless seem to involve small (although sometimes nonsignificant) costs. Einstein, McDaniel, Thomas, Mayfield, Shank, Morrisette, and Breneiser (2005) explained these findings by assuming that some people engage in monitoring on simple prospective-memory tasks whereas others perform these tasks automatically. They tested this explanation by carrying out the following experiment. Participants were presented with sentences such as:

The warrior's armor makes him —— to any blows that he may undergo in battle.

IMPERVIOUS.

Their main task was to decide whether the final word in capital letters correctly completed the blank in the sentence. This task was sometimes performed on its own and sometimes performed at the same time as a prospective memory task. This involved detecting a target word (e.g. *medicine*) occurring anywhere in the sentence.

Einstein et al. (2005) found that 56 out of 104 participants performed the main task more slowly when it was combined with the prospective memory task, suggesting that they might have engaged in monitoring on the latter task. However, 44 participants performed the main task as least as quickly when it was combined with the prospective memory task as when it was performed on its own. These participants apparently did not engage in capacity-consuming monitoring while performing the prospective-memory task. In spite of this lack of monitoring, these participants performed the prospective-memory task very well. They detected 93% of the targets, which is very similar to the 95% detection rate showed by participants who were monitoring. Thus, a substantial proportion of people can perform at least some prospective-memory tasks in an automatic fashion without using monitoring.

Einstein et al. (2005) found another way of comparing the PAM theory and the multiprocess theory. Here is what happened on each trial of their Experiment 5:

1. A target item was presented for the prospective memory task.
2. Seven items were rated for imagery.
3. Lexical decisions (word vs. nonword) were made for 18 items.
4. Seven additional items were rated for imagery.

Participants had to press a key whenever they detected the target word (prospective-memory task) while performing the imagery rating task. However (and this is the most important part of the experiment), participants were explicitly told to ignore the prospective-memory task while performing the lexical-decision task.

Of central theoretical interest was to see what happened when the target word on the prospective-memory task was presented while participants were carrying out the lexical-decision task. According to the PAM theory, there should have been no intention to perform the prospective-memory task. As a result, there should have been no deliberate monitoring, and so the presentation of the target word should not have disrupted performance on the lexical-decision task. According to the multiprocess theory, by contrast, automatic processes occur without intention. As a consequence, presentation of the target word should have activated the processes involved in the prospective-memory task and this in turn would produce disruption of lexical-decision performance. There was a significant slowing of 55 ms on the lexical-decision task to prospective-memory targets compared to control items, a finding that is more consistent with the multiprocess view.

In sum, there is general agreement that successful performance of prospective-memory tasks often involves extensive use of monitoring including the use of preparatory attentional processes. However, it seems likely that this is more true when people try to remember intentions over a short period of time (as in the laboratory) rather than over long periods of time (as is often the case in real life). The evidence favors the notion that monitoring is not invariably involved in successful prospective-memory performance and is thus more in line with the predictions of multiprocess theory than of PAM theory. It is likely that we sometimes use relatively automatic processes requiring little or no processing capacity to perform prospective-memory tasks. As is assumed by multiprocess theory, the processes we use in prospective memory vary between those that are very demanding (e.g. monitoring) and those that impose very few demands (e.g. relatively automatic ones) depending upon the precise nature of the prospective memory task.

SUMMARY

There is an important distinction between prospective and retrospective memory, but remembering and forgetting in the real world often involve a mixture of both. Anxious individuals tend to have relatively poor prospective memory. Patients with obsessive-compulsive disorder believe that their prospective memory is very poor and this leads them to check repeatedly that they have carried out their intentions. In fact, it is likely that that their repeated checking reduces their confidence in their prospective memory ability.

Detailed analysis of airplane incidents and accidents indicates that failures of prospective memory are often involved but that failures of retrospective memory are extremely rare. Many of the failures of prospective memory occur when pilots are interrupted while carrying out a plan of action and then do not produce a new plan or intention to deal with the changed situation.

We can distinguish between event-based and time-based prospective memory tasks. With both types of task, performance is worse when the task is poorly specified than when it is well specified because more processing resources are required in the former case.

Older adults perform less well than younger adults on laboratory time-based and event-based prospective memory tasks. This is especially the case when overall processing demands are high, because the working memory system is less efficient in older adults. However, older adults often outperform younger adults on naturalistic prospective memory tasks, probably because they spend more time planning how to remember to perform them.

According to the preparatory attentional and memory processes theory, successful prospective memory always requires a capacity-demanding monitoring process and retrospective memory. As predicted from this theory, performance on prospective memory tasks is typically better when full attention is devoted to the task than when it is not. According to multiprocess theory, it is an exaggeration to claim that active monitoring is always involved in successful prospective memory performance. There is evidence that at least some people can perform some prospective memory tasks in an automatic way without monitoring, for example, when the cue and the to-be-performed target action are strongly associated or the cue is conspicuous.

FURTHER READING

- Dismukes, K., & Nowinski, J. (in press). Prospective memory, concurrent task management, and pilot error. In A. Kramer, D. Wiegmann, & A. Kirlik (Eds.), *Attention: From theory to practice*. New York: Oxford University Press. This chapter provides fascinating insights into the causes of aircraft accidents, showing clearly that failures of prospective memory are of special importance.

- Einstein, G. O., & McDaniel, M. A. (2005). Prospective memory: Multiple retrieval processes. *Current Directions in Psychological Science*, 14, 286–290. Gilles Einstein and Mark McDaniel discuss their influential multiprocess theoretical approach to prospective memory in simple terms.

- Ellis, J. A., & Cohen, G. (2008). Memory for intentions, actions, and plans. In G. Cohen & M. A. Conway (Eds.), *Memory in the real world* (3rd edn). Hove, UK: Psychology Press. Judi Ellis and Gillian Cohen discuss a wide range of issues relating to prospective memory in this chapter.

- Kliegel, M., McDaniel, M. A., & Einstein, G. O. (2007). *Prospective memory: Cognitive, neuroscience, developmental, and applied perspectives*. Hove, UK: Psychology Press. There are contributions from the world's leading experts on prospective memory in this very comprehensive edited book. The preparatory attentional and memory processes theory is presented in detail by the theorists responsible for its development.

CHAPTER 16

IMPROVING YOUR MEMORY

Michael W. Eysenck

Nearly everyone complains about their memory. In spite of the power and elegance of the human memory system, it is by no means infallible and we have to learn to live with that fallibility. It seems to be much more acceptable to complain of a poor memory, and much more acceptable to blame a social lapse on "a terrible memory," than to attribute it to stupidity or insensitivity. How much do we actually know about our own memories? Obviously, we need to remember our memory lapses in order to know just how bad our memories are. One of the most amnesic patients ever tested by one of us (Alan Baddeley) was a woman suffering from Korsakoff's syndrome, which is memory loss following chronic alcoholism. The test involved presenting her with lists of words. After each list, she commented with surprise on her ability to recall the words, saying, "I pride myself on my memory!" In fact, she performed very poorly on the recall test compared to other people. She seemed to have forgotten just how bad her memory was!

One of the central problems in trying to evaluate our own memory is that in doing so we are effectively comparing it with other people's memories. Typically, we do not really know how good or bad other people's memories are, so it is very easy to have a distorted view of our own. Evidence that many of us have poor memories for important information comes from the study of passwords. Brown, Bracken, Zoccoli, and Douglas (2004) found that 31% of their sample of American

students admitted to having forgotten one or more passwords. As Brown et al. (2004, p. 650) pointed out, "We are faced with a continuing dilemma in personal password construction between security and convenience: Fool the password hacker and you are likely to fool yourself." They found that 45% of students avoided this dilemma by using their own name in password construction, which hardly seems the way to have a secure password!

Brown et al. (2004) provided tips to people constructing passwords. If security is important, select a password that is a transformation of some memorable cue involving a mixture of letters and symbols. In addition, keep a record of passwords in a place to which only you have access (e.g. a safe deposit box). Of course, you then need to remember where you have put your passwords! Research by Winograd and Soloway (1986) provides some guidance here. Students found it harder to remember the locations at which objects had been hidden when the locations were unlikely (e.g. hiding jewelry in the oven) than when they were likely (e.g. hiding a thermometer in the medicine chest).

TECHNIQUES TO IMPROVE MEMORY

In this section of the chapter, I focus on some of the many techniques that can be used to improve your memory. I start by considering which mnemonic aids people use in their everyday lives. After that, we will have a look at the feats of some memory experts, which might provide insights into the strategies underlying outstanding memory. Finally, I discuss some of the most important techniques that have been developed specifically to enhance people's memory.

Mnemonic aids

John Harris (1980) carried out a survey to discover what types of mnemonic aid people use most often to assist their memory. The questionnaire that he used (in modified form) appears below (Box 16.1), and was administered by him to a group of university students and a sample of housewives. Compare your

---

Box 16.1 A modified version of Harris's (1980) questionnaire

How often do you use these memory aids?

Rate your use of each of the memory aids below with a score of 0 to 6, using the following scoring system:

0 = Never use
1 = Used less than three times in the last 6 months
2 = Used less than three times in the last 4 weeks
3 = Used less than three times in the last 2 weeks
4 = Used three to five times in last 2 weeks
5 = Used six to ten times in last 2 weeks
6 = Used eleven or more times in last 2 weeks

Two or more "average" scores indicate large differences between individuals, with each of the numbers being given by a subgroup of those tested.

Questions		Your rating	Students	Housewives
1	*Shopping lists.*		3,2,1	3,4,5
2	*First-letter memory aids.* For example the first letters of "Richard of York Gave Battle in Vain" give the first letters of the rainbow.		1	0,1
3	*Diary.*		1,6	6
4	*Rhymes.* For example, "In fourteen hundred and ninety-two Columbus sailed the ocean blue" helps you to remember the date 1492.		0	0
5	*The place method.* Items to be remembered are imagined in a series of familiar places. When the recall is required, one "looks" at the familiar place.		0,1	0,1
6	*Writing on hand* (or any other part of your anatomy or clothing).		0	0
7	*The story method.* Making up a story that connects items to be remembered in the correct order.		2,3	4,3,2
8	*Mentally retracing a sequence of events or actions* in order to jog your memory; useful for remembering where you lost or left something, or at what stage something significant happened.		5,6	1,5,6
9	*Alarm clock* (or other alarm device) for waking up only.		0,1	4,0
10	*Cooker timer* with alarm for cooking only.		0	0
11	*Alarm clock* (or other alarm devices such as watches, radios, timers, telephones, calculators) used for purpose other than waking up or cooking.		0	0

12 *The pegword method.* "One is a bun, two is a shoe, three is a tree," etc, as a method of remembering lists of items in correct order. 12 ☐ ⊙ 0 ⊙ 0

13 *Turning numbers into letters.* For remembering telephone numbers, for example. 13 ☐ ⊙ 1,2,5,6 ⊙ 2,3

14 *Memos.* For example, writing notes and "To do" lists for yourself. 14 ☐ ⊙ 0 ⊙ 0

15 *Face–name associations.* Changing people's names into something meaningful and matching them with something unusual about their face. For example, red-bearded Mr Hiles might be imagined with hills growing out of his beard. 15 ☐ ⊙ 1 ⊙ 1,0

16 *Alphabetical searching.* Going through the alphabet letter by letter to find the initial letter of a name. For example, does a particular person's name begin with A…B…Ah yes? C! C for Clark… 16 ☐ ⊙ 0 ⊙ 6

17 *Calendars, wall charts, year planners, display boards, etc.* 17 ☐ ⊙ 2 ⊙ 3

18 *Asking other people to remember things for you.* 18 ☐ ⊙ 2 ⊙ 3,4,5

19 *Leaving objects in special or unusual places so that they act as reminders.* 19 ☐ ⊙ 0 ⊙ 0

use of mnemonic aids to those of Harris's two groups. The figures given are the most frequently chosen categories (in descending order where not equal). In general terms, Harris found that his two groups had a similar pattern of mnemonic use, but there were some minor differences. For example, housewives seemed less inclined to write on their hands than students, but more inclined to write on calendars.

Harris discovered that nearly everyone in his study showed some use of mnemonic aids, but these were overwhelmingly *external* aids such as diaries, calendars, lists, and timers. In 1990, Douglas Herrmann and Susan Petro reported asking a group of people what external memory aids they found most helpful. Some of the most useful were traditional aids such as calendars, appointment books, and alarm clocks. Beeping keychains (a lost key can be

Harris (1980) discovered that nearly everyone in his study showed some use of mnemonic aids, such as diaries, calendars, lists, and timers.

summoned by clapping the hands) were found to be fairly helpful, as were telephone answering machines and watches and calendars with "reminder" features.

In recent years, there has been an enormous growth in the availability of commercial memory aids, often based on new developments in microelectronics. For example, the humble diary or day book is in danger of becoming obsolete as it is replaced by the portable personal computer complete with keyboard and screen.

If we return to the study by Harris (1980), one of the interesting features of his findings was that very few *internal* mnemonics were reported by Harris's participants. Such mnemonics (which are covered shortly) are often very useful in situations like examinations where external memory aids are not permitted. Most memory-training courses focus on internal mnemonics. What we have in mind here are courses of the kind devised as "never-fail systems to help you to remember everything." What do such systems involve? Although the present book does not aim to be a primer for memory training, it is appropriate to discuss at least some of the more popular mnemonic systems. However, before we do that, we will consider mnemonists or memory experts. We might be able to gain useful insights from them into the kinds of strategies that could greatly improve our own memory.

Memory experts

You have probably heard about the amazing memory feats that can be performed by extremely gifted individuals. Some of these feats are so remarkable that you might have suspected that the claims made were grossly exaggerated. There have undoubtedly been some charlatans, but solid evidence of truly remarkable memory powers has been obtained from some individuals.

The Russian, Shereshevskii, was possibly the most extraordinary of all the mnemonists. He had a truly amazing memory that relied heavily on imagery. This remarkable man was studied over a period of years by the Russian psychologist, A. R. Luria, who wrote a fascinating book about him, The *Mind of a mnemonist* (Luria, 1968). Shereshevskii was

first discovered when he was a journalist. His editor noticed that however complex the briefing instructions he was given before going out on a story, he never took notes. In spite of this, he could repeat anything that was said to him word for word, a feat he simply took for granted. His editor, realizing that he was a very unusual case, sent him along to see Luria, who gave him a series of increasingly demanding memory tests. There seemed to be no limit to the amount of information he could commit to memory—lists of more than 100 digits, long strings of nonsense syllables, poetry in unknown languages, complex figures, elaborate scientific formulae. According to Luria (1968), "He could repeat such material back perfectly, even in reverse order, and even years later!"

What was the secret of Shereshevskii's amazing memory? He had quite remarkable imagery. Not only could he rapidly and easily create a wealth of visual images, he also had an amazing capacity for **synesthesia**, which is the capacity for a stimulus in one sense to evoke an image in another. A small amount of synethesia is very common. For example, most people have a slight tendency to associate high-pitched sounds with bright colors and low-pitched sounds with more somber hues. In Shereshevskii's case, the amount of overlap was enormous. When presented with a tone with a pitch of 2000 cycles per second, he said, "It looks something like fireworks tinged with a pink-red hue. The strip of color feels rough and unpleasant, and it has an ugly taste— rather like that of a briny pickle … you could hurt your hand on this." Numbers resembled people, with one being "a proud well-built man" and two "a high-spirited woman."

Shereshevskii became a professional mnemonist, giving demonstrations of his extraordinary memory on stage. However,

KEY TERM

Synesthesia: The tendency for one sense modality to evoke another.

although his remarkable synesthesia was very advantageous to him, it also presented problems. For example, if someone coughed while the material to be remembered was being read out, the cough would impress itself on his memory as a blur or puff of steam, which threatened to get in the way of subsequent recall. Sometimes Shereshevskii became almost overwhelmed by the rich imagery that he generated, so that he found it very difficult to understand even simple prose: "Each word calls up images; they collide with one another, and the result is chaos. I can't make anything out of this. And then there's also your voice … another blur … then everything's muddle."

You might be envying Shereshevskii's memory powers. However, the fact that he found it extremely difficult to forget anything meant that his memory was cluttered up with all sorts of information he didn't want to recall. Eventually, he hit on a very simple solution—he imagined the information he wished to remember written on a blackboard and then imagined himself rubbing it out. Strange to relate, this worked perfectly!

Naturals vs. strategists

Why is it that some people have memories that are far better than those of the rest of us? Is it simply that they are "naturally" gifted, or is it rather that they have devoted much time to developing effective mnemonic techniques? Wilding and Valentine (1994) discovered that some memory experts are naturals whereas others rely heavily on various memory strategies. They took advantage of the fact that the World Memory Championships were being held in London (they were both working at Royal Holloway, University of London at the time) to assess the memory performance of the contestants as well as members of the audience who showed outstanding memory abilities.

Wilding and Valentine (1994) classified their participants into two groups: (1) *strategists*, who reported frequent use of memory strategies; and (2) *naturals*, who claimed naturally superior memory ability from early childhood,

and who possessed a close relative exhibiting a comparable level of memory ability. They used two kinds of memory task:

1. *Strategic tasks* (e.g. recalling names to faces) that seemed to be susceptible to the use of memory strategies. Recalling names to faces might not seem like a strategic task, but later I will consider clever strategies for enhancing people's ability to associate names with faces.
2. *Nonstrategic tasks* (e.g. recognition of snow crystals).

There were important differences between the strategists and the naturals (Figure 16.1). The strategists performed much better on strategic tasks than on nonstrategic ones, whereas the naturals did well on both kinds of memory tasks. The data are plotted in percentiles, so we can see how the two groups compared against a normal control sample (the 50th percentile is the average person's score). Easily the most impressive memory performance (surpassing that of more than 90% of the population) was obtained by strategists on strategic tasks. This should provide hope and encouragement to all of us that an excellent memory can be developed through training.

Maguire, Valentine, Wilding, and Kapur (2003) used brain imaging to study superior

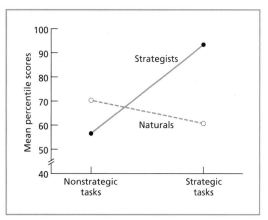

Figure 16.1 Memory performance strategists and naturals on strategic and nonstrategic tasks. Based on data in Wilding and Valentine (1994).

memorizers, most of whom had performed outstandingly well at the World Memory Championships. These superior memorizers and control participants memorized three-digit numbers, faces, and snowflakes, with the superior memorizers outperforming the controls most with the three-digit numbers and least with the snowflakes. Maguire et al.'s key finding was that during learning the superior memorizers had significantly more activity than the controls in areas of the brain involved in spatial memory and navigation. It is probably relevant that 90% of the superior memorizers reported using the method of loci (discussed shortly) on some or all of the memory tasks. This method involves visualizing to-be-remembered information at various points along a known route, and so makes extensive use of spatial memory.

Ericsson (e.g. 2003) has consistently argued that individuals with exceptional memory (rather than merely very good memory) are made rather than born. In other words, the secret of their success is that they have all spent numerous hours developing effective strategies. An apparent exception is Rajan Mahadevan, who has a remarkable ability to remember numbers. For several years, he held the world record for memorizing the maximum number of digits of *pi*, having produced 31,811 digits in just under 4 hours. When tested in the laboratory, he was found to have a digit span of 59 digits for visually presented digits and 63 for heard digits (Thompson, Cowan, Frieman, Mahadevan, Vogl, & Frieman, 1991). According to Thompson et al. (1991), Rajan is endowed with a naturally superior basic memory capacity. When most people (including memory experts) are remembering strings of digits, they typically divide them up into groups of about three or four digits. This makes sense, because that corresponds to attentional capacity. However, Thompson, Cowan, and Frieman (1993) claimed that Rajan divided digit strings into groups of ten to fifteen digits, and that he did this because his basic memory capacity was far greater than that of other people. They accepted that

Rajan developed various strategies to allow him to remember over 30,000 digits of *pi*, but argued strongly that the essence of his memory superiority stemmed from his extraordinary basic memory capacity.

Ericsson, Delaney, Weaver, and Mahadevan (2004) carried out several experiments on Rajan, and reported several findings suggesting that he doesn't in fact have an unusually large basic memory capacity. For example, they assessed his symbol span using ten symbols (e.g. ?, @, #, and *). His initial symbol span was only six symbols, which is the same as college students. With practice, he managed to increase his symbol span to nearly 30. However, he achieved this by recoding each symbol into a different digit, and then using his usual strategies to remember the resulting string of digits. In addition, Rajan's performance is only average on several other tasks, including remembering the position and orientation of images of various objects (Biederman, Cooper, Fox, & Mahadevan, 1992) and remembering word lists and stories (Thompson et al., 1993). These findings (especially those of Ericsson et al., 2004) cast strong doubt on the notion that Rajan has an innately superior memory capacity.

If Rajan's basic memory capacity is only average, how does he manage to have a digit span that is something like nine times greater than most people's? Ericsson et al. (2004) obtained relevant evidence in a study on digit span. Rajan reported using various mnemonic associations and patterns to group digits together. For example, "52" was remembered by thinking "1952 Wechsler's book," "007" by thinking "James Bond," and "2025" by thinking "45×45."

Some strategists have spent hundreds (or even thousands) of hours developing their memory skills. Dominic O'Brien devoted 6 years of his life to becoming world memory champion in the early 1990s (he went on to win the World Memory Championships eight times). One of his greatest feats was achieved in May 2002 at Simpson's, a restaurant in central London. He spent 12 hours memorizing

54 packs of playing cards (2808 cards) shuffled together and presented one card at a time. When he tried to recall all of the cards in order, he was correct with 2800 cards, with a tiny error rate of 0.3%

What motivated Dominic O'Brien? According to him:

I can now be introduced to a hundred new people at a party and remember all their names perfectly. Imagine what that does for your social confidence. My memory has helped me to lead a more organized life. I don't need to use a diary any more: appointments are all stored in my head. I can give speeches and talks without referring to any notes. I can absorb and recall huge amounts of information (particularly useful if you are revising for exams or learning a new language). And I have used my memory to earn considerable amounts of money at the blackjack table.
(O'Brien, 1993, p. 6)

Dominic O'Brien's exceptional memory abilities depended at least in part on his enormous skills in elaborative encoding and recoding.

One of the most extraordinary feats of memory ever accomplished was performed by Akira Haraguchi, a 60-year-old Japanese mental health counselor, who first came to prominence in 1995 when he recited *pi* to an amazing 83,431 decimal places, almost doubling the previous record. On 4 October 2006, he smashed his own record by reciting *pi* to 100,000 digits! It took him over 16½ hours to do this in a hall in Kisarazu, Japan. He was remarkably modest about his latest achievement: "The figure 100,000 is just an extension of the previous record … I'm certainly no genius. I'm just an ordinary old guy." It emerged that the essence of his memorizing strategy involves rhyming the numbers with Japanese words to make them more meaningful.

Mnemonic techniques

Every self-help book designed to improve your memory provides many examples of effective mnemonic techniques (e.g. McPherson, 2004). Indeed, there are more such techniques than you could shake a stick at. What we will do here is to focus on a few of the most important mnemonic techniques assessing their strengths and limitations. Our discussion is divided up into those mnemonics that rely mostly on visual imagery and those that are primarily word-based. Bear in mind, however, that the distinction is only a relative one—many mnemonic techniques involve a combination of words and images.

As you read about the various mnemonic techniques, you might find yourself wondering *why* these techniques are so effective. What I have done is to describe the techniques before having a concluding section titled, "Why do mnemonic techniques work?" If you want to know the answer at any point, simply read this later section, which starts on p. 368.

Visual imagery mnemonics: Method of loci

Mnemonics based on visual imagery have been common at least since classical times. According to Cicero, writing in the first century BC, the first such mnemonic was devised by the Greek poet Simonides in about 500 BC. A Greek who had won a wrestling victory at the Olympic Games gave a banquet at his house to celebrate. Simonides was invited to attend the banquet and to give a recitation in honor of the victor. Shortly after completing his eulogy, Simonides was called away. This was lucky for him, because just after he left, the floor of the banqueting hall collapsed, killing and mutilating the guests. Many of the bodies were unrecognizable. How were the victims' relatives to identify them and give them a decent burial? Simonides found that he could quite easily remember where most of the guests had been at the time he left, and so was able to identify the bodies. This set him thinking: If his visual memory was so good, could he not use it to help himself recall other material? He therefore devised a system in which he visualized a room in great detail, and then imagined various items in special places in the room. Whenever he needed to remember what these items were, he would "look" at the appropriate location in his mind's eye and mentally recall. The system (known as the *method of loci*) became popular with classical orators such as Cicero and has continued in use to the present day. As you will find if you give it a serious trial, it operates very effectively and easily (Box 16.2).

One of us (Alan Baddeley) has used the method of loci very often in student laboratory classes and it almost invariably works extremely well. Although it is much easier to use with concrete words such as the names of objects it is still effective in remembering abstract words such as *truth*, *hope*, and *patriotism*. The use of imagery can be prevented by introducing an interfering spatial task, so don't try to use this method while skiing down a mountain or driving a car!

The method of loci is very effective. Bower (1973) compared recall of five lists of twenty nouns each for groups using or not using the method of loci. The former group recalled 72% of the nouns on average against only 28% for the latter group. Kondo, Suzuki, Mugikura,

---

Box 16.2 Method of loci: How it works

First of all, think of 10 locations in your home, choosing them so that the sequence of moving from one to the next is an obvious one; for example, front door to entrance hall to kitchen to bedroom, and so on. Check that you can imagine moving through your 10 locations in a consistent order without difficulty. Now think of 10 items and imagine them in those locations. If the first item is a pipe, you might imagine it poking out of the letterbox in your front door, and great clouds of smoke billowing into the street. If the second is a cabbage, you might imagine your hall obstructed by an enormous cabbage, and so on. When it comes to recall, all you need to do is to re-walk mentally the route around your house.

Now try to create similarly striking images associating your 10 chosen locations with the words below:

shirt	eagle	paperclip	rose	camera
mushroom	crocodile	handkerchief	sausage	mayor

The same set of locations can be used repeatedly, as long as only the most recent item in a particular location is remembered. Earlier items in that location will suffer from the usual interference effects, unless of course you deliberately link them into a coherent chain.

Try to recall the 10 items listed two paragraphs ago. No, don't look! Rely on the images you created at various points around you.

It is certainly possible to create a system that has more than 10 locations; this was true of classical mnemonic systems and of the complex and somewhat mystical systems developed during the Middle Ages. Ross and Lawrence (1968) discovered that people using the method of loci could recall more than 95% of a list of 40 or 50 items after a single study trial.

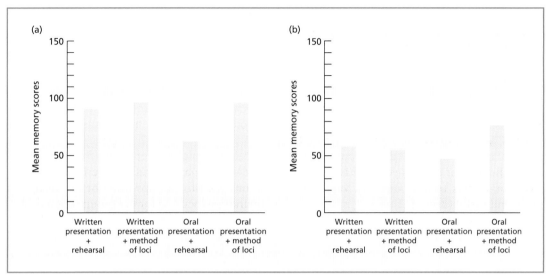

Figure 16.2 (a) Memory performance at a short retention interval as a function of type of presentation (written vs. oral) and learning strategy (rehearsal vs. method of loci). (b) Memory performance at a 1-week retention interval as a function of type of presentation and learning strategy. Data from De Beni et al. (1997).

Abe, Takahashi, Iijima, and Fujii (2004) also found that the method of loci enhanced memory. In addition, they used brain imaging to assess the effects of using the method of loci on brain activation. Several brain areas (e.g. right inferior frontal gyrus; middle frontal gyrus) were more activated when learners were using the method of loci rather than their habitual techniques. The finding that there was more brain activation when the method of loci was used suggests that the encoding process is more elaborate and variegated when it is used.

In spite of its effectiveness, the method of loci is limited in some ways. For example, it can be difficult to recall any given item without working your way through the list in sequence until you come to the item you want. It is also frequently argued that the method of loci is not useful when people are trying to learn material in the real world. De Beni, Moè, and Cornoldi (1997) attempted to address this criticism. They presented a 2000-word text orally or in written form to students who tried to remember as much as possible by either using the method of loci or rehearsing parts of the text. Memory was tested shortly after presentation

and 1 week later. With oral presentation of the material the method of loci led to greatly increased recall at both retention intervals (Figure 16.2). Thus, the method of loci was very effective when there was a lecture-style presentation. In contrast, there was no effect of the learning method when the text was presented in written form. Presumably the method of loci was ineffective with written presentation because the visual nature of the presentation interfered with the use of visual imagery within the method of loci.

Did De Beni et al. (1997) manage to show that the method of loci is useful in the real world? Not entirely. It is true that they used a situation that is somewhat more like the real world than previous researchers. However, the task of trying to remember a 2000-word text verbatim is not something any of us often tries to do!

Visual imagery mnemonics: Pegword system

The pegword system resembles the method of loci in that it relies on visual imagery and allows you to remember sequences of 10 unrelated items in the correct order. First of all you have to memorize 10 pegwords. As each pegword rhymes with a number from one to ten, this is relatively easy. Try it for yourself.

One = *bun* Two = *shoe* Three = *tree* Four = *door* Five = *hive* Six = *sticks* Seven = *heaven* Eight = *gate* Nine = *wine* Ten = *hen*

Having mastered this, you are ready to memorize 10 unrelated words. Suppose these are as follows: *battleship, pig, chair, sheep, castle, rug, grass, beach, milkmaid, binoculars*. Take the first pegword, *bun* (rhyming with one), and form an image of a bun interacting in some way with *battleship*. You might, for example, imagine a battleship sailing into an enormous floating bun. Now take the second pegword, *shoe*, and imagine it interacting with *pig*, perhaps a large shoe with a pig sitting in it. Pegword three is *tree*, and the third item is *chair*, so you might imagine a chair wedged in the branches of a tree. Work through the rest of the items, forming an appropriate inter-active image in each case. We are reasonably confident that when you have completed the task, you will be able to recall all 10 items in the correct order given that we don't spend much of our time trying to remember 10 unrelated items in a given order.

All three authors of this book have tried the pegword technique, and were relieved to find that it worked for us! There is also experimental evidence that it is very effective. For example, Morris and Reid (1970) found that twice as many words were recalled when the technique was used than when it was not. However, there are some limitations associated with the use of the pegword technique. First, it requires extensive training for it to be effective. Second, it is easier to use with concrete than with abstract material. For example, it is not easy to form interactive images involving abstract concepts such as "morality" or "insincerity." Third, there are some doubts as to how useful it is in everyday life.

There are clear similarities between the pegword method and the method of loci.

The main difference is that the pegword system uses numbers rather than locations, and bridges the gap between number and image by means of a rhyme: one is a bun, two is a shoe, three is a tree, and so on. An inter-mediate system developed by Henry Herdson in Cambridge during the seventeenth century relied on a series of visual images, the shape of which resembled that of various numbers. Hence *one* might be represented by a candle or a tower, *two* by a swan, *three* by a trident, and so on. The first object would then be imagined interacting with a candle in some way, the sec-ond with a swan, and so on. An elaboration of this system, combining it with a location mne-monic, was used by the late eighteenth-century mnemonist Gregor von Feinaigle.

Visual imagery mnemonics: Remembering names

Most people have problems remembering names. When being introduced to someone new, we tend to look at them and make whatever initial remarks are appropriate, with the result that their name often "goes in one ear and out the other." As you have probably found, it can be socially embarrassing if you have to admit that you have completely forgotten someone's name.

You can try to remember people's names based on a visual imagery mnemonic. You start by searching for an imageable substitute for the person's name (e.g. Eysenck becomes "ice sink"). Then some prominent feature of the person's face is selected, and the image is linked with that feature. For example, the nose might be regarded as a tap over the sink. Brief training in this method has been found to improve recall of names to faces by almost 80% (Morris, Jones, & Hampson, 1978) under laboratory conditions.

The imagery mnemonic for learning names works well in the peace and calm of the laboratory. However, that doesn't necessarily mean that it is also effective in real-life social conditions in which being involved in conversation might make it difficult to find the time to construct good imagery mnemonics. Morris, Fritz, Jackson, Nichol, and Roberts (2005) invited first-year university students to attend a party having received instructions about learning the names of the other students there. One group was instructed in use of the imagery mnemonic. A second group was told to try to retrieve the names at increasing intervals after first hearing them (expanded retrieval practice). There was also a control group told simply to learn people's names. Between 24 and 72 hours after the party, the students were given the task of writing the names under the photographs of the students who had been at the party.

The findings obtained by Morris et al. (2005) were clear-cut. Students in the expanded retrieval practice condition recalled 50% more names than those in the control condition (24 vs. 16, respectively). The imagery mnemonic was even less effective than no specific memorizing strategy, leading to an average recall of only 12 names. Thus, putting

Morris et al.'s (2005) study found that the imagery mnemonic was even less effective than no specific memorizing strategy in facilitating the recall of names. © Falko Updarp/zefa/Corbis.

in the effort to recall the names of people you have just met at a party or other social occasion pays considerable dividends in terms of long-term memory.

Verbal mnemonics

Although mnemonics used during classical times relied mainly on visual imagery, this was by no means the case in later times. For example, the Puritans favored verbal systems over those based on visual imagery. They did so for a rather curious reason: They regarded images as wicked and liable to give rise to "depraved carnal affections"!

In Victorian times, there was an emphasis on students having to memorize vast numbers of facts, such as the dates of accession of kings and queens. It is thus no surprise to discover that the Victorians devised various verbal mnemonics to assist students confronted by the need to engage in rote learning. For example, a Yorkshire headmaster, the Reverend Brayshaw, published a book in 1849 entitled *Metrical mnemonics applied to geography, astronomy and chronology* containing a selection of rhymes incorporating more than 2000 dates and numerical facts drawn from physics, astronomy, history, and geography. His preferred system involved substituting consonants for particular numbers and then using the consonants to create words. Brayshaw's code was as follows:

1	2	3	4	5	6	7	8	9	0	00
B	D	G	J	L	M	P	R	T	W	St
C	F	H	K		N	Q		V	X	
			S			Z				

You can use this code to turn a number sequence into a word by simply selecting one of the appropriate consonants for each digit, inserting vowels where necessary. For example, 1914 (the year the First World War started) can be represented by using the consonants CTBS to produce the words CAT BASE. In fact, since all the dates used by Brayshaw were later than AD 1000, he ignored the initial

1000. Here are some examples of his rhymes that give the dates of English kings:

- By MeN, near Hastings, William gains the crown   1066
- A RaP in Forest New brings Rufus down   1087
- Gaul's CoaSt first Henry hates, whose son is drowned   1100

The vital information about a date is always given in the second or second and third word in the line, and the line is completed by incorporating the name of the monarch and some striking feature about him/her. Fortunately, rote memorization of dates no longer plays much part in the teaching of history. However, the system could prove useful if you are struggling to memorize a large number of telephone numbers, PIN numbers, and zip codes (post codes).

There are many other situations in which verbal mnemonics are useful and still widely used. Suppose, for example, that you want to remember the colors of the spectrum (red, orange, yellow, green, blue, indigo, and violet). You start with the first letters of the colors (ROYGBIV), and use those first letters to construct a sentence (e.g. Richard Of York Gave Battle In Vain). Medical students learning anatomy sometimes seem to be required to perform as much rote learning as Brayshaw's students, and still buy books of mnemonics to help them. One of the best-known anatomy mnemonics refers to the names of the cranial nerves: On Old Olympia's Towering Top A Finn And German Vault And Hop (olfactory, optic, oculomotor, trochlear, trigeminal, abducens, facial, auditory, glossopharyngeal, vagus, accessory, and hypoglossal). The assumption is that medical students know the particular names but cannot reliably retrieve them in the correct order.

One of the most effective verbal mnemonics is the story method. It is used to remember a series of unrelated words in the correct order by linking them together within the context of a story. Note that the story method often involves the use of visual imagery as well as producing sentences. We will show this method at work with the 10 words we used to illustrate use of the pegword technique (*battleship, pig, chair, sheep, castle, rug, grass, beach, milkmaid, binoculars*):

> In the kitchen of the *battleship*, there was a *pig* that sat in a *chair*. There was also a *sheep* that had previously lived in a *castle*. In port, the sailors took a *rug* and sat on the *grass* close to the *beach*. While there, they saw a *milkmaid* watching them through her *binoculars*.

Bower and Clark (1969) showed that the story method can be extremely effective. They gave their participants the task of recalling 12 lists of 10 nouns each in the correct order when given the first words of each list as cues. Those who had constructed narrative stories recalled 93% of the words compared to only 13% for those who didn't do so. The story method is limited in that it requires fairly extensive training—I took a few minutes to construct the story given above! Another limitation is that you generally have to work your way through the list if you want to find a given item (e.g. the seventh one).

Why do mnemonic techniques work?

The success of techniques such as the method of loci, the pegword method, and the story method owes much to the fact that they allow us to make use of our knowledge (e.g. about the layout of the world around us; about the sequence of numbers). However, the full story of what is involved is more complicated than that—detailed knowledge isn't always enough. Suppose, for example, that we asked taxi drivers and students to recall lists of streets in the city in which they lived. You might imagine that the taxi drivers (with their superb knowledge of the spatial layout of the city's streets) would always outperform the students. In fact, that is *not* the case. Kalakoski and Saariluoma (2001) asked Helsinki taxi drivers and students to recall lists of 15 Helsinki street names in the order presented. In one condition, the streets were connected and were presented in an order forming a spatially continuous route through the city. In this condition, the taxi drivers recalled 87% of the street names correctly compared to only 45% by the students. In another condition, the same street names (all from the same part of Helsinki) were presented in a random order. In this condition, the taxi drivers recalled 70% of the street names compared to 46% for the students. However, when nonadjacent street names taken from all over Helsinki were presented in a random order, there was no difference in recall between the taxi drivers and the students.

What can we conclude from the above study by Kalakoski and Saariluoma (2001)? The taxi drivers obviously knew considerably more than the students about the spatial structure of Helsinki's streets. This knowledge could be used effectively to facilitate learning and retrieval when all the streets were fairly close together in that spatial structure. However, the taxi drivers couldn't use their special knowledge effectively to organize the to-be-remembered information when the street names to be remembered were distributed randomly around the city.

Why are techniques such as the method of loci, the pegword method, and the story method so effective? According to Ericsson (1988), there are three requirements to achieve very high memory skills:

1. *Meaningful encoding*: The information should be processed meaningfully, relating it to pre-existing knowledge. This is clearly the case when you use known locations (the method of loci) or the number sequence (pegword method), or when taxi drivers use their knowledge of their own town or city. This is the encoding principle.
2. *Retrieval structure*: Cues should be stored with the information to aid subsequent retrieval. The connected series of locations

or the number sequence both provide an immediately available retrieval structure, as does the knowledge of spatial layout possessed by taxi drivers. This is the retrieval structure principle.
3. *Speed-up*: Extensive practice allows the processes involved in encoding and retrieval to function faster and faster. The importance of extensive practice can be seen in the generally superior memory for street names shown by taxi drivers compared to students in the study by Kalakoski and Saariluoma (2001). This is the speed-up principle.

We can see the above principles at work in a study by Ericsson and Chase (1982) on participant SF, who was a student at Carnegie-Mellon University and was paid to practice the digit-span task for 1 hour a day for 2 years. The digit span (the number of random digits that can be repeated back in the correct order) is typically about six or seven items and ten is exceptional. However, this individual eventually attained a span of 80 items.

How did SF do it? He reached a digit span of about 18 items by using his extensive knowledge of running times (encoding and retrieval principles). For example, if the first few digits presented were "3594," he would note that this was Bannister's time for the mile, and so those four digits would be stored away as a single chunk or unit. He then increased his digit span to 80 items by organizing those chunks into a hierarchical structure and by extensive practice (the speed-up principle). Sadly, this outstanding digit span did not generalize to other memory tasks; SF had only average letter and word spans.

PREPARING FOR EXAMINATIONS

Students of psychology should find it easier than other students (at least in theory!) to develop good study skills. This is because psychological principles are at the heart of study skills. For example, study skills are designed to promote effective learning and remembering, and learning and memory are key areas within psychology. We will consider the issue of study skills in some detail. We will also consider some motivational issues, because motivation is important if students are to study effectively.

Study skills

How can students preparing for examinations develop effective study skills? Part of the answer to this question can be found by considering individual differences in learning styles. There is plentiful evidence that some learning styles are more effective than others in allowing students to remember information that will enhance their examination performance (Richardson, Eysenck, & Warren Piper, 1987). Here, we consider the three learning styles identified by the Study Process Questionnaire (Biggs, 1987), which was subsequently revised by Biggs, Kember, and Leung (2001):

1. *Surface*: Emphasis on rote learning of ideas and facts; little interest in the content of what is being learned. Items focus on issues such as poor motivation for study and simply learning important information by heart.
2. *Deep*: Emphasis on meaning, relating ideas to evidence and integrating information from various sources. Items focus on issues such as obtaining a clear understanding of the material and spending extra time to find out more about interesting topics.
3. *Strategic*: Emphasis on finding study techniques that achieve the best grades; using information about assessment procedures "to play the examination game." Items focus on issues such as studying the fewest topics needed to do well on examinations and picking up useful tricks that will maximize marks.

It is worth noting that there is some overlap between the deep and surface learning styles assessed by the Study Process Questionnaire

and the distinction between deep and shallow processing emphasized in the levels of processing approach (Craik & Lockhart, 1972; see Chapter 5).

What has typically been found is that the deep learning style predicts good examination performance whereas the surface learning style predicts poor performance (see Entwistle, 1987, for a review). McManus, Richards, Winder, and Sproston (1998) considered the final examination performance of medical students at the University of London. The strategic learning style was the one most positively associated with examination performance, closely followed by the deep learning style. As expected, the surface learning style was negatively associated with examination performance, perhaps in part because students who adopt this style often devote less time and effort to studying than do other students. The take-home message from research on learning

When it comes to preparation for exams, a deep learning style (full comprehension of the subject matter) predicts a good performance whereas the surface learning style predicts poor performance.

styles is that it is important to understand fully the meaning of what you are studying (deep learning) and to be fully aware of what is going to be involved when you are assessed (strategic learning).

We can make some headway in understanding what is involved in effective studying by focusing on various learning styles. However, there is more to effective studying than simply adopting an appropriate learning style. For example, the SQ3R approach (Morris, 1979) provides a broader perspective on effective studying. SQ3R stands for Survey, Question, Read, Recite, Review, and these represent the five stages in effective reading. We now consider these five stages with respect to the task of reading a chapter of this book:

1. The *Survey stage* involves obtaining an overall view of the way in which the information in the chapter is organized. The chapter summary is probably the easiest way to achieve that goal. If you read a chapter lacking a summary, then you could look through the chapter to find out what topics are discussed and how they are linked to each other.
2. The *Question stage* should be applied to fairly short sections of the chapter of no more than 3000 words or so. The essence of this stage is that you should think of relevant questions to which you expect this section to provide answers.
3. The *Read stage* involves reading through each section identified at the Question stage. There are two main goals at this stage. First, you should try to answer the questions you thought of during the previous stage. Second, you should try to integrate the information provided in the section of the chapter to your pre-existing knowledge of the topic.
4. The *Recite stage* involves you in trying to remember the key ideas contained in the section of the chapter you have been reading. If you cannot remember some of them, then you should go back to the Read stage.
5. The *Review stage* occurs when you have read the entire chapter. If all has gone

well, you should remember the key ideas from the chapter, and you should be able to combine information from different sections into a coherent structure. If you cannot do these things, then go back to earlier stages in the reading process.

One of the reasons why the SQ3R approach is so effective is that it avoids what we might call the student's illusion. Many students studying for an examination convince themselves that is all is well when they skim through the chapters of a book and discover that most of the material seems familiar. In other words, they find that they have reasonable recognition memory for the material. However, there is a large difference between *recognizing* information as familiar and being able to produce it at will during an anxiety-inducing examination. In order to succeed in written examinations, you must be able to *recall* the information you need. As generations of students have discovered to their cost, good recognition memory for the material relevant to an examination is no guarantee at all that recall will be equally good. This finding is relevant to a phenomenon known as the testing effect (Box 16.3).

There is convincing evidence that there is a strong testing effect under classroom conditions. Bangert-Drowns, Kulik, and Kulik (1991) reviewed the findings from 35 classroom studies. A significant testing effect was found in 83% of these studies, and the magnitude of the effect tended to increase as the number of testing occasions went up.

How can we explain the testing effect? Bjork and Bjork (1992) addressed this issue by distinguishing between storage strength and retrieval strength. Storage strength reflects the relative permanence of a memory trace, whereas retrieval strength reflects the accessibility of any given memory trace. Retrieval is easy when retrieval strength is high, but easy retrieval does not increase storage strength. By contrast, retrieval is difficult when retrieval strength is low, but difficult retrieval increases storage strength and leads to good long-term memory. The take-home message is

Box 16.3 Testing effect (Roediger & Karpicke, 2006a)

The testing effect refers to the finding that long-retention for material is better when memory for that material is tested during the time of learning than when it is not. Convincing evidence that the testing effect is strong was reported by Roediger and Karpicke (2006a). The basic set-up was that students read a prose passage covering a general scientific topic and tried to memorize it in one of three conditions:

1. *Repeated study*: The passage was read four times and there was no test.
2. *Single test*: The passage was read three times and then students recalled as much as possible from it.
3. *Repeated test*: The passage was read once and then students recalled as much as possible on three occasions.

Finally, memory for the passage was tested after 5 minutes or 1 week.

The findings are shown in Figure 16.3. Repeated study was the most effective strategy when the final test was given 5 minutes after learning, and the repeated test condition was the least effective. However, there was a dramatic reversal of the conditions when the final test occurred 1 week after learning (this is the testing effect), and these findings are of most relevance to students preparing for an examination. What is striking is the size of the testing effect: average recall was 50% higher in the repeated test condition than the repeated study condition. That difference could easily

make the difference between doing very well on an examination and failing it!

Why do so many students prefer repeated studying to repeated testing when engaged in revision for an examination? There are three main reasons. First, repeated studying produces short-term benefits, as can be seen in Figure 16.3. Second, Roediger and Karpicke (2006a) found at the time of learning that students in the repeated study condition predicted that they would recall more of the prose passage after 1 week than did those in the repeated test condition. Third, studying tends to be less effortful and demanding than testing, and this makes it more appealing to students.

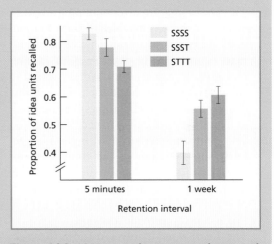

Figure 16.3 Memory performance as a function of learning conditions (S, study; T, test) and retention interval (5 minutes vs. 1 week). From Roediger and Karpicke (2006). Copyright © Blackwell Publishing. Reproduced with permission.

that putting in a considerable amount of effort to recall information on a test is well worth it because it makes the information in question more memorable in the long term.

It is worth mentioning that the notion that testing is important to memory is not something discovered by psychologists and educationalists in the twentieth century. Here is a quotation from the seventeenth-

century philosopher Francis Bacon: "If you read a piece of text through twenty times, you will not learn it by heart so easily as if you read it ten times while attempting to recite from time to time and consulting the text when your memory fails" (Bacon, 1620/2000, p. 143).

There is an important final point relating to the use of testing. Pashler, Cepeda, Rohrer, and Wixted (2005) presented their participants with 20 words from the Luganda dialect and their English translations. Presentation was followed almost immediately by testing whether the participants could recall the English translation when given each Luganda word. Some of the participants received feedback in the form of the correct response after each incorrect response whereas others did not. What was of greatest interest was correct recall 1 week later for those words that had received incorrect responses before. Correct recall for these words was almost *five* times better for those participants who had received feedback.

The findings of Pashler et al. (2005) suggest strongly that adding feedback to testing is even better than testing on its own. In practical terms,

KEY TERM

Mind map: A diagram in which words or other items are linked in various ways around a central key word.

the message is that your studying is likely to be most effective if you use flashcards, which permit self-testing *and* feedback. Whatever you do, *don't* just rely on re-reading your notes!

Mind maps

In recent years, there has been a substantial increase in a study technique based on mind maps (see Buzan & Buzan, 1993, for a comprehensive review). A **mind map** is a diagram

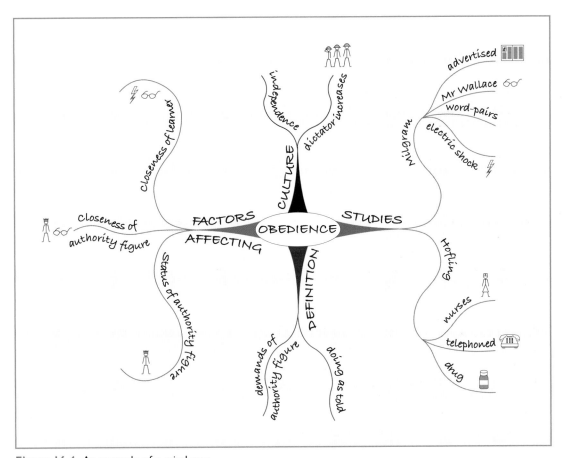

Figure 16.4 An example of a mind map.

in which, typically, a central idea is linked to several other ideas and/or concepts in various ways. A concrete example of a mind map is shown in Figure 16.4. As you can see, information is presented in a very flexible way. However, the most important concepts and words are typically written in large letters fairly close to the central concept and the less important ones written in smaller letters further away from the central concept.

Tony Buzan, and many other educationalists, argue that mind maps possess several advantages over the traditional approach based on note taking. First, students need to be actively involved in the learning process to produce satisfactory mind maps. By contrast, note taking mainly involves writing down verbatim phrases or sentences in a textbook, or recording the instructor. Second, the concepts contained within mind maps are shown as having several links or associations to each other. It is arguable that this is more realistic and useful than the linear presentation of information in texts or conventional notes. Third, each concept is typically reduced to one or two words within mind maps, thus reducing ideas to their essence. By contrast, only expert note takers manage to avoid including trivial details in their notes. Fourth, mind maps provide striking visual images that might be easier to remember than conventional notes. Fifth, many mind maps make use of several different colors to make it easy to work out which concepts belong to the same category. By contrast, conventional notes are nearly always written in a single color.

We have seen that there are various reasons why mind maps might be an effective technique to use during the learning process. As yet, there have been relatively few systematic experimental studies comparing mind maps to other forms of learning. However, the available research evidence suggests that mind maps are of real use. Farrand, Hussain, and Hennessy (2002) presented medical students with a 600-word text that they were told to learn. Half of them had been trained in the mind-map technique and the others were simply instructed to use study techniques they had learned previously. One week after learning, participants in the mind-map group recalled 10% more factual knowledge from the text than did those using pre-existing study techniques. This difference occurred even though users of mind maps had lower motivation for the technique than did those using ordinary study techniques. If ways could be found to make students more motivated when using mind maps, then the superiority of the mind-map approach over other study techniques would presumably be greater.

Budd (2004) argued that we need to take account of individual differences in learning style to explain why many students don't seem to be very motivated when using mind maps. Those students favoring a "doing" learning style felt they learned a lot from using mind maps and rated their use as highly as lectures. By contrast, students preferring a "thinking" learning style were less sure about the value of mind maps and rated lectures much more favorably.

Learning vocabulary

Most of us at some point in our lives (most frequently during the school years) find ourselves struggling to learn foreign vocabulary. As you have probably discovered for yourself, that is generally a very time-consuming and effortful business. Atkinson and Raugh (1975) found that the keyword technique was a useful way of making it easier to acquire foreign vocabulary. Learners using this technique first of all form an association between each spoken foreign word and an English word or phrase sounding like it (the keyword). After that, they create a mental image, with the keyword acting as a link between the foreign word and its English equivalent. For example, the Russian word *zvonok* is pronounced *zvah-oak* and means bell. This can be learned by using *oak* as the keyword and forming an image of an oak tree covered with bells.

In their study, Atkinson and Raugh (1975) presented their participants with 120 Russian

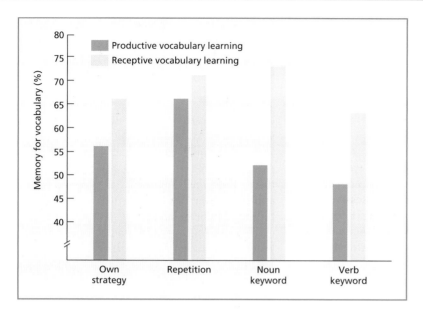

Figure 16.5 Memory for foreign vocabulary as a function of learning strategy for receptive and productive vocabulary learning. Adapted from Ellis and Beaton (1993).

words and their English equivalents. They found that the keyword technique was more effective when the keywords were provided than when learners thought of their own. When the keywords were provided, the keyword method improved memory for Russian words by about 50% over a short retention interval and by over 70% at a long (6-week) interval. Similar findings involving several other languages including Spanish, Italian, French, and Greek have been reported (see Taguchi, 2006, for a review).

The study by Atkinson and Raugh (1975) was limited in that they only considered receptive vocabulary learning (producing the appropriate English word to a foreign word). What happens when the keyword technique is applied to productive vocabulary learning (producing the right foreign word to an English word)? Ellis and Beaton (1993) provided the answer in a study of receptive and productive vocabulary learning of German words in four conditions: noun keyword; verb keyword; repetition (keep repeating the paired German and English words), and own strategy (participants used their preferred strategy). The keyword technique (especially with noun keywords) was relatively more successful with

receptive than with productive vocabulary learning (Figure 16.5).

Why was the keyword technique unsuccessful with productive vocabulary learning? What the participants had to do when presented with an English word was first to retrieve the correct keyword and then to use the keyword to produce the appropriate German word. The problem was as follows: retrieving the keyword often didn't provide sufficiently precise information to recall the German word correctly. However, there is more recent evidence suggesting that productive vocabulary learning can benefit from the keyword technique provided that it is used over a prolonged period of time. Taguchi (2006) studied students at an Australian university who were taking a 3-month course in the Japanese language. Those students trained in the keyword technique were able to recall correctly more Japanese words when presented with the English translations than were controls.

In sum, there is reasonable evidence that the keyword technique can enhance receptive and productive vocabulary learning for those trying to master a foreign language. However, the keyword technique is generally only superior to other techniques when learners have received much training in its use (McPherson, 2004). This is likely to be especially the case when it comes to learning abstract words, because it is much more difficult to generate mental images for such words than for concrete ones.

Learning verbatim

On occasion, students have to remember information verbatim (word for word). For example, English students might need to learn poems off by heart, and it is sometimes worthwhile for psychology students to learn key information (e.g. important quotations) verbatim. You can gain some insight into the processes involved in learning verbatim by hearing about the strategies used by actors and actresses. Whenever you go to a theatrical production, you have probably been very impressed by the ability of actors and actresses to remember hundreds (or even thousands) of lines when performing a play. You might have wondered whether what they say really corresponds precisely to the words written down by the playwright, but research shows that that is nearly always the case (Oliver & Ericsson, 1986). The fact that actors manage fairly rapidly to memorize a script verbatim is perplexing. There is much evidence that learners have much better memory for material that has been processed in terms of its meaning as in levels of processing theory (Craik & Lockhart, 1972; see Chapter 5). However, processing of meaning typically produces good recall of the gist of a text but not of its exact wording.

Helga and Tony Noice have contributed more than anyone else to our understanding of precisely what actors do to memorize the exact wording of a script (see Noice & Noice, 1996, for a review). Their first surprising finding was that professional actors generally do *not* start by trying to learn the exact words of the script! Instead, what they do is to focus on the needs and motivations of their characters. Helga Noice (1992) asked seven actors to describe how they went about learning a role. Her central conclusion was as follows: "They [the actors] read the script many times, trying

Noice and Noice (1996) investigated how actors memorize their scripts. They concluded that professional actors do not usually start by trying to memorize the script verbatim, but rather aim to infer the needs and motivations of their character's utterances.

to infer the motivation behind each utterance. All of the actors stressed the importance of identifying the underlying meaning and of explaining why the character uses those exact words." Thus, actors do process the meaning of a script, and they do so in such a way that they are able to understand why their character used each of the words he/she does in the play.

We can see how this works in practice by considering the following example, discussed by Noice and Noice (1996), in which an actor playing the part of a mayor has to say to a reporter, "Don't pester me now, please." The actor assumed from the word *pester* that the mayor regarded the reporter as a bothersome child, which is why that word was in the script rather than *bother* or *annoy*. The mayor softens his statement by adding "please" at the end of the sentence, because he doesn't want to alienate the reporter.

Noice and Noice (1996) examined in detail how actors go about the task of learning a script. They presented six actors with a scene from a play in which a man and a woman are having a conversation about love and possible infidelity. They were each given a tape recorder and instructed to verbalize their thoughts as they worked through the script. The actors' utterances were assigned to 12 categories. Over 40% of the utterances belonged to the category of interactions ("statements concerning mental or emotional interactions between characters in which one character affects, tries to affect, or is affected by, another character"; Noice & Noice, 1996, p. 6). The second and third most common categories of utterance (each accounting for almost 9% of the total utterances) were metastatements (general statements regarding the actor's learning process) and memorization (the reasons why some lines are easier or harder to learn).

How long-lasting is an actor's memory for a script? Schmidt, Boshuizen, and van Breukelen (2002) addressed this question in a study in which actors tried to recall their parts from Sartre's *Huis clos* (*No exit*) 5 months after a production of the play had come to a close. Some of the play was performed in the usual fashion with the actors moving around and looking at each other, but the rest of the play was performed with the actors sitting at a table with their backs turned to each other. Overall, 53% of the script was recalled verbatim, with a further 28% being recalled in the form of paraphrases that captured the meaning of the original script. In addition, 3% of what the actors said represented inferences based on the script, meaning that 85% of the text was retained in some form. The fact that most of the inaccurately recalled material from the script nevertheless captured its gist strongly suggests that actors learn lines by focusing on their meaning.

Schmidt et al. (2002) found that the actors recalled 87% of their lines (verbatim + paraphrase + inference) when actually performing the play against 81% when sitting down not looking at each other. What does this finding mean? It indicates that actors use contextual information (e.g. gestures, posture, facial expressions) provided by other actors as cues to facilitate recall of their lines. However, the fact that the beneficial effect of having access to contextual information had a fairly modest impact suggests that the cues provided by the text itself are generally strong enough to ensure that actors recall their lines.

Attention, interest, and knowledge

Many years ago, Sir Frederic Bartlett (1932) investigated the claim that the Swazi of South Africa had remarkable memory abilities. He began by asking a Swazi boy to take a message to the other end of the village. The message contained 10 elements and the journey took about 2 minutes. The boy made two major errors, about what we would expect from an American or English boy of the same age. A similar conclusion followed the testing of Swazi adults on a range of memory tests. Then a farmer suggested that one of his herdsmen should be tested on his memory for cattle. The man was asked to give a list of the cattle bought by a former employer a year previously, together with any details that he could remember. He squatted on the ground and rapidly recited a list of nine transactions, of which the following two are typical: "From Mbimbimaseko, one young black ox with a white bush on its tail, for £2 [about $4]; from Ndoda Kedeli, one young red heifer, the calf of a red cow, and with a white belly, for £1 [about $2]." The nine transactions were checked against the sales list from the farmer's records and all nine were found to be accurate with only small exceptions—one price was out by 10 shillings [about $1] and the color of one animal was discrepant. The reason for this remarkable memory for stock transactions, none of which the herdsman had conducted himself, lies in the fact that cattle were of enormous interest to the Swazi, because they played a very important role in their social structure.

Bartlett's (1932) findings are an example of one of the most important generalizations about memory—information on any given topic will be remembered much better by individuals who have great interest in it than by those who do not. Of course, it is typically the case that those who are most interested in a topic will also possess the most knowledge about it. In general terms, the more knowledge people possess about a given topic, the easier they find it to relate new information to their existing knowledge (see Chapter 5). For example, Morris, Gruneberg, Sykes, and Merrick (1981) presented their participants with made-up soccer scores. Participants' knowledge of soccer correlated +.81 with memory for these scores, indicating that knowledge was a powerful predictor of how much could be remembered.

Motivation

One of the most influential theories of human motivation is goal-setting theory. This was originally put forward by Edwin Locke (1968) and subsequently modified (e.g. Locke & Latham, 2002). The key assumption of goal-setting theory is that conscious goals have a major impact on people's motivation and behavior. More specifically, the harder the goals we set ourselves, the better our performance is likely to be. Wood, Mento, and Locke (1987) reviewed 192 studies testing that hypothesis, and concluded that it was supported in 175 of them.

Of course, motivation involves more than simply setting difficult goals. Another important factor is goal commitment. There is little point in setting yourself the goal of obtaining an excellent examination result in a course on memory if you do not fully commit and dedicate yourself to the achievement of that goal. It is also important that the goals you set yourself should be specific and clear—make sure to avoid very vague goals such as simply "doing well." Some of the key points in goal-setting theory were summarized very succinctly by Latham (2003, p. 309): the goal should be "specific, measurable, attainable, relevant, and have a time-frame (SMART)."

Goal-setting theory has proved very successful over a long period. However, it has one serious limitation. Most of the research designed to test the theory has involved situations in which a single, specific task is performed in the absence of distractions. As you will probably agree, this does not sound much like the realities of everyday life, in which we seem to spend most of our time trying to achieve multiple goals at the same time while surrounded by distractions. It certainly doesn't correspond to the lives of most students, who are trying to achieve academic success while at the same time having an active and enjoyable social life.

How can we move from goal setting to goal attainment in a world full of complications and distractions? Gollwitzer has focused on precisely this issue. His key concept is that of **implementation intentions**, which "specify the when, where, and how of responses leading to goal attainment" (Gollwitzer, 1999, p. 494; see also Chapter 15). We will consider Gollwitzer's ideas in the context of a concrete example. Suppose a student called Natalie has set herself the task of spending 4 hours on a given Saturday revising for a forthcoming examination. However, there are obstacles in the way. Natalie generally chats for several hours a day with the students she shares an apartment with, and she also likes to watch television. Thus, there is a real danger that Natalie will be distracted from her studies and so finish-up doing much less revision than she intended.

How can Natalie ensure her revision is done so she passes the examination? According to Gollwitzer's (1999) theory, this is where implementation intentions come in. Two possible implementation intentions are as follows: (1) "When one of my flatmates knocks on the door, I will tell her that I'll see

KEY TERM

Implementation intentions: Intentions specifying in detail how individuals are going to achieve the goals they have set themselves.

her in the pub at 8 o'clock"; (2) "If I discover there's something interesting on television, I'll ask my flat-mates to record it so I can watch it later." According to Gollwitzer, most goals are much more likely to be attained if individuals form implementation intentions.

Evidence that implementation intentions can reduce susceptibility to distraction was discussed by Gollwitzer (1999). College students performing arithmetic problems were presented with distracting clips of award-winning commercials. The performance of participants who focused on thinking, "I will not let myself get distracted!" was adversely affected by the distracting commercials. The implementation intention, "Whenever the distraction arises, I will ignore it!" was very effective at reducing distraction, more so than the implementation intention, "Whenever the distraction arises, I will increase my efforts at the task in hand!". If you want to prevent yourself being distracted, you should focus on forming implementation intentions that involve ignoring distractions rather than stepping up your efforts.

Further evidence supporting the importance of implementation intentions was reported by Gollwitzer and Brandstätter (1997), who gave students the goal of writing a report on how they spent Christmas Eve within 48 hours of that day. Half the participants formed implementation intentions by indicating where and when they intended to write the report. The goal of writing the report very shortly after Christmas was achieved by 75% of those who formed implementation intentions but by only 33% of those who did not.

Why are implementation intentions so effective in enhancing the chances of people achieving their goals? According to Gollwitzer (1999), forming an implementation intention is like creating an "instant habit." Our habits (e.g. always going for lunch at 1 o'clock; always meeting our friends at McDonald's) are reliably triggered by relevant cues providing information about *when* and/or *where* certain actions occur. In a similar way, implementation intentions specify where and when we are going to initiate behavior to attain our goal.

SUMMARY

Most of the mnemonic aids that people report using are external ones such as calendars, lists, and computer-based aids. Memory experts or mnemonists, however, nearly all rely heavily on internal mnemonic aids involving various strategies. In addition, some individuals with excellent memory powers seem to be naturally gifted. However, those relying on natural memory ability rarely achieve the almost incredible levels of memory performance of strategists on those memory tasks for which they have developed effective strategies.

Mnemonics based on visual imagery have been common since classical times. One of the oldest (and most effective) of such mnemonics is the method of loci. It can be used in lectures, but is more difficult to use with abstract than with concrete material. The pegword technique is also effective and also works best with concrete material. There are also numerous verbal mnemonics. For example, Brayshaw devised a code to turn historical dates into consonants that are then used to construct meaningful sentences. There is also the story method, in which the learner constructs a story to link unrelated words. There are three ingredients in most mnemonic techniques: meaningful encoding (relating what is to be learned to pre-existing knowledge); retrieval structure (cues are stored to assist subsequent retrieval); and speed-up (extensive practice allows encoding and retrieval to occur faster).

The SQ3R (Survey, Question, Read, Recite, Review) approach is very useful for students preparing for an examination. The Recite stage (requiring the learner to recall what he/she has just learned) is important, because students need to recall learned material when taking an examination. There is evidence in the testing effect that long-term memory for information is better when memory for that information is tested at the time of learning. Students can also construct mind maps, in which the associations between key ideas and concepts are displayed in a figure. Mind maps are more flexible and imageable than conventional notes. Foreign vocabulary can be learned by means of the keyword technique, in which a keyword acts as a link between a foreign word and its English equivalent. The key word technique is more effective when learning the English translation of a foreign word than the foreign translation of an English word. Research on professional actors has shown that they achieve word-for-word recall by trying to understand why their character used the precise words he/she did.

Attention and interest are important if you want to store information over long periods of time. For example, cattle are of great importance to the Swazi of South Africa, and so they remember cattle transactions in great detail. Effective motivation involves setting difficult (but achievable) goals and being committed to them. It also involves implementation intentions to minimize the chances of being distracted while working towards a goal.

FURTHER READING

- Ericsson, K. A. (2003). Exceptional memorizers: Made, not born. *Trends in Cognitive Sciences*, 7, 233–235. Anders Ericsson marshals the evidence suggesting that individuals with exceptional memory achieve their success through hard work and the development of strategies rather than simply through natural ability.

- McPherson, F. (2004). *The memory key: Unlock the secrets to remembering*. New York: Barnes & Noble Books. This book provides a reasonably thorough and balanced account of the strengths (and limitations) of numerous techniques and strategies designed to increase memory.

- Morris, P. E., & Fritz, C. O. (2006). How to … improve your memory. *The Psychologist*, 19, 608–611. Peter Morris and Catherine Fritz discuss several useful ways of improving your memory based on solid experimental evidence.

- Roediger, H. L., & Karpicke, J. D. (2006b). The power of testing memory: Basic research and implications for educational practice. *Perspectives on Psychological Science*, 1, 181–213. This article provides a thorough review and discussion of laboratory and classroom research on the effectiveness of testing in improving memory.

- Wilding, J., & Valentine, E. (1997). *Superior memory*. Hove, UK: Psychology Press. The fascinating topic of memory experts (and the strategies they use to perform outstanding memory feats) is discussed in a comprehensive way in this book.

GLOSSARY

Accessibility/availability distinction:
Accessibility refers to the ease with which a stored memory can be retrieved at a given point in time. Availability refers to the distinction indicating whether a trace is or is not stored in memory.

Activation level: The variable internal state of a memory trace that contributes to its accessibility at a given point.

Alcoholic Korsakoff syndrome: Patients have difficulty learning new information, although events from the past are recalled. There is a tendency to invent material to fill memory blanks. Most common cause is alcoholism, especially when this has resulted in a deficiency of vitamin B1.

Amygdala: An area of the brain close to the hippocampus that is involved in emotional processing.

Anterograde amnesia: A problem in encoding, storing, or retrieving information that can be used in the future.

Articulatory suppression: A technique for disrupting verbal rehearsal by requiring participants to continuously repeat a spoken item.

Associative blocking: A theoretical process hypothesized to explain interference effects during retrieval, according to which a cue fails to elicit a target trace because it repeatedly elicits a stronger competitor, leading people to abandon efforts to retrieve the target.

Associative deficit hypothesis: Proposal that the age deficit in memory comes from an impaired capacity to form associations between previously unrelated stimuli.

Autobiographical knowledge base: Facts about ourselves and our past that form the basis for autobiographical memory.

Autobiographical memory: Memory across the lifespan for both specific events and self-related information.

Autonoetic consciousness: A term proposed by Tulving for self-awareness, allowing the rememberer to reflect on the contents of episodic memory.

Binding: Term used to refer to the linking of features into objects (e.g. color red, shape square, into a red square), or of events into coherent episodes.

Cell assembly: A concept proposed by Hebb to account for the physiological basis of long-term learning, which is assumed to involve the establishment of links between the cells forming the assembly.

Change blindness: Failure to detect even quite dramatic changes in a scene, given a brief delay.

Change blindness blindness: The unduly optimistic belief that one is very rarely affected by change blindness.

Chunking: The process of combining a number of items into a single chunk typically on the basis of long-term memory.

Classical conditioning: A learning procedure whereby a neutral stimulus (e.g. a bell) that is paired repeatedly with a response-evoking stimulus (e.g. meat powder), will come to evoke that response (salivation).

Cognitive control: The ability to flexibly control thoughts in accordance with our goals, including our ability to stop unwanted thoughts from rising to consciousness.

Cohort effect: The tendency for people born at different time periods to differ as a result of historic changes in diet, education, and other social factors.

Collaborative inhibition: A phenomenon in which a group of individuals remembers significantly less material collectively than does the combined performance of each group member individually when recalling alone.

Competition assumption: The theoretical proposition that the memories associated to a shared retrieval cue automatically impede one another's retrieval when the cue is presented.

Confabulation: Recollection of something that did not happen.

Consolidation: The time-dependent process by which a new trace is gradually woven into the fabric of memory and by which its components and their interconnections are cemented together.

Context cues: Retrieval cues that specify aspects of the conditions under which a desired target was encoded, including (for example) the location and time of the event.

Context shift hypothesis: An alternative explanation for list-method directed forgetting, positing that forget instructions separate first-list items into a distinct context, which unless reinstated during the final test will make the later context a relatively ineffectual retrieval cue.

Context-dependent memory: The finding that memory benefits when the spatio-temporal, mood, physiological, or cognitive context at retrieval matches that present at encoding.

Contextual fluctuation: The gradual drift in incidental context over time, such that distant memories deviate from the current context more so than newer memories, thereby diminishing the former's potency as a retrieval cue for older memories.

Corsi block tapping: Visuo-spatial counterpart to digit span involving an array of blocks that the tester taps in a sequence and the patient attempts to copy.

Cross-sectional design: Method of studying development or aging whereby participants are sampled from different age bands and tested only once.

Cue-overload principle: The observed tendency for recall success to decrease as the number of to-be-remembered items associated to a cue increases.

Delusions: False beliefs, often found in schizophrenic patients, that seem well founded to the patient but implausible to a neutral observer.

Depth of processing: The proposal by Craik and Lockhart that the more deeply an item is processed, the better will be its retention.

Digit span: Maximum number of sequentially presented digits that can reliably be recalled in the correct order.

Direct/explicit memory tests: Any of a variety of memory assessments that overtly prompt participants to retrieve past events.

Directed forgetting: The tendency for an instruction to forget recently experienced items to induce memory impairment for those items.

Distributed practice: Breaking practice up into a number of shorter sessions; in contrast to massed practice, which comprises fewer, long, learning sessions.

Double-dissociation: A term particularly used in neuropsychology when two patient groups show opposite patterns of deficit, e.g. normal STM and impaired LTM, versus normal LTM and impaired STM.

Dual-coding hypothesis: Highly imageable words are easy to learn because they can be encoded both visually and verbally.

Dual-process theories of recognition: A class of recognition models that assumes that recognition memory judgments can be based on two independent forms of retrieval process: recollection and familiarity.

Echoic memory: A term sometimes applied to auditory sensory memory.

Elaborative rehearsal: Process whereby items are not simply kept in mind, but are processed either more deeply or more elaborately.

Electroencephalogram (EEG): A device for recording the electrical potentials of the brain through a series of electrodes placed on the scalp.

Emotion regulation: Goal-driven monitoring, evaluating, altering, and gating one's emotional reactions and memories about emotional experiences.

Encoding specificity principle: The more similar the cues available at retrieval are to the conditions present at encoding, the more effective the cues will be.

Environmental support: Characteristics of a retention test that support retrieval.

Episodic buffer: A component of the Baddeley and Hitch working memory model, which assumes a multidimensional code, allowing the various subcomponents of working memory to interact with long-term memory.

Episodic memory: A system that is assumed to underpin the capacity to remember specific events.

Event-based prospective memory: A form of prospective memory in which some event (e.g. seeing a grocery store) provides the cue to perform a given action (e.g. buying some fruit).

Everyday memory: Term applied to a movement within memory to extend the study of memory from the confines of the laboratory to the world outside.

Event-related potentials (ERP): A method using electroencephalography, in which the electrophysiological reaction of the brain to specific stimuli is tracked over time.

Expanding retrieval: A learning schedule whereby items are initially tested after a short delay, with pretest delay gradually increasing across subsequent trials.

Explicit/declarative memory: Memory that is open to intentional retrieval, whether based on recollecting personal events (episodic memory) or facts (semantic memory).

False memory syndrome: Term applied to cases, particularly of child abuse, in which the rememberer becomes convinced of an event that did not happen.

Familiarity-based recognition: A fast, automatic recognition process based on the perception of a memory's strength. Proponents of dual process models consider familiarity to be independent of the contextual information characteristic of recollection.

Flashbulb memory: Term applied to the detailed and apparently highly accurate memory of a dramatic experience.

Forgetting curve/retention function: The logarithmic decline in memory retention as a function of time elapsed, first described by Ebbinghaus.

Fragment completion: A technique whereby memory for a word is tested by deleting alternate letters and asking participants to produce the word.

Frame: A type of schema in which information about objects and their properties is stored.

Free recall: A method whereby participants are presented with a sequence of items, which they are subsequently required to recall in any order they wish.

Gestalt psychology: An approach to psychology that was strong in Germany in the 1930s and that attempted to use perceptual principles to understand memory and reasoning.

HERA (Hemispheric Encoding and Retrieval Asymmetry) hypothesis: Tulving's proposal that the encoding of episodic memories involves the left frontal lobe whereas their retrieval depends on right frontal areas.

Hippocampus: Brain structure in the medial temporal lobe that is important for long-term memory formation.

Hypermnesia: The improvement in recall performance arising from repeated testing sessions on the same material.

Iconic memory: A term applied to the brief storage of visual information.

Immersion method: A strategy for foreign language teaching whereby the learner is placed in an environment where only the foreign language is used.

Implementation intentions: Intentions specifying in detail how individuals are going to achieve the goals they have set themselves.

Implicit/nondeclarative memory: Retrieval of information from long-term memory through performance rather than explicit conscious recall or recognition.

Incidental forgetting: Memory failures occurring without the intention to forget.

Incidental learning: Learning situation in which the learner is unaware that a test will occur.

Infantile amnesia: Tendency for people to have few autobiographical memories from below the age of 5.

Inhibition: A general term applied to mechanisms that suppress other activities. The term can be applied to a precise physiological mechanism or to a more general phenomenon, as in proactive and retroactive inhibition, whereby memory for an item is impaired by competition from earlier or later items.

Intentional learning: Learning when the learner knows that there will be a test of retention.

Interference: The phenomenon in which the retrieval of a memory can be disrupted by the presence of related traces in memory.

Irrelevant sound effect: A tendency for verbal STM to be disrupted by concurrent fluctuating sounds, including both speech and music.

Latent inhibition: Classical conditioning phenomenon whereby multiple prior presentations of a neutral stimulus will interfere with its involvement in subsequent conditioning.

Levels of processing: The theory proposed by Craik and Lockhart that asserts that items that are more deeply processed will be better remembered.

Life narrative: A coherent and integrated account of one's life that is claimed to form the basis of autobiographical memory.

Longitudinal design: Method of studying development or aging whereby the same participants are successively tested at different ages.

Long-term memory: A system or systems assumed to underpin the capacity to store information over long periods of time.

Long-term potentiation (LTP): A process whereby synaptic transmission becomes more effective following a cell's recent activation.

Long-term recency: A tendency for the last few items to be well recalled under conditions of long-term memory.

Long-term working memory: Concept proposed by Ericsson and Kintsch to account for the way in which long-term memory can be used as a working memory to maintain complex cognitive activity.

Magnetic resonance imaging (MRI): A method of brain imaging that relies on detecting changes induced by a powerful magnetic field.

Magnetoencephalography (MEG): A system whereby the activity of neurons within the brain is detected through the tiny magnetic fields that their activity generates.

Maintenance rehearsal: A process of rehearsal whereby items are "kept in mind" but not processed more deeply.

Masking: A process by which the perception and/or storage of a stimulus is influenced by events occurring immediately before presentation (forward masking) or more commonly after (backward masking).

Mental time travel: A term coined by Tulving to emphasize the way in which episodic memory allows us to relive the past and use this information to imagine the future.

Mere exposure effect: A tendency for a neutral stimulus to acquire positive value with repeated exposure.

Metamemory: Knowledge about one's own memory and an ability to regulate its functioning.

Method of loci: A mnemonic technique in which the to-be-remembered items are associated with the locations (e.g. places along a walk).

Mind map: A diagram in which words or other items are linked in various ways around a central key word.

Modal model: A term applied to the model of memory developed by Atkinson and Shiffrin (1968).

Model: A method of expressing a theory more precisely, allowing predictions to be made and tested.

Mood-congruent memory: Bias in the recall of memories such that negative mood makes negative memories more readily available than positive, and vice versa. Unlike mood dependency, it does not affect the recall of neutral memories.

Mood-dependent memory: A form of context dependent effect whereby what is learnt in a given mood, whether positive, negative, or neutral, is best recalled in that mood.

Motivated forgetting: A broad term encompassing intentional forgetting as well as forgetting triggered by motivations, but lacking conscious intention.

Neuroimaging: A term applied to a range of methods whereby the brain can be studied, either in terms of its anatomical structure (structural imaging), or its operation (functional imaging).

Nonsense syllables: Pronounceable but meaningless consonant–vowel–consonant items designed to study learning without the complicating factor of meaning.

Nonword repetition test: A test whereby participants hear and attempt to repeat back nonwords that gradually increase in length.

Object memory: System that temporarily retains information concerning visual features such as color and shape.

Part-set cuing impairment: When presenting part of a set of items (e.g. a category, a mental list of movies you want to rent) hinders your ability to recall the remaining items in the set.

Personal semantic memory: Factual knowledge about one's own past.

Phonological loop: Term applied by Baddeley and Hitch to the component of their model responsible for the temporary storage of speech-like information.

Phonological similarity effect: A tendency for immediate serial recall of verbal material to be reduced, when the items are similar in sound.

Positivity bias: The tendency, increasing over the lifespan, to recall more pleasant memories than either neutral or unpleasant ones.

Positron emission tomography (PET): A method whereby radioactively labeled substances are introduced into the bloodstream and subsequently monitored to measure physiological activation.

Post-traumatic amnesia (PTA): Patients have difficulty forming new memories. Often follows a severe concussive head injury and tends to improve with time.

Post-traumatic stress disorder (PTSD): Emotional disorder whereby a dramatic and stressful event such as rape results in persistent anxiety, often accompanied by vivid flashback memories of the event.

Primacy effect: A tendency for the first few items in a sequence to be better recalled than most of the following items.

Priming: The process whereby presentation of an item influences the processing of a subsequent item, either making it easier to process (positive priming) or more difficult (negative priming).

Proactive interference: The tendency for earlier memories to disrupt the retrievability of more recent memories.

Process dissociation procedure (PDP): A technique for parceling out the contributions of recollection and familiarity within a recognition task.

Prosopagnosia: A condition, also known as face-blindness, in which there is extremely poor face recognition combined with reasonable ability to recognize other objects.

Prospective memory: Remembering to carry out some intended action in the absence of any explicit reminder to do so; see retrospective memory.

Psychogenic amnesia: Profound and surprising episodes of forgetting the events of one's life, arising from psychological factors, rather than biological damage or dysfunction.

Psychogenic fugue: A form of psychogenic amnesia typically lasting a few hours or days following a severe trauma, in which afflicted individuals forget their entire life history, including who they are.

Reality orientation training (ROT): A method of treating patients in the latter stages of dementia who have lost their orientation in time and place.

Reappearance hypothesis: The view that under certain circumstances, such as flashbulb memory and PTSD, memories can be created that later reappear in exactly the same form.

Recency effect: A tendency for the last few items in a list to be well recalled.

Recognition memory: A person's ability to correctly decide whether they have encountered a stimulus previously in a particular context.

Recollection: The slower, more attention-demanding component of recognition memory in dual process models, which involves retrieval of contextual information about the memory.

Reconstructive memory: An active and inferential process of retrieval whereby gaps in memory are filled in based on prior experience, logic, and goals.

Reductionism: The view that all scientific explanations should aim to be based on a lower level of analysis: psychology in terms of physiology, physiology in terms of chemistry, and chemistry in terms of physics.

Remember/know procedure: A procedure used on recognition memory tests to separate the influences of familiarity and recollection on recognition performance. For each test item, participants report whether it is recognized because the person can recollect contextual details of seeing the item (classified as a "remember" response) or because the item seems familiar, in the absence of specific recollections (classified as a "know" response).

Reminiscence: The remembering again of the forgotten, without learning or a gradual process of improvement in the capacity to revive past experiences.

Reminiscence bump: A tendency in participants over 40 to show a high rate of recollecting personal experiences from their late teens and 20s.

Reminiscence therapy: A method of helping dementia patients cope with their growing amnesia by using photographs and other reminders of their past life.

Repetition priming: Enhanced processing of a stimulus arising from recent encounters with that stimulus, a form of implicit memory.

Repression: In psychoanalytic theory, a psychological defense mechanism that banishes unwanted memories, ideas, and feelings into the unconscious in an effort to reduce conflict and psychic pain. Theoretically, repression can either be conscious or nonconscious.

Resource sharing: Use of limited attentional capacity to maintain two or more simultaneous activities.

Retrieval: The process of recovering a target memory based on one or more cues, subsequently bringing that target into awareness.

Retrieval-induced forgetting (RIF): The tendency for the retrieval of some target items from long-term memory to impair the later ability to recall other items related to those targets.

Retrieval inhibition hypothesis: A proposed mechanism underlying list-method directed forgetting suggesting that first-list items are temporarily inhibited in response to the instruction to forget and can be reactivated by subsequent presentations of the to-be-forgotten items.

Retrieval mode: The cognitive set, or frame of mind, that orients a person towards the act of retrieval, ensuring that stimuli are interpreted as retrieval cues.

Retrieval practice paradigm: A procedure used to study retrieval-induced forgetting.

Retroactive interference: The tendency for more recently acquired information to impede retrieval of similar older memories.

Retrograde amnesia: A problem accessing events that happened in the past.

Retrospective memory: Memory for people, words, and events encountered or experienced in the past.

Schema: Proposed by Bartlett to explain how our knowledge of the world is structured and influences the way in which new information is stored and subsequently recalled.

Script: A type of schema relating to the typical sequences of events in various common situations (e.g. going to a restaurant).

Semantic coding: Processing an item in terms of its meaning, hence relating it to other information in long-term memory.

Semantic dementia: A progressive dementia characterized by gradual deterioration of semantic memory.

Semantic memory: A system that is assumed to store accumulative knowledge of the world.

Sensory memory: A term applied to the brief storage of information within a specific modality.

Short-term memory: A term applied to the retention of small amounts of material over periods of a few seconds.

Signal detection theory: A model of recognition memory that posits that memory targets (signals) and lures (noise) on a recognition test posses an attribute known as strength or familiarity, which occurs in a graded fashion, with previously encountered items generally possessing more strength that novel items. The process of recognition involves ascertaining a given test item's strength and then deciding whether it exceeds a criterion level of strength, above which items are considered to be previously encountered. Signal detection theory provides analytic tools that separate true memory from judgment biases in recognition.

Source monitoring: The process of examining the contextual origins of a memory in order to determine whether it was encoded from a particular source.

Spatial working memory: System involved in temporarily retaining information regarding spatial location.

Spontaneous recovery: The term arising from the classical conditioning literature given to the reemergence of a previously extinguished conditioned response after a delay; similarly; forgotten declarative memories have been observed to recover over time.

Stem completion: A task whereby retention of a word is tested by presenting the first few letters.

Subjective organization: A strategy whereby a learner attempts to organize unstructured material so as to enhance learning.

Supervisory attentional system (SAS): A component of the model proposed by Norman and Shallice to account for the attentional control of action.

Synesthesia: The tendency for one sense modality to evoke another.

System consolidation: Process of gradual reorganization of the regions of the brain that support memory. Information is consolidated within the brain by a process of transfer from one anatomically based system to another.

Task switching: A process whereby a limited capacity system maintains activity on two or more tasks by switching between them.

The Peterson task: Short-term forgetting task in which a small amount of material is tested after a brief delay filled by a rehearsal-preventing task.

Think/no-think (TNT) paradigm: A procedure designed to study the ability to volitionally suppress retrieval of a memory when confronted with reminders.

Time-based prospective memory: A form of prospective memory in which time is the cue indicating that a given action needs to be performed.

Total time hypothesis: The proposal that amount learned is a simple function of the amount of time spent on the learning task.

Trace decay: The gradual weakening of memories resulting from the mere passage of time.

Transfer-appropriate processing (TAP): Proposal that retention is best when the mode of encoding and mode of retrieval are the same.

Transient global amnesia (TGA): Apparently normal individuals suddenly develop severe problems in forming and retrieving new memories. The cause is unknown and the condition tends to resolve relatively rapidly.

Traumatic brain injury (TBI): Caused by a blow or jolt to the head, or by a penetrating head injury. Normal brain function is disrupted. Severity ranges from "mild" (brief change in mental status or consciousness) to "severe" (extended period of unconsciousness or amnesia after the injury).

Typicality gradient: The ordering of the members of a category in terms of their typicality ratings.

Unconscious transference: the tendency of eyewitnesses to misidentify a familiar (but innocent) face as belonging to the person responsible for a crime.

Unlearning: The proposition that the associative bond linking a stimulus to a memory trace will be weakened when the trace is retrieved in error when a different trace is sought.

Verbal learning: A term applied to an approach to memory that relies principally on the learning of lists of words and nonsense syllables.

Visual cache: A component of Logie's model of visual working memory. It forms a counterpart to the phonological store and is maintained by the inner scribe, a counterpart to phonological rehearsal.

Visuo-spatial sketchpad: A component of the Baddeley and Hitch model that is assumed to be responsible for the temporary maintenance of visual and spatial information.

Visuo-spatial STM: Retention of visual and/or spatial information over brief periods of time.

Weapon-focus effect: The finding that eyewitnesses pay so much attention to the attacker's weapon that that they ignore and thus cannot recall other details.

Word length effect: A tendency for verbal memory span to decrease when longer words are used.

Working memory: A memory system that underpins our capacity to "keep things in mind" when performing complex tasks.

Working memory span: Term applied to a range of complex memory span tasks in which simultaneous storage and processing is required.

Working self: A concept proposed by Conway to account for the way in which autobiographical knowledge is accumulated and used.

REFERENCES

Abel, T., & Lattal, K. M. (2001). Molecular mechanisms of memory acquisition, consolidation and retrieval. *Current Opinion in Neurobiology, 11*, 180–187.

Abeles, M., & Schilder, P. (1935). Psychogenic loss of personal identity: Amnesia. *Archives of Neurology and Psychiatry, 34*, 587–604.

Addis, D. R., Moscovitch, M., Crawley, A. P., & McAndrews, M. P. (2004). Recollective qualities modulate hippocampal activation during autobiographical memory retrieval. *Hippocampus, 14*, 752–762.

Aggleton, J. P., & Brown, M. W. (1999). Episodic memory, amnesia, and the hippocampal–anterior thalamic axis. *Behavioral and Brain Sciences, 22*, 425–489.

Alberoni, M., Baddeley, A. D., Della Sala, S., Logie, R. H., & Spinnler, H. (1992). Keeping track of conversation: Impairments in Alzheimer's disease. *International Journal of Geriatric Psychiatry, 7*, 639–646.

Allen, B. P., & Lindsay, D. S. (1998). Amalgamations of memories: Intrusion of information from one event into reports of another. *Applied Cognitive Psychology, 12*, 277–285.

Allen, R. J., & Baddeley, A. D. (2008). Memory for prose: Mechanisms of binding in verbal working memory. In A. Thorn & M. Page (Eds.), *Interactions Between Short-term and Long-term Memory in the Verbal Domain.* Hove: Psychology Press.

Allen, R., Baddeley, A. D., & Hitch, G. J. (2006). Is the binding of visual features in working memory resource-demanding? *Journal of Experimental Psychology: General, 135*, 298–313.

Allport, A., Styles, E. A., & Hsieh, S. (1994). Shifting attentional set: Exploring the dynamic control of tasks. In C. Umilta & M. Moscovitch (Eds.), *Attention and Performance XV.* (pp. 421–462). Cambridge, MA: MIT Press.

Alvarez, P., & Squire, L. R. (1994). Memory consolidation and the medial temporal lobe: A simple network model. *Proceedings, National Academy of Sciences of the United States of America, 91*, 7041–7045.

Anderson, M. C., & Green, C. (2001). Suppressing unwanted memories by executive control. *Nature, 410*, 366–369.

Anderson, M. C. (2003). Rethinking interference theory: Executive control and the mechanisms of forgetting. *Journal of Memory and Language, 49*(4), 415–445.

Anderson, M. C., & Levy, B. J. (2007). Theoretical issues in inhibition: Insights from research on human memory. In D. Gorfein & C. M. MacLeod (Eds.), *Inhibition in Cognition.* Washington, DC: American Psychological Association.

Anderson, M. C., & Levy, B. J. (in press). Suppressing unwanted memories. *Current Directions in Psychological Science.*

Anderson, M. C., & Neely, J. H. (1996). Interference and inhibition in memory retrieval. In E. L. Bjork & R. A. Bjork (Eds.), *Memory. Handbook of Perception and Cognition.* (pp. 237–313). San Diego: Academic Press.

Anderson, M. C., & Spellman, B. A. (1995). On the status of inhibitory mechanisms in cognition: Memory retrieval as a model case. *Psychological Review, 102*, 68–100.

Anderson, M. C., & Weaver, C. (in press). Inhibitory control over action and memory. In L. R. Squire (Ed.), *The New Encyclopedia of Neuroscience.* Oxford: Elsevier Ltd.

Anderson, M. C., Bjork, R. A., & Bjork, E. L. (1994). Remembering can cause forgetting: Retrieval dynamics in long-term memory. *Journal of Experimental Psychology: Learning, Memory, and Cognition, 20*, 1063–1087.

Anderson, M. C., Ochsner, K. N., Cooper, J., Robertson, E., Gabrieli, S. W., Glover, G. H., et al. (2004). Neural systems underlying the suppression of unwanted memories. *Science, 303*, 232–235.

Anderson, R. C., & Pichert, J. W. (1978). Recall of previously unrecallable information following a shift in perspective. *Journal of Verbal Learning and Verbal Behavior, 17*(1), 1–12.

Andrade, J. (2005). Does memory priming during anaesthesia matter? *Anesthesiology, 103*, 919–920.

Andrade, J., Munglani, R., Jones, J. G., & Baddeley, A. D. (1994). Cognitive performance during anaesthesia. *Consciousness and Cognition*, 3, 148–165.

Andrews, B., Brewin, C. R., Ochera, J., Morton, J., Bekerian, D. A., Davies, G. M., et al. (1999). Characteristics, context and consequences of memory recovery among adults in therapy. *British Journal of Psychiatry*, 175, 141–146.

Antonini, A., Leenders, K. L., Meier, D., Oertel, W. H., Boesiger, P., & Anliker, M. (1993). T2 relaxation time in patients with Parkinson's disease. *Neurology*, 43, 697–700.

Aron, A. R., Fletcher, P. C., Bullmore, E. T., Sahakian, B. J., & Robbins, T. W. (2003). Stop-signal inhibition disrupted by damage to right inferior frontal gyrus in humans. *Nature Neuroscience*, 6(2), 115–116.

Arrigo, J. M., & Pezdek, K. (1997). Lessons from the study of psychogenic amnesia. *Current Directions in Psychological Science*, 6(5), 148–152.

Astin, A. W. (1993). *What matters in college? Four critical years revisited*. San Franciso: Jossey-Bass.

Atkinson, R. C., & Juola, J. F. (1974). Search and decision processes in recognition memory. In D. H. Kroutz, R. C. Atkinson, & P. Suppes (Eds.), *Contemporary Developments in Mathematical Psychology*. San Francisco: Freeman.

Atkinson, R. C., & Raugh, M. R. (1975). An application of the mnemonic keyword method to the acquisition of a Russian vocabulary. *Journal of Experimental Psychology: Human Learning and Memory*, 104, 126–133.

Atkinson, R. C., & Shiffrin, R. M. (1968). Human memory: A proposed system and its control processes. In K. W. Spence & J. T. Spence (Eds.), *The Psychology of Learning and Motivation: Advances in Research and Theory* (Vol. 2, pp. 89–195). New York: Academic Press.

Atkinson, R. C., & Shiffrin, R. M. (1971). The control of short-term memory. *Scientific American*, 225, 82–90.

Averbach, E., & Sperling, G. (1961). Short-term storage of information in vision. In C. Cherry (Ed.), *Information Theory* (pp. 196–211). London: Butterworth.

Baars, B. J. (1997). *In the Theater of Consciousness*. New York: University Press.

Baars, B. J. (2002). The conscious access hypothesis: Origins and recent evidence. *Trends in Cognitive Sciences*, 6(1), 47–52.

Bäckman, L., & Molander, B. (1986). Adult age differences in the ability to cope with situations of high arousal in a precision sport. *Psychology and Aging*, 1, 133–139.

Bäckman, L., & Nilsson, L. -G. (1984). Aging effect in free recall: An exception to the rule. *Human Learning*, 3, 53–69.

Bäckman, L., Almkvist, O., Andersson, J., Nordberg, A., Winblad, B., Reineck, R., & Langstrom, B. (1997). Brain activation in young and older adults during implicit and explicit retrieval. *Journal of Cognitive Neuroscience*, 9, 378–391.

Bäckman, L., Ginovart, N., Dixon, R. A., Robins Wahlin, T. B., Wahlin, A., Halldin, C., & Farde, L. (2000). Age-related cognitive deficits mediated by changes in the striatal dopamine system. *American Journal of Psychiatry*, 157, 635–637.

Bacon, F. T. (1620/2000). *Novum organum* (L. Jardine & M. Silverthorne, Trans.). Cambridge: Cambridge University Press [original work published in 1620].

Baddeley, A. D. (1964). Language habits, S–R compatibility and verbal learning. *American Journal of Psychology*, 77, 463–468.

Baddeley, A. D. (1966a) Short-term memory for word sequences as a function of acoustic, semantic and formal similarity. *Quarterly Journal of Experimental Psychology*, 18, 362–365

Baddeley, A. D. (1966b). The influence of acoustic and semantic similarity on long-term memory for word sequences. *Quarterly Journal of Experimental Psychology*, 18, 302–309.

Baddeley, A. D. (1986). *Working Memory*. New York: Oxford University Press.

Baddeley, A. D. (1993). *Your Memory: A User's Guide*. London: Sidgwick & Jackson.

Baddeley, A. D. (1996). Exploring the central executive. *Quarterly Journal of Experimental Psychology*, 49A(1), 5–28.

Baddeley, A. D. (1997). *Human Memory: Theory and Practice (revised edn)*. Hove, UK: Psychology Press.

Baddeley, A. D. (1998). The central executive: A concept and some misconceptions. *Journal of the International Neuropsychological Society*, 4, 523–526.

Baddeley, A. D. (2000). The episodic buffer: A new component of working memory? *Trends in Cognitive Sciences*, 4(11), 417–423.

Baddeley, A. D. (2001). Is working memory still working? *American Psychologist*, 56, 851–864.

Baddeley, A. D. (2007). *Working Memory, Thought and Action*. Oxford: Oxford University Press.

Baddeley, A. D., & Andrade, J. (2000). Working memory and the vividness of imagery. *Journal of Experimental Psychology: General*, 129(1), 126–145.

Baddeley, A. D., & Dale, H. C. A. (1966). The effect of semantic similarity on retroactive interference in long- and short-term memory. *Journal of Verbal Learning and Verbal Behavior, 5*, 417–420.

Baddeley, A. D., & Hitch, G. J. (1974). Working memory. In G. A. Bower (Ed.), *Recent Advances in Learning and Motivation* (Vol. 8, pp. 47–89). New York: Academic Press.

Baddeley, A. D., & Hitch, G. J. (1977). Recency re-examined. In S. Dornic (Ed.), *Attention and Performance* (Vol. VI, pp. 647–667). Hillsdale, NJ: Lawrence Erlbaum Associates.

Baddeley, A. D., & Hitch, G. J. (1993). The recency effect: Implicit learning with explicit retrieval? *Memory and Cognition, 21*, 146–155.

Baddeley, A. D., & Larsen, J. D. (2007). The phonological loop unmasked? A comment on the evidence for a "perceptual-gestural" alternative. *Quarterly Journal of Experimental Psychology, 60*, 497–504.

Baddeley, A. D., & Lieberman, K. (1980). Spatial working memory. *Attention and Performance VIII*, 521–539.

Baddeley, A. D., & Longman, D. J. A. (1978). The influence of length and frequency of training sessions on the rate of learning to type. *Ergonomics, 21*, 627–635.

Baddeley, A. D., & Warrington, E. K. (1970). Amnesia and the distinction between long- and short-term memory. *Journal of Verbal Learning and Verbal Behavior, 9*, 176–189.

Baddeley, A. D., & Wilson, B. (1986). Amnesia, autobiographical memory and confabulation. In D. Rubin (Ed.), *Autobiographical Memory* (pp. 225–252). Cambridge: Cambridge University Press.

Baddeley, A. D., & Wilson, B. (1988). Frontal amnesia and the dysexecutive syndrome. *Brain and Cognition, 7*(2), 212–230.

Baddeley, A. D., & Wilson, B. A. (1994). When implicit learning fails: Amnesia and the problem of error elimination. *Neuropsychologia, 32*, 53–68.

Baddeley, A. D., Baddeley, H., Bucks, R., & Wilcock, G. K. (2001a). Attentional control in Alzheimer's disease. *Brain, 124*, 1492–1508.

Baddeley, A. D., Bressi, S., Della Sala, S., Logie, R., & Spinnler, H. (1991a). The decline of working memory in Alzheimer's disease: A longitudinal study. *Brain, 114*, 2521–2542.

Baddeley, A. D., Chincotta, D., & Adlam, A. (2001b). Working memory and the control of action: Evidence from task switching. *Journal of Experimental Psychology: General, 130*, 641–657.

Baddeley, A. D., Chincotta, D., Stafford, L., & Turk, D. (2002). Is the word length effect in STM entirely attributable to output delay? Evidence from serial recognition. *Quarterly Journal of Experimental Psychology, 55A*, 353–369.

Baddeley, A. D., Della Sala, S., & Spinnler, H. (1991b). The two-component hypothesis of memory deficit in Alzheimer's disease. *Journal of Clinical and Experimental Neuropsychology, 13*(2), 372–380.

Baddeley, A. D., Emslie, H., & Nimmo-Smith, I. (1992). *Speed and Capacity of Language Processing Test (SCOLP)*. Bury St Edmunds, UK: Thames Valley Test Company.

Baddeley, A. D., Emslie, H., & Nimmo-Smith, I. (1994). *Doors and People: A Test of Visual and Verbal Recall and Recognition*. Bury St Edmunds, UK: Thames Valley Test Company.

Baddeley, A. D., Gathercole, S. E., & Papagno, C. (1998). The phonological loop as a language learning device. *Psychological Review, 105*(1), 158–173.

Baddeley, A. D., Grant, S., Wight, E., & Thomson, N. (1973). Imagery and visual working memory. In P. M. A. Rabbitt & S. Dornic (Eds.), *Attention and Performance V* (pp. 205–217). London: Academic Press.

Baddeley, A. D., Lewis, V. J., & Nimmo-Smith, I. (1978). When did you last...? In M. M. Gruneberg, P. E. Morris, & R. N. Sykes (Eds.), *Practical Aspects of Memory* (pp. 77–83). London: Academic Press.

Baddeley, A. D., Lewis, V. J., & Vallar, G. (1984a). Exploring the articulatory loop. *Quarterly Journal of Experimental Psychology, 36*, 233–252.

Baddeley, A. D., Lewis, V., Eldridge, M., & Thomson, N. (1984b). Attention and retrieval from long-term memory. *Journal of Experimental Psychology: General, 113*(4), 518–540.

Baddeley, A. D., Logie, R., Bressi, S., Della Sala, S., & Spinnler, H. (1986). Dementia and working memory. *Quarterly Journal of Experimental Psychology, 38A*, 603–618.

Baddeley, A. D., Papagno, C., & Vallar, G. (1988). When long-term learning depends on short-term storage. *Journal of Memory and Language, 27*, 586–595.

Baddeley, A. D., Thomson, N., & Buchanan, M. (1975). Word length and the structure of short-term memory. *Journal of Verbal Learning and Verbal Behavior, 14*, 575–589.

Baddeley, A. D., Thornton, A., Chua, S. E., & McKenna, P. (1996). Schizophrenic delusions and the construction of autobiographical memory. In D. C. Rubin (Ed.), *Constructing our Past: Autobiographical Memory*. New York: Cambridge University Press.

Baddeley, A. D., Vargha-Khadem, F., & Mishkin, M. (2001c). Preserved recognition in a case of developmental amnesia: Implications for the acquisition of semantic memory.

Journal of Cognitive Neuroscience, 13(3), 357–369.

Bahrick, H. P. (1984). Semantic memory content in permastore: Fifty years of memory for Spanish learning in school. *Journal of Experimental Psychology: General, 113,* 1–29.

Bahrick, H. P., Bahrick, P. O., & Wittlinger, R. P. (1975). Fifty years of memory for names and faces: A cross-sectional approach. *Journal of Experimental Psychology: General, 104*(1), 54–75.

Bailey, C. H., & Chen, M. (1989). Structural plasticity at identified synapses during long-term memory in Aplysia. *Journal of Neurobiology, 20*(5), 356–372.

Ball, K., Berch, D. B., Helmers, K. F., Jobe, J. B., Leveck, M. D., Marsiske, M. et al. (2002). Effects of cognitive training intervention with older adults: A randomised control trial. *Journal of the American Medical Association, 288,* 2271–2281.

Ballard, P. B. (1913). Oblivescence and reminiscence. *British Journal of Psychology Monograph Supplements, 1,* 1–82.

Baltes, P. B., & Kliegl, R. (1992). Further testing of limits of cognitive plasticity: negative age differences in a mnemonic skill are robust. *Developmental Psychology, 18,* 121–125.

Baltes, P. B., & Lindenberger, U. (1997). Emergence of a powerful connection between the sensory and cognitive functions across the adult lifespan: A new window to the study of cognitive ageing? *Psychology and Ageing, 12,* 12–21.

Banaji, M. R., & Crowder, R. G. (1989). The bankruptcy of everyday memory. *American Psychologist, 44,* 1185–1193.

Bangert-Drowns, R. L., Kulik, J. A., & Kulik, C. L. C. (1991). Effects of frequent classroom testing. *Journal of Educational Research, 85,* 89–99.

Barclay, J. R., Bransford, J. D., Franks, J. J., McCarrell, N., & Nitsch, K. (1974). Comprehension and semantic flexibility. *Journal of Verbal Learning and Verbal Behavior, 13,* 471–481.

Barnes, J. M., & Underwood, B. J. (1959). Fate of first-list association in transfer theory. *Journal of Experimental Psychology, 58*(2), 97–105.

Barnett, S. M., & Ceci, S. J. (2002). When and where do we apply what we learn? A taxonomy for far transfer. *Psychological Bulletin, 128,* 612–637.

Barnier, A. J., Conway, M. A., Mayoh, L., & Speyer, J. (2007). Directed forgetting of recently recalled autobiographical memories. *Journal of Experimental Psychology: General, 136*(2), 301–322.

Barrouillet, P., Bernardin, S., & Camos, V. (2004). Time constraints and resource sharing in adults' working memory spans. *Journal of Experimental Psychology: General, 133,* 83–100.

Bartlett, F. C. (1932). *Remembering: A Study in Experimental and Social Psychology.* New York: Cambridge University Press.

Basden, B. H., & Basden, D. R. (1996). Directed forgetting: Further comparisons of the item and list methods. *Memory, 4*(6), 633–653.

Basden, B. H., Basden, D. R., & Gargano, G. J. (1993). Directed forgetting in implicit and explicit memory tests: A comparison of methods. *Journal of Experimental Psychology: Learning, 19*(3), 603–616.

Bass, E., & Davis, L. (1988). *The Courage to Heal.* New York: Harper & Row.

Basso, A. H., Spinnler, G., Vallar, G., & Zanobia, E. (1982). Left hemisphere damage and selective impairment of auditory verbal short-term memory: A case study. *Neuropsychologica, 20,* 263–274.

Bassock, M., & Holyoak, K. J. (1989). Interdomain transfer between isomorphic topics in algebra and physics. *Journal of Experimental Psychology: Learning, Memory and Cognition, 15,* 153–166.

Bauer, P. J. (2004). Getting explicit memory off the ground: Steps toward construction of a neuro-developmental account of changes in the first two years of life. *Developmental Review, 24,* 347–373.

Bauer, P. J., Wenner, J. A., & Kroupina, M. G. (2002). Making the past present: Later verbal accessibility of early memories. *Journal of Cognition and Development, 3,* 21–47.

Bauer, P. J., Wenner, J. A., Dropik, P. L., & Wewerka, S. S. (2000). Parameters of Remembering and forgetting in the transition form infancy to early childhood: Introduction. *Monographs of the Society for Research in Child Development, 65,* 1–36.

Bayley, J. (1998). *Iris: A Memoir of Iris Murdoch.* London: Duckworth.

Beauregard, M., Chertkow, H., Gold, D., & Bergman, S. (2001). The impact of semantic impairment on word stem completion in Alzheimer's disease. *Neuropsychologia, 39*(3), 302–314.

Bechara, A., Tranel, D., Damasio, H., Adolphs, R., Rockland, C., & Damasio, A. R. (1995). Double dissociation of conditioning and declarative knowledge relative to the amygdala and hippocampus in humans. *Science, 269,* 1115–1118.

Becker, J. T. (1988). Working memory and secondary memory deficits in Alzheimer's disease. *Journal of Clinical and Experimental Neuropsychology, 10,* 739–753.

Bekerian, D. A., & Baddeley, A. D. (1980). Saturation advertising and the repetition effect. *Journal of Verbal Learning and Verbal Behavior, 19,* 17–25.

Bekerian, D. A., & Bowers, J. M. (1983). Eyewitness testimony: Were we misled? *Journal of Experimental Psychology: Learning,, Memory, and Cognition, 9,* 139–145.

Benton, S. L., Kraft, R. G., Glover, J. A., & Plake, B. S. (1984). Cognitive capacity differences among writers. *Journal of Educational Psychology, 76*(5), 820–834.

Berman, C. (2004). *Welcome to my pages on prosopagnosia.* Online. Available at: http://www. prosopagnosia. com/

Bernsten, D. (1996). Involuntary autobiographical memories. *Applied Cognitive Psychology, 10*(5), 435–454.

Berntsen, D., & Rubin, D. C. (2002). Emotionally charged autobiographical memories across the life span: The recall of happy, sad, traumatic and involuntary memories. *Psychology and Ageing, 17,* 636–652.

Berntsen, D., & Rubin, D. C. (2004). Cultural life scripts structure recall from autobiographical memory. *Memory and Cognition, 32,* 427–442.

Berntsen, D., & Rubin, D. C. (2008). The reappearance hypothesis revisited: Recurrent involuntary memories after traumatic events and in everyday life. *Memory and Cognition, 36,* 449–460.

Berntsen, D., & Thomsen, D. K. (2005). Personal memories for remote historical events: Accuracy and clarity of flashbulb memories related to World War II. *Journal of Experimental Psychology: General, 134,* 242–257.

Berry, D. C., & Broadbent, D. E. (1984). On the relationship between task performance and associated verbalizable knowledge. *Quarterly Journal of Experimental Psychology, 36A,* 209–231.

Biederman, I., Cooper, E. E., Fox, P. W., & Mahadevan, R. S. (1992). Unexceptional spatial memory in an exceptional memorist. *Journal of Experimental Psychology: Human Perception and Performance, 19,* 1162–1182.

Biggs, J. B. (1987). *The Study Process Questionnaire (SPQ): Manual.* Hawthorn, Victoria: Australian Council for Educational Research.

Biggs, J. B., Kember, D., & Leung, D. Y. P. (2001). The revised two-factor Study Process Questionnaire: R-SPQ-2F. *British Journal of Educational Psychology, 71,* 133–149.

Bjork, E. L., & Bjork, R. A. (2003). Intentional forgetting can increase, not decrease, residual influences of to-be-forgotten information. *Journal of Experimental Psychology: Learning, Memory, and Cognition, 29*(4), 524–531.

Bjork, E. L., Bjork, R. A., & Macleod, M. D. (2006). Types and consequences of forgetting: Intended and unintended. In L. Nilsson & O. Nobuo (Eds.), *Memory and Society: Psychological Perspectives.* (pp. 141–65). New York: Psychology Press.

Bjork, R . A., & Bjork, E. L. (1992). A new theory of disuse and an old theory of stimulus fluctuation. In A. Healy, S. Kosslyn, & R. Shiffrin (Eds.), *From Learning Process to Cognitive Processes: Essays in Honor of William K. Estes* (Vol. 2, pp. 35–67). Hillsdale, NJ: Lawrence Erlbaum Associates.

Bjork, R. A. (1970). Positive forgetting: The noninterference of items intentionally forgotten. *Journal of Verbal Learning and Verbal Behavior, 9*(3), 255–268.

Bjork, R. A. (1988). *Retrieval Practice and the Maintenance of Knowledge.* Oxford: Wiley.

Bjork, R. A. (1989). Retrieval inhibition as an adaptive mechanism in human memory. In H. L. Roediger & F. I. Craik (Eds.), *Varieties of Memory and Consciousness: Essays in Honour of Endel Tulving.* (pp. 309–30). Hillsdale, NJ: Lawrence Erlbaum Associates.

Bjork, R. A., & Whitten, W. B. (1974). Recency-sensitive retrieval processes. *Cognitive Psychology, 6,* 173–189.

Bjorklund, D. F., & Jacobs, J. W. (1985). Associative and categorical processes in children's memory: The role of automaticity in the development of organization in free recall. *Journal of Experimental Child Psychology, 39,* 599–617.

Blaney, P. H. (1986). Affect and memory: A review. *Psychological Bulletin, 99*(2), 229–246.

Bliss, T. V. P., & Lomo, T. (1973). Long-lasting potentiation of synaptic transmission in the dentate area of the anaesthetised rabbit following stimulation of the perforant path. *Journal of Physiology, 232,* 331–356.

Bluck, S., Alea, N., Habermas, T., & Rubin, D. C. (2005). A tale of three functions: The self-reported uses of autobiographical memory. *Social Cognition, 23,* 91–117.

Bluck, S., Levine, L. J., & Laulhere, T. M. (1999). Autobiographical remembering and hypermnesia: A comparison of older and younger adults. *Psychology and Aging, 14*(4), 671–682.

Bonanno, G. (2005). Resilience in the face of potential trauma. *Current Directions in Psychological Science, 14,* 135–138.

Bornstein, B. H., Liebel, L. M., & Scarberry, N. C. (1998). Repeated testing in eyewitness memory: A means to improve recall of a negative emotional event. *Applied Cognitive Psychology, 12*(2), 119–131.

Bornstein, R. F. (1989). Exposure and affect: Overview and meta-analysis of research, 1968–1987. *Psychological Bulletin, 106,* 265–289.

Bower, B. (1993). Sudden recall: adult memories of child abuse spark a heated debate. Online. Available at: *www.thefreelibrary.com* [accessed 5 May 2008].

Bower, G. H. (1973). How to…uh…remember! *Psychology Today, 7,* 63–70.

Bower, G. H., & Clark, M. C. (1969). Narrative stories as mediators for serial learning. *Psychonomic Science, 14,* 181–182.

Bower, G. H., Black, J. B., & Turner, T. J. (1979). Scripts in memory for test. *Cognitive Psychology, 11,* 177–220.

Bower, G. H., Clark, M. C., Lesgold, A. M., & Winzenz, D. (1969). Hierarchical retrieval schemes in recall of categorised word lists. *Journal of Verbal Learning and Verbal Behavior, 8,* 323–343.

Bower, G. H., Karlin, M. B., & Dueck, A. (1975). Comprehension and memory for pictures. *Memory and Cognition, 3,* 216–220.

Braak, H., & Braak, E. (1991). Neuropathological stageing of Alzheimer-related changes. *Acta Neuropathologica, 82,* 239–259.

Bradfield, A. L., Wells, G. L., & Olson, E. A. (2002). The damaging effect of confirming feedback on the relation between eyewitness certainty and identification accuracy. *Journal of Applied Psychology, 87,* 112–120.

Brainerd, C. J., & Mojardin, A. H. (1998). Children's and adults' spontaneous false memories: Long-term persistence and mere-testing effects. *Child Development, 69,* 1361–1377.

Brainerd, C. J., & Mojardin, A. H. (1998). Children's spontaneous false memories for narrative statements: Long-term persistence and mere-testing effects. *Child Development, 69,* 1361–1377.

Brainerd, C. J., & Reyna, V. F. (2004). Fuzzy-trace theory and memory development. *Developmental Review, 24,* 396–439.

Bransford, J. D. (1979). *Human Cognition: Learning, Understanding and Remembering.* Belmont, CA: Wadsworth.

Bransford, J. D., & Johnson, M. K. (1972). Contextual prerequisites for understanding. *Journal of Verbal Learning and Verbal Behavior, 11,* 717–726.

Braver, T. S., Cohen, J. D., Nystrom, L. E., Jonides, J., Smith, E. E., & Noll, D. C. (1997). A parametric study of prefrontal cortex involvement in human working memory. *Neuroimage, 5*(1), 49–62.

Brayshaw, T. (1849). *Metrical Mnemonics Applied to Geography, Astronomy and Chronology.* London.

Brener, R. (1940). An experimental investigation of memory span. *Journal of Experimental Psychology, 26,* 467–483.

Brewer, J. B., Zhao, Z., Desmond, J. E., Glover, G. H., & Gabrieli, J. D. E. (1998). Making memories: Brain activity that predicts how well visual experience will be remembered. *Science, 281,* 1185–1187.

Brewer, W. F. (1988). Memory for randomly sampled autobiographical events. In U. Neisser & E. Winograd (Eds.), *Remembering Reconsidered: Ecological and Traditional Approaches to the Study of Memory* (pp. 21–90). New York: Cambridge University Press.

Brewer, N., Weber, N., & Semmler, C. (2005). Eyewitness identification. In N. Brewer & K. D. Williams (Eds.), *Psychology and Law: An Empirical Perspective.* (pp. 177–221). New York: Guilford.

Brewer, W. F., & Treyens, J. C. (1981). Role of schemata in memory for places. *Cognitive Psychology, 13,* 207–230.

Brewin, C. R. (2001). A cognitive neuroscience account of posttraumatic stress disorder and its treatment. *Behaviour Research and Therapy, 39,* 373–393.

Broadbent, D. E. (1958). *Perception and Communication.* New York: Pergamon Press.

Broadbent, D. E., Cooper, P. J., & Broadbent, M. H. (1978). A comparison of hierarchical retrieval schemes in recall. *Journal of Experimental Psychology: Human Learning and Memory, 4,* 486–497.

Brooks, D. N., & Baddeley, A. D. (1976). What can amnesic patients learn? *Neuropsychologia, 14,* 111–122.

Brooks, L. R. (1967). The suppression of visualization by reading. *Quarterly Journal of Experimental Psychology, 191,* 289–299.

Brooks, L. R., & Vokey, J. R. (1991). Abstract analogies and abstracted grammars: A comment on Reber, Mathews et al. *Journal of Experimental Psychology: General, 120,* 316–323.

Brown, A. S. (1976). Spontaneous recovery in human learning. *Psychological Bulletin, 83*(2), 321–338.

Brown, A. S., Bracken, E., Zoccoli, S., & Douglas, K. (2004). Generating and remembering passwords. *Applied Cognitive Psychology, 18,* 641–651.

Brown, D., Scheflin, A. W., & Whitfield, C. L. (1999). Recovered memories: The current weight of the evidence in science and in the courts. *Journal of Psychiatry and Law, 27,* 5–156.

Brown, G. D. A., Neath, I., & Chater, N. (2007). A temporal ratio model of memory. *Psychological Review, 114,* 539–576.

Brown, I. D., Tickner, A. H., & Simmonds, D. C. V. (1969). Interference between concurrent tasks of driving and telephoning. *Journal of Applied Psychology, 53,* 419–424.

Brown, J. (1958). Some tests of the decay theory of immediate memory. *Quarterly Journal of Experimental Psychology, 10,* 12–21.

Brown, R. G., & Marsden, C. D. (1990). Cognitive function in Parkinson's disease: From description to theory. *Trends in Cognitive Sciences, 13,* 21–29.

Brown, R., & Kulik, J. (1977). Flashbulb memories. *Cognition, 5,* 73–99.

Brown, R., & McNeill, D. (1966). The "tip of the tongue" phenomenon. *Journal of Verbal Learning and Verbal Behavior, 5*(4), 325–337.

Bruce, V., Henderson, Z., Greenwood, K., Hancock, P., Burton, A. M., & Miller, P. (1999). Verification of face identities from images captured on video. *Journal of Experimental Psychology: Applied, 5,* 339–360.

Bruck, M., & Ceci, S. J. (1997). The suggestibility of young children. *Current Directions in Psychological Science, 6,* 75–79.

Bruck, M., & Ceci, S. J. (1999). The suggestibility of children's memory. *Annual Review of Psychology, 50,* 419–439.

Bruck, M., Ceci. S., Francoeur, E., & Barr, R. (1995). "I hardly cried when I got my shot!" Influencing children's reports about a visit to their pediatrician. *Child Development, 66,* 193–208.

Bruck, M., & Melnyk, L. (2004). Individual differences in children's suggestibility: A review and synthesis. *Applied Cognitive Psychology, 18,* 947–996.

Büchel, C., & Dolan, R. J. (2000). Classical fear conditioning in functional neuroimaging. *Current Opinion in Neurobiology, 10,* 219–223.

Büchel, C., Morris, J., Dolan, R. J., & Friston, K. J. (1998). Brain systems mediating aversive conditioning: An event-related fMRI study. *Neuron, 20,* 947–957.

Budd, J. W. (2004). Mind maps as classroom exercises. *Journal of Economic Education, 35,* 35–46.

Burgess, N., & Hitch, G. J. (1999). Memory for serial order: A network model of the phonological loop and its timing. *Psychological Review, 106,* 551–581.

Burgess, N., & Hitch, G. J. (2006). A revised model of short-term memory and long–term learning of verbal sequences. *Journal of Memory and Language, 55,* 627–652.

Burke, D. M., MacKay, D. G., Worthley, J. S., & Wade, E. (1991). On the tip of the tongue: What causes word finding failures in young and older adults. *Journal of Memory and Language, 30,* 542–579.

Butler, K. M., Zacks, R. T., & Henderson, J. M. (1999). Suppression of reflexive saccades in younger and older adults: Age comparisons in an antisaccade task. *Memory and Cognition, 27,* 584–591.

Butters, N., & Cermak, L. S. (1986). A case study of the forgetting of autobiographical knowledge. In Rubin D. C. (Ed.), *Autobiographical Memory* (pp. 253–272). Cambridge: Cambridge University Press.

Buzan, T., & Buzan, B. (1993). *The Mind Map Book.* London: BBC Books.

Cabeza, R., Prince, S. E., Daselaar, S. M., Greenberg, D. L., Budde, M., Dolcos, F. et al. (2004). Brain activity during episodic retrieval of autobiographical and laboratory events: An fMRI study using a novel photo paradigm. *Journal of Cognitive Neuroscience, 16,* 1583–1594.

Cahill, L., Haier, R. J., & Alkire, M. T. (1996). Amygdala activity at encoding correlated with long-term free-recall of emotional information. *Proceedings of the National Academy of Science of USA, 93,* 8016–8021.

Campoy, G., & Baddeley, A. D. (2008). Phonological and semantic strategies in immediate serial recall. *Memory, 16,* 329–340.

Caplan, D., Rochon, E., & Waters, G. S. (1992). Articulatory and phonological determinants of word-length effects in span tasks. *Quarterly Journal of Experimental Psychology, 45A,* 177–192.

Caramazza, A., & Shelton, J. R. (1998). Domain specific knowledge systems in the brain: The animate-inanimate distinction. *Journal of Cognitive Neuroscience, 10,* 1–34.

Cardena, E., & Spiegel, D. (1993). Dissociative reactions to the San Francisco Bay area earthquake of 1989. *American Journal of Psychiatry, 150,* 474–478.

Carlesimo, G. A., Perri, R., Turriziani, P., Tomaiuolo, F., & Caltagirone, C. (2001). Remembering what but not where: Independence of spatial and visual working memory in the human brain. *Cortex, 37*(4), 519–534.

Carmichael, L., Hogan, H. P., & Walter, A. A. (1932). An experimental study of the effect of language on the reproduction of visually perceived form. *Journal of Experimental Psychology, 15,* 73–86.

Carroll, M., Campbell-Ratcliffe, J., Murnane, H., & Perfect, T. J. (2007). Retrieval-induced forgetting in educational contexts: Monitoring, expertise, text integration and test format. *European Journal of Cognitive Psychology, 19*, 580–606.

Ceci, S. J., Baker, J. E., & Bronfenbrenner, U. (1988). Prospective remembering and temporal calibration. In M. M. Grunberg, P. E. Morris, & R. N. Sykes (Eds.), *Practical Aspects of Memory: Current Research and Issues* (Vol. 1). Chichester, UK: Wiley.

Cermak, L. S. (1976). The encoding capacity of a patient with amnesia due to encephalitis. *Neuropsychologia, 14*, 311–326.

Cermak, L. S., & Moreines, J. (1976). Verbal retention deficits in aphasic and amnesic patients. *Brain and Language, 3*, 16–27.

Cermak, L. S., & Reale, L. (1978). Depth of processing and retention of words by alcoholic Korsakoff patients. *Journal of Experimental Psychology: Human Learning and Memory, 4*, 165–174.

Cermak, L. S., Butters, N., & Moreines, J. (1974). Some analyses of the verbal encoding deficit of alcoholic Korsakoff patients. *Brain and Language, 1*, 141–150.

Chalfonte, B. L., & Johnson, M. K. (1996). Feature memory and binding in young and older adults. *Memory and Cognition, 24*, 403–416.

Charles, S. T., Mather, M., & Carstensen, L. L. (2003). Aging and emotional memory: The forgettable nature of negative images for older adults. *Journal of Experimental Psychology General, 132*(2), 310–324.

Charness, N. (1985). Ageing and problem-solving performance. In N. Charness (Ed.), *Ageing and Human Performance* (pp. 225–260). Chichester, UK: John Wiley.

Chase, W. G., & Ericsson, K. A. (1982). Skill in working memory. In G. H. Bower (Ed.), *The Psychology of Learning and Motivation* (Vol. 16). New York: Academic Press.

Chasteen, A. L., Park, D. C., & Schwarz, N. (2001). Implementation intentions and facilitation of prospective memory. *Psychological Science, 12*, 457–461.

Chi, M. T. (1978). Knowledge, structure and memory development. In R. S. Siegler (Ed.), *Children's Thinking. What Develops?* Hillsdale, NJ: Lawrence Erbaum Associates.

Christensen, H., Henderson, A. S., Griffiths, K., & Levings, C. (1997). Does aging inevitably lead to declines in cognitive performance: A longitudinal study of elite academics. *Personality and Individual Differences, 23*, 67–78.

Christensen, H., Kopelman, M. D., Stanhope, N., Lorentz, L., & Owen, P. (1998). Rates of forgetting in Alzheimer dementia. *Neuropsychologia, 36*, 546–557.

Chu, S., & Downes, J. J. (2002). Proust nose best: Odors are better cues of autobiographical memory. *Memory and Cognition, 30*, 511–518.

Claparède, E. (1911). Recognition et moïté. *Archives de Psychologie, 11*, 79–90.

Clare, J., & Lewandowsky, S. (2004). Verbalizing facial memory: Criterion effects in verbal overshadowing. *Journal of Experimental Psychology: Learning, Memory and Cognition, 30*, 739–755.

Clare, L., Wilson, B. A., Carter, G., Breen, K., Gosses, A., & Hodges, J. R. (2000). Intervening with everyday memory problems in early Alzheimer's disease: An errorless learning approach. *Journal of Clinical and Experimental Neuropsychology, 22*, 132–146.

Clark, D. M., & Teasdale, J. D. (1982). Diurnal variation in clinical depression and accessibility of memories of positive and negative experiences. *Journal of Abnormal Psychology, 91*(2), 87–95.

Clayton, N.S., & Dickinson, A. (1999). Scrub jays remember when as well as where and what food items they cached. *Journal of Comparative Psychology, 113*, 403–416.

Cockburn, J., & Smith, P. (1991). The relative influence of intelligence and age on everyday memory. *Journal of Gerontology, 46*, 31–36.

Cockburn, J., & Smith, P. T. (1994). Anxiety and errors of prospective memory among elderly people. *British Journal of Psychology, 85*, 273–282.

Cohen, G., & Faulkner, D. (1989). Age differences in source forgetting: Effects on reality monitoring and on eyewitness testimony. *Psychology and Aging, 4*, 10–17.

Cohen, N. J., & Squire, L. R. (1980). Preserved learning and retention of pattern-analyzing skill in amnesia: Dissociation of knowing how and knowing that. *Science, 210*, 207–210.

Colle, H. A. (1980). Auditory encoding in visual short-term recall: Effects of noise intensity and spatial location. *Journal of Verbal Learning and Verbal Behaviour, 19*, 722–735.

Colle, H. A., & Welsh, A. (1976). Acoustic masking in primary memory. *Journal of Verbal Learning and Verbal Behavior, 15*, 17–32.

Collie, R., & Hayne, H. (1999). Deferred imitation by 6- and 9-month-old infants: More evidence for declarative memory. *Developmental Psychobiology, 35*, 83–90.

Collins A. M., & Loftus E. (1975). A spreading activation theory of semantic memory. *Psychological Review, 82*, 407–428.

Collins, A. M., & Quillian, M. R. (1969). Retrieval time from semantic memory. *Journal of Verbal Learning and Verbal Behavior, 8*, 240–247.

Conrad, C. (1972). Cognitive economy in semantic memory. *Journal of Experimental Psychology, 92*, 149–154.

Conrad, R. (1960). Very brief delays of immediate recall. *Quarterly Journal of Experimental Psychology, 12*, 45–47.

Conrad, R. (1964). Acoustic confusion in immediate memory. *British Journal of Psychology, 55*, 75–84.

Conrad, R., & Hull, A. J. (1964). Information, acoustic confusion and memory span. *British Journal of Psychology, 55*, 429–432.

Conroy, R., & Salmon, K. (2006). Talking about parts of a past experience: The influence of elaborative discussion and event structure on children's recall of nondiscussed information. *Journal of Experimental Child Psychology, 95*, 278–297.

Conway, A. R. A., Cowan, N., & Bunting, M. F. (2001). The cocktail party phenomenon revisted: The importance of working memory capacity. *Psychonomic Bulletin and Review, 8*, 331–335.

Conway, M. A. (1990). *Autobiographical Memory: An Introduction*. Philadelphia: Open University Press.

Conway, M. A. (2005). Memory and the self. *Journal of Memory and Language, 53*, 594–628.

Conway, M. A., & Pleydell-Pearce, C. W. (2000). The construction of autobiographical memories in the self-memory system. *Psychological Review, 107*, 262–288.

Conway, M. A., & Tacchi, P. C. (1996). Motivated confabulation. *Neurocase, 2*, 325–338.

Conway, M. A., Cohen, G., & Stanhope, N. M. (1992). Very long-term memory for knowledge acquired at school and university. *Applied Cognitive Psychology, 6*, 467–482.

Conway, M. A., Collins, A. F., Gathercole, S. E., & Anderson, S. J. (1996). Recollection of true and false autobiographical memories. *Journal of Experimental Psychology: General, 125*, 69–95.

Conway, M. A., Pleydell-Pearce, C. W., Whitecross, S., & Sharpe, H. (2003). Neurophysiological correlates of autobiographical memory: On the unversality of the reminiscence bump. *Neuropsychologia, 41*, 334–340.

Conway, M. A., Wang, Q., Hanyu, K., & Haque, S. (2005). A cross-cultural investigation of autobiographical memory. *Journal of Cross-Cultural Psychology, 36*, 739–749.

Cordón, I. M., Pipe, M. E., Sayfan, L., Melinder, A., & Goodman, G. S. (2004). Memory for traumatic experiences in early childhood. *Developmental Review, 24*, 101–132.

Corkin, S. (1968). Acquisition of motor skill after bilateral medial temporal-lobe excision. *Neuropsychologia, 6*, 255–265.

Cosentino, S., Chute, D., Libon, D., Moore, P., & Grossman, M. (2006). How does the brain represent scripts? A study of executive processes and semantic knowledge in dementia. *Neuropsychology, 20*, 307–318.

Cowan, N. (1988). Evolving conceptions of memory storage, selective attention, and their mutual constraints within the human information-processing system. *Psychological Bulletin, 104*(2), 163–191.

Cowan, N. (1992). Verbal memory span and the timing of spoken recall. *Journal of Memory and Language, 31*(5), 668–684.

Cowan, N. (1999). An embedded-processes model of working memory. In A. M. P. Shah (Ed.), *Models of Working Memory* (pp. 62–101). Cambridge: Cambridge University Press.

Cowan, N. (2001). The magical number 4 in short-term memory: a reconsideration of mental storage capacity. *Behavioral and Brain Sciences, 24*, 87–114; discussion 114–185.

Cowan, N. (2005). *Working Memory Capacity*. Hove, UK: Psychology Press.

Cowan, N., Day, L., Saults, J. S., Keller, T. A., Johnson, T., & Flores, L. (1992). The role of verbal output time and the effects of word-length on immediate memory. *Journal of Memory and Language, 31*, 1–17.

Craik, F. I. M. (1986). A functional account of age difference in memory. In F. Klix & H. Hagendorf (Eds.), *Human Memory and Cognitive Capabilities: Mechanisms and Performances*. (pp. 409–422). New York: Elsevier Science.

Craik, F. I. M. (2005). On reducing age-related declines in memory. In J. Duncan, L. Phillips, & P. McLeod (Eds.), *Measuring the Mind: Speed, Control and Age*. (pp. 275–292). Oxford: Oxford University Press.

Craik, F. I. M., & Byrd, M. (1982). Aging and cognitive deficits: The role of attentional resources. In F. I. M. Craik & S. Trehub (Eds.), *Aging and Cognitive Processes* (pp. 191–211). New York: Plenum.

Craik, F. I. M., & Jennings, J. M. (1992). Human memory. In F. I. M. Craik & T. A. Salthouse (Eds.), *Handbook of Ageing and Cognition* (pp. 51–100). Hillsdale, NJ: Lawrence Erlbaum Associates.

Craik, F. I. M., & Lockhart, R. S. (1972). Levels of processing. A framework for memory research. *Journal of Verbal Learning and Verbal Behavior, 11*, 671–684.

Craik, F. I. M., & Tulving, E. (1975). Depth of processing and the retention of words in episodic memory. *Journal of Experimental Psychology: General, 104*(3), 268–294.

Craik, F. I. M., Byrd, M., & Swanson, J. M. (1987). Patterns of memory loss in three elderly samples. *Psychology and Aging, 2*, 79–86.

Craik, F. I., Govoni, R., Naveh-Benjamin, M., & Anderson, N. D. (1996). The effects of divided attention on encoding and retrieval processes in human memory. *Journal of Experimental Psychology: General, 125*(2), 159–180.

Craik, K. J. W. (1943). *The Nature of Explanation.* London: Cambridge University Press.

Crary, W. G. (1966). Reactions to incongruent self-experiences. *Journal of Consulting Psychology, 30,* 246–252.

Crawford, J. R., Smith, G., Maylor, E. A., Della Sala, S., & Logie, R. H. (2003). The Prospective and Retrospective Memory Questionnaire (PRMQ): Normative data and latent structure in a large non-clinical sample. *Memory, 11,* 261–275.

Crawley, R. A., & Eacott, M. J. (2006). Memories of early childhood: Qualities of the experience of recollection. *Memory and Cognition, 34,* 287–294.

Cree, G. S., & McRae, K. (2003). Analyzing the factors underlying the structure and computation of the meaning of chipmunk, cherry, chisel, cheese, and cello (and many other such concrete nouns). *Journal of Experimental Psychology: General, 132,* 163–201.

Crocker, J., & Major, B. (1989). Social stigma and self-esteem: The self-protective properties of stigma. *Psychological Review, 96*(4), 608–630.

Crovitz, H. F., & Shiffman, H. (1974). Frequency of episodic memories as a function of their age. *Bulletin of the Psychonomic Society, 4,* 517–518.

Crowder, R. G. (1971). Waiting for the stimulus suffix: Decay, delay, rhythm, and readout in immediate memory. *Quarterly Journal of Experimental Psychology, 23,* 324–340.

Crowder, R. G. (1972). Visual and auditory memory. In J. F. Kavanagh & I. G. Mattingly (Eds.), *Language by Ear and by Eye: The Relation between Speech and Learning to Read.* Cambridge, MA: MIT Press.

Crowder, R. G. (1976). *Principles of Learning and Memory.* Hillsdale, NJ: Lawrence Erlbaum Associates.

Crowder, R. G., & Morton, J. (1969). Precategorical acoustic storage (PAS). *Perception and Psychophysics, 5,* 365–373.

Crowder, R. G., & Raeburn, V. P. (1970). The suffix effect with reversed speech. *Journal of Verbal Learning and Verbal Behavior, 9,* 342–345.

Cuc, A., Koppel, J., & Hirst, W. (2007). Silence is not golden: A case for socially shared retrieval-induced forgetting. *Psychological Science, 18*(8), 727–733.

Cutler, B. L., Penrod, S. D., & Dexter, H. R. (1989). The eyewitness, the expert psychologist, and the jury. *Law and Human Behavior, 13,* 311–332.

d'Ydewalle, G., Luwel, K., & Brunfaut, E. (1999). The importance of on-going concurrent activities as a function of age in time- and event-based prospective memory. *European Journal of Cognitive*

Psychology, 11, 219–237.

Dale, H. C. A. (1973). Short-term memory for visual information. *British Journal of Psychology, 64,* 1–8.

Dalgleish, T., Spinks, H., Yiend, J., & Kuyken, W. (2001). Autobiographical memory style in seasonal affective disorder and its relationship to future sympton remission. *Journal of Abnormal Psychology, 110,* 335–340.

Dalla Barba, G., Cipolotti, L., & Denes, G. (1990). Autobiographical memory loss and confabulation in Korsakoff's syndrome: A case report. *Cortex, 26,* 525–534.

Dallam, S. J. (2001). The long-term medical consequences of childhood maltreatment. In K. Franey, R. Geffner, & R. Falconer (Eds.), *The Cost of Child Maltreatment: Who Pays? We All Do.* (pp. 1–14). San Diego, CA: Family Violence & Sexual Assault Institute.

Damasio, A. R. (1994). *Descartes' Error: Emotion, Reason, and the Human Brain.* New York: Putnam.

Damasio, A. R., Eslinger, P. J., Damasio, H., Van Hoesen, & G.W., Cornell, S. (1985). Multi-modal amnesic syndrome following bilateral temporal and basal forebrain damage. *Archives of Neurology, 42,* 252–259.

Daneman, M., & Carpenter, P. A. (1980). Individual differences in working memory and reading. *Journal of Verbal Learning and Verbal Behaviour, 19,* 450–466.

Daneman, M., & Merikle, P. M. (1996). Working memory and language comprehension: A meta-analysis. *Psychonomic Bulletin and Review, 3,* 422–433.

Dave, A. S., & Margoliash, D. (2000). Song replay during sleep and computational rules for sensorimotor vocal learning. *Science, 290,* 812–816.

Davidson, P. S. R., Cook, S. P., & Glisky, E. L. (2006). Flashbulb memories for September 11th can be preserved in older adults. *Aging, Neuropsychology, and Cognition, 13,* 196–206.

De Beni, R., Moè, A., & Cornoldi, C. (1997). Learning from texts or lectures: Loci mnemonics can interfere with reading but not with listening. *European Journal of Cognitive Psychology, 9,* 401–415.

De Renzi, E., Liotti, M., & Nichelli, P. (1987). Semantic amnesia with preservation of autobiographic memory. *Cortex, 23,* 575–597.

Deary, I. J., Whalley, L. J., Batty, G. D., & Starr, J. M. (2006). Physical fitness and lifetime cognitive change. *Neurology, 67,* 1195–1200.

Deary, I. J., Whiteman, M. C., Starr, J. M., Whalley, L. J., & Fox, H. C. (2004). The impact of childhood intelligence on later life: following up the Scottish Mental Surveys of 1932 and 1947.

Journal of Personality and Social Psychology, 86, 130–147.

DeCasper, A. J., & Fifer, W. P. (1980). Of human bonding: Newborns prefer their mothers' voices. *Science, 208,* 1174–1176.

Deeprose, C., & Andrade, J. (2006). Is priming during anesthesia unconscious? *Consciousness and Cognition, 15,* 1–23.

Deese, J. (1959). Influence of inter-item associative strength upon immediate free recall. *Psychological Reports, 5,* 305–312.

Deffenbacher, K. A. (1983). Identification evidence: A psychological evaluation: J. W. Shepherd, H. D. Ellis, & G. M. Davies. *American Journal of Psychology, 96,* 591–595.

Deffenbacher, K. A., Bornstein, B. H., Penrod, S. D., & McGorty, E. K. (2004). A meta- analytic review of the effects of high stress on eyewitness memory. *Law and Human Behavior, 28,* 687–706.

Della Sala, S., & Logie, R. H. (2002). Neurospsychological impairments of visual and spatial working memory. In A. D. Baddeley, M. D. Kopelman, & B. A. Wilson (Eds.), *Handbook of Memory Disorders* (2nd ed., pp. 271–292). Chichester, UK: Wiley.

Della Sala, S., Freschi, R., & Lucchelli, F. (1996). Retrograde amnesia: No past, new life. In P. W. Halligan & J. C. Marshall (Eds.), *Method in Madness: Case Studies in Cognitive Neuropsychiatry* (pp. 209–233). Hove, UK: Psychology Press.

Della Sala, S., Gray, C., Baddeley, A., Allamano, N., & Wilson, L. (1999). Pattern span: A means of unwelding visuo-spatial memory. *Neuropsychologia, 37,* 1189–1199.

DeMarie, D., & Ferron, J. (2003). Capacity, strategies, and metamemory: Tests of a three-factor model of memory development. *Journal of Experimental Child Psychology, 84,* 167–193.

Depue, B. E., Banich, M. T., & Curran, T. (2006). Suppression of emotional and nonemotional content in memory. Effects of repetition on cognitive control. *Psychological Science, 17*(5), 441–447.

Depue, B. E., Curran, T., & Banich, M. T. (2007). Prefrontal regions orchestrate suppression of emotional memories via a two-phase process. *Science, 317,* 215–219.

DeZeeuw, C. I. (2007). Plasticity: A pragmatic compromise. In H. L. Roediger, III, Y. Dudai, & S. M. Fitzpatrick (Eds.), *Science of Memory: Concepts* (pp. 83–86). New York: Oxford University Press.

Di Vesta, F. J., Ingersoll, G., & Sunshine, P. (1971). A factor analysis of imagery tests. *Journal of Verbal Learning and Verbal Behavior, 10,* 471–479.

Diener, E., & Diener, C. (1996). Most people are happy. *Psychological Science, 7*(3), 181–185.

Dismukes, K., & Nowinski, J. (in press). Prospective memory, concurrent task managment, and pilot error. In A. Kramer, D. Wiegmann, & A. Kirlik (Eds.), *Attention from Theory to Practice.* New York: Oxford University Press.

Dodhia, R. M., & Dismukes, R. K. (2005). *A task interrupted becomes a prospective memory task.* Paper presented at the biennial meeting of the Society for Applied Research in Memory and Cognition, Wellington, New Zealand.

Dodson, C. S., & Krueger, L. E. (2006). I misremember it well: Why older adults are unreliable eyewitnesses. *Psychonomic Bulletin and Review, 13,* 770–775.

Dolcos, F., LaBar, K. S., & Cabeza, R. (2005). Remembering one year later: Role of the amygdala and the medial temporal lobe memory system in retrieving emotional memories. *Proceedings of the National Academy of Sciences, 102,* 2626–2631.

Doody, R. S., Stevens, J. C., Beck, C., Dubinsky, R. M., Kaye, J. A., Gwyther, L. et al. (2001). Practice parameter: Management of dementia (an evidence-based review). *Neurology, 56,* 1154–1166.

Dooling, D. J., & Christiaansen, R. E. (1977). Episodic and semantic aspects of memory for prose. *Journal of Experimental Psychology–Human Learning and Memory, 3,* 428–436.

Druchman, D., & Bjork, A. (1994). *Learning, Remembering, Believing: Enhancing Human Performance.* Washington, DC: National Academy Press.

Dudai, Y. (2004). The neurobiology of consolidations, or, how stable is the engram. *Annual Review of Psychology, 55,* 51–86.

Duncan, J., & Owen, A. M. (2000). Common regions of the human frontal lobe recruited by diverse cognitive demands. *Trends in Neurosciences, 23,* 475–483.

Düzel, E., Vargha-Khadem, F., Heinze, H. J., & Mishkin, M. (2001). Brain activity evidence for recognition without recollection after early hippocampal damage. *Proceedings, National Academy of Sciences of the United States of America, 98*(14), 8101–8106.

Dywan, J., & Jacoby, L. L. (1990). Effects of aging on source monitoring: Differences in susceptibility to false fame. *Psychology and Aging, 5,* 379–387.

Eakin, D. K., Schreiber, T. A., & Sergent-Marshall, S. (2003). Misinformation effects in eyewitness memory: The presence and absence of memory impairment as a function of warning and misinformation accessibility. *Journal of*

Experimental Psychology: Learning, Memory, and Cognition, 29, 813–825.

Ebbesen, E. B., & Konecni, V. J. (1997). Eyewitness memory research: Probative vs. prejudicial value. *The International Digest of Human Behavior, Science, and the Law, 5,* 2–28.

Ebbinghaus, H. (1885), Über das Gedächtnis. Untersuchungen zur experimentellen Psychologie, Duncker & Humblot, Leipzig. [English translation by H. A. Ruger & C. E. Bussenius. In Ebbinghaus, H. (1913) *Memory: A Contribution to Experimental Psychology.* New York: Teachers College, Columbia University].

Ebbinghaus, H. (1913). *Memory: A Contribution to Experimental Psychology.* (H. A. Ruger & C. E. Bussenius, Trans.). New York: Teachers College, Columbia University.

Ehlers, A., Hackmann, A., & Michael, T. (2004). Intrusive reexperiencing in posttraumatic stress disorder: Phenomenology, theory, and therapy. *Memory, 12,* 403–415.

Eich, E., Macaulay, D., & Ryan, L. (1994). Mood dependent memory for events of the personal past. *Journal of Experimental Psychology: General, 123*(2), 201–215.

Eich, E., Macauley, D., Loewenstein, R. J., & Dihle, P. H. (1997). Memory, amnesia and dissociative identity disorder. *Psychological Science, 8,* 417–422.

Eich, J. E. (1980). The cue-dependent nature of state-dependent retrieval. *Memory and Cognition, 8*(2), 157–173.

Eichenbaum, H. (1994). The hippocampal system and declarative memory in humans and animals: Experimental analysis and historical origins. In D. L. Schacter & E. Tulving (Eds.), *Memory Systems* (pp. 143–99). Cambridge, MA: MIT Press.

Einstein, G. O., & McDaniel, M. A. (1990). Normal aging and prospective memory. *Journal of Experimental Psychology: Learning, Memory and Cognition, 16,* 717–726.

Einstein, G. O., & McDaniel, M. A. (2005). Prospective memory: Multiple retrieval processes. *Current Directions in Psychological Science, 14,* 286–290.

Einstein, G. O., McDaniel, M. A., Richardson, S. L., Guynn, M. J., & Cunfer, A. R. (1995). Aging and prospective memory: Examining the influences of self-initiated retrieval processes. *Journal of Experimental Psychology: Learning, Memory and Cognition, 21,* 996–1007.

Einstein, G. O., McDaniel, M. A., Thomas, R., Mayfield, S., Shank, H., Morrisette, N., & Breneiser, J. (2005). Multiple processes in prospective memory retrieval: Factors determining monitoring versus spontaneous retrieval. *Journal*

of Experimental Psychology: General, 134, 327–342.

Elliot, D., & Madalena, J. (1987). The influence of premovement visual information on manual aiming. *Quarterly Journal of Experimental Psychology, 39A,* 542–559.

Ellis, N. C. (1993). Rules and instances in foreign language learning: Interactions of explicit and implicit knowledge. *European Journal of Cognitive Psychology, 5,* 289–318.

Ellis, N. C. (1994). Implicit and explicit processes in language acquisition: An introduction. In N. Ellis (Ed.), *Implicit and Explicit Learning of Languages.* (pp. 1–32). London: Academic Press.

Ellis, N., & Beaton, A. (1993). Factors affecting the learning of foreign language vocabulary: Imagery keyword mediators and phonological short-term memory. *Quarterly Journal of Experimental Psychology, 46A,* 522–558.

Emerson, M. J., & Miyake, A. (2003). The role of inner speech in task switching: A dual-task investigation. *Journal of Memory and Language, 48,* 148–168.

Engle, R. W. (1996). Working memory and retrieval: An inhibition-resource approach. In J. T. E. Richardson, R. W. Engle, L. Hasher, R. H. Logie, E. R. Stoltfus, & R. T. Zacks (Eds.), *Working Memory and Human Cognition* (pp. 89–119). New York: Oxford University Press.

Engle, R. W., & Kane, M. J. (2004). Executive attention, working memory capacity and two-factor theory of cognitive control. In B. Ross (Ed.), *The Psychology of Learning and Motivation.* (pp. 145–199). New York: Elsevier.

Engle, R. W., Carullo, J. W., & Collins, K. W. (1991). Individual differences in working memory for comprehension and following directions. *Journal of Educational Research, 84,* 253–262.

Engle, R. W., Tuholski, S. W., Laughlin, J. E., & Conway, A. R. A. (1999). Working memory, short-term memory, and general fluid intelligence: A latent-variable approach. *Journal of Experimental Psychology: General, 128,* 309–331.

Englekamp, J. (1998). *Memory for Actions.* Hove, UK: Psychology Press.

Entwistle, N. (1987). A model of the teaching–learning process. In J. T. E. Richardson, M. W. Eysenck, & D. Warren Piper (Eds.), *Student Learning: Research in Education and Cognitive Psychology.* Buckingham, UK: Open University Press.

Erdelyi, M. H. (2006). The unified theory of repression. *Behavioral and Brain Sciences, 29*(5), 499–551.

Erdelyi, M. H., & Kleinbard, J. (1978). Has Ebbinghaus decayed with time? The growth of recall (hypermnesia) over days. *Journal of*

Experimental Psychology: Human Learning and Memory, 4(4), 275–289.

Ericsson, K. A. (1988). Analysis of memory performance in terms of memory skill. In R. J. Sternberg (Ed.), *Advances in the Psychology of Human Intelligence* (Vol. 4, pp. 137–179). Hillsdale, NJ: Lawrence Erlbaum Associates.

Ericsson, K. A. (2003). Exceptional memorizers: Made, not born. *Trends in Cognitive Sciences, 7,* 233–235.

Ericsson, K. A., & Chase, W. G. (1982). Exceptional memory. *American Scientist, 70,* 607–615.

Ericsson, K. A., & Kintsch, W. (1995). Long-term working memory. *Psychological Review, 102*(2), 211–245.

Ericsson, K. A., & Polson, P. G. (1988). An experimental analysis of a memory skill for dinner orders. *Journal of Experimental Psychology: Learning Memory and Cognition, 14,* 305–316.

Ericsson, K. A., Delaney, P. F., Weaver, G., & Mahadevan, R. (2004). Uncovering the structure of a mnemonist's superior "basic" memory capacity. *Cognitive Psychology, 49,* 191–237.

Ericsson, K. A., Krampe, R. T., & Tesch-Römer, C. (1993). The role of deliberate practice in the acquisition of expert performance. *Psychological Review, 100,* 363–406.

Erixon-Lindroth, N., Farde, L., Wahlin, T. B., Sovago, J., Halldin, C., & Backman, L. (2005). The role of the striatal dopamine transporter in cognitive aging. *Psychiatry Research, 138,* 1–12.

Farah, M. J. (1994). Perception and awareness after brain damage. *Current Opinion in Neurobiology, 4,* 252–255.

Farah, M. J., & McClelland, J. L. (1991). A computational model of semantic memory impairment: Modality-specificity and emergent category-specificity. *Journal of Experimental Psychology: General, 120,* 339–357.

Farah, M. J., Hammond, K. M., Levine, D. N., & Calvanio, R. (1988). Visual and spatial mental imagery: Dissociable systems of representation. *Cognitive Psychology, 20,* 439–462.

Farrand, P., Hussain, F., & Hennessy, E. (2002). The efficacy of the 'mind map' study technique. *Medical Education, 36,* 426–431.

Farrell, S., & Lewandowski, S. (2002). An endogenous model of ordering in serial recall. *Psychonomic Bulletin and Review, 9,* 59–60.

Farrell, S., & Lewandowski, S. (2003). Dissimilar items benefit from phonological similarity in serial recall. *Journal of Experimental Psychology: Learning, Memory and Cognition, 29,* 838–849.

Fernandes, M. A., & Moscovitch, M. (2000). Divided attention and memory: Evidence of substantial interference effects at retrieval and encoding. *Journal of Experimental Psychology: General, 129*(2), 155–1766.

Fernandes, M. A., & Moscovitch, M. (2003). Interference effects from divided attention during retrieval in younger and older adults. *Psychology of Aging, 18*(2), 219–230.

Finke, R. A., & Slayton, K. (1988). Explorations of creative visual synthesis in mental imagery. *Memory and Cognition, 16,* 252–257.

Fisher, R. P., & Craik, F. I. M. (1977). Interaction between encoding and retrieval operations in cued recall. *Journal of Experimental Psychology: Learning, Memory and Cognition, 3,* 701–711.

Fisher, R. P., Geiselman, R. E., Raymond, D. S., Jurkevich, L. M., & Warhaftig, M. L. (1987). Enhancing enhanced eyewitness memory: Refining the cognitive interview. *Journal of Police Science and Administration, 15,* 291–297.

Fivush, R., & Nelson, K. (2004). Culture and language in the emergence of autobiographical memory. *Psychological Science, 15,* 573–577.

Fivush, R., Gray, J. T., & Fromhoff, F. A. (1987). Two-year-olds talk about the past. *Cognitive Development, 2,* 393–409.

Fivush, R., Hudson, J., & Nelson, K. (1984). Children's long-term memory for a novel event: An exploratory study. *Merrill-Palmer Quarterly Journal of Developmental Psychology, 30,* 303–316.

Fleischman, D. A., Vaidya, C. J., Lange, K. L., & Gabrieli, J. D. (1997). A dissociation between perceptual explicit and implicit memory processes. *Brain and Cognition, 35,* 42–57.

Flynn, J. R. (1987). Massive IQ gains in 14 nations: What IQ tests really measure. *Psychological Bulletin, 101,* 171–191.

Foa, E. B., & Rothbaum, B. O. (1998). *Treating the Trauma of Rape: Cognitive Behavioral Therapy for PTSD.* New York: Guilford Press.

Foa, E. B., Rothbaum, B. O., Riggs, D. S., & Murdock, T. (1991). Treatment of posttraumatic stress disorder in rape victims: A comparison between cognitive behavioural procedures and counseling. *Journal of Consulting and Clinical Psychology, 59,* 715–723.

Freud, S. (1900). The interpretation of dreams. In J. Strachey (Ed.), *The Standard Edition of the Complete Psychological Writings of Sigmund Freud.* London: Hogarth Press.

Freud, S. (1901). *The Psychopathology of Everyday Life.* New York: W. W. Norton.

Freud, S. (1904/1938). Psychopathology of everyday life. In A. A. Brill (Ed.), *The Writings of Sigmund Freud.* New York: Modern Library.

Freud, S. (1915/1957). Repression. In *Freud's Collected Papers* (Vol. IV). London: Hogarth Press.

Freud, S. (1917). Repression. In J. Riviere (Ed.), *A General Introduction to Psychoanalysis* (p. 147). New York: Liveright.

Friedman, N. P., & Miyake, A. (2004). The relations among inhibition and interference control functions: A latent variable analysis. *Journal of Experimental Psychology: General, 133*, 101–135.

Frith, C. D. (1992). *The Cognitive Neuropsychology of Schizophrenia*. Hove, UK: Psychology Press.

Funahashi, S., Bruce, C. J., & Goldman-Rakic, P. S. (1989). Mnemonic coding of visual space in the monkey's dorsolateral prefrontal cortex. *Journal of Neuophysiology, 61*, 331–349.

Funnell, E. (1996). Response biases in oral reading: An account of the co-occurrence of surface dyslexia and semantic dementia. *Quarterly Journal of Experimental Psychology A, 49*, 417–446.

Fuster, J. M. (1954). *Memory in the Cerebral Cortex*. Cambridge, MA: MIT Press.

Gabrieli, J. D. (1998). Cognitive neuroscience of human memory. *Annual Reviews in Psychology, 49*, 87–115.

Gabrieli, J. D. E., Cohen, N. J., & Corkin, S. (1988). The impaired learning of semantic knowledge following bilateral medial temporal-lobe resection. *Brain and Cognition, 7*, 157–177.

Gabrieli, J. D. E., McGlinchey-Berroth, R., Carrillo, M. C., Gluck, M. A., Cermak, L. S., & Disterhoft, J. F. (1995). Intact delay-eyeblink classical conditioning in amnesia. *Behavioral Neuroscience, 109*, 819–827.

Gainotti, G. (2000). What the locus of brain lesion tells us about the nature of the cognitive defect underlying category-specific disorders: A review. *Cortex, 36*, 539–559.

Gais, S., Albouy, G., Boly, M., Dang-Vu, T. T., Darsaud, A., Desseilles, M. et al. (2007). Sleep transforms the cerebral trace of declarative memories. *Proceedings of the National Academy of Sciences, 104*, 18778–18783.

Galton, F. (1879). Psychometric experiments. *Brain: A Journal of Neurology, II*, 149–162.

Gardiner, J. M., Brandt, K. R., Baddeley, A. D., Vargha-Khadem, F., & Mishkin, M. (in press). Acquisition and recall of novel facts in a case of developmental amnesia. *Neuropsychologia*.

Gardiner, J. M., Brandt, K. R., Vargha-Khadem, F., Baddeley, A. D., & Mishkin, M. (2006). Effects of level of processing but not of task enactment on recognition memory in a case of developmental amnesia. *Cognitive Neuropsychology, 23*, 930–948.

Gardiner, J. M., Ramponi, C., & Richardson-Klavehn, A. (2000). Response deadline and subjective awareness in recognition memory. *Consciousness and Cognition, 8*(4), 484–496.

Garrard, P., Malony, L. M., Hodges, J. R., & Patterson, K. (2005). The effects of very early Alzheimer's disease on the characteristics of writing by a renowned author. *Brain, 128*, 250–260.

Garven, S., Wood, J. M., & Malpass, R. S. (2000). Allegations of wrongdoing: The effects of reinforcement on children's mundane and fantastic claims. *Journal of Applied Psychology, 85*, 38–49.

Gaskell, M. G., & Dumay, N. (2003). Lexical competition and the acquisition of novel words. *Cognition, 89*, 105–132.

Gathercole, S. E. (1995). Is nonword repetition a test of phonological memory or long-term knowledge? It all depends on the nonwords. *Memory and Cognition, 23*, 83–94.

Gathercole, S. E., & Alloway, T. P. (2008). *Working Memory and Learning: A Practical Guide for Teachers*. London: Sage.

Gathercole, S. E., & Baddeley, A. (1989). Evaluation of the role of phonological STM in the development of vocabulary in children: A longitudinal study. *Journal of Memory and Language, 28*, 200–213.

Gathercole, S. E., & Baddeley, A. D. (1990). Phonological memory deficits in language-disordered children: Is there a causal connection? *Journal of Memory and Language, 29*, 336–360.

Gathercole, S. E., & Pickering, S. J. (2000a). Assessment of working memory in six- and seven-year-old children. *Journal of Educational Psychology, 92*, 377–390.

Gathercole, S. E., & Pickering, S. J. (2000b). Working memory deficits in children with low achievements in the national curriculum at seven years of age. *British Journal of Educational Psychology, 70*, 177–194.

Gathercole, S. E., Lamont, E., & Alloway, T. P. (2006). Working memory in the classroom. In S. Pickering (Ed.), *Working Memory and Education*. (pp. 220–241). London: Elsevier Press.

Gathercole, S. E., Pickering, S. J., Ambridge, B., & Wearing, H. (2004a). The structure of working memory from 4 to 15 years of age. *Developmental Psychology, 40*, 177–190.

Gathercole, S. E., Pickering, S. J., Knight, C., & Stegmann, Z. (2004b). Working memory skills and educational attainment: Evidence from National Curriculum assessments at 7 and 14 years of age. *Applied Cognitive Psychology, 40*, 1–16.

Gauld, A., & Stephenson, G. M. (1967). Some experiments relating to Bartlett's Theory of Remembering. *British Journal of Psychology, 58,* 39–49.

Geiselman, R. E., Bjork, R. A., & Fishman, D. L. (1983). Disrupted retrieval in directed forgetting: A link with posthypnotic amnesia. *Journal of Experimental Psychology General, 112*(1), 58–72.

Geiselman, R. E., Fisher, R. P., MacKinnon, D. P., & Holland, H. L. (1985). Eyewitness memory enhancement in police interview: Cognitive retrieval mnemonics versus hypnosis. *Journal of Applied Psychology, 70,* 401–412.

Geraerts, E. (2006). *Remembrance of Things Past. The Cognitive Psychology of Remembering and Forgetting Trauma.* Unpublished PhD Thesis, Maastricht University, The Netherlands.

Geraerts, E., Arnold, M. M., Stephen Lindsay, D., Merckelbach, H., Jelicic, M., & Hauer, B. (2006). Forgetting of prior remembering in persons reporting recovered memories of childhood sexual abuse. *Psychological Science, 17*(11), 1002–1008.

Geraerts, E., Lindsay, D. S., Merckelbach, H., Jelicic, M., Raymaekers, L., Arnold, M. M. et al. (in press). Cognitive mechanisms underlying recovered memory experiences of childhood sexual abuse. *Psychological Science.*

Geraerts, E., Schooler, J. W., Merckelbach, H., Jelicic, M., Hauer, B. J., & Ambadar, Z. (2007). The reality of recovered memories: Corroborating continuous and discontinuous memories of childhood sexual abuse. *Psychological Science, 18*(7), 564–568.

Giambra, L. M., Arenberg, D., Zonderman, A. B., & Kawas, C. (1995). Adult life span changes in immediate visual memory and verbal intelligence. *Psychology and Aging, 10,* 123–139.

Gilbertson, M., Shenton, M., Ciszewski, A., Kasai, K., Lasko, N., Orr, S., & Pitman, R. (2002). Small hippocampal volume predicts pathologic vulnerability to psychological trauma. *Nature Neuoscience, 5,* 1242–1247.

Glanzer, M. (1972). Storage mechanisms in recall. In G. H. Bower (Ed.), *The Psychology of Learning and Motivation: Advances in Research and Theory* (Vol. 5). New York: Academic Press.

Glanzer, M., & Bowles, N. (1976). Analysis of the word-frequency effect in recognition memory. *Journal of Experimental Psychology: Human Learning and Memory, 2*(1), 21–31.

Glaze, J. A. (1928). The association value of nonsense syllables. *Journal of Genetic Psychology, 35,* 255–269.

Glenberg, A. M., Bradley, M. M., Stevenson, J. A., Kraus, T. A., Tkachuk, M. J., Gretz, A. L. et al. (1980). A two-process account of long-term serial position effects. *Journal of Experimental Psychology: Human Learning and Memory, 6,* 355–369.

Glenberg, A. M., Smith, S. M., & Green, C. (1977). Type I rehearsal: Maintenance and more. *Journal of Verbal Learning and Verbal Behavior, 16,* 339–352.

Glück, J., & Bluck, S. (2007). Looking back across the life span: A life story account of the reminiscence bump. *Memory and Cognition, 35,* 1928–1939.

Godden, D. R., & Baddeley, A. (1975). Context-dependent memory in two natural environments: On land and underwater. *British Journal of Psychology, 66*(3), 325–331.

Goernert, P. N. (2005). Source-monitoring accuracy across repeated tests following directed forgetting. *British Journal of Psychology, 96*(2), 231–247.

Goernert, P. N., & Larson, M. E. (1994). The initiation and release of retrieval inhibition. *The Journal of General Psychology, 121*(1), 61–66.

Goernert, P. N., & Wolfe, T. (1997). Is there hypermnesia and reminiscence for information intentionally forgotten? *Canadian Journal of Experimental Psychology, 51*(3), 231–240.

Gold, J. M., Murray, R. F., Sekuler, A. B., Bennett, P. J., & Sekuler, R. (2005). Visual memory decay is deterministic. *Psychological Science, 16*(10), 769–774.

Goldenberg, G. (2002). Transient global amnesia. In A. D. Baddeley, M. D. Kopelman, & B. A. Wilson (Eds.), *Handbook of Memory Disorders* (2nd edn). Chichester, UK: John Wiley.

Goldman-Rakic, P. S. (1988). Topography of cognition: Parallel distributed networks in primate association cortex. *Annual Review of Neuroscience, 11,* 137–156.

Goldman-Rakic, P. S. (1996). The prefrontal landscape: Implications of functional architecture for understanding human mentation and the central executive. *Philosophical Transactions of the Royal Society (Biological Sciences), 351,* 1445–1453.

Gollwitzer, P. M. (1999). Implementation intentions: Strong effects of simple plans. *American Psychologist, 54,* 493–503.

Gollwitzer, P. M., & Branstatter, V. (1997). Implementation intentions and effective goal pursuit. *Journal of Personality and Social Psychology, 73,* 186–199.

Gomulicki, B. R. (1956). Recall as an abstractive process. *Acta Psychologia, 12,* 77–94.

Goodwin, D. W., Powell, B., Bremer, D., Hoine, H., & Stern, J. (1969). Alcohol and recall: State-dependent effects in man. *Science, 163,* 1358–1360.

Gorman, A. M. (1961). Recognition memory for nouns as a function of abstractness and frequency. *Journal of Experimental Psychology, 61,* 23–29.

Graf, P., & Mandler, G. (1984). Activation makes words more accessible, but not necessarily more retrievable. *Journal of Verbal Learning and Verbal Behavior, 23,* 553–568.

Graf, P., Squire, L. R., & Mandler, G. (1984). The information that amnesic patients do not forget. *Journal of Experimental Psychology: Learning, Memory and Cognition, 10,* 164–178.

Grafton, S., Hazeltine, E., & Ivry, R. (1995). Functional mapping of sequence learning in normal humans. *Journal of Cognitive Neuroscience, 7,* 497–510.

Green, D. M., & Swets, J. A. (1966). *Signal Detection Theory and Psychophysics.* New York: Wiley.

Greenberg, D. L., & Rubin, D. C. (2003). The neuropsychology of autobiographical memory. *Cortex, 39,* 687–728.

Greenberg, D. L., Rice, H. J., Cooper, J. J., Cabeza, R., Rubin, D. C., & LaBar, K. S. (2005). Co-activation of the amygdala, hippocampus and inferior frontal gyrus during autobiographical retrieval. *Neuropsychologia, 43,* 659–674.

Greene, J. D. W., & Hodges, J. R. (1996). The fractionation of remote memory-evidence from a longitudinal study of dementia of Alzheimer type. *Brain, 119,* 129–142.

Greene, J. D. W., Baddeley, A. D., & Hodges, J. R. (1996). Analysis of the episodic memory deficit in early Alzheimer's disease: Evidence from the Doors and People Test. *Neuropsychologia, 34,* 537–551.

Greenough, W. T., Black, J. E., & Wallace, C. S. (1987). Experience and brain development. *Child Development, 58,* 539–559.

Groeger, J. A. (1997). *Memory and Remembering.* Harlow, UK: Addison Wesley Longman.

Gross, J., & Hayne, H. (1999). Drawing facilitates children's verbal reports after long delays. *Journal of Experimental Psychology: Applied, 5,* 265–283.

Gruneberg, M. M., Morris, P. E., & Sykes, R. N. (1978). *Practical Aspects of Memory.* London: Academic Press.

Hall, J. F. (1954). Learning as a function of word-frequency. *The American Journal of Psychology, 67*(1), 138–140.

Han, J. J., Leichtman, M. D., & Wang, Q. (1998). Autobiographical memory in Korean, Chinese, and American children. *Developmental Psychology, 34,* 701–713.

Handberg, R. B. (1995). Expert testimony on eyewitness identification: A new pair of glasses for the jury. *American Criminal Law Review, 32,* 1013–1064.

Haque, S., & Conway, M. A. (2001). Sampling the process of autobiographical memory construction. *European Journal of Cognitive Psychology, 13,* 529–547.

Harley, K., & Reese, E. (1999). Origins of autobiographical memory. *Developmental Psychology, 35,* 1338–1348.

Harris, J. E. (1980). Memory aids people – 2 interview studies. *Memory and Cognition, 8,* 31–38.

Harris, L. M., & Menzies, R. G. (1999). Mood and prospective memory. *Memory, 7,* 117–127.

Hartley, T., Maguire, E. A., Spiers, H. J., & Burgess, N. (2003). The well-worn route and the path less traveled: Distinct neural bases of route following and wayfinding in humans. *Neuron, 37,* 877–888.

Hartshorn, K., & Rovee-Collier, C. (1997). Infant learning and long-term memory at 6 months: A confirming analysis. *Developmental Psychobiology, 30,* 71–85.

Harvey, A. G., & Bryant, R. A. (2000). Memory for acute stress disorder symptoms: A two-year prospective study. *Journal of Nervous and Mental Disease, 188,* 602–607.

Hasher, L., & Zacks, R. T. (1988). Working memory, comprehension, and aging: A review and a new view. In G. H. Bower (Ed.), *The Psychology of Learning and Motivation* (Vol. 22, pp. 193–225). San Diego, CA: Academic Press.

Hasher, L., Zacks, R. T., & May, C. P. (1999). Inhibitory control, circadian arousal, and age. In D. Gopher & A. Koriat (Eds.), *Attention and Performance, XVII, Cognitive Regulation of Performance. Interaction of Theory and Application* (pp. 653–675). Cambridge, MA: MIT Press.

Hastorf, A. A., & Cantril, H. (1954). They saw a game: A case study. *Journal of Abnormal and Social Psychology, 97,* 399–401.

Hatano, G., & Osawa, K. (1983a). Digit memory of grand experts in abacus-derived mental calculation. *Cognition, 15,* 95–110.

Hatano, G., & Osawa, K. (1983b). Japanese abacus experts memory for numbers is disrupted by mechanism of action. *Journal of Clinical Psychology, 58*(1), 61–75.

Hay, J. F., & Jacoby, L. L. (1999). Separating habit and recollection in young and older adults: Effects of elaborative processing and distinctiveness. *Psychology and Aging, 14,* 122–134.

Hayne, H. (2004). Infant memory development: Implications for childhood amnesia. *Developmental Review, 24,* 33–73.

Hayne, H., Boniface, J., & Barr, R. (2000). The development of declarative memory in Human infants: Age-related changes in deferred imitation. *Behavioral Neuroscience, 114*, 77–83.

Hazeltine, E., Grafton, S. T., & Ivry, R. (1997). Attention and stimulus characteristics determine the locus of motor sequence learning: A PET study. *Brain, 120*, 123–140.

Healy, H., & Williams, J. M. G. (Eds.). (1999). *Autobiographical Memory*. Chichester, UK: Wiley.

Heath, W. P., & Erickson, J. R. (1998). Memory for central and peripheral actions and props and peripheral actions and props after varied post-event presentation. *Legal and Criminal Psychology, 3*, 321–346.

Hebb, D. O. (1949). *The Organization of Behavior*. New York: Wiley.

Heindel, W. C., Salmon, D. P., Shults, C. W., Walicke, P. A., & Butters, N. (1989). Neuropsychological evidence for multiple implicit systems: A comparison of Alzheimer's, Huntington's and Parkinson's disease patients. *Journal of Neuroscience, 9*, 582–587.

Henkel, L. A. (2004). Erroneous memories arising from repeated attempts to remember. *Journal of Memory and Language, 50*(1), 26–46.

Henkel, L. A., Franklin, N., & Johnson, M. K. (2000). Cross-modal source monitoring confusions between perceived and imagined events. *Journal of Experimental Psychology: Learning, Memory, and Cognition, 26*, 321–335.

Henry, J. D., MacLeod, M. S., Phillips, L. H., & Crawford, J. R. (2004). A meta-analytic review of prospective memory and aging. *Psychology and Aging, 19*, 27–39.

Henson, R. N. A. (1998). Short-term memory for serial order. The Start-End Model. *Cognitive Psychology, 36*, 73–137.

Herman, J., & Schatzow, E. (1987). Recovery and verification of memories of childhood sexual trauma. *Psychoanalytic Psychology, 4*, 1–14.

Herrmann, D. J., & Gruneberg, M. (1993). The need to expand the horizons of the practical aspects of memory movement. *Applied Cognitive Psychology, 7*, 553–565.

Herrmann, D. J., & Petro, S. J. (1990). Commercial memory aids. *Applied Cognitive Psychology, 4*, 439–450.

Herron, J. E., & Wilding, E. L. (2006). Neural correlates of control processes engaged before and during recovery of information from episodic memory. *Neuroimage, 30*, 634–644.

Heuer, F., Fischman, D., & Reisberg, D. (1986). Why does vivid imagery hurt colour memory? *Canadian Journal of Psychology, 40*, 161–175.

Hicks, J. L., Marsh, R. L., & Cook, G. I. (2005). Task interference in time-based, event-based, and dual intention prospective memory conditions. *Journal of Memory and Language, 53*, 430–444.

High, W. M., Levin, H. S., & Gary, H. E. (1990). Recovery of orientation and memory following closed-head injury. *Journal of Clinical and Experimental Neuropsychology, 12*, 703–714.

Hinton-Bayre, A. D., Geffen, G., & McFarland, K. (1997). Mild head injury and speed of information processing: A prospective study of professional rugby league players. *Journal of Clinical and Experimental Neuropsychology, 19*, 275–289.

Hockey, G. R. J. (1973). Rate of presentation in running memory and direct manipulation of input processing strategies. *Quarterly Journal of Experimental Psychology, 25*, 104–111.

Hodges, J. R., & McCarthy, R. A. (1993). Autobiographical amnesia resulting from bilateral paramedian thalamic infarction. A case study in cognitive neurobiology. *Brain, 116*, 921–940.

Hodges, J. R., & Patterson, K. (1995). Is semantic memory consistently impaired early in the course of Alzheimer's disease? Neuroanatomical and diagnostic implications. *Neuropsychologia, 33*, 441–459.

Hodges, J. R., Patterson, K., & Tyler, L. (1994). Loss of semantic memory: Implications for the modularity of mind. *Cognitive Neuropsychology, 11*, 505–542.

Holding, D., H. (1989). Counting backward during chess move choice. *Bulletin of Psychonomic Society, 27*, 421–424.

Hollingworth, A., & Henderson, J. M. (2002). Accurate visual memory for previously attended objects in natural scenes. *Journal of Experimental Psychology: Human Perception and Performance, 28*, 113–136.

Hopwood, J. S., & Snell, H. K. (1933). Amnesia in relation to crime. *Journal of Mental Science, 79*, 27–41.

Howard, D. V., & Howard, J. H., Jr. (1989). Age differences in learning serial patterns: Direct versus indirect measures. *Psychology and Aging, 4*, 357–364.

Howe, M. L., & Courage, M. L. (1997). The emergence and early development of autobiographical memory. *Psychological Review, 104*, 499–523.

Howe, M. L., Courage, M. L., & Edison, S. C. (2003). When autobiographical memory begins. In M. Conway, S. Gathercole, S. Algarabel, A. Pitarque, & T. Bajo (Eds.), *Theories of Memory, Vol. III*. Hove, UK: Psychology Press.

Hsi, S., Linn, M. C., & Bell, J. A. (1997). The role of spatial reasoning in engineering and the design of spatial instruction. *Journal of Engineering Education, 86*, 151–158.

Hubel, D. H., & Weisel, T. N. (1979). Brain mechanisms of vision. *Scientific American, 241,* 150–162.

Hugenberg, K., Miller, J., & Claypool, H. (2007). Categorization and individuation in the CR recognition deficit: Toward a solution to an insidious problem. *Journal of Experimental Social Psychology, 43,* 334–340.

Hull, C. L. (1943). *The Principles of Behaviour.* New York: Appleton-Century.

Hulme, C., Neath, I., Stuart, G., Shostak, L., Suprenant, A. M., & Brown, G. D. A. (2006). The distinctiveness of the word-length. *Journal of Experimental Psychology: Learning, Memory and Cognition, 32,* 586–594.

Hunter, I. M. L. (1968). *Memory.* Harmondsworth, UK: Penguin Books.

Huppert, F. A., & Piercy, M. (1978a). Dissociation between learning and remembering in organic amnesisa. *Nature, 275,* 317–318.

Huppert, F. A., & Piercy, M. (1978b). The role of trace strength in recency and frequency judgements by amnesic and control subjects. *Quarterly Journal of Experiment Psychology, 30,* 346–354.

Hyde, T. S., & Jenkins, J. J. (1973). Recall for words as a function of semantic, graphic, and syntactic orienting tasks. *Journal of Verbal Learning and Verbal Behavior, 12,* 471–480.

Hyman, I. E., Jr., & Faries, J. M. (1992). The functions of autobiographical memories. In M. A. Conway, D. C. Rubin, H. Spinnler, & W. A. Wagenaar (Eds.), *Theoretical Perpectives on Autobiographical Memory* (pp. 207–221). Dordrecht, The Netherlands: Kluwer Academic.

Ihlebaek, C., Løve, T., Eilertsen, D. E., & Magnussen, S. (2003). Memory for a staged criminal event witnessed live and on video. *Memory, 11,* 319–327.

Iidaka, T., Sadato, N., Yamada, H., Murata, T., Omori, M., & Yonekura, Y. (2001). An fMRI study of the functional neuroanatomy of picture encoding in younger and older adults. *Cognitive Brain Research, 11,* 1–11.

Irwin, D. E., & Andrews, R. V. (1996). Integration and accumulation of information across saccadic eye movements. In T. Inui & J. L. McClelland (Eds.), *Attention and Performance XVI: Information Integration in Perception and Communication* (pp. 125–155). Cambridge, MA: MIT Press.

Jacobs, J. (1887). Experiments on "prehension". *Mind, 12,* 75–79.

Jacoby, L. L. (1991). A process dissociation framework: Separating automatic from intentional uses of memory. *Journal of Memory and Language, 30*(5), 513–541.

Jacoby, L. L., & Dallas, M. (1981). On the relationship between autobiographical memory and perceptual learning. *Journal of Experimental Psychology: General, 110*(3), 306–340.

Jacoby, L. L., Bishara, A. J., Hessels, S., & Toth, J. P. (2005). Aging, subjective experience, and cognitive control: Dramatic false remembering by older adults. *Journal of Experimental Psychology: General, 134,* 131–148.

James, W. (1890). *The Principles of Psychology.* New York: Holt, Rinehard & Winston.

Jenkins, J. J., & Russell, W. A. (1952). Associative clustering as a function of verbal association strength. *Psychological Reports, 4,* 127–136.

Johnson, M. K., Foley, M. A., Suengas, A. G., & Raye, C. L. (1988). Phenomenal characteristics of memory for perceived and imagined autobiographical events. *Journal of Experimental Psychology: General, 117,* 371–376.

Johnson, M. K., Hashtroudi, S., & Lindsay, D. S. (1993). Source monitoring. *Psychological Bulletin, 114*(1), 3–28.

Johnson, M. K., Kim, J. K., & Risse, G. (1985). Do alcoholic Korsakoff's syndrome patients acquire affective reactions? *Journal of Experimental Psychology: Learning, Memory and Cognition, 11,* 22–36.

Johnson, S. K., & Anderson, M. C. (2004). The role of inhibitory control in forgetting semantic knowledge. *Psychological Science, 15,* 448–453.

Johnstone, K. M., Ashbaugh, H., & Warfield, T. D. (2002). Effects of repeated practice and contextual-writing experiences on college students' writing skills. *Journal of Educational Psychology, 94,* 305–315.

Jones, D. M. (1993). Objects, streams and threads of auditory attention. In A. D. Baddeley & L. Weiskrantz (Eds.), *Attention: Selection, Awareness and Control* (pp. 87–104). Oxford: Clarendon Press.

Jones, D. M., & Macken, W. J. (1993). Irrelevant tones produce an irrelevant speech effect: Implications for phonological coding in working memory. *Journal of Experimental Psychology: Learning, Memory and Cognition, 19,* 369–381.

Jones, D. M., & Macken, W. J. (1995). Phonological similarity in the irrelevant sound effect: Within- or between- stream similarity. *Journal of Experimental Psychology: Learning, Memory, and Cognition, 21,* 103–115.

Jones, D. M., Hughes, R. W., & Macken, W. J. (2007). The phonological store abandoned. *Quarterly Journal of Experimental Psychology, 60,* 497–504.

Jones, D. M., Macken, W. J., & Murray, A. C. (1993). Disruption of visual short-term memory by changing-state auditory simuli: The role of segmentation. *Memory and Cognition, 21*(3), 318–366.

Joormann, J., Hertel, P. T., Brozovich, F., & Gotlib, I. H. (2005). Remembering the good, forgetting the bad: Intentional forgetting of emotional material in depression. *Journal of Abnormal Psychology, 114*(4), 640–648.

Joslyn, S. L., & Oakes, M. A. (2005). Directed forgetting of autobiographical events. *Memory and Cognition, 33*(4), 577–587.

Jung, J. (1968). *Verbal Learning.* New York: Holt, Rinehart and Winston.

Kalakoski, V., & Saariluoma, P. (2001). Taxi drivers' exceptional memory of street names. *Memory and Cognition, 29*, 634–638.

Kandel, E. R. (2006). *In Search of Memory: The Emergence of a New Science of Mind.* New York: Norton.

Kane, M. J., & Engle, R. W. (2000). Working-memory capacity, proactive interference, and divided attention: Limits on long-term memory retrieval. *Journal of Experimental Psychology: Learning, Memory and Cognition, 26*(2), 336–358.

Kapur, N. (1999). Syndromes of retrograde amnesia. A conceptual and empirical synthesis. *Psychological Bulletin, 125*, 800–825.

Karpicke, J. D., & Roediger III, H. L. (2008). The critical importance of retrieval for learning. *Science, 319*, 966–968.

Kassin, S. M., Tubb, V. A., Hosch, H. M., & Memon, A. (2001). On the "general acceptance" of eyewitness testimony research. *American Psychologist, 56*, 405–416.

Kay, H. (1955). Learning and retaining verbal material. *British Journal of Psychology, 46*, 81–100.

Kemper, S. (1990). Adults' diaries: Changes made to written narratives across the life-span. *Discourse Processes, 13*, 207–223.

Kemper, S., Kynette, D., & Norman, S. (1992). Age differences in spoken language. In R. West & J. Sinnott (Eds.), *Everyday Memory and Aging: Current Research and Methodology* (pp. 138–152). New York: Springer-Verlag.

Keppel, G., & Underwood, B. J. (1962). Proactive inhibition in short-term retention of single items. *Journal of Verbal Learning and Verbal Behavior, 1*, 153–161.

Kiewra, K. A., & Benton, S. L. (1988). The relationship between information-processing ability and note taking. *Comtemporary Educational Psychology, 13*, 33–44.

Kihlstrom, J. F., & Schacter, D. L. (2000). Functional amnesia. In F. Boller & J. Grafman (Eds.), *Handbook of Neuropsychology* (Vol. 2, pp. 409–427). Amsterdam: Elsevier Publications.

Kinsbourne, M., & George, J. (1974). The mechanism of the word-frequency effect on recognition memory. *Journal of Verbal Learning and Verbal Behavior, 13*(1), 63–69.

Kintsch, W. (1980). Semantic memory: A tutorial. In R. S. Nickerson (Ed.), *Attention and Performance, Vol. VIII.* Hillsdale, NJ: Lawrence Erlbaum Associates.

Kintsch, W., & van Dyck, T. (1977). Toward a model of text comprehension and production. *Psychological Review, 85*, 63–94.

Klauer, K. C., & Zhao, Z. (2004). Double dissociaions in visual and spatial short-term memory. *Journal of Experimental Psychology: General, 133*, 355–381.

Kliegl, R., Smith, J., & Baltes, P. (1989). Testing-the-limits and the study of adult age differences in cognitive plasticity of a mnemonic skill. *Developmental Psychology, 25*, 247–256.

Kohnken, G., Milne, R., Memon, A., & Bull, R. (1999). The cognitive interview: A meta-analysis. *Psychology of Crime Law, 5*, 3–27.

Kondo, Y., Suzuki, M., Mugikura, S., Abe, N., Takahashi, S., Iijima, T., & Fujii, T. (2004). Changes in brain activation associated with use of a memory strategy: A functional MRI study. *Neuroimage, 15*, 1154–1163.

Kopelman, M. D. (1985). Rates of forgetting in Alzheimer-type dementia and Korsakoff's syndrome. *Neuropsychologia, 23*, 623–628.

Kopelman, M. D. (1987). Crime and amnesia: A review. *Behavioural Sciences and the Law, 5*, 323–342.

Kopelman, M. D. (1989). Remote and autobiographical memory, temporal context memory and frontal atrophy in Korsakoff and Alzheimer's patients. *Neuropsychologia, 27*, 437–460.

Kopelman, M. D. (1995). The Korsakoff syndrome. *The British Journal of Psychiatry, 166*(2), 154–173.

Kopelman, M. D. (2002a). Disorders of memory. *Brain, 125*(10), 2152–2190.

Kopelman, M. D. (2002b). Psychogenic amnesia. In A. D. Baddeley, M. D. Kopelman, & B. A. Wilson (Eds.), *Handbook of Memory Disorders* (2nd ed., pp. 451–472). Chichester, UK: Wiley.

Kopelman, M. D., Green, R. E. A., Guinan, E. M., Lewis, P. D. R., & Stanhope, N. (1994). The case of the amnesic intelligence officer. *Psychological Medicine, 24*, 1037–1045.

Kopelman, M. D., Wilson, B. A., & Baddeley, A. D. (1990). *Autobiographical Memory Interview.* Bury St Edmunds, UK: Thames Valley Test Company.

Kritchevsky, M., Chang, J., & Squire, L. R. (2004). Functional amnesia: Clinical description and neuropsychological profile of 10 cases. *Learning and Memory, 11*(2), 213–226.

Kuehn, L. L. (1974). Looking down a gun barrel: Person perception and violent crime. *Perceptual and Motor Skills, 39*, 1159–1164.

Kunda, Z. (1990). The case for motivated reasoning. *Psychological Bulletin, 108*, 480–498.

Kunst-Wilson, W. R., & Zajonc, R. B. (1980). Affective discrimination of stimuli that cannot be recognized. *Science, 207*, 557–558.

Kyllonen, P. C., & Christal, R. E. (1990). Reasoning ability is (little more than) working memory capacity. *Intelligence, 14*, 389–433.

Kyllonen, P. C., & Stephens, D. L. (1990). Cognitive abilities as the determinants of success in acquiring logic skills. *Learning and Individual Differences, 2*, 129–160.

Landauer, T. K., & Bjork, R. A. (1978). Optimum rehearsal patterns and name learning. In M. M. Gruneberg, P. E. Morris, & R. N. Sykes (Eds.), *Practical Aspects of Memory* (pp. 625–632). London: Academic Press.

Lashley, K. S. (1951). The problem of serial order in behaviour. In L. A. Jeffress (Ed.), *Cerebral Mechanisms in Behavior: The Hixon Symposium.* New York: John Wiley.

Latham, G. P. (2003). Goal setting: A five-step approach to behavior change. *Organizational Dynamics, 32*, 309–318.

Le Compte, D. C., & Shaibe, D. M. (1997). On the irrelevance of phonological similarity to the irrelevant speech effect. *Quarterly Journal of Experimental Psychology, 50A*, 100–118.

LeDoux, J. (1998). *The Emotional Brain.* London: Weidenfeld & Nicolson.

Lee, A. C. H., Graham, K. S., Simons, J. S., Hodges, J. R., Owen, A. M., & Patterson, K. (2002). Regional brain activations differ for semantic features but not for categories. *NeuroReport, 13*, 1497–1501.

Leichtman, M. D., Wang, Q., & Pillemer, D. B. (2003). Cultural variations in Interdependence and autobiographical memory: Lessons from Korea, China, India, and the United States. In R. Fivush & C. A. Haden (Eds.), *Autobiographical Memory and the Construction of a Narrative Self: Developmental and Cultural Perspectives* (pp. 73–98). Mahwah, NJ: Lawrence Erlbaum Associates.

Leigland, L. A., Schulz, L. E., & Janowsky, J. S. (2004). Age related changes in emotional memory. *Neurobiology of Aging, 25*(8), 1117–1124.

Leippe, M. R. (1995). The case for expert testimony about eyewitness memory. *Psychology, Public Policy, and Law, 1*, 909–959.

Leippe, M. R., Eisenstadt, D., Rauch, S. M., & Seib, H. M. (2004). Timing of eyewitness expert testimony, jurors' need for cognition, and case strength as determinants of trial verdicts. *Journal of Applied Psychology, 89*, 524–541.

Lépine, R., Barrouillet, P., & Camos, V. (2005). What makes working memory spans so predictive of high-level cognition? *Psychonomic Bulletin and Review, 12*, 165–170.

Levin, D. T., Drivdahl, S. B., Momen, N., & Beck, M. R. (2002). False predictions about the detectability of visual changes: The role of beliefs about attention, memory, and the continuity of attended objects in causing change blindness blindness. *Consciousness and Cognition, 11*, 507–527.

Levin, H. S., & Hanten, G. (2002). Post traumatic amnesia and residual memory deficit after closed head injury. In A. D. Baddeley, M. D. Kopelman, & B. A. Wilson (Eds.), *Handbook of Memory Disorders* (2nd ed., pp. 381–412). Chichester, UK: Wiley.

Levin, H. S., O'Donnell, V. M., & Grossman, R. G. (1979). The Galvaston Orientation and Amnesia Test: A practical scale to assess cognition after a head injury. *Journal of Nervous and Mental Disease, 167*, 675–684.

Levy, B. J., & Anderson, M. C. (2002). Inhibitory processes and the control of memory retrieval. *Trends in Cognitive Sciences, 6*, 299–305.

Levy, B. J., & Anderson, M. C. (2008). Individual differences in the suppression of unwanted memories: The executive deficit hypothesis. *Acta Psychologica, 127*, 623–635.

Lewandowski, S., & Oberauer, K. (in press). The word length effect provides no evidence for decay in short-term memory. *Psychonomic Bulletin and Review.*

Lewandowski, S., Brown, G. D. A., Wright, T., & Nimmo, L. M. (2006). Timeless memory: Evidence against temporal distinctiveness models of short-term memory for serial order. *Journal of Memory and Language, 54*, 20–38.

Lewis, M., & Brooks-Gunn, J. (1979). Toward a theory of social cognition: The development of self. *New Directions for Child Development, 4*, 1–20.

Lewis, M., & Ramsay, D. (2004). Development of self-recognition, personal pronoun use, and pretend play during the 2nd year. *Child Development, 75*, 1821–1831.

Light, L. L., Prull, M. W., La Voie, D., & Healy, M. R. (2000). Dual process theories of memory in older age. In T. J. Perfect & E. Maylor (Eds.), *Theoretical Debate in Cognitive Aging* (pp. 238–300). Oxford: Oxford University Press.

Lindenberger, U., & Pötter, U. (1998). The complex nature of unique and shared effects in hierarchical linear regression: Implications for developmental psychology. *Psychological Methods, 3*, 218–230.

Lindholm, T., & Christianson, S.-A. (1998). Intergroup biases and eyewitness testimony. *Journal of Social Psychology, 138,* 710–723.

Lindsay, D. S., Allen, B. P., Chan, J. C. K., & Dahl, L. C. (2004). Eyewitness suggestibility and source similarity: Intrusions of details from one event into memory reports of another event. *Journal of Memory and Language, 50,* 96–111.

Lindsay, R. C. L., & Harvie, V. (1988). Hits, false alarms, correct and mistaken identifications: The effects of method of data collection on facial memory. In M. Grunberg, P. Morris, & R. Sykes (Eds.), *Practical Aspects of Memory: Current Research and Issues, Vol. 1: Memory in Everyday Life* (pp. 47–52). Chichester, UK: Wiley.

Lindsay, R. C. L., Lim, R., Marando, L., & Cully, D. (1986). Mock-juror evaluations of eyewitness testimony: A test of metamemory hypothesis. *Journal of Applied Social Psychology, 16,* 447–459.

Linn, M. C., & Petersen, A. C. (1985). Emergence and characterization of sex differences in spatial ability: A meta-analysis. *Child Development, 56,* 1479–1498.

Linton, M. (1975). Memory for real-world events. In D. A. Norman & D. E. Rumelhart (Eds.), *Explorations in Cognition* (pp. 376–404). San Francisco: Freeman.

Locke, E. A. (1968). Toward a theory of task motivation and incentives. *Organizational Behavior and Human Performance, 3,* 157–189.

Locke, E. A., & Latham, G. P. (2002). Building a practically useful theory of goal setting and task motivation: A 35-year odyssey. *American Psychologist, 57,* 705–717.

Loess, H. (1968). Short-term memory and item similarity. *Journal of Verbal Learning and Verbal Behavior, 7,* 87–92.

Loftus, E. F. (1979). *Eyewitness Testimony.* Cambridge, MA: Harvard University Press.

Loftus, E. F. (1992). When a lie becomes memory's truth: Memory distortion after exposure to misinformation. *Current Directions in Psychological Science, 13,* 145–147.

Loftus, E. F. (1993). The reality of repressed memories. *American Psychologist, 48,* 518–537.

Loftus, E. F. (1994). Forgetting sexual trauma: What does it mean when 38% forget? *Journal of Consulting and Clinical Psychology, 62,* 1177–1181.

Loftus, E. F., & Marburger, W. (1983). Since the eruption of Mount St Helens, has anyone beaten you up? Improving the accuracy of retrospective reports with landmark event. *Memory and Cognition, 11,* 114–120.

Loftus, E. F., & Palmer, J. C. (1974). Reconstruction of automobile destruction: An example of the interaction between language and memory. *Journal of Verbal Learning and Verbal Behavior, 13,* 585–589.

Loftus, E. F., & Pickrell, J. E. (1995). The formation of false memories. *Psychiatric Annals, 25,* 720–725.

Loftus, E. F., & Suppes, P. (1972). Structural variables that determine the speed of retrieving words from long-term memory. *Journal of Verbal Learning and Verbal Behavior, 11,* 770–777.

Loftus, E. F., Loftus, G. R., & Messo, J. (1987). Some facts about weapon focus. *Law and Human Behavior, 11,* 55–62.

Logie, R. H. (1995). *Visuo-spatial Working Memory.* Hove, UK: Lawrence Erlbaum Associates.

Logie, R. H., & van der Meulen, M. (in press). Fragmenting and integrating visuo-spatial working memory. In J. R. Brockmole (Ed.), *Representing the Visual World in Memory.* Hove, UK: Psychology Press.

Logie, R. H., Cocchini, G., Della Sala, S., & Baddeley, A. (2004). Is there a specific capacity for dual task co-ordination? Evidence from Alzheimer's Disease. *Neuropsychology, 18,* 504–513.

Luciana, M., & Collins, P. F. (1997). Dopaminergic modulation of working memory for spatial but not object cues in normal humans. *Journal of Cognitive Neuroscience, 9,* 330–367.

Luck, S. J., & Vogel, E. K. (1997). The capacity of visual working memory for features and conjunctions. *Nature, 390,* 279–281.

Luria, A. R. (1959). The directive function of speech in development and dissolution, Part I. *Word, 15,* 341–352.

Luria, A. R. (1968). *The Mind of a Mnemonist.* New York: Basic Books.

Luzatti, C., Vecchi, T., Agazzi, D., Cesa-Bianchi, M., & Vergani, C. (1998). A neurological dissociation between preserved visual and impaired spatial processing in mental imagery. *Cortex, 34,* 461–469.

Lykken, D., & Tellegen, A. (1996). Happiness is a stochastic phenomenon. *Psychological Science, 7*(3), 186–189.

MacLeod, C. M. (1998). Directed forgetting. In J. M. Golding & C. M. MacLeod (Eds.), *Intentional Forgetting: Interdisciplinary Approaches* (pp. 197–218). Mahwah, NJ: Lawrence Erlbaum Associates.

MacLeod, M. D., & Macrae, C. N. (2001). Gone but not forgotten: The transient nature of retrieval-induced forgetting. *Psychological Science, 12*(2), 148–152.

Macrae, C. N., & MacLeod, M. D. (1999). On recollections lost: When practice makes imperfect.

Journal of Personality and Social Psychology, 77(3), 463–473.

Maguire, E. A., & Frith, C. D. (2003). Lateral asymmetry in the hippocampal response to the remoteness of autobiographical memories. *Journal of Neuroscience, 23,* 5302–5307.

Maguire, E. A., Valentine, E. R., Wilding, J. M., & Kapur, N. (2003). Routes to remembering: The brains behind superior memory. *Nature Neuroscience, 6,* 90–95.

Maguire, E. A., Vargha-Khadem, F., & Mishkin, M. (2001). The effects of bilateral hippocampal damage on fMRI regional activations and interactions during memory retrieval. *Brain, 124,* 1156–1170.

Maguire, E. A., Woollett, K., & Spiers, H. J. (2006). London taxi drivers and bus drivers: A structural MRI and neuropsychological analysis. *Hippocampus, 16,* 1091–1101.

Mailer, N. (2003). *The Spooky Art: Some Thoughts on Writing.* New York: Random House.

Mandler, G. (1967). Organization and memory. In K. W. Spence & J. T. Spence (Eds.), *The Psychology of Learning and Motivation: Advances in Research and Theory* (Vol. 1, pp. 328–372). New York: Academic Press.

Mandler, G. (1980). Recognizing – the judgment of previous occurrence. *Psychological Review, 87,* 252–271.

Mannes, S. M., & Kintsch, W. (1987). Knowledge organization and text organization. *Cognition and Instruction, 4,* 91–115.

Manns, J. R., & Squire, L. R. (1999). Impaired recognition memory on the Doors and People Test after damage limited to the hippocampal region. *Hippocampus, 9,* 495–499.

Mäntylä, T. (2003). Assessing absentmindedness: Prospective memory complaint and impairment in middle-aged adults. *Memory and Cognition, 31,* 15–25.

Mäntylä, T., & Nilsson, L. -G. (1997). Are my cues better than your cues? Recognition memory and recollective experience in Alzheimer's disease. *Memory, 5,* 657–672.

Marian, V., & Fausey, C. M. (2006). Language-dependent memory in bilingual learning. *Applied Cognitive Psychology, 20(8),* 1025–1047.

Marian, V., & Neisser, U. (2000). Language-Dependent recall of autobiographical memories. *Journal of Experimental Psychology: General, 129(3),* 361–368.

Markowitsch, H. J., Kessler, J., Van Der Ven, C., Weber-Luxenburger, G., Albers, M., & Heiss, W. D. (1998). Psychic trauma causing grossly reduced brain metabolism and cognitive deterioration. *Neuropsychologia, 36(1),* 77–82.

Marques, J. F., Canessa, N., Siri. S., Catricala, E., & Cappa, S. (2008). Conceptual knowledge in the brain: fMRI evidence for a featural organization. *Brain Research, 1194,* 90–99.

Marsh, E. J., Roediger III, H. L., Bjork, R. A., & Bjork, E. L. (2007). The memorial consequences of multiple-choice testing. *Psychonomic Bulletin and Review, 14,* 194–199.

Marsh, R. L., Hicks, J. L., & Landau, J. D. (1998). An investigation of everyday prospective memory and executive control of working memory. *Journal of Experimental Psychology: Learning, Memory and Cognition, 24,* 336–349.

Martin, A., & Caramazza, A. (2003). Neuropsychological and neuroimaging perspectives on conceptual knowledge: An introduction. *Cognitive Neuropsychology, 20,* 195–221.

Martin, A., & Chao, L. L. (2001). Semantic memory and the brain: Structure and processes. *Current Opinion in Neurobiology, 11,* 194–201.

Martin, A., Ungerleider, L. G., & Haxby, J. V. (2000). Category specificity and the brain: the sensory/motor model of semantic representations of objects. In M. S. Gazzaniga (Ed.), *The New Cognitive Neurosciences* (2nd edn, pp. 1023–1036). Cambridge, MA: MIT Press.

Martin, M., & Schumann-Hengsteler, R. (2001). How task demands influence time-based prospective memory performance in young and older adults. *International Journal of Behavioral Development, 25,* 386–391.

Masters, R. S. W. (1992). Knowledge, knerves and know-how: The role of explicit versus implicit knowledge in the breakdown of a complex skill under pressure. *British Journal of Psychology, 83,* 343–358.

Mather, M., & Carstensen, L. L. (2005). Aging and motivated cognition: The positivity effect in attention and memory. *Trends in Cognitive Sciences, 9(10),* 496–502.

May, C. P., Hasher, M., & Kane, M. J. (1999). The role of interference in memory span. *Memory and Cognition, 27,* 759–767.

Mayes, A. R., Holdstock, J. S., Isaac, C. L., Hunkin, N. M., & Roberts, N. (2002). Relative sparing of item recognition memory in a patient with adult-onset damage limited to the hippocampus. *Hippocampus, 12,* 325–340.

Maylor, E. A. (1996). Does prospective memory decline with age? In M. Brandimonte, G. O. Einstein, & M. A. McDaniel (Eds.), *Prospective Memory: Theory and Applications* (pp. 173–198). Hove, UK: Psychology Press.

McClelland, J. L., McNaughton, B. L., & O'Reilly, R. C. (1995). Why there are complementary learning systems in the hippocampus and neocortex: insights from the successes and failures of connectionist models of learning and memory. *Psychology Review, 102,* 419–457.

McCloskey, C. G., Wible, C. G., & Cohen, N. J. (1988). Is there a special flashbulb-memory mechanism? *Journal of Experimental Psychology: General, 117,* 171–181.

McCloskey, M. E., & Glucksberg, S. (1978). Natural categories: Well defined or fuzzy sets? *Memory and Cognition, 6,* 462–472.

McCrea, M., Guskiewicz, K. M., Marshall, S. W., Barr, W., & Randolph, C. (2003). Acute effects and recovery time following concussion in collegiate football players: The NCAA concussion study. *Journal of the American Medical Association, 290,* 2556–2563.

McDaniel, M. A., Einstein, G. O., Graham, T., & Rall, E. (2004). Delaying execution of intentions: Overcoming the costs of interruptions. *Applied Cognitive Psychology, 18,* 533–547.

McDaniel, M. A., Robinson-Riegler, B., & Einstein, G. P. (1998). Prospective remembering: Perceptually driven or conceptually driven processes? *Memory and Cognition, 26,* 121–134.

McDaniel, M. A., Roediger, H. L., III, & McDermott, K. B. (2007). Generalising test-enhanced learning from the laboratory to the classroom. *Psychonomic Bulletin and Review, 14,* 200–206.

McDonough, L., Mandler, J. M., McKee, R. D., & Squire, L. R. (1995). The deferred Imitation task as a non-verbal measure of declarative memory. *Proceedings of the National Academy of Sciences of the United States of America, 92,* 7580–7584.

McEwen, B. (1999). Stress and hippocampal plasticity. *Annual Review of Neuroscience, 22,* 105–122.

McGaugh, J. L. (2003). *Memory and Emotion: The Making of Lasting Memories.* New York: Columbia University Press.

McGeoch, J. A. (1942). *The Psychology of Human Learning: An Introduction.* New York: Longman.

McGeoch, J. A., & Irion, A. L. (1952). *The Psychology of Human Learning.* New York: Longman.

McGeogh, J. A., & McDonald, W. T. (1931). Meaningful relation and retroactive inhibition. *American Journal of Psychology, 43,* 579–588.

McKenna, P., Ornstein, T., & Baddeley, A. (2002). Schizophrenia. In A. D. Baddeley, M. D. Kopelman, & B. A. Wilson (Eds.), *The Handbook of Memory Disorders* (2nd edn, pp. 413–436). Chichester, UK: Wiley.

McKone, E. (1998). The decay of short-term implicit memory: Unpacking lag. *Memory and Cognition, 26*(6), 1173–1186.

McKone, E. (2004). Isolating the special component of face recognition: Peripheral identification and a Mooney face. *Journal of Experimental Psychology: Learning, Memory, and Cognition, 30,* 181–197.

McKone, E., Kanwisher, N., & Duchaine, B. C. (2007). Can generic expertise explain special processing for faces? *Trends in Cognitive Sciences, 11,* 8–15.

McManus, I. C., Richards, P., Winder, B. C., & Sproston, K. A. (1998). Clinical experience, performance in final examinations, and learning style in medical students: Prospective study. *British Medical Journal, 316,* 345–450.

McNamara, T. P. (1992). Priming and constraints it places on theories of memory and retrieval. *Psychological Review, 99,* 650–662.

McPherson, F. (2004). *The Memory Key: Unlock the Secrets to Remembering.* New York: Barnes & Noble.

Means, B., Mingay, D. J., Nigam, A., & Zarrow, M. (1988). A cognitive approach to enhancing health survey reports of medical visits. In M. M. Gruneberg, P. E. Morris, & R. N. Sykes (Eds.), *Practical Aspects of Memory: Current Research and Issues* (Vol. 1). Chichester, UK: Wiley.

Mechanic, A. (1964). The responses involved in the rote learning of verbal materials. *Journal of Verbal Learning and Verbal Behavior, 3,* 30–36.

Meeter, M., Murre, J. M., & Janssen, S. M. (2005). Remembering the news: Modeling retention data from a study with 14,000 participants. *Memory and Cognition, 33*(5), 793–810.

Meiser, T., & Klauer, K. C. (1999). Working memory and changing-state hypothesis. *Journal of Experimental Psychology: Learning, Memory and Cognition, 25*(5), 1272–1299.

Melton, A. W. (1963). Implications of short-term memory for a general theory of memory. *Journal of Verbal Learning and Verbal Behavior, 3,* 30–36.

Melton, A., & Irwin, J. (1940). The influence of degree of interpolated learning on retroactive inhibition and the overt transfer of specific responses. *American Journal of Psychology, 53,* 173–203.

Meltzer, M. L. (1983). Poor memory: A case report. *Journal of Clinical Psychology, 39,* 3–10.

Meltzoff, A. N. (1985). Immediate and deferred imitation in 14-month-old and 24-month-old infants. *Child Development, 56,* 62–72.

Mensink, G., & Raaijmakers, J. G. (1988). A model for interference and forgetting. *Psychological Review, 95*(4), 434–455.

Merskey, H. (1992). The manufacture of personalities. The production of multiple personality disorder. *British Journal of Psychiatry, 160*, 327–340.

Metcalf, J., & Kornell, N. (2007). Principles of cognitive science in education: The effects of generation, errors, and feedback. *Psychonomic Bulletin and Review, 14*, 225–229.

Meudell, P. R., Mayes, A., & Neary, D. (1980). Orienting task effects on the recognition of humorous material in amnesic and normal subjects. *Journal of Clinical Neuropsychology, 2*, 1–14.

Meyer, D. E., & Schvaneveldt, R. W. (1976). Meaning, memory structure, and mental processes. *Science, 192*, 27–33.

Miles, C., & Hardman, E. (1998). State-dependent memory produced by aerobic exercise. *Ergonomics, 41*(1), 20–28.

Miller, E. (1971). On the nature of the memory disorder in presenile dementia. *Neuropsychologia, 9*, 75–81.

Miller, G. A. (1956). The magical number seven, plus or minus two: Some limits on our capacity for processing information. *Psychological Review, 63*, 81–97.

Miller, G. A., Galanter, E., & Pribram, K. H. (1960). *Plans and the Structure of Behavior.* New York: Holt, Rinehart & Winston.

Miller, R., & Matzel, L. D. (2000). Memory involves far more than 'consolidation'. *Nature Neuroscience Reviews, 1*, 214–216.

Milner, B. (1966). Amnesia following operation on the temporal lobes. In C. W. M. Whitty & O. L. Zangwill (Eds.), *Amnesia* (pp. 109–133). London: Butterworths.

Milner, B. (1968). Visual recognition and recall after right temporal-lobe excision in man. *Neuropsychologia, 6*, 191–209.

Mishkin, M., Ungerleider, L. G., & Macko, K. A. (1983). Object vision and spatial vision: Two cortical pathways. *Trends in Neurosciences, 6*, 414–417.

Miyake, A., & Shah, P. (1999a). *Models of Working Memory: Mechanisms of Active Maintenance and Executive Control.* Cambridge: Cambridge University Press.

Miyake, A., & Shah, P. (1999b). Toward unified theories of working memory: Emerging general consensus, unresolved theoretical issues and future directions. In A. Miyake & P. Shah (Eds.), *Models of Working Memory: Mechanisms of Active Maintenance and Executive Control* (pp. 28–61): Cambridge University Press.

Miyake, A., Friedman, N. P., Emerson, M. J., Witzki, A. H., Howerter, A., & Wager, T. D. (2000). The unity and diversity of executive functions and their contributions to complex "frontal lobe" tasks: A latent variable analysis. *Cognitive Psychology, 41*, 49–100.

Miyake, A., Friedman, N. P., Rettinger, D. A., Shah, P., & Hegarty, P. (2001). How are visuospatial working memory, executive functioning, and spatial abilities related? A latent-variable analysis. *Journal of Experimental Psychology: General, 130*(4), 621–640.

Molander, B., & Bäckman, L. (1989). Age differences in heart rate patterns during concentration in a precision sport: Implications for attentional functioning. *Journal of Gerontology: Psychological Sciences, 44*, 80–87.

Moffat, N. (1989). Home-based cognitive rehabilitation with the elderly. In L. Poon, D. Rubin, & B. A. Wilson (Eds.), *Everyday Cognition in Adult and Later Life* (pp. 659–680). Cambridge: Cambridge University Press.

Monsell, S. (2005). The chronometrics of task-set control. In J. Duncan, L. Phillips, & P. McLeod (Eds.), *Measuring the Mind: Speed, Control, and Age.* (pp. 161–190). Oxford: Oxford University Press.

Moore, P. J., Ebbesen, E. B., & Konecni, V. J. (1994). *What Does Real Eyewitness Testimony Look Like? An Archival Analysis of Witnesses to Adult Felony Crimes.* Technical Report: University of California, San Diego, Law and Psychology Program.

Morris, C. D., Bransford, J. D., & Franks, J. J. (1977). Levels of processing versus transfer appropriate processing. *Journal of Verbal Learning and Verbal Behavior, 16*, 519–533.

Morris, J. S., Ohman, A., & Dolan, R. J. (1998). Conscious and unconscious emotional learning in the human amygdala. *Nature, 393*, 467–470.

Morris, P. E. (1979). Strategies for learning and recall. In M. M. Gruneberg & P. E. Morris (Eds.), *Applied Problems in Memory.* London: Academic Press.

Morris, P. E., & Reid, R. L. (1970). The repeated use of mnemonic imagery. *Psychonomic Science, 20*, 337–338.

Morris, P. E., Fritz, C. O., Jackson, L., Nichol, E., & Roberts, E. (2005). Strategies for learning proper names: Expanding retrieval practice, meaning and imagery. *Applied Cognitive Psychology, 19*, 779–798.

Morris, P. E., Gruneberg, M. M., Sykes, R. N., & Merrick, A. (1981). Football knowledge and the acquisition of new results. *British Journal of Psychology, 72*, 479–483.

Morris, P. E., Jones, S., & Hampson, P. (1978). An imagery mnemonic for the learning of people's names. *British Journal of Psychology, 69*, 335–336.

Morris, R. G. (1986). Short-term forgetting in senile dementia of the Alzheimer's type. *Cognitive Neuropsychology, 3*, 77–97.

Morris, R. G., & Baddeley, A. D. (1988). Primary and working memory functioning in Alzheimer-type dementia. *Journal of Clinical and Experimental Neuropsychology, 10,* 279–296.

Morris, R. G., Davis, S., & Butcher, S. P. (1990). Hippocampal synaptic plasticity and NMDA receptors: A role in information storage? *Philosophical Transactions of the Royal Society of London B, 329,* 187–204.

Morris, R. G., Garrud, P., Rawlings, J. M. P., & O'Keefe, J. (1982). Place navigation impaired in rats with hippocampal lesions. *Nature, 297,* 681–683.

Moscovitch, M. (1982). A neuropsychological approach to perception and memory in normal and pathological aging. In F. I. M. Craik & S. Trehub (Eds.), *Aging and Cognitive Processes* (pp. 55–78). New York: Plenum Press.

Mueller, J. H., & Brown, S. C. (1977). Output interference and intralist repetition in free recall. *American Journal of Psychology, 90(1),* 157–164.

Mueller, S. T., Seymour, T. L., Kieras, D. E., & Meyer, D. E. (2003). Theoretical implications of articulatory duration, phonological similarity, and phonological complexity in verbal working memory. *Journal of Experimental Psychology: Learning, Memory, and Cognition, 29(6),* 1353–1380.

Mueller-Johnson, K., & Ceci, S. J. (2004). Memory and suggestibility in older adults: Live event participation and repeated interview. *Applied Cognitive Psychology, 18,* 1109–1127.

Müller, G. E., & Pilzecker, A. (1900). Experimentalle beitrage zur lehre com gedachtnis. *Zeitschrift für Psychologie, 1,* 1–288.

Murdock Jr., B. B. (1960). The distinctiveness of stimuli. *Psychological Review, 67,* 1631.

Murdock Jr., B. B. (1967). Auditory and visual stores in short-term memory. *Acta Psychologica, 27,* 316–324.

Murphy, K., McKone, E., & Slee, J. (2003). Dissociations between implicit and explicit memory in children: The role of strategic processing and the knowledge base. *Journal of Experimental Child Psychology, 84,* 124–165.

Murray, J. D., & Burke, K. A. (2003). Activation and encoding of predictive inferences: The role of reading skill. *Discourse Processes, 35,* 81–102.

Murre, J. M. J. (1996). TraceLink: A model of amnesia and consolidation of memory. *Hippocampus, 6,* 675–684.

Nadel, L. (2007). Consolidation: The demise of the fixed trace. In H. L. Roediger III, Y. Dudai, & S. M. Fitzpatrick (Eds.), *Science of Memory* (pp. 177–182). New York: Oxford University Press.

Nadel, L., & Moscovitch, M. (1997). Memory consolidation, retrograde amnesia and the hippocampal complex. *Current Opinion in Neurobiology, 7,* 217–227.

Nadel, L., & Moscovitch, M. (1998). Hippocampal contributions to cortical plasticity. *Neuropharmacology, 37,* 431–439.

Nader, K., Schafe, G., & LeDoux, J. E. (2000). The labile nature of the consolidation theory. *Nature Neuoscience Reviews, 1,* 216–219.

Nairne, J. S. (1988). A framework for interpreting recency effects in immediate serial recall. *Memory and Cognition, 16,* 343–352.

Nairne, J. S. (1990). A feature model of immediate memory. *Memory and Cognition, 18,* 251–269.

Nairne, J. S. (2002). Remembering over the short-term: The case against the standard model. *Annual Review of Psychology, 53,* 53–81.

National Highway Safety Administration (2006). *The Impact of Driver Inattention on Near Crash/Crash Risk: An Analysis Using the 100-car Naturalistic Driving Study Date (DOTHS810–594).* Washington, DC: US Department of Transportation.

Naveh-Benjamin, M. (2000). Adult age differences in memory performance: Tests of an associative deficit hypothesis. *Journal of Experimental Psychology: Learning Memory and Cognition, 26,* 1170–1187.

Naveh-Benjamin, M., Guez, J., & Marom, M. (2003a). The effects of divided attention at encoding on item and associative memory. *Memory and Cognition, 31,* 1021–1035.

Naveh-Benjamin, M., Guez, J., & Shulman, S. (2004a). Older adults' associative deficit in episodic memory: Assessing the role of decline in attentional resources. *Psychonomic Bulletin and Review, 11,* 1067–1073.

Naveh-Benjamin, M., Guez, J., Kilb, A., & Reedy, S. (2004b). The associative memory deficit of older adults: Further support using face-name associations. *Psychology and Aging, 19,* 541–546.

Naveh-Benjamin, M., Hussain, Z., Guez, J., & Bar-On, M. (2003b). Adult age differences in episodic memory: Further support for an associative deficit hypothesis. *Journal of Experimental Psychology: Learning Memory and Cognition, 29,* 826–837.

Neath, I., & Nairne, J. S. (1995). Word-length effects in immediate memory: Overwriting trace-decay theory. *Psychonomic Bulletin and Review, 2,* 429–441.

Neath, I., & Surprenant, A. (2003). *Human Memory: An Introduction to Research, Data and Theory* (2nd edn). Belmont, CA: Wadsworth.

Neisser, U. (1967). *Cognitive Psychology*. New York: Appleton-Century Crofts.

Neisser, U. (1978). Memory: What are the important questions? In M. M. Gruneberg, P. E. Morris & R. N. Sykes (Eds.), *Practical Aspects of Memory* (pp. 3–24). London: Academic Press.

Neisser, U. (1981). John Dean's memory: A case study. *Cognition, 9*, 1–22.

Neisser, U. (1988). Five kinds of self-knowledge. *Philosophical Psychology, 1*, 35–59.

Neisser, U., & Harsch, N. (1992). Phantom flashbulbs: False recollections of hearing the news about Challenger. In E. Winograd & U. Neisser (Eds.), *Affect and Accuracy in Recall: Studies of 'Flashbulb' Memories* (pp. 9–31). New York: Cambridge University Press.

Nelson, K. (1988). Where do taxonomic categories come from? *Human Development, 31*, 3–10.

Nelson, K. (1989). *Narratives From the Crib*. Cambridge, MA: Harvard University Press.

Neshige, R., Barrett, G., & Shibasaki, H. (1988). Auditory long latency event-related potentials in Alzheimer's disease and multi-infarct demantia. *Journal of Neurology and Psychiatry, 69*, 615–636.

Neuschatz, J. S., Lampinen, J. M., Preston, E. L., Hawkins, E. R., & Toglia, M. P. (2002). The effect of memory schemata on memory and the phenomenological experience of naturalistic situations. *Applied Cognitive Psychology, 16*, 687–708.

Nickerson, R. S. (1984). Retrieval inhibition from part-set cuing: A persisting enigma in memory research. *Memory and Cognition, 12*(6), 531–552.

Nickerson, R. S., & Adams, M. J. (1979). Long-term memory for a common object. *Cognitive Psychology, 11*, 287–307.

Nilsson, L.-G. (1987). Motivated memory: Dissociation between performance data and subjective reports. *Psychological Research, 49*, 183–188.

Nilsson, L. -G., Adolfsson, R., Bäckman, L., Cruts, M., Nyberg, L., Small, B. J., & Van Broeckhoven, C. (2006). The influence of APOE status on episdoc and semantic memory: Data from a population-based study. *Neuropsychology, 20*, 645–657.

Nilsson, L. -G., Adolfsson, R., Bäckman, L., de Frias, C., Molander, B., & Nyberg, L. (2004). Betula: A prospective cohort study on memory, health and aging. *Aging, Neuropsychology and Cognition, 11*, 134–148.

Nimmo, L. M., & Lewandowski, S. (2006). From brief gaps to very long pauses: Temporal isolation does not benefit serial recall. *Psychonomic Bulletin and Review, 12*, 999–1004.

Nissen, M. J., & Bullemer, P. (1987). Attentional requirements of learning: Evidence from performance measures. *Cognitive Psychology, 19*, 1–32.

Nissen, M. J., Knopman, D. S., & Schacter, D. L. (1987). Neurochemical dissociations of memory systems. *Neurology, 37*, 789–794.

Nissen, M. J., Ross, J. L., Willingham, D. D., MacKenzie, T. B., & Schacter, D. L. (1988). Memory and awareness in a patient with multiple personality disorder. *Brain and Cognition, 8*, 117–134.

Noice, H. (1992). Elaboration memory strategies of professional actors. *Applied Cognitive Psychology, 6*, 417–427.

Noice, H., & Noice, T. (1996). Two approaches to learning a theatrical script. *Memory, 4*, 1–17.

Norman, D. A., & Shallice, T. (1986). Attention to action: Willed and automatic control of behaviour. In R. J. Davidson, G. E. Schwarts, & D. Shapiro (Eds.), *Consciousness and Self-regulation. Advances in Research and Theory* (Vol. 4, pp. 1–18). New York: Plenum Press.

Norris, D., Baddeley, A. D., & Page, M. P. A. (2004). Retrospective effects of irrelevent speech on serial recall from short-term memory. *Journal of Experimental Psychology, 30*, 1093–1105.

Nyberg, L., Sandblom, J., Jones, S., Neely, A. S., Petersson, K. M., Ingvar, M., & Bäckman, L. (2003). Neural correlates of training-related memory improvement in adulthood and aging. *Proceedings of the National Academy of Sciences, 100*, 13728–13733.

O'Brien, D. (1993). *How to Develop a Perfect Memory*. London: Pavilion Books.

O'Connell, B. A. (1960). Amnesia and homicide. *British Journal of Delinquency, 10*, 262–276.

Ochsner, K. N., Chiu, C. Y. P., & Schacter, D. L. (1998). Varieties of priming. *Current Opinion in Neurobiology, 4*, 189–194.

Oddy, M., Coughlan, T., Tyerman, A., & Jenkins, D. (1985). Social adjustment after closed head injury: A further follow up seven years after injury. *Journal of Neurology, Neurosurgery and Psychiatry, 48*, 564–568.

Oh, S.-H., & Kim, M. -S. (2004). The role of spatial working memory in visual search efficiency. *Psychonomic Bulletin and Review, 11*, 275–281.

Oliver, W. L., & Ericsson, K. A. (1986). Repeating actors' memory for their parts. In *Proceedings of the 8th Annual Conference of the Cognitive Science Society, Amherst, MA* (pp. 399–406). Hillsdale, NJ: Lawrence Erlbaum Associates.

Owen, A. M., McMillan, K. M., Laird, A. R., & Bullmore, E. (2005). N-back working memory paradigm: A meta-analysis of normative functional neuroimaging studies. *Human Brain Mapping, 25,* 46–59.

Page, M. P. A., & Norris, D. (1998). The primacy model: A new model of immediate serial recall. *Psychological Review, 105,* 761–781.

Page, M. P. A., & Norris, D. G. (2003). The irrelevant sound effect: What needs modeling, and a tentative model. *Quarterly Journal of Experimental Psychology, 56A,* 1289–1300.

Paivio, A. (1969). Mental imagery in associative learning and memory. *Psychological Review, 76,* 241–263.

Paivio, A. (1971). *Imagery and Verbal Processes.* London: Holt Rinehart and Winston.

Palmer, S. E. (1975). The effects of contextual scenes on the identification of objects. *Memory and Cognition, 3,* 519–526.

Papagno, C., & Vallar, G. (1992). Phonological short-term memory and the learning of novel words: The effect of phonological similarity and item length. *Quarterly Journal of Experimental Psychology, 44A,* 47–67.

Papagno, C., Valentine, T., & Baddeley, A. D. (1991). Phonological short-term memory and foreign language vocabulary learning. *Journal of Memory and Language, 30,* 331–347.

Park, D. C., & Puglisi, J. T. (1985). Older adults' memory for the color of matched pictures and words. *Journal of Gerontology, 40,* 198–204.

Park, D. C., Hertzog, C., Kidder, D. C., Morrell, R. W., & Mayhorn, C. B. (1997). Effect of age on event-based and time-based prospective memory. *Psychology and Aging, 12,* 314–327.

Park, S., & Holzman, P. (1992). Schizophrenics show spatial working memory deficits. *Archives of General Psychiatry, 49,* 975–982.

Parker, E. S., Cahill, L., & McGaugh, J. L. (2006). A case of unusual autobiographical remembering. *Neurocase, 12*(1), 35–49.

Parkin, A. J., & Java, R. I. (2000). Determinants of age-related memory loss. In T. Perfect & E. Maylor (Eds.), *Debates in Cognitive Aging.* Oxford: Oxford University Press.

Parkin, A. J., & Walter, B. M. (1992). Recollective experience, normal aging and frontal dysfunction. *Psychology and Aging, 7,* 290–298.

Parkinson, S. R., Inman, V. W., & Dannenbaum, S. E. (1985). Adult age differences in short-term forgetting. *Acta Psychologica, 60,* 83–101.

Pashler, H., Cepeda, N. J., Rohrer, D., & Wixted, J. T. (2005). When does feedback facilitate learning of words? *Journal of Experimental Psychology: Learning, Memory, and Cognition, 31,* 3–8.

Pashler, H., Rohrer, D., Cepeda, N. J., & Carpenter, S. K. (2007). Enhancing learning and retarding forgetting: Choices and consequences. *Psychonomic Bulletin and Review, 14,* 187–193.

Patterson, K. E., & Baddeley, A. D. (1977). When face recognition fails. *Journal of Experimental Psychology: Human Learning and Memory, 3,* 406–417.

Paulesu, E., Frith, C. D., & Frackowiak, R. S. J. (1993). The neural correlates of the verbal component of working memory. *Nature, 362,* 342–345.

Pavlov, I. P. (1927). *Conditioned Reflexes: An Investigation of the Physiological Activity of the Cerebral Cortex.* London: Oxford University Press.

Payne, D. G. (1987). Hypermnesia and reminiscence in recall: A historical and empirical review. *Psychological Bulletin, 101*(1), 5–27.

Pearson, D. G., Logie, R. H., & Gilhooly, K. J. (1999). Verbal representations and spatial manipulation during mental synthesis. *European Journal of Cognitive Psychology, 11*(3), 295–314.

Pelosi, L., & Blumhardt, L. D. (1999). Effects of age on working memory: An event-related potential study. *Cognitive Brain Research, 7,* 321–334.

Penrod, S., & Cutler, B. (1995). Witness confidence and witness accuracy: Assessing their forensic relation. *Psychology, Public Policy, and Law, 1,* 817–845.

Perfect, T. J., & Askew, C. (1994). Print adverts: Not remembered but memorable. *Applied Cognitive Psychology, 8,* 693–703.

Perfect, T. J., & Hollins, T. S. (1996). Predictive feeling of knowing judgments and postdictive confidence judgments in eyewitness memory and general knowledge. *Applied Cognitive Psychology, 10,* 371–382.

Perlmuter, L. C., Scharff, K., Karsh, R., & Monty, R. A. (1980). Perceived control: A generalized state of motivation. *Motivation and Emotion, 4,* 35–45.

Perruchet, P., & Pacteau, C. (1990). Synthetic grammar learning: Implicit rule abstraction or explicit fragmentary knowledge? *Journal of Experimental Psychology: General, 119,* 264–275.

Perry, R. J., & Hodges, J. R. (1999). Attention and executive deficits in Alzheimer's disease: A critical review. *Brain, 122,* 383–404.

Petersen, R. C., Stevens, J. C., Ganguli, M., Tangalos, E. G., Cummings, J. L., & DeKosky, S. T. (2001). Practice parameter: Early detection of dementia: Mild cognitive impairment (an evidence based review). Report of the Quality Standards Subcommittee of the American Academy of Neurology. *Neurology, 56,* 1133–1142.

Peterson, C. (2002). Children's long-term memory for autobiographical events. *Developmental Review, 22*, 370–402.

Peterson, C., & Rideout, R. (1998). Memory for medical emergencies experienced by 1- and 2-year-olds. *Developmental Psychology, 34*, 1059–1072.

Peterson, L. R., & Peterson, M. J. (1959). Short-term retention of individual verbal items. *Journal of Experimental Psychology, 58*, 193–198.

Phillips, L. H., & Henry, J. D. (2005). An evaluation of the frontal lobe theory of cognitive aging. In J. Duncan, L. H. Phillips, & P. McLeod (Eds.), *Measuring the Mind: Speed, Control and Age*. Oxford: Oxford University Press.

Pickel, K. L. (1999). The influence of context on the "weapon focus" effect. *Law and Human Behavior, 23*, 299–311.

Pillemer, D. B. (1998). What is remembered about early childhood events? *Clinical Psychology Review, 18*, 895–913.

Pinto, A. da Costa, & Baddeley, A. D. (1991). Where did you park your car? Analysis of a naturalistic long-term recency effect. *European Journal of Cognitive Psychology, 3*, 297–313.

Pitman, R., Sanders, K., Zusman, R., Healy, A., Cheema, F., Lasko et al. (2002). Pilot study of secondary prevention of post traumatic stress disorder with propranolol. *Biological Psychiatry, 51*, 189–192.

Posner, M. I., & Konick, A. F. (1966). Short term retention of visual and kinesthetic information. *Journal of Organization Behavior and Human Performance., 1*, 71–86.

Postman, L. (1971). Transfer, interference and forgetting. In J. W. Kling, & L. A. Riggs (Eds.), *Woodworth and Schlosberg's Experimental Psychology* (pp. 1019–132). New York: Holt, Rinehart and Winston.

Postman, L., & Phillips, L. W. (1965). Short-term temporal changes in free recall. *Quarterly Journal of Experimental Psychology, 17*, 132–138.

Postman, L., Stark, K., & Henschel, D. M. (1969). Conditions of recovery after unlearning. *Journal of Experimental Psychology, 82*(1, Pt. 2), 1–24.

Prentice, W. C. H. (1954). Visual recognition of verbally labelled figures. *American Journal of Psychology, 67*, 315–320.

Priestley, G., Roberts, S., & Pipe, M.-E. (1999). Returning to the scene: Reminders and context reinstatement enhance children's recall. *Developmental Psychology, 35*, 1006–1019.

Pyszora, N. M., Barker, A. F., & Kopelman, M. D. (2003). Amnesia for criminal offences: A study of life sentence prisoners. *The Journal of Forensic Psychiatry and Psychology, 14*, 475–490.

Quas, J. A., Goodman, G. S., Bidrose, S., Pipe, M. -E., Craw, S., & Ablin, D. S. (1999). Emotion and memory: Children's long-term remembering, forgetting, and suggestibility. *Journal of Experimental Child Psychology, 72*, 235–270.

Querleu, D., Lefebvre, C., Renard, X., Titran, M., Morillion, M., & Crepin, G. (1984). Réactivité du nouveau-né de deux heures de vie à la voix maternelle. *Journal de Gynécologie, Obstrétrique et Biologie de la Réproduction, 13*, 125–134.

Quinn, G., & McConnell, J. (1996a). Exploring the passive visual store. *Psychologische Beitrage, 38*(314), 355–367.

Quinn, G., & McConnell, J. (1996b). Irrelevant pictures in visual working memory. *Quarterly Journal of Experimental Psychology, 49A*(1), 200–215.

Rabbitt, P., & Abson, V. (1990). 'Lost and found': Some logical and methodological limitations of self-report questionnaires as tools to study cognitive aging. *British Journal of Psychology, 81*, 1–16.

Radomsky, A. S., Gilchrist, P. T., & Dussault, D. (2006). Repeated checking really does cause memory distrust. *Behaviour Research and Therapy, 44*, 305–316.

Rajaram, S. (1993). Remembering and knowing: Two means of access to the personal past. *Memory and Cognition, 21*, 89–102.

Ramaekers, J. G., Louwerens, J. W., Muntjewerff, N. D., Milius, H., de Bie, A., Rosenzweig, P. et al. (1999). Psychomotor, cognitive, extrapyramidal, and affective functions of healthy volunteers during treatment with an atypical (amisulspride) and a classic (haloperidol) antipsychotic. *Journal of Clinical Psycholopharmacology, 19*, 209–221.

Raz, N. (2000). Aging of the bran and its impact on cognitive performance: Integration of structural and functional findings. In F. I. M. Craik & T. A. Salthouse (Eds.), *The Handbook of Aging and Cognition* (2nd ed., pp. 91–153). Mahwah, NJ: Lawrence Erlbaum Associates.

Reber, A. S. (1967). Implicit learning of artificial grammars. *Journal of Verbal Learning and Verbal Behavior, 6*, 855–863.

Redelmeier, D. A., & Tibshirani, R. J. (1997). Association between cellular-telephone calls and motor vehicular collisions. *New England Journal of Medicine, 336*, 453–458.

Reed, J. M., & Squire, L. R. (1997). Impaired recognition memory in patients with lesions limited to the hippocampal formation. *Behavioral Neuroscience, 111*, 667–675.

Reese, C. M., & Cherry, K. E. (2002). The effects of age, ability, and memory monitoring on prospective memory task performance. *Aging, Neuropsychology, and Cognition, 9*, 98–113.

Reisberg, D., Clayton, C. L., Heuer, F., & Fischman, D. (1986). Visual memory: When imagery vividness makes a difference. *Journal of Mental Imagery, 10*, 51–74.

Rendell, P. G., & Craik, F. I. M. (2000). Virtual week and actual week: Age-related differences in prospective memory. *Applied Cognitive Psychology, 12*, S43–S62.

Rendell, P. G., & Thomson, D. M. (1999). Aging and prospective memory: Differences between naturalistic and laboratory tasks. *Journal of Gerontology: Psychological Sciences, 54*, 256–269.

Rensink, R. A., O'Regan, J. K., & Clark, J. J. (1997). To see or not to see: The need for attention to perceive changes in scenes. *Psychological Science, 8*, 368–373.

Rescorla, R. A. (2004). Spontaneous recovery varies inversely with the training-extinction interval. *Learning and Behavior: A Psychonomic Society Publication, 32*(4), 401–408.

Reuter-Lorenz, P. A. (2002). New visions of the aging mind and brain. *Trends in Cognitive Sciences, 6*, 394–400.

Ribot, T. R. (1882). *Diseases of Memory.* New York: Appleton & Co.

Riby, L. M., Perfect, T. J., & Stollery, B. (2004). The effects of age and task domain on dual task performance: A meta-analysis. *European Journal of Cognitive Psychology, 16*, 863–891.

Richardson, J. T. E., Eysenck, M. W., & Warren Piper, D. (Eds.) (1987). *Student Learning: Research in Education and Cognitive Psychology.* Buckingham, UK: Open University Press.

Richardson-Klavehn, A., & Bjork, R. A. (1988). Measures of memory. *Annual Reviews in Psychology, 39*, 475–543.

Richmond, J., & Nelson, C. A. (2007). Accounting for change in declarative memory: A cognitive neuroscience perspective. *Developmental Review, 27*, 349–373.

Rips, L. J., Shoben, E. J., & Smith, E. E. (1973). Semantic distance and the verification of semantic relations. *Journal of Verbal Learning and Verbal Behavior, 12*, 1–20.

Robbins, T., Anderson, E., Barker, D., Bradley, A., Fearneyhough, C., Henson, R. et al. (1996). Working memory in chess. *Memory and Cognition, 24*(1), 83–93.

Robinson, J. A., & Swanson, K. L. (1990). Autobiographical memory: The next phase. *Applied Cognitive Psychology, 4*, 321–335.

Roebers, C. M., & Schneider, W. (2005). Individual differences in young children's suggestibility: Relations to event memory, language abilities, working memory, and executive

functioning. *Cognitive Development, 20*, 427–447.

Roediger, H. L., & Karpicke, J. D. (2006a). Test-enhanced learning: Taking memory tests improves long-term retention. *Psychological Science, 17*, 249–255.

Roediger, H. L., & McDermott, K. B. (1993). Encoding specificity in perceptual priming. In A. Garriga-Trillo, P. R. Minon, C. Garcia-Gallego, P. Lubin, J. M. Merino, & A. Villarino (Eds.), *Fechner Day '93: Proceedings of the Ninth Annual Meeting of the International Society for Psychophysics* (pp. 227–232). Madrid, Spain.

Roediger, H. L., & McDermott, K. B. (1995). Creating false memories: Remembering words not presented in lists. *Journal of Experimental Psychology: Learning, Memory and Cognition, 21*, 803–814.

Rohrer, D., & Pashler, H. E. (2003). Concurrent task effects on memory retrieval. *Psychonomic Bulletin and Review, 10*(1), 96–103.

Rönnlund, M., & Nilsson, L.-G. (2006). Adult life-span patterns in WAIS block design performance: Cross sectional versus longitudunal age gradients and relations to demographic predictors. *Intelligence, 34*, 63–78.

Rönnlund, M., & Nilsson, L.-G. (2008). The magnitude, generality, and determinents of the Flynn effects on forms of declarative memory and visuo-spatial ability: Time-sequential analyses of data from a Swedish cohort study. *Intelligence, 36*, 192–209.

Rönnlund, M., Nyberg, L., Bäckman, L., & Nilsson, L.-G. (2005). Stability, growth and decline in adult life-span development of declarity of memory: Cross sectional and longitudinal data from a population-based sample. *Psychology and Aging, 20*, 3–18.

Rosch, E. H. (1973). Natural categories. *Cognitive Psychology, 4*, 328–350.

Rosch, E., & Mervis, C. B. (1975). Family resemblances: Studies in the internal structure of categories. *Cognitive Psychology, 7*, 573–605.

Rosielle, L. J., & Scaggs, W. J. (2008). What if they knocked down the library and nobody noticed? The failure to detect large changes to familiar scenes. *Memory, 16*, 115–124.

Ross, D. F., Ceci, S. J., Dunning, D., & Toglia, M. P. (1994). Unconscious transference and mistaken identity: When a witness misidentifies a familiar but innocent person. *Journal of Applied Psychology, 79*, 918–930.

Ross, J., & Lawrence, K. A. (1968). Some observations on memory artifice. *Psychonomic Science, 13*, 107–108.

Rothbaum, B. O., & Davis, M. (2003). Applying learning principles to the treatment of post-trauma reactions. *Annals of the New York Academy of Science, 1008*, 112–121.

Rovee-Collier, C. K. (1989). The joy of kicking: Memories, motives, and mobiles. In P. R. Solomon, G. R. Goethals, C. M. Kelley, & B. R. Stephens (Eds.), *Memory: Interdisciplinary Approaches* (pp. 151–180). New York: Springer.

Rovee-Collier, C. K., Hayne, H., & Colombo, M. (2001). *The Development of Implicit and Explicit Memory*. Amsterdam: John Benjamins.

Rovee-Collier, C. K., Sullivan, M. W., Enright, M., Lucas, D., & Fagen, J. W. (1980). Reactivation of infant memory. *Science, 208*, 1159–1161.

Roy, D. F. (1991). Improving recall by eyewitnesses through the cognitive interview: Practical applications and implications for the police service. *The Psychologist, 4*, 398–400.

Rubenstein, H., & Aborn, M. (1958). Learning, prediction, and readability. *Journal of Applied Psychology, 42*, 28–32.

Rubin, D. C. (2000). The distribution of early childhood memories. *Memory, 8*, 265–269.

Rubin, D. C., & Berntsen, D. (2006). People over forty feel 20% younger than their age: Subjective age across the lifespan. *Psychonomic Bulletin and Review, 13*(5): 776–780.

Rubin, D. C., & Kontis, T. C. (1983). A schema for common cents. *Memory and Cognition, 11*, 335–341.

Rubin, D. C., & Kozin, M. (1984). Vivid memories. *Cognition, 16*, 81–95.

Rubin, D. C., & Wallace, W. T. (1989). Rhyme and reason: Analyses of dual retrieval cues. *Journal of Experimental Psychology. Learning, 15*(4), 698–709.

Rubin, D. C., & Wenzel, A. E. (1996). One hundred years of forgetting: A quantative description of retention. *Psychological Review, 103*, 734–760.

Rubin, D. C., Groth, E., & Goldsmith, D. J. (1984). Olfactory cueing of autobiographical memory. *American Journal of Psychology, 97*, 493–507.

Rubin, D. C., Wetzler, S. E., & Nebes, R. D. (1986). Autobiographical memory across the lifespan. In D. C. Rubin (Ed.), *Autobiographical Memory*. Cambridge: Cambridge University Press.

Rugg, M. D. (2002). Functional neuroimaging of memory. In A. Baddeley, B. Wilson, & M. Kopelman (Eds.), *Handbook of Memory Disorders* (pp. 57–81). Chichester, UK: Wiley.

Rumelhart, D. E., & Ortony, A. (1977). The representation of knowledge in memory. In R. C. Anderson, R. J. Spiro, & W. E. Montague (Eds.), *Schooling and the Acquisition of Knowledge*. Hillsdale, NJ: Lawrence Erlbaum Associates.

Rundus, D. (1971). Analysis of rehearsal process in free recall. *Journal of Experimental Psychology, 89*, 63–77.

Russell, W. R. (1959). *Brain, Memory, Learning: A Neurologist's View*. London: Oxford University Press.

Russo, R., Nichelli, P., Gibertoni, M., & Cornia, C. (1995). Developmental trends in implicit and explicit memory: A picture completion study. *Journal of Experimental Child Psychology, 59*, 566–578.

Ryan, J. (1969a). Grouping and short-term memory: Different means and patterns of grouping. *Quarterly Journal of Experimental Psychology, 21*, 137–147.

Ryan, J. (1969b). Temporal grouping, rehearsal and short-term memory. *Quarterly Journal of Experimental Psychology, 21*, 148–155.

Saeki, E., & Saito, S. (2004). The role of the phonological loop in task switching performance: The effect of articulatory suppression in the alternating runs paradigm. *Psychologica, 47*, 35–43.

Sahakyan, L., & Kelley, C. M. (2002). A contextual change account of the directed forgetting effect. *Journal of Experimental Psychology: Learning, Memory, and Cognition, 28*(6), 1064–1072.

Salame, P., & Baddeley, A. D. (1982). Disruption of short-term memory by unattended speech: Implications for the structure of working memory. *Journal of Verbal Learning and Verbal Behaviour, 21*, 150–164.

Salame, P., & Baddeley, A. D. (1989). Effects of background music on phonological short-term memory. *Quarterly Journal of Experimental Psychology, 41A*, 107–122.

Salmon, D. P., & Heindel, W. C. (1992). Impaired priming in Alzheimer's disease: Neuropsychological implications. In L. R. Squire & N. Butters (Eds.), *Neuropsychology of memory* (2nd edn, pp. 179–187). New York: Guilford.

Salmon, D. P., Shimamura, A. P., Butters, N., & Smith, S. (1988). Lexical and semantic priming deficits in patients with Alzheimer's disease. *Journal of Clinical and Experimental Neuropsychology, 10*, 477–494.

Salthouse, T. A. (1991). *Theoretical Perspectives on Cognitive Aging*. Hillsdale, NJ: Lawrence Erlbaum Associates.

Salthouse, T. A. (1992). *Mechanisms of Age–Cognition Relations in Adulthood*. Hillsdale, NJ: Lawrence Erlbaum Associates.

Salthouse, T. A. (1996). The processing-speed theory of adult age differences in cognition. *Psychological Review, 103*, 403–428.

Salthouse, T. A., & Becker, J. T. (1998). Independent effects of Alzheimer's disease on neuropsychological functioning. *Neuropsychology, 12*, 242–252.

Sanders, H. I., & Warrington, E. K. (1971). Memory for remote events in amnesic patients. *Brain*, 94, 661–668.

Sapolsky, R. (1996). Why stress is bad for your brain. *Science*, 273, 749–750.

Sara, S. J. (2007). Consolidation: From hypothesis to paradigm to concept. In H. L. Roediger III, Y. Dudai, & S. M. Fitzpatrick (Eds.), *Science of Memory: Concepts* (pp. 183–192). New York: Oxford.

Sargant, W., & Slater, E. (1941). Amnesic syndromes of war. *Proceedings of the Royal Society of Medicine*, 34, 757–764.

Sasaki, K., Gemba, H., & Tsujimoto, T. (1989). Suppression of visually initiated hand movement by stimulation of the prefrontal cortex in the monkey. *Brain Research*, 495(1), 100–107.

Schacter, D. L. (1986). On the relation between genuine and simulated amnesia. *Behavioural Sciences and the Law*, 4, 47–64.

Schacter, D. L. (1987). Implicit memory: History and current status. *Journal of Experimental Psychology: Learning, Memory, and Cognition*, 13(3), 501–518.

Schacter, D. L. (1992). Priming and multiple memory systems: Perceptual mechanisms of implicit memory. *Journal of Cognitive Neuroscience*, 4, 244–256.

Schacter, D. L. (2001). *The Seven Sins of Memory: How the Mind Forgets and Remembers*. New York: Houghton-Mifflin.

Schacter, D. L., Cooper, L. A., & Delaney, S. M. (1990). Implicit memory for unfamiliar objects depends upon access to structural descriptions. *Journal of Experimental Psychology: General*, 199, 5–24.

Schacter, D. L., Harbluk, J. L., & McLachlan, D. R. (1984). Retrieval without recollection: An experimental analysis of source amnesia. *Journal of Verbal Learning and Verbal Behavior*, 23, 593–611.

Schacter, D. L., Koutsaal, W., & Norman, K. A. (1997). False memories and aging. *Trends in Cognitive Sciences*, 1, 229–236.

Schacter, D. L., Wang, P. L., Tulving, E., & Freedman, M. (1982). Functional retrograde amnesia: A quantitative case study. *Neuropsychologia*, 20(5), 523–532.

Schacter, D., & Moscovitch, M. (1984). Infants, amnesiacs, and dissociable memory. In M. Moscovitch (Ed.), *Infant Memory* (pp. 173–209). New York: Plenum.

Schacter, D., Reiman, E., Curran, T., Yun, L. S., Bandy, D., McDermott, K. B. et al. (1996). Neuroanatomical correlates of veridical and illusory recognition memory: Evidence from positron emission tomography. *Neuron*, 17, 267–274.

Schank, R. C., & Abelson, R. P. (1977). *Scripts, Plans, Goals and Understanding*. Hillsdale, NJ: Lawrence Erlbaum Associates.

Schmidt, H. G., Boshuizen, H. P. A., & van Breukelen, G. J. P. (2002). Long-term retention of a theatrical script by repertory actors: The role of context. *Memory*, 10, 21–28.

Schmidt, R. A., & Bjork, R. A. (1992). New conceptualizations of practice: Common principles in three paradigms suggest new concepts for training. *Psychological Science*, 3, 207–214.

Schmoick, H., Buffalo, E. A., & Squire, L. R. (2000). Memory distortions develop over time: Recollections of the O. J. Simpson trial verdict after 15 and 32 months. *Psychological Science*, 11, 39–45.

Schneider, W. (1999). The development of metamemory in children. *Attention and Performance*, 17, 487–514.

Schneider, W., & Pressley, M. (1998). The development of metacognition: Introduction. *European Journal of Psychology of Education*, 13, 3–8.

Schneider, W., Gruber, W., Gruber, H., Gold, A., & Opwis, K. (1993). Chess expertise and memory for chess positions in children and adults. *Journal of Experimental Child Psychology*, 56, 328–349.

Schneider, W., Knopf, M., & Stefanek, J. (2002). The development of verbal memory in childhood and adolescence: Findings from the Munich Longitudinal Study. *Journal of Educational Psychology*, 94, 751–761.

Schooler, J. W., & Engstler-Schooler, T. Y. (1990). Verbal overshadowing of visual memories: Some things are better left unsaid. *Cognitive Psychology*, 22, 36–71.

Schooler, J. W., Ambadar, Z., & Bendiksen, M. A. (1997). A cognitive corroborative case study approach for investigating discovered memories of sexual abuse. In J. D. Read & D. S. Lindsay (Eds.), *Recollections of Trauma: Scientific Evidence and Clinical Practice*. (pp. 379–88). New York: Plenum.

Schott, B. H., Henson, R. N., Richardson-Klavehn, A., Becker, C., Thoma et al. (2005). Redefining implicit and explicit memory: The functional neuroanatomy of priming, remembering, and control of retrieval. *Proceedings of the Natural Academy of Sciences of the USA*, 102, 1257–1262.

Scott, V. (1989). An empirical study of explicit and implicit teaching strategies in French. *The Modern Language Journal*, 73, 14–22.

Scott, V. (1990). Explicit and implicit grammar teaching strategies: New empirical data. *The French Review*, 63, 779–789.

Sellen, A. J., Lowie, G., Harris, J. E., & Wilkins, A. J. (1997). What brings intentions to mind? An *in situ* study of prospective memory. *Memory, 5,* 483–507.

Sergent, J., & Signoret, J. L. (1992). Varieties of functional deficits in prosopagnosia. *Cerebral Cortex, 2,* 375–388.

Shallice, T. (2002). Fractionation of the supervisory system. In D. T. Stuss & R. T. Knight (Eds.), *Principles of Frontal Lobe Function.* (pp. 261–277). New York: Oxford University Press.

Shallice, T., & Warrington, E. K. (1970). Independent functioning of verbal memory stores: A neuropsychological study. *Quarterly Journal of Experimental Psychology, 22,* 261–273.

Shaw, J. S., Bjork, R. A., & Handal, A. (1995). Retrieval-induced forgetting in an eyewitness-memory paradigm. *Psychonomic Bulletin and Review, 2*(2), 249–253.

Sheingold, K., & Tenney, Y. J. (1982). Memory for a salient childhood event. In U. Neisser (Ed.), *Memory Observed* (pp. 201–212). New York: Freeman.

Shepard, R. N., & Feng, C. (1972). A chronometric study of mental paper-folding. *Cognitive Psychology, 3,* 228–243.

Shiel, A., Wilson, B. A., McLellan, L., S., H., & Watson. (2000). *The Wessex Head Injury Matrix (WHIM).* Bury St Edmunds, UK: Thames Valley Test Company.

Shimamura, A. P., & Squire, L. R. (1991). The relationship between fact and source memory: findings with amnesic patients and normal subjects. *Psychobiology, 19,* 1–10.

Shimamura, A. P., Berry, J. M., Mangels, J. A., Rustings, C. L., & Jurica, P. J. (1995). Memory and cognitive abilities in academic professors: Evidence for successful aging. *Psychological Science, 6,* 271–277.

Shors, T. J., & Matzel, L. D. (1997). Long-term potentiation: What's learning got to do with it? *Behavioural and Brain Sciences, 20,* 597–655.

Shriver, E. R., Young, S. G., Hugenberg, K., Bernstein, M. J., & Lanter, J. R. (2008). Class race, and the face: Social context modulates the cross-race effect in face recognition. *Personality and Social Psychology Bulletin, 34,* 260–274.

Shute, V. J. (1991). Who is likely to acquire programming skills? *Journal of Educational Computing Research, 7,* 1–2.

Siegler, R. S. (1998). *Children's Thinking* (3rd edn). Upper Saddle River, NJ: Prentice Hall.

Simcock, G., & Hayne, H. (2002). Breaking the barrier? Children fail to translate their Preverbal memories into language. *Psychological Science, 13,* 225–231.

Simcock, G., & Hayne, H. (2003). Age-related changes in verbal and non-verbal memory during early childhood. *Developmental Psychology, 39,* 805–814.

Simon, H. A., & Gilmartin, K. (1973). Simulation of memory for chess positions. *Cognitive Psychology, 5,* 29–46.

Simons, D. J., & Levin, D. T. (1998). Failure to detect changes to people during a real-world interaction. *Psychonomic Bulletin and Review, 5,* 644–649.

Sirigu, A., Zalla, T., Pillon, B., Grafman, J., Agid, Y., & Dubois, B. (1995). Selective impairments in managerial knowledge following prefrontal cortex damage. *Cortex, 31,* 301–316.

Sitnikova, T., West, W. C., Kuperberg, G. R., & Holcomb, P. J. (2006). The neural organization of semantic memory: Electrophysiological activity suggests feature-based segregation. *Biological Psychology, 71,* 326–340.

Slamecka, N. J. (1968). A methodological analysis of shift paradigms in human discrimination learning. *Psychological Bulletin, 69*(6), 423–438.

Smith, E. E., & Jonides, J. (1997). Working memory: A view from neuroimaging. *Cognitive Psychology, 33,* 5–42.

Smith, E. E., & Jonides, J. (1999). Storage and executive processes in the frontal lobes. *Science, 283,* 1657–1661.

Smith, E. E., & Kosslyn, S. M. (2007). *Cognitive Psychology: Mind and Brain.* Upper Saddle River, NJ: Pearson/Prentice Hall.

Smith, E. E., Jonides, J., & Koeppe, R. A. (1996). Dissociating verbal and spatial working memory using PET. *Cerebral Cortex, 6,* 11–20.

Smith, R. E. (2003). The cost of remembering to remember in event-based prospective memory: Investigating the capacity demands of delayed intention performance. *Journal of Experimental Psychology: Learning, Memory, and Cognition, 29,* 347–361.

Smith, R. E., & Bayen, U. J. (2005). The effects of working memory resource availability on prospective memory: A formal modeling approach. *Experimental Psychology, 52,* 243–256.

Smith, S.M., & Moynan, S.C. (2008). Forgetting and recovering the unforgettable. *Psychological Science, 19,* 462–468.

Smith, S. M., & Vela, E. (2001). Environmental context-dependent memory: A review and meta-analysis. *Psychonomic Bulletin and Review, 8*(2), 203–220.

Snowden, J. S., Neary, D., & Mann, D. M. A. (1996). *Fronto-temporal Lobar Degeneration: Fronto-temporal Dementia, Progressive Aphasia, Semantic Dementia.* New York: Churchill, Livingstone.

Snowden, J., Griffiths, H., & Neary, D. (1994). Semantic dementia: Autobiographical contribution to preservation of meaning. *Cognitive Neuropsychology, 11,* 265–288.

Spector, A., Davies, S., Woods, B., & Orrell, M. (2000). Reality orientation for dementia: A systematic review of the evidence of effectiveness from randomised control trials. *The Gerontologist, 40,* 206–212.

Sperling, G. (1960). The information available in brief visual presentations. *Psychological Monographs: General and Applied, 74,* 1–29.

Sperling, G. (1963). A model for visual memory tasks. *Human Factors, 5,* 19–31.

Spiers, H. J., Maguire, E. A., & Burgess, N. (2001). Hippocampal amnesia. *Neurocase, 7,* 357–382.

Spinnler, H., Della Sala, S., Bandera, R., & Baddeley, A. D. (1988). Dementia, ageing and the structure of human memory. *Cognitive Neuropsychology, 5,* 193–211.

Spiro, R. J. (1977). Remembering information from text: Theoretical and empirical issues concerning the 'state of schema' reconstruction hypothesis. In R. C. Anderson, R. J. Spiro, & W. E. Montague (Eds.), *Schooling and the Acquisition of Knowledge.* Hillsdale, NJ: Lawrence Erlbaum Associates.

Sporer, S. L., Penrod, S., Read, D., & Cutler, B. (1995). Choosing, confidence, and accuracy: A meta-analysis of the confidence–accuracy relation in eyewitness identification studies. *Psychological Bulletin, 118,* 315–327.

Squire, L. R. (1981). Two forms of human amnesia: An analysis of forgetting. *Journal of Neuroscience, 1,* 635–640.

Squire, L. R. (1987). *Memory and Brain.* New York: Oxford University Press.

Squire, L. R. (1992a). Declarative and nondeclarative memory: Multiple brain systems supporting learning and memory. *Journal of Cognitive Neuroscience, 4,* 232–243.

Squire, L. R. (1992b). Memory and the hippocampus: A synthesis from findings with rats, monkeys, and humans: Correction. *Psychological Review, 99*(3), 582.

Squire, L. R. (1992c). Memory and the hippocampus: A synthesis from findings with rats, monkeys, and humans. *Psychological Review, 99*(2), 195–231.

Squire, L. R. (2004). Memory systems of the brain: A brief history and current perspective. *Neurobiology of learning and memory, 82,* 171–177.

Squire, L. R., & Alvarez, P. (1995). Retrograde amnesia and memory consolidation: A neurobiological perspective. *Current Opinion in Neurobiology, 5,* 169–177.

Squire, L. R., Haist, F., & Shimamura, A. P. (1989). The neurology of memory: Quantitative assessment of retrograde amnesia in two types of amnesic patient. *Journal of Neuroscience, 9,* 828–839.

Squire, L. R., Knowlton, B., & Musen, G. (1993). The structure and organisation of memory. *Annual Review of Psychology, 44,* 453–495.

Srinivas, K., & Roediger, H. L. (1990). Classifying implicit memory tests: Category association and anagram solution. *Journal of Memory and Language, 29,* 389–412.

St George-Hyslop, P. H. (2000). Piecing together Alzheimer's. *Scientific American, 283*(6), 76–83.

Stanley, W. B., Mathews, R. C., Buss, R. R., & Kotler-Cope, S. (1989). Insight without awareness: On the interaction of verbalization, instruction, and practice in a simulated process control task. *Quarterly Journal of Experimental Psychology, 41A,* 553–577.

Staubli, U., Rogers, G., & Lynch, G. (1994). Facilitation of glutamate receptors enhances memory. *Proceedings of the Natural Academy of Sciences of the USA, 91,* 777–781.

Steblay, N. M. (1997). Social influence in eyewitness recall: A meta-analytic review of line-up instruction effects. *Law and Human Behavior, 21,* 283–298.

Steblay, N. M., Dysart, J., Fulero, S., & Lindsay, R. C. L. (2001). Eyewitness accuracy rates in sequential and simultaneous line-up presentations: A meta-analytic comparison. *Law and Human Behavior, 25,* 459–474.

Stewart, E. W., Shimp, T. A., & Engle, R. W. (1987). Classical conditioning of consumer attitudes: Four experiments in an advertising context. *Journal of Consumer Research, 14,* 334–349.

Stickgold, R., LaTanya, J., & Hobson, J. A. (2000). Visual discrimination learning requires sleep after training. *Nature Neuoscience, 3,* 1237–1238.

Storm, B. C., Bjork, E. L., Bjork, R. A., & Nestojko, J. F. (2006). Is retrieval success a necessary condition for retrieval-induced forgetting? *Psychonomic Bulletin and Review, 13,* 1023–1027.

Strayer, D. L., & Johnston, W. A. (2001). Driving to distraction: Dual-task studies of simulated driving and conversing on a cellular telephone. *Psychological Science, 12,* 462–466.

Sulin, R. A., & Dooling, D. J. (1974). Intrusion of a thematic idea in retention of prose. *Journal of Experimental Psychology, 103,* 255–262.

Sumby, W. H. (1963). Word frequency and serial position effects. *Journal of Verbal Learning and Verbal Behavior, 1*(6), 443–450.

Sunderland, A., Harris, J. E., & Baddeley, A. D. (1983). Do laboratory tests predict everyday memory? *Journal of Verbal Learning and Verbal Behavior, 22,* 341–357.

Sunderland, A., Watts, K., Baddeley, A. D., & Harris, J. E. (1986). Subjective memory assessment and test performance in the elderly. *Journal of Gerontology, 41*, 376–385.

Svoboda, E., McKinnon, M. C., & Levine, B. (2006). The functional neuroanatomy of autobiographical memory: a meta-analysis. *Neuropsychologia, 44*, 2189–2208.

Taguchi, K. (2006). Should the keyword method be introduced in tertiary foreign language classrooms? *Electronic Journal of Foreign Language Teaching, 3*, 22–38.

Talarico, J. M., & Rubin, D. C. (2003). Confidence, not consistency, characterizes flashbulb memories. *Psychological Science, 14*, 455–461.

Tallis, F. (1995). *Obsessive-compulsive Disorder: A Cognitive and Neuropsychological Perspective.* Chichester, UK: Wiley.

Tam, L., & Ward, G. (2000). A recency-based account of the primacy effect in free recall. *Journal of Experimental Psychology: Learning, Memory, and Cognition, 26*, 1589–1625.

Teasdale, J. D., & Fogarty, S. J. (1979). Differential effects of induced mood on retrieval of pleasant and unpleasant events from episodic memory. *Journal of Abnormal Psychology, 88*(3), 248–257.

Thierry, K. L., & Spence, M. J. (2002). Source-monitoring training facilitates preschoolers' eyewitness memory performance. *Developmental Psychology, 38*, 428–437.

Thompson, C. P., Cowan, T., & Frieman, J. (1993). *Memory Search by a Memorist.* Hillsdale, NJ: Lawrence Erlbaum Associates.

Thompson, C. P., Cowan, T., Frieman, J., Mahadevan, R. S., Vogl, R. J., & Frieman, R. J. (1991). Rajan—a study of a memorist. *Journal of Memory and Language, 30*, 702–724.

Thompson, P. (1980). Margaret Thatcher: A new illusion. *Perception, 9*, 483–484.

Thompson, W. C., Clarke-Stewart, K. A., & Lepore, S. J. (1997). What did the janitor do? Suggestive interviewing and the accuracy of children's accounts. *Law and Human Behavior, 21*, 405–426.

Thomson, J. A. (1983). Is continuous visual monitoring necessary in visually guided locomotion. *Journal of Experimental Psychology, 9*, 427–433.

Tollestrup, P. A., Turtle, J. W., & Yuille, J. C. (1994). Actual victims and witnesses to robbery and fraud: An archival analysis. In D. F. Ross, J. D. Read, & M. P. Toglia (Eds.), *Adult Eyewitness Testimony: Current Trends and Developments.* New York: Wiley.

Tolman, E. C. (1948). Cognitive maps in rats and men. *Psychological Review, 55*, 189–208.

Towse, J. N., & Hitch, G. J. (1995). Is there a relationship between task demand and storage space in tests of working memory capacity? *Quarterly Journal of Experimental Psychology, 48A*(1), 108–124.

Towse, J. N., Hitch, G. J., & Hutton, U. (2000). On the interpretation of working memory span in adults. *Memory and Cognition, 28*(3), 341–348.

Tranel, D., & Damasio, A. R. (2002). Neurological foundations of human memory. In A. D. Baddeley, M. D. Kopelman, & B. A. Wilson (Eds.), *Handbook of Memory Disorders* (2nd ed., pp. 17–56). Chichester, UK: Wiley.

Tuckey, M. R., & Brewer, N. (2003a). How schemas affect eyewitness memory over repeated retrieval attempts. *Applied Cognitive Psychology, 7*, 785–800.

Tuckey, M. R., & Brewer, N. (2003b). The influence of schemas, stimulus ambiguity, and interview schedule on eyewitness memory over time. *Journal of Experimental Psychology: Applied, 9*, 101–118.

Tulving, E. (1962). Subjective organisation in free recall of "unrelated" words. *Psychological Review, 69*, 344–354.

Tulving, E. (1972). Episodic and semantic memory. In E. Tulving & W. Donaldson (Eds.), *Organization of Memory* (pp. 381–403). New York: Academic Press.

Tulving, E. (1979). Relation between encoding specificity and levels of processing. In L. S. Cermak & F. I. M. Craik (Eds.), *Levels of Processing in Human Memory.* Hillsdale, NJ: Lawrence Erlbaum Associates Inc.

Tulving, E. (1983). *Elements of Episodic Memory.* Oxford: Oxford University Press.

Tulving, E. (1985). How many memory systems are there? *The American Psychologist, 40*, 385–398.

Tulving, E. (1989). Memory: Performance, knowledge and experience. *European Journal of Cognitive Psychology, 1*, 3–26.

Tulving, E. (2002). Episodic memory: From mind to brain. *Annual Review of Psychology, 53*, 1–25.

Tulving, E., & Osler, S. (1968). Effectiveness of retrieval cues in memory for words. *Journal of Experimental Psychology, 77*(4), 593–601.

Tulving, E., & Pearlstone, Z. (1966). Availability versus accessibility of information in memory for words. *Journal of Verbal Learning and Verbal Behavior, 5*, 381–391.

Tulving, E., & Thomson, D. M. (1973). Encoding specificity and retrieval processes in episodic memory. *Psychological Review, 80*(5), 352–373.

Tulving, E., Kapur, S., Craik, F. I. M., Moscovitch, M., & Houle, S. (1994). Hemispheric encoding/retrieval asymmetry in episodic memory—positron emission tomography findings.

Proceedings of the National Academy of Sciences of the USA, 91(6), 2016–2020.

Tulving, E., Schacter, D. L., & Stark, H. A. (1982). Priming effects in word-fragment completion are independent of recognition memory. *Journal of Experimental Psychology: Learning, Memory and Cognition, 8,* 336–342.

Turner, M. L., & Engle, R. W. (1989). Is working memory capacity task-dependent? *Journal of Memory and Language, 28,* 127–154.

Turvey, M. T. (1973). On peripheral and central processes in vision: Inferences from an information processing analysis of masking with patterned stimuli. *Psychological Review, 80,* 1–52.

Turvey, M. T., & Kravetz, S. (1970). Retrieval from iconic memory with shape as the selection criterion. *Perception and Psychophysics, 8,* 171–172.

Twitmyer, E. B. (1902). *A Study of the Knee Jerk.* Philadelphia: Winston.

Underwood, B. J. (1948). Retroactive and proactive inhibition after five and forty-eight hours. *Journal of Experimental Psychology, 38,* 29–38.

Underwood, B. J. (1957). Interference and forgetting. *Psychological Review, 64,* 49–60.

Underwood, B. J., & Schulz, R. W. (1960). *Meaningfulness and Verbal Learning.* Chicago: Lippincott.

Vaidya, C. J., Huger, M., Howard, D. V., & Howard, J. H. (2007). Developmental differences in implicit learning of spatial context. *Neuropsychology, 21,* 497–506.

Vaiva, G., Ducrocq, F., Jezequel, K., Averland, B., Levestal, P., Brunet, A. et al. (2003). Immediate treatment with propranolol decreases post traumatic stress two mouths after trauma. *Biological Psychiatry, 54,* 947–949.

Valentine, T., Pickering, A., & Darling, S. (2003). Characteristics of eyewitness identification that predict the outcome of real line-ups. *Applied Cognitive Psychology, 17,* 969–993.

Vallar, G., & Baddeley, A. D. (1987). Phonological short-term store and sentence processing. *Cognitive Neuropsychology, 4,* 417–438.

Vallar, G., & Papagno, C. (2002). Neuropsychological impairments of verbal short-term memory. In A. D. Baddeley, M. D. Kopelman, & B. A. Wilson (Eds.), *Handbook of Memory Disorders* (2nd edn, pp. 249–270). Chichester, UK: Wiley.

Vallar, G., & Shallice, T. (1990). *Neuropsychological Impairments of Short-term Memory.* Cambridge: Cambridge University Press.

van den Hout, M., & Kindt, M. (2004). Obsessive-compulsive disorder and the paradoxical effects of perseverative behavior on experienced uncertainty. *Journal of Behavior Therapy and Experimental Psychiatry, 35,* 165–181.

Vargha-Khadem, F., Gadian, D. G., & Mishkin, M. (2001). Dissociations in cognitive memory: The syndrome of developmental amnesia. *Philosophical Transactions of the Royal Society. Series B., 356,* 1435–1440.

Vargha-Khadem, F., Gadian, D. G., Watkins, K. E., Connelly, A., Van Paesschen, W., & Mishkin, M. (1997). Differential effects of early hippocampal pathology on episodic and semantic memory. *Science, 277,* 376–380.

Velten, E. (1968). A laboratory task for induction of mood states. *Behavior Research and Therapy, 6*(4), 473–482.

Verhaeghen, P., Marcoen, A., & Goossens, L. (1993). Facts and fiction about memory aging: A quantitative integration of research findings. *Journal of Gerontology: Psychological Sciences, 48,* 157–171.

Vogel, E. K., Woodman, G. F., & Luck, S. J. (2001). Storage of features, conjunctions, and objects in visual working memory. *Journal of Experimental Psychology: Human Perception and Performance, 27*(1), 92–114.

von Wright, J. M. (1968). Selection in visual immediate memory. *Acta Psychologica, 33,* 280–292.

Vygotsky, L. S. (1962). *Thought and Language* (E. Hanfmann & G. Vakar, Trans.). Cambridge, MA: MIT Press.

Wade, K. A., & Garry, M. (2005). Strategies for verifying false autobiographical memories. *American Journal of Psychology, 118,* 587–602.

Wagenaar, W. A. (1986). My memory: A study of autobiographical memory over six years. *Cognitive Psychology, 18,* 225–252.

Wagenaar, W. A., & Groeneweg, J. (1990). The memory of concentration camp survivors. *Applied Cognitive Psychology, 4,* 77–87.

Wagner, A. D., Schacter, D. L., Rotte, M., Koutstaal, W., Maril, A., Dale, A. M. et al. (1998). Building memories: Remembering and forgetting of verbal experiences as predicted by brain activity. *Science, 281,* 1188–1191.

Waldfogel, S. (1948). The frequency and affective character of childhood memories. *Psychological Monographs, 62*(whole no. 291).

Walker, W. R., Skowronski, J. J., & Thompson, C. P. (2003). Life is pleasant— and memory helps to keep it that way! *Review of General Psychology, 7,* 203–210.

Walter, W. G. (1953). *The Living Brain.* London: Norton.

Wang, Q. (2001). Cultural effects on adults' earliest childhood recollection and self-description:

Implications for the relation between memory and the self. *Journal of Personality and Social Psychology, 81,* 220–233.

Wang, Q. (2006a). Earliest recollections of self and others in European American and Taiwanese young adults. *Psychological Science, 17,* 708–714.

Wang, Q. (2006b). Relations of maternal style and child self-concept to autobiographical memories in Chinese, Chinese immigrant, and European American 3-year-olds. *Child Development, 77,* 1799–1814.

Warrington, E. K, & Weiskrantz, L. (1970). Amnesic syndrome: Consolidation or retrieval? *Nature, 226,* 628–630.

Warrington, E. K., & Shallice, T. (1984). Category-specific semantic impairments. *Brain, 107,* 829–853.

Warrington, E. K., & Weiskrantz, L. (1968). New methods of testing long-term retention with special reference to amnesic patients. *Nature, 217,* 972–974.

Warrington, E. K., & Weiskrantz, L. (1978). Further analyses of the prior learning effect in amnesic patients. *Neuropsychologia, 16,* 169–176.

Watkins, M. J. (1978). Engrams as cuegrams and forgetting as cue-overload: A cueing approach to the structure of memory. In C. R. Puff (Ed.), *The Structure of Memory.* (pp. 347–372). New York: Academic Press.

Webb, S., Long, J., & Nelson, C. (2005). A longitudinal investigation of visual event-related potentials in the first year of life. *Developmental Science, 8,* 605–616.

Weiner, N. (1950). *The Human Use of Human Beings.* Boston: Houghton Mifflin.

Weiskrantz, L., & Warrington, E. K. (1979). Conditioning in amnesic patients. *Neuropsychologia, 8,* 281–288.

Weist, R. M. (1972). The role of rehearsal: Recopy or reconstruct? *Journal of Verbal Learning and Verbal Behavior, 11,* 440–445.

Weldon, M. S., & Bellinger, K. D. (1997). Collective memory: Collaborative and individual processes in remembering. *Journal of Experimental Psychology: Learning, Memory, and Cognition, 23*(5), 1160–1175.

Welford, A. T. (1985). Changes of performance with age: An overview. In N. Charness (Ed.), *Aging and Human Performance* (pp. 333–369). New York: Wiley.

Wheeler, M. A. (1995). Improvement in recall over time without repeated testing: Spontaneous recovery revisited. *Journal of Experimental Psychology: Learning, 21*(1), 173–184.

Wheeler, M. A., Stuss, D. T., & Tulving, E. (1997). Toward a theory of episodic memory:

The frontal lobes and autonoetic consciousness. *Psychological Bulletin, 121,* 331–354.

Wickelgren, W. A. (1964). Size of rehearsal group and short-term memory. *Journal of Experimental Psychology, 68,* 413–419.

Wilding, J., & Valentine, E. (1994). Memory champions. *British Journal of Psychology, 85,* 231–244.

Wiley, J. (2005). A fair and balanced look at the news: What affects memory for controversial arguments? *Journal of Memory and Language, 53,* 95–109.

Willander, J., & Larsson, M. (2006). Smell your way back to childhood: Autobiographical odour memory. *Psychonomic Bulletin and Review, 13,* 240–244.

Williams, H. L., Conway, M. A., & Cohen, G. (2008). Autobiographical memory. In G. Cohen & M. A. Conway (Eds.), *Memory in the Real World* (3rd ed., pp. 21–90). Hove, UK: Psychology Press.

Williams, J. M. G., Watts, F. N., MacLeod, C., & Mathews, A. (1997). *Cognitive Psychology and Emotional Disorders* (2nd edn). Chichester, UK: Wiley.

Willingham, D. B., & Winter, E. (1995). Comparison of motor skill learning in elderly and young human subjects. *Society for Neuroscience Abstracts, 21,* 1440.

Wilson, B. A. (1991). Long term prognosis of patients with severe memory disorders. *Neuropsychological Rehabilitation, 1,* 117–134.

Wilson, B. A., Baddeley, A. D., & Kapur, N. (1995). Dense amnesia in a professional musician following Herpes Simplex Virus Encephalitis. *Journal of Clinical and Experimental Neuropsychology, 17,* 668–681.

Wilson, B. A., Baddeley, A. D., & Young, A. W. (1999). LE, A person who lost her "mind's eye". *Neurocase, 5,* 119–127.

Wilson, B. A., Cockburn, J., & Baddeley, A. D. (Eds.). (1989a). *Assessment of Everyday Memory Functioning Following Severe Brain Injury.* Stoneham, MA: Butterworths.

Wilson, B. A., Cockburn, J., Baddeley, A. D., & Hiorns, R. (1989b). The development and validation of a test battery for detecting and monitoring everyday memory problems. *Journal of Clinical and Experimental Neuropsychology, 11,* 855–870.

Wilson, M. A., & McNaughton, B. L. (1994). Reactivation of hippocampal ensemble memories during sleep. *Science, 265,* 676–679.

Winocur, G. (1978). Effects of inteference on discrimination learning and recall by rats with hippocampal lesions. *Physiology and Behavior, 22,* 339–345.

Winocur, G., & Mills, J. A. (1970). Transfer between related and unrelated problems following hippocampal lesions in rats. *Journal of Comparative and Physiological Psychology, 73*, 162–169.

Winograd, E., & Soloway, R. M. (1986). On forgetting the locations of things stored in special places. *Journal of Experimental Psychology: General, 115*, 366–372.

Wise, R. A., & Safer, M. A. (2004). What US judges know and believe about eyewitness testimony. *Applied Cognitive Psychology, 18*, 427–443.

Wishart, L. R., & Lee, T. D. (1997). Effects of aging and reduced relative frequency of knowledge of results on learning a motor skill. *Perceptual and Motor Skills, 84*, 1107–1122.

Wittgenstein, L. (1958). *Philosophical Investigations*. New York: Macmillan.

Wood, R. E., Mento, A. J., Locke, A. J., & Locke, E. A. (1987). Task complexity as a moderator of goal effects: A meta-analysis. *Journal of Applied Psychology, 72*, 416–425.

Woodman, G. F., & Luck, S. J. (2004). Visual search is slowed when visuospatial working memory is occupied. *Psychonomic Bulletin and Review, 11*, 269–274.

Woods, R. T., & McKiernan, F. (1995). Evaluating the impact of reminiscence on old people with dementia. In B. K. Haight & J. Webster (Eds.), *The Art or Science of Reminiscing: Theory, Research, Methods and Applications* (pp. 233–242). Washington, DC: Taylor and Francis.

Woods, R., Spector, A., Orrell, M., & Davies, S. (2005). *Reminiscence Therapy for Dementia: A Review of the Evidence of Effectiveness from Randomised Controlled Trials*. Oxford: Update Software.

Wright, B. M., & Payne, R. B. (1985). Effects of aging on sex differences in psychomotor reminiscence and tracking proficiency. *Journal of Gerontology, 40*, 184.

Wright, D. B., & Stroud, J. N. (2002). Age differences in lineup identification accuracy: People are better with their own age. *Law and Human Behavior, 26*, 641–654.

Wyer, R. S., & Frey, D. (1983). The effects of feedback about self and others on the recall and judgments of feedback-relevant information. *Journal of Experimental Social Psychology, 19*(6), 540–559.

Yarnell, P. R., & Lynch, S. (1970). Retrograde memory immediately after concussion. *Lancet, 1*(7652), 863–865.

Yasuda, K., Watanabe, O., & Ono, Y. (1997). Dissociation between semantic and autobiographic memory: A case report. *Cortex, 33*, 623–638.

Yonelinas, A. P. (1999). The contribution of recollection and familiarity to recognition and source-memory judgments: A formal dual-process model and an analysis of receiver operating characteristics. *Journal of Experimental Psychology: Learning, Memory, and Cognition, 25*(6), 1415–1434.

Yonelinas, A. P. (2002). The nature of recollection and familiarity: A review of 30 years of research. *Journal of Memory and Language, 46*, 441–517.

Yonelinas, A. P., & Levy, B. J. (2002). Dissociating familiarity from recollection in human recognition memory: Different rates of forgetting over short retention intervals. *Psychonomic Bulletin and Review, 9*(3), 575–582.

Yuille, J. C., & Cutshall, J. L. (1986). A case study of eyewitness memory of a crime. *Journal of Applied Psychology, 71*, 291–301.

Yussen, S. R., & Levy, V. M. (1975). Developmental changes in predicting one's own span of short-term memory. *Journal of Experimental Child Psychology, 19*, 502–508.

Zacks, R. T., Hasher, L., & Li, K. Z. H. (2000). Human memory. In F. I. M. Craik & T. A. Salthouse (Eds.), *The Handbook of Aging and Cognition* (2nd edn). Mahwah, NJ: Lawrence Erlbaum Associates.

Zola-Morgan, S., Cohen, N. J., & Squire, L. R. (1983). Recall of remote episodic memory in amnesia. *Neuropsychologia, 21*, 487–500.

Zuckerman, M. (1979). *Sensation Seeking: Beyond the Optimal Level of Arousal*. Hillsdale, NJ: Lawrence Erlbaum Associates.

AUTHOR INDEX

Norman, D.A. 53
Norman, K.A. 303
Norman, S. 303
Norris, D. 31, 32, 198
Nowinski, J. 347–8
Nyberg, L. 294–5, 296, 308
Nystrom, L.E. 66

O

Oakes, M.A. 223
Oberauer, K. 29
O'Brien, D. 362–3
Ochera, J. 239
Ochsner, K.N. 175, 227–8
O'Connell, B.A. 156
Oddy, M. 261
O'Donnell, V.M. 260
Oertel, W.H. 308
Oh, S.-H. 34
Ohman, A. 89
O'Keefe, J. 87
Oliver, W.L. 376
Olson, E.A. 325–6
Omori, M. 307
Ono, Y. 115
Opwis, K. 275, 276
O'Regan, J.K. 79
O'Reilly, R.C. 258
Ornstein, T. 64
Orr, S. 153
Orrell, M. 138, 313
Ortony, A. 129–30
Osawa, K. 51
Osler, S. 169
Owen, A.M. 66, 124

P

Pacteau, C. 84
Page, M.P.A. 31, 32, 198
Paivio, A. 66, 98
Palmer, J.C. 322
Palmer, S.E. 130
Papagno, C. 32, 45–6, 47
Park, D.C. 300, 301, 352
Park, S. 64
Parker, E.S. 192–3
Parkin, A.J. 301, 306
Parkinson, S.R. 296, 306
Pashler, H. 74, 75, 372–3
Pashler, H.E. 168
Patterson, K. 124, 309–10, 311
Patterson, K.E. 329–30, 331
Paulesu, E. 64
Pavlov, I.P. 79–80, 231
Payne, D.G. 234
Payne, R.B. 304

Pearlstone, Z. 104
Pearson, D.G. 50–1
Pelosi, L. 307
Penrod, S. 325
Penrod, S.D. 328, 338, 339–40
Perfect, T.J. 81, 207, 298, 325
Perlmuter, L.C. 302
Perri, R. 37–8
Perruchet, P. 84
Perry, R.J. 313
Petersen, A.C. 50
Petersen et al. 01 309
Peterson, C. 281, 282, 284
Peterson, L.R. 22, 306
Peterson, M.J. 22, 306
Petersson, K.M. 308
Petro, S.J. 359
Pezdek, K. 230
Phillips, L.H. 307, 351
Phillips, L.W. 24, 25
Piaget, J. 271
Pickel, K.L. 327–8
Pickering, A. 328, 334
Pickering, S.J. 59, 60, 274, 275, 277
Pickrell, J.E. 151
Piercy, M. 251–2
Pillemer, D.B. 142, 285
Pillon, B. 133
Pilzecker, A. 200
Pinto, A. da Costa 25
Pipe, M.-E. 281–2, 286, 289
Pitman, R. 153
Plake, B.S. 59
PlaneCrashInfo.com 347
Pleydell-Pearce, C.W. 145, 159
Polson, P.G. 63
Posner, M.I. 33
Postman, L. 24, 25, 200, 232
Pötter, U. 306
Powell, B. 156, 177
Prentice, W.C.H. 96
Pressley, M. 276–7
Preston, E.L. 129
Pribram, K.H. 43
Priestley, G. 289
Prince, S.E. 160, 307
Pritchert, J.W. 171
Prull, M.W. 301, 303
Puglisi, J.T. 300
Pyszora, N.M. 156

Q

Quas, J.A. 281–2
Querleu, D. 271
Quillian, M.R. 13, 116–18, 119, 303
Quinn, G. 52

SUBJECT INDEX